D1535204

J. Brooks Heckert, C.P.A., is Professor Emeritus of Accounting at The Ohio State University, where he has taught for many years. Past President of the National Association of Accountants, Professor Heckert is the author of *Accounting Systems* (with Harry D. Kerrigan), *Distribution Costs* (with Robert B. Miner), and *Business Budgeting and Control* (with James D. Willson), all published by The Ronald Press Company.

James D. Willson, C.P.A., is Vice-President—Finance, Northrop Corporation. He has held financial executive positions, which encompassed the planning and control function, with several leading corporations, including Libbey-Owens-Ford Glass Company, Norris-Thermador Corporation, and the Tidewater Oil Company. He received the Lybrand Gold Medal of the National Association of Accountants for distinguished contribution to accounting literature in 1958–1959. Mr. Willson is co-author of *Business Budgeting and Control* and a Contributing Editor of the *Marketing Handbook,* published by The Ronald Press Company.

CONTROLLERSHIP

J. BROOKS HECKERT, C.P.A.
The Ohio State University

JAMES D. WILLSON, C.P.A.
Vice President—Finance
Tidewater Oil Company

SECOND EDITION

THE RONALD PRESS COMPANY · NEW YORK

Library of Congress Catalog Card Number: 63-11838
PRINTED IN THE UNITED STATES OF AMERICA

Preface

The past ten years may be characterized best as a period of extensive revolution in the financial and accounting fields. In no segment of this broad area is the evidence of change more profound than with respect to applications in both the planning and control phases of business. Increased emphasis on the analytical, investigative approach to solving management problems has seen the development of finer tools and more management-oriented attitudes by accounting-trained practitioners.

The purpose of this Second Edition is to consider some of these new and more satisfactory methods as applied to the task of the chief accounting official. This volume, in presenting an integrated and comprehensive treatment of practical controllership, places greater stress on the broad management aspects so necessary to a satisfactory execution of the financial-accounting functions. In reviewing this management-oriented philosophy, considerable space is devoted to the planning task of financial-accounting executives as a precedent to the control function.

The material presented herein is based on years of experience by the authors directly in financial management and controllership under circumstances of an extremely competitive business atmosphere. Likewise, the organization of the material reflects extensive exposure in the teaching of managerial accounting to university students, and equally close contact with the needs and attitudes of members of executive management actively engaged in business.

As in the First Edition, every effort has been made to prepare a book of practical ideas to assist financial and accounting executives in meeting the challenge of present-day business management. The numerous illustrations and examples are taken from a wide variety of industries and business situations. They have been planned to maximize the applications for not only the larger firms, but also the medium- and small-sized companies.

To their many professional associates and friends who have given advice and assistance, sometimes unknowingly, the authors take pleasure in acknowledging their indebtedness.

Naturally, any opinions expressed in this volume are those of the authors, and are not necessarily those of any company or institution with which the authors may be directly or indirectly associated.

J. Brooks Heckert
James D. Willson

January, 1963

Contents

PART VII

Other Problems of Controllership

PART I

The Broad Management Aspects of Controllership

1

Accounting and Its
Relation to Management

THE BUSINESS OBJECTIVE

The objective of business under the competitive "free enterprise" American economy has been characterized as the earning of maximum profit consistent with the longer-term growth of the company. In a broader sense, a business organization is an economic institution. It is created principally to provide the public with those goods or services which are needed or desired and are compatible with the social attitudes of the nation. In the eyes of the customers there is no reason for the existence of the business except the service it renders. If this service objective is not attained, then the organization ultimately will wither away and die.

There usually exist other collateral objectives which have social implications. For example, employers may seek to provide employees with the best possible working conditions or job security, consistent with the longer-term well-being of the business; or management may seek for itself the highest possible remuneration for guiding the business; or employees may attempt to secure the highest possible wages. But any such objectives are still dependent upon and successfully supported only by effectively meeting the principal business objective—the satisfaction of customer needs or desires.

THE MANAGEMENT TASK

If the business objective is known, then the question arises as to what function management is expected to perform in reaching the goal. It is the task of management to determine the needs and desires of consumers for goods and services, to assemble and organize the agencies of production and distribution for the satisfaction of these desires, and to direct and coordinate these agencies efficiently. This is no easy assignment. Successful accomplishment does not just happen. The exact goal must be intelli-

3

gently conceived, and the method of accomplishment must be planned and properly executed. Moreover, the task is continuous. Needs and desires are changing constantly; new products and services which will add to the consumers' well-being and enjoyment must be continuously developed and perfected; new agencies of research, production, and distribution must be developed to accomplish the desired results most efficiently.

AN ENLIGHTENED PHILOSOPHY OF MANAGEMENT

The philosophy and the practice of business management are being subjected to a most critical analysis, an analysis directed to both the scientific aspect of business practice and the ethical basis upon which such practice rests. Business management is presently contemplated both as a productive enterprise and as a social trust. Much study is being directed to an understanding of the responsibility of the business executive, for it is recognized that business executives have become a most important agency in the guidance of our economic activity. If the march of industrial progress is to continue uninterrupted, business leaders must be skillful, intelligent, and motivated by a social responsibility. Unless they possess these qualities, there is serious question whether our present economic institutions can be maintained.

COMPLEXITIES OF MANAGEMENT GREATLY INCREASED

Our economic structure has become tremendously complex and its complexities will continue to increase. A manager taking command of a modern business craft must direct its course through social and political currents, the courses of which are constantly changing and increasing in swiftness. The economic storms appear to be no less severe. His own craft is one of extremely sensitive direction and technical complexity. The instruments of direction and control are vastly improved, and the personnel at his command is more highly skilled. The seas are somewhat better charted, but upon the commander still rests the responsibility of selecting the course, equipping the vessel, and organizing the crew, coordinating its effort, and inspiring it with the heart to see the voyage through. If he lacks skill, disaster is certain. If he possesses skill but is motivated only by selfish ends, he bids fair to become an economic pirate and a menace to all legitimate commerce. Only as the ranks of business leaders are freed of both the unskilled and the greedy can the ships of commerce make their full speed toward the ports of economic well-being.

MANAGERIAL SKILL ESSENTIAL

A management job well done involves the application of sound management principles carried out by competent and experienced personnel. In fact one might ask, "If a business manager has competent and willing people to assist him, and follows sound management principles, how can he fail?" Is anything else required? The fact is that *sound management principles* encompass many factors relating to all leadership activity from initial planning to attainment of the goal. To be more specific and to indicate the scope and complexity of the management problem, it involves such action as: establishing both short- and long-range plans; defining specific corporate objectives; developing basic policies; building a sound organizational structure including the establishment of definite lines of authority and responsibility; setting performance standards; creating and maintaining good communication methods and channels within the company; measuring performance; and maintaining proper human relations with employees, stockholders, the public, and customers.

There must be continuous refinement in the science of management— more intelligent planning, better coordination and facilitation, more effective direction and control of effort, more accurate measurement of and reward for performance, and greater security for workers and investors. Wastefulness and inefficiency of management are no more to be condoned than greed. In brief, there must be a high degree of managerial skill and intelligence as well as honesty of purpose.

In this broad field, then, the question is raised as to the role accounting can and should play in developing or maintaining an effective effort.

ACCOUNTING AS AN AID TO MANAGEMENT

One of the chief aids to management in making its efforts fully productive is modern accounting. It is to the chief accounting officer, the controller, more than to any other official, that the business manager must turn for guidance in the direction, control, and protection of the business. To extend the maritime figure, the controller is not the commander of the ship—that is the task of the chief executive—but he may be likened to the navigator, the one who keeps the charts. He must keep the commander informed as to how far he has come, where he is, what speed he is making, resistance encountered, variations from the course, dangerous reefs which lie ahead, and where the charts indicate he should go next in order to reach the port in safety.

Emerson once said, "There is no more terrible sight than ignorance in action." And it was Gantt who stated, "There is no moral right to decide on a basis of opinion that which can be determined as a matter of fact." There is no place for the rabbit's-foot executive in modern business. The successful manager must know and use the instruments of guidance and control at his command. The use of modern accounting and statistical data is the means by which the business executive is able to direct and control operations which reach beyond the range of his own personal observation and supervision. There is no question that the executive who is best informed about his operations is in the best position to manage his business profitably.

BASIC CONCEPTS UNDERLYING SOUND FINANCIAL ACCOUNTING

The preceding section has emphasized accounting as an aid to management, and this thought will predominate throughout this book. It is the utilitarian viewpoint of accounting. Certainly the accounting process should stand this test of practicality. Yet a professional job cannot be done with merely this concept in mind.

The accounting process is made up of a multitude of postulates, principles, conventions, methods, and practices, some of which are of such fundamental significance that the utilitarian concept must recognize them. In other words, the most effective exercise of the professional managerial accounting function will blend business management's needs and desires on the one hand and certain important basic accounting principles on the other. Integrity and practical judgment are required in this balancing.

So that a clear understanding of the area of discussion may exist, some review of the more important accounting principles is presented to insure their conscious consideration in the development of managerial accounting practices and procedures.

Perhaps the best description of accounting is that presented by the American Institute of Certified Public Accountants: "Accounting is the art of recording, classifying, and summarizing in a significant manner, and in terms of money, transactions which are, in part at least, of a financial character, and interpreting the results thereof." In carrying out this accounting function, and to best serve in the fiduciary sense the interests of all parties involved in the business enterprise—the management, the owners, the creditors, the customers, the public—several basic concepts must be recognized and evaluated.

A fundamental assumption in the accounting process relates to the entity for which the accounting is done. Accounting is designed to record and report the financial transactions of a particular economic unit—the business enterprise—and not the economy as a whole. Further, this entity very often is separate and distinct from the parties who furnish the funds.

Still another basic principle is the cost concept. Business transactions fundamentally involve exchanges with the common means of expressing these in monetary terms. The measure at the time of exchange is cost. It is to be noted that "cost" is used rather than "value"; and value may change while cost does not. Financial accounting concerns itself most directly with such cost. Further, the cost concept inherently assumes that costs may be separated and regrouped in different combinations. That is, costs are somewhat like minute particles which, mobile in nature, can be moved about and combined or assembled to form new cost aggregates such as, for example, the change from raw materials to finished goods.

Another ground rule is the concept of immateriality which requires a practical approach in dealing with items which are inconsequential in amount. Recognition must be given to *relative* significance in a particular business enterprise. Furthermore, the effect in the aggregate must be considered. Items immaterial in a large firm may be material in a small company. Transactions immaterial individually may be significant in the aggregate.

Objectivity is another principle to be kept in mind. This is particularly true because the interests of the various groups using financial statements may be to some extent in conflict with each other. Insofar as possible, the statements should be an objective disclosure of facts, within the confines of sound accounting practice and the going-concern concept. If the various interested groups are presented information of a factual nature—to the extent that accounting is factual—then each may make its own interpretation and form its own opinion.

The principle of income determination and the need to match properly costs and income are of prime significance. The periodic reporting of income is a necessity. Yet, accountants recognize that even the annual report is at best only an interim report. Profits are not fundamentally the result of operations during any short period of time.

Conservatism is another convention of financial accounting. Because of the importance of the earnings statement, this principle should not be used as an excuse to make unwarranted or arbitrary write-offs. On the other hand, assets should not be intentionally overstated, nor liabilities understated.

The going-concern concept is a viewpoint customarily taken in statement preparation. On this basis, it is assumed that the business enterprise has continuity of life and that the periodic financial statements are test readings on the continuous stream of economic transactions of the enterprise. Liquidation values, therefore, are of secondary importance.

Perhaps consistency—the uniformity of methods and practices from period to period—should be mentioned. Where alternative methods are available, the comparability and uniformity of periodic reports require that one method be followed consistently. Further, the treatment in one area of the accounting process should be consistent with the treatment accorded in other areas. Obviously, however, there will be times when methods must be changed, as the circumstances of the company change, in order to report more properly on the operating results or financial position.

There are other accounting concepts of which the professional accounting manager should be aware, and the reader is referred to the many excellent writings on the subject.[1] It is the intention of the authors merely to touch upon them and to stress the importance of such background and thinking in properly understanding the relationship between management and the accounting function.

THE FUNCTIONS OF MANAGERIAL ACCOUNTING

It is difficult to reduce to a concise outline the functions of managerial accounting. Circumstances of business operation vary widely and the successful accounting executive must bring to his task a high degree of initiative, constructive thinking, and analytical ability. There are, however, certain basic functions toward which the accountant must direct his effort. These may be stated as follows:

1. To assist management in determining policies and in making plans for their execution
2. To assist management in the planning, direction, coordination, and control of operations
3. To maintain records and procedures which will adequately protect all interests related to the business

Each controller, in fact all supervisory accountants, in carrying out his day-to-day duties should relate his efforts to these three elements.

Responsibility accounting is the recording of transactions or events to identify them with the individual in the organization who controls the activity or is held accountable for it. It is inherently a principle which emphasizes the use of the information by management and de-emphasizes figures not related to responsibility areas. Stated in another way, the figures are personalized to the individual instead of being a hodgepodge.

In effect, the chart of accounts must be guided by and must follow the company organization chart. Costs and income are aggregated by the person accountable. For example, labor costs are accumulated by cost center for the foreman responsible for controlling such costs. Again, in a large company, inventories would be separated in terms of those responsible for the various sections.

Responsibility accounting is another example of the evolution of sound accounting. It represents an attitude not of mere recording—important though that is—but of recording with a purpose, with improvement, and with action in mind.

---

[1] For example, see "Restatement and Revision of Accounting Research Bulletins," *Accounting Research Bulletin* No. 43, and subsequent bulletins issued by the Committee on Accounting Procedure of the American Institute of Certified Public Accountants.

METHOD OF APPROACH

Very little more will be said in the remainder of this volume about generally accepted principles or practice. An understanding of these will be assumed on the part of the reader; however, the authors feel that the most effective managerial accounting work will be done if two principal viewpoints are kept in mind. One is the utility concept of accounting, specifically that a basic function of accounting is to render assistance to the operating and planning executives. This does not imply a servile attitude, but rather a recognition of a job which must be done and, quite often, as these other executives wish it done. The other desirable viewpoint is that which constantly keeps in mind the broad top-management approach to a function which is requisite to a successful business enterprise —the planning and control functions which are most effectively expressed through accounting means. Without this the best management, the most efficient factory, the most effective sales management will accomplish little. Such a viewpoint is fundamental if the accounting and financial executive is to sit in the high council of business leaders and to reach and maintain the stature in business management to which his knowledge, ability, and contribution potential should entitle him.

2

The Controllership
Function in Management

EVOLUTION IN DUTIES OF FINANCIAL EXECUTIVES

Since the turn of the twentieth century at least three factors have had a significant effect on the status of the financial executive in American business. The increased size and complexity of the industrial organization, growing governmental relationships with company affairs, and more numerous sources of capital have, among other things, made financial accountability an increasingly important consideration in the conduct of business. Consequently, the functions and responsibilities of the individual financial executive have changed.

In this period the birth and development of the separate controllership function occurred. Noticeably increased financial activities forced a wider delegation of authority and responsibility in many companies. Moreover, greater size has required more checks and balances and better internal control within the business. But perhaps most important, a demand for better management practices has brought with it the necessity for more adequate accounting and more effective management control information. Thus, for the reasons stated, the separation of the accounting function from the secretarial and financial functions was a logical growth.

In this evolution of the controllership function, it is understandable that much diversity between companies would appear. In most organizations, the certificate of incorporation, or bylaws, or resolutions by the board of directors set forth the *general* financial duties to be performed. However, that share of the total duties assigned to the controller had no generally accepted precedent and was influenced by such forces as the size of the company, industry practice, personality and ability of the controller, and prevailing opinion on the part of the chief executive and his associates as to just what should constitute the job.

AN ESSENTIAL TO THE FUNCTION

Though the scope of the position varies from company to company, yet one concept is common. In the representative company, the controller is thought of simply as the chief accountant who supervises and maintains the formal corporate financial records. He is regarded as the executive who concerns himself with general accounting, cost accounting, auditing, taxes, and perhaps insurance and statistics. Such a viewpoint is backward-looking.

It is true that the controller must engage in accounting activities; yet he must not restrict his role to the recording function. More properly, he is expected to extend his accounting function to its management applications. Essential to the proper fulfillment of the controllership function is an attitude of mind which energizes and vitalizes the financial data by applying it to *future* company activities. It is a forward-looking concept—a trained analytical approach, which brings balance to the management planning and control system. The controller's viewpoint should be the management viewpoint—one which guides management's thinking to the most profitable combination of operations.

This modern concept of controllership is the one stressed in this book and is more fully described in this chapter.

VARIOUS TITLES APPLIED TO POSITION

Numerous titles are applied to the position of chief accounting officer: chief accountant, office manager, chief clerk, auditor, comptroller, and controller. The duties are frequently assumed by the treasurer, assistant treasurer, secretary, or assistant secretary. In recent years, with the growing development of the accounting and statistical function and the increased emphasis on the control aspect of the task, there has been a rather general acceptance of the term *controllership,* particularly in larger concerns. This would seem to be a proper choice since the title of "controller" denotes, more clearly than the others, the full responsibility of the position. "Controller" is the title accepted in this book as signifying the position of the chief accounting and statistical officer.

There have been some indications that the use of the word "controller" is unfortunate in that he does not *control* the business. His function is that of reporting and advising, of providing valuable control mechanisms. The operating men in the company do the real controlling, if any is done. The sole area where a controller might be said to control is with respect to his departmental expenses. Under such circumstances, it would seem a more appropriate title might be "Director of Planning and Controls." As will be seen, it is a better description of the management functions.

CONTROLLERSHIP PRINCIPLES APPLICABLE TO ALL TYPES AND SIZES OF CONCERNS

One of the obstacles to the development of the controllership function is the feeling on the part of executives that their particular business is *different* and does not lend itself to modern control methods.

Basically the problems of management cannot vary much between industries and concerns. There are always the problems of determining policies, of planning for future action, of organization, of direction of sales effort and control of sales cost, and of control of production and production costs. Workers must be employed in competition with other firms; they must be trained and supervised, and their performance closely checked; materials must be purchased in proper quantities, at proper times, and investment in inventories must be closely controlled; suitable physical equipment must be selected, maintained, and replaced; finances must be arranged and kept in proper balance as between fixed and working funds; and finally all factors must be properly coordinated. Such problems are not peculiar to any business; they are common problems which form the basis of the management task. Few businesses have "peculiar" problems of accounting procedure and control.

It is true that certain peculiarities do exist in the detailed operations of certain types of business and with regard to the economic and political restrictions which surround them. Utilities, insurance companies, brokerage houses, hotels, amusement concerns, financial institutions, department stores, and chain organizations present examples of certain peculiarities of organization and procedure, but here again the basic problems are similar. The controller who understands thoroughly the basic problems of accounting control can readily apply them to his industry and concern.

Moreover, the controllership function is not restricted to large companies. A business need not reach any considerable size before a qualified controller can find ample opportunity to establish his usefulness and value to his company. There are still thousands of small concerns which need the services of an accountant who envisions the full opportunity of the task.

With this general background relating to controllership, a discussion of specific functions is in order.

CONTROLLERSHIP FUNCTION AS DEFINED BY FINANCIAL EXECUTIVES INSTITUTE [1]

One of the most comprehensive definitions of the controllership function is that developed by the Committee on Ethics and Eligibility Standards of

---

[1] Formerly Controllers Institute.

the Financial Executives Institute, and approved by its National Board of Directors in September, 1949, as follows:

1. To establish, coordinate and maintain, through authorized management, an integrated plan for the control of operations. Such a plan would provide, to the extent required in the business, cost standards, expense budgets, sales forecasts, profit planning, and programs for capital investment and financing, together with the necessary procedures to effectuate the plan.

2. To measure performance against approved operating plans and standards, and to report and interpret the results of operations to all levels of management. This function includes the design, installation and maintenance of accounting and cost systems and records, the determination of accounting policy and the compilation of statistical records as required.

3. To measure and report on the validity of the objectives of the business and on the effectiveness of its policies, organization structure and procedures in attaining those objectives. This includes consulting with all segments of management responsible for policy or action concerning any phase of the operation of the business as it relates to the performance of this function.

4. To report to government agencies, as required, and to supervise all matters relating to taxes.

5. To interpret and report on the effect of external influences on the attainment of the objectives of the business. This function includes the continuous appraisal of economic and social forces and of governmental influences as they affect the operations of the business.

6. To provide protection for the assets of the business. This function includes establishing and maintaining adequate internal control and auditing, and assuring proper insurance coverage.

BASIC CONTROLLERSHIP FUNCTIONS

The Institute's definition is broad in its concept, and outlines the major area of activity. In order to facilitate discussion, the authors will use the points covered as a base, and recast them with a somewhat more restricted functional segregation, as a controller might see them when he considers his specific responsibilities in day-to-day operations. There is always some commingling of functions, but the following breakdown of controllership activities will be useful. They include:

1. The *planning function,* including the establishment and maintenance of an integrated plan of operation through authorized management channels, both short- and long-term, compatible with the corporate objectives, the testing thereof, the required revisions thereof, and the requisite system and procedures

2. The *control function,* including the development, testing, and revision by appropriate means, of satisfactory standards against which to measure actual performance, and assistance to management in encouraging conformance of actual results to standards

3. The *reporting function,* which includes the preparation, analysis, and interpretation of financial facts and figures for the use of

management, and encompasses an evaluation of such data with reference to company and departmental objectives and methods, and external influences; and as appropriate, the preparation and presentation of reports to such third parties as governments and governmental agencies, shareholders, creditors, customers, the general public, and others

4. The *accounting function,* including the establishment and maintenance of the corporate, divisional, and plant general accounting and cost accounting operations, together with the systems and methods embracing the design, installation, and custody of all books of account, records, and forms required to record objectively financial transactions, and to conform them to sound accounting principles with adequate internal control

5. *Other related functions of primary responsibility,* including supervision and operation of such areas as taxes, encompassing federal, state, and local matters and relationship with tax agents and auditors; auditing, both internal aspects and relationship with independent auditors; insurance, both adequacy of coverage and maintenance of records; standard practice instructions and systems and procedures, both development and maintenance; record retention programs; financial public relations; and, finally, the coordination of all clerical and office systems and facilities throughout the company

For reasons previously discussed, there exist many deviations from this general list of *basic* functions. It should be stressed, however, that the above duties of a primarily fiscal nature should not be diluted by the inclusion of operating functions such as purchasing. Effective over-all planning and control functions are too important to the successful conduct of business.

The Planning Function. The establishment and maintenance of an integrated plan of operation has been described as a major function of the controller. The business objective is profit, and planning is necessary to fulfill it, for profits do not "just happen." Visualize, then, the role of the modern controller in business planning.

First, he has a responsibility to see that a plan exists, and that it is supported by all levels of management. The implication of an integrated plan is that all parts will mesh together and support the business objective. For this reason, all members of management must participate willingly. It must be the *company* plan and *not* the controller's plan. He will act as *coordinator* in the various stages, in translating the base to monetary terms, and in putting the plan together in financial terms—finally expressed as a statement of forecast income and expense and a statement of estimated financial condition, together with supporting schedules.

Assuming the recognition of the need for a plan, and the desire by all management to participate, then the controller has a responsibility to determine that the parts in and of themselves are sound, and that they fit together. For example, he should, as a staff officer, ascertain that:

1. The sales plan or forecast supports known corporate policies and objectives (market areas, types of product, etc.)
2. The sales plan appears realistic
3. The production plan or schedule supports the sales program
4. The production plan is within facility capabilities
5. The cost and expense levels and relationships are proper

When the total plan is put together, the controller should test or appraise its adequacy and report to the chief executive on his findings. It must be judged on an over-all basis:

1. In the light of past experience, is it realistic?
2. Does it reflect economic conditions which are expected to prevail in the period of the plan?
3. In terms of management policy, have lines designated to be discontinued been discontinued on a practical basis—with regard to inventory disposal considerations, etc.?
4. Does it meet requirements of return on investment and such other broad tests as may be applicable?

Some of the testing and analysis will be accomplished as preliminary plans are formulated, and the rest will await the total picture. But, however and whenever it is done, the controller is counselor and coordinator. He advises and suggests. Final responsibility for the over-all program must rest with the chief executive; and responsibility for each operating function must be that of the applicable officer. Thus, the vice-president for sales is responsible for the sales program. But this staff relationship should not deter the controller from making his considered observations.

The Control Function. The management function of control is the measurement and correction of performance so that business objectives and plans are accomplished. Management control seeks to compel conformance to plan or standard. In this function, also, the controller assists. He does not enforce control, except in his own department, but he provides information which the functional executive is expected to use to achieve the required performance.

Activities in this control area absorb a great deal of time of the controller's staff. Some information is provided from hour to hour, or from day to day; other data are prepared from week to week or from month to month, as circumstances require. For example, in larger companies, hourly or daily information on labor performance may be helpful, or weekly manufacturing expense figures may be needed.

In approaching problems relative to the control function, a broad view usually is helpful. The end result of the control function is not merely a report on performance. Rather it should involve:

1. Assistance in setting standards for control
2. Evaluation of standards, including related analysis
3. Reporting short-term actual and standard performance
4. Developing trends and relationships to assist the operating executives
5. Ascertaining that the system and procedure, through constant review, are providing the required, most helpful data, on the most practical and economic basis

A little reflection will indicate that a manager cannot control the past. He may study past action to determine place and cause of deviation. But here, as in planning, the best kind of control is forward-looking. This the controller must keep in mind as he participates in the control function, giving constant thought to steps which might be taken before the operating action to assure "on-standard or desired performance." This might be called *preventive* control.

The Reporting Function. Insofar as it concerns internal management, the reporting function is closely related to both the planning and the control functions. Reporting is essential to make planning and control effective. Yet the reporting function is not merely one of presentation of tabulations and is not wholly routine although some phases become routinized. Moreover, the management which makes decisions often cannot be kept adequately informed solely from periodic statements regardless of how well-designed they may be. The reporting function encompasses the *interpretation* of the figures, and the controller's duty is not discharged until management actually understands the facts.

The reporting function with the requisite interpretation is an opportunity to bring life and meaning to the figures.

Prior comments have related to management reporting, and this is perhaps the most interesting area. Yet, information must be provided to a rather wide field. The controller will be called upon to furnish data of a financial or statistical nature to such other groups as:

Shareholders of the company (annual and quarterly reports)
Creditors—banks, suppliers, other financing institutions
Stock Exchanges
Employees and the general public
Customers

U. S. Government and agencies thereof:

Securities and Exchange Commission
Internal Revenue Service
Department of Commerce
Department of Labor
Federal Trade Commission

State and local governments and agencies

The Accounting Function. The systematic recording of financial transactions is often regarded as the principal function of the controller. Important as this is, the authors stress in this text the management aspects
of accounting. In fact, within the limits explained in Chapter 1, the controller may well take the viewpoint of the businessman first and then
that of the accountant.

Because the strictly accounting considerations are well-known, little
additional comment is necessary. The controller is expected to apply,
in a practical manner, sound accounting principles and practices within
his company. He is expected to keep abreast of technology so that he
can provide management with needed information on the most economical
and feasible basis. He is also expected to develop and maintain records
and procedures, including adequate internal control, so that reports properly reflect the financial condition of the company and the operating
results.

A MORE DETAILED LIST OF FUNCTIONS

In the preceding sections, the authors have attempted to outline and explain the *general* functional areas of the controller. With this background,
the following listing of detailed controllership functions compiled by the
Financial Executives Institute takes on added meaning:

1. The installation and supervision of all accounting records of the
   corporation
2. The preparation and interpretation of the financial statements
   and reports of the corporation
3. The continuous audit of all accounts and records of the corporation wherever located
4. The compilation of production costs
5. The compilation of costs of distribution
6. The taking and costing of all physical inventories
7. The preparation and filing of tax returns and the supervision of
   all matters relating to taxes
8. The preparation and interpretation of all statistical records and
   reports of the corporation
9. The preparation, as budget director, in conjunction with other
   officers and department heads, of an annual budget covering all

activities of the corporation, for submission to the board of directors prior to the beginning of the fiscal year. The authority of the controller, with respect to the veto of commitments or expenditures not authorized by the budget, shall, from time to time, be fixed by the board of directors.

10. The ascertainment currently that the properties of the corporation are properly and adequately insured

11. The initiation, preparation, and issuance of standard practices relating to all accounting matters and procedures and the coordination of systems throughout the corporation, including clerical and office methods, records, reports, and procedures

12. The maintenance of adequate records of authorized appropriations and the determination that all sums expended pursuant thereto are properly accounted for

13. The ascertainment currently that financial transactions covered by minutes of the board of directors and/or the executive committee are properly executed and recorded

14. The maintenance of adequate records of all contracts and leases

15. The approval for payment (and/or countersigning) of all checks, promissory notes, and other negotiable instruments of the corporation which have been signed by the treasurer or such other officers as shall have been authorized by the bylaws of the corporation or from time to time designated by the board of directors

16. The examination of all warrants for the withdrawal of securities from the vaults of the corporation and the determination that such withdrawals are made in conformity with the bylaws and/or regulations established from time to time by the board of directors

17. The preparation or approval of the regulations or standard practices required to assure compliance with orders or regulations issued by duly constituted governmental agencies

ORGANIZATIONAL STATUS

The review of the controllership duties indicates the broad scope of the position. In this area, as in all other management positions, the proper climate must exist if the plant is to grow and prosper. The status of the controller—regardless of his title—must be such that his function is given full expression. The function of the fact-finding and intelligence officer exists in every business, large or small. It may be fully exercised whether the title is that of chief accountant, secretary, or controller; but it is of such commanding importance in the modern era of business that it should stand in a coordinate relationship to the position of all other major functional executives. If the controller is fully qualified to do his work properly he will have no difficulty in maintaining his standing with other major executives; indeed, he bids fair to render a service to his concern second in importance only to that of the chief executive. This is evidenced by the increasing number of controllers who in recent years have been advanced to the position of chief executive.

While all these things are true, the evolution of the separate controllership function is relatively new compared to the secretarial or treasury functions. In view of this, among other things, the Financial Executives Institute felt that a statement as to the organizational status of the controller might prove a useful guide. Accordingly, its Board of Directors accepted this codification:

1. The controller should be an executive officer at the policy-making level responsible directly to the chief executive officer of the business. His appointment or removal should require the approval of the Board of Directors.

2. The controller should be required by the Board of Directors to present directly periodic reports covering the operating results and financial conditions of the business, together with such other information as it may request.

3. The controller should preferably be a member of the Board of Directors, and all other top policy-making groups. At a minimum he should be invited to attend all meetings of such groups with the right to be heard.

It is hoped and expected that proficiency and salesmanship gradually will cause these concepts to be widely accepted.

SOURCE OF THE CONTROLLER'S AUTHORITY

A clear definition of duties, authority, and responsibility is generally regarded as a prerequisite to good performance. Certainly in large companies, and perhaps in smaller ones, the scope of the controller's authority and responsibility can be established in one of three ways: (1) in accordance with the bylaws of the corporation, (2) by resolution of the executive committee, or (3) by general order of the president.

Bylaw provisions vary considerably in length and content in dealing with the controllership function. In essence, however, most state that "the controller shall be the principal officer in charge of the accounts of the company." Further, most provisions also contain the statement that "he shall have such other powers and duties as may be assigned to him by the Board of Directors, or by the Executive Committee, or by the President." An example of a bylaw provision, very complete as to the duties of the controller's office, is that of the United States Steel Corporation:

Powers, Authorities, and Duties of the Comptroller.—The Comptroller shall be the principal officer in charge of the accounts of the Company and

a. Shall establish and maintain, or cause to be established and maintained, all accounting, including cost accounting, policies, and the methods and procedures of carrying out such policies.

b. He shall be responsible for the design, installation, custody and operation of all accounting, including cost accounting, books, records, and forms of the Company.

c. He shall prepare, or cause to be prepared, all checks, drafts, and other orders for the payment of money for authorized disbursements, or for the transfer of funds, of the Company, except as may be otherwise provided in respect of any special or limited bank account under and pursuant to the provisions of these By-Laws. He shall not prepare or countersign, or permit the countersigning of, any such checks, drafts, or other orders for the payment of money of the Company if such payment is in excess of an amount properly authorized by any rule or regulation established by the Board of Directors or by any officer having authority to establish such rule or regulation.

d. He shall examine and audit, or cause to be examined and audited, all financial and business records and all receipts and disbursements of the Company, including all books and accounts of all officers and agents of the Company who are charged with the receipt and disbursement of money or material or who have jurisdiction over labor. He shall make, or cause to be made, such examination and audit with established regularity, and as often as dictated by good business methods and practices.

e. He shall audit or investigate, or cause to be audited or investigated, any matter the audit or investigation of which may be requested of him by or at the instance of the Board of Directors or the President.

f. He shall analyze and check, or cause to be analyzed and checked, and assist other officers of the Company in analyzing and checking, the policies and activities of the Company, as revealed by the records. He shall also assist other officers in determining future policies and plans by developing and interpreting facts and applying good business judgment to the conclusions to be deduced from such facts.

g. He shall prepare and interpret, or cause to be prepared and interpreted, all statistical records and reports and all financial statements and reports of the Company whether for internal or external use.

h. He shall establish and maintain, or cause to be established and maintained, budget control and the consolidation and coordination of budgets.

i. He shall take and evaluate, or cause to be taken and evaluated, all physical inventories and all matters relating thereto.

j. He shall be responsible for all matters relating to taxes and shall prepare and file, or cause to be prepared and filed, all tax returns and other papers relating to taxes.

k. He shall place and effect, or cause to be placed and effected, all insurance, including employees' indemnity bonds, in order adequately and properly to safeguard the properties and business of the Company and in accordance with policies established by the Board of Directors or by officers whose function it is to establish the same.

l. He shall determine, or cause to be determined, that all expenditures against appropriations are made pursuant to and in accordance with proper authorization and are properly accounted for, and shall have authority over the establishment and maintenance of proper and adequate records of authorized appropriations.

m. He shall be responsible for the approval of the auditing and accounting provisions of all contracts, leases, and agreements of the Company and the maintenance of adequate records thereof.

n. He shall coordinate, or cause to be coordinated, the clerical and office systems and facilities throughout the Company.

o. He may delegate actual performance of any of his work to other departments in the interest of efficiency and economy. Such delegation will not, however, affect his responsibility for and authority over policies, methods, or procedures, or the accuracy and results of any work so delegated.

p. He shall render to the Board of Directors, whenever requested by it, an account of his transactions as Comptroller.

q. Whenever requested by the President or the Board of Directors or independent auditors designated by or under authority of the stockholders he shall exhibit his books and accounts to them or to any of them during business hours.

r. He shall give a bond, in such form and in such amount and with such sureties as the Board of Directors may require and approve.

CHARACTERISTICS OF THE CONTROLLERSHIP TASK

Now that his functions have been defined, it might prove helpful to turn the spotlight on the man who must perform them.

There are certain characteristics and requirements of the controllership function which the controller should keep constantly before him. The most important of these are noted in the following paragraphs.

1. The controller is chiefly a staff executive whose primary function is to gather and interpret data which will be of assistance to other general and functional executives in the determination of sound policies and their successful execution. As with all staff positions a high degree of initiative is required. The controller cannot expect on the whole that the various executives will come to him requesting information for their own guidance. To a certain extent this will be done but in a large measure he must of his own initiative determine the need of such executives. He must anticipate and foresee the problems which will arise and the information which will be needed for their consideration.

2. The controller must see through the eyes of the other executives, that is, he must see the problems as they see them. The final responsibility for directing the work of salesmen and getting sales results rests upon the sales manager. To a certain extent the sales manager must undertake this task in his own way. It is not so much a matter of the information which the controller feels he would need, were he the sales manager, as it is a determination of what the sales manager himself will need to do the work as he plans to do it. This does not mean, of course, that the controller should not suggest new and different methods of approach to the problems of the various executives and analyses of data likely to be useful; but it does mean that the controller must give painstaking study to the methods actually employed by the various functional executives and relate his analytical effort to those methods.

Many controllers spend far too much time in their own departments and far too little in studying the departments which they are assisting to control. There is no lack of problems. Every executive as he sits at his desk day-by-day is faced with perplexing tasks which he feels he could perform to much better advantage if certain facts were before him. The controller who can anticipate and supply this need is the one upon whom dependence and reliance will be placed.

3. The information must be supplied in the language and for the understanding of the person for whom it is intended. This may range from elaborate statistical charts to brief narrative statements. The controller should err, if at all, in the direction of simplicity. No data should ever be given to an executive as a matter of formality. There should be a definite purpose in mind and the relation of the data to that purpose should be as clear as it can possibly be made. No work of interpretation should be left for the executive which can be safely done by the controller.

4. The controller must translate absolute facts and statistics into trends and relationships. Business is so dynamic in its character that to guide it the trends and relationships of the various forces at play must be grasped quickly. It is not the fact that sales in West Virginia were lower this December than last, or that they were lower than in November, or that they were either higher or lower, that is of interest. It is the relation of sales results to sales potential and effort and the trend of this relationship in this territory that are the guiding considerations. It is readily conceivable that sales may be much lower and results much more satisfactory.

5. The viewpoint of the controller must be that of the future. There is no chance to control the past; the profits and losses of the past cannot be changed. The controller must be able to make the most exacting analyses of past performance and results without losing sight of the fact that such analyses are of value only insofar as they reveal the proper course in the future.

6. The information supplied must be timely. Business currents change swiftly. There must be a quick analysis of past operations. The results of January's sales effort must be known in time to guide the plans for February, the off-standard factory operations of today must be known in time to correct them tomorrow. Facts which come too late to be acted upon are useless. They constitute the spoiled work of the controller's department. In many concerns this clerical spoilage runs very high.

7. The controller should follow up his studies and interpretations. Executives are busy and inclined to delay matters not requiring immediate attention. If the records clearly reveal unsatisfactory results or adverse trends, even though of minor consequence, they should be followed through until executive action results. It is not what the controller sees in his study of the organization but what executives act on that

eventually reduces cost, improves operations, and increases profits. The controller cannot force action but he can usually secure it by keeping important matters before the executives until satisfactory action is taken.

8. The controller must assume the position of a counselor rather than that of a critic. As his investigation reveals weakness in the work of major and minor executives, his attitude must be, "Here is something which we can improve," rather than, "Here is something for which you should be criticized." If the controller acquires the distinction of being the company's chief detective, his usefulness will end. If, on the other hand, he is awaited by the other executives as a welcome counselor, the avenues will be open for the full exercise of his responsibility.

9. Above all things, the controller must be fair. Occasions arise when he must give adverse reports on the work of other executives and employees. In a broad sense his department is charged with the task of measuring the performance of all employees. In this work he must be fair and impartial, if not for the preservation of his own integrity, at least for the protection of his job, for no other defect will so quickly destroy his usefulness.

10. In some concerns, particularly smaller ones, the controller may require some selling ability in the marketing of his product. This, however, is largely a matter of the quality of the product. There are few executives who do not welcome assistance if it is the type they can understand and if they have confidence in its value. If, for example, a controller can tell the superintendent of the grinding department that he can save $100 a month by seasoning his grindstones six months longer, he will have no difficulty in getting a hearing. Some executives are far more ready to use accounting and statistical data than others and far more capable of its interpretation. For those untrained in its use the controller must go to unusual pains to set forth his findings in usable form.

11. While realizing the full purpose of his task, the controller must also realize its limitations. Statistical information, no matter how accurately collected, analyzed, and interpreted, is not a substitute for executive ability. It is of tremendous value in business and, other things being the same, the company with the best-informed executives will outstrip its rivals. There are, however, many questions upon which the controller can make little contribution. The success or failure of the business may hinge upon shrewdness of investments, engineering ingenuity, matters of style, etc., concerning which the controller may be able to make only a small contribution.

Moreover, the value of accounting and statistical data must be weighed against the cost. It may be interesting to know how much of each of ten major products is sold to a particular customer or by a particular salesman every month, but unless these data can be used definitely to further the sales program to an extent that justifies the cost of securing them, the effort results in a loss. Or if the same results could have been obtained by an occasional test rather than by a continuous analysis, the accounting task is inefficiently performed.

QUALIFICATIONS OF THE CONTROLLER

The foregoing summary of the characteristics and requirements of the controllership task indicates the breadth of training required for the position. More specifically the qualifications of the controller are:

1. A general understanding of the industry of which his company is a part and of the social, economic, and political forces directly related thereto
2. A thorough knowledge of his own company, its history, policies, program, organization, and, to a considerable extent, its technical operations
3. An understanding of the basic problems of organization, planning, and control
4. An understanding of the basic problems of production, distribution, finance, and personnel management
5. The ability to analyze and interpret accounting and statistical data in such a manner that they become a basis for action
6. The ability to express ideas clearly in writing (using proper English)
7. A thorough knowledge of accounting principles and procedure and the ability to direct statistical inquiry

If these qualifications are coupled with a reasonable amount of tact, constructive imagination, and initiative, and a spirit of fairness, helpfulness, and sincerity, the controller will have no difficulty in developing his function to its full importance.

Certain other qualities, no more essential to the work of the controller than to that of other executives, but nonetheless of tremendous value in controllership, are the ability to get along with people, the ability to exercise unlimited patience, the ability to respect other men's ideas and opinions, and the practice of thinking problems through to the end.

PROFESSIONAL SOCIETIES

One other suggestion seems in order. Any controller or aspiring controller should keep in mind the many benefits to be gained through association with competent practitioners. There are several fine organizations which not only make significant contributions to accounting literature, but also provide opportunity for discussion and personal contact. Perhaps the outstanding professional group in controllership is represented by the Financial Executives Institute, and its research arm, Financial Executives Foundation.

Other organizations which are a source of information on controllership and accounting functions include:

National Association of Accountants
American Institute of Certified Public Accountants
System and Procedures Association
National Society for Business Budgeting
National Office Management Association

Because controllers are members of management, their professional activities may go beyond accounting societies. The various meetings, seminars, and other gatherings of the American Management Association, or the National Industrial Conference Board, to mention only two, with the related excellent management literature will assist in developing a better-rounded management approach.

3

An Over-All Appraisal of the Business

A BROAD MANAGEMENT VIEWPOINT

The first part of this volume is devoted to the broad management aspects of controllership. If the controller is to be management oriented, if, indeed, he is to best serve *all* management, then obviously he must be able objectively to take an over-all look at the business. He must be familiar with its strength and weaknesses. He must understand the inter-relationship of the functions of the organization. Just as any prudent buyer of a business must appraise it carefully in all its important aspects, so also the controller lays the best foundation for doing an effective job by having a broad understanding of the business of which he is a part.

THE BUSINESS INGREDIENTS

This matter of reviewing or appraising a business from the over-all vantage point may be approached in any one of several ways. However, the following factors or ingredients must be evaluated during the process of analysis:

1. *The Objectives and Policies.* These factors have to do with the purpose of the business and its parts, and the guiding principles or rules of action to be followed in achieving that purpose.
2. *The Organization.* This element is concerned with the employees, including the organizational structure, i.e., the relationship to one another and the duties, authorities, and responsibilities of each.
3. *The Products.* These are the means of satisfying customer demands. Many of the other factors are heavily influenced by them.
4. *The Market.* This factor has to do with the customers, their location, and the extent and nature of their wants.
5. *The Distribution Program.* This element relates to ways and means of getting the products to market.

6. *The Production Plan.* This factor relates to the all-inclusive segment of the facilities in which the product is manufactured, and the techniques used in the process.

7. *The Research and Development Program.* This has reference to the efforts and effectiveness in creating new products, or improving existing products or product applications.

8. *The Finances.* This factor includes the acquisition and optimum use of capital needed in the enterprise.

9. *The Control System.* This element includes the methods or techniques used in developing and guiding the functions so as to achieve the business objective.

An understanding of the nature, importance, interrelationship, and effectiveness of each of these factors in his company should facilitate the more useful functioning of the controller.

BUSINESS OBJECTIVES AND POLICIES

In the controller's review of his company, he should be concerned not with a *general* business objective, but with the more specific objective of *his company,* and the policies of operation. Quite obviously, a company must know what it wants to accomplish. The controller should attempt to seek out management's real goals. Are they in writing? Not only should the company objective be known, but also there should exist specific objectives for each operating division: marketing, production, research, engineering, accounting, etc.; and if the company is organized on a decentralized basis, each operating group ought to have a goal. Further, the objective of each group should be in tune with the over-all company objective.

An example of an over-all company goal might be "An intelligent, well-established industrial enterprise, organized to return continual maximum benefits, in the light metal fabrication field, to customers, employees, and shareholders." A subsidiary goal might include the attainment of x dollars of sales by the year 19xx. The specific goal of each sales function in the autonomous divisions should support these objectives.

If the company objectives are not in writing, then the controller should encourage such action.

Company policies should support the company objectives. Business policies may be classified as general, major, or minor. General policies, of course, govern the conduct of the business as a whole; they are the basic principles which the company proposes to follow. As an example, a general policy might be expressed in these words: "The company will confine its business to the continental United States." General policies will relate to both internal and external matters.

Major policies govern performance and control of the principal functions of the business. Thus, for an ultimately successful operation there must be sales policy, purchasing policy, engineering policy, etc. An example of a purchasing policy may be: "No division must necessarily purchase parts from other divisions of the company."

Finally, minor policies will relate to the activities of a department or segment of a major division, etc. For example, the policy of a division credit department may be: "The maximum credit extension, without home office approval, to a C class appliance dealer, will be $5,000."

In his review, the controller should be aware of the existence or absence of written policies of the company, and should attempt to conduct his planning and control, or other controllership functions, within the confines of sound policy.

THE ORGANIZATION

Many of the problems of business relate to organization—or lack of it. The ability to stand away from the trees and study the forest of organization—its strong and weak points—should be valuable in effective planning and control work. The interrelationship of the various groups, the duties and responsibilities of each position are important considerations in the effectiveness of planning and control systems.

An organization may be defined as a group of individuals, under leadership, working toward a common goal. This is the dynamic, the vital part of the business, upon which all else chiefly depends. Andrew Carnegie is reported to have said, "Take away my mills, but leave me my organization and I will be back in business in a year." Some of the basic problems of business arise by reason of organizational troubles. The business functions must be properly segregated, and the relationship between functions and organizational groups must be clearly defined. Some of the specific points bearing on the problem are:

1. *Organization Chart.*
   a. Has an organization chart been prepared?
   b. Are the line and staff relationships evident?

2. *Manual of Organization.* Is a manual in existence which, in detail, outlines for supervisory personnel at least the following:
   a. Title of position,
   b. Position to which responsible,
   c. General functions and responsibility,
   d. Detailed duties and responsibilities?

3. *Standard Practice Instructions.* Are such aids available as to the repetitive and routine functions, indicating (a) the responsibility of the several departments, and (b) the procedure to be followed?

4. *Selection of Personnel.* What basis is used?
5. *Training of Personnel.* Has any program been established for either formal or informal training?
6. *Coordination of Functions.* How is coordination attained?

THE PRODUCTS

The management audit or review can very logically begin with the product line. For the most effective selling force, a skillfully developed advertising program, an efficient production group, the best equipped plant, and an excellent organization in general will be unable to secure a satisfactory return on investment if the product line is basically one which cannot secure consumer acceptance under such circumstances as to return a proper share of profits. The analysis of the product line or lines must include several phases:

1. *Trends in Sales Volume.* These should be known and explained, and not merely as an over-all sales pattern. Rather, in each territory and for each product the trend should be determined and analyzed as to cause.
2. *Competitive Advantages.* Such a comparison should reveal the weak and strong points of each product. The advantages may not necessarily be restricted to the product itself, but may relate to customer service, etc. Knowledge of these points may disclose sales arguments which may be used more effectively.
3. *Gross Margins.* An analysis of gross margins will reveal the more important products from a gross profit viewpoint.
4. *Completeness of Line.* Consideration of these phases may reveal deficiencies and the cause of wasted sales effort. However, smart merchandising does not necessarily require that all sizes, colors, etc., be handled.
5. *Prices.* This phase of the audit should cover three avenues:
   a. Does the price provide the necessary margin?
   b. Is the price competitive?
   c. Is the price such as to secure the greatest *profit?* The turnover as well as individual unit margin must be considered.
6. *Product Diversification.* Is only one industry served, and is the consumption seasonal? Can other products be fitted into the line so as to promote stability of employment and operations?
7. *Quality.* What is trade opinion on this factor? Does analysis of returns and allowances support the results of field reports?
8. *Design and Styling.* What are the prevailing opinions on this point? Should a market study be made on this aspect?
9. *Identification.* Through the use of brand names, trademarks, method of packaging, and similar devices, is the company securing the maximum transfer of goodwill between products?

Answers to such product considerations as the foregoing will provide a sound basis for business planning. Moreover, such a review can be instrumental in changing the objective of the company as to the area of activity.

THE MARKET

After a thorough understanding of the product has been secured, the next logical spot for study is the market in which it must be sold. Successful marketing of a product requires a good product, properly priced, and an effective method of selling and distribution. Market knowledge is thus seen to be essential in any business planning.

Information about the market may be secured from two sources: (1) a study of the internal records of the company, and (2) the analysis of data from external sources. Both the qualitative considerations of the market—information as to customer characteristics, such as who buys what, and how—as well as the quantitative phases—how much of and where the product is to be sold—must be critically studied. Suggestive of the market information which a company should possess are the following:

1. *Data on Present Customers.* These may be secured through an analysis of internal records:
   a. Who buys
   b. Location
   c. Volume of sales for each
   d. Profitability
   e. Size of orders
   f. Method of delivery
2. *Seasonal or Cyclical Characteristics.* Secured from industry sales data as well as company records.
3. *Market Potentials.* A determination of reasonably expected sales volume by products, by territory, by industry, and by customers is essential to the intelligent direction of selling effort. Such data may be developed from government and industry data in conjunction with internal records.
4. *Customer Purchasing Habits, Buying Preferences, Etc.* May be secured through field surveys.
5. *Competitive Activity.* Usually secured through sales channels, trade paper reports, and similar sources.
6. *Technical Advances.* Such developments may affect the demand for the product, whether in the same line or in competitive product types.

This information is fundamental to the development of a sound marketing plan.

THE DISTRIBUTION PROGRAM

With a knowledge of the product and the market, the effectiveness of reaching that market must then be examined. This sphere of activity is generally known as sales management, and involves a great many considerations. Suggestive of the subjects to be covered in the review or audit are these:

1. *Selection and Training of Salesmen.* What is the program? Its cost? How does it compare with competitive practice?
2. *Selection of Channels of Distribution and Methods of Sale.* Are the methods as effective as those used by competition? Are the number and types of outlets adequate? What is the relative profitability of the various channels or methods of sale employable?
3. *Determination of Sales Quotas.* Are they related to market potentials? On what basis are they changed?
4. *Sales Territories.* Is full coverage provided? Is the company selling in territories too far from home—uneconomical territories?
5. *Routing of Salesmen.* Are the men economically routed? Does a supervisor aid them? How are calls planned?
6. *Advertising and Sales Promotion Aids.* Are the programs correlated with the sales effort? Is the coverage adequate? Is there coverage where no sales outlets are available?
7. *Salesmen's Compensation.* Does the basis of compensation provide incentive? Does the method secure the type of salesman the company wants? Is there a definite relationship between such compensation and desired sales volume?
8. *Price Policies.* How are prices set? Is provision made for an adequate margin? How is price competition met? On what basis are prices set when business volume is low? How are differing costs of production recognized in quantity brackets?
9. *Other Sales Policies.*
   a. On returns and allowances
   b. On entertainment
   c. As to use of company cars
   d. As to terms of sale
10. *Distribution Costs.* Are the following costs known?
    a. Distribution costs by territories, by salesmen, by product, or such segment as may be applicable
    b. Costs per dollars of sales, per call
    c. Freight equalization by areas
    d. By functions, such as warehouse handling, credits and collections, packaging, order handling
    Have distribution cost standards been set, such as number of calls per day, dollars of sales per call, cost per mile traveled?

Such information will reveal the strong and weak points of the company from the marketing viewpoint.

THE PRODUCTION PLAN

When the major characteristics of the product, its market, and the program for reaching that market are known, the next logical area of study is the plan for manufacturing the product. There are three major subdivisions:

1. Materials, parts, and supplies.
2. Plant and facilities.
3. Production process.

Among the topics which need to be considered are the following:

1. *Materials, Parts and Supplies.*
   a. Relative share of cost represented by raw materials or purchased parts
   b. Sources of raw material and their adequacy
   c. Program of reviewing materials and searching for cheaper substitutes
   d. Competitive position in regard to raw materials
   e. Method of inventory control

2. *Plant and Facilities.*
   a. *Location:*
      1) Location of manufacturing facility in relation to major market. Are freight costs, including freight equalization, high?
      2) Location in relation to raw materials. Again, the problem of freight costs arises.
      3) Location of warehouse facilities in relation to market.
   b. *Layout and adequacy:*
      1) Layout of equipment. Is plant layout such as to avoid or minimize back-handling of material in the manufacturing process?
      2) Adequacy of space. Is there adequate space for the storage of raw materials and finished goods? Or must expensive public warehousing be used? Is sufficient space made available for the service departments?
      3) Plant capacity. What is normal capacity? Maximum? In relation to market?

3. *Production Process.*
   a. Extent of time and methods study. Is there a planned program for cost reduction?
   b. Method of determining and revising bill of material

   c. Existence of incentive plan for hourly labor as well as super-vision

   d. Production control system

   e. Labor rates in relation to market

   f. Inspection and quality control methods

   g. Maintenance program—existence of preventive maintenance program, knowledge of maintenance cost by piece of equipment, etc.

   h. Relative production costs as compared to competitors

Such a review should reveal the strength and weakness of the production facilities and methods.

RESEARCH AND DEVELOPMENT PROGRAM

To an increasing degree the life of a business enterprise is dependent upon an adequate program for the development and improvement of the company's products. While the chemical industry is often given as a prime example, the principle is applicable to most industries. These points will provide a background for appraisal of this function:

1. What new or improved products have been developed in the past five years? What share of total sales do they represent?

2. What is the nature of the research program? Are *specific* projects assigned for research purposes and periodically reviewed as to progress? Are probable benefits measured against cost?

3. What is the extent of correlation between the research department and the sales department as to new products? Is there a smooth transfer from a laboratory product status to a commercial status?

4. How do the expenditures for research and development compare with industry or competition as to total amount or per cent of sales dollar?

5. To what extent are independent laboratories used to add flexibility to the research staff?

FINANCIAL STRENGTH AND ORGANIZATION

Financial or accounting controls will be reviewed in succeeding chapters. Discussion here relates to the non-control phases. In brief, sufficient financial strength must be available to carry out the sales, production, and research programs. As a general survey of this aspect, the following matters should be checked:

1. *Soundness of Financial Structure.*

   a. Sources of working capital

   b. Analysis by use of ratios

   c. Nature of indebtedness

   d. General credit standing

2. *Return on Investment.*
    a. Adequacy as related to total assets used in business
    b. Adequacy as related to net worth

THE CONTROL SYSTEM

The last important business factor to be considered in a management audit is the control system. Preceding sections have dealt with a review of the specialized functions of the enterprise—distribution, manufacturing, research, and finance. Yet, it is not enough that each of these activities be seemingly well-performed in and of itself. Management must *know* that these tasks are being efficiently executed; there must be little guesswork. Furthermore, each activity must be kept in balance with the related activity. For example, the production program must keep step with the sales program. Inventories must be kept ample to meet customer needs, but should not become unduly high. And how are these things accomplished? Just as the mortar binds the bricks in a building, so also the accounting control system provides the information and procedures for the proper guidance of the business and the coordination and proper integration.

Why is such a system necessary? When the enterprise is small, direct or *personal* observation and control may be exercised by the owner or manager. However, as the size of the organization grows, this high degree of personal contact between each individual employee and the manager is largely lost. Another means of control becomes necessary, and this means is an adequate reporting system. Fundamentally, the process becomes one of:

1. Setting a standard of measurement
2. Comparing actual and standard performance
3. Ferreting out the cause of variance
4. Taking the necessary corrective action

The standards must be set by those best qualified by experience to judge exactly what constitutes good, acceptable performance. Actual results must be reported by an independent and unbiased agency—the accounting department—and compared with the standard. From appropriately designed reports, those whose performance is being measured must be advised of their progress. Similarly, management is advised of the degree of performance, trends, and relationships. Through the use of such reports, management is enabled to plan, supervise, evaluate, and coordinate the activities of the various departments or divisions.

Accounting control of operations is the use of accounting and statistical reports as part of a well-conceived plan to maintain the pressures necessary for efficiency, and to expose unfavorable trends or variations. Thus, it can be seen that such control is a necessary ingredient in modern business management.

SUMMARY

The business factors discussed in the preceding sections are, in the opinion of the authors, fundamental. An understanding of each of these, as practiced in his company, would give each accounting executive or controller a sound foundation on which to build his contribution as part of a sound management team. Without this perspective his efforts must indeed be relegated to a narrower, more specialized, and less fruitful area of activity.

4

Some Over-All Yardsticks
of Financial Performance

THE NEED FOR SOME OVER-ALL TESTS

Much of the discussion in this book is devoted to planning and control of specific parts of the business enterprise. Yet, each of these areas is but a segment of the business. While the controller necessarily must consider each function in the business, it is still desirable that over-all tests or measurements be used. The fact that each individual area might appear to be satisfactory does not necessarily warrant the conclusion that the entire business is moving properly toward its objective. Further, if management is to do a good job, it must have readily available ways and means of judging its over-all performance. Then too, the financial community rather continuously attempts to judge the financial capabilities of those companies in which it has an interest. These same groups seek techniques of making their determinations simply and quickly, without the necessity of reviewing a mass of detail.

Under the circumstances, the need for simple over-all yardsticks is understandable. It is expected that the controller will select the ones most suitable for his company.

AN OUTLINE OF SOME GENERAL YARDSTICKS

Under free enterprise capitalism, and within the scope of social objectives of the business enterprise, management is expected to make a profit. One might say that management is expected to make the optimum *money* on *money* over a period of time. This goal serves as the underlying clue to the more important over-all tests of financial performance.

Some suggested broad yardsticks which company management may utilize in judging its performance, whether by itself or in relationship to competitors, other companies, or other industries, are as follows:

1. *Profitability*
   a. Per cent return on net sales
   b. Per cent return on owner equity
   c. Per cent return on total capital employed

2. *Growth*
   a. Per cent increase in sales
   b. Per cent increase in earnings per common share

Although emphasis in this chapter is on the total business picture, these same controls or tests may be effectively applied to individual segments of the business, such as divisions or product groups or subsidiaries.

These ratios apply to actual results which may be compared readily with actual results of other business concerns. They are in addition to the forecasting or budget comparisons described in Part II, which provide another type of over-all business control principally for internal applications.

LIMITS TO THE USE OF OVER-ALL TESTS

Useful though they are, statistical guides are not the ultimate measures of management ability. Mere figures cannot tell the entire story, and those who use them should be aware of their limitations. For example, these percentages cannot take into account the relative difficulties of the task; the possibility that the management with the best ratios is also the management with the easiest job. Further, a wise management may be laying the groundwork for sound growth. Consequently, a company may not be shown at its best in statistical compilations over a short-term period. In the reverse situation, a company showing good performance in these measurements may be omitting some function, such as research and development, which is essential to its long-term growth.

Concisely stated, it is important that the figures be properly interpreted and that they be regarded as measures of *financial* performance and not of the entire gamut of the management field.

PER CENT RETURN ON NET SALES

One of the most commonly encountered measures of profitability is the relationship of net income to net sales. The ratio, usually expressed as a percentage, indicates what share of the sales dollar is translated into profit. The trend of this relationship is important and should be watched by management.

The widespread use of the income-to-sales ratio permits easy comparison with other companies or with industry performance. The interim and annual reports to shareholders of publicly held corporations facilitate measurement against individual business concerns. In addition, the Federal Trade Commission and the Securities and Exchange Commission are important sources for broad industry averages.[1] Among private groups which also supply useful information are Dun & Bradstreet, Inc., the National Industrial Conference Board, the U. S. Chamber of Commerce, trade associations, and other credit agencies.

Profit as a per cent of net sales has much value, but alone it is an insufficient measure of profitability. That business which produces the highest per cent of net profit to sales (or profit before income taxes to net sales) may not be giving the best financial performance. After all, the measurement of net income against net sales is but one yardstick of profitability.

PER CENT RETURN ON OWNER EQUITY

Another broad profit guide is the relationship of net income to stockholder equity. Where only common stock is outstanding the percentage is determined by dividing net income by the total ownership equity, however described. If preferred stock exists, then earnings must be reduced by preferred stock dividends and related to only the equity of the common shareholders.

A great many business executives feel that the ultimate test of stewardship is the amount of net income produced in relationship to shareholders' capital. For the *owners* of the business this is certainly an important test. The trend should be watched from year to year. In fact, the controller might do well to compare the current year, as well as the forecast, with the past year and the past five years' average.

It may be seen that the financial structure of the business enterprise may have an important bearing on this ratio. Through judicious use of cheaper creditor funds, for example, the return on shareholder capital may be multiplied. This is known as trading on the equity, or leverage.

In using this ratio, as in all others, consideration must be given to the existing circumstances. Thus, if stockholder funds have just been put into a new $20,000,000 chemical plant not yet in operation, then adjustment might be made when comparing rate of return to that of a competitor who has had all facilities "on stream" for a year or so. A companion ratio to return on shareholder equity, also useful in financial circles, is cash flow per dollar of equity. Cash flow is defined as net income plus depreciation and depletion (non-cash book charges).

[1] See "Quarterly Financial Report for Manufacturing Corporations," Washington, D. C.: U. S. Government Printing Office.

RETURN ON CAPITAL EMPLOYED

It is the opinion of the authors that one of the best and most effective over-all measures of financial performance is the ratio of earnings to total capital employed. In fact, if only one simple yardstick could be used, this is the one that should be selected.

Return on capital employed is computed by dividing the net income of the business by the capital employed, and expressing the quotient as a per cent. An underlying assumption in using this guide is that profit, not as an absolute amount but as a return on capital, is the important criterion in judging performance. The goal of management, under such a philosophy, is not to maximize profits alone, but to maximize the return from the *capital devoted to the business*. It logically follows, also, that attention is to be focused on the *use* of capital in generating profit, and not on the *source* of the funds. Management, indeed, is expected to use with equal diligence all assets, regardless of the origin.

Parenthetically, it may be added that the concept has much usefulness in testing the desirability of capital expenditures, in financial planning, and in measuring both division performance and profitability of product lines.

FORMULA FOR RETURN ON CAPITAL EMPLOYED

The factors which affect the rate of return on total investment, and their relationship to each other, are illustrated in Fig. 1. It can be seen that there are two principal elements: (1) earnings on net sales, expressed as a percentage, and (2) turnover. Why consider each element separately?

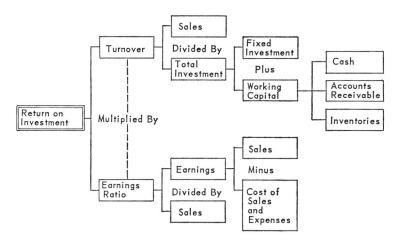

Fig. 1—The Relationship of Major Factors Influencing Return on Investment.

Why not simply divide net income by total investment to determine the rate of return? The answer is that return on capital employed responds to movement in each of these factors, and each therefore must be analyzed. If there has been no change in selling price, then any improvement in the profit-sales ratio indicates cost reduction. If, on the other hand, there is no change in selling price or in total investment, then an improvement in turnover indicates that capital is being utilized more effectively; that management is securing more sales volume out of the same working capital and plant. The management which can control both of these relationships has done much to control over-all corporate financial performance.

The use of two factors has sometimes been a source of confusion. Let us review the formula in algebraic form and then follow it through in two examples. The formula might be set forth in this manner:

$$\frac{\text{Sales}}{\text{Investment}} \times \frac{\text{Profit}}{\text{Sales}} = \text{Return on Investment}$$

or cancel out sales:

$$\frac{\cancel{\text{Sales}}}{\text{Investment}} \times \frac{\text{Profit}}{\cancel{\text{Sales}}} = \frac{\text{Profit}}{\text{Investment}} = \text{Return on Investment}$$

Now assume a company with these results:

Net Sales	$2,000,000
Capital Employed	1,000,000
Net Income	200,000

Applying the formula, it can be determined not only that the return is 20%, but also that the turnover was 2, and earnings on sales was 10%.

$$\frac{\text{Sales}}{\text{Investment}} = \text{Turnover} = \frac{\$2,000,000}{\$1,000,000} = 2$$

$$\frac{\text{Net Income}}{\text{Sales}} = \% \text{ Profit on Sales} = \frac{\$200,000}{\$2,000,000} = 10\%$$

Turnover × Earnings as a % of Sales = Return on Investment

$$2 \times 10\% = 20\%$$

Now assume the company is able to accomplish these results:

Net Sales	$3,000,000
Investment	1,250,000
Net Income	270,000

Then, what is the return on capital employed?   Has the company improved in its use of capital, and why?

$$\text{Turnover is calculated: } \frac{\$3,000,000}{\$1,250,000} = 2.4 \text{ times}$$

$$\text{\% Return on Net Sales is determined: } \frac{\$270,000}{\$3,000,000} = 9\%$$

Consequently, the return on investment is 2.4 × 9% or 21.6%.

This was achieved through a 20% higher turnover rate and a 10% drop in rate of net income to sales.

It would be logical to review competitive results to form an opinion as to the optimum or most desirable turnover rates and the optimum profit per cent of net sales.   The next step would be to determine what improvement this management should make, longer-term results considered.

It might be well to keep a chart showing trends as in Fig. 2.   If month-to-month results are plotted, it is desirable to average the capital employed at the beginning and end of the period and to annualize the earnings.

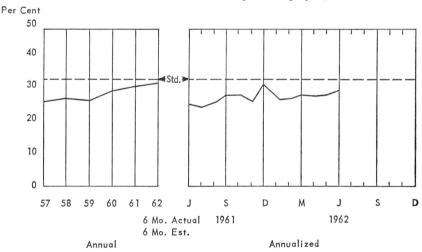

The Illustrative Company

COMPARATIVE RETURN ON CAPITAL EMPLOYED
(Income as Per Cent of Capital Employed)

Fig. 2—Comparative Return on Capital Employed.

The Johnson Company
Sales Revenue

Description	Current Year Annualized		Last Year	2 Years ago
	Actual	Forecast		
Net Sales ($M)	37,896	37,000	35,011	34,260
Less: Non-recurring items	560	—	211	40
Price changes	70	70	300	260
As adjusted	37,266	36,930	34,500	33,960
Increase (Decrease) from Prior Year	2,766		540	1,070
% Change	8.1		1.6	3.3

Fig. 3—Worksheet for

3 Years ago	4 Years ago	5 Years ago				
33,190	31,010	29,660				
— 300	— 100	— 100				
32,890	30,910	29,560				
1,980	1,350					
6.4	4.6					

Summary Sales Analysis.

DEFINITION OF CAPITAL EMPLOYED

One point needing further clarification is "capital employed." Much has been written on just what should be included and the basis of valuation. It is the experience of the authors, however, that it should include the sum total of all of the assets used in the business. In short, it is the "total assets" figure at the bottom of the conventional statement of financial condition, adjusted for assets not used in earning the operating results, e.g., investments in and advances to other enterprises, marketable securities, assets held primarily for long-term appreciation, fixed assets completed and not in operation, and perhaps goodwill. On this basis of computation, fixed assets would be included at their depreciated value. Some authorities advocate the inclusion of fixed assets at gross value. Conventionally, however, depreciation is treated as an expense, reducing the net income. If the cost of fixed assets is not reduced by cumulative depreciation, then in effect it is expected the enterprise will continue earning a return on something already expensed, and this does not seem logical. Also, funds made available through depreciation charges are re-invested either in other fixed assets or in working capital. Moreover, such treatment does not place the heavy burden on worn-out or obsolete assets which perhaps incur heavy maintenance costs. Furthermore, within a company, when the assets reflected in published financial statements are used, there is more ready acceptance of the return-on-capital-employed figure.

A valuation problem sometimes arises as to the use of original cost in contrast to replacement cost. Proponents of replacement value argue that such a basis is necessary to combat the instability of our economy, and that business managers should match current earnings against current costs of capital. In this and related problems, choice of a base should depend upon company thinking, the nature of the assets, the use to be made of the ratio. While the authors support the total assets (net of depreciation) as the most practicable base, including facility of comparison with competition and industry figures, consistency in treatment is to be emphasized. Trends are significant in making observations.

PER CENT INCREASE IN SALES

In addition to the profitability indexes discussed, consideration might well be given to the growth picture. One measure of growth is in net sales. Many business executives want to know how sales volume has changed in each of the past five years. This rate of increase can be measured against competition and industry to judge relative performance.

Within the controller's own company some more useful refinements may be developed, for example:

1. The share of sales gains due to higher prices vs. movement of more units
2. The share due to abnormal or "windfall" conditions

An illustration of a simple worksheet form which the controller can prepare is shown in Fig. 3. Of course, mere sales volume is not sufficient. Consideration must be given to the quality of sales as reflected in the profits earned.

PER CENT INCREASE IN PER SHARE EARNINGS

This introduces another measure of growth—the change in earnings. Earnings are a relative thing, and must therefore be judged against competitive or industry performance. Moreover, in an age of expansion by acquisition, sometimes a percentage change from year to year does not take into account earnings from acquired companies purchased through exchange of stock. Hence, some thought should be given to this growth as reflected in per share earnings. Other things being equal, a large share of aggregate net income brought down to *per share* net income indicates either avoidance of dilution, or the wise use of borrowed capital, or the intelligent employment of plowed-back earnings.

Therefore, not only should net income in the absolute and its year-to-year changes be considered, but also the changes per share of common stock outstanding.

A variation of earnings per share, useful to the financial group, is the change in cash flow per common share from year to year.

SUMMARY

The emphasis in this chapter has been on the return-on-capital-employed concept as the best measure of management's financial performance. In addition, other supplementary ratios have been suggested as over-all guides which shed some light on the progress being made by management in improving the company's position.

The use of a *few* sound relationships has much to recommend it, in contrast to the deluging of top management with many ratios and trends. The controller, indeed, may maintain a chart book which is exhaustive in its scope and which is primarily an analytical tool for *his own use,* to better explain to management the background and reasons for the conditions. Perhaps periodically he may discuss more detailed trends with top management, or with the second echelon of management. In general, emphasis should be on *analysis* by the controller to the degree he feels necessary, but *simplicity* in what is presented to management.

The value of some of the more detailed relationships as a means of comparing performance or condition and as applied to certain segments of the business is explained in the next chapter.

5

Financial and Operating Ratios, Trends, and Relationships

USE OF RATIOS

In order to know relative progress or relative condition, it is necessary to have some measures of comparison. And what is more natural than for business management to want to compare itself with competition—either individual companies or industry averages? Some of these comparisons will be used only by financial management, and others will be valuable to over-all and functional executives in other fields.

Almost anyone with some knowledge and experience in financial matters can review one or more of a series of statements and arrive at some logical conclusions about the business. However, the use of dollar figures by themselves is very often misleading. For example, an annual net income of $5,000,000 may sound quite large. Yet if one is given further information that such net income is but ¼ % of sales or ⅛ % of the net worth, then a better perspective is secured.

This difficulty in using absolute amounts has led to the adoption of ratios as a more understandable means of measuring trends and relationships. Experience has shown that proportions or relationships are at least as significant as the dollar figures. Use of ratios can make the financial statements more meaningful to management.

RATIOS AVAILABLE

Some *over-all* measures of performance are discussed in Chapter 4. In addition, a sizable number of ratios have been developed for analyzing financial statements with particular reference to a specific segment of a business. Some of the more common ones are explained in the following paragraphs.

For discussion purposes, three main groups of ratios may be distinguished: (1) financial ratios, (2) financial-operating ratios, and (3) operating ratios. In addition, there are numerous miscellaneous ratios.

Financial ratios as here used are those expressing a relationship between the various items on the same balance sheet. Some of the more commonly used financial ratios are:

   a. Current assets to current liabilities
   b. Cash, receivables, and marketable securities to current liabilities
   c. Net worth to total assets
   d. Net worth to fixed assets

Financial-operating ratios express a relationship between certain balance sheet items and items in the statement of income and expense. A few of the more widely used are:

   a. Net sales to receivables
   b. Cost of goods sold to inventory
   c. Net sales to current assets
   d. Net sales to working capital
   e. Net sales to plant investment
   f. Net sales to total assets
   g. Maintenance expense to fixed assets
   h. Depreciation to fixed assets
   i. Net income to net worth

Operating ratios express a relationship between different items in the statement of income and expense. Included in this category are the following:

   a. Sales deductions to gross sales
   b. Gross profit to net sales
   c. Cost of goods sold to net sales
   d. Operating expenses to net sales
   e. Net income to net sales
   f. Salaries and wages to net sales
   g. Sales discounts to net sales
   h. Purchase discounts to purchases
   i. Indirect labor expense to direct labor

Finally, there is a group of miscellaneous ratios which permits useful comparisons:

   a. Number of times fixed charges are earned
   b. Dividends to net profit
   c. Earnings per share of common stock

  d. Book value of common stock
  e. Average amount of fixed assets per employee
  f. Average stockholder investment per employee
  g. Average hourly wage rate
  h. Average yearly wage per employee

NEED FOR STANDARD RATIOS

As is discussed in Part III, an important factor in control of performance is comparison with a proper measuring stick. So also, in analyzing financial and operating relationships, and in judging the significance of trends, much the same need exists. Ratio and trend analysis tends to lose a great deal of its significance except when judged by proper standards—standard ratios.

A number of standards of comparison may be available to the controller. Because each industry has its own characteristics which influence the operating and financial relationships, it is more desirable to use measures of the particular industry than those of business generally. The standards of comparison may include any or all of the following:

  1. Ratios of the individual industry of which the company is a member
  2. Ratios of competing companies, particularly the more progressive ones
  3. Past experience of the company itself
  4. General relationships developed by the controller or others, based on observation and past experience

Such standards as these do not have the exactness of factory standards set by time and motion studies, and should be considered in this light when evaluating a company's position. Though a ratio may depart substantially from the standard, the first impression of a weak position may not be supported. Differences in accounting policy, geographic location, depreciation or amortization policy, credit policy, ownership vs. leasing of properties, or integration vs. buying of many processed materials—all these may substantially affect the ratios. The specific condition of the business may result in very different ratios. Such factors must be properly weighed in comparing a single company's position with ratios which usually are averages.

Standard ratios are available from several sources. These include the Securities and Exchange Commission, publications of Dun & Bradstreet, Inc., private institutions of business research, and Moody's Manuals.

Since many published standard ratios are averages, and are thus greatly influenced by extremely high or low figures, the controller may consider creation of his own standards. If such a project is undertaken, sound principles of statistical compilation should be followed. Though arithmetic averages can be used, it may be found desirable to calculate the median or modal figures. Again, the interquartile range may be found most useful.

TRENDS EXPRESSED BY PERCENTAGES

Before reviewing in detail some of the ratios commonly employed in evaluating financial statements, it may be well to consider some of the simpler and more effective tools available for use. Financial statements can be studied in a number of different ways—in addition to a review of the absolute data. One already mentioned is the relationship between figures in the same statement or in the related operating statement. Another is the compilation of trends by means of percentages. Still a third method is the preparation of percentage statements.

Controllers are often so deeply engrossed in the current problems that they fail to watch trends. It is occasionally no small source of amazement to find some very revealing figures with little expenditure of effort—through the use of trend percentages. The technique is somewhat similar to that used in calculating index numbers. A base period is selected and given a weighting of 100. Each similar item in other periods is related to the comparable value of the base period. It is a simple division problem. An increase will result in a percentage greater than 100; and a decrease, in a percentage less than 100. Selection of the base period is important, for it must be typical or representative. Otherwise, comparisons will give evidence of extreme conditions when such are not the case.

As a practical matter, it may not be desirable or necessary to apply such a technique to all the items in a statement, but rather only to those values which should bear some relationship to each other. Thus the cost of goods sold should show a certain relationship to sales; or accounts receivable should increase somewhat in proportion to an increase in sales. Further, in planning the use of trend statements, the absolute data are not to be ignored. A major increase percentagewise may be insignificant from a dollar standpoint, and little time should be wasted in considering such an item.

The raw data from which trends may be determined, and which usually should be a part of any interpretative report, are illustrated in Figs. 4 and 5. The trend statement is developed simply by dividing each yearly value by that of the base year (or multiplying by the reciprocal), and results in data similar to Fig. 6. In this example, 1956 has been selected as a normal business year.

ILLUSTRATIVE INTERPRETATION OF TRENDS

The financial statements of The Plastic Corporation show, for example, the growth in current assets, current liabilities, and net worth. But it is not easy to determine whether or not the inventories and receivables have increased unduly. Figure 6, the trend percentages, facilitates a quick comparison, when used in conjunction with Figs. 4 and 5.

The Plastic Corporation

CONDENSED COMPARATIVE STATEMENT OF FINANCIAL CONDITION

As of December 31, 1956 Through 1962

Description	1956	1957	1958	1959	1960	1961	1962
ASSETS							
Current Assets							
Cash	$ 20,000	$ 25,000	$ 25,000	$ 50,000	$ 40,000	$ 30,000	$ 35,000
Receivables, Net	80,000	83,000	83,000	84,000	117,000	134,000	137,000
Marketable Securities	10,000	10,000	10,000	—	—	—	—
Inventories	90,000	92,000	93,000	92,000	128,000	145,000	151,000
Total Current Assets	200,000	210,000	211,000	226,000	285,000	309,000	323,000
Fixed Assets							
Land and Buildings, Net	20,000	20,000	19,000	20,000	25,000	24,000	24,000
Machinery and Equipment, Net	80,000	81,000	81,000	103,000	142,000	146,000	160,000
Total Fixed Assets	100,000	101,000	100,000	123,000	167,000	170,000	184,000
Total Assets	$300,000	$311,000	$311,000	$349,000	$452,000	$479,000	$507,000
LIABILITIES AND NET WORTH							
Liabilities							
Current Liabilities							
Accounts Payable	$ 40,000	$ 41,000	$ 43,000	$ 42,000	$ 82,000	$110,000	$120,000
Accrued Salaries and Wages	5,000	6,000	3,000	7,000	10,000	12,000	10,000
Accrued Taxes	15,000	16,000	19,000	22,000	13,000	17,000	18,000
Total Current Liabilities	60,000	63,000	65,000	71,000	105,000	139,000	148,000
Mortgage Payable	30,000	25,000	20,000	40,000	45,000	45,000	65,000
Total Liabilities	90,000	88,000	85,000	111,000	150,000	184,000	213,000
Net Worth							
Capital Stock	100,000	100,000	100,000	100,000	170,000	170,000	180,000
Earned Surplus	110,000	123,000	126,000	138,000	132,000	125,000	114,000
Total Net Worth	210,000	223,000	226,000	238,000	302,000	295,000	294,000
Total Liabilities and Net Worth	$300,000	$311,000	$311,000	$349,000	$452,000	$479,000	$507,000

Fig. 4—Comparative Statement of Financial Condition.

The Plastic Corporation

CONDENSED COMPARATIVE STATEMENT OF INCOME AND EXPENSE

For the Years Ended December 31, 1956 Through 1962

Description	1956	1957	1958	1959	1960	1961	1962
Net Sales............	$400,000	$420,000	$422,000	$428,000	$510,000	$590,000	$620,000
Cost of Goods Sold....	265,000	270,000	275,000	281,000	368,000	421,000	437,000
Gross Profit.........	135,000	150,000	147,000	147,000	142,000	169,000	183,000
Operating Expenses....	100,000	103,000	104,000	105,000	125,000	147,000	159,000
Operating Profit......	35,000	47,000	43,000	42,000	17,000	22,000	24,000
Other Income and Expenses......	5,000	4,000	6,000	3,000	4,000	3,000	4,000
Profit Before Taxes......	40,000	51,000	49,000	45,000	21,000	25,000	28,000
Federal Income Taxes......	8,000	10,000	12,000	13,000	6,000	10,000	11,000
Net Profit...........	$ 32,000	$ 41,000	$ 37,000	$ 32,000	$ 15,000	$ 15,000	$ 17,000

Fig. 5—Comparative Statement of Income and Expense.

The Plastic Corporation

SELECTED COMPARATIVE PERCENTAGES

For the Period 1956 Through 1962

(1956—100%)

	1956	1957	1958	1959	1960	1961	1962
FINANCIAL CONDITION (As of 12/31)							
Cash	100	125	125	250	200	150	175
Receivables, Net	100	104	104	105	146	167	171
Inventories	100	102	103	102	142	161	168
Total Current Assets	100	105	106	113	143	155	162
Fixed Assets	100	101	100	123	167	170	184
Total Assets	100	104	104	116	151	160	169
Current Liabilities	100	105	108	118	175	232	247
Long-Term Debt	100	83	67	133	150	150	217
Capital Stock	100	100	100	100	170	170	180
Surplus	100	112	115	125	120	114	104
Total Net Worth	100	106	108	113	144	140	140
STATEMENT OF INCOME AND EXPENSE							
Net Sales	100	105	106	107	127	147	155
Cost of Goods Sold	100	102	104	106	139	159	165
Gross Profit	100	111	109	109	105	125	136
Operating Expenses	100	103	104	105	125	147	159
Operating Profit	100	134	123	120	49	63	69
Net Profit	100	128	116	100	47	47	53

Fig. 6—Trend Statement, Using Percentages.

For the period 1956–59 the company experienced a gradual growth in net sales so that sales in the year 1959 were 107% of 1956. Cost of goods sold also increased some, but at a slower rate. Consequently, the gross profit margin was more favorable—109% of the 1956 base year. This condition was not unreasonable because of the fixed element in the cost of sales. A further analysis would reveal how important a role the volume increase played. Operating expenses increased somewhat; but the corporation also experienced a growth at a slower rate than net sales. The combined effect of these favorable factors was a rise in operating profit to 134% in 1957, and 120% in 1959, as compared with the base year.

This growth was also evidenced in the balance sheet. The total net worth, all of it in the earned surplus section, gradually grew larger so that in 1959 it was 113% of the 1956 level. The current assets were in relatively good shape in that the rate of increase in receivables and inventories was less than that of net sales or cost of sales, thus evidencing a faster turnover. To be sure, there was a tendency to allow current liabilities to increase at a faster rate than sales, but this was largely the result of increasing state income taxes. Further than that, the current ratio was well over 2 to 1. The mortgage payable was reduced until 1959, when an expansion began.

This expansion made itself felt in 1960 through 1962. Beginning in 1960 several unfavorable trends developed. Net sales increased tremendously; but the cost of sales climbed at an even higher rate, so that the gross profit suffered correspondingly. Here, again, further analysis would provide information as to the effect of volume. Operating expenses were not well controlled in that they kept pace with the rate of sales increase in 1961 and surpassed it in 1962. These factors, together with heavier taxes, reduced net profit to 53% of the 1956 level, despite sales in 1962 of 155% of the 1956 level. To compound errors, as it were, the company continued dividend payments at a rate higher than net profit. The effect was to permit a reduction of earned surplus from 125% in 1959 to only 103% in 1962.

The sales expansion was accompanied by, or resulted from, the physical plant growth. While some funds were secured through the issuance of additional capital stock, an increase in long-term debt was permitted. Current liabilities grew at a more rapid rate than sales or current assets with a result that in 1962 they were 247% of the 1956 level, whereas current assets were only 162% of this same base period. While the current ratio was not as favorable in the latter years, the cash and receivables were more than adequate to cover the current liabilities. This is some indication that the best use of funds was not made in the early period. However, it is to be observed that the rate of increase in receivables and inventories is substantially greater than the corresponding increase in net sales. A net sales percentage of 155 in 1962 compares to 171 and 168 for receivables and inventories, respectively, for the same period. This indicates a tendency

Comparative Statement of Financial Condition

SELECTED CHEMICAL COMPANIES

As of December 31, 1959

	The Dow Company		The Santo Company		Cyanamid, Inc.	
	Amount	%	Amount	%	Amount	%
ASSETS						
Current Assets						
Cash	$ 150,000	2.45	$ 300,000	3.68	$ 410,000	6.90
Receivables	900,000	14.71	1,665,000	20.44	930,000	15.66
Inventories	750,000	12.26	1,105,000	13.57	775,000	13.05
Other	100,000	1.63	10,000	.12	5,000	.08
Total Current Assets	1,900,000	31.05	3,080,000	37.81	2,120,000	35.69
Fixed Assets						
Land and Buildings, Net	120,000	1.96	175,000	2.15	200,000	3.37
Machinery and Equipment, Net	4,100,000	66.99	4,890,000	60.04	3,620,000	60.94
Total Fixed Assets	4,220,000	68.95	5,065,000	62.19	3,820,000	64.31
Total Assets	$6,120,000	100.00	$8,145,000	100.00	$5,940,000	100.00
LIABILITIES AND NET WORTH						
Current Liabilities						
Accounts Payable	$ 205,000	3.35	$ 410,000	5.03	$ 507,000	8.54
Accrued Salaries and Wages	42,000	.69	89,000	1.09	92,000	1.55
Accrued Taxes	575,000	9.39	865,000	10.62	705,000	11.87
Total Current Liabilities	822,000	13.43	1,364,000	16.74	1,304,000	21.96
Long-Term Liabilities	–	–	120,000	1.48	400,000	6.73
Total Liabilities	822,000	13.43	1,484,000	18.22	1,704,000	28.69
Net Worth						
Capital Stock	$3,500,000	57.19	3,000,000	36.83	2,750,000	46.30
Capital Surplus	500,000	8.17	–	–	–	–
Earned Surplus	1,298,000	21.21	3,661,000	44.95	1,486,000	25.01
Total Net Worth	5,298,000	86.57	6,661,000	81.78	4,236,000	71.31
Total Liabilities and Net Worth	$6,120,000	100.00	$8,145,000	100.00	$5,940,000	100.00

Fig. 7—Comparative Statement of Financial Condition—Amounts and Percentages.

toward a slower turnover in these categories. Further analysis is desirable to determine the cause.

The above comments are an extremely simple illustration of the use of trend percentages as an assistance in interpreting financial statements.

PERCENTAGE STATEMENTS

The controller may often be interested in comparing the financial statements of different companies in the same industry, and in checking the distribution of expenses in the income and expense statement or assets and liabilities in the balance sheet. This is accomplished more readily by using percentages instead of the actual dollars. Such a method is another approach in analyzing statements—the use of percentage components, often called common-size statements.

Most companies employ this analysis in some degree for the income and expense statements for internal management purposes and usually include percentages relating all costs, expenses, and income to the net sales. The use of percentages on the balance sheet is less extensive. In any event the technique is merely that of considering the total assets, and total liabilities and net worth in the balance sheet, and the net sales in the statement of income and expense, as each equal to 100%. All other items in the statement are related, as percentages, to the base. The same approach may be used for subsections of a statement. Such a device will indicate the distribution of the items, but will not give evidence of growth or decline. Thus, cash may be 2% of the total assets in one year, and only 1% in another year. It cannot be concluded that less cash is available, because the total assets may have expanded considerably while the cash remained about the same.

PERCENTAGE STATEMENTS ILLUSTRATED

Common-size statements may be prepared for a company and comparisons made from month to month and from year to year. Another application is the comparison with competing companies. Such statements are illustrated in Figs. 7 and 8. Some of the significant features in evaluating the comparative strength of the companies which are revealed more clearly by the use of percentages are:

Statement of Financial Condition

1. The Dow Company has only 2.45% of its assets in cash, while Cyanamid, Inc. has 6.90%. The former may have too small a cash balance to operate most effectively. Reference to other years' experience will indicate the trend. Further analysis may be necessary to determine a reasonable amount.
2. The Santo Company has a much heavier proportion of its property in the form of receivables—20.44% as compared with only

Comparative Statement of Income and Expense
SELECTED CHEMICAL COMPANIES
For the Year Ended December 31, 1959

	The Dow Company		The Santo Company		Cyanamid, Inc.	
	Amount	%	Amount	%	Amount	%
Net Sales	$4,300,000	100.00	$7,100,000	100.00	$5,900,000	100.00
Cost of Goods Sold	3,010,000	70.00	5,360,500	75.50	4,307,000	73.00
Gross Margin	1,290,000	30.00	1,739,500	24.50	1,593,000	27.00
Operating Expenses						
Administrative and General	86,000	2.00	177,500	2.50	118,000	2.00
Selling and Advertising	172,000	4.00	248,500	3.50	177,000	3.00
Research and Development	172,000	4.00	71,000	1.00	177,000	3.00
Total Operating Expenses	430,000	10.00	497,000	7.00	472,000	8.00
Operating Profit	860,000	20.00	1,242,500	17.50	1,121,000	19.00
Other Income (net)	4,300	.10	35,500	.50	5,900	.10
Profit Before Federal Income Taxes	864,300	20.10	1,278,000	18.00	1,126,900	19.10
Provision for Federal Income Taxes	516,000	12.00	766,800	10.80	672,600	11.40
Net Profit	$ 348,300	8.10	$ 511,200	7.20	$ 454,300	7.70

Fig. 8—Comparative Statement of Income and Expense—Amounts and Percentages.

14.71% for Dow Company and 15.66% for Cyanamid. The trend of receivables and sales may be compared for several years to determine whether or not this particular year is out of line. The turnover of receivables is about 4.25 for Santo and 4.8 for Dow. This can be some indication that the credit and collection policy of the latter is more efficient.

3. The investment in inventories is proportionately much the same for each of the companies. In fact Dow would appear in a slightly more favorable position in that it has the smallest share of assets in inventories. However, a comparison of turnover rates indicates a "turn" of only 4 times for Dow; 4.85 times for Santo; and 5.56 times for Cyanamid. If these inventories are representative for the year, then Dow appears to have an overinvestment in this category. Further analysis is desirable.

4. A relatively larger share of Dow properties is in the form of fixed assets—68.95%, contrasted to 62.19% for Santo and 64.31% for Cyanamid. Further analysis of turnover as measured by the relationship of cost of sales to plant investment reveals a serious overinvestment in fixed assets. Trends should be studied. Further analysis is indicated.

5. The Dow Company is the most conservatively financed corporation of the three. Whereas 86.57% of its capital is furnished by the owners, only 71.31% of Cyanamid capital is from stockholders.

6. The current liabilities of Cyanamid, Inc. are 21.96% of total liabilities and net worth; but only 13.43% and 16.74% respectively of the capital for Dow and Santo is furnished by current creditors.

Statement of Income and Expense

1. From the standpoint of gross margin, Dow is in the most favorable position. The average gross margin was 30% of sales; but Santo secured a gross of only 24.5% of net sales. Cyanamid was somewhat better with a margin of 27%. Trends should be analyzed.

2. However, ten cents out of every sales dollar of Dow is used for operating expenses. This offsets some of the advantages of the higher gross, for operating expenses of Santo were only 7% of net sales; and those of Cyanamid were 8% of net sales.

It will be observed that 4% of net sales is spent by Dow for research and development activity—much more than Santo, which spent only 1%—and more than the 3% expended by Cyanamid. This may be the reason for the higher gross margin. Also, it may indicate a forward-looking management.

FINANCIAL RATIOS

CURRENT RATIO

One of the most widely used ratios, particularly among credit men, is the current ratio. It is calculated by dividing the total current assets of a company by the total current liabilities. For example, a firm having current assets of $290,000 and current liabilities of $110,000 is said to have a current ratio of 2.64 to 1. Expressed in another manner, the current ratio is 264%, or current assets are 264% of current liabilities.

A ratio of 2 to 1 has long been considered as reflecting a satisfactory condition. The ratio is presumed to measure in some degree the liquidity of the business, or the ability of the concern to meet its current obligations. It must be realized, of course, that the type of business as well as the seasonal characteristics may affect the current ratio. Therefore, it would be unwise to conclude, without further review, that a current ratio of less than 2 to 1 was unsatisfactory. Again, it can be seen that the ratio is only one indicator. A company might have a very high current ratio and be in a poor liquid condition in that a heavy inventory might make up most of the current assets. Further, the accounts receivable might be questionable. The controller will realize that (1) other relationships in the current asset group must be considered and (2) in his own company current assets should be properly valued.

QUICK RATIO

A supplemental ratio to the current ratio is known variously as the "quick" ratio or "acid test." This is the relationship of cash plus receivables plus marketable securities to the current liabilities.

$$\frac{\text{Cash} + \text{Receivables} + \text{Marketable securities}\ (\$300,000)}{\text{Current liabilities} \qquad\qquad (\$250,000)}$$
$$= \text{Quick ratio} = 1.2$$

The "quick" assets are 120% of the current liabilities. Such a relationship permits a better estimate than the current ratio of the immediate ability of the business to meet its current obligations. Inventories are not included because it would take time to sell and/or convert the materials into finished goods for sale.

A quick ratio of 100% is usually considered a satisfactory current financial condition. Trends are important, however, and any evidence of a decline should be checked thoroughly.

DISTRIBUTION OF CURRENT ASSETS

Component percentages may be used in evaluating current assets. Favorable or unfavorable trends can be readily detected through the use of a common-size statement. The following tabulation of the current assets of a business points out tendencies that need to be checked:

Description	1958	1959	1960	1961	1962
Cash	3.6%	3.4%	3.0%	2.7%	2.6%
Accounts Receivable, Net	34.2	35.3	35.7	36.0	37.1
Notes Receivable	4.1	4.0	4.3	4.0	2.0
Temporary Investments	3.9	2.7	2.0	—	—
Inventories	54.2	54.6	55.0	57.3	58.3
Total	100.0%	100.0%	100.0%	100.0%	100.0%

RATIO OF NET WORTH TO TOTAL ASSETS

Although current creditors are most interested in the immediate or short-term debt-paying ability, the stockholders, bondholders, and other long-term creditors are concerned with the long-term financial condition. One ratio which measures this condition is the relationship of net worth to total assets (or to total liabilities and net worth). It reflects the share of total assets which has been financed by the stockholders. A creditor would be interested in seeing a high ratio since a greater margin of safety would exist for creditors as the proportion of capital furnished by the owners rose. Owners, also, would be desirous, under many circumstances, of increasing the ratio with a consequent reduction in pressure to meet interest and principal payments.

The ratio, of course, can be increased through reducing the indebtedness, selling more capital stock, or retaining a greater share of the earnings in the business.

A high ratio of net worth to total assets reflects conservatism in company financing. Where earnings fluctuate to any considerable extent, perhaps such conservatism is desirable. It may not be the most profitable method of financing, however. The principle of "trading on the equity" might be advantageously used by the stockholders. This simply involves the use of borrowed funds in anticipation of a rate of return much higher than the cost of such borrowed capital.

Figure 9 illustrates two situations, one where trading on the equity was profitable, and another where it was not. For example, in 1959 a return of 4% was earned on the total investment of $1,000,000. Since the bondholders were paid a return of 5%, a net return of only 3.3% was realized by the common stockholders. However, in 1960, when an average return of 8% was secured, the rate for the common stockholders was considerably higher since only 5% was paid for borrowed funds. Trading on the equity was profitable for the stockholders in 1960.

Description	1959	1960
Long-Term Capital		
Bonds (5%)...	$ 400,000	$ 400,000
Common Stock.....................................	600,000	800,000
Total...	1,000,000	1,200,000
Income		
Net Income Before Interest on Bonds.................	40,000	96,000
Interest on Bonds................................	20,000	20,000
Net Income for Common Stockholders...............	$ 20,000	$ 76,000
Return on Total Investment..........................	4.0%	8.0%
Return on Common Stock Equity.....................	3.3%	9.5%

Fig. 9—Trading on the Equity.

RATIO OF NET WORTH TO FIXED ASSETS

The relationship of the net worth to fixed assets gives some indication as to whether or not the stockholders have furnished any share of the working capital. In instances where the net worth is less than, or equal to, the fixed assets, it is obvious that the working capital is being furnished by creditors. Quite obviously, also, this determination can be made by checking the dollar amounts in the balance sheet. However, the ratio is useful in indicating trends over a period of time.

To some analysts, a low ratio of net worth to fixed assets is evidence of overinvestment in fixed assets. The ratio may decline, not because of overexpansion, but because of dividend payments or operating losses. Perhaps more reliable guides as to overexpansion are the ratios of plant turnover and earning power.

FINANCIAL AND OPERATING RELATIONSHIPS

Financial ratios are useful in evaluating the security of investment, perhaps more from the quantitative standpoint. Financial and operating relationships bring more qualitative factors into play, and provide the management with valuable guides as to actual conditions. Some of the more commonly used ones are discussed here.

RATIO OF NET SALES TO RECEIVABLES

The investment in customers' accounts and notes receivable should bear a reasonable relationship to net sales. This factor, often called the turnover of receivables, is measured by dividing the net sales (or net credit sales, where data are available and credit sales do not account for most of the sales) by the receivables at the end of the period. For example,

$$\frac{\text{Net sales}}{\text{Customers' accounts and notes receivable}} \quad \frac{(\$1,100,000)}{(\$200,000)} = 5.5$$

The reserve for bad debts is not deducted as this would understate the investment in receivables.

The above calculation may be interpreted somewhat as follows: Receivables have been "turned over," or collected, 5.5 times during the year. If the industry standard turnover ratio is eight, then the company has too low a turnover. Such a condition may be the result, among other things, of overextension of credit, ineffective collection policies, too liberal a credit policy, or ineffective credit investigation. Further analysis should be made of the trend within the business.

If the ratio is divided into 300, it will be found that the 54.5 days of average days' sales are uncollected. Comparison of this with the terms of net 30 days gives an indication of poor performance.

The above ratio may also be stated as indicating that (1) net sales are 550% of customers' accounts and notes receivable, and (2) for every $5.50 of net sales during the year, $1.00 is still uncollected.

TURNOVER OF INVENTORIES

This relationship reveals how many times during the period the inventories are sold or used and replaced. The turnover of finished goods would be measured:

$$\frac{\text{Cost of goods sold}}{\text{Average finished inventory}} \quad \frac{(\$290,000)}{(\$40,000)} = \text{Turnover of 7.25 times}$$

The turnover of raw materials would be calculated thus:

$$\frac{\text{Raw material issues}}{\text{Average raw material inventory}} \quad \frac{(\$120,000)}{(\$14,000)} = \text{Turnover of 8.57 times}$$

These ratios may be divided into the number of business days per year to determine the number of days of inventory on hand.

Use of average inventories may be misleading if the business is seasonal. Under such circumstances, it might be desirable to check the monthly turnover rates, for considerable fluctuation may be revealed. Further, some interesting questions of inventory control will arise. For example, if a beginning inventory of $30,000 was adequate to provide for sales of $40,000 in January, then why is a beginning inventory of $60,000 needed to provide for sales of only $50,000 in July?

All the facts must be secured by the controller before drawing conclusions about inventories. Higher inventories may be secured in anticipation of a price rise, or in view of increased sales in the following period. Also, turnover rate cannot be considered by itself. A high turnover could be secured by lowering prices or by a disproportionate increase in selling and advertising expense. Too low an inventory turnover rate might prompt a detailed analysis of inventories to find the types of goods which are slow-moving, and corrective action could then be suggested.

TURNOVER OF CURRENT ASSETS

A general indication of the efficiency and profitability of use of current assets can be secured by three relationships. The turnover of current assets can be measured by dividing the sum of the cost of goods sold and operating expenses (less depreciation and amortization charges, for more accuracy) by the average of the total current assets at the beginning and end of the accounting period. Closely related to turnover is the profitability which can be calculated by dividing the net income by the average current assets. From these, the profitability per turn can be determined. Trends are important in measuring a company by this means. This method is illustrated by the figures shown on page 63.

The company achieved an increased turnover of current assets, and because of a tremendously higher volume and greater markup, was able to report a much higher profitability in the use of current assets.

		1959	1960	1961
Net Sales		$300,000	$350,000	$450,000
Cost of Sales and Operating Expenses (exclusive of depreciation)	(a)	250,000	287,500	367,500
Depreciation		22,000	22,500	22,500
Total Costs and Expenses		272,000	310,000	390,000
Net Income	(b)	28,000	40,000	60,000
Current Assets				
Beginning of year		88,000	92,000	87,700
End of year		92,000	87,700	105,160
Average	(c)	$ 90,000	$ 89,850	$ 96,430
Turnover of Current Assets $(a \div c)$	(d)	2.78	3.20	3.81
Profitability of Current Asset Turnover $(b \div c)$	(e)	31.11%	44.52%	62.22%
Rate of Profit per Turn $(e \div d)$		11.19%	13.91%	16.33%

RATIO OF NET SALES TO WORKING CAPITAL

An increase in sales volume is usually accompanied by an increase in receivables and inventories. Because of this relationship, analysts have developed the ratio of net sales to working capital as a measure of the efficiency in the use of working capital.

Such a ratio has limited use because of the many factors influencing working capital. A low turnover may result from heavy inventories or receivables. But it might be the effect of a large cash balance. A high ratio could be the result of favorable turnovers of receivables and inventories. But it might also reflect inadequate working capital—current assets kept high through a substantial increase in current liabilities which may mature before the inventories can be converted into cash.

RATIO OF NET SALES TO PLANT INVESTMENT

An indication of any tendency toward overexpansion, or the degree of plant utilization, is the ratio of net sales to operating fixed assets. It is calculated as follows:

		1959	1960	1961
Net Sales	(a)	$900,000	$950,000	$1,000,000
Fixed Assets (net)	(b)	$325,000	$320,000	$ 380,000
Ratio of Sales to Fixed Assets (a ÷ b)		2.77	2.97	2.63

Since sales are influenced by markups, it is desirable to use the cost of goods manufactured if the information is available.

This ratio should be considered with the operating profit in determining the effect of investment in plant and equipment.

RATIO OF NET SALES TO TOTAL ASSETS

A general gauge of management efficiency is the relationship of net sales to total assets used in the business. Presumably, the greater the volume of business done, the greater the efficiency in the use of the assets. However, this condition should be considered in relation to profits. High volume does not necessarily mean high profits.

RATIO OF REPAIRS AND MAINTENANCE TO FIXED ASSETS

Maintenance expense is a major item in most companies, and increases in importance as the investment in machinery and equipment grows. The ratio of repairs and maintenance expense to fixed assets is a valuable guide in checking maintenance policy. In periods of low profits, some managements tend to defer maintenance, allowing the equipment to get into a state of disrepair, in an effort to continue reporting profits. This policy tends to increase long-run maintenance expense and probably property losses. For external analysis, such information often is not available.

RATIO OF DEPRECIATION TO FIXED ASSETS

This ratio is a rough check on the adequacy of the depreciation policy. It furnishes a simple means of comparison with other companies. Differences in accounting policy, maintenance policy, and the share of fixed assets owned have their effect on the ratio.

RATIO OF NET PROFIT TO NET WORTH

To the owners of a business, one of the most important general measures is the relationship of net profit after taxes to the stockholders' equity. Since the objective of business is net profit, this ratio is one measure of achievement. A high ratio may be the result of any one of several factors: efficient management, good general business conditions, and advantageous use of creditors' funds (trading on the equity).

OPERATING RATIOS AND TRENDS

To be sure, the controller is concerned with the financial ratios for credit and investment purposes; and he must watch the utilization of capital and assets as measured by financial and operating relationships. However, a much greater share of his time and energy will be devoted to a study of operating ratios and the concomitant analysis which will be found necessary. Analysis of operating data gets into the very bowels of the business. Some of the more common ratios are described here.

RATIO OF SALES RETURNS AND ALLOWANCES TO GROSS SALES

The ratio of returns and allowances to gross sales is of value in accounting for variations in net profit because it reflects a cause of change in gross margin through reducing the sales income. The relationship is an indication of the pressure on the sales force for price concessions, and a weather-vane of customer satisfaction. Increases in this ratio usually signify not only lost sales but also higher freight costs because of returns and increased expense in adjusting and handling such matters.

RATIO OF GROSS PROFIT TO NET SALES

The ratio of gross profit to net sales is usually expressed as a percentage of net sales. Most controllers find it a very pertinent ratio and analyze it each month. The business must secure a gross profit high enough to cover operating expenses and return a normal profit. Where significant changes occur, they must be analyzed as to cause, and corrective action recommended. Changes in the volume of sales, manufacturing costs, and the mixture of products sold will affect this ratio.

It may be found desirable to calculate for the monthly statements the standard gross margin percentage by major product groups as well as the actual margin.

A low gross margin may be evidence among other things of intense price competition, poor pricing policies, or insufficient volume to cover fixed manufacturing costs adequately.

In analyzing statements the trend of the gross margin should be watched. The determination of the gross margin percentage, illustrated in Fig. 10, is but a step in analyzing the reason for changes.

Reference to the dollar amounts in Fig. 10 indicates a gradual increase in sales volume and margins and a decrease in variances until 1960. But the basic weakness is better illustrated in a review of the margin in relation to net sales, and the trend percentages. From 1950 through 1959 there was a rather general decline in both standard margin and actual gross profit, as related to net sales. Some of the decline in standard gross was offset by increased efficiencies. However, in 1960 the situation permitted a restoration of the standard gross margin of 32% of net sales and an actual manufacturing profit of 30.5% of net sales. The lowered margins are also reflected in the trend percentages in that the manufacturing profit, as related to 1950, lagged behind the sales growth until 1960, when it ran ahead. The two rates of growth were identical in 1961.

RATIO OF OPERATING EXPENSES TO NET SALES

A widely used device for internal management purposes, as well as external analysis, is the measurement of operating expenses against net sales. This review can be made by individual types of expense, groups of expenses, or total functional expense in relation to net sales. The resulting percentages indicate in part the ability of the management to adjust expenses to varying sales volumes.

Of course, merely measuring such expenses in relation to net sales can be extremely misleading in that sales volume may account for the lower ratio, and management might interpret the results as stemming from increased efficiency. It therefore becomes important that the controller compare trend percentages and absolute data as well as percentage of expense to net sales. One such analysis is illustrated in Fig. 11.

This illustration can be interpreted somewhat as follows: Over-all selling expenses increased from $256,000 in 1957 to $310,000 in 1961, an increase of $54,000. The direct selling expense increased by $36,000, whereas advertising and sales promotion expense was $18,000 higher in 1961 compared to 1957. However, such expenses did not increase in direct proportion to sales. While total selling expense was 31.22% of net sales in 1957, four years later such expense was only 30.10% of net sales. This is not necessarily an indication of efficiency, because certain

The Jones Company

STATEMENT OF COMPARATIVE GROSS PROFIT

For the Years 1950–1961

Year	Net Sales	Standard Cost of Sales	Standard Gross Margin	Variances	Manufacturing Profit	Percentage of Net Sales		Trend Percentages	
						Standard Gross Margin	Manufacturing Profit	Net Sales (1950 = 100%)	Manufacturing Profit (1950 = 100%)
1950	$ 322,000	$218,960	$103,040	$ 6,440	$ 96,600	32.00%	30.00%	100.00	100.00
1951	310,000	211,575	98,425	5,425	93,000	31.75	30.00	96.27	96.27
1952	300,000	207,000	93,000	6,000	87,000	31.00	29.00	93.17	90.06
1953	327,000	222,360	104,640	9,810	94,830	32.00	29.00	101.55	98.17
1954	330,000	227,700	102,300	8,250	94,050	31.00	28.50	102.48	97.36
1955	350,000	243,250	106,750	5,250	101,500	30.50	29.00	108.70	105.07
1956	396,000	277,200	118,800	3,960	114,840	30.00	29.00	122.98	118.89
1957	522,000	370,620	151,380	2,610	148,770	29.00	28.50	162.11	154.01
1958	687,000	496,700	190,300	6,870	183,430	27.70	26.70	213.35	189.89
1959	993,000	714,960	278,040	4,965	273,075	28.00	27.50	308.39	282.69
1960	1,029,000	699,720	329,280	15,435	313,845	32.00	30.50	319.57	324.89
1961	1,222,000	837,070	384,930	18,330	366,600	31.50	30.00	379.50	379.50

Fig. 10—Statement of Comparative Gross Profit, Including Trend Percentages.

expenses are largely fixed in nature, and should not increase as sales become higher.

Reference to the percentage of net sales will indicate that the following expenses took a larger share of the sales dollar in 1961 than in 1957:

	% Net Sales	
	1957	1961
DIRECT SELLING EXPENSE		
Salaries—Supervisory	3.05	3.20
Commissions	2.44	2.72
Rent	1.46	1.75
Samples	.49	.87
Telephone and Telegraph	.73	.78
ADVERTISING AND SALES PROMOTION EXPENSE		
Supplies	.73	.87
Magazine Advertising	4.27	4.61

These expenses, which increased at a rate faster than net sales, were offset by other expenses which actually decreased, or increased at a slower rate than net sales.

The rate of growth is also indicated by the trend percentages. Whereas net sales in 1961 were 125.61% of 1957 sales, total selling expenses were only 121.09% of the base period. The largest increase, 225%, occurred in sample expense, which, from a dollars-of-expenditures viewpoint is not as significant as the 132% increase in supervisory salaries. Rent expense is 150% of the 1957 level.

From a control standpoint, those expenses which increased at a relatively high rate should be analyzed to determine what reductions can be effected—or whether the company is receiving full value for moneys paid out. Standard ratios and individual expense standards are useful in evaluating results of such analysis.

RATIO OF NET INCOME TO NET SALES

A business should earn a reasonable net profit in relation to sales as well as capital invested. This ratio is valuable for over-all control purposes, and is usually incorporated in the periodic internal statements. It is discussed in Chapter 3.

MISCELLANEOUS RATIOS

NUMBER OF TIMES FIXED CHARGES ARE EARNED

The ratio of number of times fixed charges are earned is used to indicate the margin of safety for the bondholder. It is determined by dividing the net profit after taxes by the interest on fixed indebtedness, including

The Distributing Company, Inc.

COMPARATIVE STATEMENT OF SELLING EXPENSES

For the Years 1957 Through 1961

	1957		1958		1959		1960		1961	
	Amount	%	Amount	%	Amount	%	Amount	%	Amount	%
NET SALES	$820,000		$870,000		$960,000		$910,000		$1,030,000	
SELLING EXPENSES										
Direct Selling Expense										
Salaries—Supervisory	$ 25,000	3.05	$ 26,000	2.99	$ 28,000	2.92	$ 30,000	3.30	$ 33,000	3.20
Salaries—Salesmen	48,000	5.86	47,500	5.46	48,000	5.00	50,000	5.49	48,000	4.66
Salaries—Clerical	14,000	1.70	14,500	1.67	15,000	1.56	15,000	1.65	17,000	1.65
Commissions	20,000	2.44	26,000	2.99	32,000	3.33	27,000	2.97	28,000	2.72
Traveling	35,000	4.27	37,000	4.25	40,200	4.20	40,000	4.40	39,500	3.84
Rent	12,000	1.46	15,000	1.72	15,000	1.56	15,000	1.65	18,000	1.75
Office Supplies	7,000	.85	6,000	.69	6,500	.68	6,000	.66	6,500	.63
Samples	4,000	.49	4,500	.52	6,000	.62	6,500	.71	9,000	.87
Telephone and Telegraph	6,000	.73	6,800	.78	7,900	.82	7,500	.82	8,000	.78
Depreciation	3,000	.37	3,000	.34	3,000	.31	3,000	.33	3,000	.29
Total Direct Selling Expense	174,000	21.22	186,300	21.41	201,600	21.00	200,000	21.98	210,000	20.39
Advertising and Sales Promotion										
Salaries	15,000	1.83	16,500	1.90	16,500	1.72	16,500	1.81	17,500	1.70
Traveling	9,000	1.10	8,000	.92	10,000	1.04	9,000	.99	10,000	.97
Supplies	6,000	.73	6,500	.75	7,500	.78	8,500	.93	9,000	.87
Newspaper Advertising	15,000	1.83	15,000	1.72	17,500	1.82	16,000	1.76	15,000	1.46
Magazine Advertising	35,000	4.27	38,000	4.37	36,500	3.80	38,000	4.18	47,500	4.61
Miscellaneous Advertising	2,000	.24	3,000	.34	2,000	.21	2,000	.22	1,000	.10
Total Advertising and Sales Promotion	82,000	10.00	87,000	10.00	90,000	9.37	90,000	9.89	100,000	9.71
Total Selling Expense	$256,000	31.22	$273,300	31.41	$291,600	30.37	$290,000	31.87	$ 310,000	30.10

TREND PERCENTAGES	%	%	%	%	%
Direct Selling Expense					
Salaries—Supervisory	100.00	104.00	112.00	120.00	132.00
Salaries—Salesmen	100.00	98.96	100.00	104.17	100.00
Salaries—Clerical	100.00	103.57	107.14	107.14	121.43
Commissions	100.00	130.00	160.00	135.00	140.00
Traveling	100.00	105.71	114.86	114.29	112.86
Rent	100.00	125.00	125.00	125.00	150.00
Office Supplies	100.00	85.71	92.86	85.71	92.86
Samples	100.00	112.50	150.00	162.50	225.00
Telephone and Telegraph	100.00	113.33	131.67	125.00	133.33
Depreciation	100.00	100.00	100.00	100.00	100.00
Total Direct Selling Expense	100.00	107.07	115.86	114.94	120.69
Advertising and Sales Promotion					
Salaries	100.00	110.00	110.00	110.00	116.67
Traveling	100.00	88.89	111.11	100.00	111.11
Supplies	100.00	108.33	125.00	141.67	150.00
Newspaper Advertising	100.00	100.00	116.67	106.67	100.00
Magazine Advertising	100.00	108.57	104.29	108.57	135.71
Miscellaneous Advertising	100.00	150.00	100.00	100.00	50.00
Total Advertising and Sales Promotion	100.00	106.10	109.76	109.76	121.95
Total Selling Expense	100.00	106.76	113.91	113.28	121.09
Net Sales	100.00	106.10	117.07	110.98	125.61

Fig. 11—Comparative Statement of Selling Expenses—Per Cent of Sales and Trend Percentages.

discount amortization. When more than one issue of bonds is to be considered, the margin on each can be determined separately. The method of calculating the margin is as follows:

		1961	1962	1963 (Estimated)
Net Income Before Fixed Charges	(a)	$62,000	$79,000	$110,000
Interest on First Mortgage Bonds	(b)	5,000	5,000	7,000
Balance	(c)	57,000	74,000	103,000
Interest on Debentures	(d)	7,000	7,000	6,000
Balance	(e)	$50,000	$67,000	$ 97,000
Number of Times Charges Are Earned				
First Mortgage Bonds $(c \div b)$		11.40	14.80	14.71
Debentures $[e \div (b + d)]$		4.17	5.58	7.46

Some analysts do not deduct the interest charges before making the calculation. When so determined, one time must be omitted when measuring the real margin.

EARNINGS PER SHARE OF COMMON STOCK

A common ratio in financial circles is the earnings per share of common stock. Essentially, this is calculated by deducting from the net income any dividends for preferred stock, and dividing the result by the number of shares of common stock outstanding at the end of the period. The earnings per share of common stock can be expressed also as a percentage of the par value or market value of the stock.

BOOK VALUE OF COMMON STOCK

The book value of common stock is determined by dividing the total net worth of the corporation by the number of outstanding shares of common stock, provided there is no preferred stock issued and outstanding. If more than one class of stock is outstanding, it is necessary to segregate the capital and surplus according to the respective rights of each; and then divide each equity by the outstanding shares to arrive at the book value.

PRESENTING THE ANALYSIS

The only purpose in making a ratio analysis is to point out significant trends and secure corrective action if in order. While particular situations may demand a different approach, the normal line of procedure would be somewhat as follows:

1. Determine what ratio should be presented. The significant ratios should be selected which will serve to point out all aspects of the particular weakness to be corrected.

2. Determine the trend of the selected ratios over a reasonable period of time.
3. To the extent possible, secure ratios for comparative purposes. These may include similar ratios of competing companies, or industry ratios.
4. Present the ratios in suitable form.
5. Interpret the data in an accompanying report, pointing out unusual features and suggesting corrective action.

A variety of means is available for presenting the information in an interesting and attention-getting form. Since the data lend themselves to interpretation, it is desirable that the controller include a brief narrative. However, ratios can be presented: (1) in narrative form only; (2) in tabular form; (3) in graphic form; or (4) in supplementary tables and graphs as part of a narrative report.

Pie charts and percentage bar charts are very suitable for graphically presenting component percentages. Trends can be shown by simple straight-line graphs or bar charts.

6

Organization for Effective Controllership

NEED FOR SOUND ORGANIZATION

In the over-all review of the business, one of the basic factors discussed was organization. When controllership is viewed in its broadest aspects, consideration must be given to the basic problems of organization in both the company and the controller's division.

Experience in observing many well-managed enterprises will usually lead to the conclusion that it is not individual genius that achieves good operation. Rather, it is the organized efforts of a group of individuals. Through organization the tasks are divided in such a manner that the work can be done properly, the performance supervised, and the results controlled. It might be said also that no chief executive can know the true capabilities of his company until it is properly organized.

As a business grows in size, communication becomes increasingly complex. Administration is more difficult and cumbersome; consequently, attention must be paid to planning and developing a sound organization. Proper organization in itself is not always a cause of success or failure. But it is a requisite for the highest degree of success that conditions will otherwise permit.

Readers are referred to the many fine publications on matters of organization. In this chapter, the authors highlight some of the conditions which the accounting executive must consider in the execution of his task.

ORGANIZING FOR CONTROL

The accounting division must be properly organized if the accounting and statistical functions are to be most effective; records and methods alone are not enough, for well-applied human effort is required to accomplish the task. The principles of organization for the accounting family are no different from those applicable to all other functions of the business. The particular type of organization suitable in a specific case depends upon the size of the concern, the nature of the operations, the location and extent of operations, the probabilities of expansion, and, to a limited degree, the personal characteristics and training of the executive group as a whole. No set plan of organization can be successfully superimposed upon all types of concerns or even upon all concerns with the same general type of operations. However, certain guiding principles apply with uniformity to all concerns.

An effective organization may be defined as a group of individuals who are cooperating successfully toward a common objective. In building such a team the controller must weigh three factors:

1. The organizational structure—a proper grouping of functions to promote cooperation most effectively and a determination of the proper relationship between all such groups
2. The proper delegation of responsibility and authority to the supervisors
3. The selection of the right people for the right job

The degree of success in securing the correct answer for each of these factors will determine the success of the accounting division as a whole.

The final test of the effectiveness of this division will depend upon its ability to:

1. Provide the required services
2. Provide such services at a minimum of cost
3. Develop competent personnel

TYPICAL ORGANIZATIONAL PROBLEMS FOR THE CONTROLLER

Sooner or later, and particularly as the company grows in size, the controller will be faced with decisions on problems of an organizational nature, such as:

1. As a general matter, the proper organizational structure to facilitate the effective performance of the controllership functions
2. The functions to be performed in the home office, and those best performed in the division office, or factory office, or regional sales office, etc.
3. The nature of the relationship between the company controller and each division controller, viz., line or staff
4. The proper segregation of functions within the home office controller's department
5. The extent of delegation of authority and responsibility

Some suggestions on these points are made in the sections which follow.

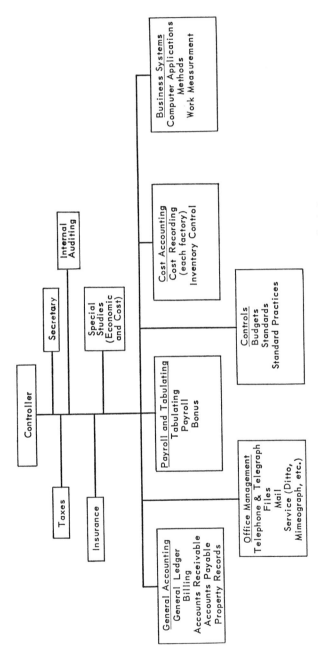

Fig. 12—Typical Organizational Chart of the Controller's Department.

ORGANIZATIONAL STRUCTURE FOR CONTROLLER'S DIVISION

No one organizational structure fits all needs; no one plan may be said to be ideal. However, certain patterns have been found practical. The basic problem is to decide how the functions may best be assembled for the most effective results. This, in turn, will depend on how information is used and the function of the controller. Other factors having a bearing on the solution are the nature of the business, the experience and personalities of the staff and executives, custom, extent of mechanization, management philosophy, physical location of plants and sales offices, etc.

A typical organizational structure for a central controller's department is illustrated in Fig. 12. Some comments on special features of the grouping may be helpful.

1. *Office management functions are grouped under one department head.* These are the general services which are largely routine and require little accounting knowledge or skill. The main problem is one of organizing the flow of work and following up on the work of numerous clerks. Rather complete delegation of this somewhat routine task leaves the controller's time available for matters requiring a higher degree of skill and managerial talent. In some companies central stenographic service would be in this department, as well as billing and other related functions.

2. *The budget and standards functions are segregated from other departments.* This relieves the staff from any recording duties and permits them to follow through on points of excess cost, and other special studies related to determining what constitutes good performance or what reasons caused deviations from acceptable levels. A different type of personality is needed in dealing with the factory or other operating department personnel from the one needed to record historical costs.

3. *A separate department is established for internal auditing.* This is a further example of complete separation of the responsibility for maintaining records from an activity of an investigational nature. It tends to make the studies more objective. The internal auditor may also make special studies, and assist the public accountants in connection with annual or special audits.

4. *A special department is established for special economic and/or cost studies.* The interpretation of data is a function which should remain under the direct supervision of the controller. A special staff is used to gather the necessary information and prepare the details. Such an organizational structure frees the interpretative staff from the operating detail.

It is to be emphasized that rapid changes in the science of electronic data processing may profoundly affect the organizational structure.

A CENTRALIZED VS. DECENTRALIZED ACCOUNTING ORGANIZATION

Companies with branch plants are among those chiefly concerned with the problem of decentralization. Decentralization as here used relates to the trend to increased delegation of authority to subordinate operating officials at remote locations. Centralization, of course, relates to the trend toward increased executive control from the home office. Quite clearly, the matter may transcend merely the accounting organization and extend to the entire company, through every major function.

There are an infinite number of possibilities as to centralization or decentralization of accounting functions. On the one extreme is the highly centralized organization in which all records are maintained in the home office. The control and subsidiary ledgers are kept there. The sole accounting function at the factory or branch is an accumulation of the documents of original entry—the production lot sheets, material requisitions, time cards, and perhaps invoices and receiving reports. These are summarized and transmitted monthly, or on some other periodic basis, to the general offices. At the other extreme is the completely decentralized operation. Each plant or each warehouse may operate as though it were an independent company. A complete set of books is maintained; monthly statements are prepared at the branch and sent to the home office for consolidation. In between these extremes are a great number of combinations. Thus, there may be a decentralized billing procedure with centralized accounts receivable records. Or there may be a centralized disbursements department with decentralized account distribution. Similarly, there are wide differences in the treatment of payrolls. As a matter of fact, with the use of factory ledger accounts and the complementary general and factory ledger control accounts, a great number of choices can be made as to accounts to be centralized and those to be decentralized. Each method has its advantages as well as its problems.

There are probably five basic considerations which influence the decision as to the degree of centralized accounting structure:

1. The management philosophy as to divisional responsibility
2. The availability of operating data
3. The size of operating divisions or units
4. The geographic location of the operating units
5. The economies of the situation

These major factors are briefly reviewed.

Management Philosophy. As business expands to embrace several plants, each of which produces several distinct products or is a step in a complete integration, the philosophy may develop that the best operating results are obtained by creating an autonomous unit. Under this management theory, each divisional manager has complete authority over all matters affecting his operation; and this includes the accounting function. On such a basis, each division is generally complete in all respects, and the division's management is judged on the over-all profit results of the operation. The home office or administrative staff deals only with over-all policy or matters of company-wide application. Such a philosophy might apply, for example, to the *divisions* of The Ford Motor Company, but might not extend to the separate plants within each division.

This same accounting concept has considerable appeal, and has been applied even where the management is not judged on the over-all profit results, and where the home office takes a more active part in the local operations. Thus, sales methods, purchasing policies, credit extension, inventory policies, and other matters may be directed or modified by top management. Moreover, the detailed expenses and income may be subject to close scrutiny through the means of periodic reports. Clearly, the same management philosophy does not apply here, although the accounting may be decentralized to give the divisional manager a certain control over the activity. Undoubtedly there are instances where the divisional manager would be glad to be relieved of the accounting responsibility if the needed information were forthcoming. Undoubtedly, also, the practice of decentralization has been applied on this managerial concept when not warranted.

Availability of Operating Information. Whether the local management is independent or not, it may need accounting information to control the business adequately. This matter involves two separate questions: (1) What information must be available on a division or plant basis? (2) Where should such information be prepared? For it does not follow that, because data are required at the division level, they must be prepared at this same level.

In judging what information should be segregated by division, an important consideration is the placement of responsibility. Just who is responsible for the particular items—plant management or home office? For example, whether or not accounts receivable should be recorded on a divisional basis would depend on who is responsible for credit extension. If credit approval and follow-up is a divisional matter, then records should be segregated accordingly. If it is a home office charge, then a divisional classification would seem unnecessary. Fixed asset data perhaps need be made available only periodically, and divisional management could be advised through reports prepared either at the home office or at the division level.

There is, of course, a definite need for operating data. Here timing is an important factor. Whether the needs can be met by a centralized accounting organization will depend on the circumstances. Perhaps the factory data for labor, material, and expense control must be prepared locally, while selling and administrative costs are centralized. In any event, the home office must thoroughly know the operations, and the degree of coordination between branch and general office must be great, if the latter organization is to do the accounting and reporting.

Size of Operating Unit. In some cases the operating unit will be large enough so that all or most of the accounting functions can be carried out efficiently on a decentralized basis. Factors to be weighed include: degree of internal control which can be achieved; availability of competent personnel; degree of utilization of mechanical or electronic equipment; availability of office space; and the nature and number of accounting decisions to be resolved.

Geographical Location. As a generalization, the farther away an operation is from the home office, the smaller the unit which would justify decentralization on the basis of geography only—to avoid or minimize delays and other complications. If a unit is only overnight mail service away, centralization of items might be more desirable than if the plants were on opposite coasts. If closeness of customer contact is important and the sales are largely restricted to the local area, perhaps decentralization of accounts receivable or billings might be desirable. Again, closeness of contact with suppliers might be a controlling factor in the decentralization of the purchasing function and accounts payable.

Economy of Operation. If there is no compelling need for decentralization, then the matter may be resolved on an economy basis. Under these circumstances the tendency of the local unit to maintain records rather than rely on general office reports should not be overlooked. This duplication of effort should be avoided. In approaching the problem of economy, the controller will, of course, probably need an objective survey of accounting methods. The survey should emphasize the activity by accounts rather than merely the nature of the accounting function. In considering economy, the extent of machine accounting can be an important factor.

ADVANTAGES OF DECENTRALIZATION—A SUMMARY

Many controllers tend to favor a centralized organization if at all practical, because they feel better enabled to control accounting activities. There have been, however, some sad experiences with centralization; and furthermore the theoretical savings have not been realized or have been offset by other costs not quite as readily apparent. It is felt desirable, therefore, to emphasize the advantages of decentralization, recognizing, however, that decentralization is not always the best form of operation.

The advantages of decentralization may be noted as follows:

1. From a psychological viewpoint, decentralization tends to increase the initiative of local management. The control responsibilities are more keenly felt.
2. Local organization of data avoids some excuses for inactivity or poor performance because "the report was too late" or "the report was wrong." This factor is partly psychological as to its benefits.
3. Duplication can be eliminated—particularly where the branch or plant retains records so as to have current information or to "check up" on the home office report. Of course, if the records are maintained to have current data available, this may be some indication that the wrong record was centralized.
4. Under ordinary circumstances, speedier results can be attained. When the entire operation is under local control, every effort will be made to secure timely data. This should contribute to closer cost control.
5. Wider accounting responsibility in the field is a means of training field personnel for promotions and generally results in a sounder organization.
6. Competent personnel can as readily prepare data for home office use as can the central organization. With an objective accountant on the job, perhaps even a better reporting of facts can be secured. Decentralization need not be a means of denying the necessary data for executive control. For example, copies of the same reports going to divisional management could go also to home office management.
7. Decentralization is not in opposition to uniformity. It adds some flexibility and still permits the application of accounting policies and practices through the use of standard forms and standard practice manuals.

The advantages of decentralization, in a general way, are the disadvantages of centralization. However, some advantages of a centralized organization may be emphasized:

1. Permits greater flexibility in the utilization of existing personnel and facilities, including the ability to meet peak loads
2. Frequently permits the utilization of mechanical equipment that might not be justified in a decentralized situation
3. May permit the utilization of more qualified personnel, particularly in the higher executive echelon, because of increased responsibilities

The extent to which these advantages may *not* be realized in a decentralized organization depends in large part on the size of the local unit.

DELEGATION OF RESPONSIBILITY AND AUTHORITY

A difficult problem confronting every controller, indeed any executive, relates to the extent to which he can delegate responsibility and authority. He is charged with the responsibility for a large number of duties to which he cannot give his personal attention. He *must* therefore pass on authority to accomplish certain tasks, and place the responsibility for execution—although in the final analysis the controller is still responsible. Only by such delegation can he free himself to devote his time and energy to those matters which will best serve the interests of management.

What duties, then, should be delegated? As a general statement, the controller should reserve for himself the broader duties, those of wide application, such as decisions relating to accounting policy and practice. He should assign to others those matters which are smaller in scope. Moreover, he must delegate sufficient duties so that he is not burdened with details. Such delegation of authority, incidentally, has the advantage of developing the confidence and judgment of junior executives. On the other extreme, the controller should not get so far away that he loses touch with significant developments.

Because of the nature of his duties, the controller has a great personal responsibility to the management, the stockholders, and the government for the facts and figures issued by the accounting division. No delegation of authority can pass on this responsibility to others. However, it is suggested that any delegation of duties be accompanied by a thorough explanation of the accounting philosophy and business objectives to be followed. This practice should assist the controller in better securing the type of accomplishment desired.

Some examples may assist in clarifying what type of work may and should be delegated. All matters relating to routine operation of the accounting departments may be delegated to the department heads; only matters not covered by procedures or established policy need be referred to the controller. Again, as to accounting departments, all changes in budget structures, salaries, additional personnel, new procedures, accounting policy, or basic changes in reports should be reviewed by the controller; and all other aspects of operations might be delegated. As another more specific illustration, all special cost studies involving large expenditures or matters of basic management policy—such as purchase of a new production site or change in major product emphasis—should be handled by the controller. In contrast, routine cost determinations, such as formulation costs or parts costs for limited application, might be delegated to the cost accountant. As another general rule, cost studies requested by top-level management should be channeled through the controller's department. Although the details may be worked out by others, the controller should at least thoroughly review the interpretation.

THE CONTROLLER'S AUTHORITY OVER ACCOUNTING AND STATISTICAL ACTIVITIES

An organizational problem to be clearly resolved involves the controller's authority in a twofold manner: (1) where the branch offices or plants are on a decentralized accounting basis, what should be the authority of the corporate controller as related to the divisional manager and the divisional controller, and (2) what should be the authority of the controller (central office or divisional) as to accounting, statistical, or other office activities not under his department? The general answer to both questions is that the controller should have *functional* control and responsibility for *all* such records. While the divisional controller may report to the divisional manager, for example, the corporate controller should have the right to prescribe methods and procedures if the need should arise. Also, records kept by the factory or sales staff should be subjected to the same functional control.

While the records can be physically located in the departments with which associated—in the sales department as to sales statistics, and in the factory as to production records—there are definite advantages to be gained by placing all accounting, statistical, and office procedure under one chief accounting officer. If the job is well done, the following benefits should be realized:

1. Duplication of effort can be avoided
2. Clerical expense can be reduced as the result of centralized and more efficient supervision
3. All records and statistical data can be made available to all departments
4. Accounting and statistical data will be interpreted better, and figure-facts will be more objectively presented

PART II

The Planning Function of Controllership

7

The Nature of
Total Corporate Planning

PLANNING AND THE BUSINESS OBJECTIVE

The objective of business is the earning of a net profit—a profit consistent with the company's responsibilities to its employees, customers, and owners. Only by earning a profit through selling goods and services at a fair price, while paying fair and reasonable wages, can a business justify its existence. Only then will employees be reasonably secure in their jobs. And only through the earning of such profits will capital flow into the industry. Generally, from profits alone may come higher salaries and wages, lower prices, and better products through research. Over a long term, such achievements do not stem from businesses which are losing money.

But profits do not merely happen. They are primarily the result of skillful planning. Profits result from the effort of managements which can organize all the forces of a business enterprise into a well-coordinated team whose objective is the earning of a profit.

MANAGEMENT EMPHASIS DIFFERS

There are several kinds of managements operating American business today, and by no stretch of the imagination are they all "profit-minded." First, there exists a sales-minded management which, with its sales contests, quotas, slogans, and advertising, is interested in how *much* it can sell, not whether the products are profitable. Closely related is the volume-minded management which thinks merely in terms of volume. "Just get enough volume and the profit will take care of itself." Then there is the price-minded management which believes that by lowering the price the sales will "roll in." These managements have in common the emphasis on sales volume, although from different approaches. In addition there is a factory-minded management whose sole objective is efficient production. It will have the latest and best equipment, regardless of cost. There is also the finance-minded management which places the chief emphasis on financial manipulation, reorganization, mergers, etc., rather than on sales and production. Again the financial emphasis may be on conservatism. The management rarely takes any chances. Suggestions are weighed in great detail. Management is ultraconservative; it will pinch pennies and lose dollars (profits). To most controllers it is obvious that all these factors must be considered in relation to each other. All factors must be balanced; and the management "in balance" is the profit-minded management. It recognizes that profits are the result of exacting planning for potential profit as well as the ability to meet changing conditions.

PLANNING AND CONTROL DEFINED AND DIFFERENTIATED

Some of the best information on the management function of planning and control is that prepared by the Financial Executives Institute of America and its related organizations. The Institute's National Technical Committee on Management Planning and Control has developed this meaningful definition:[1]

Management planning and control refers to the organization, techniques and procedures whereby long-and-short-range plans are formulated, considered and approved; responsibility to meet changing conditions is provided; progress in working the plan is reported; deviations in operation are analyzed; and corrective action, required to reach the desired objective, is taken.

In interpreting this definition, there are several aspects to be kept in mind. First, planning and control are *management* functions, to be participated in by a great many of business management and not a select few. Second, planning refers to the preparation of a scheme, or predetermination of a course of action, in such reasonable detail that it reaches down quite far in the management structure, and influences actions. It includes forecasting sales, determining inventory levels, scheduling production, estimating costs and expense levels. It involves the making of decisions concerning new products, research and development, merchandising methods, labor contract rates, sources of material procurement, and organization. In short, it implies the attempt to anticipate all major problems to be faced by the business during the planning period. Third, it involves making decisions *ahead of time,* but provides for a revision in plans if this seems desirable. It is also evident that planning does not involve merely forecasting a condition or result. Emphasis is on *action* to take

[1] *Management Planning and Control: The H. J. Heinz Approach* (New York: Controllership Foundation, Inc., 1957), p. viii.

advantage of a situation and to change circumstances if such steps seem prudent.

The effectiveness of this business planning is to be measured by the degree to which it stimulates continuous and imaginative effort toward the objective—and not merely by the extent to which planned and actual results coincide.

It is to be observed that planning precedes control. Control, in this context, involves action to conform to the plan or to other predetermined objectives. This phase of the controllership function is discussed in Part III.

PLANNING AND CORPORATE GROWTH

In the financial market place, the investor today places a premium on "growth companies." Capable young men tend to seek out these same corporations that appear to be "going places." What is this attribute possessed by such companies that distinguishes them from others? In general, it might be said that growth companies are those organized to cope successfully with the future. They are not so overwhelmed by the compelling day-to-day operating problems that planning ahead is generally ignored.

Indeed, the success of a dynamic growth company may in part be laid to a planned attack on the future. A significant amount of time is spent by its management in properly answering these four pertinent questions:

1. What conditions are likely to prevail in the future?
2. What is the position of the company in the light of these trends?
3. What are the opportunities that will open?
4. What should the company do?

It can be seen that growth depends on an attitude of mind which recognizes the need for continuous planning, and not one motivated by the mood of the day. When the need is recognized, the management commits itself to a coordinated, systematic planning for profit. It accumulates the available facts and applies the latest scientific tools in using these facts and judgments in matching company resources against the opportunities. Company growth and, very often, company survival depend on adequate planning.

PERIOD OF THE PLAN

Business planning, broadly speaking, may be viewed as composed of two major segments: (1) short-term planning, which encompasses a planning period from one month to a year, or perhaps to as much as five years, and (2) long-term planning, which covers a span of time from five years up to twenty or thirty years.

Short-term planning is rather specific and detailed. For the immediate month or three months, it concerns itself rather concretely with activity levels in each cost or profit center, building or combining the cost, income, and profit plans into a specific total corporate picture. However, as this plan reflects expected operations over the near term of, let us say, the ensuing nine months, the coverage, while still dealing with each responsibility center, is inclined to be somewhat specific as to cost center, but less detailed as to specific model of product. Averages may be used to give a sufficiently clear picture until precise plans must be formulated.

On the other hand, long-range planning usually by nature is order-of-magnitude. It concerns itself chiefly with rather broad ranges or bands. It is translated into major segments of the business, and not each specific cost center. It might be said that the long-range plan is broad and perhaps fuzzy. As the time span comes closer, it is brought more clearly into focus and the details are discernible. Both types of planning are necessary, and both employ somewhat the same principles. One flows into the other. The short-term plan must fit into the long-term plans; the short-range plan and objective must constantly be progressing toward the longer-term corporate goal.

ADVANTAGES OF PLANNING

Business management involves the intelligent use of capital and labor to produce the optimum profit. It would indeed be a foolish manager who would invest millions of dollars in plant and equipment without a reasonable study of probable future market conditions, including advancing technology which might make a process obsolete, in an effort to evaluate the probabilities of not only recovering the investment, but also earning a fair return on the investment. Intelligent planning causes the organization to study, to analyze, to consider carefully the possibilities, alternatives, and consequences of any given proposal. This is, indeed, one of the intangible but principal advantages. Such a scientific approach to business problems may produce many benefits from well-conceived plans, including these:

1. *The return on investment is increased.* In considering alternative choices, the more desirable projects are selected with a resultant higher return on the capital employed.
2. *Profits tend to be improved and stabilized.* For the same reason as above, the relative risks are considered, and the odds of a successful plan are increased. Moreover, if peaks and valleys in opera-

tions can be determined in advance, the economies of leveling-out the operations may be studied and improvements planned.

3. *More effective group efforts are achieved.* Each individual participating in the plan-making knows the corporate objectives, and the way the company is going. His efforts are more effective because he feels he is part of the management group. Also, the final plans express the combined judgment of the entire organization, eliminating bias which might otherwise exist.

4. *An improved financing program is made possible.* With adequate planning, the extent of required funds is known. The most desirable means of securing the financing can be considered in the ample time which exists. Under such circumstances, banks and financing institutions become more receptive. Further, the company is not forced to agree to borrowing terms considered unwarranted when the circumstances permit discussions with several competitive sources.

5. *Better industrial relations are developed.* Sound planning must give consideration to the development and training of supervisory management and all other personnel. Such longer-term projects, together with stabilized employment and provision for personal growth, contribute to better industrial relations.

6. *Improved long-term procurement of materials and supplies results.* The best type of planning will take into account availability of materials, technological improvements, etc. Such far-sighted programs permit the execution of sounder contracts and development of alternative sources.

7. *More effective sales or merchandising programs are made possible.* With an informed knowledge of short- and long-term trends in the market, recognition of this intelligence can be given in advertising and sales promotion programs, in the order of product introduction and phasing-out. Consideration can be given to activity in the light of the longer trends. The sales route becomes smoother and more direct.

8. *A more intelligent research program is encouraged.* Generally speaking, research funds are ill-spent if projects are turned off and on rather haphazardly, dependent upon the immediate prospect of earnings and cash. Continuity and consistent application over a period of years very often are necessary. Looking down the road, or looking ahead over the hills and valleys—in other words, planning—is required to give the necessary stability and perspective to an intelligent research program.

These are but a few of the gains to the conduct of business which are achieved by a recognition of the need for planning.

SCOPE OF PLANNING DISCUSSION

This chapter on corporate planning is intended to review briefly the basic philosophy of the function, including the purpose, need, and benefits. It is not intended to discuss in detail the technique. Several excellent books are available on the subject.[2]

There may be an advantage, however, in commenting on the broad aspects of presenting, reviewing, and evaluating the business plan and the role of the controller therein.

TYPICAL STEPS IN EXPRESSING THE PLAN

A business plan usually is presented in financial terms. This is the common language of business, and it is by financial means that the acceptability of the program is measured. For this purpose a soundly conceived plan would give consideration to at least four basic factors: (1) earnings, (2) financial condition, (3) cash flow, and (4) capital expenditures. The general or master plan, therefore, should include the related four basic statements:

1. *Statement of Estimated Income and Expense.* This should be presented in reasonable detail, by months or quarters, and in a format which reveals the important relationships.
2. *Statement of Estimated Financial Condition.* This statement should indicate the expected financial condition at the critical periods of the program. In practice, a quarterly balance sheet and year-end projection of financial condition usually suffice.
3. *Statement of Estimated Cash Flow.* The purpose of this statement is, of course, to reflect the adequacy of cash for operating and capital needs.
4. *Summary of Proposed Plant and Equipment Appropriations and Expenditures.* This statement indicates by general category and perhaps by degree of expected profit (return on investment) or relative need, planned capital expenditures for the period under review.

These four primary expressions of the business program usually are supported by as detailed a plan as circumstances require for each function or activity.

Typical detailed plans would indicate the following (in a manufacturing company):

1. *Sales budget.* The plan would indicate the units by type of product to be sold; unit selling price; and aggregate sales volume by

[2] See, for example, J. Brooks Heckert and James D. Willson, *Business Budgeting and Control,* New York: The Ronald Press Company, 1955.

months or other appropriate period of the forecast. Further refinements would include a plan of sales by territories, estimated returns, and allowances—all on a responsibility basis.

2. *Quantitative manufacturing budget.* This program, taking into account the desired inventory levels and sales program, would outline the required quantity of manufacture of each product by month or other time interval.

3. *Materials or purchases budget.* Based on beginning inventory of raw materials and components, etc., quantity of manufacture, and desired ending inventory, the required purchases would be calculated. Such planning would reflect purchases by major material component, e.g., steel, electric motors, and groupings of other lesser materials.

4. *Direct labor forecast.* Also based on units to be manufactured, the required direct labor would be determined. Consideration might be given to standard man-hours, expected degree of efficiency, probable wage increases, etc.

5. *Manufacturing expense forecast.* Recognizing by responsibility the fixed and variable nature of expenses, the experienced or expected degree of efficiency, the probable level of manufacturing expenses by month (usually built up by cost center) would be ascertained.

6. *Cost of goods sold estimate.* The determination of the material, labor, and manufacturing expenses permits a calculation of the cost of goods sold to support the earnings statement in the most meaningful format.

7. *Administrative and general expense forecast.* In a manner similar to that applied to manufacturing expenses, by applicable period and by responsibility, the expected general and administrative expenses for the period are estimated.

8. *Selling expenses forecast including advertising and sales promotion.* These expenses, by responsibility area, needed to support the sales budget, are estimated by period and/or program, in a manner consistent with the other expense forecasts.

9. *Research and development expense budget.* These expenses may be outlined by major project and by period.

10. *Other income and expense forecast.* This phase of the plan includes those items of income and expense not expressly contained in the other functional areas.

Each major function, identified on a responsibility accounting basis,[3] is considered in the light of all related activity, and plans are made accordingly. For example, manufacturing levels are set with the sales volume in mind. Purchases of raw materials and components are directly related to manufacturing quantities and optimum inventory levels under

[3] See explanation on p. 8.

the expected conditions. Advertising and sales promotion must support the planned sales activity. All these functions, and the capital expenditures budget, must be modified to fit within the financial capabilities of the company. Truly, the need for a coordinated plan can be seen.

Each segment of the total plan is the basis of the accounting which translates the tentative plan into the over-all company picture of operations and financial condition. It is done in much the same way as the actual accounting is handled. Thus, the sales forecast or budget becomes the basis for the net sales figures in the income statement and the addition to accounts receivable. Giving proper recognition to lead or lag, the expense forecast becomes the basis for changes in accruals and prepayments, and in accounts payable, etc., as well as the income results. The cash flow statement gives recognition to experience or plans for collection of receivables and disbursements required to meet obligations incurred.

EVALUATING THE PLAN

Once the various segments of the forecast have been combined and expressed as a complete company picture, it becomes necessary to judge or evaluate the plan. Is it realistic? Is it within the financial capabilities of the company? Is the return on investment adequate? Questions such as these must be asked. For it is usually not sufficient to prepare the initial forecast and conclude that it represents the best plan for the coming period.

The plan must be compared with some measuring stick. In the typical enterprise, a comparison is made with the preceding year or period. However, another more useful device for evaluation of plans is through break-even analysis.[4]

Once the areas of weakness are studied and appropriate adjustments decided upon, the plan is revised. In actual practice, many discussions are held with functional executives and department heads to correct seemingly out-of-line conditions. Such a process may require several revisions in plans.

The final plan is ordinarily submitted by the chief executive for approval of the board of directors. Once approval is secured, the steps are set in motion to achieve the corporate goal.

REVISION OF THE PLAN

Business is dynamic and conditions change. Every effort may be made to meet the forecast, but occasionally outside forces are such that, despite all reasonable prudence, it appears the plan is unattainable. Under such circumstances, the business plan must be revised. Perhaps capital ex-

[4] Discussed on pp. 113 to 116.

penditures need to be sharply reduced to avoid corporate borrowing and enable the company to live within the available means. Or, drastic slashes may be necessary in personnel and related expenses to avoid a disastrous loss. Continuous vigilance is required, supported by intestinal fortitude, to make the indicated changes in order to best serve the longer-term interests of employees, shareholders, creditors, and customers.

ROLE OF CONTROLLER IN PLANNING

The controller is the skilled analyst of the business, the interpreter of the figures. But his is not a disjointed or disconnected function. He may investigate and report upon matters which are solely production problems or sales problems. For example, he may determine the extent and cause of excess labor by department or cost center. However, there are many problems, including profit planning, which involve the broad aspects of the business. In approaching these problems, the controller can employ a broad perspective because the accounts reach into every department of the company. In fact, this situation should permit him to observe trends and relationships which those who deal with only one function cannot see. It follows, therefore, that he can and should retain the initiative in bringing many problems and recommended solutions to the attention of management. He should be a spark plug when it comes to planning for profits. He should not and cannot wait until some other executives bring up the matters for investigation.

The very essence of controllership in its highest form is coordination— the bringing together of all viewpoints in a proposed plan of action which, when approved or modified by executive management, becomes the accepted practice. In performing this function, the controller should study the business at all times and at all points, continually formulating or planning what controls, what line of action is most desirable from a profit-earning standpoint. He must seek and secure the cooperation of all the executives in bringing together for management discussion the results of an investigation. To accomplish this task, he must understand how costs behave in relation to volume. His work requires a thorough basic knowledge of the business, a well-organized accounting department which can carry on day-to-day routines with a minimum of his own supervision, and a keen study of all available financial and statistical information pertaining to his own company and related business. Much depends on the ability and personality of the man himself.

8

Profit Planning—
Its Method

BASIC APPROACH IN PROFIT PLANNING

A fundamental objective of business management is to find the most profitable course to which effort should be directed, and to hold the enterprise to that course. This, indeed, is planning and control of profits. Thus, the term "profit planning" has become associated with the flexible budget technique of planning and controlling operations. This involves, basically, a recognition of the fact that some costs or expenses vary with production or sales volume, while others are "time" costs and are more or less independent of volume. Changes in "time" or fixed costs are accomplished generally by management action. In terms of application, the utilization of cost and income data in determining what to produce and at what price to sell is all embodied in profit planning. Moreover, it involves the concept of variable costs and marginal income as contrasted with the use of conventional total costs.

It is not the purpose of the authors to review budgetary procedures, but rather to point out applications or problems associated with the cost-volume-profit relationship in business. Profit planning is here being restricted to special phases or applications of planning and control, and does not involve the detailed techniques concerned with cost segregation.

GENERAL COMMENTS ON THE COST-VOLUME-PROFIT RELATIONSHIP

Most business decisions involve the selection of alternatives—whether to accept certain business at a specified price or not, whether to sell aggressively products A or B, whether to expand in territory X or Y. In all these decisions, as well as many others, three factors must be considered: volume, costs, and profit. An understanding of the relationship among these three forces, and of the probable effect that any change in sales volume would have on the business, should be extremely helpful to management in a broad variety of problems involving planning and control. The interrelationship of costs, volume, and profits makes up what may be described as the profit structure of a company. Through the knowledge and intelligent use of such information, it is possible to predict the effect of any number of contemplated actions.

The data used in a review of this relationship may come from several channels and may differ considerably in adaptability or usefulness. In companies where a rather complete sales analysis is made, and where flexible budgets and standard costs are available, the records will provide the necessary information in readily usable form. Costs in all probability will have been segregated into the fixed and variable elements. If such sources are not available, then the conventional historical records might be utilized. Much analysis may be necessary to isolate the effect of changes in volume, selling prices, and variable costs. Moreover, if cost control has been poor, then the relationship between volume and costs will be difficult to detect and the margin of error will be high. Stated in other words, the accuracy of the results will depend greatly on the reliability of the data and the validity of the assumptions.

Very often, for investment or credit purposes, published financial statements are used as source data in studying the effect of volume on the business. It should be kept in mind that such statements are usually highly condensed and give little indication of the factors which may greatly influence the results—such as change in product mixture. Consequently, the extent of reliability is very limited.

THE BREAK-EVEN CHART

The profit structure of a company is often presented in the familiar break-even chart form. By such a presentation, management can understand the interrelationship of costs, profit, and volume much more readily than by tables. The simple chart illustrated in Fig. 13 is based upon the following assumptions:

1. That prices will remain unchanged
2. That fixed costs will remain the same up to the maximum capacity of the plant
3. That variable costs will vary in direct ratio to volume
4. That federal income taxes will be 50% of all income before taxes

Figure 13 clearly presents the following information for management:

1. Fixed costs of the business are $50,000 monthly.
2. Under present tax laws, and with present facilities, the maximum net profit is $25,000 per month, or $300,000 per year.

3. At present prices, a monthly sales volume of $100,000, or 50,000 units, is required to break even. This makes no provision for dividends to the stockholders.
4. To realize a net profit of $10,000 per month will require a sales volume of $140,000 per month.
5. Plant capacity expressed in sales dollars under existing prices and processes is $200,000 per month.

It may be observed that the net profit is measured by the vertical line between sales income and federal income taxes. Income taxes have been figured only from the break-even point.

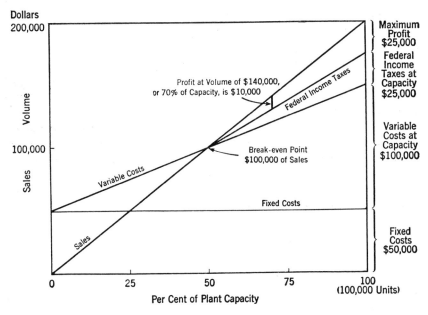

Fig. 13—Break-Even Chart Illustrating the Interrelationship of Costs, Volume, and Profit.

Another means of showing the relationship between net profit and sales volume is illustrated in Fig. 14. It can be seen that some of the essential cost factors are not disclosed.

A break-even chart which illustrates not only the operating factors but also the dividend requirements is shown in Fig. 15.

Needless to say, in most businesses the cost-volume-profit relationship is more complex than can be shown in any single break-even chart. This is discussed later. Moreover, it is not necessary to draw a chart to find the

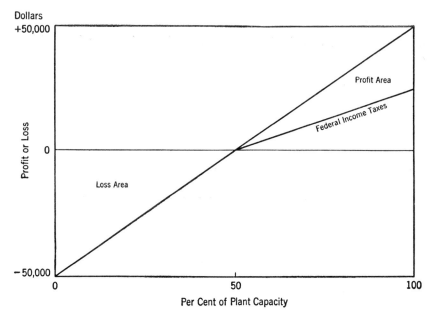

Fig. 14—Graphic Presentation of Relationships Between Sales Volume and Profit
or Loss.

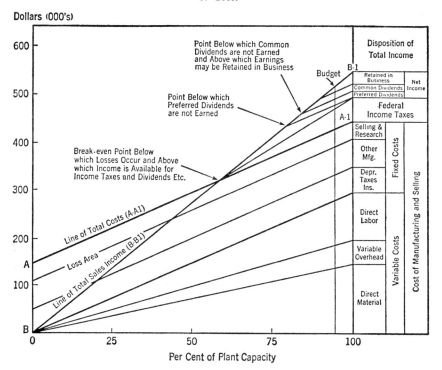

Fig. 15—Break-Even Chart Illustrating Sales Income and Its Disposition.

break-even point of a business. This can always be done by a simple calculation:

$$\text{Break-even point} = \frac{\text{Aggregate fixed expense}}{\text{Ratio of variable income to sales}}[1]$$

CHANGES IN SALES REVENUE

In analyzing the revenue factor, the controller may find it necessary to consider three aspects of the problem:

1. Treatment of difference between sales and production volume
2. Changes in the composition of sales
3. Changes in sales prices

When past experience is being analyzed, a problem is presented where the sales volume is greatly different from the production volume, with a corresponding change taking place in the finished goods inventory. And adjustment must be made because two different indexes of activity are being used—the production volume for variable manufacturing costs, and sales volume for certain selling and other expenses. The solution lies in converting to a common basis, namely, the sales dollar. First, manufacturing costs must be analyzed or compared to physical production converted to a sales basis—the sales value of production. Next, the non-manufacturing costs are measured against the sales value. The costs can then be superimposed on each other at the respective levels, and the total costs for various levels of activity can be determined.

CHANGES IN SALES MIXTURE

Most companies have a variety of product lines, each making a different contribution toward fixed expenses. Changes in the break-even point as well as the operating profit can result from shifts in the mixture of products sold, even though the sales prices are unchanged and the total dollar sales volume meets expectancy. Such results can occur also from changes in distribution channels or sales to different classes of customers if the rearrangement affects the contribution of the product over and above variable costs. Actually, when a break-even chart is used, an underlying assumption is that the proportion of each product sold, or sales through each channel of distribution, is unchanged. Very often this does not happen; the proportionate drop is not the same for all products. The higher-priced lines, for ex-

---

[1] Variable income represents sales income less the variable expense applicable to such sales.

ample, may decline much more rapidly than others. Such changes must be recognized in evaluating the data.

The effect of a change in sales mixture can be illustrated by the following calculations.

Assume the following proportion of sales among three products, the indicated variable costs, fixed costs, and profit:

	Sales		Variable	Marginal Income Over Variable Costs	
Product	%	Amount	Costs	Amount	% of Net Sales
A	40.00	$ 4,000.00	$2,600.00	$1,400.00	35.00
B	50.00	5,000.00	4,000.00	1,000.00	20.00
C	10.00	1,000.00	875.00	125.00	12.50
Total	100.00	$10,000.00	$7,475.00	2,525.00	25.25
Fixed Costs				1,200.00	
Operating Profit				$1,325.00	

The break-even point can be calculated as follows:

$$\frac{\$1,200}{.2525} = \$4,752$$

If, however, sales increase on the higher-margin items, the break-even point would naturally decrease. Such a change is illustrated as follows:

	Sales		Variable	Marginal Income Over Variable Costs	
Product	%	Amount	Costs	Amount	% of Net Sales
A	60.00	$ 6,000.00	$3,900.00	$2,100.00	35.00
B	35.00	3,500.00	2,800.00	700.00	20.00
C	5.00	500.00	437.50	62.50	12.50
Total	100.00	$10,000.00	$7,137.50	2,862.50	28.625
Fixed Costs				1,200.00	
Operating Profit				$1,662.50	

The break-even point would be:

$$\frac{\$1,200}{.28625} = \$4,192$$

This break-even point has dropped by $560 only as a result of the changes in sales mixture.

CHANGES IN SALES PRICE

On the typical break-even chart the sales value is represented by a line which starts at zero and proceeds upward as the volume increases. Sales value equals unit selling price times number of units. It can be understood that the slope of the line changes if the unit sales price changes. The effect of a 10% increase in selling prices is illustrated in Fig. 16.

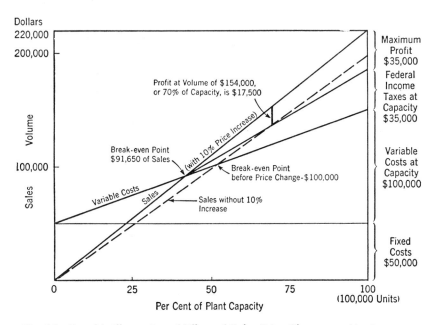

Fig. 16—Graphic Illustration of Effect of Sales Price Change on Net Income.

Quite often some of the variable costs—commissions or royalties, for example—are related to the sales price. Consequently, the variable cost line as well as the sales value line might change as a result of selling price changes. In Fig. 16 it has been assumed that variable costs relate only to units sold and not to value. As a direct result of the increase in selling price, the break-even point has dropped from $100,000 to $91,650, or by 8.35%.

It should be clear that a change in selling price affects the break-even point and the relationship between income and variable costs. The controller should also be aware that a change in selling price may have an even greater effect upon marginal income than a corresponding percentage increase in variable costs. For example, in the following illustration, a 10%

drop in selling prices is equivalent to an 11.1% increase in variable costs as regards the break-even point and marginal income:

	At Present Selling Prices		With a 10% Reduction in Sales Price		Equivalent Increase in Variable Costs	
	Amount	% of Net Sales	Amount	% of Net Sales	Amount	% of Net Sales
Sales	$50,000	100.00	$45,000	100.00	$50,000	100.00
Variable Costs	20,000	40.00	20,000	44.44	22,222	44.44
Marginal Income ...	30,000	60.00	25,000	55.56	27,778	55.56
Fixed Costs	15,000	30.00	15,000	33.33	15,000	30.00
Operating Profit	15,000	30.00	10,000	22.23	12,778	25.56
Break-even Volume..	$25,000		$27,000		$27,000	

Sales were reduced by 10% of $50,000 to a level of $45,000. As variable costs were not changed, these costs as a per cent of sales are 44.44%, or an increase of 11.1% (44.44 − 40 = 4.44; 4.44 ÷ 40 = 11.1%). Relating the revised variable cost as a per cent of net sales to the original $50,000 of sales produces a variable cost of $22,222. This is 11.1% higher than original variable cost.

CHANGES IN COSTS

Interpretation of the effect of changes in the cost level presents some interesting problems as well as opportunities for the controller.

An increase or decrease in the amount of fixed cost has a twofold effect: (1) the operating profit is changed by a like *amount* and (2) the break-even point is changed by a like *percentage*. To illustrate, assume a case where fixed costs are reduced by $10,000 or 33⅓%. The operating profit and break-even points would be thus:

	Present		Fixed Costs Reduced by $10,000	
	Amount	% of Net Sales	Amount	% of Net Sales
Net Sales	$200,000	100	$200,000	100
Variable Costs	120,000	60	120,000	60
Marginal Income	80,000	40	80,000	40
Fixed Costs	30,000	15	20,000	10
Operating Profit	50,000	25	60,000	30
Break-even Point Sales	$ 75,000		$ 50,000	

With a reduction of $10,000 in fixed costs, the operating profit naturally increased by a like amount. Moreover, fixed costs were reduced 33⅓%, and so the break-even point also declined by 33⅓%, or from a $75,000 sales volume to $50,000.

This calculation assumes that no change would take place in variable costs, but in practice a change in fixed costs may be accompanied by a change in the variable. For example, installation of a labor-saving device may increase depreciation and maintenance charges while at the same time decreasing direct labor costs and related payroll charges. Such possibilities must be considered. Needless to say, if an increase in fixed costs is

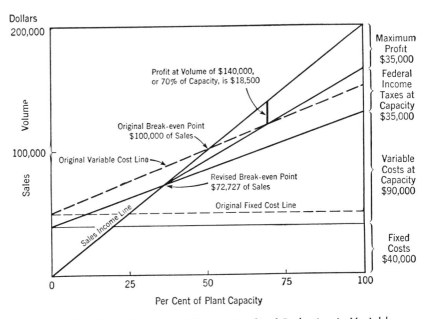

Fig. 17—Chart Illustrating Effect on Profit of Reduction in Variable and Fixed Costs.

being discussed, the probability of an increased sales volume should be reviewed. Furthermore, it would be well to examine possible alternatives, such as subcontracting or renting of space and equipment in lieu of purchasing. Acquisition of permanent assets will decrease the concern's ability to adjust its costs to lower levels should a reduced sales volume ever necessitate such action. Opportunities for the reduction of fixed expenses should not be overlooked in any attempt to reduce costs. A lowering of *fixed* costs increases the margin at any sales level, and, by reducing the break-even point, enables the company to withstand a greater drop in income before losses appear.

Changes in unit variable costs or expenses, of course, also affect the break-even point as well as the marginal income factor (discussed in the next section). Perhaps most cost reduction programs center about this category. A great many possibilities are open. For example, changes in the type of material used, or the purchase price of material, or the amount of scrap or waste can affect variable material costs. Changes in manufacturing processes, hourly labor rates, plant layout, or employee training methods, or the introduction of incentive payments can all affect the labor costs. General economic conditions may influence the ability of a firm to reduce variable costs. Very often the reduced sales volume permits more effective maintenance of equipment in the shutdown periods. Then, too, in such periods the labor turnover rate and material prices are usually reduced. Of course, such conditions may force sales price reductions on the company's own products.

The effect of reduced fixed and variable costs is graphically illustrated in Fig. 17.

MARGINAL INCOME RATIO AND MARGIN OF SAFETY

In any review of the interrelationship of costs and volume, one of the most significant figures is the marginal income ratio. This may be defined as the residual value after deducting the variable cost from net sales, expressed as a percentage of the net sales. The marginal income ratio represents the share of the sales dollar remaining to cover fixed expenses, income taxes, and net profit. It is indeed a highly useful figure, for it can be employed to determine readily the break-even point or the added income resulting from increased sales volume. To illustrate, if sales are to be increased by $30,000 and the marginal income ratio is 40%, then such sales should result in additional income before taxes, all other factors unchanged, of $12,000 (40% of $30,000). To determine the break-even sales volume, it is necessary merely to divide total fixed costs by the marginal income ratio, as mentioned earlier. The marginal income ratio is useful, also, in determining how low a price may be quoted, or what sales volume is required to support a salesman in a territory. It is probably a much more useful figure than the break-even point. Where the marginal income ratio is high, a change in sales volume has a tremendous effect on profit. Thus, an increase of $100,000 in sales will increase operating profit by $60,000 for a company with a 60% marginal income ratio, but only $20,000 for a firm with a 20% marginal income ratio. A high ratio, of course, may carry with it high fixed charges. Incidentally, if the controller can prepare the income and expense statements to indicate the marginal income, the use of such statements will be greatly enhanced.

Another figure often used in conjunction with cost-volume-profit analyses is the margin of safety. It is defined as the excess of actual or budgeted sales over the break-even sales volume, and is a measure of the extent to which sales may drop before losses appear. The profit strength of a business might be said to be proportionate to the distance between its existing sales volume and its break-even point. Over the period of a business cycle, as between any two companies of the same size with the same percentage of net profit on present sales volume, the one with the greater margin of safety may have the greater earning power.

ANALYSIS BY PRODUCTS

Since most companies have more than one product or product line, a large number of business decisions relate to *individual* product lines. For this reason, it is desirable to apply the cost-volume-profit analysis to specific product lines so that management can better understand the effect upon profits of changes in volume of selected products, or of the relative proportion of products sold.

The same technique which is applied to over-all operations can be applied to individual product lines. Decisions reached from such studies should be a guide in determining which products should be sold aggressively (or emphasized because of profits, or sold through a particular channel of distribution); which products should be continued but not promoted, merely because of some contribution toward fixed expense; and which lines or commodities should be discontinued or replaced by more profitable lines. Obviously, general economic conditions, relative supply and demand, and the long-range effect on customer relationships are some non-cost factors which must be weighed.

In making any profit analyses the reliability of the results depends in part upon the organizational structure and the extent or type of analysis made. To illustrate, a product manufactured in one plant and requiring all the plant's facilities, which is then marketed through its own separate sales organization, presents few cost allocation problems. Only part of the general administrative expenses need be allocated to the line. Quite in contrast to such a situation is a product whose production and distribution facilities are shared by many other items. In such a case the allocation of fixed and indirect costs requires careful attention, for the reliability of break-even points is greatly dependent upon the manner in which such common costs or expenses are distributed to product lines. If, on the other hand, the objective is not the determination of break-even points but rather a knowledge of marginal income by products, then no allocation of fixed costs would be necessary. The development of variable costs, depending on usage, would be relatively simple. And many companies predicate important decisions on the relative contribution of each line to fixed costs and profit.

Any controller who has had the task of determining an over-all break-even point for his company, and then has determined the break-even point by product lines, has perhaps been confused by the fact that the sum of the individual break-even points usually did not equal the over-all break-even point—unless the sales figures for each break-even point bore the same relationship to total sales as the individual break-even points bore to the over-all break-even point. Such a condition is well explained as follows: [2]

A business with three products has calculated break-even points for the individual products as follows:

	Product			
	A	B	C	Totals
Sales	$30	$25	$80	$135
Variable Costs	12	10	60	82
Fixed Costs	6	30	10	46
Break-Even Sales	10	50	40	100(by cross-footing)
				117(by computation from totals above)

The break-even point calculated on an over-all basis is found to exceed the break-even point obtained by summing individual product break-even points. However, if sales of each product have been at the break-even volume for that product, individual break-even points could be cross-footed, to obtain the break-even point based on total sales of the three products combined as illustrated below:

	Product			
	A	B	C	Totals
Sales	$10	$50	$40	$100
Variable Costs	4	20	30	54
Fixed Costs	6	30	10	46
Sales to Break-Even	10	50	40	100

The reason for the difference between the two sets of figures lies in the fact that the sales mix is not the same. Thus, in the first example, the products are sold in proportions of 22%, 19%, and 59%, whereas in the second they are sold in proportions of 10%, 50%, and 40%. When total sales differ from the break-even volume but the distribution among the three products is in the same proportions of 10%, 50%, and 40%, the individual product break-even points add up to the over-all break-even point as shown below:

	Product			
	A	B	C	Totals
Sales	$20	$100	$80	$200
Variable Costs	8	40	60	108
Fixed Costs	6	30	10	46
Sales to Break-Even	10	50	40	100

The effect of such changes in mix is exerted on the break-even point through changes in the over-all marginal income ratio. Unless individual product marginal income ratios are weighted by sales figures in the ratio of the individual product break-even volumes, a different over-all marginal income ratio and hence a different over-all break-even point results.

[2] "The Analysis of Cost-Volume-Profit Relationships," *NACA Bulletin,* December, 1949, pp. 539–40.

Where several product lines are being analyzed, the controller may find it advantageous to prepare break-even charts for each product if they are useful to the executives in profit planning. The relative profitability can be determined by observing the slope of the profit line, assuming the same relative scale is used. It is rather difficult to construct a break-even chart for all products combined, which would be of much practical significance. Some companies have used charts similar to Fig. 18. Obviously, all the factors cannot be presented.

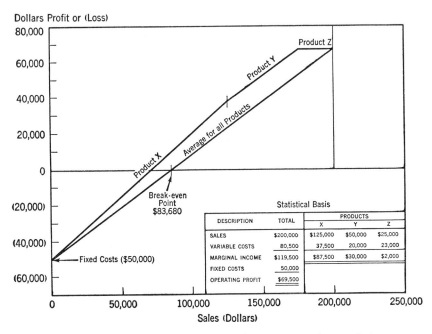

Fig. 18—Profitability of Products in Relation to Break-Even Point.

APPLICATION OF COST-VOLUME-PROFIT ANALYSIS

Even if the controller is fully aware of all the ramifications of the cost, volume, and profit relationship, the question arises as to how he can best put this information to work for management. The principal use of the data, of course, is in planning and policy-making decisions. Its chief value lies in the facility with which volume can be treated as a variable factor. Through applying such information, it is fairly simple to determine at various ranges of volume exactly what the effect on profits will be of contemplated changes. The traditional income and expense statement simply does not permit this.

A great variety of questions are asked in the management of a business, such as:

1. What will be the profit or loss at x sales level?
2. What additional sales volume will be needed to meet the fixed charges arising from the proposed plant expansion program?
3. What is the possibility of earning a profit on x product?
4. What sales volume is required to earn a certain designated profit?
5. At a sales level of x per month, what reduction in fixed and variable costs must be made to earn a profit, before taxes, of some designated amount?
6. What will be the effect of adding a second shift operation?
7. What effect will a 15% increase in sales volume have on profits?

For questions such as these, the controller should find the answers very easily through the analyses just described. Stated positively, a thorough understanding and analysis of cost-volume-profit data can provide information for such uses as:

1. Sales and Pricing Policies
   a. Determination of profit which will result from any given volume of sales
   b. Analysis of effect of changes in selling prices
   c. Effect of change in product mixture
   d. Additional sales volume needed to support a salesman in a territory, or a warehouse, etc.
   e. Lowest prices at which business may be accepted to utilize facilities and contribute something toward net profit
   f. The particular products to be emphasized to reflect the greatest net profit

2. Financial and Production Problems
   a. Interpretation of proposed or alternative budgets and effect of suggested cost and other changes—when the goals are not satisfactory to management
   b. Determination of unit costs at various volume levels
   c. Determination of probable effect of investment in new plant and equipment
   d. Determination of most profitable use of scarce materials
   e. Assistance in choice between subcontracting work or manufacturing certain articles

3. General
   a. General understanding of profit structure of the business, and effect of volume changes—for the major executives
   b. General educational purposes for plant supervision

Some of these applications are discussed in the following pages.

SELECTING THE MOST PROFITABLE PRODUCTS

When all the productive facilities of a company are fully occupied, and when the demand is much greater than supply, a decision must be reached as to the products to be manufactured. The long-term customer reactions, the availability of material, and the probable continued price differential between different products must be weighed. But relative costs and profit should be important factors in the decision. Whether one or many products are manufactured, the principle is valid. Of course, where several products are manufactured by different processes and in different departments, the bottleneck department should be considered separately.

Description	Product A	Product B
PER HUNDRED POUNDS		
Selling Price...	$35.00	$ 28.00
Costs		
Variable:		
Material...	18.00	16.00
Labor and Overhead..............................	8.00	5.33
Total Variable..............................	26.00	21.33
Fixed..	5.00	3.33
Total Cost..	31.00	24.66
Operating Profit....................................	4.00	3.34
Marginal Profit......................................	$ 9.00	$ 6.67
PER MACHINE HOUR		
Rate of Production (cwt.).............................	10	15
Operating Profit ($4.00 times 10; and $3.34 times 15)........	$40.00	$ 50.10
Marginal Profit ($9.00 times 10; and $6.67 times 15)........	$90.00	$100.05

Fig. 19—Computation of Marginal Profit per Unit of Product and per Machine-Hour.

In earlier sections the importance of marginal income was emphasized; and the greatest marginal income is desirable because it usually results in the highest net profit. However, when considering marginal income, the greatest income per piece or per pound is not the sole factor, for the effect of the rate of production must be reckoned with. To be specific, refer to Fig. 19. The greatest marginal profit per unit of sale, per hundredweight, is realized on product A. Product B returns only $6.67 marginal income per unit. If only this *unit* marginal contribution were considered, the business would not be making the best use of the facilities. When the operating hour is taken into account, product B returns 11.12% more than A— $100.05 per machine hour as compared with $90 for product A.

In making decisions of this nature, other cost factors must be kept in mind; e.g., cost of carrying inventories and receivables, changes in the relationship of fixed and variable expense.

THE MINIMUM SELLING PRICE

In theory, perhaps, each product should yield a net profit. However, under our competitive economy this does not usually happen. Some products bear their own direct costs, a full share of indirect expenses, and return a net profit. Others may carry only a partial share of their indirect costs. In any event, the objective is to secure the greatest over-all profit. When all the available capacity is not being utilized, the problem arises as to the lowest price to be charged which will still contribute something to the over-all profit. The obvious answer is recovery of variable costs, taking into account any additional maintenance or other costs. Such costs set the floor, and anything above this is making a contribution toward fixed expenses. The concept of fixed and variable costs is necessary to such a determination. Obviously, the controller should be realistic or conservative in the segregation of costs. Further, any legal implications—e.g., the possibility of violating the Robinson-Patman Act—must be reviewed.

UNIT COSTS AT DIFFERENT VOLUME LEVELS

Another application of the cost-volume-profit relationship is in the determination of unit costs. Suppose, for example, that management desires to know what the unit cost would be at various sales volume levels, with prices remaining fixed. It may be assumed that, in the illustration at hand, the selling price is $2 per unit. What would be the unit cost were the sales to be increased to $240,000? It is assumed that the present sales consist of 50,000 units and that the present unit cost is $2.40, consisting of $.80 of fixed costs and $1.60 of variable costs.

The proposed volume is 120,000 units ($240,000 ÷ $2). The new unit cost would then be:

$$\frac{\text{Fixed costs}}{\text{Proposed unit volume}} + \text{Present variable unit cost}$$

$$= \frac{\$40,000}{120,000} + \$1.60$$
$$= \$\ .333 \ + \$1.60$$
$$= \$1.933$$

At a sales volume of $240,000, the unit cost is $1.933.

INCREASED SALES VOLUME TO OFFSET REDUCED SELLING PRICES

In the same illustration, let it be assumed that the sales department insists that the present low volume is due to the fact that the company's prices are out of line with those of competing concerns or with competing products. A reduction of 10% in selling prices is advised. What percentage increase in volume will be necessary to yield a profit of $5,000 if selling prices are reduced 10%?

The assumptions are the same as those mentioned previously, except for the change in prices. In this case, the solution is:

Increased Sales Volume Required to Offset Reduced Selling Price

$$= \frac{\text{Profit desired plus fixed costs}}{1 - \left(\dfrac{\text{Present variable ratio}}{1 - \text{Proposed percentage reduction in selling price}} \right)}$$

$$= \frac{\$5,000 + \$40,000}{1 - \dfrac{\dfrac{\$80,000}{\$100,000}}{1-.10}} = \frac{\$45,000}{1 - \dfrac{.8}{.9}}$$

$$= \frac{\$45,000}{.111111} = \$405,000$$

Therefore, a sales volume of $405,000, or 225,000 units, must be secured to produce a profit of $5,000 if prices are reduced by 10%. If this goes beyond the capacity of the plant, such a program is impossible without further increase in fixed costs.

MOST PROFITABLE USE OF SCARCE MATERIALS

Another interesting application of the cost and profit relationship is the determination of the best use of restricted or scarce materials. Assume, for example, that only partial requirements are available of a chemical common to five products. How should the ingredient "X" be distributed, considering only the greatest net profit to the company? It is assumed that rates of production are about the same, and that all products are manufactured with the same facilities. The solution is evident from the following example:

	Unit				
Product	Selling Price	Variable Cost	Marginal Income Contribution	Pounds of "X" per Lb. of Product	Marginal Profit per Lb. of "X"
1	$2.00	$1.00	$1.00	.5	$2.00
2	2.50	1.50	1.00	.3	3.33
3	4.00	2.50	1.50	.5	3.00
4	3.00	1.00	2.00	1.5	1.33
5	5.00	2.50	2.50	2.0	1.25

Product 2 yields the greatest profit per pound of "X" and these requirements should be met first, all other factors being equal.

ADVISABILITY OF PLANT EXPANSION

Break-even and related data are helpful when considering plant expansion. The following information would be useful in arriving at a decision:

1. The relative break-even points
2. The sales volume required to earn existing profits
3. The sales volume required to net a fair return on the investment
4. The maximum profit

Assume the following present average earnings statement (monthly) of the company:

Net Sales	$500,000
Costs and Expenses	
Variable (60% Net Sales)	300,000
Fixed	100,000
Total	400,000
Net Profit Before Taxes	100,000
Federal Income Taxes (50%)	50,000
Net Profit	$ 50,000

Increased fixed costs with plant expansion — $50,000
Additional income desired on investment — $5,000
Maximum production in new plant — $300,000

Using the available data, these determinations can be made:

1. *Break-Even Points.*

    Present facilities:

$$\frac{\text{Fixed costs}}{\text{Marginal income ratio}} = \frac{\$100,000}{.40} = \$250,000 \text{ sales volume}$$

    Proposed:

$$\frac{\text{Present} + \text{Additional fixed costs}}{\text{Marginal income ratio}} = \frac{\$150,000}{.40} = \$375,000 \text{ sales volume}$$

2. *Sales Volume Required to Earn Existing Profit.*

$$= \frac{\text{Present fixed costs} + \text{Additional fixed costs} + \text{Existing profit}}{\text{Marginal income ratio}}$$

$$= \frac{\$100,000 + \$50,000 + \$100,000}{.40}$$

$$= \frac{\$250,000}{.40}$$

$$= \$625,000 \text{ sales volume}$$

3. *Sales Volume to Net a Fair Return on Added Investment.*

Assume a fair return on the added investment to be $5,000 (monthly) after federal income taxes, or $10,000 before.

Then a fair return equals at least existing profit plus the above return.

$$= \frac{\text{Present fixed costs} + \text{Additional fixed costs} + \text{Existing profit} + \text{Return on added investment}}{\text{Marginal income ratio}}$$

$$= \frac{\$260,000}{.40}$$

$$= \$650,000 \text{ sales volume}$$

4. *Maximum Earnings with New Plant.*

Net Sales ($500,000 + $300,000)	$800,000
Costs and Expenses	
Variable (60% of Net Sales)	480,000
Fixed	150,000
Total	630,000
Net Profit Before Taxes	170,000
Federal Income Taxes (50%)	85,000
Net Profit	$ 85,000

These computations may be summarized as follows:

Item	Present	Prospective	Increase
Break-even Sales Volume (Monthly)	$250,000	$375,000	$125,000
Sales Volume to Earn Existing Profit	500,000	625,000	125,000
Sales Volume to Earn 6% on New Plant Cost ..	—	650,000	—
Maximum Profit	50,000	85,000	35,000
Sales Volume to Earn Maximum Profit	500,000	800,000	300,000

The management must consider the possibility of increasing sales by $125,000 monthly to maintain existing profits. It must also weigh the probability of sales remaining at least $125,000 higher, for profits before income taxes will be reduced by $50,000 per month if the expansion is made but sales continue at the present level. Sales must be increased by $125,000 just to retain existing profits, but this disadvantage may be offset by the higher potential earnings of $35,000 per month.

Incidentally, these calculations illustrate the variety of simple arithmetical formulas which may be helpful in profit planning and control.

BREAK-EVEN ANALYSIS TO EVALUATE A FORECAST [3]

The discussion of the cost-volume-profit technique has been applied in large part to segments of the business—to individual products, or areas, or projects such as a new plant. Yet, the same approach can be useful in judging the business plans of a division or a company. Typically, a projection is compared with some past year, usually the immediately preceding year, to determine whether or not it appears satisfactory. Such a comparison has value. It may be a gauge of the adequacy of the sales volume and, in a general way, it may raise questions about cost or expense levels. However, such a comparison is not as sharp a tool as is available. Most of the time, the sales level and product mix in the forecast year will not be identical with that of the past year. Therefore, it may be difficult to measure more precisely the propriety of the costs and expenses in relationship to sales volume. To further complicate the problem, management, when looking at a higher sales volume and a net income which appears more favorable, tends to be less critical. In most instances, if net income expressed as a per cent of sales is greater than the preceding year, the forecast is gleefully pronounced satisfactory.

Why not use a superior tool which permits a more effective evaluation of the volume factor? Once management has agreed upon a reasonable sales objective, a volume for the year under forecast, then it becomes practical to measure the proposed forecast against the break-even structure, i.e., to apply the break-even economic structure of the company to the projected sales volume. Essentially, this means that management should decide upon a reasonable cost-profit-volume relationship and that this standard should be used as a measure of the forecast. The results of the application of the break-even factors, as shown in Fig. 20, to a projected sales volume (standard profit structure) and the comparison of such results with the aggregate costs and expenses as set forth in an illustrative forecast, are shown in Fig. 21. It is to be noted that percentage relationships are developed to aid in detecting out-of-line conditions. The exhibit portrays one of the basic considerations in the preparation of forecasts, i.e., that the company must not be allowed to develop or assume a less favorable cost structure. Hence, it is necessary to apply some over-all tests quite distinct, for example, from individual departmental budget performance.

The greatest dollar increase and relative increase is in prime material costs. This 5% or $250,000 increase must be analyzed to determine whether the cost increase results from changes in product mix or from cost increases in any given product line. The initial break-even application has isolated this apparently excessive cost relationship. Now it should be

---

[3] Adapted in part from James D. Willson, "Practical Applications of Cost-Volume-Profit Analysis," *NAA Bulletin*, March, 1960, pp. 5–18.

The Sample Company
Profit Structure

Description	Fixed Costs	Variable Costs Total	Variable Costs % Net Sales	Combined
Net Sales				$10,000,000
Costs and Expenses				
Direct Material		$4,000,000	40.00%	
Direct Labor		1,000,000	10.00	
Manufacturing Expenses	$ 500,000	1,000,000	10.00	
Selling Expenses	400,000	100,000	1.00	
Research and Development Expenses	250,000	50,000	.50	
General and Administrative Expenses	150,000	50,000	.50	
	$1,300,000	$6,200,000	62.00%	7,500,000
Profit Before Income Taxes				$ 2,500,000

Fig. 20—Standard Profit Structure.

The Sample Company
Break-even Analysis of Forecast
Fiscal Year 1960

Description	Application of Standard Profit Structure	Tentative Forecast	Forecast Over (Under) Standard Amount	Forecast Over (Under) Standard %
Net Sales	$12,500,000	$12,500,000		
Cost of Sales				
Direct Material	5,000,000	5,250,000	$250,000	5.00%
Direct Labor	1,250,000	1,310,000	60,000	4.80
Manufacturing Expenses	1,750,000	1,820,000	70,000	4.00
Total	8,000,000	8,380,000	380,000	4.75
Gross Margin	4,500,000	4,120,000	(380,000)	(8.44)
Operating Expenses				
Selling	525,000	540,000	15,000	2.86
Research and Development	312,500	310,000	(2,500)	(.80)
General and Administrative	212,500	190,000	(22,500)	(10.59)
Total	1,050,000	1,040,000	(10,000)	(.95)
Profit Before Taxes	$ 3,450,000	$ 3,080,000	$370,000	(10.72%)
Other Data				
Break-even Point	$ 3,421,050	$ 3,714,290	$293,240	8.6%
Marginal Income Ratio	.38	.35		

Fig. 21—Comparison of Standard and Forecast Profit Structure.

114

analyzed in more depth and a decision made as to an acceptable plan. Perhaps the product mix is not the optimum believed to be attainable in the forecast year. Perhaps action can be taken on cost increases to reduce or eliminate them.

The Sample Company

PROFIT GRAPH

(Standard and Forecast)

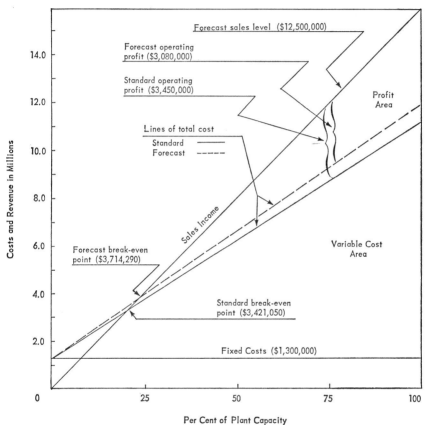

Fig. 22—Profit Graph Comparing Standard and Forecast Performance.

Second, the next largest *relative* increase, amounting to $60,000, is in direct labor. A similar analysis should be made to localize the cause and seek an improvement in the plan.

Next, manufacturing expenses have increased by 4%, or $70,000. Departmental budgets should be reviewed to determine the areas of greatest increase and their causes. Management must then decide what corrective

The Toledo Manufacturing Company

STATEMENT OF INCOME AND EXPENSE BY PRODUCT LINES
For the Month Ended November 30, 1961

	ALL PRODUCTS		PLASTIC MOLDINGS			PAINTS			DISHWARE		
	Amount	% of Net Sales	Amount	% of Net Sales	Per Cwt.	Amount	% of Net Sales	Per Cwt.	Amount	% of Net Sales	Per Cwt.
SALES											
Gross Sales	$146,835		$143,575		$20.65	$1,210		$10.26	$2,050		$62.00
Less: Returns and Allowances	7,750		7,742			4			4		
Net Sales	139,085	100.0	135,833	100.0		1,206	100.0		2,046	100.0	
COST OF SALES											
AT STANDARD											
Variable											
Material	62,792	45.1	60,913	44.8	9.26	539	44.7	4.58	1,340	65.5	40.61
Manufacturing Expense	16,145	11.6	15,977	11.8	2.43	105	8.7	.89	63	3.1	1.91
Royalties	69	—	—	—	—	—	—	—	69	3.4	2.09
Total Variable Cost	79,006	56.7	76,890	56.6	11.69	644	53.4	5.47	1,472	72.0	44.61
Fixed	8,245	6.0	8,169	6.0	1.24	45	3.8	.40	31	1.4	.94
Total	87,251	62.7	85,059	62.6	12.93	689	57.2	5.87	1,503	73.4	45.55
Standard Manufacturing Profit	51,834	37.3	50,774	37.4	7.72	517	42.8	4.39	543	26.6	16.45
OVER OR (UNDER) STANDARD											
Material and Freight—Price	(137)	(.1)	(133)	(.1)	—	(3)	(.3)	(.03)	(1)	—	(.03)
Material Usage	3,215	2.3	3,186	2.3	.48	4	.4	.03	25	1.2	.76
Variable Labor and Manufacturing Expense	14,112	10.2	13,833	10.2	2.10	269	22.3	2.29	10	.5	.30
Subtotal	17,190	12.4	16,886	12.4	2.58	270	22.4	2.29	34	1.7	1.03
Fixed Manufacturing Expense	5,023	3.6	4,977	3.7	.77	27	2.2	.22	19	.9	.58
Total	22,213	16.0	21,863*	16.1	3.35	297	24.6	2.51	53	2.6	1.61
MANUFACTURING PROFIT	29,621	21.3	28,911	21.3	4.37	220	18.2	1.88	490	24.0	14.84
OPERATING EXPENSE											
Administrative	3,107	2.2	3,034	2.3	.45	27	2.2	.23	46	2.2	1.38
Selling and Advertising	17,484	12.6	17,075	12.5	2.59	151	12.5	1.29	258	12.6	7.80
Research and Development	6,761	4.9	6,603	4.9	1.00	59	5.0	.50	99	4.9	3.00
Total	27,352	19.7	26,712	19.7	4.04	237	19.7	2.02	403	19.7	12.18
Operating Profit or (Loss)	2,269	1.6	$ 2,199	1.6	$ .33	$(16)	(1.5)	$(.14)	$ 87	4.3	$ 2.66
Other Income (net)	6,205	4.4									
Profit Before Federal Income Taxes	8,474	6.0									
Federal Income Taxes	3,389	2.4									
Net Profit	$ 5,085	3.6									
Net Shipments—Pounds	673,835		657,775			11,760			3,300		
Production—Pounds	688,800		654,244			34,563			1,000		

* See Fig. 24 for details.

Fig. 23. Statement of Income and Expense with Segregation of Fixed and Variable Manufacturing Costs.

action must be taken. If, for example, the increase is in maintenance expense, is it sound to defer projects? What is the best approach when considering the longer-term interests of the business? Similar analyses should be made of the other expense areas. If expenses are *under* the standard, the accountant should ascertain that no omissions have been made erroneously.

It is to be observed that the break-even point has risen by 8.6% to $3,714,290. Perhaps a better way to state the case is that the forecast is based on a somewhat changed cost structure. This change may be shown graphically as in Fig. 22. The solid lines indicate the acceptable cost-volume-profit structure and the dotted lines reveal the condition as planned in the forecast. Incidentally, any change in this relationship can be readily shown on the graph, whether in sales, variable costs, or fixed expense.

In poor economic weather, a reasonable margin of safety is necessary. Accordingly, in the Sample Company, if management agrees that the standard profit structure must be maintained, every element should be analyzed and explored by the accountant so that the final business plan for the ensuing year retains the characteristics of this structure. As an alternative, once the most satisfactory cost-volume-profit relationship is determined, including the proper product mix, then the possibility of securing additional sales volume to offset cost increases is to be considered.

A WORKABLE STATEMENT OF INCOME AND EXPENSE

The conventional statement of income and expense can be quite misleading. In practice, managements have been known to take action on the basis of such statements, when the action was unwarranted on the basis of actual facts. Companies have discontinued products which showed losses on the conventional statements only to find that the loss increased as a result of the discontinuance. Further, goods have been sold at prices below cost in the belief that added volume would reduce the costs and result in a profit. Of course, the controller may explain that action should not be taken on the strength of a monthly statement of income and expense, which is very true. He may emphasize that all the facts should be marshaled in making a decision—which means a detailed analysis. But the fact remains that some executives may take corrective action, however ill-advised, after seeing the monthly statement. It behooves the chief accounting official to devise a form of statement which may be a little more informative or helpful in giving some clues, and which will give a better perspective of the situation. Basically, of course, this merely means making a distinction between fixed and variable costs or expenses. One such statement for internal management purposes is illustrated in Fig. 23. The contribution of each product line toward fixed expenses and profits is shown, and a great deal of information can be gleaned from the supplementary data shown

The Toledo Manufacturing Company

COMPARISON OF ACTUAL AND STANDARD MANUFACTURING COSTS

OF PLASTIC MOLDINGS

For the Month Ended November 30, 1961

Description	Actual	Standard	Actual (Over) or Under Standard
PRICE			
Material	$ 41,277	$41,370	$ 93
Freight	3,061	3,101	40
Total	44,338	44,471	133
MATERIAL USAGE			
Yield	2,730	–	(2,730)
Containers	3,519	3,292	(227)
Inventory Shortages	229	–	(229)
Total Material Usage	6,478	3,292	(3,186)
DIRECT LABOR AND MANUFACTURING EXPENSE			
Variable			
Direct Labor			
Preforming	2,174	2,001	(173)
Molding	16,861	10,179	(6,682)
Polishing	2,941	2,147	(794)
Packing	6,987	2,830	(4,157)
Total Direct Labor	28,963	17,157	(11,806)
Manufacturing Expense			
Preforming	873	862	(11)
Molding	2,016	1,698	(318)
Polishing	910	920	10
Packing	2,110	1,742	(368)
Receiving	1,847	1,074	(773)
Shipping	1,994	1,427	(567)
Total Manufacturing Expense	9,750	7,723	(2,027)
Total Variable Direct Labor and Manufacturing Expense	38,713	24,880	(13,833)
Fixed Expense			
Direct Overhead	1,204	1,016	(188)
General Manufacturing Overhead	677	623	(54)
Depreciation*	11,806	7,118	(4,688)
Property Taxes and Insurance	850	803	(47)
Total Fixed Expense	14,537	9,560	(4,977)
Total Direct Labor and Manufacturing Expense	53,250	34,440	(18,810)
Total	$104,066	$82,203	$(21,863)

* Includes $4,123 applicable to prior months.

Fig. 24—Comparison of Actual and Standard Manufacturing Costs.

thereon. Such a statement may be supported by other schedules giving the details of actual and standard manufacturing expenses, as in Fig. 24. Where desirable, a statement of cost of goods manufactured can be prepared using the same principle of segregating fixed and variable costs.

SOME PRACTICAL GENERALIZATIONS

The primary purpose in any analysis of the cost-volume-profit relationship is to permit the planning of larger profits in the future. Such reviews may disclose basic weaknesses in the profit structure and assist in suggesting remedies. Because the field is so broad, it is felt desirable to summarize some generalizations which should be clearly understood by the controller, and by other members of management as well. These general comments are:

1. A change in the *amount* of *fixed* costs changes the break-even point by a similar percentage and the operating profit by a like amount, but does not affect the marginal income ratio.
2. A change in the selling price changes the break-even point and marginal income ratio. Such a change, percentagewise, may be quite different in the effect on the marginal income ratio than a similar percentage change in variable costs.
3. A change in variable costs, likewise, changes the break-even point and marginal income ratio.
4. When the marginal income ratio is high, large profits may result from comparatively small increases in sales volume above the break-even point. For the same reason, small declines in revenue will cut sharply into profits. By like token, a low marginal income ratio requires considerable change in sales volume to reflect any significant change in profits.
5. A high margin of safety indicates that a substantial drop in sales volume can take place before losses develop.
6. When certain conditions exist, some general conclusions as to points of attack can be suggested. For example:
   a. A high marginal income ratio with a low margin of safety probably indicates an excess of fixed costs for the sales volume. The remedy lies in either reducing such fixed costs or increasing the sales volume.
   b. A low marginal income ratio and a low margin of safety may indicate that selling prices are too low, or variable costs are too high. If prices are as high as competition will allow, then variable costs should be combed for possible reductions.

STATISTICAL TECHNIQUES FOR PLANNING

Business is complex; and the decisions faced by management become increasingly difficult as more alternatives need to be considered. The many products, the many processes, the constant change simply accentuate the pressure for the most modern techniques in the planning and forecasting area. Speed is necessary if adequate attention is to be paid to the various possible courses of action. Moreover, once a business plan has been conceived, a review every three months may be too infrequent. As one month closes, and as more information about probable conditions in the following thirty days is available, management wants to know the outlook for the succeeding period.

An analysis of such alternatives and the need for constant projections into the future places a tremendous burden on the accounting staff unless statistical techniques are utilized. The break-even analysis approach must be combined with linear programming, statistical decision theory, and the use of electronic computers if a satisfactory planning job is to be done. The controller must add these latest mathematical techniques to his know-how.

9

Profit Planning—
An Application

AN ILLUSTRATIVE ANALYSIS

When net losses crop up or when profits are not satisfactory, and such a condition appears to persist, the task of making a critical review of the operations may well fall to the controller. He should encourage the preparation of such an analysis for it represents an opportunity to render a real service. Illustrated in this section is an analysis prepared as the basis for executive discussion by the officers of an integrated chemical company. In this case, it is assumed that the company has operated heavily in the red in one of three divisions, and the management can see no immediate prospects of improving the condition.

The general steps in the analysis, while partially evident from accompanying figures, are outlined as follows:

1. The operations for the past year were reviewed to secure some indication of the nature of the costs, and the points of apparent waste or excessive costs

2. Unit standard costs, budgets, and variances were analyzed and segregated into their fixed and variable elements

3. Sales were analyzed to determine a representative product mixture, by certain commodity groups

4. With known product mixture, total costs and income at capacity were determined

5. On the basis of information determined in step 4 above, profit graphs were prepared

6. Within each product group, marginal income for each product was determined so as to suggest a more profitable sales mixture

7. The data were interpreted in a narrative report containing recommendations for improvement

The remainder of this chapter reproduces in full the report prepared by the controller.

CHEMICAL MANUFACTURING CORPORATION
CHICAGO DIVISION
Report on Profit Potential and Break-even Points

GENERAL COMMENTS

Operations at the Chicago Division for the year ended December 31, 1960, resulted in a net loss of $730,142.

It may be taken for granted that the past year was one of experimentation and inefficiency which might be expected normally as a part of the start-up cost of a new plant. However, the question which now can be asked is: "What is the normal profit expectancy, now that operating experience has been gained?" Other questions frequently posed include these:

1. Would the company as a whole have lost less if the Chicago Division had not operated?

2. What are the earning possibilities of the Division?

3. What are the break-even points of the three major product lines?

4. What action can be taken to minimize losses or increase profits?

It is hoped that some of the facts and opinions expressed in this report will stimulate thinking as to possible corrective action.

OPERATIONS FOR THE YEAR 1960

A summary of operating results is presented in Fig. 25. The net loss of $730,142 represents 35.95% of net sales. It will be observed that the standard gross margin is only 13.25% of net sales, and that it was insufficient to cover the operating expenses. If the plant had operated close to capacity the excess fixed costs of $268,082 would have largely disappeared. Furthermore, the additional income, even at a low margin rate, probably would have been sufficient to offset a major share of the excess manufacturing costs and operating expenses. Even at the higher volume level, the results would have been disappointing.

However, the over-all company losses for the year would have been greater if the Chicago Division had not operated. This results from the

Chemical Manufacturing Corporation—Chicago Division
STATEMENT OF INCOME AND EXPENSE

For the Year Ended December 31, 1960

		Amount	Percent of Sales
Net Sales...		$2,030,958	100.00
Cost of Sales			
At Standard:			
Material.........................	$1,515,062		
Variable Expense..................	82,705		
Fixed Expense....................	164,022	1,761,789	86.75
Standard Gross Margin............................		269,169	13.25
Over Standard:			
Material.........................	168,305		
Variable Expense..................	135,182		
Fixed Expense....................	268,082	571,569	28.14
Manufacturing Loss.................................		302,400	14.89
Operating Expenses................................		441,639	21.74
Operating Loss.....................................		744,039	36.63
Other Income (Net).................................		13,897	.68
Net Loss...		$ 730,142	35.95

Fig. 25—Statement of Income and Expense.

fact that the sales income was greater than the direct out-of-pocket charges. A balance was available to cover either a share of the general office expenses, or Illinois Division expenses, or the depreciation and insurance costs which would have continued. The net advantage of operating the Chicago Division was $185,646, calculated as follows:

Net Sales		$2,030,958
Other Income (Net)		13,897
Total		2,044,855
Deduct:		
Direct Out-of-Pocket Costs		
Material	$1,683,367	
Expenses	175,842	1,859,209
Income in Excess of Out-of-Pocket Costs		$ 185,646

Chemical Manufacturing Corporation—Chicago Division

STATEMENT OF ESTIMATED INCOME AND EXPENSE

At Plant Capacity (5-Day Week) For One Month

Description	PAINTS			AMMONIA DERIVATIVES			COKE BY-PRODUCTS			TOTAL		
	Amount	Per Cwt.	% Net Sales	Amount	Per Cwt.	% Net Sales	Amount	Per Cwt.	% Net Sales	Amount	Per Cwt.	% Net Sales
Net Sales Before Freight Allowance..	$282,050	$19.6742	105.26	$103,617	$19.8500	104.81	$118,820	$26.0000	103.96	$504,487	$20.9105	104.86
Less: Freight Allowance..	14,099	.9835	5.26	4,754	.9107	4.81	4,521	.9893	3.96	23,374	.9688	4.86
Net Sales..	267,951	18.6907	100.00	98,863	18.9393	100.00	114,299	25.0107	100.00	481,113	19.9417	100.00
Cost of Sales												
Variable..	231,657	16.1591	86.45	75,621	14.4868	76.49	70,308	15.3847	61.51	377,586	15.6506	78.48
Fixed..	16,010	1.1168	5.98	9,442	1.8088	9.55	13,554	2.9659	11.86	39,006	1.6168	8.11
Total Cost of Sales..	247,667	17.2759	92.43	85,063	16.2956	86.04	83,862	18.3506	73.37	416,592	17.2674	86.59
Manufacturing Profit..	20,284	1.4149	7.57	13,800	2.6437	13.96	30,437	6.6602	26.63	64,521	2.6743	13.41
Operating Expenses..	19,823	1.3827	7.40	7,603	1.4565	7.69	8,368	1.8311	7.32	35,794	1.4836	7.44
Operating Profit..	$ 461	$ .0322	.17	$ 6,197	$ 1.1872	6.27	$ 22,069	$ 4.8291	19.31	$ 28,727	$ 1.1907	5.97
Pounds Manufactured and Sold..	1,433,600			522,000			457,000			2,412,600		

NOTES:
(1) Variable expenses shown above are those indicated in Fig. 30, except that freight costs have been deducted from sales (and not included in cost of sales) to arrive at a net sales figure consistent with the usual statement presentation.
(2) Reference is made to the appended comments which are an integral part of this report.

Fig. 26—Statement of Estimated Income and Expense by Product Line.

This gain is reconciled with the net loss in this manner:

Allocated Expenses

Illinois Division Expenses	$ 510,859
General Offices Expenses	214,114
Total Allocated Expenses	724,973
Continuing Fixed Charges—Depreciation, etc.	190,815
Total Costs	915,788

Deduct:

Income in Excess of Out-of-Pocket Costs	185,646
Net Loss	$ 730,142

It is to be observed that the fixed charges of $190,815 would not have been incurred if the Chicago Division properties had not been purchased, and that they will continue until the property is either fully depreciated or disposed of. Moreover, the income in excess of out-of-pocket expenses, an amount of $185,646, was almost enough to cover the continuing fixed charges.

PROSPECTS FOR THE FUTURE

The severe losses of last year have prompted a thorough review of future possibilities. After extensive discussions with the General Sales Manager and Works Manager, together with a critical analysis of present sales trends and expected cost levels, it appears that present plans would result in an operating profit, at plant capacity, of $28,727 per month or $344,724 per year. While this is more encouraging than a loss of $730,142, yet over-all profit is only 5.97% of net sales. The condensed statement by product lines is shown in Fig. 26. A most serious aspect is the almost total lack of profit, even at capacity levels, on our most voluminous product—paints. Quite in contrast, the coke by-products show a possible operating profit of 19.31% of net sales at capacity.

The Chicago Division, of course, has not yet attained 100% of plant capacity sales volume.

PROFIT POTENTIALS AT VARIOUS VOLUME LEVELS

Because the Division may experience several different monthly sales and production levels, it has been felt desirable to construct profit graphs so that the operating profit on any of the three product lines may be anticipated with a reasonable degree of accuracy. These are illustrated in Figs. 27, 28, and 29. The probable profit or loss at any selected volume level is

Thousands of Dollars

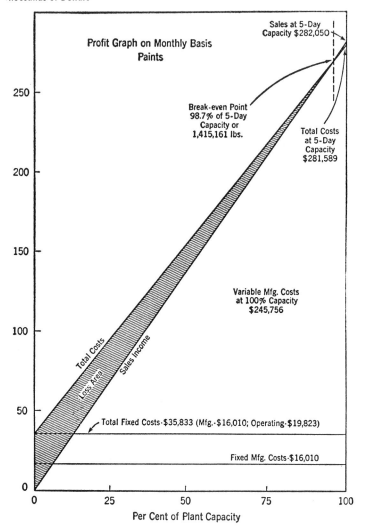

Fig. 27—Break-Even Chart—Paint Works.

Thousands of Dollars

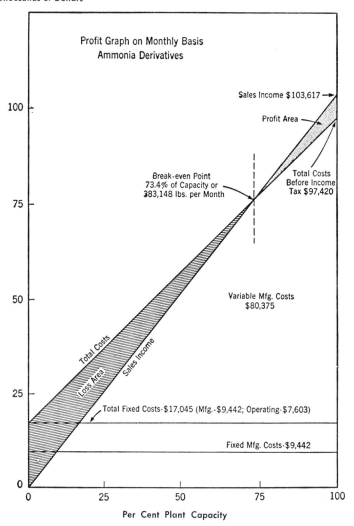

Fig. 28—Break-Even Chart—Ammonia Plant.

Thousands of Dollars

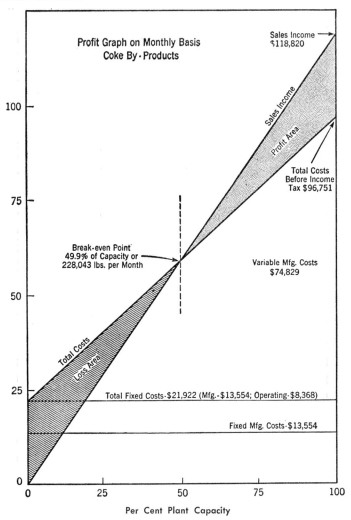

Fig. 29—Break-Even Chart—Coke By-Product Plant.

measured by the vertical difference between the sales income line and total cost line at that level. For example, at a 50% plant capacity level, the operating profit or loss would be about as follows:

Product	Sales Volume at 50% Level	Monthly Operating Profit or (Loss)
Paints	$141,025	$(17,687)
Ammonia Derivatives	51,810	(5,423)
Coke By-Products	59,410	73
Total	$252,245	$(23,037)

These figures have been calculated, but a close approximation can be read on the graphs.

These charts also indicate the break-even points at which income balances expense. The break-even points are quite dissimilar:

	Break-even Point		
	% of Five-	Sales per Month	
Product	Day Capacity	Pounds	Dollars
Paints	98.7	1,415,161	$278,423
Ammonia Derivatives ...	73.4	383,148	76,094
Coke By-Products	49.9	228,043	59,249

The details of costs and income on which these break-even points are predicated are set forth in Figs. 30, 31, and 32.

The chief problem of the Chicago Division centers about the paint line, where a plant capacity operation is required in order to avoid a loss. This is, indeed, a disturbing condition; and the remaining comments relate chiefly to this product line.

PAINTS—RECOMMENDATIONS

In reviewing the profit structure, a detailed analysis was made of each of the more popular items in each product group. The total income and standard variable costs are outlined in Fig. 30. The hundredweight data and marginal income per machine or kettle hour are shown in Fig. 33. It will be observed that items 103 and 105 contribute the greatest income over variable expense, per machine hour, to help meet the fixed expenses, income taxes, and profit. It would seem desirable, and is possible in the opinion of the General Sales Manager, to increase the proportion of sales of these two items. As items 102 and 104 contribute the lowest marginal income, these should not be promoted. Of course, until the system is at capacity, every drum of paint sold helps reduce losses or increase profits.

Chemical Manufacturing Corporation—Chicago Division

BREAKDOWN BY PRODUCT OF VARIABLE INCOME AND COSTS

USED IN DEVELOPMENT OF PROFIT GRAPH

Product	SALES		VARIABLE COSTS (STANDARD)								Marginal Income
	Pounds	Value	Freight	Material	Shipping	Drums	Processing	Material Handling	Royalties	Total	
PAINTS											
101	235,200	$ 47,040.00	$ 2,312.73	$ 34,958.48	$ 141.12	$ 2,373.87	$ 924.81	$ 367.85	$ —	$ 41,078.86	$ 5,961.14
102	235,200	47,040.00	2,312.73	37,600.48	141.12	2,373.87	928.57	489.92	—	43,846.69	3,193.31
103	336,000	67,200.00	3,303.89	46,783.97	201.60	3,391.25	1,501.58	593.38	—	55,775.67	11,424.33
104	156,800	34,496.00	1,541.81	27,408.48	94.08	1,582.58	653.86	190.04	—	31,470.85	3,025.15
105	313,800	53,346.00	3,085.60	35,005.65	188.28	3,167.18	1,264.30	560.45	—	43,271.46	10,074.54
106	156,800	32,928.00	1,541.81	23,697.81	94.08	1,582.58	568.09	266.87	14.11	27,765.35	5,162.65
Total Paints	1,433,800	282,050.00	14,098.57	205,454.87	860.28	14,471.33	5,841.21	2,468.51	14.11	243,208.88	38,841.12
AMMONIA DERIVATIVES											
205	78,300	14,877.00	713.16	9,703.41	46.98	341.70	541.84	80.34	—	11,427.43	3,449.57
206	208,800	41,760.00	1,901.75	26,307.76	125.28	911.20	1,426.10	152.84	—	30,824.93	10,935.07
207	156,600	31,320.00	1,426.31	20,492.83	93.96	683.40	1,027.45	158.48	—	23,882.43	7,437.57
208	78,300	15,660.00	713.16	11,708.67	46.98	341.70	485.15	58.96	113.61	13,468.23	2,191.77
Total Ammonia Derivatives	522,000	103,617.00	4,754.38	68,212.67	313.20	2,278.00	3,480.54	450.62	113.61	79,603.02	24,013.98
COKE BY-PRODUCTS											
301	343,000	89,180.00	3,393.30	42,062.78	205.80	4,372.91	3,352.48	1,919.43	—	55,306.70	33,873.30
303	114,000	29,640.00	1,127.80	12,536.92	68.40	1,453.39	1,290.94	621.19	—	17,095.64	12,541.36
Total Coke By-Products	457,000	118,820.00	4,521.10	54,599.70	274.20	5,826.30	4,643.42	2,540.62	—	72,405.34	46,414.66
Total Variable Income and Costs—All Products	2,412,800	$504,487.00	$23,374.05	$328,267.24	$1,447.68	$22,575.63	$13,965.17	$5,459.75	$127.72	$395,217.24	$109,269.76

COST DATA USED IN PROFIT GRAPH

	Paints	Ammonia Derivatives	Coke By-Products	Total
Variable Costs, as above	$243,209	$79,603	$72,405	$395,217
Deduct:				
Costs Assumed to Be Fixed in Nature	1,168	696	929	2,793
Net	242,041	78,907	71,476	392,424
Add:				
Assumed Material Losses—1%	2,055	682	546	3,283
Assumed Overrun on Standards (20% of Processing and Handling)	1,660	786	1,436	3,882
Assumed Short-Term Excess Costs	—	—	1,371	1,371
Total Variable Costs	$245,756	$80,375	$74,829	$400,960

Fig. 30—Detail of Variable Income and Expense for Use in Profit Graph.

DETAIL OF MONTHLY FIXED COSTS
USED IN DEVELOPMENT OF PROFIT GRAPH

Item	PRODUCT			Total	Comments
	Paints	Ammonia Derivatives	Coke By-Products		
MANUFACTURING					
DIRECT					
Depreciation—Buildings	$ 1,408	$ 537	$ 710	$ 2,655	Actual Expense—1960
Depreciation—Machinery and Equipment	4,818	2,363	2,783	9,964	Actual Expense—1960
Property Insurance	62	23	31	116	Actual Expense—1960
Real and Personal Property Taxes	815	306	386	1,507	Actual Expense—1960
Building Costs (Heat, Lighting, Janitor Service, etc.)	2,184	833	1,100	4,117	Average Budgeted Cost—1961; allocated to products on cubic ft. basis
General Plant Costs	826	1,116	1,530	3,472	Average Budgeted Cost—1961; allocated to products on forecasted conversion cost basis
Control Laboratory	952	1,287	1,765	4,004	Average Budgeted Cost—1961; allocated to products on forecasted conversion cost basis
Vacuum Boilers (Labor and Related Costs)	624	208	–	832	Actual Expense—1960
Total Direct Manufacturing Expense	11,689	6,673	8,305	26,667	
ALLOCATED					
General Works Cost	2,106	1,591	2,499	6,196	Budgeted Cost—1961
Boiler House Fixed Costs	47	82	1,221	1,350	Budgeted Cost—1961
Total Allocated Costs	2,153	1,673	3,720	7,546	
Total Fixed Manufacturing Expense Before Adjustments	13,842	8,346	12,025	34,213	
Add:					
Share of Undistributed Water and Steam Costs	1,000	400	600	2,000	Expected Experience—1961 budget
20% of Processing Costs Assumed to Be Fixed	1,168	696	929	2,793	
Total Fixed Manufacturing Costs for Construction of Profit Graph	16,010	9,442	13,554	39,006	
OPERATING EXPENSES					
Administrative, Selling, and Advertising, Technical, etc. per Fig. 32	19,823	7,603	8,368	35,794	
Total Fixed Expense for Construction of Profit Graph	$35,833	$17,045	$21,922	$74,800	

Fig. 31—Detail of Monthly Fixed Costs for Use in Profit Graph.

131

Chemical Manufacturing Corporation—Chicago Division

DETAIL OF MONTHLY OPERATING EXPENSES

USED IN DEVELOPMENT OF PROFIT GRAPH

Item	PRODUCT			Total	Comments
	Paints	Ammonia Derivatives	Coke By-Products		
DIRECT					
Advertising and Sales Promotion	$ 1,587	$1,146	$ 975	$ 3,708	Budget—1961
Selling	7,743	2,717	3,124	13,584	
Technical Service	1,126	395	456	1,977	
Research	1,701	597	686	2,984	
Total Direct Operating Expense	12,157	4,855	5,241	22,253	
ALLOCATED					
Administrative	840	295	338	1,473	Based on Budget—1961; allocated to Chicago Division on forecasted net sales for 1961
Advertising and Sales Promotion	412	144	166	722	
Selling	1,097	385	442	1,924	
Technical Service	1,653	580	667	2,900	
Research	858	301	347	1,506	
Engineering	565	198	229	992	
Patents	439	154	177	770	
Total Allocated Operating Expense	5,864	2,057	2,366	10,287	
Total Operating Expense Before Adjustment	18,021	6,912	7,607	32,540	
Add:					
Assumed 10% Overrun on Budget	1,802	691	761	3,254	
Total Operating Expense for Construction of Profit Graph	$19,823	$7,603	$8,368	$35,794	

Fig. 32—Detail of Monthly Operating Expenses for Use in Profit Graph.

Chemical Manufacturing Corporation—Chicago Division

COMPARATIVE UNIT COSTS AND INCOME

| | Sales Price | Variable Costs | | | | Marginal Income | Fixed Costs and Expenses | Operating Profit or (Loss) | Per Machine Hour | |
		Material	Con-tainer	Other	Total				Pro-duction (lbs.)	Marginal Income
PAINTS										
101	$20.00	$14.8633	$1.0093	$1.5929	$17.4655	$2.5345	$4.2681	$(1.7336)	1,032	$26.16
102	20.00	15.9866	1.0093	1.6464	18.6423	1.3577	3.5458	(2.1881)	884	12.00
103	20.00	13.9238	1.0093	1.6668	16.5999	3.4001	3.5666	(.1665)	943	32.06
104	22.00	17.4799	1.0093	1.5815	20.0707	1.9293	3.6981	(1.7688)	775	14.95
105	17.00	11.1554	1.0093	1.6248	13.7895	3.2105	3.1721	.0384	852	27.35
106	21.00	15.1134	1.0093	1.5848	17.7075	3.2925	3.5831	(.2906)	774	25.48
AMMONIA DERIVATIVES										
205	19.00	12.3926	.4364	1.7654	14.5944	4.4056	3.8752	.5304	963	42.43
206	20.00	12.5995	.4364	1.7270	14.7629	5.2371	3.7995	1.4376	947	49.60
207	20.00	13.0861	.4364	1.7281	15.2506	4.7494	3.7313	1.0181	985	46.78
208	20.00	14.9536	.4364	1.8108	17.2008	2.7992	3.5728	(.7736)	1,032	30.40
COKE BY-PRODUCTS										
301	26.00	12.2632	1.2749	2.5863	16.1244	9.8756	4.7988	5.0768	895	88.39
302	26.00	10.9973	1.2749	2.7266	14.9988	11.0012	3.9772	7.0240	831	91.42

Fig. 33—Comparative Unit Costs and Income.

Chemical Manufacturing Corporation—Chicago Division

Paints

DETERMINATION OF STANDARD MARGINAL INCOME AT CAPACITY

Product	Present Sales Mixture			Change in Sales Mixture			10% Reduction in Cycle Time		
	(000's) Pounds	% Total	Marginal Income	(000's) Pounds	% Total	Marginal Income	(000's) Pounds	% Total	Marginal Income
101	235.2	16.4	$ 5,961.14	235.2	16.6	$ 5,961.14	261.3	16.3	$ 6,725.34
102	235.2	16.4	3,193.31	117.0	8.3	1,588.51	130.4	8.1	1,821.95
103	336.0	23.5	11,424.33	461.0	32.6	15,674.47	512.0	31.8	17,637.38
104	156.8	10.9	3,025.15	77.5	5.4	1,495.21	86.0	5.4	1,695.06
105	313.8	21.9	10,074.54	400.0	28.3	12,842.00	444.6	27.6	14,453.06
106	156.8	10.9	5,162.65	124.6	8.8	4,102.46	173.1	10.8	5,761.98
Total.......	1,433.8	100.0	$38,841.12	1,415.3	100.0	$41,663.79	1,607.4	100.0	$48,094.77

Fig. 34—Statement of Standard Marginal Income Giving Effect to Changes in Products Sold and Manufacturing Efficiency.

Thousands of Dollars

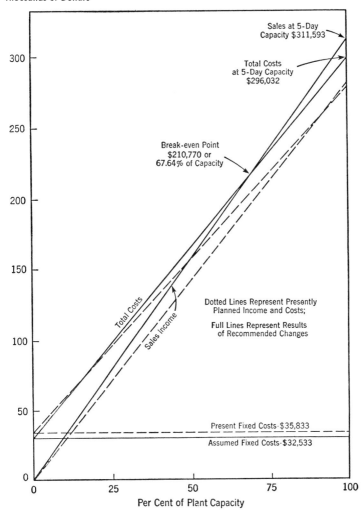

Fig. 35—Profit Graph, Giving Effect to Changes in Income and Costs—
Paint Works.

A review of sales indicates that 85% of the volume is secured from 15% of the customers. Furthermore, from what information we piece together it appears our operating expenses are out-of-line with our competitors. There is some indication, also, that the cycle time in production is on the high side. The Works Manager is of the opinion that reductions can be made in production time. Such improvement would, of course, reduce the variable cost per hundredweight and increase the plant capacity and therefore the potential marginal income.

On the basis of available information, it is recommended that immediate steps be taken to:

1. Reduce selling expenses (fixed costs) by $3,300 per month through the release of three salesmen. The remaining staff can readily cover our large volume customers and contact other possible users.
2. Emphasize the more profitable products, increasing the proportion of 103 and 105.
3. Concentrate on a reduction of cycle times by 10%.

The effect of each successive action, detailed in Fig. 34 as to marginal income, would be as follows:

Action		Break-even Sales Volume (Monthly)	Monthly Operating Profit at Capacity
Present plans	(a)	$278,400	$ 461
Reduce fixed expenses by $3,300 per month	(b)	252,800	3,761
Change sales mixture to higher proportion of profitable items, plus (b)	(c)	214,000	9,131
Reduce cycle time by 10%, plus (b) and (c)		210,770	15,561

The accomplishment of these objectives would result in a net profit of 5.0% of sales at capacity.

The profit graph on paints, with these changes incorporated, would appear as in Fig. 35. As a long-range program, research should be intensified on material costs so as to increase the margin of selling price over such costs. Since the net profit as a percentage of investment, even with the improved results, would not be satisfactory, perhaps consideration can be given to new product lines with higher margins that could advantageously be manufactured in the paint facilities.

Further details can be made available as requested.

CONTROLLER

10

Planning and Analysis for Acquisitions and Mergers

ACQUISITIONS AS RELATED TO CORPORATE OBJECTIVES

Corporate objectives may be achieved by several means, and effective planning must consider the alternative routes available to a given company. The corporate goals of growth—with emphasis on increased earnings—and stability can be attained strictly by internal methods, yet such growth usually requires a great many years. Consequently, it is understandable that many firms look to acquisitions and mergers for a solution to some of their problems.

Motives which prompted acquisitions in the 1950's and appear to apply in the 1960's are varied. For some concerns, this avenue is a means of accomplishing in part these purposes:

1. Diversifying—for growth, or to counteract a declining market, or to offset seasonal factors
2. Broadening product lines
3. Acquiring research and development capabilities
4. Creating or securing profitable new products
5. Integrating so as to assure an adequate supply of raw materials
6. Broadening markets, including previously untapped areas
7. Improving management by replacing aging capabilities, or filling voids in talents
8. Eliminating obsolete plants, or duplication of facilities
9. Providing sufficient working capital
10. Developing or securing new lines of credit and general funds for expansion possibilities
11. Achieving maximum advantage of tax or other legislation

Thus it can be seen that by proper combinations, and with the proper planning and analysis, business is enabled to use its surplus management skill, if any, its surplus productive capacity, its available sales know-how, and other assets to enhance its competitive position and to achieve some of its corporate objectives.

This chapter is intended to highlight some of the more important steps or considerations in achieving an effective acquisition posture. Emphasis, of course, is placed on those aspects important in the role of the controller or financial officer. It does not deal extensively with special considerations such as antitrust problems, other basic legal problems, or specialty aspects in which financial skill is not a prime requisite.

INGREDIENTS OF A SUCCESSFUL ACQUISITION PROGRAM

There is no simple formula by which every risk may be evaluated and which assures that every acquisition will be a sound one. It has been observed, however, that many companies which have done well in this field have been effective to the extent that they have been thorough in preparing, organizing for, and implementing a plan for wise selection. Provision should be made for the following actions:

1. *Define the corporate objectives for long-range development.* A mere general statement is insufficient. Plans ought to be specific enough to include a five- or ten-year projection of sales growth for each product line by area. Also, it should incorporate the expected earnings, desired rate of return on investment, and the financial plan which makes the growth possible.

Very often the mere existence of such a plan, intelligently conceived, will attract a selling company when its absence would negate the sale— particularly when the seller desires a pay-off in future years and not immediately.

2. *Develop a program and schedule by which the objective will be achieved.* Mere hoped-for goals and optimistic projections are not enough. The objective must be supplemented by a specific program and a schedule which indicates *how* and *when* the program reasonably can be attained.

3. *Provide a coordinated and effective staff group to review and evaluate plans and prospects.* Sound acquisitions require a staff which devotes sufficient time to the problem. An occasional effort is not enough.

4. *Establish specifications which potential to-be-acquired companies must meet.* These are the measuring sticks or guides as to the requisites which the candidate should possess. Basically, of course, the specifications would stipulate the fields of interest, which should be identifiable from the corporate objectives statement. An illustrative list for a company in heavy machinery manufacture might include:

a. Power gardening equipment
b. In-plant material handling equipment
c. Pumps and related hydraulic equipment
d. Automotive servicing equipment
e. Ground launching systems for missiles

In addition, the statement should include those qualifications to best fit into the acquiring company, possibly including offsets to inherent weaknesses of the purchaser. For example, these standards might be required:

a. Demonstrated earning ability over the past five years
b. A continually increasing sales volume
c. Competent, self-sufficient research and engineering departments
d. A net worth of at least five million dollars
e. Absence of any long-term debt

5. *Secure the ability to analyze critically one company as compared to another.* Very often several prospects may be available. The company which has the business acumen to select the best partner has a distinct advantage. The analytical ability of the controller and his staff indeed can prove to be most beneficial.

6. *Develop the most effective method of acquiring the business.* The best means of accomplishing the acquisition must be used. Included are the most desirable manner of financing and the route which minimizes the tax consequences. In some instances, determination of the best method will be the only advantage which one firm might have as against another—and the more favorable end results for both parties will stem solely from the route used. Here also, the controller's financial, accounting, and tax knowledge are important contributions to a successful venture.

7. *Recognize the human element in acquisitions.* This facet is important and critical. An acquiring company should attempt to secure the full talents of the acquired. Failure to do so deprives a business of an important asset.

Perhaps the need for the steps outlined above seems self-evident. Yet the authors have known corporate executives who desired diversification for their business, but whose approach was made on a rather haphazard basis, consisting largely of reviewing those firms which came to them— often the least desirable. A more effective approach is to define the fields of interest and screen the potential candidates to the most desirable two or three opportunities. Acquisition then becomes a matter of analysis and salesmanship.

PRELIMINARY REVIEW OF PROSPECT

The prior comments have indicated the *general* approach to a sound acquisition. Assuming that a company has been selected which, after a preliminary screening, appears to meet the specifications of the buyer, then the next step is in order. This is usually a face-to-face meeting between principals or their representatives. This, too, is somewhat preliminary in nature and involves a determination of these general points:

1. Does it appear the seller is sincere in his desire to sell?
2. Do the general discussions confirm the statistical findings, etc., that the company meets the broad criteria of the acquiring company?
3. Does it appear the seller will put a value on his business, and is it even remotely reasonable?
4. Do the principals want to continue in business and are they compatible with the management of the acquiring company?
5. Does a mutually satisfactory basis for dealing seem to exist?

If these general explorations disclose nothing of significance which is negative, then the way is opened for further analysis.

EVALUATING THE PROSPECT

Evaluating the company is no easy task. The matching of values of two businesses to determine an equitable exchange of equities or other suitable consideration requires special and careful analysis. Though one firm may have a less favorable earnings history than another, certain franchises, or patents, or production facilities may be of special importance to the acquiring company. Again, one corporation may own a modern plant, be well located with respect to raw materials and markets, but may lack sales know-how. In contrast, another business may possess a superb nationwide sales organization and an excellent product, but be burdened with obsolete manufacturing facilities. Still another company may have acquired an excellent research organization, and the question arises as to how this is evaluated. Much judgment is required to weigh earnings against assets and organization. Obviously, when this stage is reached, much analysis must be undertaken.

The kinds of information to be gathered will depend on the particular situation. Many man-hours ordinarily will be spent in collecting and organizing all of the pertinent facts which are considered necessary to arrive at a fair estimate of the value of the business. The company to be acquired may be seeking the same data with respect to the acquiring company.

The primary areas of investigation ordinarily will include the following:

1. Management and personnel
2. Market and product
3. Manufacturing facilities and processes
4. Research and patents, etc.
5. Finances

While each acquisition team should develop its own approach to an analysis of the business, the following checklist used by the Rockwell Manufacturing Company indicates the many aspects to a complete study:

A. *General*

1. Statement of proposed transaction and objectives.
2. History of business and general description.
3. List of officers and directors; affiliation.
4. Stock distribution—number, principal holders, etc.
5. Organization chart.
6. Policy manual.

B. *Financial*

1. Latest audited financial statements.
2. Last available financial statements.
3. Ten-year summary financial statements.
4. Projected operating and financial statements.
5. Full description of securities, indebtedness, investments, and other assets and liabilities other than normal day-to-day accounts.
6. Chart of accounts and/or description of accounting practices relative to inventories, fixed assets, etc.
7. List of bank accounts, average balances.
8. Credit reports from banks and Dun & Bradstreet.
9. Federal income tax status: i.e., excess profits tax credit, any loss or unused B.P.T. credit carry-forwards, latest year audited, any deficiency claims, etc.
10. Summary of state and local tax situation: i.e., applicable taxes, unemployment tax rate, any deficiency claims, etc.
11. Tax status of proposed transaction: recommendation for best method of acquisition.
12. Complete list of insurance policies, including description of coverage and cost; workmen's compensation rate.
13. Statement of responsible officer of business as to unrecorded or contingent liabilities.
14. Nature of inventory.

C. *Sales*

1. A brief description and history (if any) of the product line.
2. A ten-year record of product sales performance.
3. A long-range forecast of growth or contraction trends for the industry of which the product line is a part.
4. A three-to-five-year forecast of anticipated demand for the product.
5. An estimate of the industry's ability to supply present and anticipated demand.
6. A three-to-five-year forecast of sales expectations for this company (share of the market).
7. An analysis of the effect of anticipated increased volume and/or cost reduction on:
   (a) Product demand and share of the market.
   (b) Market saturation and over-capacity.

8. An analysis of the effect of the geographic location of the new facility on:
   (a) Product demand and share of the market.
   (b) Distribution costs (freight savings, warehousing, etc.).
   (c) Competitive position.
9. A review of present sales management, selling force, advertising and sales promotion policies for adaptability and adequacy in relation to new facility.
10. A review of present competitors and competitive practices including:
    (a) Description of *competitive* products.
    (b) Location.
    (c) Estimated share of market.
    (d) Pricing policies.
    (e) Methods of distribution.
11. An analysis of present and/or probable pricing policies for the product line considering:
    (a) Competitive position.
    (b) Cost pricing.
12. An analysis of present and potential domestic and export customers.
    (a) Major types of customers and per cent of sales to each.
    (b) Geographical location.
    (c) Buying habits.

D. *Manufacturing*
   1. Description and layout of plant and property.
   2. List of principal machine tools—age and condition.
   3. Opinion re maintenance and "housekeeping."
   4. Utilities—availability, usage, rate.
   5. Estimated total annual fixed cost.
   6. Organization, departmentalization.
   7. Transportation facilities.
   8. Description of area, including climate, hazards from flood, etc.
   9. Opinion re adequacy of auxiliary equipment—tools, patterns, material, handling equipment, etc.
   10. Detail expense schedule.
   11. Building codes, zoning laws and restrictions.

E. *Purchasing*
   1. Principal materials used.
   2. Relation of material costs to sales.
   3. Purchasing methods.
   4. List of principal suppliers, items, location.
   5. Inbound freight costs.
   6. Work load—last twelve months.
      (a) Number of purchase orders issued.
      (b) Value—purchase orders issued.
      (c) Value of outstanding commitments.

F. *Research and Engineering*
   1. Description and condition of facilities.
      (a) Drafting room and office.

    (b) Experimental room.
    (c) Laboratory.
    (d) Special test equipment.
2. Engineering personnel—quality and quantity of technical talents—employed—unemployed.
3. Product designs—evaluation, condition of drawings.
4. Patents and trade-marks—coverage, existing applications, litigation.

G. *Labor*

1. Number, sex, age and color—present employees.
2. Direct, indirect, administrative: number and cost.
3. Number of potential job applicants from surveys or census.
4. Determination of types of skills available in the area from state employment service and other sources.
5. Location and availability of students from high schools and technical schools.
6. Union—copy of contract.
7. Labor relations history.
8. Appraisal of working conditions.
9. Statistics on turnovers: reasons.
10. Description of incentive system: average rates incentive and hourly.
11. Employment and personnel policies.
12. Accident frequency.
13. Ratio of total labor cost to sales.
14. Pension and welfare plans.
15. Appraisal of transportation, community recreation facilities, housing.
16. Evaluation of labor situation in area.

FINANCIAL ANALYSIS AND PRESENTATION

Based on a thorough analysis of the financial data, it is ordinarily desirable to summarize the findings or conclusions for full consideration by management. Differing conditions and differing interests will influence the content of the financial section of the report as well as the scope of review. The following are, however, suggested as steps to be taken in preparing material for effective presentation:

1. Adjust financial data for abnormalities in earnings.
2. Make appropriate corrections where a question arises as to a suitable basis of accounting.
3. Aside from the special adjustments in 1 and 2 above, recast the financial statements of the to-be-acquired company on the same format as the acquiring firm. Among other things, this approach may insure better understanding by the management.
4. Reconcile the various analytical schedules so as to uncover unexplained adjustments. As examples, the earned surplus analyses should be reconciled to the income statements. Again, perhaps the funds statement should be "tied into" the earnings reports. Or,

Western Producing Corporation and Southern Refining Company

SALES, EARNINGS, AND CASH FLOW

For the Years 1956–1965

In Thousands of Dollars

	Net Sales		Pre-Tax Earnings		Net Income		Cash Flow *	
	Amount	% Increase Preceding Year	Amount	% Net Sales	Amount	% Net Sales	Amount	% Net Sales
WESTERN PRODUCING CORPORATION								
Actual								
1956	184,216	2.72	18,230	9.90	13,611	7.39	28,319	15.37
1957	189,817	3.10	18,493	9.74	13,809	7.27	29,877	15.74
1958	190,066	.10	17,894	9.41	12,202	6.42	28,067	14.77
1959	197,430	3.87	20,311	10.29	14,666	7.43	31,412	15.91
1960	204,684	3.67	22,430	10.96	16,427	8.03	33,660	16.44
Total	966,213	—	97,358	—	70,715	—	151,335	—
Average	193,243	2.64	19,472	10.08	14,143	7.32	30,267	15.66
Forecast								
1961	208,310	1.77	20,831	10.00	15,415	7.40	32,288	15.50
1962	216,990	4.17	22,784	10.50	16,057	7.40	33,633	15.50
1963	226,300	4.29	23,762	10.50	16,746	7.40	35,077	15.50
1964	239,800	5.97	26,378	11.00	17,745	7.40	37,169	15.50
1965	253,670	5.78	27,904	11.00	18,772	7.40	39,319	15.50
Total	1,145,070	—	121,659	—	84,735	—	177,486	—
Average	229,014	4.28	24,332	10.62	16,947	7.40	35,497	15.50
SOUTHERN REFINING COMPANY								
Actual								
1956	107,660	1.96	8,612	8.00	4,218	3.92	6,318	5.87
1957	108,320	.61	9,430	8.71	4,706	4.34	6,988	6.45
1958	107,899	—	8,976	8.32	4,491	4.16	6,619	6.13

1959	115,660	3.34	10,866	9.56	5,403	4.75	7,562	6.65
1960	117,432	3.32	10,311	8.78	5,011	4.27	7,184	6.12
Total	554,971	—	48,195	—	23,829	—	34,671	—
Average	110,994	2.29	9,639	8.68	4,766	4.29	6,934	6.25
Forecast 1961	118,980	1.32	10,110	8.50	5,000	4.20	7,140	6.00
1962	122,820	3.23	11,050	9.00	5,280	4.30	7,490	6.10
1963	124,200	1.12	11,800	9.50	5,590	4.50	7,575	6.10
1964	129,030	3.89	12,260	9.50	5,805	4.50	7,870	6.10
1965	134,610	4.32	12,790	9.50	6,055	4.50	8,210	6.10
Total	629,640	—	58,010	—	27,730	—	38,285	—
Average	125,928	2.73	11,602	9.21	5,546	4.40	7,657	6.08
MERGED COMPANIES								
Historical 1956	291,876	2.50	26,842	9.20	17,829	6.11	34,637	11.87
1957	298,137	2.15	27,923	9.37	18,515	6.21	36,865	12.37
1958	297,965	—	26,870	9.02	16,693	5.60	34,686	11.64
1959	311,090	4.40	31,177	10.02	20,069	6.45	38,974	12.53
1960	322,116	3.54	32,741	10.16	21,438	6.66	40,844	12.68
Total	1,521,184	—	145,553	—	94,544	—	186,006	—
Average	304,237	2.51	29,111	9.57	18,909	6.22	37,201	12.23
Projection 1961	327,290	1.61	30,941	9.45	20,415	6.24	39,428	12.05
1962	339,810	3.52	33,834	9.96	21,337	6.28	41,123	12.10
1963	350,500	3.15	35,562	10.15	22,336	6.37	42,652	12.17
1964	368,830	5.23	38,638	10.49	23,550	6.39	45,039	12.21
1965	388,280	5.27	40,694	10.48	24,827	6.39	47,529	12.24
Total	1,774,710	—	179,669	—	112,465	—	215,771	—
Average	354,942	3.67	35,934	10.12	22,493	6.34	43,154	12.16

* Net income plus depreciation, depletion, and amortization, if applicable.

Fig. 36—Comparative Sales, Earnings, and Cash Flow Data for Merger Study.

the plant and equipment analyses should be cross-referenced to the related balance sheets and reserve analyses, etc.

5. When the analyses have been completed, the report may be prepared, including this information:

   a. Summary commentary on:

     1) Advantages and disadvantages of the acquisition or merger

     2) Adjustments or findings which require explanation

     3) Concise statement of financial results as reflected more fully in the accompanying schedules

   b. The following suggested financial schedules:

     1) Summary of sales, earnings, and cash flow, for each of the companies, and on a pro-forma basis for the consolidation of a reasonable past period (five years) and projection (also five years). Relating sales to per cent increase and other factors to sales may be helpful. A suggested schedule is shown in Fig. 36.

     2) Summary of pertinent equity information, including book value, earnings, dividends, and market price, as in Fig. 37.

     3) A summary statement of financial condition of each participant, and pro-forma for the group. This preferably should include a projection for several years in advance. In specialized industries, such as extractive, where reserves and other values are not fully reflected in the balance sheet, appropriate comparative data should be provided.

     4) A cash flow statement of the group for several past and projected years.

     5) Appropriate detailed statements of income and expense (by product line, etc.).

     6) A summary comparison of the principal tangible factors to be considered in arriving at a price. This subject is discussed in detail in the next section.

DETERMINING THE PRICE

The objective of the financial review, of course, is to determine with reasonable accuracy exactly what is being acquired, and to secure some measure of a fair price. To reiterate, there is no single formula. Rather, judgment must be used in weighing the various factors. The purpose of the acquisition has an important bearing. For example, in circumstances where current return is fundamental, the past or prospective dividend outlook may be paramount. If long-term growth is singularly important, then prospective earnings loom large in the picture. Again, if immediate cash is the objective of the seller, then the liquidity and market value of the consideration is most significant.

Very often it is desirable to summarize the various factors or measures of worth and indicate the relationship between companies. Such a schedule is shown below:

COMPARATIVE FACTORS IN PROPOSED MERGER

Evidence of Value	Company A	Company B	Relationship Ratio/Share
Five-year average earnings/share	$ 3.60	$ 3.90	.92 to 1
Five-year average dividends/share	1.80	1.90	.95 to 1
Market price (recent before merger influence)	54.00	51.40	1.03 to 1
Book value/share	11.37	17.89	.64 to 1
Net current assets/share	8.96	7.12	1.26 to 1

These are the factors usually taken into account in arriving at a stock exchange ratio. The weighting, a matter of judgment and bargaining power, depends on the opinion of both buyer and seller. In the above example, if earnings, market price, and net current assets are the important factors in the eyes of both buyer and seller, there is a strong probability that one-for-one will be the stock exchange ratio.

TAX CONSIDERATIONS OF ACQUISITIONS AND MERGERS

On the basis that sound economic reasons exist for a purchase and sale of a business, it is important that the parties to the transaction clearly understand the tax effects of the many available routes by which a transfer may be consummated.

Tax laws change so much that there is little merit in discussing the tax consequences of the present laws, which may not be in existence when the reader becomes involved in an acquisition. Only some general observations will be made.

It should be recognized that the tax effect of a transaction may call for an adjustment in selling price. For example, if a buyer insists on a taxable transaction, the selling shareholders may insist on an increase in price to cover the tax. Again, it may be desirable to have an "open-end" arrangement whereby upon the attainment of a given sales volume or earnings, additional stock will be issued by the purchaser to the selling corporation or its shareholders—so handled to be non-taxable.

Choice must be made between a taxable and non-taxable transaction, and this may appear strange. Who would ever want a taxable acquisition?

From the acquiring corporation's standpoint, a taxable transaction may be strongly preferred. If the transaction is non-taxable, the acquiring corporation succeeds to the tax basis of the assets in the hands of the acquired corporation, regardless of their present values or of the price it must pay for them. In a taxable transaction, however, the acquiring

Western Producing Corporation and Southern Refining Company
SELECTED SHAREHOLDER DATA
1956–1965

		No. of Shares Issued (000)	Common Equity at Year-End		Dividends Paid		Earnings Applicable (a) to Common		Market Price Per Share	Price Earnings Ratio
			Amount ($M)	Per Share ($)	Amount ($M)	Per Share ($)	Amount ($M)	Per Share ($)		
WESTERN PRODUCING CORP.										
Actual	1956	2,000	220,000	110.00	6,000	3.00	13,611	6.81	81.70	12.
	1957	"	227,809	113.96	6,000	3.00	13,809	6.90	89.70	13.
	1958	"	234,011	117.00	6,000	3.00	12,202	6.10	88.50	14.5
	1959	"	242,077	121.04	6,600	3.30	14,666	7.33	110.00	15.0
	1960	"	251,904	125.95	6,600	3.30	16,427	8.22	140.00	17.0
	Total	—	—	—	31,200	15.60	70,715	35.36	—	—
	Average	2,000	235,160	117.59	6,240	3.12	14,143	7.07	101.98	14.3
Forecast	1961	2,000	260,719	130.36	6,600	3.30	15,415	7.71	131.00	17.0
	1962	"	270,176	135.10	6,600	3.30	16,057	8.03	136.50	17.0
	1963	"	280,322	140.17	6,600	3.30	16,746	8.37	142.25	17.0
	1964	"	290,867	145.43	7,200	3.60	17,745	8.87	150.80	17.0
	1965	"	301,639	150.82	8,000	4.00	18,772	9.39	159.60	17.0
	Total	—	—	—	35,000	17.50	84,735	42.41	—	—
	Average	2,000	280,745	140.38	7,000	3.50	16,947	8.48	144.03	17.0
SOUTHERN REFINING CO.										
Actual	1956	1,000	90,000	90.00	2,000	2.00	4,218	4.22	50.50	12.
	1957	"	92,706	92.71	2,000	2.00	4,706	4.71	61.25	13.
	1958	"	95,197	95.20	2,000	2.00	4,491	4.49	58.40	13.
	1959	"	98,600	98.60	2,000	2.00	5,403	5.40	75.50	14.
	1960	"	101,111	101.11	2,500	2.50	5,011	5.01	75.10	15.
	Total	—	—	—	10,500	10.50	23,829	23.83	—	—
	Average	1,000	95,523	95.52	2,100	2.10	4,766	4.77	64.15	13.4

Forecast 1961	1,000	103,611	103.61	2,500	2.50	5,000	5.00	75.00	15.
1962	"	106,391	106.39	2,500	2.50	5,280	5.28	84.50	16.
1963	"	109,481	109.48	2,500	2.50	5,590	5.59	89.50	16.
1964	"	112,786	112.79	2,500	2.50	5,805	5.81	93.00	16.
1965	"	115,841	115.84	3,000	3.00	6,055	6.06	97.00	16.
Total	—	—	—	13,000	13.00	27,730	27.74	—	—
Average	1,000	109,642	109.64	2,600	2.60	5,546	5.55	87.80	15.8
MERGED COMPANIES (b)									
Historical 1956	2,600	310,000	119.23	8,000	3.08	17,829	6.86		
1957	"	320,515	123.28	8,000	3.08	18,515	7.12		
1958	"	329,208	126.62	8,000	3.08	16,693	6.42		
1959	"	340,677	131.03	8,600	3.30	20,069	7.72		
1960	"	353,015	135.78	9,100	3.50	21,438	8.25		
Total	2,600	—	—	41,700	—	94,544	—		
Average	2,600	330,683	127.19	8,340	3.20	18,909	7.27		
Projected 1961	2,600	364,330	140.13	9,100	3.50	20,415	7.85		
1962	"	376,567	144.83	9,100	3.50	21,337	8.21		
1963	"	389,803	149.92	9,100	3.50	22,336	8.59		
1964	"	403,653	155.25	9,700	3.73	23,550	9.06		
1965	"	417,480	160.55	11,000	4.22	24,827	9.55		
Total	2,600	—	—	48,000	—	112,465	—		
Average	2,600	390,367	150.14	9,600	3.70	22,493	8.65		

(a) For simplicity, illustration assumes no preferred stock issued.
(b) Exchange ratio of .6 share of Western Producing for each share of Southern Refining.

Fig. 37—Selected Shareholder Data for Merger Discussions.

corporation must allocate its purchase cost among the assets acquired [whether it acquires them directly or through acquisition of stock and subsequent liquidation of the acquired corporation under I.R.C. § 334(b)(2)] under technical rules and on the basis of the present values of the assets acquired. Any remaining balance of the purchase cost is considered to be goodwill. Depreciable assets of the acquired corporation will often have a present value greatly in excess of their depreciated tax basis on the books of that corporation. A taxable transaction will enable the acquiring corporation to step up the tax basis of these assets, sometimes to a level even higher than original cost, and to begin the depreciation cycle all over again. If the acquiring corporation foresees a sale of certain assets of the acquired corporation, this stepped-up basis will also have the effect of limiting taxable gain on the sale.

The question of income tax consequences is obviously of immediate interest to the selling shareholders. In general, a capital gain or loss to these shareholders is recognized upon acquisition of their shares if

1. The entire purchase price is paid in cash, or
2. There is a cash down payment and the balance is to be paid in cash over a period of time, or
3. The consideration is part cash and part stock, or
4. The consideration (except in certain statutory mergers) includes non-voting stock or debt securities, whether or not any cash is paid.

In view of the desire of the selling shareholders to avoid immediate capital gains or income tax, the law is quite specific. The method of combining corporations without income tax consequences to the shareholders of the acquired corporation are rigidly limited. The three available methods take their abbreviated names from subdivisions (A), (B), and (C) of I.R.C. § 368(a)(1) as follows:

1. The "A type" is the statutory merger or consolidation. This usually means that a corporation is merged by operation of law into another corporation (or that two corporations are consolidated to form a new corporation) upon compliance with procedures covered in detail by the merger (or consolidation) statutes of the states of incorporation.
2. The so-called "B type" or "stock-for-stock" transaction involves the acquisition by one corporation, solely in exchange for its voting stock, of the stock of another corporation if, immediately after the acquisition, the acquiring corporation has control of the acquired corporation. Under I.R.C. § 368(c), control is defined as "the ownership of stock possessing at least 80 percent of the total combined voting power of all classes of stock entitled to vote and at least 80 percent of the total number of shares of all other classes

of stock of the corporation." Section 368(a)(1)(B) applies whether or not the acquiring corporation already had control immediately before the acquisition.

3. The designated "C type" refers to the stock-for-assets transaction in which the acquiring corporation, in most instances solely in exchange for voting stock, acquires substantially all the assets of another corporation. The acquiring corporation may assume the liabilities of the corporation whose assets it acquires (but not debt created as part of the reorganization) without jeopardizing the non-taxable status of the exchange. A part of the plan of reorganization in these cases involves the subsequent liquidation of the corporation whose assets have been acquired and distribution to its shareholders of the acquiring corporation's stock.

There are, of course, many other aspects of the problem. Also, hybrid arrangements have been created which are partially taxable. The authors' principal objective is to make the reader aware of the wisdom of carefully checking on tax consequences.

SCIENTIFIC TECHNIQUES

In this scientific age it is not unusual to perform some analysis, but actually to rely a great deal on intuition or "feeling." Yet the more complex a potential merger, the greater the need to use scientific techniques. Such methods can be applied in evaluation just as they have been utilized in inventory management. And the greater the number of factors, the greater the possibility of error, and the corresponding need for mathematical or computer assistance.

Operations research methodology should be helpful in structuring the decision, and the reader is referred to appropriate sources.[1]

---

[1] For example, see Roger R. Crane, "The Place of Scientific Techniques in Mergers and Acquisitions," *The Controller,* July, 1961, pp. 326–29 and 340–42.

PART III

Accounting Control and Planning of Operations

11

General Problems of Accounting Control— Standards

MEANING OF ACCOUNTING CONTROL

Planning, one of the primary business management functions, was discussed in Part II. This section, and the one following, are concerned with the control function, and, to a lesser degree, with the planning function, of management.

Control can be defined as the regulating or confining of business activities, in accordance with a plan, so that the objectives of the business may be attained. In small plants or organizations the manager or owner personally can observe and control all operations. By means of daily trips through the factory, he is able to pick out the good workmen from the poor and to spot the efficient or inefficient operations. He is able to observe whether the raw material inventories are adequate or too large, and whether material is flowing smoothly through the production line. He can detect costly and inefficient processes and make the necessary changes. In a similar fashion, he can check the sales orders and see whether goods are being shipped promptly. Through his intimate knowledge of the business and his constant talks with the salesmen and customers, he can discern the effectiveness of sales effort.

However, as the organization grows, this close contact or supervision by the owner or manager is necessarily lost in large degree. Other means of control become necessary—accounting and statistical reports. By the use of reports, management is enabled to plan, supervise, evaluate, and coordinate the activities of the various departments and divisions. Accounting control of operations is the use of such tools, as part of a well-conceived plan, to maintain the pressures necessary for efficiency and to expose unfavorable variations or trends. It is the control of costs or expenses through the use of accounts. It is the guidance and regulation of business activity through the measurement of performance by means of accounting and statistical records and reports. However, the effective application of these accounting controls often must extend to the related phase of planning, which is before-the-fact control. Moreover, the system of records which establishes accountability must be considered as a prerequisite to this accounting control.

EXTENT OF ACCOUNTING CONTROL

Effective control implies a vigilance that extends to every operation of the business—every function, every department, every territory, every man. For example, it assumes a knowledge of the cash receipts and disbursements, and the judicious use and protection of the business funds, as well as the probable trend of flow. Accounting control encompasses a review of receivables and the avoidance of losses through faulty credit and collection procedures. It includes the planning and checking of inventories to prevent disruption of production or shipments, or losses from obsolescence or other factors. It involves the determination of borrowed capital needs on an intelligent and well-planned basis. It requires *all* the necessary facts on performance of the manufacturing, selling, financial, or research functions. The degree of success in utilizing labor and material to produce the finished article must be known. The effectiveness of sales effort in each territory or for each product must be subjected to review by the owners or managers of the business. Control can and should relate to every classification in the statement of financial condition and to each item in the statement of income and expense. In short, accounting control may extend to practically all activities of the business. Operating controls may precede accounting controls, and accounting controls alone are not enough, but in almost all fields of business endeavor the accounting system —the accounting controls—can be a powerful assistance to intelligent management.

NEED FOR STANDARDS

As American industry developed, the need arose for increased efficiency in conducting the business enterprise. Consequently the more efficient or aggressive executive sought more effective means of regulating his activities. It was no longer sufficient to know the cost to manufacture or sell. The question became "Are we manufacturing as economically as we should?" or "Are our selling costs too high?" Thus, it became a matter of measuring performance. The measurement of performance presupposes a yardstick of desirable or planned results with which actual results may be compared. In this desire for a measuring stick, it was natural to compare current performance with performance in the past month or year. Such a comparison did point out trends, but it also served to perpetuate inefficiencies. A comparison of current costs with past costs was a good measuring stick only if these historical costs represented effective and efficient performance. Furthermore, changes in the price level, in processes, and in the relative volume of production and sales tended to limit the value of historical costs in determining what current costs ought to be.

But there were also other compelling needs for something more than historical costs. Aside from cost control, for the purpose of planning and pricing, management was in need of costs not distorted by accidental performance of a worker, poor quality material, and the like. During this time of rapid industrial growth the scientific management movement came into its own, with the development of physical or engineering standards to plan manufacturing operations and evaluate the effectiveness with which work was being done. The worth of a carefully predetermined standard was recognized. Engineering standards, expressed in financial terms, became cost standards; these standards, based on careful study as to what it ought to cost to perform the operation by the best method, became a much more reliable yardstick with which to control costs.

It can thus be seen that standards are the *very basis* of accounting control. Standards provide the tools with which to judge performance. Parts III and IV of this book deal with control of the various elements in the financial statements, e.g., sales, distribution costs, inventories, and surplus. The use of standards is as adaptable to the control of income or expense as to the control of assets or liabilities. Because standards are the foundation of accounting control, they are reviewed preparatory to a detailed discussion of the elements to be controlled.

DEFINITION OF STANDARDS

A standard of any type is a measuring stick, or the means by which something else is judged. Webster's *New Collegiate Dictionary* defines a standard as "that which is set up and established by authority as a rule for the measure of quantity, weight, extent, value or quality." The standard method of doing anything can usually be described as the best method devised, as far as humanly possible, at the time the standard is set. It follows that the standard cost is the amount that should be expended under normal operating conditions. It is a predetermined cost scientifically determined in advance, in contrast to an actual or historical cost. It is not an actual or average cost, although past experience may be a factor in setting the standard.

Since a standard has been defined as a scientifically developed measure of performance, it follows that at least two conditions are implied in setting the standard:

1. *Standards are the result of careful investigation or analysis of past performance, and take into consideration expected future conditions.* They are not mere guesses; they are the opinions, based on available facts, of the men best qualified to judge what performance should be.
2. *Standards may need review and revision from time to time.* A standard is set on the basis of certain conditions. As these conditions change, the standard must change; otherwise it would not be a true measuring stick. Where there is really effective teamwork, and particularly, where standards are related to incentive payments, the probability of change is great.

Most of the above comments on standards relate to that phase of the definition on which there is general agreement. There are, however, differences of opinion which seem to relate principally to the following points:

1. Whether a standard should be (a) a *current standard,* that is, one which reflects what performance should be in the period for which the standard is to be used, or (b) a *basic standard* which serves merely as a point of reference.
2. The level at which a standard should be set—an *ideal* level of accomplishment, a *normal* level, or the *expected* level.

Where standard costs are carried into the formal records and financial statements, the current standard is generally the one used. Reference to the variances immediately indicates the extent to which actual costs departed from what they should have been in the period. A basic standard, on the other hand, does not indicate what performance should have been. Instead, it is somewhat like the base on which a price index is figured. Basic standards are usually based on prices and production levels prevailing when the standards are set. When once established, they are permanent and remain unchanged until the manufacturing processes change. Thus, they are a stationary basis of measurement. Improvement or lack of improvement involves the comparison of ratios or percentages of actual to the base standard.

The level at which standards should be set is discussed later in this chapter under the subject of standards for cost control.

ADVANTAGES OF STANDARDS

It has already been mentioned that standards arose, as part of the scientific management movement, from the necessity of better control of manufacturing costs. The relationship between this need and the advantages of standards is close. However, the benefits from the use of standards extend beyond the relationship with cost control to all the other applications, such as price setting or inventory valuation. Therefore, it may be well to summarize the principal advantages of standards, and the related scientific methods, by the four primary functions in which they are used:

1. *In Controlling Costs:*

   a. *Standards provide a better measuring stick of performance.* The use of standards sets out the area of excessive cost which otherwise might not be known or realized. Without scientifically set standards cost comparison is limited to other periods which in themselves may contain inefficiencies.

   b. *Use of the "principle of exception" is permitted, with the consequent saving of much time.* It is not necessary to review and report upon all operations, but only those which depart significantly from standard. The attention of management may be focused on those spots requiring corrective action.

   c. *Economies in accounting costs are possible.* Clerical costs may be reduced because fewer records are necessary and simplified procedures may be adopted. Many of the detailed subsidiary records, such as production orders or time reports, are not necessary. Again, if inventories are carried as a standard value, there is no need of calculating actual costs each time new lots are made or received. Still further, much of the data for month-end closing can be set up in advance with a reduction in peak load work.

   d. *A prompter reporting of cost control information is possible.* Through the use of simplified records and procedures and the application of the exception principle, less time is required to secure the necessary information.

   e. *Standards serve as incentives to personnel.* If an employee has a fair goal, he will tend to work more efficiently with the consequent reduction in costs. This applies to executives, supervisors, and workers alike.

2. *In Setting Selling Prices:*

   a. *Better cost information is available as a basis of setting prices.* Through the use of predetermined standards, costs are secured which are free from abnormal distortions caused by excess spoilage and other unusual conditions. Furthermore, the use of standard overhead rates eliminates the influence of current activity. A means is provided to secure, over the long run, a full recovery of overhead expenses, including marketing, administrative, and research expense.

   b. *Flexibility is added to selling price data.* Through the use of predetermined rates, changes in the product, or processes, can be quickly reflected in the cost. Furthermore, adjustments to material prices or labor rates are easily made. Again, the use of standards requires a distinction between fixed and variable costs. This cost information permits cost calculations on different bases. Since pricing is sometimes a matter of selection of alternatives, this flexibility is essential.

c. *Prompter pricing data can be furnished.* Again, the use of predetermined rates permits the securing of information more quickly.

3. *In Valuing Inventories:*

   a. *A "better" cost is secured.* Here, too, as in pricing applications, a more reliable cost is secured. The effect of idle capacity, or of abnormal wastes or inefficiencies, is eliminated.

   b. *Simplicity in valuing inventories is obtained.* All like product is valued at the same cost. This not only assists in the recurring monthly closings but also is an added advantage in pricing the annual physical inventory.

4. *In Budgetary Planning:*

   a. *Determination of total standard costs is facilitated.* The standard unit costs provide the basic data for converting the sales and production schedules into total costs. The unit costs can readily be translated into total costs for any volume or mixture of product by simple multiplication. Without standards, extensive analysis is necessary to secure the required information because of the inclusion of non-recurring costs.

   b. *The means is provided for setting out anticipated substandard performance.* A history of the variances is available, together with the causes. Since actual costs cannot be kept exactly in line with standard costs, this record provides the basis for forecasting the variances which can reasonably be expected in the budget period under discussion. This segregation permits a determination of realistic operating results without losing sight of unfavorable expected costs.

TYPES OF STANDARDS NEEDED

STANDARDS FOR ALL BUSINESS ACTIVITY

Managerial control extends to all business functions—selling, production, finance, and research. It would appear highly desirable, therefore, to have available standards for measuring effort and results in all these activities. The word "standard" in much of the accounting literature applies to manufacturing costs. But the fact remains that the principles underlying the development of standards can and should be applied to many non-manufacturing functions. In the authors' experience, business executives generally do not question the need or desirability of standards for the control of administrative, distribution, and financial activities; they do, however, recognize the difficulties involved. Of course, some activities are more susceptible to measurement than others, but application of some standard is generally possible.

STANDARDS FOR INDIVIDUAL PERFORMANCE

Costs are controlled by people. It is through the action of an individual, or group of individuals, that costs are corrected or reduced to an acceptable level. It is by the efforts of the individual salesman that the necessary sales volume is secured. It is largely through the operational control of the departmental foreman that labor efficiency is maintained. As a result, any standards, to be most effective, must relate to specific phases of performance rather than merely general results. In a manufacturing operation, for example, standards should relate to the quantity of labor, material, or overhead in the execution of a particular operation—rather than the complete product cost standard. In the selling field, a sales quota must be set for the individual salesman, perhaps by product, and not just for the branch or territory.

Thus, the setting of standards and measurement of performance against such yardsticks fit into the scheme of "responsibility accounting" as reviewed in Chapter 1.

Keeping in mind these general comments, specific types of standards can now be examined.

MATERIAL QUANTITY STANDARDS

In producing an article, one of the most obvious cost factors is the quantity of material used. Quantitative standards, based upon engineering specifications, outline the kind and quantity of material which should be used to make the product. This measuring stick is the primary basis for material cost control. This quantity standard, when multiplied by the unit material price standard, results in the cost standard. Where more than one type of material is involved, the sum of the individual material cost standards equals the total standard material cost of the product.

MATERIAL PRICE STANDARDS

To isolate cost variances arising out of excess material usage from those arising because of price changes, it is necessary to establish a material price standard. Usually this price standard represents the expected cost instead of a desired or "efficient" cost. In many companies this price is set for a period of a year, and although actual cost may fluctuate, these changes are not reflected in the standard unit cost of material used. In other words, every piece of material used is charged with this predetermined cost.

LABOR QUANTITY STANDARDS

The labor content of many products is the most costly element. But whether it is the most costly or not, it is usually important. And because we are dealing with the human element, the labor cost is one of the most variable. It is indeed a fertile field for cost reduction and cost control.

For these reasons it is necessary to know the amount of labor needed to produce the article. The technique is that of determining the time needed to complete each operation when working under standard conditions; hence, time and motion study is involved.

LABOR RATE STANDARDS

The price of labor is generally determined by factors outside the complete control of the individual business, perhaps as a result of union negotiations or the prevailing rate in the area. In any event, it is desirable to have a fixed labor rate on each operation to be able to isolate high costs resulting from the use of an excess quantity of labor. Also, the utilization of labor within a plant is within the control of management and some rate variances arise from actions controllable by it. Examples are the assignment of the wrong men (too high a rate) to the job, or the use of overtime.

The standard time required, when multiplied by the standard rate, gives the standard labor cost of the operation.

MANUFACTURING OVERHEAD EXPENSE STANDARDS

One of the many problems which most controllers must resolve is that of determining standards for the control of manufacturing overhead as well as absorption into inventory. The determination of these standards is somewhat more complicated than in the development of material or labor standards. Several conditions are responsible:

1. Manufacturing overhead consists of a great variety of expenses, each of which reacts in different fashion at varying levels of plant activity. Some costs, such as depreciation, remain largely independent of plant activity; others vary with changes in production, but not in direct proportion. Examples are supervisory labor, maintenance, and clerical expense. Still other overhead expense varies directly with, and proportionately to, plant volume. This may include certain supplies, indirect labor, and fuel expense.
2. Control of overhead expenses rests with a large number of individuals in the organization. For example, the chief maintenance engineer may be responsible for maintenance costs; the factory account-

ant for factory clerical costs; foremen in productive departments for indirect labor.

3. The proper estimate of the rate and amount of production must be made to serve as the basis of setting standard rates. An improper level of activity not only affects the statement of income and expense but also gives management an erroneous picture of the cost of an insufficient volume of business and distorts inventory values.

Overhead expenses are best controlled through the use of a flexible budget (discussed in Chapter 16). Use of this means of analysis and control permits a realistic segregation of overhead variances as to cause: (1) volume, (2) rate of expenditure, and (3) efficiency of use.

Standards for manufacturing overhead can be expressed in total amount budgeted by type of expense as well as unit standards for each item, such as power cost per operating hour or supplies per man-hour.

SALES STANDARDS

Sales standards are for the purpose of controlling sales operations, rewarding merit, and stimulating sales effort. The most common form of standard for a territory, branch, or salesman is the sales quota, usually expressed as the dollar or physical volume of sales assigned. Other illustrative types of standards found useful in directing sales effort are:

Number of calls to be made per period
Number of new customers to be secured
Average size of order to be secured
Amount of gross profit to be secured

DISTRIBUTION COST STANDARDS

Just as production standards have been found useful in controlling manufacturing costs, so an increasing number of companies are finding that distribution cost standards are a valuable aid in properly directing selling effort. The extent of application and degree of completeness of distribution cost standards will differ from production standards; but the potential benefits from the use of such standards are equally important.

Some general standards can be used in measuring distribution effort and results; however, more effective standards are those measuring individual performance. Some illustrative standards are:

Selling expense per unit sold
Selling expense as a per cent of net sales
Cost per account sold
Cost per call
Cost per day
Cost per mile of travel
Cost per sales order

In addition to general or individual performance standards, another type of control relates to budgets for selling expenses. The procedure for setting budgets is similar to that used in the manufacturing division.

ADMINISTRATIVE EXPENSE STANDARDS

As a business increases in size or volume, there is a tendency for administrative expenses to increase proportionately. The same need for managerial control exists in this field, therefore, as in manufacturing or distribution. This control can be exercised through budgets as well as through unit standards of performance. The general approach to control of administrative expense is essentially no different than the approach to control of selling and general manufacturing expense.

Illustrative examples of types of standards are as follows:

Function	Standard Unit of Measurement
Traffic	Cost per shipment; cost per ton mile
Filing	Cost per item handled
Bookkeeping	Cost per posting
Billing	Cost per invoice rendered
Credit and collection	Cost per collection; per cent of bad debt losses to net sales
Dictation	Cost per letter transcribed

OTHER STANDARDS

The preceding discussion has dealt largely with standards applicable to expense or income. By the same token, standards exist for measurement of the effective utilization of the assets or credit of a company. Some illustrative yardsticks already reviewed are:

1. Current ratio (current assets to current liabilities)
2. The "acid test" (cash + receivables + marketable securities to current liabilities)
3. Inventory to current liabilities
4. Inventory turnover (merchandise cost of sales to average finished goods inventory)
5. Operating ratio (operating expense to net sales)
6. Net sales to receivables

SETTING THE STANDARDS

WHO SHOULD SET THE STANDARDS?

Standards should be set by those who are best qualified by training and experience to judge what good performance should be. It is often a joint process requiring cooperation between the staffs of two or more divisions of the business. Fundamentally, the setting of standards requires careful study and analysis. The controller and his staff, trained in analysis, and possessing essential records on the various activities, are in an excellent position to play an important part in the establishment of yardsticks of performance.

Since standards are yardsticks of performance, they should not be set by those whose performance is to be measured. Sufficient independence of thought should exist. Of course, the standards should be reviewed with those who will be judged by them, and any suggestions considered. However, final authority in establishing the standard should be placed in other hands.

Exactly which staff members cooperate in setting standards depends on the standards under consideration. Material quantity standards, for example, are generally determined by the engineers who are familiar with the operation methods employed as well as the product design. Assisting the engineers may be the production staff and the accounting staff. The production men can make valuable contributions because of their knowledge of the process. Furthermore, permitting the production staff to assist usually enlists their cooperation in making the standards effective. The accounting department assists by providing necessary information on past experience.

The determination of material price standards is usually the responsibility of both the purchasing and accounting departments. The purchasing department may indicate what expected prices are. These should then be challenged by the accounting department, taking into account current prices and reasonably expected changes. In other instances the accounting department sets the standards, based again on current prices, but takes into consideration the opinion of the purchasing department as to future trends.

Quantitative labor standards are usually set by industrial engineers through the use of time and motion study. This is properly an engineering function in that a thorough background of the processes is necessary. On occasion the accounting department furnishes information of past performance as a guide. Standard labor rates are set by the department having available the detailed job rates and other necessary information—typically the cost department. The cost department must also translate the physical standards into cost standards.

Manufacturing overhead standards, too, are often a matter of cooperation between the accounting and engineering departments. Engineers may be called upon to furnish technical data, such as power consumption in a particular department, or maintenance required, or type of supplies necessary. However, this is then costed by the accounting staff. In other instances the unit standards or budgets may be set in large part on past experience. The role played by the accountant tends to be much greater in the establishment of overhead standards since he is familiar with the techniques of organizing the data into their most useful form for cost and budget reporting.

Setting the standards for distribution activities is best done through the cooperation of sales, sales research, and accounting executives. Reliance is placed on the sales staff for the supplying of information pertaining to market potentials and sales methods. The accountant contributes the analysis and interpretation of past performance, trends, and relationships. The sales and accounting executives jointly must interpret the available data as applied to future activity.

Unit standards for the measurement of administrative expense are often determined on the basis of time and motion study by the industrial engineers. For example, a study might be made of the time required to dictate and transcribe a typical letter or to post a shipment. Where standardization is not feasible, past experience is the guide. In many instances the accountant either costs the data or sets the standard based on experience.

Financial and operating ratios may be set by the controller on the basis of experience in the particular company, special analysis of the factors involved, or information secured from trade associations or other external sources.

METHOD OF SETTING STANDARDS

Those aspects of setting standards which are beyond the sphere of accounting responsibility are adequately covered in engineering and production management literature. The more detailed phases of standards are reviewed in the chapters dealing with control of expenses, income, assets, or other subject matter. Only the general steps taken in the establishment of standards are briefed in this section.

Any outline of procedure regarding standards is basically only the application of clear thinking to the problem. The various phases involved in the setting of standards may be summarized as follows:

1. *Recognition of the Need for a Standard in the Particular Application.* Obviously, before action is taken, the need should exist. This need must be acknowledged in order that the problem can be attacked.
2. *Preliminary Observation and Analysis.* This involves "getting the feel" of the subject, recognizing the scope of the problem, and securing a general understanding of the factors involved.
3. *Segregation of the Function, or Activity, and/or Costs in Terms of Individual Responsibility.* Since standards are to control individual actions, the outer limits of the responsibility of each individual must be ascertained in the particular application.
4. *Determination of the Unit of Measurement in Which the Standard Should Be Expressed.* To arrive at the quotient, the divisor is necessary. And in many applications, the base selected can be one of many.

5. *Determination of the Best Method.* This may involve time and motion study, a thorough review of possible materials, or an analysis of past experience. It must also involve consideration of possible changes in conditions.

6. *Statement or Expression of the Standard.* When the best method and the unit of measurement have been determined, the tentative standard can be set.

7. *Testing of the Standard.* After analysis and synthesis and preliminary determination, the standard must be tested to see that it meets the requirements.

8. *Final Application of the Standard.* The testing of a standard will often result in certain compromises or changes. When this has been effected, when the best judgment of all the executives concerned has been secured, then and only then can the standard be considered set and ready to be applied.

USE OF STANDARDS FOR CONTROL

CONTROL—A PSYCHOLOGICAL PROBLEM

It is well to set standards for cost control, but the mere setting of standards by no means assures control of costs. Costs are held within limits by human beings—with all their weaknesses and frailties, with all their prejudices and stubbornness. The fact remains, therefore, that to get the greatest good from standards they must be "sold" to the people who use them. The yardsticks should be accepted with enthusiasm as a goal to be met. This enthusiasm must be sustained through a well-founded realization that the standards are fair and reasonable.

Many are the times when the controller or his staff may be called upon to justify or defend a standard. He must use all of his selling ability in securing acceptance. When standards can be shown clearly to be unreasonable, he must demonstrate his readiness to make the necessary adjustments.

TECHNIQUE OF COST CONTROL

In the final analysis, the objective of cost control is to secure the greatest amount of production or results of a desired quality from a given amount of material, manpower, effort, or facilities. It is the securing of the best result at the lowest possible cost under existing conditions. In this control of performance, the first step is the setting of standards of comparison; the next step is the recording of actual performance; and the third step is the comparing of actual and standard costs as the work progresses. This last step involves:

1. Determining the variance between standard and actual
2. Analyzing the cause of the variance

3. Taking remedial action to bring unfavorable actual costs in line with the predetermined standards

Control is established through prompt follow-up, before the unfavorable trends or tendencies develop into large losses. It is important that any variances be determined quickly, and it is equally important that the unfavorable variance be stated in terms which those responsible will understand. The speed and method of presentation have a profound bearing on the corrective action which will be taken, and, hence, on the effectiveness of control.

WHO SHOULD CONTROL COSTS?

Costs must be controlled by individuals, and the question is raised as to who should control costs—the controller, as representing accounting personnel; or the operating executive in charge of the activity—manufacturing, sales, or research—to be cost-controlled. It has already been explained that operational control preceded accounting control. And in many thousands of small businesses, operating control is the only type used. It may be said, further, that cost control is not primarily an accounting process, although accounting plays an important part. Control of costs is an operating function. The controller, in the capacity of an operating executive, may control costs within the accounting department. Beyond this, the function of the controller is to report the facts on other activities of the business so that corrective action may be taken, and to inform management of its effectiveness in cost control. The part played by the controller is advisory or facilitative in nature.

In many instances the development of the standards to be used in measuring performance is largely the work of non-accountants—whether product specifications, operational methods, time requirements, or other factors. Likewise, decision as to the corrective action to be taken is generally up to the operating personnel. However, the controller is in an excellent position to stimulate and guide the interest of management in the control of costs through the means of reports analyzing out-of-line conditions. His work is usually confined to summarizing basic information, analyzing results, and preparing intelligently conceived reports. It follows that he must produce reports that a non-accounting-trained executive or operator can understand and will act upon. To do this, he must be thoroughly conversant with the operating problems and viewpoints. In large degree, then, the effectiveness of any cost control system depends on the degree of coordination between the accounting control personnel and the operating personnel. One presents the facts in an understandable manner; the other takes the remedial action.

At this time it is well to point out again that cooperation at all levels is essential in control of costs. Cooperation is secured, in part, through the application of correct management policies. The use of standards, when fully understood, should be of great assistance in securing this cooperation, for the measuring stick is based on careful analysis, and not preconceived ideas or rule-of-thumb methods.

THE LEVEL OF THE STANDARD

Since one of the primary purposes of a standard is as a control tool—to see that performance is held to what it should be—it is necessary to determine at what level the standard should be set. Just how "tight" should a standard be? While there is no clear-cut line of demarcation among them, the three following levels may be distinguished:

1. The ideal standard
2. The average of past performance
3. The attainable good performance standard

The ideal standard is the one representing the best performance that can be attained under the most favorable conditions possible. It is not a standard which is expected to be attained, but rather a goal toward which to strive in an attempt to improve efficiency. Hence, variances are always unfavorable and represent the inability to reach the ideal level of efficiency. The use of an unattainably tight standard confuses the objectives of cost reduction and cost control. Cost reduction involves the finding of ways and means to achieve a given result through improved design, better methods, new layouts, new equipment, better plant layout, etc., and therefore results in the establishment of new standards. If the standards set are more restrictive than currently attainable performance, the lower cost will not necessarily result until cost reduction has found the means by which the standard may be attained. Ideal standards, then, are not highly desirable as a means of cost control.

Standards are frequently set on the basis of what was done in the past, without adjustments to reflect improved methods or elimination of wastes. A standard set on this basis is likewise a poor measuring stick in that it can be met by poor performance. Hence, the very inefficiencies which standards should disclose are obscured by the loose standard.

A third level at which a standard may be set is the attainable level of good performance. This standard includes waste, or spoilage, lost time, and other inefficiencies only to the extent that they are considered impractical of elimination. This type of standard can be met or bettered by efficient performance. It is a standard set at a high level, but is attainable with reasonably diligent effort. Such a standard would seem to be the one most effective for cost control purposes.

THE POINT OF CONTROL

Since costs are controlled by individuals, it follows that the accounting classifications must reflect both standard and actual performance in such a manner that individual performance can be measured. As stated previously, "responsibility accounting" must be adopted. Provision must be made for the accumulation of costs by cost centers, or cost pools, or by departments which follow organizational structure. Furthermore, this cost accumulation must reflect, first, only those costs which are direct as to the specific function being measured. Allocations and re-allocations may be made for product cost *determination* and for certain other *planning* applications, but this is not desirable for cost *control*. If a great many prorations are made, it is often difficult to determine where the inefficiency exists, or the extent of it. Therefore, it is desirable from a cost control standpoint to collect the costs at the point of incurrence.

If, as in some companies, allocated costs are reflected in control reports, it is desirable to separate them from direct expenses or costs. Some companies show allocated costs so that the department manager will be aware of the cost of the facilities or services they use.

Discussion of the point of control of costs involves, in addition to placement of responsibility, the matter of timing. Costs must be controlled not only at the point of incurrence but also, preferably, at or before the time of incurrence. Thus, if a department on a budget basis processes a purchase requisition and is advised at that time of the excess cost over budget, perhaps action can be taken then—either delaying the expenditure until the following month or getting a cheaper yet satisfactory substitute. Again, material control is best exercised at the point of issuance. Only the standard quantity should be issued. Or, in the case of purchases, the price and type are best controlled at the time of purchase.

WHAT COSTS SHOULD HAVE STANDARDS?

From the viewpoint of standards for cost control, a question may be raised as to the extent to which attempts should be made to set standards. Factors to be considered include the relative amount of cost, and the degree of control possible over the cost.

It may be stated that standards should be set for all cost items of a significant or material amount. In many cases, the more important the cost, the greater is the opportunity or need for cost control. With such items as overhead, it may be necessary to combine certain elements, but so far as practicable a standard should be set to measure performance.

Another factor to be considered is the degree of control possible or needed or desired over the cost. At first blush, it might appear that little control can be exercised over some types of cost, such as depreciation, salaries of key personnel, or personal property taxes. However, the fact is that most costs can be controlled by someone. The time and place and method of control of costs generally considered as "fixed" may differ from control of material, direct labor, or variable overhead expense, but a certain degree of control is possible. Control of the fixed charges may be exercised in at least two ways:

1. *By limiting the expenditure to a predetermined amount.* For example, depreciation charges are controlled through the acquisition of plant and equipment. Any control must be exercised at the time of purchase or construction of the asset. This is usually done by means of an appropriation budget, which is a type of standard. A similar plan can be applied to the group of salaried personnel generally considered as a part of the fixed charges. In many instances, control of this type of expense or expenditure is a top-management decision. It may be observed, however, that control at this high level does exist.

2. *By securing the proper utilization of the facilities and organization represented by the fixed charges.* The controller can assist in this task by properly isolating the volume costs, or cost of idle equipment. An acceptable standard might be the per cent of plant utilization as related to "normal." In the monthly statement of income and expense, the lack of volume costs should be set out as part of the effort to direct management's attention to the excess costs and to a consideration of ways and means of reducing personnel, if necessary, or increasing volume through other products, intensified sales activity, etc.

PROCEDURE FOR REVISING STANDARDS

REVISION OF STANDARDS

Whether standards are used for cost control or the related function of budgetary planning, or whether standards are for the purpose of price setting or inventory valuation, they must be kept up to date in order to be most useful. Revision appears desirable when important changes are made in material specifications or prices, methods of production, or labor efficiency or price—from the viewpoint of manufacturing operations. Changes in the methods or channels of distribution, or basic organizational or functional changes, would necessitate standard changes in the selling, research, or administrative activities. Stated in other terms, current standards must be revised when conditions have changed to such an extent that the standard no longer represents a realistic or fair measure of performance.

It is obvious that standard revisions should not be made for every change —only the important ones. However, the constant search for better methods and for better measurements of performance subjects every standard to possible revision. The controller constantly must be on the alert as to the desirability of adjusting standards to prevent the furnishing of misleading information to management.

A PROGRAM FOR STANDARD REVISION

The changing of standards is time-consuming and may be expensive. For this reason, it should not be treated in a haphazard manner. It is desirable to plan in advance the steps to be taken in revising standards. Through the use of an orderly program for constant review and revision of standards, the time and money spent on standard changes can be less and the effort more productive.

In planning the program of standard revision, the ramifications of any changes should be considered. For example, changes in manufacturing standards usually necessitate changes in inventory values. Accordingly, it may appear desirable to review the standards at the end of each fiscal year and make the necessary changes. In a chemical plant with which the authors are familiar, a review of material price standards is made every quarter. In this instance, the selling price of the finished product is sympathetic to changes in commodity prices. This more frequent revision results in cost information which is more useful to the sales department. In some companies a general practice is to change standards whenever basic selling price changes occur. This results in a more constant standard gross profit figure by which to judge sales performance. In considering frequent changes, however, the expense should be weighed against the benefits. In this connection, the value for cost control should be matched against the lessened degree of comparability of the variances from period to period.

Judgment should be exercised as to the necessity for, and extent of, change in the records. For example, general changes in labor rates, raw material costs, standard overhead rates, or product design may dictate a complete revision of product and departmental costs, extending through every stage of manufacture. On the other hand, a change in one department, or in one part, or in a small assembly might necessitate the change of only one standard for control purposes. The difference between old and new, with respect to other stages of manufacture, or the finished product cost, could be temporarily written off as a variance until the time is ripe for a complete product standard revision.

RECORDING STANDARDS

IMPORTANCE OF ADEQUATE RECORDS

If the controller is to serve management most effectively and if the business is to have the advantage of accurate, reliable, and prompt cost information, then an adequate recording of the facts is necessary. This principle is as applicable to recording standards and standard costs as it is to actual costs—perhaps even more so. The degree of intelligence applied to the form and method of recording determines in large measure that (1) the data underlying the development and revision of standards will be available as needed, (2) the facts relating to operating efficiency will be ascertainable and accurately analyzed, (3) the information will be made available on an economical basis, and (4) the records will have the necessary flexibility to meet promptly the needs of the various applications of the standards.

Work Order & Lot No. 1424	LotQuan. 250	Spares	Adj.	Quan. to Make 250	Part Number 2611012				
SCHEDULE	550	555	560	561	562				
DISPATCH ROUTING	03	10	31	97	98	45			

Part Name Fitting Vert. Stab. Hinge		Part Number 108-2611012-0		Sheet of
Material Specs 26 ST	Raw Mat'l-Req'd Size FM 108-8211002	B M Item No. 01132	Unit FT	Unit Part 230
Material Description Rextrusion SP 4760		Change Schedule M	Revision Date 1-30-51	

OP. NO.	DEPT. W.	STA.	OPERATION DESCRIPTION	TOOL SYMBOL	TOOL ORDER#	STANDARD TIME SET-UP	STANDARD TIME OPERATING
10	60	502	Cut 2.76 long			.0071	.0040
20	60	302	Drill (4) .191 .194 dia. holes	J	29948		
			and (1) .254 .250 hole				.0257
30	30	306	Route angles and radus	RE	29949		.0010
35	45	304	Barrel burr				.0020
40	45	301	Clean				.0103
50	45	306	Alodize				.0100
		108-2312050-0		1	1		

Fig. 38—Standard Operation Sheet—Fabrication.

TYPES OF RECORDS NECESSARY

In the manufacturing function the records incident to the establishment and use of standards may be classified into four basic groups:

1. Physical specifications which outline the required material and the sequence of manufacturing operations which must be performed
2. Details of standard or budgeted overhead based on normal capacity
3. Standard cost sheets for each product and component part; these sheets indicate standard cost by elements
4. Variance accounts which indicate the type of departure from standard

The extent and form of these records depend on the size and characteristics of the business. In an assembly-type operation, for example, there

Detroit Chemical Company

PRODUCT STANDARD COST SHEET

Effective Date 2/1/62   Type 672C

RAW MATERIALS:

Code No.	Description	Formula	Standard Raw Material Cost Per Cwt.	Standard Raw Material Cost Total	Finished Product Cwt. Cost
3001	Crystal Urea	3393	$ 4.800	$163	$ 3.335
4005	Formaldehyde (47½%)	4377	6.010	263	5.380
803	Extender "W"	500	4.800	24	.491
119	Accelerator "T"	48	25.000	12	.245
201	Formic Acid—90%	2	17.200	–	–
202	Chemical "P"	45	1.605	1	.021
209	Sodium Nitrate	5	5.010	–	–
210	Calcium Phosphate	91	7.217	7	.143
221	Ammonium Chloride	113	3.280	4	.082
272	Barium Sulfate	182	7.275	13	.266
	Charged Weight	8756			9.963
	Yield (lbs.)	4888	$ 5.562	$487	
33	Containers (300 lb.)				1.027

MANUFACTURING EXPENSE (Incl. Direct Labor):

	Base	Hourly Rate Variable	Hourly Rate Fixed	Total Expense Variable	Total Expense Fixed	Cwt. Cost Variable	Cwt. Cost Fixed
51 Kettle Room	3.81 hr.	$20.614	$5.210	$ 79	$20	$1.616	$.409
21 Boiler		4.173	–	16	–	.327	–
27 Building		2.308	.298	9	1	.184	.020
30 Quality Control		2.277	–	9	–	.184	–
35 Materials Handling		2.775	–	11	–	.226	–
Direct Overhead	5%				7		.143
General Manufacturing Overhead	14%				20		.409
Total Manufacturing Expense and Direct Labor				$124	$48	$2.537	$.981

Grand Total Manufacturing Costs.................$14.508

would be a product specification for each part. These in turn would form the basis for cost sheets on subassemblies and assemblies. This type of operation might lend itself to a punched card application. An example of a standard operational record is shown in Fig. 38. In this instance the standard operational sheet is produced on tabulating equipment and serves as (1) the production order, (2) the count ticket to evaluate the day's production in terms of standard labor hours, and (3) the means of determining the standard cost of the part, when priced at standard. These same sheets are summarized to obtain assembly and product costs. With the necessary details of the standard, substitution of parts is easily accomplished to determine the standard cost of various modifications of the basic product.

On the other hand, a simple one-stage chemical process might involve a single cost sheet for each product (Fig. 39). Supporting the product cost sheet, of course, are specification sheets (formula) and technical data on the standard cost per operating hour in the processing departments.

DISTRIBUTION AND ADMINISTRATIVE ACTIVITIES

In most firms, the records for standards on distribution or administrative activities are not as well developed as those on manufacturing operations. They generally represent a collection of statistical data, often in worksheet form, from which unit comparisons of actual and standard activity are made. These will be discussed in subsequent chapters.

INCORPORATION OF STANDARD COSTS IN ACCOUNTS

Some concerns use standard costs for statistical comparisons only, and do not incorporate them in the books of account. This is particularly true of non-manufacturing expenses—commercial expense, research expense, financial expense. Most firms which use standard manufacturing costs prefer to record them in the cost accounts as part of the double-entry system. The incorporation of standard costs in the accounts has the advantage of reducing clerical effort. If the standard costs are not incorporated in the books, they ordinarily would not be used for inventory costing, but they may be used for cost control, budgetary planning, and pricing.

APPLICATION OF STANDARD COSTS

Even though standard costs are incorporated in the accounts, there is considerable difference as to the period in the accounting cycle when the standards should be recorded. While there are several variations in accounting treatment, the distinction may be twofold:

1. Recognition of standard cost at time of cost incurrence
2. Recognition of standard cost at time of cost completion

The first method charges work in process at standard cost, while the second method develops the standard cost at the time of transfer to the finished goods account. Recognition of costs at incurrence would imply a recording of material price variance at time of purchase, and material usage variance at time of usage or transfer to work in process. However, many firms record material at actual cost and recognize price variances only as the material is used. This practice permits a write-off of excess costs proportionate to usage, so that unit costs tend to approximate the actual cost each month.

STATISTICAL SAMPLING AS RELATED TO CONTROL

The use of standards for control purposes does not imply that a 100% or complete enumeration or check is necessary. The statistical technique of sampling may be applied to good advantage. If the cost of obtaining the data is high, the sampling approach should be considered. Control limits may be computed by statistical methods; and as long as the sampling stays within the stated ranges the process would be considered as under control. If, however, the waste extends outside the permissible deviation, then management action would be required.

As an example, assume that the past acceptable experience indicates 105 pounds per hour of Chemical A is generated as scrap. On the basis of statistical techniques, also assume that control limits of 87 and 117 pounds were established. If the hourly scrap generation of Chemical A is more than 87 pounds and less than 117 pounds, the process may be said to be under control. If it is less than 87 pounds the management would be expected to seek out the cause of improvement. If the waste becomes more than 117 pounds, then remedial steps should be taken.

The statistical approach is applicable in many areas and not merely in processing operations. For example, acceptable ranges may be established for inventory levels. Again, it may be used as a control device in measuring the proportion of delinquent accounts receivable.

12

Control of Sales

PROBLEMS OF SALES MANAGEMENT

LACK OF SCIENTIFIC SALES MANAGEMENT

The field of sales management is one of the last bastions to fall under the attack of the scientific method. Indeed, in many companies the sales manager still operates by rule of thumb or by hunch. A primary distinction between the older sales management and modern sales management is the emphasis on securing as many facts as practicable before making decisions or undertaking action. Another characteristic of the new sales approach is the objective of securing the greatest *profit* consistent with the long-range objectives of the company, and not merely the highest sales volume.

If the controller does a first-rate job, he can be an important influence in promoting sound decisions in many phases of sales management by encouraging the sales executive to depend more and more on objective analyses of sales and distribution costs.

NATURE OF SALES MANAGEMENT PROBLEMS

The problems of any management function are multitudinous, and sales management is no exception. In fact, the problems are greater because sales executives generally have been late in adopting a scientific approach. The controller must be aware of the problems and their implications if he is to assist most effectively.

Since the field of sales management is broad, those matters needing solution are correspondingly extensive. Some are recurring and constantly plague every sales manager; others, when once settled, can be forgotten. While some problems are basic, others are routine. Accordingly, any attempt to classify them is subject to limitations, but the listing which follows is indicative of the fundamental problems. Generally, all problems will fall within the categories listed.

1. *Product.* What product is to be sold, and in what quantity? Is it to be the highest quality in its field or lower? Is the product to be a specialty or a staple?

2. *Pricing.* At what price is the article to be sold? Shall the company follow a policy of meeting any and all price competition? What are the terms of sale to be granted?

3. *Distribution.* To whom shall the product be sold, i.e., shall the firm sell directly to the ultimate consumer, or through others, such as wholesalers? What channels of distribution should be used?

4. *Method of Sale.* How shall the goods be sold? Is it to be by personal solicitation, advertising, or direct mail? What sales promotion means shall be used?

5. *Organization.* How shall salesmen be selected, and how shall they be trained? What is to be the basic organizational setup? Are there to be branch offices? Will sales supervisors handle all lines of product, or will each specialize? Into what departments shall the sales organization be divided? How many salesmen should be employed?

6. *Planning and Control.* How are sales territories to be set up? Shall sales standards be used as measuring sticks of performance? How will salesmen be compensated—salary, commission, bonus? What controls will be employed?

Problems relating to these six categories are found in every company, regardless of size. The solutions to many depend, in large part, on the facts available within each organization.

THE CONTROLLER AND SALES MANAGEMENT PROBLEMS

The final solution to sales management problems must, of course, rest largely with the chief sales executive. However, an intelligent executive will always seek any assistance available. In this respect, the controller can help by bringing to bear a scientific, analytical approach. While doing this, he is expected to use judgment as well as imagination. It should be realized that the solution in one firm may not be the solution in another. It should be realized further that the answers to today's problems may not be the answer tomorrow—for industry is dynamic. The controller is of value primarily in getting the facts—he is the fact-finder. In presenting the facts, though, he will have to merchandise or sell his product; his approach must be one that invites reception.

The degree of assistance the controller can render in solving the previously mentioned sales problems is indicated in the following outline.

1. *Problems of Product.* The initial selection of the product, or consideration of changes in the line, sizes, and colors should generally be based on collective judgment of the marketing considerations by the sales manager, of production problems by the manufacturing executive, and of cost

considerations by the controller. Costs are not the only factor in the decision, but they are an important factor. The chief accounting official should be able to indicate the probable margin on the product, as well as the margins on alternative choices. He should also be able to indicate the probable effect of volume on the margin, or the effect of changes in quality, composition, and manufacturing processes on the cost to make or sell.

In his constant reviews of sales trends by product, the controller may be able to identify unfavorable trends which might call for a change in product.

2. *Problems of Price.* Again, while cost is not the only determining factor, it must be considered in establishing a realistic price schedule. The controller must furnish this information in all of its ramifications. Marginal or differential costs, out-of-pocket costs, or cost differences which can be justified under the Robinson-Patman Act are all phases which must be considered in developing price data—whether for competitive bids or establishing price lists for the usual type of sale.

By reviewing sales volume and checking prices, the controller may be able to spot unfavorable developments in instances where the individual salesman has considerable latitude in setting a selling price. As production costs change, with differing margins, he may wish to bring this to the attention of the sales executive for consideration as to price changes. He should be able to render considerable assistance in setting price brackets for different sizes of orders.

3. *Problems of Distribution.* Toward the solution of these problems, too, the controller contributes the cost analysis necessary, as well as a review of statistics for unfavorable trends. He is able to provide indications of the selling cost through the various channels of distribution. He should be on the alert for major changes in sales trends through particular channels or margins thereon. He frequently has a chance to show ingenuity in analysis regarding types and sizes of accounts and orders to be sought. Questions of policy on which he should provide many of the facts, for example, relate to:

a. The minimum order to be accepted
b. Restriction of sales effort on large volume accounts which purchase only low-margin products, or which are unprofitable because of special laboratory service
c. Desirability of servicing particular types of accounts through jobbers, telephone, mail order, etc.
d. Discontinuance of aggressive sales effort on accounts where annual sales volume is too low
e. Best location for branch warehouses

4. *Problems Relating to Method of Sale.* The assistance of the controller is somewhat limited on matters relating to method of sale. It is the

task of the sales manager to select that which will best accomplish the purpose in the long run. Probably the largest field in which the accountant can help is in furnishing information on past costs and in preparing cost estimates. He would, for example, be able to estimate the cost of sample distribution and point out what past costs have been, if samples were used. He may have useful data on advertising programs. If tests are made to determine the best method of sale, the controller can gather and help interpret the costs. In the long run, of course, the best selling method is that which secures the greatest volume at the least cost.

5. *Problems of Organization.* In this field, too, the controller can be of limited assistance only—chiefly in cost analysis. For example, based on information from the sales executive as to potential sales, he might determine whether it appears profitable to hire additional salesmen for a territory. Again, he may provide comparative cost data on different forms of organizational structure, and attendant changes in sales policy.

6. *Problems of Planning and Control.* So numerous are the applications where the controller can be of assistance in planning and controlling sales effort that only a few can be indicated. Whereas he is able to aid the sales executive in solving some of the previously mentioned problems through special studies, yet in the planning and control fields many of his functions are repetitive. Suggestive of the contributions by the accounting official are the following:

a. *Sales budgets and quotas.* Detailed records and knowledge as to distribution of sales by territory, product, and customer, coupled with the knowledge of the sales manager on product changes and trends, provide basic information necessary in an intelligent setting of sales budgets, quotas, and standards. The controller also may provide services in connection with forecasting and market studies.

b. *Distribution expense budgets and standards.* A history of past expenses as recorded in the accounting department provides much needed data in setting budgets and standards for the measurement and control of selling effort.

c. *Monthly or periodic income and expense statements:*
1) By territories
2) By commodities
3) By methods of sale
4) By customers
5) By salesmen
6) By organization or operating divisions

These and other analytical statements can provide a vast amount of useful information. The disclosure of the contribution to net profit of each territory or other factor analyzed, over and above the direct expense, may reveal spots of weakness.

d. *Special analyses to reveal conditions needing correction, or as an audit of performance:*

1) Sales incentive plans. The probable cost of various plans as applied to the business and degree to which they are mutually profitable for company and salesman. A determination as to whether or not they direct salesmen's efforts toward the most profitable products.

2) Branch and warehouse expense. Periodic reviews and comparison of expense, in relationship to sales, earnings of the activity, cwt. of material handled, etc.

3) Entertainment expense. Analysis of entertainment expense by customer, with emphasis on the necessity for entertainment, cheaper methods accomplishing the objective—all with reference to the profitability of the account.

4) Salesmen's salaries. Review of salesmen's salaries in relation to other salaries, and as part of a salary evaluation program, to see that the payments are in line with company policy and classification of salesmen.

CONTROL OF SALES

Just what is implied by the phrase "control of sales"? For this discussion it involves the required analysis and study, together with subsequent action, of actual performance, policies, and methods required to secure the desired sales volume, at reasonable expense, which produces those gross margins needed to achieve the expected return on investment. The optimum net income is realized only when a proper relationship exists among these four factors: (1) *investment in working capital and facilities,* (2) *volume of sales,* (3) *operating expenses,* and (4) *gross margins.* The accounting control of sales, therefore, relates to the reports analyzing sales activity which brings to light undesirable trends and relationships, or departures from goals, budgets, or standards in the manner best calculated to secure corrective action.

The controller and his staff may assist in improving the sales picture through the use of several analytical techniques:

1. Analysis of past sales performance—as to both price and volume—to ferret out unfavorable developments, points of weakness, or trends

2. Assistance to sales management in the determination of suitable over-all sales budgets, and reporting on conformance to plan

3. Assistance to sales management in setting sales performance standards so as to measure performance

4. Preparation of sound cost and investment analyses for use in establishing product prices

Some of these functions are discussed in the following section.

SALES ANALYSIS

GETTING AT THE FACTS

The stress sometimes placed on sales volume can be misleading. If a business were to ignore the profit factor, it could probably secure any desired volume. Through the cutting of prices, through the spending of huge amounts on direct selling expense or sales promotion or advertising, volume itself could be secured. Yet, what good would result? It is obvious that the implied factor is *profitable* sales volume.

If business is to achieve profitable sales, it must know where the areas of greatest profit are. This means both sales analysis and cost analysis. There is little doubt that the analysis of sales has reached different peaks of achievement in different firms and industries. Many large companies devote a great deal of time to this phase of marketing control, and have well-developed programs. A large number of medium-sized or small firms have little or none. It is also probably true that the sales executive in consumer goods lines has many more facts than the industrial marketing executive.

Yet the evidence is unmistakably clear in any business of size that overall or average figures are not enough. Such generalities are of little value in directing sales effort. They are reminiscent of the man who drowned in twenty feet of water because he heard that the Missouri River *averaged* three feet in depth. The shallows and sand bars as well as the areas of good sailing must be known.

TYPES OF SALES ANALYSIS NEEDED

What is needed, then, is detailed analysis to guide sales effort. Some required analysis relates solely to past sales performance as such. Other studies involve the determination of trends by comparison with previous periods. Still other reviews show the relationship to budget or standard, to gross profit, or selling expense, or net profit. Analyses may be expressed in physical units, or dollar volume, or both.

The types of analysis frequently used are:

1. Commodity—type of product sold, colors, sizes, price lines, style, quality (reclaimed material, odd lot, first quality)
2. Territory—area used for sales direction—states, cities, counties, other marketing areas
3. Channel of distribution—wholesalers, retailers, brokers, agents
4. Method of sale—direct mail, house call, ad or coupon, delivered vs. non-delivered
5. Customer—domestic vs. foreign, industrial vs. ultimate consumer, private vs. governmental, tabulated according to volume of purchases

6. Size of order—average size of individual purchase
7. Terms of sale—cash, C.O.D., regular charge account, instalment, lay-away
8. Organization—branches, departments
9. Salesman—either individual or groups

These analyses may be developed, not merely as to sales, but through gross profit to profit after direct selling expense, or ultimately to the net profit of the segment being measured.

Other analyses relating to unrealized sales may also be useful, for example:

1. Orders received
2. Unfilled orders
3. Cancellations
4. Lost sales

These studies may be used as an integral part of sales planning, or to eliminate reasons for ineffective effort. Analysis of orders may be important where production is made to order. For example, all sales of a given size or type may be summarized to necessitate only one production run in the period.

Many subanalyses can be prepared. Thus, management may want to know not merely the over-all sales by product but the product sales in each territory.

The controller may find that the sales manager can use certain of these analyses monthly or periodically—for example, sales by territory, by product lines, or by salesman. Other analyses may be made only as a special investigation, when it is expected the tabulation will reveal out-of-line conditions. In any event, it is his responsibility to design and install procedures and records in such a fashion that the maximum information is made available with the minimum of time and effort, both clerical and analytical. It is axiomatic that in many situations the company getting the information most quickly is in a better competitive position.

This information will answer the typical questions of an analytical sales executive: What was sold? Where was it sold? Who sold it? What was the profit?

DEDUCTIONS FROM SALES

In any analysis of sales the importance of sales deductions should not be overlooked. While reviews may relate to net sales, the clue to substandard profits may lie in the deductions—high freight cost, special allowances, or discounts. These factors may reveal why unit prices appear low.

Useful analyses and reports on sales deductions can be prepared. For example, an informative summary may be compiled to indicate the general types and amounts of sales deductions, viz., returns, freight allowances, price adjustments, or customer sales policy adjustments. It may be helpful, also, to prepare an analysis of deductions by responsibility—the manufacturing division for defective product, the traffic department for erroneous freight allowances, the sales division for allowances to retain customer goodwill.

TYPICAL CONDITIONS FOUND BY SALES ANALYSIS

In many businesses it will be found that a large proportion of the sales volume is done in a small share of the product line. Likewise, a relatively small proportion of customers will provide the bulk of the volume. Such conditions reflect the fact that only a very small part of the selling effort is responsible for most of the business. This information should prove useful to the sales executive. It might permit the concentration of sales effort and the consequent reduction in selling expense. Again, it might mean a change in territorial assignments of men. Where product analysis reveals unsatisfactory conditions, a simplification of the product line may be indicated. While the line may not be limited to only volume items, many sales managers are beginning to realize that not all sizes, all colors, and all varieties need be carried. Smart executives will let their competitors have the odd sizes or odd colors, and concentrate on the more profitable articles. After all, the economies of production also must be considered in developing the product line.

ILLUSTRATIVE USE OF SALES ANALYSIS—BUDGET APPLICATION

Some examples will help in illustrating certain of the benefits to be gained from sales analysis.

Assume a case where the sales executive has just been advised by the accountant that sales for the month then ended total $125,000. Assume further that this is $15,000 lower than the preceding month and that the aggregate volume failed by $25,000 to meet the commitment to the chief executive. What can the sales manager do with merely the information that sales were $125,000? The answer, of course, is that he can't do very much. He is in the position of a hunter who has a shotgun but needs a high-powered rifle. His controller has done a poor job.

Now assume that an analysis of sales by territories is made available. The results might be as shown in the following set of figures. This analysis gives the sales executive some useful information. Instead of prodding the managers of all territories, he can concentrate his efforts on the poor performers—B, D, and C, probably in just that order.

Territory	Total Sales Actual	Total Sales Budget	Over or (Under) Budget Value	Over or (Under) Budget %
A	$ 15,000	$ 12,500	$ 2,500	20.00
B	50,000	70,000	(20,000)	(28.56)
C	10,000	12,500	(2,500)	(20.00)
D	25,000	37,500	(12,500)	(33.33)
E	13,000	8,500	4,500	52.94
F	12,000	9,000	3,000	33.33
Total .	$125,000	$150,000	$(25,000)	(16.67)

If more than one salesman is assigned to a territory, a further analysis of the substandard territories could prove useful. While territory B, for example, was badly under budget, it could well be that some of the salesmen did a good job. The picture might appear thus:

TERRITORY B—ANALYSIS BY SALESMAN

Salesman	Total Sales Actual	Total Sales Budget	Over or (Under) Budget Value	Over or (Under) Budget %
Knight	$17,000	$14,000	$ 3,000	21.43
Black	11,500	15,000	(3,500)	(23.33)
Smith	8,500	20,500	(12,000)	(58.54)
Jones	8,000	16,000	(8,000)	(50.00)
Nesser	5,000	4,500	500	11.11
Total ...	$50,000	$70,000	$(20,000)	(28.56)

It is evident that something went wrong in the areas covered by Smith, Jones, and Black. Where did they fall down? A subanalysis of the sales by Smith might reveal the following:

Product	Sales Potential	Sales Actual	Sales Budget	Over or (Under) Budget Value	Over or (Under) Budget %
Urea molding compound	$20,000	$2,500	$12,000	$(9,500)	(79.17)
Alkyd molding compound ...	4,000	500	3,600	(3,100)	(86.11)
Hard resins	1,000	1,000	900	100	11.11
Powdered glue	6,000	4,500	4,000	500	12.50
Total	$31,000	$8,500	$20,500	$(12,000)	(58.54)

Now we are beginning to get at the root of the trouble! Smith has done much better than expected on hard resins and glue. He is getting what sales management feels is his maximum share of hard resin sales in the territory. While he can get still a greater share of the potential sales, he actually exceeded his budget. However, Smith has performed very poorly on molding compound. A review of his call reports indicates that he isn't calling on the important users of molding compound. For example, he is completely overlooking the molders of electrical fixtures, yet this is where the greatest potential lies. His sales, as an analysis by customers shows, have been only to molders of bottle caps and the like. Now the sales manager has the facts and can take corrective action; and the controller can feel that his analysis has been useful.

ANOTHER ILLUSTRATIVE USE OF SALES ANALYSIS

In many businesses, budget applications are not developed to the point of sales by product by salesman. Further, it must be realistically recognized that such applications may contain errors in themselves. Aside from these matters, however, it is well to be aware of sales analyses which are useful without relating to budgets. One such analysis is by customers. Assume, for example, that a sales analysis by customers shows the following:

SALES BY CUSTOMERS—COMPARATIVE

Month of April, 1963

Customer's Name	Location State	Location City	Commodity Class	Sales This Month	Sales Year to Date	Sales Last Year to Date
American Aviation Co. . .			1	$ 119	$ 520	$ 219
			2	403	1,680	1,742
			3	1,680	6,792	12,420
				2,202	8,992	14,382
Baker Aeronautics Co. . .			1	5,420	34,916	14,820
			2	110	319	410
			3	8,600	27,816	45,389
				14,130	63,051	60,619
Cavanaugh Supply Co. . .			1	120	419	317
			2	316	1,117	817
			3	922	4,214	3,210
				1,358	5,750	4,344
Grand Total				$17,691	$77,794	$79,345

If this comparative sales report is to be of maximum use, the sales executive must, of course, be reasonably familiar with the business conditions in each territory and the general level of activity of his customers. If he is also familiar with the gross profit of each class of product, then an intelligent use of the report can be made in guiding sales effort. Assume that the most profitable products are 3, 2, and 1 in that order; and assume, further, that the business level of American Aviation Co. and Baker Aeronautics Co. is about 10% higher than last year, while Cavanaugh Supply Co. is a relatively small but growing firm.

Just what story does this simple analysis tell?

1. As to American Aviation Co.: Although business is generally higher, our share is only 62.5% of last year's business. Furthermore, the major decline is in our most profitable line. Also, an actual increase has taken place in the least profitable product. It is up to the sales manager to find out why we are not getting our share of the volume. Is our service poor? Is the competitor undercutting our prices? Or are there large inventories of "3" which are being reduced? Perhaps sales effort must be increased on the sales of commodity "3."

2. As to Baker Aeronautics Co.: Total sales volume is generally what might be expected. However, two basic weaknesses in trend present themselves:
   a. Our company is losing heavily in sales of commodity "3," our most profitable line, although the additional volume is picked up on the less desirable class "1" business.
   b. We are not securing the same relative share of class "2" business as the other products. Since we know approximately what proportion of customer business is in each class, it is evident that all class "2" purchases are not being made from us. Sales effort should be directed toward finding out why the class "3" sales have declined so much, and how to get that business. Also, sales effort should be directed toward getting all or most of the class "2" business.

3. As to Cavanaugh Supply Co.: This account, while small, appears to be growing satisfactorily. Also, the relative proportion of each product seems about right in that area. No special action need be taken.

These are highly simplified examples, but they do illustrate what an analysis can show and how it can be used in guiding sales effort. Possibly with each monthly report, the controller might find it desirable to highlight the important trends and spots of weakness—the application of the exception principle.

OTHER USES OF SALES ANALYSIS

The illustrative examples point the way to use of analysis in correcting substandard performance in terms of individual salesmen as related to planned sales or to customer purchases. Other uses, however, have been mentioned. Some of these benefits or applications are summarized below:

1. For sales planning and setting of quotas. Past experience is a factor.
2. For inventory control. To properly plan inventories, a business should be familiar with past sales and probable future trends in terms of seasonal fluctuations and type of product.

SALES REPORT

PRODUCT ☐
CUSTOMER ☐
SALESMAN ☒
LOCATION ☐

DESCRIPTION	SALES-MAN NO.	ITEM CODE OR CUST. NO.	CURRENT SALES	CURRENT GROSS PROFIT * INDICATES LOSS	SALES/YEAR-TO-DATE THIS YEAR	SALES/YEAR-TO-DATE LAST YEAR	SALES/YEAR-TO-DATE INCREASE DECREASE "CR"	GROSS PROFIT/YEAR-TO-DATE THIS YEAR	GROSS PROFIT/YEAR-TO-DATE LAST YEAR	GROSS PROFIT/YEAR-TO-DATE INCREASE DECREASE "CR"
G W ADAMS	1		2887 31	6519 6	5834 30	3854 05	4448 90	1370 30	955 01	2748 0
O T MATSON	2		257885	62077	769342	497932	271410	132560	835 00	49060
G F PRICE	3		94600	21787	217540	221726	4186 CR	32000	46750	14750 CR
T D STRUCHER	4		203660	48153	425712	254721	170991	97560	53275	44285
C D SUTTER	5		115850	29454	121562	215015	93453 CR	41000	52530	11530 CR
D T TALBOT	6		462700	97508	896510	962800	800230	157240	110001	46240
H T WAILES	7		142793	35417*	311000	217230	93770	62010	375 10	24500
H V WEBER	8		1309172	35250	541053	558560	17507 CR	113560	102900	10660

Fig. 40—Analysis of Sales and Gross Profit by Salesman.

3. For the setting of certain sales standards. Here, also, past experience is a factor.
4. For the better distribution of sales effort in territories. It may well prove that the business is concentrating its effort in too restrictive an area. Consideration of potential sales, competitive conditions, and cost factors may dictate a wider coverage. Again, analysis might reveal that the territory is not being fully covered.
5. For better direction of sales effort on products. A study of sales and the potentials may reveal the restriction of sales effort to certain products, to the neglect of other and more profitable ones. Also, a comparison of sales by product with previous periods will reveal trends. If the trends are away from the more profitable lines, corrective action may be called for.
6. For better direction of sales effort as to customers. Analysis by customers should reveal trends as to types of merchandise purchased by each customer. Also, comparison with sales of a similar period for the previous year will reveal facts on whether or not the company is making headway in securing the maximum amount of profitable business from the customer. Analysis by customer account, coupled with other information and discussions with the sales manager, will show certain accounts which cannot possibly provide a profitable volume, even if developed. This, too, may permit greater utilization of sales effort elsewhere.

SALES AND GROSS PROFIT ANALYSIS

Sales attention, as previously stated, should be focused on *profitable* volume. To do so, the sales executive must be furnished with profit facts. For this reason gross profit analysis in many cases goes hand in hand with sales analysis. An analysis of sales and gross profit by salesman is illustrated in Fig. 40. A high gross profit does not necessarily signify a high net profit—the cost to sell may be excessive. But within certain confines, a knowledge of gross profit is a guide in selecting the spots for concentration of sales effort.

One other aspect of gross profit deserves comment. Variations in gross profit may result from changes in selling price, product sales mixture, returns, or volume—largely controlled by the sales executive—or from changes in manufacturing efficiency—controlled by the production executive. These facts should be recognized when reviewing changes in gross profit. The causes should be isolated. If a standard cost system is in operation, this process is simplified somewhat. In this case, the best measure of sales performance will be *standard* gross profit. When the standard eliminates the manufacturing efficiency factor, then the sales department is generally responsible for the result, as well as the volume variance. Gross profit is discussed in more detail in Chapter 13.

LIMITATIONS OF SALES ANALYSIS

Enough has been said to indicate the limitations of sales analysis. To begin with, no amount of sales analysis can be a substitute for the alert and dynamic leadership of an aggressive sales executive. Sales analysis is merely a tool for his use. It should be further evident from the discussions that analysis of actual sales must be used in conjunction with other factors—sales potentials, budgets, or standards, as well as previous performance to detect trends; manufacturing costs; and operating expenses.

While sales volume can be used extensively in measuring or studying sales performance, those who use the figures must remember constantly that high volume does not necessarily mean high profits. A business does not earn an equal profit on all products. Thus, where a variety of products is handled, all with widely varying margins, the sales volume alone is of less significance than where fewer products, each with approximately the same margin, comprise the makeup of sales.

However, despite the limitations and simple though they may seem, analyses of sales are an integral part of intelligent sales guidance.

MECHANICS OF SALES ANALYSIS

To be most useful to the sales manager, any sales analysis must be reported promptly. From the business viewpoint, it must be produced economically. Accuracy, as every controller knows, is essential. These requirements, as well as such factors as the size of the business and the complexity of the problem, influence the means of collecting the data.

In those firms with a relatively small sales volume or number of sales invoices, the analysis is usually handled initially through a sorting of the original sales invoices, shipping memos, or like documents. These may be summarized daily and entered on columnar worksheets. The particular analysis wanted, i.e., by product, territory, or salesman, will govern the setup of the worksheet. Sometimes the pegboard method or keysort cards are used where it is felt that manual methods are best adaptable.

When the number of sales transactions is so great as to justify mechanical means, then computer or tabulating equipment can be used advantageously. Thus, by proper coding, analyses and subanalyses by customer, salesman, territory, product, etc., may be quickly prepared. Illustrations of such reports are given later in this chapter.

SALES STANDARDS [1]

DEFINITION OF SALES STANDARDS

In the preceding chapter, a standard was defined as a scientifically developed measure of performance. It was further noted that standards can be adapted to the measurement of sales performance in somewhat the same way they have been used to judge performance in the factory. The primary requirements in developing tools for the sales executive are threefold:

1. *Sales standards are the result of careful investigation and analysis of past performance, taking into consideration expected future conditions.* Sales standards represent the opinion of those best qualified to judge what constitutes satisfactory performance. Judgment as to detailed operations must rest largely with the sales executives. Opinions as to expected general business conditions and market potentials should represent the combined judgment of the executive staff, including the chief executive, the sales manager, and the controller.
2. *They must be fair and reasonable measures of performance.* Nothing will be so destructive of morale as a sales quota, or any other standard, set much too high. Experience shows that such standards will be ignored. The standards must be attainable by the caliber of salesman which the company expects to be representative of its selling staff.
3. *They will need review and revision from time to time.* As sales conditions change frequently, so the measuring stick must change.

PURPOSE OF SALES STANDARDS

In frequent discussions with sales managers, the authors find expressions of opinion that sales standards are not welcome. Some sales executives feel that sales standards are an attempt to substitute impersonal statistics for sales leadership. There is no substitute for dynamic and far-sighted sales executives; there is no intent that sales standards in any way replace personal guidance. But sales standards do provide management with its most important tool of sales control, its only basis for fairly rewarding merit, and its chief stimulating device. As a tool of control they reveal weaknesses in performance which, if properly analyzed as to causes, open the way for correction and strengthening. As a basis for rewarding merit they result in a fairer and more accurate relationship between

[1] Adapted from J. Brooks Heckert and James D. Willson, *Business Budgeting and Control,* 2d ed. (New York: The Ronald Press Co., 1955), pp. 122–26.

compensation and performance. As a stimulating device they provide each salesman and executive with a goal of accomplishment and with assurance of fair reward.

NATURE OF SALES STANDARDS

The sales standards may be expressed in terms of effort, results, or the relation of effort to result. For example, a salesman may be required to make three calls a day or fifteen calls per week. If he makes this number of calls, he meets this particular standard of effort. Again, he may, as a result of these calls, be expected to secure ten orders for every fifteen calls, or a certain dollar volume per call. If he does this, he meets this particular relationship standard. Or he may simply be asked to secure a certain dollar volume from a given territory, regardless of the number of calls made or the orders and sales per call. If he does this, he meets this particular standard of results.

Again, the standards may involve a relationship between selling cost and sales results. For example, in a retail furniture store, the standard may require that one prospective customer be attracted to the store for every $2 expended in advertising, or that $1 of sales be secured for every 7 cents expended for advertising. If these goals are achieved, those responsible for the advertising expenditures are meeting the standards of advertising results.

ILLUSTRATIONS OF SALES STANDARDS

While the applicability of sales standards to various industries and types of trading concerns may differ, suggestive standards which the controller may consider discussing with the sales manager are outlined below.

Standards of Effort

Number of calls to be made per period
Number of calls to be made on prospective customers
Number of dealers and agencies to be established
Number of units of sales promotional effort to be used, e.g., demonstrations or pieces of direct mail sent

Standards of Results

Percentage of prospects to whom sales are to be made
Number of customers to whom new articles are to be introduced or sold
Number of new customers to be secured
Amount of dollar volume to be secured
Number of physical units to be sold
Amount of gross profit to be secured

Amount of profit to be secured (here profit is frequently considered as the excess of gross profit over the expenses which are subject to the control of the salesperson or executive to whom the standard is to apply)

Amounts to be sold to individual customers (especially larger customers)

Dollar or physical volume of individual products or product classes to be sold

Percentage of gross profit to be returned (where there is a varied line or where the salesman has price latitude)

Average size of order to be secured

Relation of sales deductions to gross sales

Standards Expressing Relationship of Effort and Result

Number of orders to be received per call made

Number of new customers to be secured per call made on prospects

Number of inquiries or orders to be received per unit or per dollar of sales promotional effort expended

Relation of individual direct selling expense items to volume or gross profit

Relation of sales administration or supervision costs to volume or gross profit

REVISION OF SALES STANDARDS

There are some standards of sales performance which can be set with a high degree of exactness. The number of calls which a salesman should make, the percentage of prospects to whom sales should be made, and the physical units which should be sold to each customer are illustrative of performances which frequently lend themselves to accurate measurements. On the other hand, there are many factors in sales performance which are so governed by conditions beyond the control of the salespeople that the standards must be promptly revised to meet important changes in such conditions. Where a salesman is given some latitude in price setting, his gross profit percentage may vary with competitive conditions beyond his control. Strikes, droughts, and floods may suddenly affect the sales possibilities in a particular territory. If the sales standards are to be effective measures of sales performance, they must be promptly revised as conditions change. Careless measurement of performance soon leads to discouragement, resentment, and disinterest in the task.

USE OF SALES STANDARDS

As stated above, the purposes of sales standards are to control sales operations, to reward merit, and to stimulate sales effort. The standards in themselves are of limited value except as they are made effective in the accomplishment of such purposes. To make the standards so effective requires that:

The variations between actual and standard performance be promptly determined

The causes of such variations be investigated and explained

The responsibility for the variations be definitely fixed

The individuals held responsible be given full opportunity to present their explanations

Prompt action be taken to correct any weaknesses revealed

The method of compensation shall provide a fair and accurate reward for performance

SALES QUOTAS AS STANDARDS

The most widely used sales standard is the sales quota. As usually constituted, the sales quota is the amount of dollar or physical volume of sales assigned to a particular salesman, department, branch, territory, or other division as a measure of satisfactory performance. The quota may, however, involve other considerations, such as gross profit, new customers, collections, or traveling expense, thereby representing something of a composite or collective standard of performance.

The quota does not differ in its purpose and use from other sales standards as discussed above. Its applicability to various types of concerns depends largely upon the extent to which sales and other results are actually affected by the direct efforts of the salespeople involved; and the extent to which such results are affected by other factors, such as expenditures for advertising, special sales promotion, styles, and acceptability of products. Where the former is the dominant factor, sales quotas constitute a valuable type of sales standard.

BASIS OF SALES QUOTAS

Generally speaking, sales quotas are of value only to the extent that they are based upon known facts relative to sales possibilities. They must not be based upon the greed of the company or upon fanciful ideas of what might be done, but upon actual facts relating to past sales, sales in allied industries, population, buying power, or territorial conditions. The sales representative should be thoroughly informed as to the method of arriving at his quota and convinced that the amount of sales assigned to him is entirely justified according to the existing conditions. Then, and only then, will he exert his full effort to meet his quota.

The quota should not be thought of primarily as a basis for contests. The salesperson should consider his quota as representing a careful measurement of his task rather than a temporary target at which to shoot.

Actual experience with sales quotas, as with all standards, will reveal that sales representatives react to them somewhat differently, particularly at first. Some are stimulated to their highest efficiency, while others are discouraged. Some sales executives place considerable emphasis upon this human element in setting their quotas. In general, however, good men will, in the long run, respond favorably to intelligently devised quotas, particularly when compensation is fairly adjusted to performance.

The objection sometimes raised, that efforts are lessened after quotas are reached, is seldom valid if performance is properly rewarded. The chief difficulty arises when quotas are exceeded as a result of some fortuitous circumstance in which the sales representative has had no part or for which his share of the credit is uncertain. The solution here usually rests with extreme fairness in handling individual cases and with the development of confidence in the knowledge and integrity of sales executives.

The method of establishing sales quotas is still unsatisfactory in many concerns. The matter is frequently given insufficient study and the results are ineffective. There has, however, been a vast improvement in such methods in recent years and alert controllers have made a substantial contribution to this improvement.

It should be noted in setting quotas that past performance is greatly influenced by conditions beyond the control of the individual salesman. Hence, a quota set when business is poor is likely to result in undue reward to the salesman. Conversely, one set when business is good is likely to prove too high to serve as an effective incentive.

METHOD OF EXPRESSING QUOTAS

Insofar as practicable, quotas should be broken down into their detailed elements. This helps to show the sales representative where, how, and to whom the goods should be sold. To illustrate, a certain company gives each of its sales representatives the following details relative to his sales quota:

1. The proportion of the quota assigned to each product of the line
2. The part of the quota which represents an expected increase in business from new customers
3. The part of the quota which represents an expected increase in business among old customers
4. The part of the quota which is to be secured in cities of various sizes
5. The part of the quota assigned to particular kinds of outlets or classes of customers
6. The part of the quota to be secured from special or exceptional sources
7. The distribution of the quota by months

While such a plan entails considerable work, it tends to balance the sales effort and to assist the sales representative in directing his work most effectively.

It should be realized that such details require the necessary detailed analysis of past performance by the controller's staff. Furthermore, such detail is indicative of a well-developed program. Many firms, particularly the small and medium-sized, will express quotas in general terms only—so many dollars of sales or so many over-all units. Where quotas are relatively new, the controller should proceed cautiously and develop the details gradually so that the sales executives can be guided step by step. Only when the data are available and the sales staff realizes the advantages of detailed planning can the quota type of standard serve most usefully.

It frequently happens that the quota cannot be fairly expressed directly in money or physical volume. For example, a sale of $100 of class A goods may deserve more credit than a like amount of class B goods, or a sale to a new customer may deserve more credit than a similar sale to an old customer. In such cases the quota may be expressed in points which give effect to a weighting for different types of sales performance. Thus, a sale of $100 class A goods may be counted as 10 points, whereas $100 of class B goods would be counted as only 5 points. The "point" system may likewise be extended to include other types of service, such as calls on new prospects, demonstrations, or collections.

The final requirement for effective standards is an adequate method of compensation as a reward for good performance.

SALES REPORTS

EFFECTING SALES CONTROL

Fundamentally, control is the prompt follow-up of unfavorable trends or conditions before they develop into large losses. In the small business, the owners or manager can exercise current control of sales through a review of orders received, etc. In the larger businesses, however, such personal contact must be supplemented by reports which indicate current conditions and trends as well as current performance.

It is the function of the controller, of course, to furnish the sales executives with the sales facts. However, it is one thing to furnish the information; it is quite another thing to see that it is understood and acted upon. To assure the necessary understanding, the controller must adapt the report to his reader. Information for the needs of the chief executive will be different from that for the sales manager; and reports for subordinate sales executives will differ even more. The extent of the information required and the form of presentation will depend on the capabilities of the individual, the type of organization, the responsibilities of the man, and the philosophy of sales management. A general discussion of report preparation is presented in Chapters 28 and 29.

NATURE OF SALES REPORTS

Sales executives are prone to disregard figures, particularly reports with a vast amount of statistical data. Accordingly, the controller should modify the report to suit the situation. In some instances, the best method of getting results will be to write a short memo or narrative report, pointing out deficiencies and asking questions about them or suggesting action. Perhaps a personal visit will be feasible. In other instances a chart or graph will effectively get the point across. Where a great many facts must be given, however, statistical comparisons must be presented.

CONTENT OF SALES REPORTS

The matters which may be included in a sales report cover a broad front. Such reports might contain the following:

1. Actual sales performance, with month or year to date figures
2. Budgeted sales for both the period and year to date
3. Comparison of actual sales by firm with industry figures, including percentages of total
4. Analysis of variances between budgeted and actual sales, and reasons for differences
5. Sale-cost relationships, such as cost per order received
6. Sales standards—comparison of actual and quota sales by salesman
7. Unit sales price data
8. Gross profit data

These data often may be expressed in physical units or in dollars. Aside from actual or standard sales performance, some may relate to orders, cancellations, returns or allowances, or lost sales.

ILLUSTRATIVE FEATURES IN SALES REPORTS

The content of sales reports must be varied to suit the needs and personality of the reader. Reports to the chief executive and major sales official, for example, should present the over-all view of the operation. A simple comparison of actual and budgeted sales by major product line, as shown in Fig. 41, may quickly summarize the sales picture. Sales managers are usually interested in measuring the company performance against industry, as illustrated in Fig. 42. A graphic comparison of actual sales similar to Fig. 44 may be useful; or a percentage graph might be found informative.

Plastics Manufacturing Company

COMPARATIVE STATEMENT OF SALES

Month of April, 1962

Product	Month			Year to Date		
	Budgeted Sales	Actual Sales	Over or (Under) Budget	Budgeted Sales	Actual Sales	Over or (Under) Budget
COATING COMPOUNDS						
Alkyds........	$ 50,000	$ 52,315	$ 2,315	$ 190,000	$ 201,325	$ 11,325
Hard Resins...	20,000	17,819	(2,181)	85,000	82,300	(2,700)
Ureas........	320,000	321,510	1,510	1,410,000	1,520,000	110,000
Total......	390,000	391,644	1,644	1,685,000	1,803,625	118,625
MOLDING COMPOUNDS						
Alkyds........	190,000	197,410	7,410	860,000	812,520	(47,480)
Ureas........	25,000	22,820	(2,180)	82,000	71,900	(10,100)
Melamines....	415,000	472,320	57,320	1,560,000	1,611,000	51,000
Total......	630,000	692,550	62,550	2,502,000	2,495,420	(6,580)
Grand Total...	$1,020,000	$1,084,194	$64,194	$4,187,000	$4,299,045	$112,045
% of Budget......			106.3			102.7

Remarks:

Fig. 41—Comparison of Budgeted and Actual Sales by Product Line.

Sales executives also find trend reports on product lines to be of value. A percentage bar chart, illustrated in Fig. 43, would be particularly significant if the profit by product group is greatly different. Trends in sales volume are easily shown by vertical bar charts similar to that pictured in Fig. 44. Sales managers typically need information on the probable future course of sales. For this purpose, timely reports summarizing the orders-on-hand picture are helpful. Such a report—which may be desired daily, weekly, or monthly—is illustrated in Fig. 45.

The graphs and reports presented thus far have been rather simple in nature. While reports always should be understood, in many cases, particularly in larger companies, they must be more analytical or detailed in nature. Moreover, for control purposes and adopting the concept of "responsibility reporting," the performance of each segment of the sales organization should be made known to the supervisor responsible. It follows, therefore, that reporting must be available for each division, district, area, branch, or salesman. A typical branch report is illustrated in Fig. 46, and is very brief. However, as reports relate to increasingly lower levels of management, such information can become massive in extent. Therefore, while data may be periodically prepared on each segment of the organization, it has been found practical to apply the "exception principle" in a great many cases. This method eliminates data where performance was satisfactory, and details only that which did not reach acceptable levels. An example is Fig. 47, indicating only those salesmen who were 5% or more under budget. Another report prepared on only out-of-line performance is that shown in Fig. 48. Only customers on which a loss was realized are listed. It is to be noted that two profit or loss computations are made: (1) actual out-of-pocket losses, using the direct costing concept, and (2) gross loss, wherein all fixed and allocated charges are considered.

FREQUENCY OF REPORTS

The frequency of any report will depend on the individual requirements of each executive or staff member—whether daily, weekly, monthly, or quarterly. For example, the top executive and general sales manager may want a daily report on sales, orders received, and orders on hand; or a weekly report may suffice; or a report may be wanted daily during a critical period, and less frequently thereafter.

Regardless of the period used, *prompt reporting* is essential. Reports should be regularly scheduled for a definite issue date.

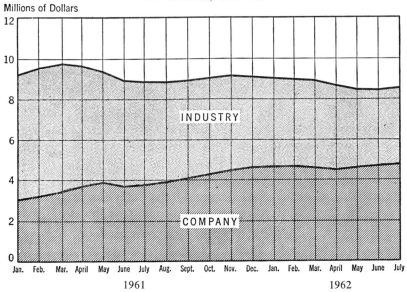

The Alpha Manufacturing Company, Inc.
COMPARISON OF COMPANY AND INDUSTRY SALES,
BY MONTHS, 1961–62

Fig. 42—Graphic Comparison of Company vs. Industry Sales.

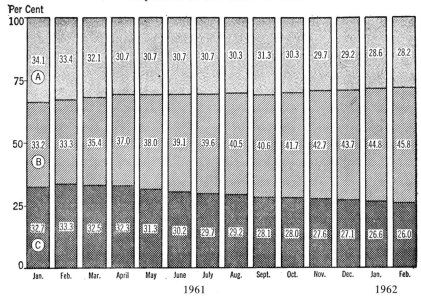

The Toy Manufacturing Company
SALES OF PRODUCT LINES, BY MONTHS
Expressed as Per Cent of Total

Fig. 43—Percentage Breakdown of Net Sales by Product Line.

200

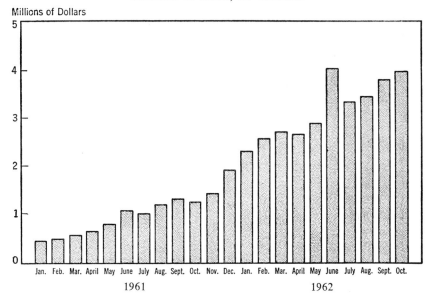

Fig. 44—Graphic Presentation of Sales Trend.

Jones Aviation Company

SUMMARY OF ORDERS ON HAND

July, 1962

Description	Orders On Hand June 30, 1962	Orders Received	Orders Canceled	Orders Filled	Orders On Hand July 31, 1962	
					Units	Value*
Cabin Liner......	22	7	–	9	20	$2,000,000
Crusair..........	45	19	–	12	52	2,600,000
Voyager..........	118	93	–	97	114	1,140,000
Voyager—S.W.....	97	112	5	105	99	1,080,000
Trainer....... ...	208	242	2	220	228	684,000
Total........	490	473	7	443	513	$7,504,000

* Sales Price.

Fig. 45—Report on Sales Order Activity.

SHEET ___ OF ___

GENERAL MANUFACTURING COMPANY

COMPARISON OF BUDGETED AND ACTUAL SALES BY BRANCH

REPORT No. 7 DATE December

DESCRIPTION	BRANCH NUMBER	NET SALES THIS MONTH	SALES BUDGET THIS MONTH	VARIANCE THIS MONTH	NET SALES YEAR TO DATE	SALES BUDGET YEAR TO DATE	VARIANCE YEAR TO DATE
BOSTON	1	1443564	1500000	56436 CR	19056325	18000000	1056325
CHICAGO	4	2348217	2000000	348217	25637940	24000000	1637940
CLEVELAND	7	2607686	2500000	107686	32642950	30000000	2642950
DETROIT	10	1112667	1000000	112667	10912624	12000000	1087376 CR
BALTIMORE	12	425835	500000	74165 CR	7316940	6000000	1316940
HOUSTON	13	495133	500000	4867 CR	6923423	6000000	923423
LOS ANGELES	16	592329	500000	92329	5730916	6000000	269084 CR
NEW ORLEANS	19	442174	500000	57826 CR	6612213	6000000	612213
NEW YORK	22	4094685	4000000	94685	50364912	48000000	2364912
PHILADELPHIA	25	1007489	1000000	7489	13064175	12000000	1064175
PITTSBURGH	28	935731	1000000	64269 CR	10316942	12000000	1683058 CR
SAN FRANCISCO	31	913875	1000000	86125 CR	12316431	12000000	316431
ST. LOUIS	34	662284	500000	162284	6014314	6000000	14314
FACTORY	58	279504		279504	1210640		1210640
		17361173	16500000	861173	208120745		10120745

Fig. 46—Comparison of Budgeted and Actual Sales by Branch.

General Manufacturing Company

SALES ANALYSIS BY SALESMAN—UNDER BUDGET 5% OR MORE—YEAR TO DATE

DISTRICT PITTSBURGH

April 1962 and Year to Date

Description	Salesman No.	Current Month			Year to Date			"Lost Gross"
		Actual Sales	Under Budget * Amount	%	Actual Sales	Under Budget * Amount	%	
PERFORMANCE SATISFACTORY		$ 827,432	$112,610 *	15.8 *	$4,623,096	$497,830 *	12.1 *	
UNDER BUDGET PERFORMANCE:								
Abernathy	2609	32,016	1,760	5.2	102,600	6,300	5.8	$ 1,520
Bristol	2671	17,433	1,390	7.4	61,080	4,270	6.5	1,080
Caldwell	2685	19,811	1,320	6.2	70,100	4,600	6.2	1,150
Fischer	2716	24,033	1,470	5.8	84,390	5,090	5.7	1,270
Gordon	2804	8,995	480	5.1	31,600	1,810	5.4	450
Inch	2827	27,666	1,820	6.2	97,010	5,930	5.8	1,480
Long	2982	4,277	600	12.3	15,020	900	5.7	230
Mather	3007	39,474	3,800	8.8	138,400	8,540	5.8	2,150
Owens	5066	43,189	4,400	9.6	151,800	9,080	5.6	2,270
Subtotal		216,894	17,040	7.3	752,000	46,520	5.8	$11,600
District Total		$1,044,326	$ 95,570 *	10.1 *	$5,375,096	$451,310 *	9.2 *	

* Better than budget.

Fig. 47—Exception Reporting—Salesman Performance.

General Manufacturing Company

SALES ANALYSIS BY CUSTOMER—GROSS LOSSES ONLY

DISTRICT CALIFORNIA

Year to Date Through June 30, 1962

(Dollars in Thousands)

Customer	Customer No.	Net Sales	Direct Costs	Gain * or Loss over Direct Costs		Gross Margin * or Loss	
				Amount	% Net Sales	Amount	% Net Sales
MARGINS SATISFACTORY		$224,390	$156,430	$67,960 *	30.3 *	$37,301 *	16.6 *
GROSS LOSSES YR. TO DATE:							
American Steel Co.	839	127	94	33 *	25.9 *	13	10.2
Barrett Machine Corp.	876	243	246	3	1.2	62	25.5
Benson Mfg. Co.	11314	182	189	7	3.8	23	12.6
Central Heating Co.	207	24	20	4 *	16.7 *	12	50.0
Fagan Steel, Inc.	436	281	307	26	9.3	56	19.9
Jones Iron Co.	920	19	22	3	15.8	9	47.4
Luckey Bridge Corp.	800	76	70	6 *	7.9 *	6	7.9
Oppowa Metals Co.	392	32	43	11	34.4	20	62.5
Subtotal		984	991	7	.7	201	20.4
District Total		$225,374	$157,421	$67,953	30.2	$37,100	16.5

Fig. 48—Sales Analysis by Customers—Exception Basis.

PRODUCT PRICING—POLICY AND PROCEDURE

PRICES IN A COMPETITIVE ECONOMY

From the economic viewpoint, prices are the regulator of our economy in that they determine the distribution of goods and services. Over the long run, when prices in a given industry are insufficient to provide an adequate return, capital and labor tend to shift to more attractive fields. In the individual business, also, skill in setting prices has a tremendous impact on the profitability of the operation and therefore on its economic life.

Product pricing is a difficult area in which to make decisions because of the many forces at play. It is so complex a subject that it is not ordinarily a one-man job or a one-activity job. Rather, the combined talents of marketeer, accountant, engineer, and economist may be needed. It might be said that pricing is one-third computation and two-thirds judgment. From the accounting viewpoint, however, the one-third computation is an essential aid to the judgment factor. Factors which influence prices include market conditions, costs of manufacturing and distribution, plant capacity, competitive activity, capital investments, financial liquidity, government pressures, and a multitude of others. It is therefore understandable that there exists a diversity of approaches to the problem. But this situation presents an equally valid reason to attempt to set out some guiding principles.

PRICES AND THE CONTROLLER

The accountant's contribution to control of sales is in most cases largely *after the fact*. That is, comparisons of actual performance are made with budget, or forecast, or standard; or, sales data are analyzed to reveal unfavorable trends and relationships. In the field of product pricing, however, the controller may be able to exert *preventive* accounting control —before the occurrence. He may bring facts to bear on the problem before unwise decisions are made. This activity is closely related to profit planning as well as control. The influence of prices on company profits is obvious; and the finest controls on costs and expenses will not succeed in producing a profit if selling prices are incorrectly set. If the controller is charged with a responsibility for protecting the assets of the company, or of exercising the control function on costs and expenses, or on capital expenditures, then he should also play an important role in price determination.

And just what should his function be in price determination and related accounting control? It is hoped he will not be merely a source of information, providing data only when requested, and even then in the form and of the content specified. In many companies, it is questionable whether the pricing officials are fully aware of the kind of facts required. Therefore, the controller should be expected to show some initiative and supply intelligent information from his legitimate sphere of activity. More specifically, the chief accounting official ordinarily can be of assistance by performing the following functions:

1. Help establish a pricing policy which will be consistent with the corporate objectives—for example, earning the desired return on investment
2. Provide unit cost analysis, in proper form, as one factor in price setting
3. Project the effect upon earnings of proposed price changes and alternatives
4. To the extent necessary or practicable, gather pertinent information on competitive price activity (this may be the function of the market research group or economics department in some companies)
5. Analyze the historical data on prices and volumes to substantiate probable trends as they may influence proposed price changes
6. Determine for management, on a regular basis—such as the monthly operations report—the influence on profit of changes in price, product mix, sales volume, etc.; in other words, focus attention on the price problem where such action may bring about intelligent direction

Some of these procedures are reviewed in the sections which follow.

COST BASIS FOR PRICING

There is a great tendency to either underrate or overrate costs as a factor in setting prices. Frequently the statement is heard that "prices are based on competition." Less often the statement is made that "prices are based on costs." There are certainly circumstances where these comments apply. Rarely, however, can costs be ignored entirely.

It is obvious that over any extended period no business can consistently sell all or most products at less than cost—cost which results from production and distribution functions and the related service activities. It is further recognized as a highly desirable condition that a profit be made on every product, in every territory, on the business with every customer. While this may not always be practicable, the closer such conditions are approached, the more certain or assured is the net profit. Hence, it is apparent that adequate cost information is absolutely indispensable.

In summary, costs may be viewed as the point of departure or starting place in product pricing. And the role to be played by the cost factor depends upon the circumstances. If the product is built to customer order, and is not a stock item, costs will be more important. Further, if competition is weak or if the company is a price leader, cost information will play a larger part than if the opposite situations exist. Also, elasticity of demand influences the weighting of costs in that (1) an inelastic demand probably will cause costs to be a greater factor, and (2) costs at various volume levels must be studied so as to maximize earnings.

The question then arises, "What kind of costs are required?" For different purposes, different costs may be desirable. One kind of cost may be suitable for a short-range decision, and quite another type for longer-term purposes. Moreover, for pricing, the usual historical cost approach may not meet the requirement. In summary, then, the controller is expected to be aware of the several costing methods and the limitations of each, and to select that concept most suited to the purpose at hand.

Before reviewing several alternative costing techniques, some general observations are desirable. First, prices relate to the future. Therefore, costs to be used in determining prices must be prospective and not retrospective. Recognition should be given to cost levels expected to prevail in the period under review. Probable raw material and labor costs should be considered. Prospective changes in process ought to be reflected in the cost estimates. The probable effect of inflation should not be ignored. In this forecasting or projecting, the modern scientific tools should be employed to the extent practicable—statistical sampling, basic economic principles, analysis as to price levels, etc. Secondly, some consideration at least should be given to the replacement cost of capital assets. Reflection will make clear that prices ought to provide for the replacement of existing assets at the market cost. Third, the modern concept of fixed and variable costs, of direct and indirect costs, of total vs. incremental costs should be used where practical.

Finally, it should be obvious that *all* costs related to a product should be considered, and not merely cost to manufacture. It defeats the purpose if manufacturing costs are carefully calculated, but selling or other expenses are applied as an over-all per cent without regard to the direct expense and effort specifically applicable to the product.

Although many costing methods or variations are in use, there are three basic approaches that warrant discussion:

1. Total cost method
2. Marginal or direct cost method
3. Return on capital method

As a prelude to reviewing costing methods, it seems desirable first to review an example of the influence of costs on profit at differing volume levels. Further, the role of competitive conditions and demand in relation to costs needs to be understood.

ELASTICITY OF DEMAND

In exercising judgment on prices, elasticity of demand should be given proper weighting in any cost-profit-volume calculations. Normally the pricing executives will have some general knowledge of the extent to which demand will react to changes in price. However, to provide supplemental assurance, perhaps controlled experimentation will be helpful in gauging this factor. If demand is relatively inelastic, and competitive

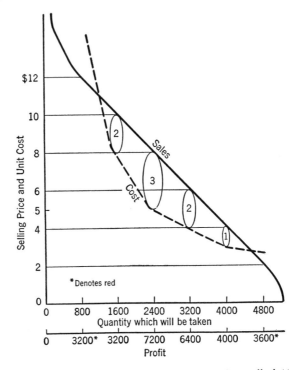

Fig. 49—Method of Setting Selling Price in a Controlled Market.

conditions permit, then it may be possible to pass cost increases on to the customers. Under such circumstances, the controller can show the effect of cost changes on profits and the desirability of effecting price changes. If demand is highly elastic, and the market is somewhat non-competitive, unit costs can be employed to determine the optimum price with which to produce the optimum profit.

Under such circumstances, it is desirable to determine the sales price which will produce the greatest net profit over a long period of time. Too high a profit over a short term might invite competition or governmental regulation.

Where conditions approach monopoly, it is perhaps of interest to review a typical procedure in setting selling prices. Basically, an estimate is secured from the sales manager as to the probable number of units which can be sold at various price levels. Then the unit cost and total cost at the corresponding production level are calculated. That volume at which the greatest total profit is secured can then be determined.

Figure 49 illustrates the application of this procedure. Here it is suggested that the unit selling price may be set at $12, $10, $8, $6, $4, or $2. Estimates are then made as to the number of units which can be sold at each price. These are indicated by the *sales* line. Thus, it is estimated that 1,600 units can be sold at a price of $10 per unit, whereas 4,000 units can be sold at a price of $4. Likewise, the *cost* line shows the estimated total unit cost (including interest on investment) at each volume level. Thus, it is estimated that the unit cost will be $5 when volume reaches 2,400 units. The spread between selling price and cost constitutes the unit profit, which, multiplied by the number of units, gives the total profit at various price levels. At a price of $10, the profit will be $2 per unit, the volume 1,600 units, and the total profit $3,200. At a price of $8, the total profit will be $7,200. At a price of $6, the total profit will be $6,400. It is apparent here that the greatest profit will be made at a unit price of $8.

TOTAL COST METHOD

Now let us consider the three more important costing techniques, the first of which is the total cost or full cost method. Under this concept the cost of the individual product is determined, and to this figure is added the desired profit margin. Such a margin is usually expressed as a percentage of either the cost or the selling price. As an example, the proposed selling price might be calculated as shown below:

	Unit Cost and Selling Price	
	Product A	Product B
Costs and Expenses		
Raw Material (Quantity × Expected Purchase Cost)	$10.00	$ 3.00
Direct Labor (Hours × Expected Hourly Rate)	4.00	8.00
Manufacturing Overhead (150% of Direct Labor)	6.00	12.00
Total Manufacturing Cost	20.00	23.00
Research and Development Expense (10% of Manufacturing Cost)	2.00	2.30
Selling and Advertising Expense (20% of Manufacturing Cost)	4.00	4.60
General and Administrative Expense (10% of Manufacturing Overhead)	.60	1.20
Total Cost	26.60	31.10
Desired Profit Margin (25% of Total Cost)	6.65	7.78
Proposed Selling Price	$33.25	$38.88

In this illustration, costs were used as the basis for determination of the markup, as well as the charge for each of the non-manufacturing expense levels. As an alternative, each cost element could have been calculated in relation to the proposed selling price. Thus, the profit margin might have been expressed in the formula as 20% of the selling price; and expenses might have been treated in the same manner.

Such a method has at least two advantages: (1) It is simple in application, and (2) it bases selling prices on all costs expected to be incurred—thus tending to assure full cost recovery, if the product sells and if the costs are generally as estimated. Over the longer run, all costs must be recovered.

From the cost viewpoint at least four disadvantages exist in using such a method exclusively:

1. It fails to distinguish between out-of-pocket costs and total costs. In the short run and with available plant capacity, there will be circumstances when business should be accepted on something less than a total cost basis.

2. It does not recognize the inability of all products to return the same rate of profit. Moreover, it fails to distinguish the elements of cost which create the profit, some of which cannot be expected logically to generate the same rate of income. For example, a product which is largely purchased materials may not reasonably return the same percentage of profit on total cost as one constituted mainly of labor and a consequent higher relative share of factory overhead and management talent.

3. The method does not recognize the optimum profit potential. The effect of elasticity in demand and the consequent point of greatest return, as described on page 209, are ignored.

4. This method of calculating tends to encourage a constant overhead application per cent to the exclusion of volume factor likely to be applicable.

The cost calculations can be modified to overcome the second objection. Then, too, several computations can be made to compensate partially for differing volumes.

THE MARGINAL COST METHOD

The marginal cost approach to prices gives recognition to the "incremental" or "marginal" costs of the product. These are costs directly associated with the product, which would not be incurred if the product were not manufactured or sold. Any selling price received above this floor represents a contribution to fixed expense and/or profit.

The application of this principle to products A and B described in the full cost method might produce a picture as follows:

	Unit Cost	
	Product A	Product B
Raw Materials	$10.00	$ 3.00
Direct Labor	4.00	8.00
Variable Manufacturing Expense	1.50	2.00
Variable Selling Expense	1.50	1.90
Variable Administrative Expense	.30	.40
Total Variable or Incremental Cost	17.30	15.30
Fixed Expense Directly Applicable to Product	2.50	3.10
Total Direct Costs	$19.80	$18.40

In this tabulation incremental costs have been segregated from direct expenses of a fixed nature applicable to the product; and these direct costs have been identified separately from the allocated costs of a fixed nature.

If the product must be sold for the incremental costs or less, then the company would earn no less a profit, or possibly even a higher profit, by *not* manufacturing and selling such product. Full consideration must be given, of course, to related profit results, viz., sales of other products to the customers, etc., if the withdrawal of a given product would in fact cause loss of the other business. From the longer-range viewpoint, the minimum price to be charged would be that covering all direct costs, and for the company to continue in business over the longer term, all costs must be recouped.

It can be appreciated that marginal and direct cost data—before allocated continuing costs—are of value in any one of several situations:

1. Where additional sales may be made at reduced prices, over and above direct costs, to another class of customer, viz., private brand business, or under another trade name, etc.
2. Where idle plant capacity can be utilized only at reduced prices, and in other than regular sales outlets
3. Under circumstances where these added sales at reduced prices do not create problems in the regular market place

The use of marginal costs are for short-term decisions only. The great danger is the tendency to secure a larger and larger volume of sales on an incremental basis, with an ultimate deteriorating effect in the market and a large share of business which does not return its full and proper share of all costs. Furthermore, under such conditions there is no return on capital employed from the products priced at not more than total costs.

RETURN ON CAPITAL EMPLOYED METHOD

From the profit viewpoint, the most desirable costing method is that which maximizes the return on total capital employed. This is the approach that has been given more attention in recent years. It is to be noted that under the two costing procedures reviewed above, no consideration has been given, for example, to the capital invested in manufacturing or sales facilities, or in working capital. Yet, as discussed in Chapter 4, the real test of business efficiency is the rate of return on total capital employed. Growth generally takes place only when the product yields a reasonable return on the funds devoted to it. If the business objective is to maximize return on capital, then, as a starting point at least, the price of each product required to achieve the desired rate of return should be known.

This method of determining markup over total costs for the desired per cent return on capital, rather than markup for a per cent return on costs (or per cent of net sales) has considerable merit in the opinion of the authors. Some of the capital employed is fixed in nature, such as plant and equipment. But a share of the investment—primarily current assets—is a variable of volume and prices. For example, accounts receivable will be higher as sales volume and sales prices are higher. Investment in inventory will increase or decrease as volume changes and as manufacturing costs and raw material prices fluctuate. In view of the variables, a formula may be employed to calculate the sales price required to produce a planned return on capital employed:

$$\text{Unit Price} = \frac{\dfrac{\text{Cost} + (\text{Desired \% Return} \times \text{Fixed Capital})}{\text{Annual Sales Volume in Units}}}{1 - \left(\dfrac{\text{Desired \%}}{\text{Return}}\right)\left(\dfrac{\text{Variable Capital Expressed}}{\text{as \% of Sales Volume}}\right)}$$

In the formula:

Cost represents total cost of manufacturing, selling, administrative, research, etc.

% return represents that rate desired on capital employed (before income taxes).

The fixed capital represents plant and equipment although some of the current assets might be placed in this category.

The variable capital represents the current assets which are a function of volume and prices.

Applying some assumptions, a unit price on product A may be calculated as follows:

$$\frac{\dfrac{\$2,660,000 + (.20 \times \$300,000)}{100,000}}{1 - (.20 \times .30)} =$$

$$\frac{\$2,720,000/100,000 \text{ units}}{1 - .06} = \frac{27.20}{.94}$$

$$= \$28.936$$

The proof is computed in this manner:

Income and Costs
Sales (100,000 units at $28.936)	$2,893,600
Costs	2,660,000
Income Before Taxes	$ 233,600

Capital Employed
Variable (30% of $2,893,600)	$ 868,080
Fixed	300,000
Total Capital Employed	$1,168,080
20% Return on Invested Capital of $1,168,080 (Fractions Ignored)	$ 233,600

The above illustration is intended to show the method of determining unit sales prices to provide a target or planned return on investment. Although applied to a single product, the percentages used were those of the product class or group of which product A is one segment.

APPLYING THE RETURN ON CAPITAL CONCEPT

The above simple example purposely avoided some of the controversial or problem areas in using the return on capital concept. Some brief observations on the subject may prove helpful.

Under this procedure, total capital employed is considered to include all assets used in manufacturing and selling the product (including related services). It is immaterial how the funds were provided—whether by debt or equity. The management of a company should effectively use all capital, whether owner supplied or creditor supplied.

Another question often raised is the basis of valuation of assets. Should replacement value be considered? Should fixed assets be included on a gross or depreciated basis? Essentially policies of valuation will have no appreciable effect on price determination. Recognition can be provided directly or indirectly in the rate of return objective. Consistency is the important consideration.

In a multiproduct company, a problem to be solved is the allocation of capital employed to the various product lines. Upon reflection, this need not be a major stumbling block. Just as controllers have been allocating costs to products for years, so also they can allocate capital on a reasonable basis consistent with the facts of the particular business. Some suggested methods of prorating capital to product lines are these:

Item	Possible Bases
Cash	In ratio to total product cost
Accounts Receivable	In ratio to sales, adjusted for significant differences in terms of sale
Raw Material	In ratio to actual or expected usage
Work in Process	In ratio to actual or expected usage
Finished Goods	In ratio to cost of manufacture
Fixed Assets	In ratio to conversion costs (labor and variable manufacturing overhead) or labor hours—either actual, normal, or standard

ANOTHER FACET TO COSTS FOR PRICING PURPOSES

Still another economic concept useful in pricing is termed the "conversion cost theory of value." In essence, this view holds that profits are, or should be, earned commensurate with the effort and risk inherent in converting raw materials into finished products. This approach has merit, particularly in situations where relative material content varies widely by product. For example, if one product is largely an assembly of purchased parts, and another requires extensive processing in expensive facilities, application of the same markup to each probably would result in a price too high on the assembly item and too low on the fabricated product. Differences in types of costs may therefore need to be recognized. A combined use of the return on capital concept and direct costs may be illustrative.

Assume the following is a typical pricing and profit planning problem:

1. A given product line R is made up of products of varying material content.
2. $24,000,000 are the gross assets employed for the line.
3. Management desires a 20% return (before taxes) on the capital employed.
4. The pertinent profit data are as follows:
   a. Period (fixed or continuing) expenses are $6,000,000.
   b. The P/V (profit to volume, or contribution margin) ratio is 30%.
   c. Direct materials and conversion expenses are, on the average, in a 4-to-3 ratio.
   d. Material turnover is twice a year.

With these premises it is necessary to calculate:

1. The sales volume needed to produce the desired rate of return
2. The markup to be applied on each of the direct cost factors in the product line

Net sales and aggregate costs by element may be determined in this manner:

Required operating profit (20% of $24,000,000)		$ 4,800,000
Add: Continuing or period expenses		6,000,000
Required margin over direct costs		10,800,000
Required Sales [$10,800,000 ÷ 30% (P/V ratio)]		36,000,000
Deduct: Margin		10,800,000
Direct costs		25,200,000
Segregated on a 4-to-3 ratio as follows:		
Direct material	$14,400,000	
Conversion	10,800,000	$25,200,000

Inasmuch as the material turnover is two times per year, the investment is $7,200,000 ($14,400,000 ÷ 2). Twenty per cent of this figure is $1,440,000. Consequently, the additive factor is 10% ($1,440,000 ÷ $14,400,000), and the portion of sales revenue needed to provide a 20% return is $15,840,000 ($14,400,000 + $1,440,000).

The additive factor on conversion costs may be determined by the difference method as follows:

Total Required Income (Sales)	$36,000,000
Less: Direct Material and related profit additive	15,840,000
Balance attributable to conversion factor	$20,160,000

Thus the conversion markup is 1.867 ($20,160,000 ÷ $10,800,000).

If the direct costs of product R162 in the line are known, the target or "ideal" selling price is then determined in this fashion:

	Unit Direct Cost	Factor	Unit Selling Price
Direct Material	$16.10	1.100	$17.71
Conversion	20.30	2.867	58.20
Total	$36.40		$75.91

Such proposed prices are a starting point only—they must be considered in relationship to competitive prices.

General Manufacturing Company
COMPARATIVE PRICING INFORMATION
Product S219   Product Line S

Earnings Data

Line	Description	Present Amount	Present % Net Sales	Proposed Amount	Proposed % Net Sales
1	Unit Sales	100,000		140,000	
2	Net Sales	$200,000	100.00	$259,000	100.00
3	Direct Costs				
4	Material	80,000	40.00	105,000	40.54
5	Conversion	60,000	30.00	84,000	32.43
6	Selling	10,000	5.00	14,000	5.41
	Total	150,000	75.00	203,000	78.38
7	Contribution Margin	50,000	25.00	56,000	21.62
8	Period Costs	30,000	15.00	30,000	11.58
9	Pre-Tax Income	$ 20,000	10.00	$ 26,000	10.04
	Capital Employed				
	Current Assets	$ 30,000		$ 34,000	
	Fixed Assets	15,000		15,000	
	Total	$ 45,000		$ 49,000	
	Return on Capital	44.4%		53.1%	
	Capital Turnover	4.4		5.3	
	Per Cent of Product Line	7.9		11.1	
	Per Cent of Capacity	4.8		6.7	
	Per Cent of Market	5.0		7.0	

Unit Data

Description	Present	Proposed
Selling Prices		
Company	$2.00	$1.85
Competition A	1.90	
B	1.80	
C	1.60	
Material	.80	.75
Conversion	.60	.60
Selling	.10	.10
Total	1.50	1.45
Margin over Direct Costs	.50	.40
Period Costs	.30	.214
Pre-Tax Income	$ .20	$ .186
Per Cent of Market		
A	7.4	6.4
B	8.9	8.4
C	11.3	10.8

Comments:
(1) Pre-tax income increases, as does return on investment.
(2) Market position requires more aggressive action. Proposal approved from financial and marketing viewpoints. J.D.W. G.F.G.

Action:
Price changed; material contracts executed.
J.R.G.

SUMMARIZED INFORMATION FOR EXECUTIVE ACTION

As previously stated, the setting of product prices is a combination of calculation and judgments. It is the task of the controller to present for management's judgment all pertinent facts based on using that costing method which, in the considered opinion of all concerned, is most applicable to the company situation. It can be further understood that each basis of price determination has some merit. Giving proper recognition to the advantages of each, the chief accounting officer should select those facts which appear most salient. A suggested format is shown in Fig. 50.

13

Control of
Distribution Costs

GENERAL ASPECTS OF DISTRIBUTION COSTS

DEFINITION OF DISTRIBUTION COSTS

In a broad sense, distribution costs may be defined as the costs incident to all activities from the time the goods are produced, or from the time of purchase in a non-manufacturing concern, until they are in the hands of the consumer—the cost to sell. This would include, then, the applicable share of general administrative and financial expenses. For the purpose of this discussion, however, it is limited to those expenses, exclusive of general administrative and financial expense, which are usually under the control of the sales manager. These may include the following general classifications:

1. *Direct Selling Expense.* All the direct expense of salesmen, branch sales offices, sales supervision, and sales service—the expenses generally incident to solicitation of orders.

2. *Advertising and Sales Promotional Expense.* All advertising expenditures; all expenses incident to sales promotion, market development, and publicity.

3. *Transportation Expense.* All transportation charges on outbound goods to customers and on returned sales; and expenses of maintenance and operation of outward transportation facilities.

4. *Warehousing and Storage.* All expense of warehousing, storing, and handling of goods properly chargeable against distribution.

5. *General Distribution Expense.* All expenses of market research; expense of distribution accounting, if applicable; and all other expenses related to distribution functions under the control of the sales manager and not mentioned above.

SIGNIFICANCE OF DISTRIBUTION COSTS

In most businesses the cost of distribution is becoming an increasingly important factor; in fact, in many concerns it constitutes the major cost. As a general statement, during the last half-century the manufacturing costs have gone down while the distribution costs have gone up. To a certain degree, of course, the greater selling expense with its resulting volume has permitted many of the manufacturing economies. Yet, it is becoming increasingly clear that the successful business must exert just as much effort toward the intelligent direction of sales effort as it has toward production effort. There is every reason to believe that the upward trend of distribution costs in the individual business concern can be limited, or perhaps even decreased, by the same type of analysis and control which has proved so successful in the factory. It is, indeed, a fertile field for the sales manager and controller jointly to develop methods of cost control which may have a significant bearing on that all important figure—the net profit.

FACTORS INCREASING THE DIFFICULTY OF COST CONTROL

Any controller who tackles the matter of distribution cost control will find that the problems usually are much more complex than those relating to production costs. First, the psychological factors require more consideration. In selling, the attitude of the buyer as well as the salesman is variable; and competitive reaction cannot be overlooked. This is in sharp contrast to production where the worker is generally the only human element. Moreover, in marketing activities the methods are more flexible and more numerous than in production; and several agencies or channels of distribution may be used. Such conditions make the activities more difficult to standardize than production activities. Also, the constant changes or switches in method of sale or channel of distribution are factors which make it harder to secure basic information. Even when the information is secured great care must be used in interpretation. Finally, the nature of the activities requires different types of costs than might be needed in production. Where the joint or indirect costs bulk large, the analyses may take the direction of additional, relative, or marginal costs under various prescribed circumstances.

Such conditions create problems which may test the ingenuity of the controller.

THE SALES MANAGER AND DISTRIBUTION COSTS

The sales manager is responsible for two primary functions in a business: (1) the requisite sales volume of the right products, and (2) the control of distribution costs. These may seem like two diametrically opposed objectives. However, the situation may be described as a problem of balance: If more money is spent for distribution effort, what does the business receive in return? Usually the sales manager will be under continuous pressure to increase sales and yet reduce selling expenses. It is obvious, then, that he must be in a position to know whether distribution costs really are too high, and if they are too high, just where—what salesman? what territory? what expense? The sales effort must be wisely guided, and if this is to be done the controller must provide the necessary facts. The sales manager must have an intelligent analysis of distribution costs as a basis on which to work. Marketing decisions must be based on adequate knowledge.

BASIC APPROACH IN CONTROL OF DISTRIBUTION COSTS

The many variables already mentioned in connection with distribution costs should make it fairly obvious that the problem of control is complex and difficult. In production cost control, a usual procedure is to compare actual and standard or budgeted expenses, and exert continuous pressure on actual expenses until they are brought in line with the standard or budget. To an extent this can be done with respect to distribution costs, particularly those of a routine, repetitive, and non-selling nature, such as order handling or warehousing. But by and large, a more positive approach is necessary to avoid an injurious curtailment of necessary distribution services. That approach consists in securing the greatest possible effectiveness in the selling or marketing operations.

As a matter of experience, any controller will find many occasions when suggestions that selling costs be reduced will arouse resentment on the part of the sales force. But almost any sales manager will listen when the approach is that of getting more distribution effort and results for the same money. Unit selling costs can be effectively reduced by getting greater volume from the same sales force, whether by securing larger orders, more customers, or otherwise. This does not obviate the fact that there will be many instances where costs must and will be reduced, but it does emphasize the consideration necessary as to the effect on sales volume of reduced distribution costs.

Since emphasis in the marketing operations is in large measure directed to securing more effective results—that is, more earnings per dollar of distribution cost—it can be seen that much of the study and effort will be applied in a preventive way. Comparative margins and distribution costs may be used in setting *future* action, in changing plans to secure improved results.

DISTRIBUTION COST ANALYSIS

WHY ANALYZE DISTRIBUTION COSTS?

Distribution costs are analyzed for three primary purposes: (1) cost determination, (2) cost control, and (3) the planning and direction of distribution effort. Perhaps the least important of these is cost determination. Yet costs must be ascertained in order to establish selling prices, formulate distribution policies, and prepare various operating statements. However, the most important purpose is to supply the marketing executives with the necessary information in the planning, direction, and control of distribution effort. Sales plans must be developed on the basis of those programs or projects which seem to offer a reasonable return. Sales effort must be directed along the most profitable channels, and inefficiencies eliminated. The what, when, and where questions of sales direction must be answered. An analysis of distribution costs will not provide all the answers to all the sales manager's problems, but it can play an important part in making decisions.

TYPES OF ANALYSES

There are three basic methods of analyzing distribution costs:

1. By nature of expense or object of expenditure
2. By functions or functional operations performed
3. By the manner of application of distribution effort

The effective direction and control of sales effort usually require all of these various types of analysis if the sales manager is to be furnished with the necessary information.

ANALYSIS BY NATURE OF EXPENSE

Generally the ledger accounts in even the smallest companies provide for a recording of distribution costs by nature of expense or object of expenditure. For example, salaries, payroll taxes, supplies, rent, traveling expense, and advertising space are usually set out in separate accounts. This is often the first, and sometimes the only, analysis made of distribution costs.

Such an analysis does provide some information for cost control purposes, general though it may be. With the type of expense segregated month by month, it is possible to follow trends and compare the expense with the previous month and with the same month last year. The ratio of the expense to net sales can also be determined. But a comparison with other periods serves to perpetuate inefficiency, and weaknesses will be revealed only in extreme instances.

It should be clear that an analysis by nature of expense is of limited value only. The cost of distribution *generally* is known. Yet the controller cannot tell the sales manager his traveling expense is too high, or that too much is being spent on advertising. He must be told whose selling expenses are too high, and how it is known they are too high. The points of high cost must be clearly defined and responsibility placed, and possibly even the solution suggested. The controller cannot expect cooperation from the sales manager or chief executive on the basis of generalities. The excess cost of specific operations or the excess cost of securing particular results must be set out if an intelligent effort is to be made in reducing the cost or improving the effectiveness of the effort.

The limitation of analysis by nature of expense, from a control standpoint, is obvious. And since the information provided is very general, it serves little useful purpose for the direction of sales effort.

ANALYSIS BY FUNCTIONAL OPERATIONS

An analysis which has been found useful, particularly for the *control* of distribution costs, is that by functions or functional operations. It is of assistance in measuring the performance by individual responsibility, especially in those applications where the organization is complex or large.

The approach is substantially similar to that used in analyzing production costs, and may be outlined as follows:

1. Establish the functional operations which are to be measured, taking care to see that the functions are properly segregated in terms of individual responsibility. Some illustrative functional operations are:

   a. Salesmen's calls on prospects or customers
   b. Shipments from warehouse
   c. Circular mailing

2. Provide for a cost segregation of these functions. In this connection the classification should provide for those costs which are direct as to the function. For *cost determination,* perhaps cost allocations should be made. Generally, however, for *cost control,* emphasis must be on the direct expenses only. Thus in a small branch warehouse such expenses as the indirect labor, supervisory salaries, and fuel should be known, but these costs should be distinct from the allocated share of the regional sales office expense.

3. Establish units of measurement of functional service to the extent practicable. For example, the pounds of shipments might be the measure of the shipping expense; or the number of salesmen's calls might serve as one measurement of direct field selling expense.

4. Calculate a unit cost of operation by dividing the total controllable functional cost by the number of units.

5. Take corrective action if out-of-line conditions appear. This situation may become more readily apparent if standards are established, and actual performance is measured against them.

It will be appreciated that this method cannot be applied to all distribution costs, but it may extend to a considerable portion.

The functional approach is useful in control and also in analysis by manner of application. For example, if an analysis is being made by territories, it is necessary to record the number of functional units of the particular activity used in that territory, and then simply multiply this number by the unit cost to arrive at a fair cost of the function for each territory.

A specific application of the functional analysis in controlling costs is discussed in the section of this chapter dealing with standards.

ANALYSIS BY MANNER OF APPLICATION

It is one thing to have an efficient organization from the standpoint of performance of the individual functions, and quite another thing to see that the performance is so directed and coordinated as to be productive of the most fruitful results. For example, the controller might well show the sales manager that the cost per call is very reasonable, or that the cost per cwt. of handling material in the New York warehouse is below standard. Yet he must go much further in his analysis. It is as important, perhaps even more important, that the controller provide information as to income or results achieved in relation to effort or cost expended. By and large, sales effort must relate to sales possibilities, and these factors must be brought into proper balance. Analysis by manner of application is primarily for the purpose of providing information in the direction of sales effort. The income from a particular factor is being measured against the cost applied against the factor. This type of analysis indicates the distribution cost of different territories, products, customers, channels of distribution, methods of sale, or salesmen. Depending on the problem, the controller must counsel with the sales manager and decide which ones are most useful. These analyses probably will extend to various subanalyses. For example, the breakdown of territorial costs among different products distributed or expected to be distributed might be necessary.

In making any analysis by manner of application, an important consideration is the proper segregation of costs. The value of the cost study will depend in large part on this factor. For this type of analysis, distribution costs may be divided into three main groups: direct costs, semidirect costs, and indirect costs. As the name implies, direct costs are those immediately identified with a segment and need no allocation. For example, in an analysis by salesman, the field expense of salary, traveling expense, and entertainment incurred by that salesman is direct. However, in an analysis by product these expenses might be semidirect or indirect. Expenses which are direct in one application are usually not in another. Ordinarily, the classification of accounts is such that one application is direct for many of the expenses.

Semidirect costs are those related in some measurable way with the particular segments under study. The variability factor which is responsible for the amount of the expense is known and recorded quantitatively, and the costs may be distributed in accordance with the service required. Thus the cost factor of the warehousing function might be pounds handled. The order-handling costs might relate to number of item-lines. Stated in other terms, the basis of allocation is less arbitrary than a basis selected at random, such as net sales; and the cost results are therefore of more significance. This might be said to be the distinction between the semidirect costs and those other common or joint costs here designated as indirect.

Indirect expenses are a general charge against the business and must be allocated on a more or less arbitrary basis. No simple measure is available to identify the expense with one territory or product, as distinguished from any other. In practice this may be found to be due as much to records kept as to the nature of the expense. Common examples are institutional advertising or the salaries of general sales executives. There perhaps is little relationship between institutional advertising and the sales in the Western territory as contrasted with the Middle Atlantic territory. There might be little relationship between the costs of general sales administration and sales of product X as compared with product Y. Of course, where it is practical for the general sales executive to keep a time record, the allocation of the expense may be less arbitrary, and of more significance.

For distribution cost analysis, as for any intelligent analysis, the type of costs most suitable will depend upon the purpose of the study. For long-term decisions total costs should be known; hence, allocated costs need to be identified. If, on the other hand, decisions are of limited scope and for a short period, such as the sale to a private brand customer for the next year, then perhaps only direct expenses ought to be considered. The advisability of making arbitrary allocations of indirect costs may be questioned. It is most important, however, that those who use the figures are knowledgeable as to limitations.

THE CONTRIBUTION MARGIN APPROACH

In making a choice between alternative business decisions, usually some costs are unaffected regardless of the conclusions reached. For this reason, among others, it has been found practical to isolate and identify those costs which do change to the exclusion of those costs which do not. The contribution margin approach adopts this concept, although such a segregation may be made in a total cost study as well.

The "contribution margin" is calculated by deducting from sales income those costs which are incurred in obtaining that segment of the sales income being analyzed. It may be the sales and costs of a given territory, or product, or customer, and need not relate to the company's entire sales of the period. These costs may be described as those costs which would not be incurred if the segment being reported upon were not present. Such costs are sometimes known also as variable costs or as direct costs. As costs are defined in the preceding section, the costs deducted would include all direct costs plus, in some instances, the semidirect costs. The inclusion of the latter would depend on the extent to which some of the content is fixed or continuing in nature. As an example, if the bulk of warehousing expense is variable, the period expense content, such as the foreman's salary, might be ignored. In such a case, the entire semidirect costs for the warehousing function might be included. (As a practical matter, the authors assume in all illustrations of semidirect costs that such costs relate basically to an activity factor and would be reduced generally in proportion to volume.)

The costs and expenses not deducted from sales income in computing contribution margins are those not changed in total amount by the decision under review. The contribution margin, therefore, is the contribution that the activity under question makes toward meeting the fixed or continuing expenses and profit. The use of such an approach does not ignore the period costs. Rather, it recognizes that (1) the separation of the common expenses in relation to the business decision at hand serves little useful purpose, and (2) emphasis should be placed on the "contribution" or provision made by the segment toward the joint expenses and profit.

The contribution margin approach and the related "direct costing" have these several advantages:

1. Measurement of the immediate gain to the company's over-all profit by the transaction or segment under review
2. Facilitation of management's decision because those costs to be changed are already separated from costs not affected
3. Avoidance of errors and controversy which arise by reason of cost allocations and allocation methods
4. Simplicity of application since direct costs usually are identifiable more readily than total costs including the necessary allocations
5. Data can be secured much more quickly and with less effort

In practice, marginal costs are used for short-term tactical decisions—and their value can be appreciated. However, over the longer term, a business must recover total costs and a reasonable profit if it is to survive. Under the circumstances, there is no good reason why the total cost method and contribution margin approach cannot be used jointly. Such a statement would indicate the immediate profit effect of the business decision; and, by inclusion of the joint or pooled costs, can reveal the operating income picture.

Management's needs and the judgment of the controller will ordinarily dictate the type of costing most adaptable. For reasons of prudence, sometimes distribution costs will be segregated on a contribution basis whereas manufacturing costs will be shown in total. An example of such a situation would be in circumstances where top management adopts the viewpoint that a sale must always recoup all manufacturing expenses plus, at a minimum, the direct selling expenses.

Some illustrations of the marginal cost approach are presented later in this chapter.

TECHNIQUE OF ANALYSIS BY MANNER OF APPLICATION

There has been sufficient experience with distribution cost analysis by manner of application to prove the value of the technique. While the degree of refinement may vary in different companies, the general approach may be outlined as follows:

1. Determine which analysis or analyses needs to be made. The analyses which can be made are suggested on pages 182–83 relating to sales analysis. However, others might be needed in a particular application, such as an analysis by method of delivery. Again, some may be recurring and others may be made only as weaknesses are indicated.
2. Classify distribution costs as to those which are direct, semidirect, and indirect.
3. Select and apply the allocation bases to the semidirect and indirect expenses. This includes a segregation and proper treatment of variable, as contrasted with fixed, costs where such a segregation is a factor.
4. Prepare the analysis and commentary for the use of the proper executive. This will involve the following steps in arriving at significant cost and profit relationships:
   a. Determine the gross profit by segment (e.g., territory, product, size of order, etc.)
   b. Accumulate the direct expense by segment, and deduct this from gross profit to arrive at *profit after direct expense*
   c. Distribute the semidirect expenses, and deduct these to arrive at *profit after semidirect expense*
   d. Prorate the indirect expense to arrive at the final net profit (in some instances steps *c* and *d* will be combined)
   e. Prepare the necessary subanalyses to pinpoint the conditions needing correction

These comments should indicate the principles and technique involved so that any controller can proceed to prepare the facts necessary in his particular situation.

Comments on the need and use of certain analyses by manner of application are made hereafter.

ANALYSIS BY TERRITORIES

A territory may be defined, for this purpose, as any geographical area, whether city, trading area, county, state, or sales district, which is used by a company for sales planning, direction, or analysis. Where, or in which territory, goods are sold has a great effect on the net profit. There are striking variations between territories as to sales potentials, as to net profit, and as to gross margins. If goods are sold f.o.b. a central point and at the same price, the gross profit, of course, is unchanged. But if the product is sold on a delivered price basis, the gross margin is different because of transportation charges. In different areas the consumers' wants and needs are different, and this factor affects the total gross margins. Even aside from these considerations, experience has shown that the distribution costs—the costs to sell—are different in different territories. The cost to sell in densely populated New York is much different from the cost to sell in western Texas. Because of all these dissimilar conditions, businessmen must have an analysis of distribution costs by territories. Such information permits the sales manager to rearrange sales effort where necessary, and direct sales effort into the most profitable areas. Control of distribution costs is facilitated through this same analysis, perhaps with the aid of distribution cost standards. Sales planning, of course, with respect to new territories and new markets is affected by distribution cost considerations.

Not every concern will find analysis by territories necessary. It applies largely in those instances where a large geographical area is covered. Thus, a manufacturer covering a national market would greatly benefit from such an analysis, whereas a retail store probably would not. Exactly what type of territorial analysis need be made depends on the problem and type of organization. If a territorial sales executive is largely responsible for costs and results, a complete analysis by this responsibility area is desirable. Or if the problem is one of costs to sell in small towns vs. cities, such a segregation is to be made.

An illustrative statement of income and expense by territories is shown in Fig. 51.

Once the points of weakness are discovered through analysis, it remains to take corrective action. Some of the possibilities are:

1. Reorganization of territories to permit effort more nearly in line with potentials
2. Rearrangement of territorial boundaries to reduce selling expense, secure better coverage, etc.
3. Shifting of salesmen
4. Increased emphasis on neglected lines or customers in territory
5. Change in method of sale or channel of distribution (shift from salesman to agent, etc.)

The P Company

STATEMENT OF INCOME AND EXPENSE BY TERRITORIES

For the Month Ended January 31, 1962

Description	TOTAL Amount	TOTAL % of Net Sales	WEST Amount	WEST % of Net Sales	MIDDLE WEST Amount	MIDDLE WEST % of Net Sales	MIDDLE ATLANTIC Amount	MIDDLE ATLANTIC % of Net Sales	NEW ENGLAND Amount	NEW ENGLAND % of Net Sales
GROSS SALES	$840,000		$50,000		$390,000		$240,000		$160,000	
Less:										
Freight	35,359		4,200		13,500		10,750		6,909	
Returns	5,000		750		1,050		1,840		1,360	
Allowances	10,650		670		3,890		3,750		2,340	
Total Sales Deductions	51,009		5,620		18,440		16,340		10,609	
Net Sales	788,991	100.00	44,380	100.00	371,560	100.00	223,660	100.00	149,391	100.00
Cost of Sales	550,127	69.73	31,066	70.00	241,514	65.00	167,745	75.00	109,802	73.50
Gross Profit	238,864	30.27	13,314	30.00	130,046	35.00	55,915	25.00	39,589	26.50
Direct Selling Expenses	45,568	5.78	2,219	5.00	16,720	4.50	20,129	9.00	6,500	4.35
Profit After Direct Selling Expenses	193,296	24.49	11,095	25.00	113,326	30.50	35,786	16.00	33,089	22.15
Semidirect Expenses	17,854	2.26	1,000	2.25	7,800	2.10	6,330	2.83	2,724	1.82
Profit After Semidirect Expenses	175,442	22.23	10,095	22.75	105,526	28.40	29,456	13.17	30,365	20.33
Allocated Share of General Expenses	15,780	2.00	888	2.00	7,431	2.00	4,473	2.00	2,988	2.00
Net Profit Before Income Taxes	$159,662	20.23	$ 9,207	20.75	$ 98,095	26.40	$ 24,983	11.17	$ 27,377	18.33
OTHER DATA										
Units Sold	36,692		2,000		17,333		10,550		6,809	
Sales Potential	$850,000		$85,000		$400,000		$225,000		$140,000	
% of Potential	92.8		52.2		92.9		99.4		106.7	

6. Changes in physical facilities (warehouses, etc.) in territory
7. Elimination of unprofitable territories (potentials of area and out-of-pocket costs vs. allocated costs considered)
8. Change in advertising policy or expenditure in territory

ANALYSIS BY COMMODITIES

In our dynamic and competitive economy, the design or style or type of product a firm sells may change constantly. The tremendous strides of research, among other factors, are repeatedly bringing new products into the market. Hence, every company is sooner or later faced with the problem of what products it should sell. Will the firm sell the best or the cheapest line? Will it promote the use of a new plastic? Should it introduce a silent airplane motor? The answer to questions like these are twofold. First, through market analysis a determination must be made as to what the consumer wants and what price he will pay. Then, through cost analysis it must be determined whether or not the company can make and sell the article at a profit. Therefore, an analysis by products is desirable.

Many firms, in their urge to increase sales volume so as to better utilize facilities and personnel, often add new products to the line. Sometimes these new products "fit" into the line and permit certain economies. Often, however, the different products require services in varying degree. For this reason, too, an analysis by product is necessary to determine the cost to sell, as well as the net profit.

Generally speaking, sales effort should be directed toward those products with the greatest net profit possibilities, and cost analysis is necessary to know just which products these are. This is not to state that a company should drop a low-margin item; it may be contributing more than out-of-pocket costs, or it may be necessary for customer convenience. Furthermore, there may be little possibility of selling a high-margin item to a customer. For example, there may be no chance of selling to a paint manufacturer any quantity of a high-profit glue instead of a low-margin paint vehicle. There are more factors than merely cost considerations in selling. But such conditions must be watched and held within reasonable limits. Distribution cost analyses by commodity, then, are of use in the direction of sales effort.

Many controllers may find, in making product cost analyses, that the net profit on an entire line of products is not great enough, or even that losses are being sustained. When such conditions are revealed, steps are usually taken to increase that margin because the firm may not be in a position to drop an entire line. This is but another way of saying that analysis is a means of controlling costs, because the manufacturing costs or distribution costs may be too high.

The Best Company

STATEMENT OF INCOME AND EXPENSE BY PRODUCTS

For the Month Ended June 30, 1962

Description	All Products Amount	All Products % of Net Sales	A Amount	A Per Cwt.	B Amount	B Per Cwt.	C Amount	C Per Cwt.	D Amount	D Per Cwt.
Gross Sales	$27,890		$14,600	$14.60	$620	$12.40	$11,040	$13.80	$1,630	$16.30
Less: Sales Deductions	1,295		600	.60	25	.50	640	.80	30	.30
Net Sales	26,595	100.0	14,000	14.00	595	11.90	10,400	13.00	1,600	16.00
Variable Cost of Sales	8,100	30.5	5,000	5.00	300	6.00	2,400	3.00	400	4.00
Profit After Direct Mfg. Costs	18,495	69.5	9,000	9.00	295	5.90	8,000	10.00	1,200	12.00
Direct Distribution Expense	1,255	4.7	500	.50	25	.50	640	.80	90	.90
Semidirect Distribution Expense (Variable)	3,355	12.6	800	.80	185	3.70	1,840	2.30	530	5.30
Contribution Margin	13,885	52.2	7,700	7.70	85	1.70	5,520	6.90	580	5.80
Fixed Expenses										
Manufacturing	4,900	18.4	3,000	3.00	100	2.00	1,600	2.00	200	2.00
Distribution	1,170	4.4	600	.60	30	.60	480	.60	60	.60
Total	6,070	22.8	3,600	3.60	130	2.60	2,080	2.60	260	2.60
Profit or (Loss) Before Income Tax	$ 7,815	29.4	$ 4,100	$ 4.10	$(45)	$(.90)	$ 3,440	$ 4.30	$ 320	$ 3.20
OTHER DATA										
Hundredweight Sold	1,950		1,000		50		800		100	
Average Sale per Call (when sold)	$348.63		$486.67		$124.00		$736.00		$54.33	
Number of "No Sale" Calls	20		10		3		4		3	
Lack of Volume Manufacturing Costs	$2,800		$ 600		$ 500		$ 1,400		$ 300	

Fig. 52—Statement of Income and Expense by Products.

Finally, product cost analyses are helpful in setting selling prices when the company is in a position to use costs as a major guide. Such analyses are desirable in conjunction with determining maximum price differentials to particular customers, as permitted under the Robinson-Patman Act.

It is probably self-evident to most controllers or accountants that a product analysis of distribution costs should be made when the characteristics of the commodity or their methods of distribution are such that a uniform basis of allocation is not indicative of the effort or cost to sell. Thus, pounds or units of sale or sales dollars may be a fair measure of selling expense. But there are numerous circumstances when such an apportionment is inaccurate or misleading:

1. *If there are differences in the time or amount of sales effort required.* Thus product A which sells at $.60 each may require about three times the effort of product V which sells at $.30 each. Neither sales dollar nor units would be a fair basis. Perhaps one product would require a high degree of technical assistance with frequent call-backs as compared with another. Again, specialty salesmen may merchandise one product while a general line salesman may handle another. All such circumstances result in different costs to sell, and should be so reflected in the analyses.

2. *If there are differences in method of sale.* Obviously, if one product is sold exclusively by mail order, and another by salesmen, the selling cost cannot be prorated on a sales dollar or unit basis.

3. *If there are differences in the size of order.* When one product is sold in ten-pound lots, while another is sold in tank cars, many of the distribution costs can be different.

4. *If there are differences in channels of distribution.* One product may be sold directly to retailers while another is distributed through wholesalers. Here, also, there is a difference in distribution cost.

The analysis by commodities ordinarily will reveal areas of weakness about which corrective action can be taken in some degree, such as:

1. Shifting emphasis of sales effort to more profitable lines, or bringing effort in line with sales potential
2. Adjusting sales prices
3. Eliminating certain unprofitable lines, package sizes, colors, etc.
4. Adding product lines related to "family," with consequent sharing of fixed distribution expense
5. Changing method of sale or channel of distribution
6. Changing type, amount, and emphasis of advertising
7. Revising packages, design, quality, etc.

A statement of income and expense which incorporates the contribution margin concept by products is shown in Fig. 52.

The Best Company

STATEMENT OF INCOME AND EXPENSE BY CUSTOMER CLASS

For the Month Ended April 30, 1962

Description	TOTAL		RETAILERS		JOBBERS		MAIL ORDER HOUSES	
	Amount	% of Net Sales	Amount	% of Net Sales	Amount	% of Net Sales	Amount	% of Net Sales
Gross Sales	$1,220,000		$690,000		$220,000		$310,000	
Less: Sales Deductions	33,000		20,000		3,000		10,000	
Net Sales	1,187,000	100.0	670,000	100.0	217,000	100.0	300,000	100.0
Cost of Goods Sold	957,600	80.7	503,800	75.2	187,700	86.5	266,100	88.7
Gross Profit	229,400	19.3	166,200	24.8	29,300	13.5	33,900	11.3
Direct Customer Distribution Costs	108,300	9.1	82,400	12.3	20,800	9.6	5,100	1.7
Profit Remaining After Direct Costs	121,100	10.2	83,800	12.5	8,500	3.9	28,800	9.6
Indirect Customer Distribution Costs	53,400	4.5	40,900	6.1	8,900	4.1	3,600	1.2
Net Profit or (Loss) After Distribution Costs (and before Federal Income Taxes)	$ 67,700	5.7	$ 42,900	6.4	$ (400)	(.2)	$ 25,200	8.4

Fig. 53—Statement of Income and Expense by Customer Class.

ANALYSIS BY CUSTOMERS

It is no secret that many manufacturers or distributors carry unprofitable accounts or customers. Such a condition may result from a philosophy of "get the volume," or from insufficient gumption to do something about the status quo, or probably because the sales executive just doesn't have sufficient knowledge about his marketing costs.

Yet, it costs more to sell to some types of customers than to others, and more to one customer within a type than another. Some customers require more services than others, such as warehousing, delivery, or financing. Some customers insist on different prices, particularly where different size orders or annual purchases are factors. Again, the type of products sold to some classes differs from others. All these are reasons why analyses by customers are necessary to measure the difference in net profit. Aside from use in direction of sales effort, these analyses serve in setting prices and controlling distribution costs.

In most firms the analyses by customers will not be continuous. Perhaps the sales manager will be interested in whether money is being made on a particular account; or changes may be contemplated only on certain groups of accounts. On these occasions special analyses can be made.

While analyses may be made by individual customers, particularly when there are a few high-volume accounts, by and large the analyses will relate to certain groups or categories. The two basic factors in selecting the classification to be used are the amount of distribution services required, for this is the primary reason for differences in distribution costs, and the practicability of segregating the distribution costs. Classifications which have proved useful are:

1. Amount of annual purchases
2. Size of orders
3. Location
4. Frequency of salesmen's calls
5. Type of agent (retailer, wholesaler, or jobber)
6. Credit rating of customers

In making an analysis by classification of customer, one approach is to segregate all customers in the applicable group and determine total costs for each group. This may often be time-consuming. Another method involves a sampling procedure, wherein representative customers in each category are selected and the cost of servicing them is determined. A modification of this approach is to make a thoroughly detailed analysis in some areas, and a sample run in other areas.

It will be appreciated that relatively few distribution cost items can be charged directly to customers, and that allocations must be made. Statistical data from various reports will be found necessary, viz., the number of calls made to customers or customer classes, the time spent with customers, or the number of orders.

Presentation of the analysis by customers may take the form of an income and expense statement as shown in Fig. 53. This example classifies customers according to type, but a similar analysis could be made by annual volume of sales.

The Roth Company

SELECTED CUSTOMER ANALYSIS ON A SALES UNIT BASIS

For the Six Months Ended June 30, 1962

| | By Calls of Field Force | | | | Proposed Centralized Phone Order Desk |
	Customer W	Customer X	Customer Y	Customer Z	Customer Z
NET SALES	$10.09	$10.16	$10.13	$10.21	$10.21
DIRECT COSTS					
Manufacturing	8.07	8.09	8.08	8.08	8.08
Transportation	.11	.12	.14	.18	.18
Warehousing	.02	.02	.02	.04	.04
Selling	.09	.10	.09	.22	.09
Total	8.29	8.33	8.33	8.52	8.39
CONTRIBUTION MARGIN	$ 1.80	$ 1.83	$ 1.80	$ 1.69	$ 1.82
Units Sold	1,200	1,090	800	390	390
Aggregate Contribution	$2,160	$1,995	$1,440	$ 559	$ 710

Fig. 54—Customer Analysis on Contribution Margin Basis.

Occasions will arise when a decision must be made whether the business with a specific customer should be continued, or whether the method of sale to him ought to be changed. The use of unit analysis of individual customers, the contribution margin concept, and an alternative method of sale for small customers are illustrated in Fig. 54. In this instance, changing the selling method from field calls to a phone basis resulted in retention of valuable business and securing a contribution margin in line with normal operating requirements. Other data may be presented in graphic or statistical form, as in Fig. 55, and Fig. 57, on page 250.

An analysis by customers will provide information of great value to the sales manager. It will give a clear view of the number of accounts in various volume brackets and the average value of orders. In using this information for corrective action, consideration must be given to potential volume and the absorption of fixed production costs. But it will furnish facts for executive discussion as to

1. Discontinuance of certain customer groups
2. Price adjustments
3. Need for higher margin for certain groups
4. Change in method of sale

ANALYSIS BY SIZE OF ORDERS

Another analysis which may be made advantageously in many business concerns is that by size of orders. It has been recognized for some time that one of the causes of both high distribution costs and unprofitable sales is the small order—generally not because it is small in itself, but because the prices are not high enough to cover the costs and leave a profit. There are many instances where small orders cannot be discontinued. But again,

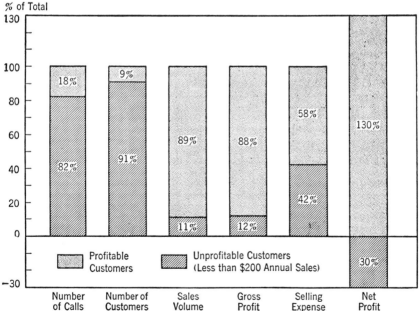

COMPARISON OF PROFITABLE AND UNPROFITABLE CUSTOMERS
NUMBER OF CASES, NUMBER OF CUSTOMERS, SALES VOLUME,
GROSS MARGIN AND SELLING EXPENSE

Based on Annual Sales Volume

Fig. 55—Comparative Data on Profitable and Unprofitable Accounts.

the problem can be solved. Corrective action can be taken; it can be brought under control. Obviously the first step a controller must take is to get the facts through an analysis of distribution costs by size of order.

The problem is naturally more important in some concerns than in others, particularly where the order-handling costs are relatively large or fixed.

By and large, the procedure for analyzing distribution costs by size of order is similar to that for other analyses. It involves segregating costs by factor of variability, and applying the factors. In this case, certain costs will be recognized as fixed for all sizes of orders; others will vary with the money volume; and still others will vary with physical volume. By way of general suggestion, the steps to be followed might be:

1. Determine the size of the order groups to be studied; e.g., below $25, $25 to $50, etc.
2. Classify the costs according to: (a) those which vary with the size of the order, e.g., packing; (b) those which are uniform for orders of all sizes, e.g., accounts receivable bookkeeping; and (3) those which must be considered as general overhead with no direct relation to orders, e.g., certain advertising and supervision costs
3. Identify the factors which appear to govern the amount of the variable expense (that expense which varies with the size of the order) applicable to orders of different sizes; e.g., dollar value, weight, or handling time
4. Apply the factors of variability to the variable expenses and add the uniform costs, thereby arriving at a direct cost of orders by sizes
5. Apply the overhead costs by some suitable factor, such as hundredweight or dollar value, to arrive at the total order cost

A condensed illustrative analysis is shown on page 253.

OTHER ANALYSES

There are other analyses which may prove useful in a particular concern, for example:

1. *By Channels of Distribution.* Useful where a choice in channel of distribution may be made, in order to direct sales into the most profitable channel. The analysis needs to be made from time to time as cost trends change.
2. *By Methods of Sale.* The same comments are applicable as in the case of analysis by channels of distribution.
3. *By Salesmen.* For the purpose of measuring the salesmen's performance in terms of profit, and to better direct salesmen in their activity.
4. *By Organization or Operating Divisions.* Useful where there are separate and distinct selling divisions. Such an analysis is used to measure performance of the divisional executive. Examples are

analyses by departments in a department store; by stores in a retail chain store company; or by branches in a manufacturing organization.

USING MATHEMATICAL TECHNIQUES

The analyses indicated herein are only illustrative. The many variables and alternatives in the distribution or marketing function can indeed make the task of analyzing seem overwhelming. Problems to be solved include warehouse locations, transportation routes, most economical shipment pattern, and a host of others. To perform the needed review, and to effect economies in these functions, use of mathematical formulas or "models" can be most helpful. By using mathematical symbolization and techniques, the many relationships and quantities can be expressed and dealt with.

INTERPRETING THE RESULTS OF ANALYSIS

It has already been stated that the primary purpose of distribution cost analysis is to supply the marketing executives with the necessary information for the planning, direction, and control of distribution effort. The preceding section has suggested the technique and purpose or use of various analyses. It is clear, however, that these methods and studies will be varied as the controller finds necessary, in order to fit the purposes which he has in mind.

He must be alert to the pitfalls or limitations of any figures prepared. Perhaps the problem will be attacked from several sides. In some cases only the variable marketing expenses (or even production costs) will be used, whereas in others both the fixed and variable will be included. Again, in making recommendations based on the distribution cost analysis, the decisions reached must consider every possible effect on every activity of the business. For example, the conclusion that a certain territory must be dropped must consider the net effect on profit—the change in factory volume with the same fixed expense, and resulting differences in unit costs.

DISTRIBUTION COST STANDARDS

STANDARDS AND CONTROL

The very foundation of distribution cost control lies in the correlation of sales effort with the potential, and the use of analysis to avoid misdirection. Though this may be done, and though the income and expense statement may reveal a satisfactory result for a time, still this is not enough. We must know that the business is being operated efficiently; and this requires measuring sticks—standards.

A complete analysis of past operations must be taken as a starting point. By this we may determine that 1,000 calls have been made by salesmen in a given territory, at a cost of $5 per call, and with certain sales results.

But the questions are left unanswered as to how many calls should have been made by the salesmen, and what the cost per call should have been. These also must be ascertained if effective control of sales effort is to be exercised. We may know that 1,000 orders have been handled at a clerical cost of 50 cents per order; but we need to know also what the cost would have been if the clerical work had been efficiently directed. In brief, we need standards by which to judge the distribution performance and signal its weaknesses. Knowing in detail what it has been is not enough; we need also to know in detail what it should be in the immediate future.

CAN STANDARDS BE ESTABLISHED FOR DISTRIBUTION ACTIVITY?

It would be foolish to contend that all distribution activity can be highly standardized. In fact, it is never possible completely to standardize production activities. Just exactly what results should be obtained from a dollar expended for advertising or direct sales effort when developing a new territory or a new product; or just what costs will be necessary to accomplish certain definite ends pertaining to customer goodwill is frequently problematical. But it would be equally foolish, and a fatal management error, to evade the fact that standards can be successfully applied to a vast amount of the distribution activity. If no one is competent to judge what distribution effort is necessary to secure certain results and what it will cost to do it, then management must indeed be in a helpless position.

While a new venture may be undertaken here and there on something of an experimental basis, the entire distribution effort will scarcely be directed along such lines continuously. It is hardly to be expected that an intelligent executive will direct a million dollars into distribution effort in the vain hope that profit will result at the end of the year. Rather, he may be expected to provide for the continuous measurement of individual and group performance as expressed in costs and results. He will want to know when billing clerks are wasting time, when automotive equipment is too costly, when direct mail pieces fail to "pull," when bad debt losses are excessive, when warehouse labor hours are too high, when long-distance telephone costs are exorbitant, and when salesmen produce insufficient orders. If these cost and performance factors are not under constant control, his hope of profit is almost certain to be unfulfilled. But such control implies standards and depends entirely upon the establishment and use of standards. Warehouse labor hours never appear too high in the absolute. They become too high only when measured against what they should be under the circumstances—only when a standard is applied.

While it must be admitted that it is difficult to establish standards for some distribution activities; that psychological factors are relatively more, and physical and mechanical factors relatively less, influential than in production; that relatively more depends upon the judgment of executives and relatively less upon objective measurements; and that a somewhat greater tolerance must be allowed in the consideration of variances; yet it should be understood that this applies only to a part of the distribution activity. Much of the distribution activity is fully as measurable as production. There is no important difference, for example, between the method of establishing standards for order handling, warehousing, shipping, delivery, and clerical work and the methods employed in production. Even those distribution activities which are largely affected by psychological factors, such as advertising and personal selling, are usually capable of reasonably accurate measurement when the activities are continuous or repetitive.

TYPES OF DISTRIBUTION COST STANDARDS

Distribution cost standards may be either (1) of a very general nature, and applicable to distribution functions as a whole, or by major divisions, or (2) units which measure individual performance. Illustrative of the former are:

1. Selling cost as a per cent of net sales
2. Cost per dollar of gross profit
3. Cost per unit sold
4. Cost per sales transaction
5. Cost per order received
6. Cost per customer account

Standards such as these are useful indicators of trends for the entire distribution effort. Furthermore, such standards can be applied to individual products, territories, branches, or departments.

However, these general standards do not necessarily indicate points of weakness in terms of individual responsibility. If costs are to be controlled, the performance of the individual must be measured. Hence, it is necessary to set standards for controllable costs of individual cost items or functions. In warehousing, for example, standards might be set for direct labor as:

Cost per item handled
Cost per pound handled
Cost per shipment
Cost per order filled

Similar standards might be set for shipping supplies, or mule and truck expense. In the direct sales field, standards might be set for salesmen's automobile expense in terms of:

Cost per mile traveled
Cost per day
Cost per month

Again, entertainment expense standards might relate to cost per customer or cost per dollar of net sales.

OTHER CONSIDERATIONS IN SETTING
DISTRIBUTION COST STANDARDS

The controller has a joint responsibility with the sales executives in setting distribution cost standards. In fulfilling this responsibility, it is well that he keep in mind the complications. For example, in manufacturing there is usually only one standard cost for the product. There are, however, many standard costs for distribution of the same article. Thus the cost per call may be different in every territory or sales district. Even in the same territory the standard cost to sell to different classes of customers may vary.

By and large, the same principles applicable to manufacturing expense standards apply to distribution costs. Thus, standards will require revision when operating conditions change materially. Also, where fixed elements of cost are included in the standards, the effect of volume must be recognized.

HOW TO SET THE DISTRIBUTION COST STANDARDS

When the need for standards has been "sold" to the sales executive, the detailed work of setting standards can proceed.

The first step in setting the distribution cost standards is to classify the costs according to functions and activities expressive of individual responsibility. How far such classification can and should be carried depends, of course, on the nature of the business, its size, methods of operation, and internal organization. The cost of such major functions as direct selling, advertising, transportation, warehousing, credit and collection, and financing can be separated in most businesses and subjected to individual study and control. Even such a general classification as this is not universal. For example, in a baking concern doing a house-to-house business, the functions of direct selling and credit and collection are merged, since the work is done by the same men under the same supervision.

The costs of the major functions should be further classified by individual activities which make up the functional service. For example, the credit and collection costs may be separated into credit approvals, posting charges, posting credits, preparing customers' monthly statements, writing collection letters, etc.

The second step is to select units or bases of measurement through which the standards can be expressed. Such units or bases will vary with the type of measurement which is to be applied; thus the measurement may apply to effort used, to cost, to results achieved, or to the relationship of these factors. To illustrate, a salesman may be expected to make a given number of calls per day. This constitutes a measure of effort used and the unit of measure is the call. The cost of writing orders in the order department may be measured in terms of number of orders or order lines [1] written. This is a measure of cost and the unit of measurement is the order or order line. The salesman may be expected to produce a certain number of orders or to secure a certain number of new accounts. This is a measure of results and the units of measurement are orders and new accounts. Finally, a salesman may be required to hold his direct costs within 8% of his sales volume. Here the measurement is in terms of the relationship of particular costs to results in sales volume and the basis of measurement is the ratio of one to the other.

While such specific units of measurement are not available for all distribution activities, some basis must be selected before the standards can be applied. Where specific units are not available, more inclusive or composite bases must be used. For example, the entire credit and collection cost may be measured by the number of accounts carried; or the entire advertising cost may be measured by its ratio to dollar sales volume.

The third step is to analyze past experience relative to the cost of the functions and specific activities involved with a view to selecting the best experience and indications as to the best procedure. This may involve intensive study of individual methods of procedure and operation similar to that employed in the development of production standards.

The fourth step is to consider the effect on costs of expected changes in external conditions and of the sales program as planned. If increased sales resistance is expected, an estimate must be made as to its effect on such costs as advertising and direct selling. If the program calls for a lengthening of the instalment credit period, the effect on the financing cost must be estimated.

The final step is to summarize the judgment of those executives, division heads, department heads, and salesmen whose experience and training qualify them to judge the measures of satisfactory performance. The standards set must be the final expression of such judgment, based upon an intelligent study of past experience and future outlook.

Standards as finally set will result in much overlapping. Thus a standard cost may be applied to the warehousing function as a whole. Within this general function many individual cost standards may be applied which relate to specific activities such as clerical costs of order handling and physical assembling.

Finally, different standards must frequently be set for different territories, products, channels of distribution, classes of customers, departments, etc., wherein different conditions prevail.

[1] By order line here is meant the writing of one line on a sales order; e.g., "200 ½″ Malleable Iron Nipples No. 682 at $8.00 = $16.00."

ADDITIONAL INFORMATION NEEDED

To establish and use distribution cost standards successfully, a concern must accumulate and have available a considerable amount of information relative to distribution activities and the cost factors pertaining to such activities. This includes a considerable body of information not available in the regular accounting records. Permanent records must be designed for regularly recording and accumulating these data in readily usable form. Just as it is now the custom to record regularly such production factors as labor hours, chargeable hours, idle hours, machine hours, power loads, and number of operations, records must likewise be made of the distribution factors.

Illustrative of such distribution data are the following:

1. Analyses of sales in physical units
2. Number of sales transactions classified as to size, hour of day, etc.
3. Number of quotations made
4. Number of orders classified as to size, period in which received, etc.
5. Number of order lines written
6. Average number of salesmen
7. Number of salesmen-days
8. Number of calls on old and new customers
9. Number of days of salesmen's travel
10. Number of miles of salesmen's travel
11. Average number of customers classified as to location, annual volume, etc.
12. Number of labor hours of salespeople, advertising and display people, warehouse workers, truck drivers, delivery men, maintenance workers, clerical workers, etc.
13. Number of returns and allowances classified as to cause
14. Number of units of advertising space or time used in the various advertising media
15. Number of advertising pieces mailed: letters, circulars, folders, calendars, etc.
16. Number of pieces of advertising material distributed: window cards, store displays, inserts, etc.
17. Number of samples distributed
18. Number of demonstrations made
19. Number of inquiries received
20. Number of new customers secured
21. Number of shipments
22. Analyses of shipments in physical units
23. Dollar value of shipments
24. Number of ton-mile units of shipping
25. Number of deliveries
26. Number of parcels delivered

27. Number of miles of truck operation
28. Number of shipping claims handled
29. Physical volume of goods handled in warehouses
30. Average size of physical inventory carried
31. Rates of turnover in dollars and physical units
32. Average number of accounts carried
33. Number of invoices
34. Number of invoice lines
35. Number of remittances received
36. Number of credit letters sent
37. Average number of days accounts are outstanding
38. Average amount of receivables carried
39. Number of mail pieces handled
40. Number of postings
41. Number of letters written—distribution sections
42. Number of units filed
43. Number of tabulating cards punched

Many of the above items must be further classified by territories, commodities, and departments to supply the full information needed.

Such information will be found useful for many purposes in the direction of distribution activity but is essential to a program of standards. Many concerns have in the past neglected to accumulate and use such information. It is not uncommon to find a concern which has the most exacting records of a production machine—the date of its purchase, full detail as to its cost, working hours, number and cause of idle hours, and cost of maintenance—almost to the point of a complete diary of the machine's daily routine over a long period of years. During the same time, the concern may have been employing a salesman whose total cost through the years has greatly exceeded the cost and maintenance of the machine, but little detailed record of his activities has been kept. How he has spent his time, the number of calls made, the number of prospects interviewed, orders received, gross profit, and even the type of goods sold have not always been recorded. The salesman's activity report can provide some of these data.

With many concerns the distribution information is entirely too meager. More information must be collected if the distribution program is to be wisely directed.

USE OF STANDARDS FOR CONTROL

The essence of control is the prompt follow-up of unfavorable trends before they develop into large losses. Once the standards are determined, the stage is set for action. The controller compares actual and standard performance and reports the results to the sales executive. Illustrative applications are set forth in the next chapter.

14

Applications of Control of Distribution Costs

APPLIED CONTROL OF DISTRIBUTION COSTS

GENERAL

It will bear repeating that a number of business concerns that have achieved a reasonable degree of success in maintaining distribution costs at a satisfactory level in relation to sales have used three basic tools:

1. Estimates of market potentials by territories, products, and types of customer, so that selling effort could be directed where the greatest sales potential lay
2. Analysis of distribution costs to reveal the areas of unprofitability, in order to study the causes and take corrective action so as to make the selling effort profitable
3. Application of sales and distribution cost standards to measure the degree of efficiency with which the distribution activity is being performed

The purpose of this section is to explain how the controller may use the control mechanisms at his command. He must secure the facts and interpret them; and the sales executive must use such information in conjunction with his appraisal of the sales problems. As to control of distribution costs, the objective is to secure effective use of the distribution dollars, and not necessarily to whittle down any and all costs. In view of the many applications possible, the illustrations presented herein should be regarded as suggestive only.

SALES POTENTIALS AND SALES EFFORT

A positive method of reducing the cost of selling as related to results, and one which any controller should be able to "sell" to the sales manager, is that of bringing sales effort in line with potential sales. It merely means going where the sales possibilities are the greatest—the product, the customer, the territory. Too often the salesman sells the product easiest to sell. The result is lost sales volume and an unbalanced sales pattern. Market planning permits a comparison of actual volume and gross profit with potentials, and the direct sales expense of getting the business. Areas or products where a company is not getting its share of the business, or where the direct selling expense is too great for the gross margin available, can be located.

Assume, for example, that an analysis of sales and potentials reveals something like the following:

Product and Territory	Share of Market Potential ("Par")	Actual Volume	% of Potential	Volume Deficiency
WONDER CLEANING FLUID				
Territory A	$100,000	$ 50,000	50.0	$50,000
Territory B	50,000	45,000	90.0	5,000
Territory C	30,000	35,000	116.7	(5,000)
Territory D	10,000	5,000	50.0	5,000
Total	190,000	135,000	71.1	55,000
SOLVENT X				
Territory E	60,000	50,000	82.2	10,000
Territory F	40,000	20,000	50.0	20,000
Territory G	50,000	45,000	90.0	5,000
Territory H	20,000	21,000	105.0	(1,000)
Total	$170,000	$136,000	80.0	$34,000

It is apparent that the company is not getting what is considered a fair share of the possible business of Wonder Cleaning Fluid in territories A and D, or to a lesser extent in B; or its fair share of Solvent X sales in territories E, F, and G. The weaker spots have been isolated. With this information the sales manager can go to the A salesman and tell him that his sales are 50% of what is expected. The substandard results may be due to insufficient coverage, or inefficient applications of sales effort. A review of the number of sales calls and the number of customers will give some indication of the reason.

It should be recognized that the relative dollar profits should be considered in shifting sales effort. A 10% deficiency in one large territory might signify more lost profit than a 30% deficiency in another.

The comparison of potential and actual sales reveals two territories where the company is securing apparently more than its share of the business— Cleaning Fluid in territory C; and Solvent X in territory H. It might well be that this is being done at an excessive selling cost; that too much selling effort is being applied. Sound selling policy might dictate the transferring of some of the men from territory C to territory F. Through this means, a greater sales volume may be realized. Redistribution of selling effort can increase volume and reduce costs.

Another application of the use of sales potentials will illustrate means of increasing sales volume with the minimum of cost. Generally speaking, the apportionment of sales effort involves the balancing of sales possibilities with the proper amount of effort to secure the maximum profit. A choice of alternatives is usually faced by the sales executive. In making the selection, the actual gross profit should be measured against the potential gross profit and the direct sales expense which would be involved in getting the additional business. Assume, for illustrative purposes, that the controller working with the sales executive develops a picture something like this:

Product and Territory	Potential Volume	Actual Volume	Volume De-ficiency	Rate of Gross Profit	"Lost Gross"	Estimated Additional Direct Selling Expense	Estimated Net Gain or (Loss)
PRODUCT X							
Ter. 1	$ 250,000	$225,000	$ 25,000	20%	$ 5,000	$ 5,500	$ (500)
Ter. 2	90,000	60,000	30,000	20	6,000	4,000	2,000
Ter. 3	360,000	220,000	140,000	10	14,000	16,000	(2,000)
Ter. 4	45,000	40,000	5,000	20	1,000	500	500
Ter. 5	100,000	60,000	40,000	25	10,000	3,000	7,000
Total	845,000	605,000	240,000	15%	36,000	29,000	7,000
PRODUCT Y							
Ter. 6	90,000	45,000	45,000	50%	22,500	12,500	10,000
Ter. 7	25,000	15,000	10,000	50	5,000	6,000	(1,000)
Ter. 8	80,000	70,000	10,000	30	3,000	2,700	300
Ter. 9	110,000	70,000	40,000	30	12,000	12,000	—
Ter. 10	50,000	30,000	20,000	60	12,000	6,000	6,000
Total	355,000	230,000	125,000	44%	54,500	39,200	15,300
Grand Total	$1,200,000	$835,000	$365,000	25%	$90,500	$68,200	$22,300

In this example, competitive prices and freight costs from the manufacturing branches have produced differing gross profits. Also, intense competition in some areas is assumed to make selling relatively more expensive. The conclusions are fairly clear, if the estimated cost to sell and the potentials are reliable:

1. It would pay immediately to intensify sales effort in territories 2 and 5 for product X, and in territories 6 and 10 for product Y.
2. The excess cost to sell in territories 1, 3, and 7 makes it unwise to place added effort there. Perhaps a cheaper form of solicitation, such as direct mail advertising or phone calls, might secure some additional volume at low cost.

This simple example illustrates the advantage of the analytical approach to sales planning.

These analyses may relate to products, territories, or customers. Recourse can be made to other data in determining the cause of not securing potential, or of not securing it on an economical basis.

ANALYSIS BY SALESMEN

Another positive means of reducing distribution costs is through an analytical review of unprofitable, or relatively less profitable, performance so as to discover the reasons and take corrective action. One such analysis is by salesmen. Assume an analysis of a three-month period showed the results as illustrated in Fig. 56. An interpretation by the controller could be highly illuminating.

Salesman Adams is the high-volume man. However, despite this volume he produced an operating profit of only 8% of net sales. To begin with, he was very lenient with his customers in that he approved very liberal allowances, and accepted a great deal of merchandise returned without thorough review to see if the complaints were justified. This added cost of handling orders is also reflected in the allocated general selling expense of 7% of net sales. Salesman Adams is a very heavy spender, and his selling expenses were 13% of net sales. A thorough review of these expense reports will reveal some of the cause: Does he entertain too much? Or is it an expensive territory in which to sell? (Expense standards would be useful.) Is he properly routed? Also, his gross margin is less, not only because of allowances but because he cuts prices to the limit in order to secure volume. Adams achieved 125% of quota, but the sales effort was too expensive.

In contrast, Salesman Brown had gross sales of only 60% of those of Adams. However, he returned a greater operating profit. He had less returns and allowances. His selling expenses were about average. However, he isn't getting the business he should in that he attained only 80% of his quota, and he should get 34% of the potential sales of the company instead of an actual of only 20.5%. A review of calls or size of orders taken may reveal the difficulty.

Caldwell returned the greatest dollar operating profit as well as the highest operating profit as a per cent of sales. He had relatively few returns or allowances; he kept the field selling costs quite low; and he concentrated on the high-profit numbers. Despite a sales volume lower than anyone except Erney, he turned in greater profits. He slightly exceeded his quota. Also, sales efforts are about in line with the potential.

Davis exceeded his quota by 10% and also turned in a much higher share of actual sales than the potential share. In doing this he kept field selling expenses reasonably well in line.

From a volume standpoint, Salesman Erney didn't do too well. He sold only 75% of his quota. However, he did return a good margin—

The Right Company

Statement of Income and Expense by Salesmen

For the Three Months Ended March 31, 1962

Item	ADAMS Amount	% of Net Sales	BROWN Amount	% of Net Sales	CALDWELL Amount	% of Net Sales	DAVIS Amount	% of Net Sales	ERNEY Amount	% of Net Sales	TOTAL Amount	% of Net Sales
Gross Sales..............	$250,000		$150,000		$116,600		$200,000		$53,000		$769,600	
Less:												
Returns..............	20,000		2,000		2,000		8,000		1,000		33,000	
Allowances..........	10,000		1,000		2,000		4,000		500		17,500	
Freight..............	5,000		3,000		2,600		4,000		1,500		16,100	
Total Deductions..........	35,000		6,000		6,600		16,000		3,000		66,600	
Net Sales...............	215,000	100.0	144,000	100.0	110,000	100.0	184,000	100.0	50,000	100.0	703,000	100.0
Cost of Sales...........	150,500	70.0	100,800	70.0	66,000	60.0	128,800	70.0	32,500	65.0	478,600	68.1
Gross Profit...........	64,500	30.0	43,200	30.0	44,000	40.0	55,200	30.0	17,500	35.0	224,400	31.9
Field Selling Expense........	27,950	13.0	14,400	10.0	8,800	8.0	18,400	10.0	4,500	9.0	74,050	10.5
Profit After Field Selling Expense..	36,550	17.0	28,800	20.0	35,200	32.0	36,800	20.0	13,000	26.0	150,350	21.4
Allocated General Product Selling Expense........	15,050	7.0	7,200	5.0	4,400	4.0	11,040	6.0	2,500	5.0	40,190	5.7
Profit After General Product Selling Expense........	21,500	10.0	21,600	15.0	30,800	28.0	25,760	14.0	10,500	21.0	110,160	15.7
Share of General Expense........	4,300	2.0	2,880	2.0	2,200	2.0	3,680	2.0	1,000	2.0	14,060	2.0
Operating Profit Before Income Tax	$17,200	8.0	$18,720	13.0	$28,600	26.0	$22,080	12.0	$9,500	19.0	$96,100	13.7
Other Data												
% of Quota.......	125		80		105		110		75			
Net Sales, % of Total......	30.6		20.5		15.6		26.2		7.1		100.0	
Potential, % of Total.......	19.1		34.0		14.9		19.1		12.8		100.0	

Fig. 56—Statement of Income and Expense by Salesmen.

35% of net sales—higher than the average. Selling expenses and returns and allowances were kept in line—perhaps too much so. His territory is very competitive and selling expenses are expected to be somewhat higher. A review of sales reports may indicate the low volume was the result of insufficient calls.

With this information, the sales manager can take corrective action.

The illustration in Fig. 56 reflects an operating profit for every salesman. Obviously there will be many instances when a salesman does not return a profit—instances where he fails to cover not only general operating overhead or allocated selling expense but also every bit of the field selling expense. For example, assume the results of an analysis by a salesman as follows:

Sales		$100,000
Cost of Sales		
Fixed	$15,000	
Variable	55,000	70,000
Gross Profit		30,000
Field Selling Expense		32,000
Net Loss After Direct Expense		2,000
Semidirect Distribution Expense		3,000
Net Loss After Semidirect Distribution Expense		5,000
Indirect Distribution Expense		1,000
Net Loss Before Taxes		$ 6,000

Over the long run, of course, every salesman is expected to cover all expense and contribute a net profit. However, it will be observed that in the above example, the company gained, even though a loss after field selling expense resulted—a gain measured by the excess of fixed manufacturing expense ($15,000) over the net loss after field selling expense ($2,000) or a net gain of $13,000. This gain might be considered reduced to the extent that any part of the semidirect distribution expense could have been avoided if this salesman's business were not handled.

Mention should be made of the fact that analysis of distribution costs by salesman provides the sales manager with a tool to persuade the individual salesman. If, for example, the average gross profit of a salesman is known, and if the typical field selling expense is available, then the sales manager can tell Salesman Jones just how much business he must get to cover his direct selling expenses. With an average gross margin of 30%, and fixed selling expense of $2,400 per month, the salesman must produce net sales of $8,000 just to "break even" ($2,400 ÷ 30%). Similar calculations can be made for other desired contributions toward expense.

CUSTOMER COST ANALYSIS

Analysis of distribution costs by customers can take several approaches, all of which might furnish astonishing facts for the sales executive. The review need not extend to the point of determining net profit or loss, although this ultimately would be useful. For example, a simple comparison of number of calls and sales produced would interest the sales manager. A classification of customer groups on the basis of annual purchases might appear as in Fig. 57.

The X Y Z Company
ANALYSIS OF SALES AND NUMBER OF CALLS IN RELATION TO AMOUNT OF ANNUAL PURCHASES

For the Year 1962

Amount of Annual Purchases	Accounts Number	Accounts % of Total	Calls Number	Calls % of Total	Sales Amount	Sales % of Total
$50,000 and over............	8	.4	144	.6	$ 560,000	9.2
$40,000–$49,999.............	4	.2	144	.6	210,000	3.5
$30,000–$39,999.............	20	1.0	768	3.2	635,000	10.5
$20,000–$29,999.............	68	3.4	816	3.4	1,830,000	30.2
$ 5,000–$19,999.............	182	9.1	2,088	8.7	1,274,000	21.0
$ 4,000–$ 4,999.............	282	14.1	3,696	15.4	1,184,000	19.5
$ 1,000–$ 3,999.............	150	7.5	1,944	8.1	185,000	3.1
$ 500–$ 999.............	62	3.1	792	3.3	43,400	.7
$ 400–$ 499.............	20	1.0	288	1.2	8,500	.1
$ 300–$ 399.............	104	5.2	1,392	5.8	35,300	.6
$ 200–$ 299.............	168	8.4	2,208	9.2	40,800	.8
Subtotal................	1,068	53.4	14,280	59.5	6,006,000	99.2
$ 100–$ 199.............	306	15.3	3,192	13.3	42,100	.7
$ 1–$ 99.............	432	21.6	4,464	18.6	8,600	.1
No Sales...................	194	9.7	2,064	8.6	–	–
Subtotal	932	46.6	9,720	40.5	50,700	.8
Total or Average............	2,000	100.0	24,000	100.0	$6,056,700	100.0

Fig. 57—Analysis of Sales and Number of Calls in Relation to Amount of Annual Purchases.

Such a tabulation reveals that 40.5% of the sales effort (number of calls) produced only .8% of the total business. Obviously, the effort is being misdirected. Figure 57 might be simplified by showing only the percentages, if it is felt the information would be more understandable.

Normally, the next step could be a further detailed analysis of gross margins and operating profit by customer classification. Expenses would be classified into functional cost groups, as discussed on pages 222–23, and allocated to customers, perhaps as follows:

Functional Cost Groups	Basis of Allocation to Customers
Direct and Semidirect:	
1. Field Selling Expense (sales-men's salaries and traveling expense)	Number of salesmen's calls
2. Freight—Outgoing	Direct
3. Billing and Order Handling	Number of invoices
4. Credit and Collections	% sales (weighted)
5. Dealer Helps (advertising)	Number of calls (weighted)
Indirect:	
6. Branch Office Expense	Number of calls (weighted)
7. Home Office Expense	Sales volume

The result of such allocations and other cost applications in a typical company might produce a picture similar to that shown in Fig. 58.

The Illustrative Company

ANALYSIS OF OPERATING PROFIT OR LOSS BY AMOUNT OF ANNUAL PURCHASES

For the Year 1962

Customer Group (Amount of Annual Purchases)	Number of Calls % of Total	Sales % of Total	Gross Profit % of Sales	Direct and Semidirect Selling Expense % of Sales	Balance Remaining % of Sales	Indirect Selling & Operating Expense % of Sales	Operating Profit or (Loss) % of Sales
$50,000 and over.	.10	5.40	16.9	3.0	13.9	1.0	12.9
$40,000–$49,999..	.83	10.32	17.4	3.1	14.3	1.0	13.3
$30,000–$39,999..	.75	6.54	19.3	3.2	16.1	1.3	14.8
$20,000–$29,999..	3.84	3.12	23.0	3.1	19.9	1.2	18.7
$10,000–$19,999..	4.70	2.50	24.1	2.9	21.2	1.1	20.1
$ 5,000–$ 9,999..	9.32	18.22	25.4	3.1	22.3	1.9	20.4
$ 4,000–$ 4,999..	6.77	14.30	26.0	3.6	22.4	1.7	20.7
$ 3,000–$ 3,999..	2.97	9.64	27.5	4.3	23.2	1.6	21.6
$ 1,000–$ 2,999..	3.86	8.43	28.3	5.5	22.8	1.5	21.3
$ 500–$ 999..	5.77	6.07	29.5	7.9	21.6	2.1	19.5
$ 400–$ 499..	6.20	3.50	30.2	7.7	22.5	2.1	20.4
$ 300–$ 399..	5.86	3.25	31.5	11.9	19.6	2.2	17.4
$ 200–$ 299..	7.30	2.25	30.7	13.2	17.5	2.1	15.4
$ 100–$ 199..	13.53	4.36	31.0	29.3	1.7	10.3	(8.6)
$ 1–$ 99..	18.70	2.10	31.1	38.0	(6.9)	12.8	(19.7)
No Sales........	9.50	–	–	–	–	–	–
Total or Average.	100.00	100.00	25.0	3.8	21.2	1.6	19.6

Fig. 58—Analysis of Operating Profit or Loss by Amount of Annual Purchases.

Commentary to the sales manager might stress these facts:

1. As a group, customers yielding sales less than $200 per year are unprofitable—with losses running as high as 19.7% of net sales (on the average for a customer group)
2. The unprofitable customers were 43% of the total (not shown in illustration) and required 32.23% of our total number of calls, yet produced only 6.46% of total sales
3. Prospects to whom no sales were made received 9.50% of our calls, and resulted in 8.7% of our selling expense (not shown)
4. While gross profit increased on smaller purchases, it was not sufficient to cover added selling expense

Before dropping any customers from the sales lists, the matter should be reviewed in detail with the salesman. No customer should be dropped if potential yield is sufficient to return a profit.

Another step in planning for the reduction of a group of unprofitable customers might be the calculation of the savings, somewhat as follows:

Item	Total Selling and Operating Expense Allocated	Estimated Expenses to Be Eliminated	Estimated Expenses Which Cannot Be Eliminated
Salesmen's Salaries	$ 4,300	$3,200	$1,100
Traveling Expense	2,700	2,000	700
Warehousing	3,100	2,100	1,000
Order Handling	1,800	900	900
Credit and Collections	400	100	300
Bad Debts	400	400	—
Branch Office Overhead	1,300	200	1,100
Total	$14,000	8,900	$5,100
Gross Margin on Abandoned Business		3,000	
Net Addition to Profit		$5,900	

In this situation it is assumed some reduction in personnel and other costs can be made. This may mean that the reorganization will result in shift of selling emphasis to other areas.

From simple calculations, other useful information can be gleaned. For example, assume a case where the sales calls are all about equal in length. By the easy process of dividing total field selling expense by the number of calls, the average cost per call in an area can be determined. Assume this to be $15. If the average gross margin is 30% of sales, then the sales dollars per call must average $50 to cover just the direct selling expense. If the typical number of calls is six per year, then at least $300 annually in sales must be secured to cover the cost of calling on the customer. If potential business above this figure is not there, then fewer calls should be made or other sales methods used.

ANALYSIS BY SIZE OF ORDER

The analysis of distribution costs by size of order is closely related to analyses by customers and commodities. Often the small-volume customers are also the small-order customers; or the reason for lack of profit on particular customers may result from the small orders just as much as from the type of product sold to them.

Analyses by size of order can include statistical analyses to apprise the sales manager of the nature of his sales makeup, and permit comparison of average order size by salesmen, or show the relative amount of business by order size and as related to number of accounts. Other analyses can relate to the distribution costs by order size, or can be developed still further to the point of profit or loss.

One use of such an analysis is to determine the minimum order which may be accepted. For example, suppose a review indicates the following minimum cost of handling an order (based on the minimum functional units).

Function	Cost per Order
Order Taking	$3.25
Packing and Shipping	2.16
Delivery	.45
Clerical—Bookkeeping	.15
Credits and Collections	.08
Subtotal	6.09
General Overhead	.22
Total	$6.31

If the average gross margin is 30%, then the loss on this assumed $1.00 order is $6.01 ($6.31 minus $.30). If the salesman's call were eliminated, i.e., assuming a phone or mail order at $.15, the loss might be $2.91 ($6.31 − $3.10 = $3.21 order cost, less $.30 gross = $2.91). It would appear that the minimum order that could be profitable would be $21.03 ($6.31 ÷ 30%). However, as certain costs might vary with sales volume this factor would have to be considered.

An analysis by size of orders might produce these results:

Size of Order (in Pounds)	Gross Margin	Selling Expense	Operating Profit or (Loss)
Under 25	$.080	$.16	$(.08)
25– 50	.060	.12	(.06)
50– 100	.050	.049	.001
100– 200	.040	.036	.004
200– 300	.035	.025	.010
300– 500	.033	.019	.014
500–1,000	.032	.017	.015

It is apparent from this analysis that orders of less than 50 pounds are unprofitable. With this determination, it is then a matter of whether such small orders can be discontinued.

Similar analyses may be made which indicate functional cost per size of order—such as direct selling expense, warehousing expense, delivery expense, or billing expense.

ANALYSIS BY COMMODITIES

Analyses by product may be presented in any one of several ways, depending on the problem to be solved. Some analyses, for example, may emphasize sales distribution while others may extend to the point of operating profit or loss. Some might show trends and relationships, while others would indicate values.

A statement of income and expense by products, prepared on the basis of principles discussed earlier, is illustrated in Fig. 52. In this instance product D was added by the sales department on the general theory that it costs little extra to sell another product. While this viewpoint perhaps has merit over the short run, over the long run the product must be measured against contribution which might be made by marketing other products and must cover not only variable costs but its proper share of fixed expense.

The following comments may be made pertaining to Fig. 52. Product D has a much higher unit gross margin than the other products, a factor which heavily influenced the sales department to add the line. However, the distribution cost was very high—because of several factors: (1) Sales per call were much smaller, even though the time per call for all products was much the same. The product was consumed in smaller quantities, and found a large share of the sales in small-dealer outlets. (2) Much time was spent in attempting to find new customers. For these reasons, the higher gross margin was more than offset by higher distribution costs. It was found that the extra time spent on product D was adversely affecting the sales of other products. Also, in the opinion of the sales manager, a decrease in price would have little effect on volume. On the basis of the information made available through analysis, the sales manager found it advisable to de-emphasize sales of D, and to concentrate on other product sales.

While the principal purpose of Fig. 52 is to illustrate an instance where high gross profit does not result in high net profit before taxes, some other observations may be made. It will be noted that product B resulted in a net loss. This item is a newly developed product which has great potential and therefore should not be dropped. It is worth noting that the net loss of $.90 per cwt. is less than the fixed manufacturing expense of $2.00; and that the line is contributing something over and above the variable manufacturing expense and total distribution costs. Also, it might reasonably be anticipated that with volume increase, the distribution cost per cwt. will decrease.

Figure 52 well could reflect *standard* cost of sales for presentation to the sales manager in order to avoid influencing the gross margin by reason of lack of volume manufacturing costs or manufacturing inefficiencies. However, since we may, in this case, consider the sales executive responsible for unabsorbed fixed manufacturing costs because of inability to get sufficient sales, this information might be shown as supplementary data.

ANALYSIS OF SALES, MARGIN, AND OPERATING PROFIT OR LOSS,
BY PRODUCT GROUP

For the Month Ended March 31, 1962

Product Group	TOTAL			PER HUNDREDWEIGHT			
	Net Sales	Gross Margin	Operating Profit or (Loss)	Net Sales	Gross Margin	Distri- bution Cost	Operating Profit or (Loss)
A..............	$ 43,000	$ 7,740	$ 6,450	$ 14.50	$ 2.61	$ .44	$ 2.17
B..............	26,000	10,400	8,320	17.50	7.00	1.40	5.60
C..............	129,000	32,250	23,220	10.00	2.50	.70	1.80
D..............	30,000	6,000	4,800	20.00	4.00	.80	3.20
E..............	8,000	1,600	1,360	20.00	4.00	.60	3.40
F..............	17,000	5,610	5,100	60.00	19.80	1.80	18.00
G..............	4,000	2,000	1,600	100.00	50.00	10.00	40.00
H..............	2,000	1,000	(800)	100.00	50.00	90.00	(40.00)
Total or Average	$259,000	$66,600	$50,050	$ 13.22	$ 3.40	$ .85	$ 2.55

Fig. 59—Condensed Analysis of Operating Profit or Loss by Product Group.

In some instances it may be desirable merely to summarize for the sales manager the pertinent data as to profit or loss by product, rather than present accounting details, as in Fig. 59.

Trends are often important in making decisions on products. In many instances changes in selling price and manufacturing costs over a period of time signal desired switches in selling effort. Such an analysis is presented in Fig. 60. Product X has lost considerable ground as a profit producer during the eleven-year period. If the other company lines are relatively much more profitable and employ the same manufacturing facilities, it would appear desirable to switch to other products.

TREND OF SALES AND OPERATING PROFIT, PER HUNDREDWEIGHT

PRODUCT X

For Selected Years from 1952 to 1962

	Year					
Item	1962	1961	1960	1957	1953	1952
Net Sales	$14.50	$14.95	$15.30	$15.50	$15.40	$15.60
Variable Cost of Sales	11.50	11.45	11.60	11.60	11.40	11.50
Gross Margin	3.00	3.50	3.70	3.90	4.00	4.10
Direct Selling Expenses	2.80	2.20	1.80	1.70	1.22	1.20
Contribution Margin	$ .20	$ 1.30	$ 1.90	$ 2.20	$ 2.78	$ 2.90
OTHER DATA:						
% of Total Sales of Company	19	21	26	24	51	60
Total Sales of Product X (00's)	$ 423	$ 408	$ 398	$ 474	$ 508	$ 495

Fig. 60—Trend of Sales and Contribution Margin—Product X.

CONTROL THROUGH FUNCTIONAL ANALYSIS

The analysis of distribution costs by manner of application facilitates the reduction of distribution costs through the better direction of sales effort. However, the question "Are the costs too high?" still may not be answered. Thus, an analysis by salesmen may reveal that field selling expense is a satisfactory per cent of net sales; but it may be demonstrated that the cost per call was excessive, or that automobile expense per mile traveled was too high. To secure some indication as to the level of costs, an analysis by functions may be necessary.

Such an analysis, for example, may be useful in judging the reasonableness of automobile expense. However, the fixed and variable nature of the expenses must be recognized. Thus the measurement should not be of total automobile expense where the mileage driven varies greatly from month to month. Depreciation expense should be kept separate, and perhaps a comparison of actual and standard expense for gasoline, oil, and repairs could be made. The standard would be set based on such factors as the type of car driven, the extent of in-town and out-of-town driving, and the general expense level of the area. A simple report to the sales executive could take the form shown in Fig. 61.

It would be necessary, also, to scrutinize the number of functional units consumed—miles, in this case—to detect excessive miles traveled per month or per call. A similar approach may be taken with respect to entertainment expense. Again, the entire cost of a particular function, such as calling on prospects, may be treated in similar fashion.

The Jones Company
ANALYSIS OF AUTOMOBILE EXPENSE
Month of January, 1962

						Cost per Mile Driven		
	Type of Expense				Miles			(Over) or Under Standard
Salesman	Gas & Oil	Repairs	Other	Total	Driven	Actual	Standard	
Austin.....	$110.20	$10.90	$ –	$121.10	4,844	$.025	$.025	$ –
Brown.....	29.50	5.20	2.00	36.70	992	037	.040	.003
Elliston....	70.30	6.40	19.50ª	96.20	3,103	.031	.025	(.006)
Jones......	42.60	–	–	42.60	1,469	.029	.030	.001
Lucas.....	47.90	–	–	47.90	1,597	.030	.035	.005
Total..	$300.50	$22.50	$21.50	$344.50	12,005	$.029	$.030	$.001

ª New tire and tube.

Fig. 61—Comparison of Actual and Standard Costs of Variable Automobile Expense.

BUDGETARY CONTROL IN GENERAL

Closely related to control through individual standards of performance is the technique of budgetary control as related to the operation as a whole. Basically it involves the determination of the amount of distribution cost necessary to sell the quantity of product called for in the sales budget, and the comparison of actual costs with the estimate. It can be said that individual standards of performance supplement budgetary control in that the latter can be realistically developed only when it is known what individual performance to expect.

The degree of refinement varies greatly in different business firms. Some companies plan or estimate a more or less fixed amount of expense each month which a salesman or branch office or other unit of responsibility shall not exceed. This is adjusted only as policies change, or as major shifts in sales volume seem to warrant corresponding short-term (longer than one month) changes in the expense allowance. In other firms the distribution costs are segregated into their fixed or variable components, and allowances granted according to some unit of measurement—a technique very similar to functional anlysis. For example, salary costs might be considered independent of activity, while entertainment expense might be related to sales or number of calls.

CONTROL OF ADVERTISING AND PROMOTION EXPENSE

While the planning and control of marketing expense is difficult, some types of cost present a greater problem of measurement than others. One such area is the advertising and sales promotion function. Consider some typical questions:

1. What should a company's total advertising budget be for the next year?
2. What share of the total budget should be expended for spot television announcements? For national television programs? For spot radio announcements?
3. How much should be spent on newspaper advertising? On national magazine advertising?
4. What sum should be spent on point-of-sale aids?

Newer mathematical techniques and probability studies can be of assistance in evaluating some risks which now are handled intuitively. Aside from this brief comment there are several guides or techniques frequently used in determining how much to budget for advertising and sales promotion expense:

1. Past experience expressed as the ratio of such expense to sales
2. Maximum allowable after provision for adequate return on investment, and available from cash generation
3. Test market evaluation to determine what results reasonably could be expected from specified amounts of advertising expense
4. Amount required for specific campaigns or objectives, viz., introduction of a new product
5. Amount spent by competitors

Most companies resort to an appropriation or fixed type budget as the primary control device. Once the amount to be spent is determined, the control aspects consist in keeping management informed currently, often monthly, of actual expenditures and commitments (perhaps revocable and irrevocable) so as to avoid overrunning the budget.

CONTROL OF DISTRIBUTION COSTS—SUMMARY

It has probably become evident from the discussion that a satisfactory level of marketing costs is achieved through two means: (1) increased operating efficiency and (2) better planning. Analysis is necessary to achieve both.

It is by the joint efforts of the chief sales executive and the controller that this objective is reached. The controller can prepare the analyses to assist in the planning and direction of sales effort, but it requires the addition of the knowledge and willingness of the sales manager to make the tools fully effective. If the willingness is present, there is little reason why the goal cannot be achieved. For example, the controller may suggest that entertainment expense is too high, that perhaps lunches instead of dinners with customers will secure the sale. Yet the sales manager must be convinced before action is taken. Furthermore, a fully cooperative sales staff will suggest, under its own steam, means of reducing selling costs or getting better results.

DISTRIBUTION COST REPORTS

GENERAL

The purpose of distribution cost reports is to get action—action in the better direction of sales effort and the control of costs. The principles of report preparation discussed later in Chapters 28 and 29 are applicable to distribution cost reports.

The form of reports, whether graphic, tabular, or narrative, will depend in part on the preference of the sales executives who use them. The subject matter or content will depend on the purpose of the report, the executives who will receive and use it, and the particular conditions at the time. Since there is such a variety of problems, there is great opportunity for the controller and his staff to exercise ingenuity and resourcefulness in the effective presentation and interpretation of distribution cost data. The field is ripe for presenting reports which motivate the selling group.

CONTENT OF DISTRIBUTION COST REPORTS

Because control of distribution costs involves the effective utilization of services as well as the reduction of costs per se, the subjects of reports are varied in scope. Some suggested contents are as follows:

1. *Total actual costs* compared with actual costs of previous periods, or budgeted costs. This presentation can be by departmental responsibility and by nature of expense item, or by any other segment, such as territory, product, channel of distribution, customer group.
2. *Unit cost comparisons* between actual and standard or budget, or actual of previous periods. This category includes a vast statistical assortment, such as cost per call, cost per order, cost per mile traveled.
3. *Comparative, quantitative, unit statistical data,* such as number of calls made, number of adjustments, number of deliveries, number of orders typed. These data can present actual compared to budget, standard, or previous periods.
4. *Comparison of costs and results,* such as income and expense statements by salesmen and territories.

MANUFACTURING COMPANY   BUDGET REPORT

MONTH___January___

DEPT. HEAD___J. Jones___
DEPARTMENT___SUMMARY #1___   NO.___

DESCRIPTION	CURRENT MONTH			YEAR TO DATE		
	BUDGET	ACTUAL	(OVER)/UNDER	BUDGET	ACTUAL	(OVER)/UNDER
ANALYSIS OF THE SALES DIVISION BY DEPARTMENTS						
GENERAL						
200 General Sales	$ 7,911	$ 8,123	$ (212)			
202 Billing & Filing	1,428	1,433	(5)			
220 New York Office	2,524	2,493	31			
230 Chicago Office	548	561	(13)			
240 New Jersey Warehouse	1,760	2,180	(420)			
	14,171	14,790	(619)			
LUBRICANTS						
300 General	12,390	12,441	(51)			
301 Chicago	1,805	1,614	191			
302 Toledo	865	935	(70)			
303 Middle Atlantic	2,075	2,136	(61)			
304 Rochester	1,125	985	140			
305 New England	2,060	2,355	(295)			
	20,320	20,466	(146)			
PAINTS AND LACQUERS						
400 General	6,426	6,592	(166)			
401 Milwaukee	1,173	993	180			
402 Toledo	2,232	2,575	(343)			
408 South Central	955	1,185	(230)			
409 South Atlantic	2,243	2,679	(436)			
	13,029	14,024	(995)			
CRUCIBLES						
500 General	3,552	3,550	2			
501 Chicago	1,398	1,200	198			
502 Toledo	2,517	2,626	(109)			
503 Middle Atlantic	1,559	1,449	110			
506 West Coast	1,333	1,514	(181)			
507 Cincinnati	795	729	66			
	11,154	11,068	86			
TOTAL SALES DEPARTMENTS	$ 58,674	$ 60,348	$(1,674)			
% REALIZATION			97.2%			
TOTAL SALES DEPARTMENTS	$ 58,674	$ 60,348	$(1,674)			
ADVERTISING & SALES PROM.	17,172	17,117	55			
TOTAL DEPARTMENT PERFORMANCE	$ 75,846	$ 77,465	$(1,619)			
% REALIZATION			97.9%			
COMMENTS:						

ISSUED BY THE ACCOUNTING DEPT. ___Feb. 16,___

Fig. 62—Actual and Budgeted Selling Expense by Department.

ILLUSTRATIVE DISTRIBUTION COST REPORTS

A simple tabulated report which informs the general sales manager of the cost performance of his organization is illustrated in Fig. 62. In this case budgeted and actual costs are compared. Each department manager receives reports showing a similar comparison by cost item. Another illustrative form of budget report in shown in Fig. 63. This type is applicable where expenses are controlled on an appropriation basis, such as advertising and sales promotion.

The P Company

STATUS OF ADVERTISING AND SALES PROMOTION
EXPENDITURES AND COMMITMENTS

As of January 31, 1962

		Expenditures and Commitments			
	Project Budget	Actual Expenditures to 1/31/62	Outstanding Commitments	Total	Balance Available for Use or Transfer
PUBLICATION ADVERTISING					
U. S. News—3/15/62	$ 10,000	$ 3,000	$ 4,000	$ 7,000	$ 3,000
Fortune—3/62	40,000	—	30,000	30,000	10,000
Business Week—2/9/62	10,000	5,000	2,000	7,000	3,000
Unallocated	60,000	—	—	—	60,000
Total	120,000	8,000	36,000	44,000	76,000
CATALOGS AND BOOKLETS					
Parts Catalog	10,000	7,000	3,200	10,200	(200)
Flying Notes	5,000	–	–	–	5,000
Ride in the Sky	20,000	2,000	3,000	5,000	15,000
Total	35,000	9,000	6,200	15,200	19,800
DISPLAYS AND EXHIBITS					
National Aircraft Exhibit	12,500	–	–	–	12,500
Flying Farmers Show	2,500	2,200	200	2,400	100
National Aircraft Show	20,000	–	4,000	4,000	16,000
Unallocated	5,000	–	–	–	5,000
Total	40,000	2,200	4,200	6,400	33,600
SALES PROMOTION					
Radio Project	10,000	800	2,800	3,600	6,400
Television Project	25,000	2,000	4,000	6,000	19,000
Ignition Project	40,000	1,000	16,000	17,000	23,000
Unallocated	–	–	–	–	–
Total	75,000	3,800	22,800	26,600	48,400
ADVERTISING ADMINISTRATION					
Applied Through Current Month	2,000	2,000	–	2,000	–
Unallocated	23,000	–	–	–	23,000
Total	25,000	2,000	–	2,000	23,000
Total Advertising and Sales Promotion	$295,000	$25,000	$69,200	$94,200	$200,800

Fig. 63—Expenditures and Commitments for Advertising and Sales Promotion Expense.

Illustrative statements of income and expense are presented in Figs. 51–53 and 56.

A simple statistical statement on cost per call is shown in Fig. 64. The same data are shown graphically in Fig. 65.

A simple vertical bar chart which indicates trend and comparison with industry figures is shown in Fig. 66.

The X Y Z Company
COST PER SALESMAN'S CALL
For the Month Ended January 31, 1962

Salesman	Number of Calls	Total Field Selling Expense	Actual Cost per Call	Standard
PRODUCT A				
Jones........................	23	$ 814	$35.39	$30.00
Brown........................	16	935	58.44	45.00
Black........................	17	786	46.24	50.00
Green........................	24	985	41.04	35.00
Total or Average..............	80	3,520	44.00	
PRODUCT B				
Ray..............	37	708	19.14	20.00
Bones........................	42	729	17.36	20.00
Bearing.......................	29	632	21.79	20.00
Crown............	36	711	19.75	20.00
Jasper.......................	32	819	25.59	20.00
Total or Average..............	176	3,599	20.45	
Grand Total....................	256	$7,119	$27.81	

Fig. 64—Standard and Actual Cost per Salesman's Call.

ACCOUNTING FOR DISTRIBUTION COSTS

ANALYSIS AND USE OF FORMAL ACCOUNTS

Various approaches to cost analysis have been suggested for use in meeting distribution cost problems. Some of these studies need to be continuous and others need be made only occasionally. Certain of the reviews embrace the entire operation while others make use of the sample or test basis. Under such circumstances it is clear that these findings need not be recorded in the books of account. The cost data used in the analysis should be reconciled with, or tied into, the data already recorded in the accounts, but it is not necessary to make entries in the ledgers.

Usually the books of account will contain distribution costs on a basis

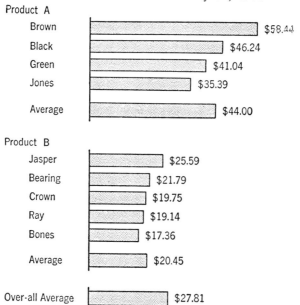

The X Y Z Company

For the Month Ended January 31, 1962

Product A

Brown	$58.44
Black	$46.24
Green	$41.04
Jones	$35.39
Average	$44.00

Product B

Jasper	$25.59
Bearing	$21.79
Crown	$19.75
Ray	$19.14
Bones	$17.36
Average	$20.45

Over-all Average — $27.81

Fig. 65—Graphic Illustration of Cost per Salesman's Call.

The Best Company

COMPARISON OF DISTRIBUTION COSTS WITH INDUSTRY

As a Per Cent of Net Sales

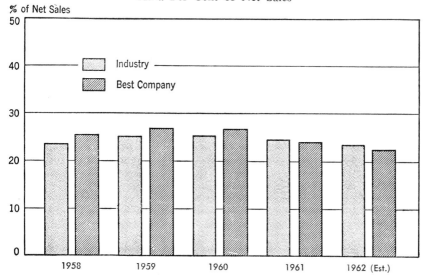

Fig. 66—Comparative Distribution Costs of Company vs. Industry.

263

which will immediately serve analytical purposes, viz., an analysis by territories or organizational divisions. All other analyses will necessarily involve reworking of the costs recorded in the usual manner.

THE ACCOUNTING PLAN

A problem which must be resolved by the controller is whether distribution costs should be recorded under the "actual" or "standard" plan. The actual plan basically involves the inclusion as expense of that period of all distribution expenditures, even though some of the marketing effort is actually directed toward sales to be secured in a subsequent period. There are exceptions in that expenditures which can be definitely related to future periods, such as advertising space not yet run, are occasionally deferred. By and large, however, distribution expenditures are written off to expense as incurred. This is the plan commonly used in business. Such a practice is founded in conservatism, guards against errors in human judgment and honesty, and recognizes the rather intangible nature of expenditures for distribution costs.

In businesses which are highly seasonal in nature, the monthly statements prepared on an actual basis, without deferring any expense, would have little value. Furthermore the statements, if prepared only with information contained in the books of account, would be practically useless in controlling operations. Because of these disadvantages, some companies have adopted the standard cost plan.

STANDARD COST METHOD

The standard cost method as applied to distribution costs is the same as the term implies in production cost accounting. Under such a system the expenditures for the month or other accounting period are segregated into three groups:

1. Those chargeable against current operations as standard costs
2. Those chargeable against current operations as variances or departures from standard performance
3. Those which may be deferred to subsequent periods in accordance with sound accounting practice

Under this method, variances from standard are analyzed as to cause and responsibility, and are recorded in the accounts. The accounts, then, serve to guide management in the control of operations.

WHICH METHOD TO USE?

Each of the accounting plans has its advantages and disadvantages, and the controller must decide which is more appropriate in his firm. Some companies have found it advantageous to use the standard cost plan for some distribution functions, such as warehousing, delivery, and order handling, and to use the actual plan for functions which are less routine.

A major objective of the controller is to furnish the marketing executives with the information required for the effective planning, direction, and control of sales effort. It has been demonstrated that standards are useful for this purpose, but whether such standards are reflected in the books of account is primarily of academic interest only. The main concern of the accountant is to secure and interpret the necessary information. This can be done just as readily through statistical analysis as through the books of account.

INTERPRETATION OF DISTRIBUTION COST VARIANCES

While it is beyond the scope of this volume to review the bookkeeping aspects of distribution costs, it is felt necessary to discuss some ramifications of distribution cost variances. Several general observations can be made.

In many companies the usual practice, at best, is to explain the difference between budgeted and actual distribution costs each month. While the method of determining the budget allowances may differ, such difference is usually not a full measure of the gain or loss to the firm. It is desirable to know the cost results due to failure to attain planned sales volume. For this reason a standard distribution cost is preferable.

This standard, which may be different for each product or territory, basically represents the relationship of expected (budgeted) selling expense to anticipated sales volume. It may be expressed conveniently as a per cent of net sales, and detailed by accounts.

The use of a standard distribution cost has the advantage of tying together the functional units of service to the expected sales volume. For example, if a traveled distance of 15,000 miles per month at $.03 per mile for gasoline and oil is expected to achieve a sales volume of $150,000, the cost and units of service can be translated into a per cent of sales, as an element of standard costs. In this case the per cent would be .3% (15,000 × $.03 = $450 total standard cost, and $450 ÷ $150,000 = .3%).

Application of a standard distribution cost may create a variance because of seasonal or calendar characteristics of the business. For example, while average sales may be $150,000 per month, the budget may call for only $100,000 of sales in January, but $200,000 in June. Each month may still require traveling 15,000 miles. Such a condition will give rise to a variance due to the method of applying the standard to seasonal conditions.

An example will best explain the variances, and show the relationship of functional unit costs and the standard distribution cost. An illustrative form of analysis sheet which a controller might use in preparing his

The Best Company—Territory Y

ANALYSIS OF DISTRIBUTION COSTS OVER OR (UNDER) STANDARD

Month of March, 1962

Description	Budgeted Expense for Month (A)	Actual Expenditure (B)	Standard Expense for Actual Sales Volume (C)	Actual Over or (Under) Standard (B-C) (D)	EXPLANATION OF EXCESS				
					Applicable to Other Periods (Deferred) (E)	Failure to Meet Budgeted Sales (F)	Functional Services Over or (Under) Planned (G)	Functional Rate Over or (Under) Planned (H)	Application of Standards (I)
DIRECT SELLING COST									
Salesmen's Salaries	$ 3,000	$ 3,000	$1,800	$1,200	$1,000	$ 200	$ —	$ —	$ —
Traveling Expense	1,600	1,710	720	990	—	80	300	(190)	800
Automobile Expense (gas, oil, and repairs)	300	240	270	(30)	—	30	(60)	—	—
Entertainment	500	495	180	315	—	20	50	(55)	300
Total	5,400	5,445	2,970	2,475	1,000	330	290	(245)	1,100
ADVERTISING AND SALES PROMOTION	10,000	10,000	6,000	4,000	3,333	667	—	—	—
WAREHOUSING AND STORAGE									
Hourly Labor	300	306	270	36	—	30	—	6	—
Supplies	20	36	18	18	—	2	—	16	—
Power	10	9	9	—	—	1	—	(1)	—
Truck Expense	20	18	18	—	—	2	—	(2)	—
Depreciation	300	300	180	120	100	20	—	—	—
Total	650	669	495	174	100	55	—	19	—
TOTAL TERRITORIAL DISTRIBUTION COST	$16,050	$ 16,114	$9,465	$6,649	$4,433	$1,052	$290	$(226)	$1,100

OTHER DATA	Units	Dollars
Actual Monthly Sales	180,000	$ 90,000
Budgeted Monthly Sales	200,000	100,000
Average Budgeted Monthly Sales	300,000	150,000

Fig. 67—Analysis of Distribution Costs vs. Standard.

commentary for the sales manager is shown in Fig. 67. Explanations of the budgeted and standard cost and variances are detailed by account.

Salesmen's Salaries. The expected salaries for the sales crew for one year is $36,000, or $3,000 per month, and the budget allowance is made on this basis. Budgeted annual sales are $1,800,000, so that salaries are 2% of sales used to develop the standard cost. The standard cost for the illustrated monthly sales is therefore 2% of $90,000, or $1,800.

Since the budgeted sales are only $100,000, or 66⅔% of the average monthly sales of $150,000, it is reasonable to relate 33⅓% of the fixed salary cost to sales for other periods. Hence, $1,000 of the excess cost is attributable to the seasonal factor (33⅓% × $3,000 = $1,000).

Actual sales were $10,000 under budget ($100,000 − $90,000). The share of excess cost due to failure to achieve planned sales volume is $200, or the "lost" sales times the standard cost rate ($10,000 × 2%).

Inasmuch as functional units of service were not used in measuring this cost, there are no further variances.

Traveling Expense. The planned calls for this month required 160 man-days on the road at a standard cost of $10 per day. The budget was set on this basis.

The standard rate for traveling expense was based on 120 man-days at $10 to produce $150,000 of sales, or the equivalent of .8% of sales. The standard expense shown in Fig. 67, therefore, represents $90,000 × .8%, or $720.

Traveling expense is not very fixed and is not considered applicable to future periods. Therefore, no variance appears in column E.

The volume loss again represents the amount of sales under budget multiplied by the standard rate, or $80 ($10,000 × .8%).

While 160 man-days of travel were planned, actually 190 were taken. Excess usage therefore cost $300 (190 − 160 × $10 per day = $300).

However, the actual cost was only $9 per day. Therefore, a savings of $190 was realized because of efficient spending ($1 × 190 man-days).

Finally, the actual and planned performance must be related to the standard to account for all variance:

Planned travel over standard (160 − 120 = 40 excess at $10 per day) $400
Planned sales volume under standard
   ($150,000 − $100,000 = $50,000 × .8%)   400
                                                                    ——
Total variation due to manner of application $800
                                                                    ════

Automobile Expense. It was expected that 10,000 miles would be traveled during the month. At the standard rate of $.03 per mile, a budget of $300 resulted.

Normal experience resulted in establishing a standard of .3% of sales, based on 15,000 miles of travel (cost $450) to produce $150,000 of sales. The standard expense for the actual sales volume for the month was therefore .3% of $90,000, or $270.

Again, the cost of insufficient sales volume resulted in excess automobile expense of $30 ($10,000 at .3%).

During the month only 8,000 miles were traveled, with a resulting savings of $60 (10,000 − 8,000 = 2,000 miles × $.03 = $60).

Expenses were kept within the standard rate per mile and no rate variance was experienced.

Once more there were seasonal and similar factors to consider, each of which canceled the other costwise:

Planned mileage under standard mileage (15,000 − 10,000 × $.03) resulted in a gain of	$(150)
Planned sales were under average with resulting higher cost ($150,000 − $100,000 × .3%)	150
Net difference	$ 0

Entertainment Expense. This expense application is based on number of customers to be entertained, at a standard rate of $5 each. The principle is the same as for traveling expense, and therefore need not be discussed.

Advertising and Sales Promotion Expense. This expense is handled on an appropriation basis. Since it is fixed in nature, the accounting treatment is similar to salesmen's salaries.

Warehousing and Storage. All warehousing and storage expense except depreciation is handled strictly on a weight basis. Hourly labor expense will illustrate the determination of variances.

It was planned to handle 200,000 pounds at $.15 per cwt. so that a budget of $300 was set. However, only 180,000 pounds were handled with the resulting standard cost of $270. The deficiency in pounds (a volume variance) amounted to $30 (20,000 pounds at $.15 per cwt.). The only other excess cost can be attributed to excess spending ($306 − $300).

Some question may be raised as to whether this type of operation should be allowed a budget on planned shipments, or only on actual materials handled. This treatment can vary, according to circumstances. In this instance it is assumed the union contract did not permit layoffs sufficient to offset the reduction in work load.

Depreciation is a fixed expense and is handled in principle the same as salaries. Since it is not controllable by the branch manager, the budget allowance always equals actual.

15

Control of Manufacturing Costs—Direct Material and Direct Labor

GENERAL ASPECTS OF MANUFACTURING COSTS

PROBLEMS OF THE MANUFACTURING EXECUTIVE

To those unfamiliar with production methods, it might seem that once the determination is made as to the product or products to be sold and the quantities required, then the remaining task is simple: proceed to manufacture the articles. As compared with the selling task, it is true that many more of the elements are subject to the control of the executive, that the psychological factors may be less pronounced, and that the variables are fewer. But the job is by no means easy, and many problems constantly plague those responsible for economically manufacturing the product. The controller must gain a clear understanding of these problems if he is to provide adequate information for effective control. While the scale of operations and the type of organization influence the problems, they may be classified generally into the following groups:

1. Physical Property
   a. Selection and layout of buildings, machinery, and equipment
   b. Maintenance of equipment and facilities

2. Planning
   a. Product design
   b. Development and selection of technical processes
   c. Methods and standards development
   d. Planning and scheduling of production operations

3. Production
    a. Employment, training, and control of labor
    b. Selection, handling, and routing of materials
    c. General direction of production operations, and coordination with other departments
    d. Inspection of product
    e. Control of manufacturing costs

OBJECTIVES OF MANUFACTURING COST ACCOUNTING

The relationship between these production management problems and the work of the controller will be clarified by defining the purposes of manufacturing cost accounting and the necessary cost analysis that is a part of the process. The objective must be defined if a practical technique is to be developed and effectively utilized. While the purposes may vary as to importance in different organizations, they may be summarized as follows:

1. For control of costs
2. For planning
3. For price setting
4. For inventory valuation

Control of costs is a primary use of manufacturing cost accounting and analysis. This involves a segregation of material costs, labor costs, and manufacturing expenses by responsibility and the measurement of these costs against predetermined standards. For example, the actual direct labor hours consumed in the assembly of an airplane wing may be compared with what the man-hours should have been, and corrective action taken, if in order.

Closely related to cost control is the use of cost data for effective planning. Some of the same information used for cost control purposes can be applied in a different manner for the planning of manufacturing operations. Thus the standards used for control of manufacturing expenses can be used to plan these expenses for a future period, perhaps with adjustments to reflect past experience as to costs in excess of standard. Cost analysis can be utilized, as a part of the planning process, to determine the probable effect of different courses of action—a comparison of costs to manufacture with the cost to buy a cog wheel, for example. The use of costs in planning would, of course, extend beyond the manufacturing operations.

A third purpose is for establishing selling prices. As previously stated, while the cost to manufacture and sell is not the sole factor in setting prices, it is an important consideration indeed. Intelligent sales and pricing policies require all the facts as to costs.

Finally, manufacturing cost accounting is necessary to calculate the value of inventories, which is a prerequisite to an accurate determination of the cost of goods sold in the statement of income and expense. It should be stated, however, that the techniques for this purpose alone would not be as detailed or refined as those which are essential for the control or planning objectives of cost accounting.

THE CONTROLLER AND MANUFACTURING MANAGEMENT PROBLEMS

For the chief production executive, as for the chief sales executive, the controller is the fact-finder as to costs. It is his responsibility to see that factory management is furnished with sufficient cost information to effect proper control and planning. This requires not only that prompt and accurate information be made available but also that the facts be interpreted. Merely to present the facts is not enough, because the ordinary production executive is not, and should not be expected to be, aware of all the ramifications of cost information before it is thoroughly explained to him. The controller is faced with the job of educating the factory operating staff as to the use and limitations of cost figures. In doing this, he will find it advisable to "sell" them a sound cost philosophy. These comments apply at every level of supervisory responsibility; and the chief accounting officer should make certain that the necessary degree of understanding and cooperation exists between his staff and their counterparts in the operating departments if he is to be fully effective.

To carry out this responsibility to the production executives, the controller must assure himself that adequate procedures exist within his own organization for the collection or recording of the basic information. Also, he must be alert to make provisions for additional or alternative cost information as the needs of the factory executives change. And change they will. In fact, the controller can be a force in this change by calling the attention of the production staff to out-of-line conditions. As certain operations become "on-standard," emphasis will switch to areas where further improvement can be made.

Some specific examples of cost information the accountant can secure and interpret for the production staff will illustrate how he is the fact-finder:

Comparison of actual and standard man-hours or labor costs
Comparison of budgeted and actual manufacturing expense
Comparison of actual and standard material costs
Comparative cost of different manufacturing processes
Maintenance cost of different pieces of equipment (for assistance in determining when to purchase new machines)
Standard man-hours required for anticipated production schedule

In order to best serve the production staff, the controller must build up a strong and efficient organization which is aware of the production viewpoint. It has been demonstrated too many times that if the accountants do not or cannot furnish essential information with sufficient promptness, then the production staff will soon begin to rely on its own engineers. Such a development is not in the best interests of most business firms for several reasons. To begin with, many engineers simply have not been exposed to cost data sufficiently to be aware of the significance of cost factors, and decisions founded on *some* of the facts may result. Secondly, in most instances these same engineers have other work which they might be doing to better utilize their abilities and from which the company could derive more benefit. This is intended in no way to belittle the work of the engineer, but it does recognize the specialization in each of the two fields. Generally speaking, many of the special cost investigations require the joint effort of both engineer and accountant, and each must shoulder his full responsibility. Finally, such a development often leads to several sources of information, rather than one central source. This becomes confusing when several sets of so-called facts are presented, as is often the case under these circumstances.

TYPES OF MANUFACTURING COST ANALYSIS

The question will arise often as to what type of cost data should be presented. Just how should production costs be analyzed? This will depend, of course, on the purpose for which the costs are to be used, as well as the cost experience of those who use the information.

Unit costs or total costs may be accumulated in an infinite variety of ways. The primary segregation may be by any one of the following:

Product or class of product	Process
Operation	Customer order
Department	Worker responsible
Machine or machine center	Cost element

Each of the primary segregations may be subdivided a number of ways. For example, the out-of-pocket costs may be separated from the continuing costs, those which would be incurred whether or not a particular order or run was made. Again, production costs might be segregated between those which are direct or indirect; that is, those which are attributable directly to the operation and those which are prorated. Thus the material used to fashion a cup might be direct, while the power used to operate the press would be indirect. Sometimes the analysis of costs will differentiate between those which vary with production volume and those which are constant within the range of production usually experienced. For example, the direct labor consumed may relate directly to volume while depreciation remains unchanged. The controller must use his judgment and experience in deciding what type of analysis is necessary to present the essential facts.

THE MANUFACTURING COST ACCOUNTING PLAN

EVOLUTION OF THE PLAN

One of the primary duties of the controller is to develop a cost system or accounting plan which will serve the needs of the business with a minimum of expense. The needs of the business involve a variety of interests. First, the requirements of management itself as to control and planning information must be known or anticipated. This is sometimes difficult to determine, for management often does not know what it will need or what is available. Hence the controller must exercise his best judgment. Another consideration is the requirements of internal control so as to prevent the loss of property through fraud or plain error. Again, the taxing authorities and other governmental agencies have certain requirements to be complied with. Finally, the nature of the product or processes is an important factor in the development of the manufacturing cost accounting plan.

TYPES OF COST SYSTEMS

Experience in cost determination in the various industries has given rise to cost systems which are characteristic of the kind of manufacturing activity. Thus, for the assembly or fabrication type of operation the job order type of cost system has been developed, and costs are secured for each separate job or order. For the process industries, exemplified by flour milling or oil refining, the process cost system, which determines the total cost by department, has been developed. The cost per unit of production is simply the departmental cost for the period divided by the units processed through the department. Such accounting is predicated on the thesis that the average cost is representative or typical. The controller is presumed to be familiar with each of these systems.

In many plants both types of costing may be found. For example, in a steel mill the process system may be applied to the direct production departments. Maintenance costs, in contrast, may be handled on a job order basis. Each system has several possible modifications.

Superimposed on either a job order or process cost system may be either an actual cost or standard cost method of accounting.

FACTORY ACCOUNTS AND GENERAL ACCOUNTS

A subject closely allied to the selection or operation of the manufacturing cost accounting system is the relationship of the factory cost accounts to the general accounts. The question arises as to whether the factory cost accounts should be coordinated with or tied into the general accounts. A decision on this matter has an important bearing on the accuracy of the monthly profit and loss statements and balance sheets. Modern management expects financial reports which are reasonably accurate and free of the possibility of major and unexpected year-end adjustments. The mere coordination of the general books and the factory accounts is no absolute assurance that the statements are accurate. But it does provide additional controls and reduces the chance of error. Generally such integration provides that disbursements related to production are accounted for as inventory values or losses in manufacture. Usually such a condition also results in more accurate costs which tend to produce better and more informative financial statements. This becomes increasingly true as the operations of the business become larger and more complex.

When the factory and general accounts are not coordinated, several methods may be used in preparing statements. All expenditures for material used and labor and overhead costs are often charged to a work-in-progress account. The cost of sales is determined by relieving inventory with the estimated product cost. The verification of the inventory is accomplished with an annual physical inventory. Another alternative is to take a physical inventory monthly and charge off any inventory differences to cost of sales. Such a procedure, of course, requires care in making the cutoff as to recorded liabilities. It is entirely possible to secure acceptable statements under such conditions, particularly if the procedure is carried out by someone familiar with the factory operations and sound accounting practice. By and large, however, it is desirable to integrate the factory and general accounts.

MATERIAL COSTS—ACCOUNTING AND CONTROL

SCOPE OF MATERIAL CONTROL

Direct material, as the term is used by cost accountants, refers to material which can be definitely or specifically charged to a particular product, process, or job, and which becomes a component part of the finished product. The definition must be applied in a practical way, for if the material cannot be conveniently charged as direct or if it is an insignificant item of cost, then it would probably be classified as *indirect* material and allocated with other manufacturing expenses to the product on some logical basis. While this section deals primarily with direct material, certain of the control phases relate also to indirect material.

In its broadest phase, material control is simply the providing of the required quantity and quality of material at the required time and place in the manufacturing process. By implication, the material secured must not be excessive in amount, and it must be fully accounted for and used as intended. Thus, it is evident that the extent of material control is broad and should cover many phases or areas of control, such as plans and specifications; purchasing; receiving and handling; inventories; usage; and scrap, waste, and salvage. In each of these phases of control, the controller has certain responsibilities and can make contributions toward an efficient operation.

NEED FOR MATERIAL ACCOUNTING AND CONTROL

Because material is such a large cost item in most manufacturing concerns, effective utilization is an important factor in the financial success or failure of the business. Proper accounting for and control of materials have the following advantages:

1. Reduce inefficient use or waste of materials
2. Reduce or prevent production delays by reason of lack of materials
3. Reduce the risk from theft or fraud
4. Reduce the investment in inventories
5. May reduce the required investment in storage facilities
6. Provide more accurate interim financial statements
7. Assist buyers through a better coordinated buying program

BASIC APPROACH TO MATERIAL COST CONTROL

With respect to materials, as with other costs, control in its simplest form involves the comparison of actual performance with a measuring stick—standard performance—and the prompt follow-up of adverse trends. However, it is not simply a matter of saying "350 yards of material were used, and the standard quantity is only 325," or "The standard price is $10.25 but the actual cost to the company was $13.60 each." Many other refinements or applications are involved. The standards must be reviewed and better methods found. Or checks and controls must be exercised before the cost is incurred. The central theme, however, is still the use of a standard as a point of measurement.

While the applications will vary in different concerns, some of the problems or considerations which must be handled by the controller are as follows:

1. Purchasing and Receiving
   a. Establishment and maintenance of internal checks to assure that materials paid for are received and used for the purpose intended.
   b. Audit of purchasing procedures to ascertain that bids are received where applicable.
   c. Comparative studies of prices paid for commodities with industry prices or indexes.

    d. Measurement of price trends on raw materials.

    e. Determination of price variance on current purchases through comparison of actual and standard costs. This may relate to actual purchases at time of receipt. The same approach may be used in a review of current purchase orders to advise management in advance as to effect on standard costs.

    f. Preparation of standard quantities to buy, based on production program. This may be a tabulating run, or simple manual extensions of needs.

2. Usage

    a. Comparison of actual and standard quantities used in production

    b. Preparation of standard cost formulas (to emphasize major cost items, and as part of a cost reduction program)

    c. Preparation of reports on spoilage, scrap, and waste as compared with standard

    d. Calculation of costs to make vs. costs to buy

This list only suggests some of the methods available to the controller in dealing with material cost control.

SETTING MATERIAL QUANTITY STANDARDS

Because an important phase of material control is the comparison of actual usage with standard, the controller is interested in the method of setting these quantitative standards. In the first place, he can render assistance by contributing information as to past experience. Second, he should act as a check in seeing that the standards are not so loose as to bury poor performance on the one hand, and that they represent realistic but attainable performance, on the other.

Standards of material usage may be established by at least three procedures:

1. By engineering studies to determine the best kind and quality of material, taking into account the product design requirements and production methods

2. By an analysis of past experience for the same or similar operations

3. By making test runs under controlled conditions

While a combination of these methods may be used, best practice usually dictates that engineering studies be made. To the theoretical loss must be added a provision for those other unavoidable losses which it is impractical to eliminate. In this decision, past experience will play a part. Past performance alone, of course, is not desirable in that certain known wastes may be perpetuated. This engineering study, combined with a few test runs, should give fairly reliable standards.

REVISION OF MATERIAL QUANTITY STANDARDS

Standards are based on certain production methods and product specifications. It would be expected, therefore, that these standards should be modified as these other factors change, if such changes affect material usage. For the measuring stick to be an effective control tool, it must relate to the function being measured. However, the adjustment need not be carried through as a change in inventory value, unless it is significant.

USING THE QUANTITY STANDARDS FOR COST CONTROL

The *sine qua non* of material quantity control is to know in advance how much material should be used on the job, frequently to secure information as to how actual performance compares with standard during the progress of the work, and to take corrective action where necessary. The supervisor responsible for the use of materials, as well as his superior, should be aware of these facts. At the lowest supervisory level, details of each operation and process should be in the hands of those who can control usage. At higher levels, of course, only over-all results need be known.

The method to be used in comparing the actual and standard usage will differ in each company, depending on a number of conditions. Some of the more important factors which will influence the controller in applying control procedures as to material usage are:

1. The production method in use
2. The type and value of the materials
3. The degree to which cost reports are utilized by management for cost control purposes

One of the most important considerations is the nature of the production process. In a job order or lot system, such as an assembly operation in an aircraft plant, where a definite quantity is to be produced, the procedure is quite simple. A production order is issued, and a bill of material or "standard requisition" states the exact quantity of material needed to complete the order. If parts are spoiled or lost, it then becomes necessary to secure replacements by means of a non-standard or excess usage requisition. Usually the foreman must approve this request, and consequently the excess usage can be identified immediately. A special color (red) requisition may be used, and a summary report issued at certain intervals for the use of the production executives responsible.

If production is on a continuous process basis, then periodically a comparison can be made of material used in relation to the finished product. Corrective action may not be as quick here, but measures can be taken to avoid future losses.

Just as the production process is a vital factor in determining the cost accounting plan, so also it is a consideration in the method of detecting material losses. If losses are to be localized, then inspections must be made at selected points in the process of manufacture. At these various stations, the rejected material can be counted or weighed, and costed if necessary. When there are several distinct steps in the manufacturing process, the controller may have to persuade the production group of the need and desirability of establishing count stations for control purposes. Once these stations are established, the chief contribution of the accountant is to summarize and report the losses over standard.

Another obvious factor in the method of reporting material usage is the type and value of the item itself. A cardinal principle in cost control is to place primary emphasis on high-value items. Hence, valuable airplane motors, for example, would be identified by serial number and otherwise accurately accounted for. Items with less unit value, or not readily segregated, might be controlled through less accurate periodic reporting. An example might be lumber. The nature and value of the materials determine whether the *time* factor or the *unit* factor would be predominant in usage reporting.

Management is often not directly interested in *dollar cost* for control purposes, but rather only in *units*. There is no difference in the principle involved, but merely in the application. Under these conditions, the controller should see that management is informed of losses in terms of physical units—something it understands. In this case, the cost report would be merely a summary of the losses. Experience will often show, however, that as the controller gives an accounting in dollars, the other members of management will become more cost-conscious.

The essence of any control program, regardless of the method of reporting, however, is to follow up on substandard performance and take corrective action.

LIMITED USEFULNESS OF MATERIAL PRICE STANDARDS

In comparing actual and standard material costs, the use of price standards permits the segregation of variances arising from excess usage from those incurred by reason of price changes. By and large, however, the material price standards used for inventory valuation cannot be considered as a satisfactory guide in measuring the performance of the purchasing department. Prices of materials are affected by so many factors outside of the business that the standards represent merely a measure of what prices are being paid as compared with what was expected to be paid.

A review of price variances may, however, reveal some informative data. Exceedingly high prices may reveal special purchases for quick delivery because someone had not properly scheduled purchases. Or higher prices may reveal shipment via express when freight shipments would have been satisfactory. To generalize, the exact cause for any price variance must be ascertained before valid conclusions can be drawn. Some companies have found it advisable to establish two standards—one for inventory valuation and quite another to be used by the purchasing department as a goal to be attained.

SETTING MATERIAL PRICE STANDARDS

Practice varies somewhat as to responsibility for setting price standards. Sometimes the cost department assumes this responsibility on the basis of a review of past prices. In other cases, the purchasing staff gives its estimate of expected prices, which is subject to a thorough and analytical check by the accounting staff. Probably the most satisfactory setup is through the combined effort of these two departments.

OTHER APPLICATIONS OF MATERIAL CONTROL

By using a little imagination, every controller will be able to devise simple reports which will be of great value in material control—whether in merely making production men aware of the high-cost items of the product, or in stimulating a program of cost reduction. For example, in a chemical processing plant, a simple report detailing the material components cost of a formulation could be used to advantage. Another report is illustrated in Fig. 68, wherein the standard material cost of an assembly-type operation, in this case a missile, is given.

Where the products are quite costly, and relatively few in number, it may be found useful to provide management periodically with the changes in standard prices, as well as an indication as to the effect of price changes on the standard cost of the product. Such statements may stimulate thinking as to material substitutions, or changes in processes or specifications.

LABOR COSTS—ACCOUNTING AND CONTROL

LABOR ACCOUNTING UNDER PRIVATE ENTERPRISE

Under our modern industrial economy, one of the most important factors in the success of a business is the maintenance of a satisfactory relationship between management and employees. The controller and his staff can do much to encourage and promote such a relationship, whether it is such a simple matter as seeing that the payroll checks are ready on time or whether it extends to the development of a wage system which rewards meritorious performance.

Aside from this fact, labor accounting and control are assuming more importance. Labor costs have generally increased; the share of the sales dollar which is received by employees for wages has grown. Likewise, those costs which are usually closely related to labor costs have grown by

The Missile Manufacturing Company

STATEMENT ON UNIT STANDARD MATERIAL COSTS

For the Month of June, 1962

Description	Standard Cost 5/31/62	Changes		Standard Cost 6/30/62	Remarks
		Increases	Decreases		
Power Unit	$ 820.00	$30.00	$ —	$ 850.00	Price increased by manufacturer
Raw Stock Aluminum	277.40	—	—	277.40	
Fabric	142.60	—	—	142.60	
Paint	127.54	—	22.54	105.00	Installation of electric equipment
Steel Tubing	117.50	—	—	117.50	
Stabilizer	106.22	—	—	106.22	
Instruments	93.14	—	1.14	92.00	New altimeter
Hardware	92.20	—	—	92.20	
Radio Equipment	91.20	—	—	91.20	
Exhaust Stock	34.17	—	—	34.17	
Steel Small Parts	76.16	—	—	76.16	
Synthetic Small Parts	14.20	—	—	14.20	
Plastic	19.06	—	.06	19.00	
Rubber	12.00	—	—	12.00	
Aluminum Forging	32.14	—	2.00	30.14	Substitute "R" forging
Raw Stock Steel	43.15	—	—	43.15	
Directional Control Component	39.15	—	—	39.15	
Battery	18.00	—	—	18.00	
Cushion	14.70	—	—	14.70	
Miscellaneous Trim Parts	22.13	—	—	22.13	
Total	$2,192.66	$30.00	$25.74	$2,196.92	

Fig. 68—Detail of, and Changes in, Standard Material Costs.

leaps and bounds—costs for longer vacations, more adequate health and welfare plans, pension plans, increased Social Security taxes. For all these reasons, the cost of labor is more significant.

The objectives of labor accounting may be outlined as follows:

1. A prompt and accurate determination of the amount of wages due the employee
2. The analysis and determination of labor costs in such a manner as may be needed by management; e.g., by product, operation, department, or category of labor
3. The segregation for control purposes of favorable or unfavorable conditions or trends and developments in labor efficiency

CLASSIFICATION OF LABOR COSTS

With the increasing trends to automation, to continuous process type of manufacturing, and to integrated machine operations under which individual hand operations are replaced, the traditional accounting definition of *direct labor* must be modernized. As a practical matter, where labor is charged to a cost center and is directly related to the main function of that center, whether it is direct or indirect labor is of no consequence. Rather, attention must be directed to *labor* costs. Perhaps the primary considerations are measurability and materiality rather than physical association with the product. For planning and control purposes, then, any factory wages or salaries which are identifiable with a directly productive department as contrasted with a service department, and are of significance in that department, are defined as manufacturing labor.

All other labor will be defined as indirect labor, treated as overhead expense, and discussed under manufacturing expenses.

WHAT DOES LABOR COST CONTROL INVOLVE?

Perhaps the fundamental basis for effective labor control is the development and retention of a cooperative attitude between labor and management. Certainly, cost control must be founded on human engineering of this type. From an accounting viewpoint, however, labor control revolves about the measurement of actual performance against a suitable yardstick or standard, and the follow-up of reasons for departure from this standard. Success of the project depends on an adequate wage system, and effective qualitative and quantitative standards.

THE CONTROLLER'S CONTRIBUTION TO CONTROL

In controlling direct labor costs, as with most manufacturing costs, the ultimate responsibility must rest with the line supervision. Yet this group must be given assistance in measuring performance, and certain other policing or restraining functions must be exercised. Herein lie the primary duties of the controller's organization. Among the means at the disposal of the chief accounting executive for his part in labor control are the following:

1. Institute procedures to limit the number of employees placed on the payroll to that called for by the production plan
2. Provide preplanning information for use in determining standard labor crews by calculating required standard man-hours for the production program
3. Report hourly, daily, or weekly standard and actual labor performance
4. Institute procedures for accurate distribution of actual labor costs, including significant labor classifications to provide informative labor cost analyses
5. Provide data on past experience with respect to the establishment of standards
6. Keep adequate records on labor standards and be on the alert for necessary revisions
7. Furnish other supplementary labor data reports, such as:
   a. Hours and cost of overtime premium, for control of overtime
   b. Cost of call-in pay for time not worked, to measure efficiency of those responsible for call-in by union seniority
   c. Comparative contract costs, i.e., old and new union contracts
   d. Average hours worked per week, average take-home pay, and similar data for labor negotiations
   e. Detailed analysis of labor costs over or under standard
   f. Statistical data on labor turnover, length of service, training costs
   g. Union time—cost of time spent on union business

SETTING LABOR PERFORMANCE STANDARDS

The improvement of labor performance and the parallel reduction and control of costs require labor standards—operating time standards and the related cost standards. Setting labor performance standards is a highly analytical job which requires a technical background of the production processes as well as a knowledge of time study methods. This may be the responsibility of a standards department, industrial engineering department, or cost control department. Occasionally, though rarely, it is under the jurisdiction of the controller. Establishment of the standard operation time requires a determination of the time needed to complete each operation when working under standard conditions. Hence, this study embodies working conditions, including the material control plan, the production planning and scheduling procedure, and layout of equipment and facilities. After all these factors are considered, a standard can be set by the engineers.

An example will serve to illustrate how the industrial engineers or standards men coordinate their work with that of the accountant. Assume that in the grinding system of a powder plant, the industrial engineers establish the following requirements through time study:

Required Crew per Shift:
1 Drum Dumper
2 Mill Operators
1 Packer
½ Handler

Makeup of Operating Hours:

Actual processing	6.5
Cleaning	.5
Maintenance, conflict, etc.	1.0
Total	8.0

Lbs. to be handled per shift (8 hours) — 1,600

Lbs. per man-hour (standard) $\left(\dfrac{1,600}{4\frac{1}{2} \times 8}\right)$ — 44.4

Upon receipt of the information and after review by the accounting staff, the standard labor cost would be calculated (on standard cost sheets):

Operator	No.	Man-Hours	Rate per Man-Hour	Total Cost
First Shift				
Drum Dumper	1	8	$1.60	$ 12.80
Mill Operators	2	16	1.75	28.00
Packer	1	8	1.50	12.00
Handler	½	4	1.40	5.60
Second—Third Shifts				
Drum Dumper	2	16	1.65	26.40
Mill Operator	4	32	1.80	57.60
Packer	2	16	1.55	24.80
Handler	1	8	1.45	11.60
Total				$178.80
Direct Labor Cost per Cwt. ($178.80 ÷ 48)				$ 3.725

The rates applied are those from the union contract. If the agreement called for premium payments on Sundays as such, for example, this would have to be considered.

REVISION OF LABOR PERFORMANCE STANDARDS

Generally, performance standards are not revised until a change of method or process occurs. Since standards serve as the basis of control, the accounting staff should be on the alert for changes put into effect in the factory but not reported for standard revision. If the revised process requires more time, the production staff will usually make quite certain that their measuring stick is modified. However, if the new process requires less time, it is understandable that the change might not be reported promptly. Each supervisor naturally desires to make the best possible showing. The prompt reporting of time reductions might be stimulated through periodic review of changes in standard labor hours or costs. In other words, the

Johnson Manufacturing Company

WEEKLY LABOR REPORT

Week Ended December 28, 1962

Department	Units Reported (a)	Actual Hours	Standard Hours	(Over) or Under Standard	MAN–HOURS (Over) or Under Standard Due to			
					Training	Lack of Material	Machine Breakdown	Low Production
25 Stamping (b)............	16,320	153	194	41	–	–	–	41
26 Foundry (b).............	4,390	56	103	47	–	–	–	47
27 Paint...................	12,800	30	25	(5)	–	–	(5)	–
41 Subassembly A..........	18,920	366	384	18	(5)	(2)	–	25
42 Final Assembly..........	17,777	106	120	14	–	(6)	–	20
44 Receiving and Shipping..	44,310	323	271	(52)	(16)	–	–	(36)
Total.........		1,034	1,097	63	(21)	(8)	(5)	97
Per Cent (Over) or Under Standard...............				5.7	(1.9)	(.7)	(.5)	8.8

NOTES (a) Equivalent units per 6/12/62 letter.
(b) Standards for Departments 25 and 26 are in process of review.

Distribution: J.R.M.
J.A.M. (2)
L.L.B. (6)
R.E.H.
File

Issued by Cost Department— January 2, 1963.

Fig. 69—Weekly Labor Report.

current labor performance of actual hours compared to standard should be but one measure of performance; another is standard time reductions, also measured against a goal for the year.

It should be the responsibility of the controller to see that the standards are changed as the process changes in order to report true performance. If a wage incentive system is related to these standards, the need of adjusting for process changes is emphasized. An analysis of variances, whether favorable or unfavorable, will often serve to indicate revisions not yet reported.

While standard revisions will often be made for control purposes, it may not be practical or desirable to change product cost standards. The differences may be treated as cost variances until they are of sufficient magnitude to warrant a cost revision.

OPERATING UNDER PERFORMANCE STANDARDS

Effective labor control through the use of standards requires *frequent* reporting of actual and standard performance. Furthermore, the variance report must be by *responsibility*. For this reason the report on performance is prepared for each foreman as well as the plant superintendent. The report may or may not be expressed in terms of dollars. It may compare man-hours or units of production instead of monetary units. But it does compare actual and standard performance.

Some operations lend themselves to daily reporting. Through the use of tabulating equipment or other means, daily production may be evaluated and promptly reported upon. A simple form of daily report, available to the plant superintendent by 10.00 A.M. for the preceding day's operations, is shown as follows:

————— PLANT
DAILY LABOR REPORT
(Date)
For Day Ending at 4:00 P.M. on —————

	Department	Man-Hours		% Standard to Actual
		Actual	Standard	
51	Fabricating	2,322	2,360	101.6
52	Subassembly	1,846	1,821	98.6
53	Painting	492	500	101.6
54	Assembly	3,960	4,110	103.8
55	Polishing	2,120	2,060	97.2
56	Packing	970	1,320	136.1
	Total	11,710	12,171	103.9

If required, the detail of this summary report can be made available to indicate on what classification and shift the substandard operations were performed. Another report, issued weekly, which details the general reason for excess labor hours is illustrated in Fig. 69.

USE OF LABOR RATE STANDARDS

Generally speaking, labor rates paid by a company are determined by external factors. The rate standard used is usually that normally paid for the job or classification as set by collective bargaining. If standards are set under this policy, no significant variances should develop because of base rates paid. There are, however, some rate variances which may be created and which are controllable by management. Some of these reasons, which should be set out for corrective action, include:

1. Overtime in excess of that provided in the standard
2. Use of higher-rated classifications on the job
3. Failure to place men on incentive
4. Use of crew mixture different from standard (more higher classifications and fewer of the lower)

The application of the standard labor rate to the job poses no great problem. Usually this is performed by the accounting department after securing the rates from the personnel department. Where overtime is contemplated in the standard, it is necessary, of course, to consult with production to determine the probable extent of overtime for the capacity at which the standard is set.

It should be mentioned that the basic design of the product will play a part in control of costs by establishing the skill necessary, and therefore the job classification required, to do the work.

CONTROL THROUGH PREPLANNING

The use of the control tools previously discussed serves to point out labor inefficiencies *after* they have happened. Another type of control requires a determination as to what should happen and makes plans to assure, to the extent possible, that it does happen. It is forward-looking and preventive. This approach, which embodies budgetary control, can be applied to the control of labor costs. For example, if the manpower requirements for the production program one month hence can be determined, then steps can be taken to make certain that excess labor costs do not arise because too many men are on the payroll. This factor can be controlled; thus the remaining factors are rate and quality of production and overtime. Overtime costs can be held within limits through the use of authorization slips.

The degree to which this preplanning can take place depends on the industry and particular conditions within the individual business firm. Are business conditions sufficiently stable so that some reasonably accurate planning can be done? Can the sales department indicate with reasonable accuracy what their requirements will be over the short run? An application might be in a machine shop where thousands of parts are made. If production requirements are known, the standard man-hours necessary can be calculated and converted to manpower. For example, tabulating equipment may be utilized to determine standard man-hours by department. Where experience reveals that standard efficiency cannot be attained, an allowance would be made for the predicted degree of efficiency. Thus, if 12,320 standard man-hours are needed for the planned production, but efficiency of only 80% is expected, then 15,400 actual man-hours must be scheduled. This requires a crew of 385 men (40 hours per week). Steps should then be taken to assure that only this number is authorized on the payroll. Of course, the probable requirements, say one month from now, must be kept in view.

Application of preplanning can be extended to the entire payroll procedure. For example, a work schedule by man can be punched and furnished to the factory. Exceptions to planned attendance can be shown on the schedule, and incorporated into the final tabulating cards for payroll determination.

A SPECIAL LABOR APPLICATION

A method in connection with a punched card accounting system, which may be used in labor control, is known as "mark-sensing." Basic accounting data are placed on tabulating cards by using pencil marks with heavy graphite content. A special reproducing punch converts the marks to punched holes at a high rate of speed with the consequent elimination of manual key punching. Thus in labor accounting, the timekeepers may be provided with prepunched cards as to department, operation, and employee. The cards are then marked for quantity of work or for hours of attendance, as in Figs. 70 and 71. These data may then be converted to punched holes. The prepunched data plus the information "marked" on the card by the timekeeper provide the basic information for issuance of labor control reports and for labor distribution computations.

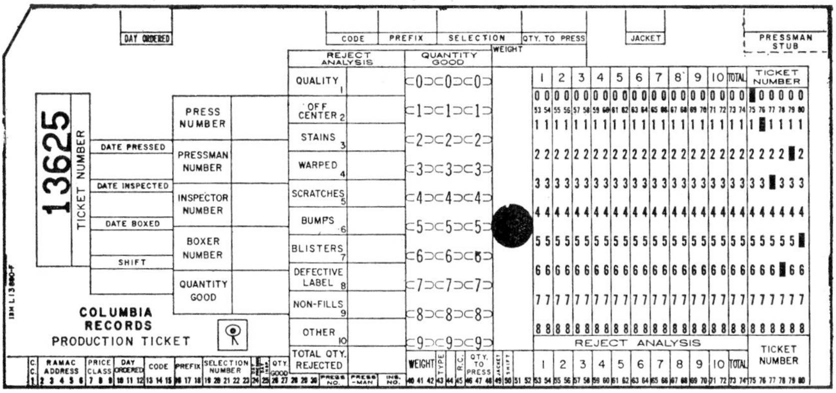

Fig. 70—Production Count Card for "Mark-Sensing" Application.

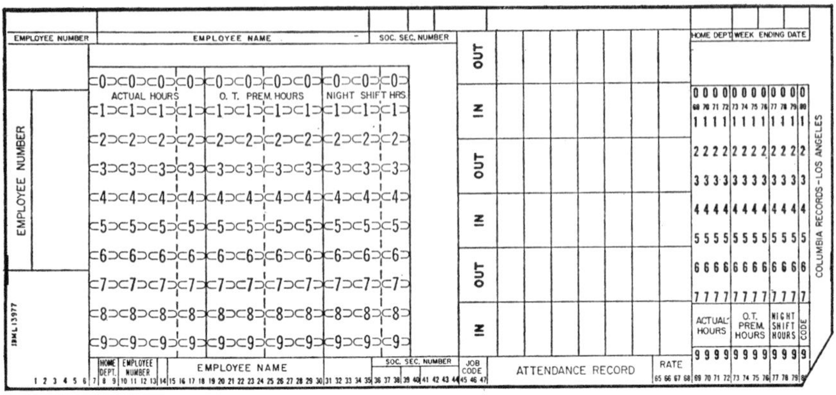

Fig. 71—Attendance Card for "Mark-Sensing" Application.

LABOR ACCOUNTING AND STATUTORY REQUIREMENTS

One of the functions of a controller is to see that the company maintains the various payroll and other records required by the Social Security program, Internal Revenue Service, or other governmental agencies, both federal and state. While it is beyond the scope of this book to delve into all the details, some general comments are believed to be in order.

FEDERAL LAWS DIRECTLY AFFECTING PAYROLLS

Four major federal laws or regulations directly affect payroll accounting:

1. The Fair Labor Standards Act of 1938, usually called the Wage and Hour Law
2. The Federal Insurance Contributions Act, commonly known as the Federal Old Age and Benefits Act
3. The Federal Unemployment Tax Act
4. The U.S. Treasury Department, Internal Revenue Service, Regulation 120, relating to the collection of income tax on wages at the source

Various federal publications and other references are available to explain the details. Information is available elsewhere as to the recording, collection, and other requirements of state laws on the subject. While generalizations can be dangerous, it is believed that compliance with most laws will require three essential records:

1. The payroll register
2. The employees' earnings record
3. The employees' time record

LABOR INCENTIVE PLANS

PURPOSE OF WAGE INCENTIVE PLANS

In all labor relations, perhaps the most important factor is wages. On the one hand, the employee seeks a weekly wage as high as possible without unduly long hours or excessive fatigue. On the other hand, the employer wants to secure unit cost as low as possible. In a competitive economy the provision of satisfactory wage levels for employees and the maintenance of adequate profit margins present a severe challenge to present-day business management. However, wage incentives can play a vital part in realizing both of these objectives.

Before getting involved in the details of incentive plans, it is well to recognize that although incentives can play an important part in controlling costs, they are not a substitute for management. Such plans do not, in themselves, control costs; they are only an aid, if wisely administered.

There are two basic plans of wage payment: (1) payment for *time* worked, and (2) payment for the *amount* of work accomplished. Any others are a combination or offshoot of these. The first, payment according to time worked, is known as the day-work or time-work plan; the second is known as a wage incentive or piecework plan. Although many types of wage incentive plans have been created, all have two chief purposes:

1. To secure the best efforts from the worker in getting more production and yet safeguard the employer against rising unit labor costs
2. To provide for the worker an additional reward for increased productivity

THE CONTROLLER'S RELATIONSHIP TO WAGE INCENTIVE PLANS

The controller of a company is interested in wage incentive plans for several reasons. In the first place, the calculation of the amount of incentive wage usually falls under his supervision. He and those directly involved must be intimately familiar with every aspect of the plan in order to assure that the correct payment is made. Furthermore, the wider the knowledge of incentive systems, the more likely it is that intelligent suggestions for improvements will be made. Any controller with a detailed knowledge of the wage incentive system will probably raise numerous questions bearing on the proper interpretation of the plan.

From a broader viewpoint, the controller should be interested in ways and means of reducing costs; and wage incentive plans can be an important force in this direction. Experience has revealed that incentive systems are one of the most fruitful avenues of securing cooperation between management and labor in reducing waste and meeting or bettering standard performance. The accounting official must watch for evidence that the plan is effective in this cost reduction; that it is working in the way intended and to the extent deemed necessary. Finally, in most organizations the controller should be an adviser or have an important voice in the selection of the wage incentive system to be installed. To carry out this responsibility requires a knowledge of the methods in use or available.

TYPES OF INCENTIVE SYSTEMS

Because the benefits of an incentive system wherein men are rewarded financially for their efforts have been generally recognized, a variety of plans has been developed. Incentive plans have been adopted for general executives, departmental executives, foremen, and salesmen as well as the direct production workers. Incentives for supervisory personnel are discussed on pages 312–13. It is sufficient to state here that supervision has a very important bearing on productivity of the direct workers, and the possibilities of an incentive plan for the supervisory group should not be overlooked.

For application to production workers a great variety of wage incentive plans has been developed—some involving a measurement of the individual worker, and others, where this was not adaptable, concerned with the measurement of a group of workers. Essentially the many plans differ, among other things, in the extent to which the employer and employee share in the savings of labor and overhead costs, the matter of guaranty of earnings, and the method or level in which the incentive changes. In any particular application, of course, the plan to be adopted should be that one which will produce the lowest cost over the long run.

REQUIREMENTS FOR SUCCESSFUL WAGE INCENTIVE OPERATIONS

Just as the ground should be prepared before the seeds are planted, so also the planning and preparation should be complete for the best results from a wage incentive system. Some bonus systems have been fruitful without much of this planning. But a vigorous management often can get results in poor soil so that the results might be achieved not because of the incentive plan itself but because of management. To avoid the pitfalls of inadequate preparation, the practical requirements considered essential for the operation of an incentive system are outlined for the controller who is advising line management.

1. *A wage incentive system should be based upon standards of performance—time and motion studies, job evaluation, and merit rating.* Independent time and motion studies should be made to determine just how long a job should take. This study should include consideration of the working conditions, cover more than one employee, and include several

manufacturing operations. Job evaluation requires the analysis of the job to determine the requirements of those who fill it, and therefore the relative worth in comparison with other jobs in the plant. Merit rating is the determination and classification of differences in individual employees. It can be seen that all three aspects are factors in determining what a worker should be paid. This analytical approach is necessary to avoid the limitation of a man's earnings by some preconceived ideas as to what performance should be, and to avoid continuance of past habits of an inefficient nature.

2. *The incentive plan should be understood by all employees before installation (or hiring).* To secure this understanding it may be desirable to provide all men with a simple written statement as to how the plan works, including examples of how wage earnings are calculated. Also, employees should be encouraged to ask questions about the plan.

3. *All direct labor tasks should be on an incentive basis.* If *all* direct labor operations are not placed on an incentive basis, those omitted from the plan will not be well done. This is a natural consequence if an individual is taken from a job on which he can earn additional wages and placed on one where he knows his increased efforts will bring no additional direct reward.

4. *Only standard or acceptable quality production should be considered in determining the bonus.* The employee should receive credit only for good units produced, in order to focus sufficient attention on quality. To do otherwise would invite material losses in addition to the lost labor and burden from other cost centers.

A corollary of this principle is the necessity for an adequate inspection system, not only as to incoming material but also at various points throughout the process. Incoming raw material must be inspected to prevent labor and overhead losses from work on faulty material, because the workman cannot be penalized for results beyond his control. Also, inspections are necessary throughout the manufacturing process to determine just where losses occur so as to give proper credit to the operations prior to spoilage.

It may be mentioned that some plans give an additional reward for less spoilage than standard, so that quality and quantity of production are emphasized by a separate incentive.

5. *When the standard is once set, it should not be changed unless the method changes.* Employees should not feel that management changes standards merely to reduce their earnings. Changes in the process, or in machinery used, or in materials may make standard revisions necessary. Management, however, must show the employee why changes were made.

6. *The incentive program must be fairly and intelligently administered.* This involves a variety of requirements. Prompt attention must be given to complaints. When unusual matters arise, fair decisions should be made as to the point at issue. A sufficient number of checks must be maintained

throughout to see that the plan is administered correctly for both the company and the employee. The foreman in direct charge must know the plan thoroughly and be able to answer all questions intelligently, and seek advice where necessary. Materials must be kept flowing and counts made without stopping the line. Supervisors and timekeepers must be on the alert to watch and recognize difficulties and take the necessary action. In short, every obstacle which prevents the maximum production as intended under the incentive program must be removed and remain removed.

7. *It is highly desirable that indirect personnel share in the incentive plan.* This practical observation stems from the principle that *all* production operations should be placed on a standard basis, coupled with the fact that the effectiveness of direct labor is often greatly influenced by the performance of indirect labor which assists it. The primary difficulty in applying the principle is that of selecting a basis on which indirect personnel should share. Just how can their performance be measured?

Part of the answer lies in recognizing the threefold character of indirect personnel:

a. Those who "police" the system, such as inspectors and timekeepers, and whose judgment must remain unbiased, and not be influenced adversely in the company's interest. This group cannot participate in a bonus for which they are the judges.

b. Those indirect employees whose work can be directly related to specific direct labor operations. This might include oilers, maintenance mechanics, setup men, material movers, and scrap handlers. These individuals might participate in a bonus related to the effectiveness of the direct labor groups they serve.

c. Those indirect workers who cannot be directly related to a specific direct labor function. The incentive for this group might be based on plant-wide performance and modified by the budget performance of their own group.

As a further general comment relative to inclusion of indirect personnel, it is often observed in practice that the exclusion of this group results in disgruntled employees if all do not have the opportunity to share in the incentive rewards.

8. *A high reward should be paid for performance above standard.* The difference between the standard rate of pay and the incentive rate must be great enough to be a real incentive. Some people advocate that all direct labor savings should go to the employee on the ground that to do otherwise would have him feel the company is benefiting by his extra effort. Under these circumstances, when all direct labor savings inure to the employee, the company gains through reduced unit overhead costs.

9. *Individual incentives should be used wherever it is possible to do so.* Where an employee can measure his own performance, and knows that his

earnings increase through his own productivity, an incentive system can be most effective. There are many instances, such as in continuous chemical processes, where individual performance cannot be measured. Under these circumstances a group bonus plan usually can be applied.

These nine requirements relate immediately and directly to the incentive system. Obviously, other conditions must exist when a wage incentive program is in operation, conditions which are present in any well-run business, whether there is an incentive system or not. These include clear definitions of responsibility and authority, continuous flow of materials, proper organizational structure, sound procedures, good morale, and sound business planning.

In the installation of an incentive plan other problems will arise which cannot be discussed here. But it is obvious that complete coordination must exist so that a management control tool does not become a "management headache." Observation of the fundamentals, coupled with good judgment as to detailed problems that will arise, should permit a reduction in actual unit costs.

The two basic factors in wage payment plans are time and speed. Management is interested in both. Time is important because it may govern the cost of operating machinery as well as influence the compensation to employees. The use of machinery is determined in part by the relative profitability of the various alternatives. Speed, too, is important, but not at the sacrifice of quality. Incentive plans vary in the relative importance of each factor. Several excellent publications are available which describe some of the more common plans.

RELATIONSHIP OF COSTING STANDARDS AND INCENTIVE STANDARDS

When an incentive wage plan is introduced into an operation already on a standard cost basis, a problem arises as to the relationship between the standard level at which incentive earnings commence and the standard level used for costing purposes. Moreover, what effect should the wage incentive plan have on the standard labor cost and standard manufacturing expense of the product? To cite a specific situation, a company may be willing to pay an incentive to labor for performance which is lower than that assumed in the cost standard (but much higher than actual experience). If such a bonus is excluded from the cost standard, the labor cost at the cost standard level will be *understated*. Further, there may be no offsetting savings in manufacturing expense since the costs are incurred to secure performance at a *lower* level than the cost standard. These statements assume, of course, that the existing cost standard represents efficient performance even under incentive conditions. On the other hand, if the effect of the incentive plan is to increase sustained production rates well above those contemplated in the cost standards, it may be that the product will be *overcosted* by using present cost standards, and that these standards are no longer applicable. How should the cost standards be set in relation to the incentive plan?

In reviewing the problem, there are several generalizations which may be made. First, there is no necessary relationship between standards for incentive purposes and standards for costing purposes. The former are intended to stimulate effort while the latter are used to determine what the labor cost of the product should be. One is a problem in personnel management while the other is strictly an accounting problem. With such dissimilar objectives, the levels of performance could logically be quite different.

Then, too, the matter of labor costing for statement purposes should be differentiated from labor control. As we have seen, labor control may involve non-financial terms—pieces per hour, pounds per man-hour, etc. Labor control can be accomplished through the use of quantitative standards. Even if costs are used, the measuring stick for control need not be the same as for product costing. Control is centered on variations from performance standards and not on product cost variations.

A thorough consideration of the problem, the authors believe, results in the conclusion that labor standards for costing purposes should be based on normal expectations from the operation of a wage incentive system under standard operating conditions. The expected earnings under the bonus plan should be reflected in the standard unit cost of the product. It does not necessarily follow that the *product* standard cost will be higher than that used before introduction of the incentive plan. It may mean, however, that the direct labor cost will be higher by reason of bonus payments. Yet, because of increased production and material savings, the *total* unit standard manufacturing cost should be lower.

16

Control of Manufacturing Costs—Expense

MANUFACTURING OVERHEAD—ACCOUNTING AND CONTROL

NATURE OF MANUFACTURING OVERHEAD

Manufacturing overhead has several distinguishing features as compared with direct material or manufacturing labor. It is a collective term encompassing innumerable items of cost. This wide variety of expenses includes depreciation, property taxes, insurance, indirect labor, supplies, repairs, power, water, payroll taxes, and many others. The individual items of cost making up this composite called expense or overhead behave in differing ways as plant activity increases or decreases. Some tend to fluctuate proportionately as business activity changes, while others remain static or fluctuate but not in direct relationship to the change in activity. Finally, control of overhead rests with many individuals in the organization. The maintenance foreman, for example, controls maintenance labor, supplies, and repairs, while the utility foreman controls his supplies, coal, etc. Other costs are controlled at higher levels through decisions by top management—depreciation, insurance, taxes, and supervisory salaries. Control of manufacturing overhead is divided indeed.

In the last few decades, manufacturing overhead has become a relatively more important cost. As the investment in machinery has grown, with a decrease in direct labor, the importance of depreciation expense, power, and similar items has increased.

PROBLEMS OF MANUFACTURING OVERHEAD ACCOUNTING AND CONTROL

The nature of manufacturing overhead raises several major problems of procedure, the solving of which must rest largely on the shoulders of the controller. Decisions must be arrived at because they affect cost control as well as cost determination. Some of these problems involve decisions as to:

1. Method to be used in establishing departments or cost centers for the accumulation of actual costs and a determination of excess costs
2. Methods of allocating costs to products or departments for cost determination
3. Determination of the level of activity to be used in measuring volume costs or establishing standard costs
4. Allocation of manufacturing expense to operating periods

APPROACH IN CONTROL OF MANUFACTURING OVERHEAD

The diverse cost items in overhead and the divided responsibility open the road to many excessive costs. Furthermore, the fact that many cost elements seem to be quite small and insignificant in terms of units of consumption, or cost per unit, often encourages neglect of proper control. Increases in clerical help may be required with business at higher levels, but many times there is a lag or delay in eliminating that help when no longer needed. Other examples include: use of too many pairs of gloves; lights left burning unnecessarily; excessive man-hours for maintenance; long-distance phone calls when telegrams or air-mail letters would have been equally effective; use of high-grade supplies when lower grades would serve the purpose; printing of special forms when standard forms would suffice. All these examples indicate possible sources of waste that must be watched.

Though these factors may complicate somewhat the control of manufacturing overhead, the basic approach to this control is fundamentally the same as that applying to direct costs: the setting of standards, the measurement of actual performance against these standards, and the taking of corrective action when those responsible for meeting standards repeatedly fail to reach the goal. Standards may change at different volume levels; or stated in other terms, they must have sufficient flexibility to adjust to the level of operations under which the supervisor is working. To this extent the setting and application of overhead standards may differ from the procedure used in the control of direct material and direct labor. The degree of refinement and extent of application will vary with the cost involved. The controller should make every attempt to apply fair and meaningful standards. He must not err in thinking that little is needed or that nothing can be accomplished.

DEPARTMENTALIZATION OF OVERHEAD

One of the most essential requirements for either adequate cost control or accurate cost determination is the proper classification of accounts. Control must be exercised at the source, and since costs are controlled by individuals, the primary classification of accounts must be by individual responsibility—"responsibility accounting." This generally requires a breakdown of expenses by factory departments, which may be either productive departments or service departments, such as maintenance, power, or tool crib. Sometimes, however, it becomes necessary to divide the expense classification more finely so as to secure a proper control or costing of products—to determine actual expenses and expense standards by cost center. This decision as to the degree of refinement will depend largely on whether improved product costs result or whether better expense control can be achieved.

A cost center, which is ordinarily the most minute division of costs, is determined on one of the following bases:

1. One or more similar or identical machines
2. The performance of a single operation or group of similar or related operations in the manufacturing process

The separation of operations or functions is essential because a foreman may have more than one type of machine or operation in his department— all of which affect costs. One product may require the use of expensive machinery in a department while another may need only some simple hand operations. The segregation by cost center will reveal this cost difference. Different overhead rates are needed to reflect differences in services or machines required.

FIXED AND VARIABLE EXPENSES

Another important step in the control of manufacturing overhead is the segregation of costs into two groups—fixed or variable. Truly variable costs increase or decrease in direct proportion to the volume of work within the plant. Control is exercised by keeping the expense within the limits determined for the particular level of activity. Fixed costs do not vary with activity, but remain much the same over a relatively short period of time. Control over this type of expense rests largely with general executives who determine policy with respect to plant investment, inventory level, and size of organization. It will be observed that failure to distinguish between these two types of expense can result in failure to control overhead. Why? Because it cannot be determined then whether increased costs result from higher unit fixed costs as a result of lower volume or from failure to keep variable costs within proper bounds.

The segregation of fixed and variable expense permits the adoption of the "flexible budget"—a budget that provides allowances which vary with the activity of the department involved. Contrasted with this flexible budget is the "fixed" budget which is planned for a particular level of activity. Rarely does activity remain at one level, or, indeed, at the level anticipated. Therefore, unless provision is made for the change in activity, the budget can be of little value as a control tool when volume is at another level.

Sometimes a separate classification of manufacturing expenses is recognized—semivariable expenses, which vary with volume of production, but not in direct proportion. To control these expenses two techniques are available. One method is to determine for each semivariable expense in each department just what the cost should be at various operating levels. For example, if the expected range is between 60% and 90% of capacity, costs could be budgeted at every 5% level—65%, 70%, 75%, etc. The budget applicable to the actual volume level would be selected, and interpolated between the 5% range if thought desirable. Then actual costs would be compared periodically with the budget, and corrective action taken.

Another method of applying budgetary control to semivariable expenses is to resolve them into their fixed and variable portions and treat each accordingly. The fixed portion could be considered the necessary expense at the lower level of the expected volume, and the difference between this and the higher level could be treated as variable.

DETERMINING FIXED AND VARIABLE EXPENSE COMPONENTS

With the knowledge that adequate control of manufacturing overhead cannot be successful without the application of a flexible standard which recognizes differences in volume of activity, the next subject is the method or approach. The aim, of course, is to establish total fixed costs by responsibility, plus the variable unit standard cost to be applied to the level of activity reached. If both are known, the total standard cost can be determined. A good starting point is a review of past experience. This review should encompass not only total costs but also various measures of activity. It is necessary to determine how much costs vary, as well as the best tool or factor for measuring activity. To illustrate, past activity may be related to standard direct labor hours, actual direct labor hours, machine hours, units of production, etc.

Another consideration is the degree of refinement necessary. If costs are properly segregated by responsibility, perhaps the review need extend only to total departmental costs and not to individual items of expense. On this basis, a fixed budget of $3,200 per month, and a variable expense allowance of $4.20 per standard labor hour might be established for the fabrication department. Under this approach, the exact way in which the supervisor spends his budgeted cost is a matter for his judgment. In other cases, it may be found desirable to analyze each type of departmental expense. This will often reveal more information about the expense behavior in the department and permit the development of a better budget. All these individual costs can be totaled to arrive at an over-all measuring stick of the department, or they can be applied individually.

Review of past experience must be supplemented by good judgment in applying the data to future periods. Changes in wage rates, material costs, or supervisory staff, for example, must be considered in modifying the data for standard purposes.

A simple analysis of the tabulated data on manufacturing overhead, and a knowledge of operating conditions, will usually permit some immediate conclusions as to whether expenses are fixed or variable. The fixed costs should be classified into those fixed by general management decisions and those currently fixed as a result of decisions by the production executives. Illustrative of the twofold segregation of fixed manufacturing expenses are the following:

1. Fixed by general management decisions
   a. Depreciation on buildings and machinery
   b. Real and personal property taxes on buildings, equipment, and inventories
   c. Insurance—property and liability
   d. Salaries of production executives
   e. Pensions
   f. Patent amortization

2. Fixed by production executive decisions
   a. Salaries of factory supervisory staff
   b. Factory administrative expense
   c. Safety and welfare expenses
   d. Engineering department expense

Costs are classified as fixed, obviously, if the review of the expenses by elements from month to month indicates that about the same amount is incurred. Other expenses are either variable or semivariable. If a division of the total cost of one type by the factor of variability results in about the same unit cost at each level of activity, then the expense can be classified as variable. Typical examples of variable manufacturing expenses are:

Royalties (on units of production)	Power
	Salvage expense
Small tool expense	Testing expense
Transportation tax	Supplies

A large number of expenses will be found to contain both fixed and variable elements—the semivariable costs. Examples are:

Payroll taxes and insurance	Telephone and telegraph expense
Repairs and maintenance expense	Factory office salaries and expense

The illustrative separation of the fixed and variable elements of a manu-facturing expense is shown below. Assumptions for the example are:

1. At a level of 50% of normal capacity, the maintenance department expense is $40,000 per month, while experience shows that at a level of 80% of capacity, the cost is $64,000.
2. The variable factor or measuring stick is standard man-hours of production.
3. At an 80% capacity, the standard man-hours are 160,000.

The variable costs may be considered to be $24,000, and the variable budget allowance $.40 per standard man-hour, calculated as follows:

	Capacity	
% Normal Activity	Standard Man-Hours	Cost
80%	160,000	$64,000.00
50	100,000	40,000.00
Variable	60,000	$24,000.00
Unit Variable Cost ($24,000 ÷ 60,000)		$ .40

On such a budget structure (assuming a portion is to be treated as fixed) the maintenance department allowance for a month of 120,000 standard man-hours of production will be:

Fixed portion	$40,000
Variable ($.40 × 120,000 − 100,000)	8,000
Total	$48,000

It will be observed that the variable allowance is granted only for standard man-hours in excess of what was considered the lowest probable level of activity. However, the entire cost might be treated as variable with the same budget (120,000 × $.40 = $48,000).

GRAPHIC DETERMINATION OF FIXED AND VARIABLE COSTS

The use of only two or a few points to determine the variable expense is of limited value since only a few levels are considered. If more accuracy is desired, another convenient approach is the use of a scatter chart. Assume, for illustrative purposes, that the following data on personnel department costs are available, adjusted for wage differences and similar factors.

Month	Reference	Factory Standard Man-Hours	Total Departmental Costs
January	(1)	20,000	$6,100
February	(2)	16,000	5,300
March	(3)	13,000	4,700
April	(4)	14,000	4,900
May	(5)	17,000	5,200
June	(6)	19,000	6,000
July	(7)	21,000	6,200
August	(8)	23,000	6,300
September	(9)	25,000	6,800
October	(10)	22,000	6,100
November	(11)	18,000	5,900
December	(12)	19,000	5,800

These points are then plotted on a chart as shown in Fig. 72, each point being numbered for reference purposes. The vertical axis represents the dollar costs, while the horizontal axis represents the factor of variability—standard man-hours in the illustration. After the points are plotted, a line

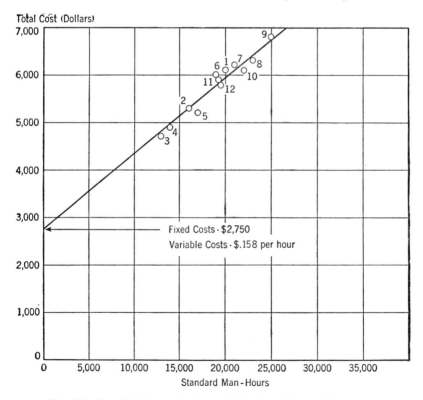

Fig. 72—Graphic Determination of Fixed and Variable Costs.

The General Corporation
HEATER DIVISION
Manufacturing Expense Budget

Department _____ Fabrication
Department Head _____ Ship

Year _____ 1963
Normal Activity _____
Base _____
Standard Labor Hours _____ 85,000

Account	PER CENT OF NORMAL ACTIVITY							
	60%	70%	80%	90%	100% (N.A.)	110%	120%	130%
Salaries								
General Foremen	$ 700	$ 700	$ 700	$ 700	$ 700	$ 700	$ 700	$ 700
Foremen	1,100	1,500	1,900	2,200	2,200	2,200	2,600	2,600
Clerks, etc.	700	700	950	950	950	950	950	1,200
Subtotal	2,500	2,900	3,550	3,850	3,850	3,850	4,250	4,500
Hourly Labor—Indirect	1,500	1,750	2,000	2,250	2,500	2,500	2,750	3,000
Fuel	350	400	430	470	510	530	570	620
Power	2,620	3,020	3,430	3,870	4,300	4,740	5,140	5,320
Water	210	220	230	240	250	260	270	280
Maintenance and Repairs	1,630	1,875	2,050	2,250	2,500	2,790	3,070	3,660
Supplies	270	315	360	405	450	495	540	585
Mule Expense	140	180	190	200	210	230	260	270
Traveling	70	70	100	100	100	100	120	120
Telephone and Telegraph	70	80	90	100	100	100	110	120
Cartons and Containers	150	175	200	225	250	275	300	325
Recreation and Welfare	30	40	50	50	50	60	60	60
Miscellaneous	120	130	150	160	175	190	200	210
Subtotal	9,660	11,155	12,830	14,170	15,245	16,120	17,640	19,070
Depreciation—Building	900	900	900	900	900	900	900	900
Depreciation—Machinery and Equipment	1,800	1,800	1,800	1,800	1,800	1,800	1,800	1,800
Property Taxes	1,200	1,200	1,200	1,200	1,200	1,200	1,200	1,200
Insurance	350	350	400	400	400	400	400	450
Total	$13,910	$15,405	$17,130	$18,470	$19,545	$20,420	$21,940	$23,420

of best fit may be drawn by inspection—drawn in such a manner that about one-half of the points are above it and the other half below. Any highly variant items should be disregarded. For a higher degree of refinement the method of least squares may be used instead of inspection.

The point at which the line of best fit intersects the vertical axis indicates the fixed cost which might be expected if the plant was in an operating condition, but producing nothing. The total cost at any level of activity is determined by reading the chart. For example, at a level of 25,000 standard man-hours, the budgeted expense would be $6,700. This is made up of $2,750 fixed and $3,950 variable elements. The variable rate is $.158 per standard man-hour.

In reviewing the chart it can be seen that the slope of the line indicates the degree of variability. Thus a horizontal line would represent a fixed cost, whereas a line which goes through the point of origin indicates a completely variable cost. Sometimes in constructing a chart the points show no tendency to arrange themselves along a line. If this situation does exist, then either the control of costs has been absent or a poor choice has been made as to the factor of variability. Use of another factor should be tested to ascertain the cause. Incidentally, the chart may be used as a tool in illustrating the degree of success in controlling costs, the extent of accomplishment being measured by the closeness of actual expense to the line of budgeted expense.

ANOTHER TYPE OF FLEXIBLE BUDGET

Some companies have found it convenient in their budgetary control methods not to express the allowance as a fixed amount plus a variable rate per factor of variability. Rather, they prefer to set out the total budget for each level of activity within the probable range. Such a budget presentation is shown in Fig. 73. If proper analysis is made, the step-up nature of certain of the expenses is clearly indicated.

OTHER ASPECTS OF APPLYING BUDGETS

In applying budgetary control in his company, an alert controller will discover means of making the budget more workable in the eyes of those who use it. Some of the modifications or adaptations of the principles are briefly mentioned here.

It is quite natural for the accountant to prepare budgets in terms of value. Sometimes, however, a monetary unit has little significance to production men. In the control of maintenance costs, for example, some plant superintendents think in terms of man-hours. If this is more understandable, the budget can easily be converted to maintenance man-hours per standard labor man-hour, or other factor variability. The budgeted allowances of other expenses may be expressed in units of consumption—kilowatt-hours of power, pounds of steam, dozens of gloves, etc.

One of the purposes of budgetary control is to maintain expenses within the limits of income. To this end, common factors of variability are *standard* labor hours or *standard* machine hours—bases affected by the quantity of approved production. If manufacturing difficulties are encountered, the budget allowance of all departments on such a base would be reduced. The controller might hear many vehement arguments by the maintenance foreman, for example, that he should not be penalized in his budget because production was inefficient; or that plans once set, cannot be changed constantly because production does not come up to expectations. Such a situation may be resolved in one of at least two ways: (1) the forecast standard hours could be used as the basis for the variable allowance, or (2) the maintenance foreman could be informed regularly if production, and therefore the standard budget allowance, will be under that anticipated. The first suggestion departs somewhat from the income-producing source, but does permit a budget allowance within the limits of income and does not require constant changes of labor force over a very short period. The second suggestion makes for more coordination between departments although it injects the element of instability to a slight degree.

Extraordinary or unanticipated expenditures of a manufacturing expense nature must frequently be made. These may fall well without the scope of the usual budget, even when the cumulative yearly condition is considered. In such instances, and if the expenditure is considered necessary and advisable, a special budget allowance may be made over and above the usual budget—something superimposed on the regular flexible budget structure.

Another point should not be overlooked by the accounting staff: the important consideration is not *how* flexibility is introduced into the standard or budget, but rather that it *is* injected. Whether charts or tables are used to determine the allowable budget on a more or less automatic basis or whether the budget is adjusted monthly or quarterly on the basis of special review in relation to business volume is not too essential, because either method can be successfully employed. The major consideration is that of securing an adequate measuring stick which also keeps expenses at the proper level in relation to activity or income.

REVISION OF MANUFACTURING EXPENSE BUDGETS

By and large the expense structure of a company does not change greatly within a year. For this reason, it is practical to review the budgets annually and make necessary revisions. However, if basic organizational changes or changes in processing take place, it is obvious that budgets must be revised with such an occurrence if they are to be effective control tools.

NORMAL ACTIVITY

A significant consideration in the control of manufacturing overhead expense through the analysis of variances is the level of activity selected in setting the standard costs. Furthermore, this factor has an important bearing on product standard costs. It should be obvious that the fixed element of unit product costs is greatly influenced by the total quantity of production assumed. Of equal importance is the necessity of a clear understanding by management of the significance of the level selected, because in large part it determines the "volume" variance.

Generally speaking, there are three levels on which fixed standard manufacturing overhead may be set:

1. The expected sales volume for the year, or other period, when the standards are to be applied
2. Practical plant capacity, representing the volume at which a plant could produce if there were no lack of orders
3. The normal or average sales volume, here defined as normal capacity

Some general comments may be made as to each of these three levels. If expected sales volume is used, all costs are adjusted from year to year. Consequently certain cost comparisons are difficult to make. Furthermore, the resulting statements fail to give management what may be considered the most useful information as to volume costs. Standard costs would be higher in low-volume years, when lower prices might be needed to get more business, and lower in high-volume years, when the increased demand presumably would tend toward higher prices. Another weakness is that the estimate of sales used as a basis would not be too accurate in many cases.

Practical plant capacity as a basis tends to give the lowest cost. This can be misleading because sales volume will not average this level. Generally there will always be large unfavorable variances, the unabsorbed expense.

Normal sales volume or activity has been defined as the utilization of the plant that is necessary to meet the average sales demand over the period of a business cycle, or at least long enough to level out cyclical and seasonal influences. This base permits a certain stabilization of costs and the recognition of long-term trends in sales. Each basis has its advantages and disadvantages, but normal capacity would seem to be the most desirable under ordinary circumstances.

Where one product is manufactured, normal capacity can be stated in the quantity of this unit. In those cases where many products are made, it is usually necessary to select a common unit for the denominator. Productive hours are a practical measure. If the normal productive hours for all departments or cost centers are known, the sum of these will represent the total for the plant. The total fixed costs divided by the productive hours at normal capacity results in the standard fixed cost per productive hour.

TREATMENT OF SERVICE DEPARTMENT COSTS

Most companies are faced with the problem of how to distribute the costs of service departments, such as steam, power, and maintenance, and the other indirect departments, such as works administration and planning and scheduling. Since such indirect departmental costs constitute a large share of general factory overhead, the selection of the proper base or bases is important not only from a cost determination but also from a cost control standpoint.

It is fundamental that a functional or proportional relationship exist between the bases used to allocate the service costs and the costs which are to be allocated. In other words, the resulting distribution must be a fair measure of the benefits received or services rendered. For many indirect or service departments there is an obviously logical method or base for distributing expenses, whereas an arbitrary basis must be used for others. Thus, power costs may be distributed in proportion to kilowatt-hours consumed; maintenance costs may be allocated on the basis of actual man-hours used; and building costs can be prorated on a square or cubic footage basis. On the other hand, the expense of works administration, or planning and scheduling, may be arbitrarily distributed on a man-hours, payroll dollars, or total processing cost basis in the absence of a better base.

From a practical viewpoint it is preferable to get as simple a method as possible, even though not theoretically correct. Yet, when large sums are involved, it is perhaps desirable to consider the nature of the indirect expenses as related to plant activity. In those instances where some costs are fixed and others are variable, it may be well to allocate these two types of costs on different bases: the fixed may be allocated on a standard or normal activity basis while the variable element can be prorated in proportion to actual activity. Powerhouse costs are a typical example. Since the plant is presumably built to handle normal capacity, the fixed costs of depreciation, taxes, insurance, and supervision could be allocated in proportion to steam consumption at normal capacity. The more variable expenses, such as fuel, hourly labor, and repairs, could be allocated on the basis of pounds of steam used each month.

It was stated earlier that the method of allocating service department costs has a direct bearing on cost control. This is related to whether actual or standard costs are distributed to departments using the service. From a cost control viewpoint, the service department supervisor should be held responsible for any costs over his budget. The departments using the services should be charged at a *standard* rate for the actual services used, differentiating between the fixed and variable costs, of course. In this manner the using department can be held fully responsible for excess service costs in that department since no share of the inefficiencies or wastes of the service department is charged against the productive department. From the cost control viewpoint, the service supervisor is responsible for efficiently operating his department at whatever level of service required by the using departments, and as measured by the flexible budget applied to the level of activity. The productive departmental supervisors, on the other hand, are responsible for the quantity of service consumed.

In cost determination, it will be necessary to allocate the variances created in the service departments, possibly in proportion to the standard costs already distributed. While this may be done for top-management purposes, these variances should not be reflected in the statements used for control purposes.

ROLE OF ACCOUNTING DEPARTMENT

Much has been said about the technique of setting manufacturing expense budgets or standards, but little mention has been made as to *who* prepares the budgets and applies them. This duty is usually delegated to the controller and his staff, and understandably so. Past experience is an important factor in setting expense budgets. An analysis of expenses and their behavior in relation to volume is required, and the principal source of information is the accounting records. The accountants are the best qualified to make these analyses of the historical information. Then, too, the accounting staff usually possesses the necessary technical qualifications for organizing the data into the desired shape. Furthermore, the approach must be objective, and the independent position of the accounting department makes it suitable for the setting of fair standards or budgets.

While the controller "carries the ball" in preparing the budgets, he is only part of the team. Successful control of manufacturing expenses requires the cooperation of the operating departments' supervisors who are charged with the responsibility of meeting their budgets. For this reason, among others, each supervisor should agree to his budget before it is put into effect. Moreover, his experience and knowledge of operating conditions must be utilized in the preparation of the budget. The controller and his staff act as coordinators in seeing that the job gets done reasonably well and that it is accomplished on time.

SECURING CONTROL OF OVERHEAD

As previously stated, the basic approach in controlling factory overhead is to set standards of performance and operate within the limits of these standards. Two avenues may be followed to accomplish this objective: one involves the preplanning or preventive approach; the other, the after-the-fact approach of reporting unfavorable trends and performance.

Preplanning can be accomplished on many items of manufacturing overhead expense in somewhat the same fashion as discussed in connection with direct labor. For example, the crews for indirect labor can be planned just as well as the crews for direct labor. The preplanning approach will be found useful where a substantial dollar cost is involved for purchase of supplies or repair materials. It may be found desirable to maintain a record of purchase commitments, by responsibility, for these accounts. Each purchase requisition, for example, might require the approval of the budget department. When the budget limit is reached, then no further purchases would be permitted except with the approval of much higher authority. Again, where stores or stock requisitions are the source of charges, the department manager may be kept informed periodically of the cumulative monthly cost, and steps may be taken to stop further issues, except in emergencies, as the budget limit is approached. The controller will be able to find ways and means of assisting the department operating executives to keep within budget limits, through providing this kind of information.

The other policing function of control is the reporting of unfavorable trends and performance. This involves an analysis of expense variances. Here the problem is somewhat different as compared with direct labor or material because of the factor of different levels of activity. Overhead variances may be grouped into the following classifications:

> Controllable by departmental supervision
> > Rate or spending variance
> > Efficiency variance
> Responsibility of top management
> > Volume variance

It is important, of course, to recognize the cause of variances if corrective action is to be taken. For this reason the variance due to business volume must be isolated from that which is controllable by the departmental supervisors.

ANALYSIS OF EXPENSE VARIANCES

The exact method and degree of refinement in analyzing variances will depend on the desires of management and the opinion of the controller as to requirements. However, the volume variance, regardless of cause, must be segregated from the controllable variances. Volume variance may be defined, simply, as the difference between budgeted expense for current activity and the standard cost for the same level. It arises because production is above or below normal activity and relates primarily to the fixed costs of the business. The variance can be analyzed in more detail as to whether it is due to seasonal causes, the number of calendar days in the month, or other causes.

The controllable variances may be defined as the difference between the budget at the current activity level and actual expenses. They must be set out for each cost center and analyzed in such detail that the supervisor knows exactly what caused the condition. At least two general categories can be recognized. The first is the rate of spending variance. Simply stated, this variance arises because more or less than standard was spent for each machine hour, operating hour, or standard labor hour. This variance must be isolated for each cost element of production expense. An analysis of the variance on indirect labor, for example, may indicate what share of the excess cost is due to (1) overtime, (2) an excess number of men, or (3) use of higher-rated men than standard. The analysis may be detailed to show the excess by craft and by shift. As another example, supplies may be analyzed to show the cause of variance as (1) too large a quantity of certain items, (2) a different material or quality being used, or (3) higher prices than anticipated.

Another general type of controllable variance is the production or efficiency variance. It represents the difference between actual hours used in production and the standard hours allowed for the same volume. It can be seen that such a loss involves all elements of overhead. Here, too, the controller should analyze the causes, usually with the assistance of production personnel. The lost production might be due to mechanical failure, poor material, inefficient labor, or lack of material. Such an analysis points out weaknesses and paves the way to corrective action by the line executives.

BUDGET REPORT

MONTH___January___

DEPT HEAD_____
DEPARTMENT___Melting Room___ NO.___No. 110___

DESCRIPTION	CURRENT MONTH			YEAR TO DATE		
	BUDGET	ACTUAL	(OVER)/UNDER	BUDGET	ACTUAL	(OVER)/UNDER
CONTROLLABLE EXPENSES						
01 Labor-Hourly-St. Time	$ 589	$ 669	$ (80)			
08 Vacation Pay	23	26	(3)			
97-98 Payroll Taxes	17	22	(4)			
11 Power	56	26	30			
39 Repairs – Materials	47	–	47			
" Labor & Overhead	289	132	157			
Modifications-Materials	–	34	(34)			
40 Supplies	144	225	(81)			
TOTAL CONTROLLABLE EXPENSES	$ 1,168	$ 1,137	$ 30			
NON-CONTROLLABLE EXPENSES						
Depreciation, Taxes & Ins.	615	615	–			
TOTAL DIRECT EXPENSES	$ 1,783	$ 1,752	$ 30			
PRODUCTION (LOSS)/GAIN – DIRECT						
Over-all						
349 Opt. Hrs.						
205 Std. Hrs.						
(144) Hrs. @ $4.690/Hr.			(675)			
Pounds – (421,200)						
TOTAL DIRECT EXPENSE (LOSS)/GAIN			$(644)			
PRODUCTION (LOSS)/GAIN – SERVICE DEPARTMENTS			–			
TOTAL DEPARTMENT PERFORMANCE			$(644)			
Cwt. (Loss)			$(.11)			

Comments: Good Production   598,195 lbs.

  Std. Lbs/Opt. Hr.   2,925

  Actual Lbs/Opt. Hr. 1,714

ISSUED BY THE ACCOUNTING DEPT.___February 13,___

Fig. 74—Budget Report—Manufacturing Expenses—Chemical Plant.

ILLUSTRATIVE PROCEDURE

Perhaps the best way in which to indicate what the accounting staff can do in analyzing overhead variances is to give an example. Figure 74 illustrates a budget report covering the activities of a department foreman and is intended to reveal overhead losses and gains for which the foreman is responsible. Several features may be pointed out:

1. The expenditure or rate variance is shown as an over- or under-budget condition, item by item in the top section of the report. The budget allowance for the controllable expenses is the result of multiplying the operating hours by the standard rate per cost item.
2. The efficiency or production variance is shown in total only, since the correction depends solely on increasing the rate of production per hour.
3. In order to keep the foreman aware of the fixed costs, these are shown, but without any gain or loss. The volume variance is shown on a report for the top-management level only.

It is not enough merely to give the foreman a report such as this. He must know exactly why the important gains or losses occurred. Furthermore, there must be a continuous follow-up to see that unfavorable conditions are removed. The follow-up is handled through a checking of the weekly or daily labor, maintenance, or other reports. An example of the detail given to this foreman for his use is as follows:

EXCESS LABOR:

Cause	Date	Shift	Hours		Amount
Extra training time					
Kettle operators	1/17–18	3	16		$32.00
Overtime					
Kettle operators	1/12	2	6	$18.00	
Helpers	1/13	1	3	4.50	
Loaders	1/14	3	1	1.50	24.00
Extra manpower					
Kettle operators	1/19	2	8	16.00	
Kettle operators	1/23	1	8	16.00	32.00
Absenteeism					
Kettle operators	1/20	3	4		(8.00)
Net excess					$80.00

The foreman gets a complete and detailed report on repairs and modifications, so he knows the cause, by repair order, of these gains or losses.

Details of the supplies could be reported in this manner:

Item	Units	Usage			Unit Price	Total (Gain) or Loss
		Actual	Standard	Excess		
Filtercel	lbs.	500	400	100	$.10	$10.00
Cleaning Fluid	quarts	50	25	25	.30	7.50
Brooms	each	3	1	2	.50	1.00
Rags	lbs.	50	20	30	.05	1.50
Solvent "B"	lbs.	350	100	250	.20	50.00
Solvent "C"	lbs.	50	60	(10)	.50	(5.00)
Solvent "D"	lbs.	100	60	40	.25	10.00
Miscellaneous (less than $.50 each)						6.00
Total						$81.00

With this information, the foreman can explain to his supervisor why he exceeded the standard cost, and what he is doing to bring the costs in line.

The single largest source of loss, of course, is the production loss. This, too, may be summarized as to cause:

Cause	Hours	Cost
Low rate of production	105	$492
Lack of heat	12	56
Lack of material	8	38
Mechanical failures	16	75
Absenteeism	3	14
Total	144	$675

Responsibility can be placed for these stoppages and corrective action taken.

INCENTIVES TO REDUCE COSTS

It has been stated repeatedly throughout these pages that costs are controlled by individuals. In the control of manufacturing expenses, no less than direct labor and material, a most important factor is the foreman. He is the representative of management who is on the scene and can immediately and directly influence the use of men and materials. Reports showing his performance are of great assistance. However, the experience of many companies has shown that standard costs and budgets are even a more effective tool when related to incentives or financial rewards. Usually this incentive takes the form of a percentage of the savings or a percentage of the foreman's salary. If John Jones can keep costs 10% under the budget and knows that he will consequently get a bonus equal to 10% of his salary, this is a powerful force to operate his department on an efficient basis. Since favorable variances in one month may be offset by unfavorable developments during other months, some companies using an incentive plan for supervision relate the bonus in part to cumulative performance.

MANUFACTURING OVERHEAD APPLICATION

Aside from problems involving control of overhead, and the setting of budgets or standards, the controller must concern himself with other aspects of manufacturing overhead. One such consideration is the manner of applying overhead to products. The direct material or direct labor chargeable against a product can be determined quite accurately. Manufacturing expenses, on the other hand, do not apply to any specific product and must therefore be distributed on a somewhat arbitrary basis. It can be realized that the correct method of overhead application, or costing, is extremely important if management is to have accurate product costs, inventories, and pricing data.

It is beyond the scope of this book to review all the phases of overhead application, but it is thought desirable to comment briefly on certain of the methods. The more commonly used bases of allocation are:

1. Rate per machine hour
2. Rate per direct labor hour
3. Rate per direct labor dollar
4. Percentage of direct material cost
5. Percentage of prime cost
6. Rate per unit of product

These bases can be used in conjunction with actual, estimated, or standard factors.

The primary purpose, of course, is to secure the best cost. The problem of the controller, then, is to select that method which most accurately reflects the services received. For example, where expensive machinery, and not direct labor, is the predominant cost factor, then the direct labor dollar base would not be desirable. Since many costs are related to time, machine hours might be an acceptable base for allocations.

DEPARTMENTAL VS. OVER-ALL BURDEN RATES

Another question of overhead allocation concerns the degree to which these costs should be subdivided. Should an over-all or blanket rate be used, or should a departmental or cost center rate be used? Usually the more detailed the cost breakdown, the higher is the clerical expense. But since proper costing is the primary requirement, there are many cases where the blanket rate is not satisfactory. A single or over-all overhead rate generally can be applied if:

1. Only a single product is manufactured, or
2. Several products are manufactured but each travels through all departments and consumes the same amount of time

Where these conditions do not exist, a blanket rate can result in the overcosting of some products and the undercosting of others.

REPORTS FOR MANUFACTURING EXECUTIVES

SCOPE OF COVERAGE

The supervisory staff of the production organization extends over several levels of authority and responsibility from the assistant foreman, foreman, general foreman, division head, plant superintendent, etc., up to the works manager. Likewise the matters which they control relate to materials, labor, and overhead, and each of these subjects has special aspects to be reported upon. It is obvious, then, that production reports must cover a wide field of both reader and subject matter. Effective production control is possible only when the production executives are aware of the necessary facts related to the plant operations; and the higher the executive the more he must rely on reports instead of personal contacts and observations. As a result, a system of reports has been developed in most industrial organizations for presenting the pertinent facts on the production activities.

TYPES OF REPORTS ON ACTUAL PERFORMANCE

The reports will differ from industry to industry and from company to company so that no standardized reports can be set for business generally. However, they may be divided into two general categories according to their purpose. These may be classified as (1) control reports and (2) summary reports. As the name implies, control reports are issued primarily to highlight substandard performance so that corrective action may be taken promptly. These reports deal with performance at the occurrence level and are therefore usually detailed in nature and frequent in issuance. On the other hand, summary reports show the results of performance over a longer period of time, such as a month, and are an over-all recapitulation of performance. They serve to keep the general executives aware of factory performance and are, in effect, a summary of the control reports.

Indicative of the subjects which the reports to production executives may cover are the following:

Material
    Inventories
    Spoilage and waste
    Unit standard costs
    Material consumed
    Actual vs. standard usage

Labor
    Total payroll
    Unit output per man-hour
    Total production in units
    Average hourly labor rates
    Overtime hours and costs
    Bonus costs
    Turnover
    Relationship of supervisory personnel to direct labor
    Actual and standard unit and total labor costs

Overhead
    Actual vs. budgeted costs
    Idle facilities
    Maintenance costs
    Supplies used
    Cost of union business
    Subcontracted repairs
    Ratio of indirect to direct labor

PRESENTATION OF DATA

It is the experience of the authors that most production executives will make good use of data bearing on their operations provided certain fundamental rules are followed:

1. The reports should be expressed in the language of the executive who is to use them and in the form preferred by him.
2. Reports should be submitted promptly enough to serve the purpose intended. Control reports are of little value if issued too late to take corrective action.
3. The form and content of the report should be in keeping with the responsibility of the executive receiving it. Minor executives are interested in details while higher executives are interested in departmental summaries, trends, and relationships.

Some of the reports prepared by the accounting department will be on costs, and others will be expressed in non-financial terms. Some may be narrative while others will be in tabular or graphic form. But all should follow the principles set forth above.

ILLUSTRATIVE REPORTS

Some illustrative reports commonly used in industry are presented here. Figure 75 shows an exception type of cost report furnished daily to the foreman showing reasons for substandard performance. Only substandard performance is listed. He is expected to take immediate steps to eliminate the causes of excess labor costs. An example of a plant report submitted daily to the superintendent is illustrated in Fig. 148 on page 556. Graphic presentation of the trend of labor efficiency for top executives is shown in Fig. 76.

SECTIONAL COST REPORT				
No. 842 Date Jan. 18,			Dept. L. I. M.	Sec. 5 Brackets
Actual Labor Cost for Day,	$100.37		Budget, $90.15	
Ck. No.	Operations Delinquent	Actual	Budget	Remarks
15	Rough Bore and Face	$5.04	$3.89	Operator Slow
18	Drill Stud Holes	2.94	1.77	Man on Woman's Job
23	Face and Fit	6.64	5.56	Too high rated operator
71	File	2.50		Extra Operation— Rough Material
84	Bore and Face 2nd	1.18	.54	Extra set-up needed
87	Complete Fit	4.72	1.88	Slow on account of poor material
92	Clean and Paint	1.56	.72	Rough work— poor material
Balance of Section Meets Standard		$24.58	$14.36	
		75.79	75.79	
	Total	$100.37	$90.15	
Foreman	Action Completed			

Fig. 75—Daily Labor Cost Report.

Material usage reports can take several forms. Excess material usage may be summarized daily as to cause, and a report made to the plant superintendent. Again, a weekly scrap report may be informative, as in Fig. 77. The trend of excess usage may be graphically portrayed.

A departmental budget report on overhead expenses is presented in Fig. 74 on page 310. Over-all reports on manufacturing costs are shown in Figs. 78 and 79. These reports are used as the basis for action by the budget committee.

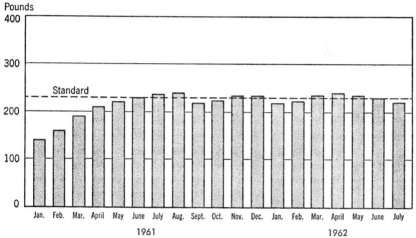

Fig. 76—Trend of Production Over or Under Standard.

The Novelty Manufacturing Company
SCRAP REPORT—STAMPING DEPARTMENT
For the Week Ended November 23, 1962

Part No.	Name	Production	Scrap	% Scrapped	Cost	Reason
647C	Hinge........	12,320	207	1.68	$ 8.28	
871R	Ring.........	8,620	73	.85	3.65	
1422	Flap.........	3,110	672	2.16	282.24	Defective die
1816	Support.......	8,520	40	.47	16.00	
1871	Spoon........	11,890	90	.76	1.80	
2167	Ruler........	1,245	–	–	–	
2173	Cap "R"......	14,505	1,070	7.38	107.00	Substitute material
2271	Cap "T"......	8,140	72	.88	21.60	
	Total				$ 440.57	
	Cost of Scrap—Year to Date				$18,497.12	

Fig. 77—Weekly Scrap Report.

Page 1

AUTOMOTIVE MANUFACTURING
COMPANY

Period March,

MANUFACTURING DIVISION
BUDGET SUMMARY

CLASSIFICATION	CURRENT MONTH				YEAR TO DATE	
	BUDGET	ACTUAL	(OVER)/UNDER	% REAL.	(OVER)/UNDER	% REAL.
Direct Labor						
Factory (See Page 2)	$ 94,363	$100,107	$(5,744)	94.3	$(11,975)	94.2
Shipping	1,120	1,069	51	104.8	222	110.2
Engineering	5,346	4,108	1,238	130.1	1,592	117.6
Tool Manufacturing	6,358	5,654	704	112.5	1,275	111.1
Contingency	1,660	-	1,660	-	4,472	-
Total	108,847	110,938	(2,091)	98.1	(4,414)	98.1
Expense (See Page 3)						
Division Departments	52,450	52,057	393	100.8	3,646	103.5
Works Departments	46,559	47,570	(1,011)	97.9	210	100.2
Non-Departmentalized Expense	53,752	56,176	(2,424)	95.7	10,509	111.1
Contingency	6,745	-	6,745	-	13,660	-
Total	159,506	155,803	3,703	102.4	28,025	109.6
Plant Over-all Performance - CCIP	268,353	266,741	1,612	100.5	23,611	104.5
Material & Other Costs (See Page 4)						
Direct Material	471,349	462,515	8,834	101.9	13,042	101.5
Other Manufacturing Costs	4,818	5,497	(679)	87.6	(542)	94.4
Engineering Other Charges	-	-	-	-	627	-
Tool Manufacturing Charges	657	4,178	(3,521)	15.7	(3,968)	24.9
Subcontract Charges	14,435	14,644	(209)	98.6	(461)	98.5
Total	491,259	486,834	4,425	100.9	8,698	101.0
Total Manufacturing Costs	$759,612	$753,575	$6,037	100.8	$32,309	102.3

Comments:

Statistics:
% Division Activity   91.6
% Expense to Direct Labor   140.4
Expense Rate per Hour $ 1.96
% Moving
      CCIP Realization   99.2

ISSUED BY THE ACCOUNTING DEPT. ____4/9/____

Fig. 78—Manufacturing Division Budget Summary.

5759 Reconnaissance Model 140 Airplanes and Spares

Description	CURRENT MONTH			CUMULATIVE PROJECT TO DATE					INDICATED COST AT COMPLETION BASED ON PERFORMANCE TO DATE		
	Actual A	Budget B	(Over) or Under C	Completed Work D	Work in Process at 2/28/63 E	Total Actual F	Allowed Budget G	(Over) or Under H	Est. Cost at Completion I	Adjusted Budget J	(Over) or Under K
MANUFACTURING COST											
1 Direct Manufacturing Labor...	$102,167	$99,193	$(2,974)	$3,467,233	$129,544	$3,596,777	$3,390,015	$(206,762)	$3,641,568	$3,432,373	$(209,195)
2 Direct Manufacturing Expense.											
3 Subcontracted Production....											
4 Direct Material.											
5 Other Charges and Transfers..											
6 Total Manufacturing Cost.											
ENGINEERING, & TOOLING											
7 Initial Engineering..........											
8 Maint. and Design Change Eng.											
9 Initial Tooling.............											
10 Maint. and Design Change Tool.											
11 Total Eng. and Tooling Cost											
OTHER:											
12 General and Adminstrative Exp.											
13 Total Project Cost.......											
14 Sales Income.											
15 Profit or (Loss)...........											
16 % of Net Sales............											
UNITS PRODUCED|											
17 Labor Equivalent Units......											
18 Subcontract Equivalent Units..											
19 Material Equivalent Units....											
20 Completed Airplanes.........											
UNIT COST											
21 Direct Manufacturing Labor...											
22 Direct Manufacturing Expense.											
23 Subcontracted Production....											
24 Direct Material.											
25 Other Charges and Transfers..											
26 Initial Engineering..........											
27 Maint. and Design Change Eng.											
28 Initial Tooling.............											
29 Maint. and Design Change Tool.											
30 General and Administrative...											
31 Total Unit Cost...........											
32 Rev. per Standard Ship.											
33 (Over) or Under Revenue											

Issued by the Accounting Department—March 6, 1963.

Fig. 79—Project Budget Report.

17

Planning and Control of Research and Development Costs

DEFINITION OF RESEARCH AND DEVELOPMENT

Research is here considered in the more restricted sense as related to the physical sciences. It is defined as the activity or function involved in the laboratory to secure or discover new products or processes. Development as used here denotes the functions carried on to put the results of research on a commercial basis. In other words, the discussion here is concerned with that work normally supervised or controlled by the vice-president or the director of research and development.

ORGANIZATION FOR RESEARCH AND DEVELOPMENT

Because research and development are assuming more significance in our modern industrial economy, it is perhaps well to describe the major activities usually making up the research and development function.

Very often the director of research and development reports to the president of the company. Under his supervision may be found four basic but related fields of activity:

1. Research
2. Patents
3. Product and process engineering
4. Development

The activities of these four fields must be coordinated if the business is to accomplish its objective of discovering and utilizing new products and processes. First, the specific idea must be conceived; and this is the purpose of fundamental research—to find new products or processes or to improve existing ones. The research group conducts laboratory or small-scale experiments to secure the basic method or product on which the other groups will work. Also, the research division may advise the other three divisions on technical problems.

The patent division obtains all patents on company inventions, reviews patent data and literature, etc., and either conducts or assists the legal department in conducting all patent litigation. As the work of the other research and development activities results in patentable ideas, it is obviously important for a company to protect these rights. Hence, detailed and careful studies must be undertaken to secure sound patents. Perhaps it is well to inject here the thought that reduced costs achieved through less thorough patent searching and less careful wording of patents can prove to be a foolish economy.

Once an idea or product or process has reached the stage where serious consideration is to be given either to pilot plant or to large-scale operations, it becomes a project of the engineering division. Generally, this division operates the pilot plant and secures the necessary data for an evaluation of large-scale operation. Likewise, it will specify the types of equipment and processes necessary in commercial production. Finally, the development division enters the picture. This division studies the market in an effort to determine present and potential demand for the product, as well as supply, so as to assist in determining the size of commercial facilities. The development division may also distribute samples to the field. When commercial production is started, it may assist the salesmen until the product is well-established and final responsibility for sales is transferred to the sales department.

The exact type of organization depends, of course, on the size of the operation. In many small concerns these functions are not departmentalized. On the other hand, in some large companies the quality control function may be added as another activity under the director of research.

NATURE OF RESEARCH AND DEVELOPMENT COSTS

Under our competitive economy, industrial firms grow and prosper by inventing or developing new products, by improving existing products, or by developing new processes which reduce the cost of production. This must be done, over the long run, to insure a reasonable return on the investment. It is simply not enough to do reasonably well that which is now being done, for competitors would pass by such a business. Improvement is the intangible attribute which distinguishes the progressive company from the one on the road of decline. Over the longer term, the growth and existence of a business enterprise, then, can be seen to depend to a significant degree on research and development.

In a certain sense, the moneys spent on research and development, which are quite different from many expenses, are like insurance policy premiums—premiums for insurance to protect the assets of the business. Some may be short-term policies whereas others may extend over a period of years. These characteristics must be remembered by the controller when he evaluates an expenditure—an expenditure designed to protect the company and to increase the comforts or enjoyments of life for many people.

Research and development costs cover a variety of expenses. An important cost, of course, is the salaries and related taxes and insurance of the staff. Supplies for the laboratories and pilot plant will bulk large. Traveling expense and professional fees may be incurred. Other expenses will be of the usual nature: supplies, repairs and maintenance, depreciation, power, telephone and telegraph, laundry, dues and subscriptions.

CAN RESEARCH AND DEVELOPMENT COSTS BE CONTROLLED?

Because of the nature of research and development activities, the question arises: What can be done to control the related costs, that is, to keep them within defined limits? Furthermore, what can be done to assure that research is actually effective? After all, the relationship between expenditures and results can be quite remote and not apparent over a short period of time. Moreover, the projects might be completely dissimilar to other past operations. Under these circumstances the controller might well conclude that little control need be exercised; that very little can be done.

Yet, mature reflection can hardly avoid the realization that management has the same responsibility to secure all the facts about the research and development activity as for any other activity, and to use these facts as a basis for judging the efficiency of the operation. Further, over the long term, perhaps even the short, the business must live within its income. Hence, these conditions require at least certain minimum accounting and control.

When research and development become major functions, as they now are in a great many companies, there is a need for managerial planning and control to direct effort into what appear to be the more fruitful channels and to assure that costs stay within predetermined limits.

In attempting to establish very simple accounting control techniques, many a controller has run into resistance from the technical personnel. This may range from grudgingly furnishing certain information, usually with statements that "research men should not waste their time by worrying about costs or budgets, or keeping time records" to a downright refusal to assist in any way with time distribution because it "interferes with research." Such an attitude arises from a fear, often well-founded, that information provided from accounting sources will harm or hinder research and development activities. This fear must be removed through demonstrations by the controller that cost data, when properly used, can be made to aid and assist the research department, whether in "selling" the benefits of a research project to management or for departmental control purposes.

When properly approached, few top-notch research men will disagree with the premise that management has a right to determine how much will be spent; that management should be advised of the progress being made, financial and otherwise; and that research activities should be governed by well-thought-out opinions of projects to be pursued. In the final analysis, the necessity for certain controls must be accepted, but the proper application or interpretation of accounting information is a required corollary.

CONTRIBUTIONS OF THE CONTROLLER TOWARD COST CONTROL

What techniques are available for control of research and development costs, and just what part can the controller play? The nature of research and development costs is quite varied, and the control problems within each business organization may be quite different. There are, however, three rather distinct approaches to control that may be utilized, either individually or collectively:

1. *Control of Effectiveness Through Planning and Measurement of Results.* This approach may be applied in the planning phases of research and development activities. Before a specific project is undertaken, an analysis should be made to estimate the probable savings resulting from a successful application, in comparison with the estimated cost of research. A similar approach can be used, when the research and development are completed, to point out to management whether the research expenditures actually were worth the effort or produced the estimated savings.
2. *Control of Expenditures.* Provision can be made for recording actual expenditures and making quite certain that such outlays are kept within the budget limitations.
3. *Functional Control Through Application of Standards.* For some limited research and development activities, just as in production or distribution, standards can be established. A comparison of actual and standard performance can be made, and corrective action taken as found necessary.

On each of these phases, the controller has the responsibility of making objective reports and analyses for the guidance of the research director as well as other members of management. It should be appreciated that the information he collects, when intelligently used in cooperation with the director of research, can be of considerable aid in planning and policy determination as well as for control of costs. Among the types of reports which might be prepared for any one of several purposes are these:

1. Statement of estimated project costs, and relative rates of return
2. Comparison of actual and budgeted expenses by departmental responsibility
3. Statement of project costs, indicating actual expenditures, commitments, and unexpended balances
4. Post-audit statement of research costs comparing expenses with actual vs. predicted savings or earnings
5. Selected statistical data, including
   a. Ratio of departmental or total salaries to man-hours, and comparison with standard or past months
   b. Number of tests per man-day, including comparison with standard
   c. Relationship of research and development costs, by products and in total, to net sales

ESTABLISHING THE RESEARCH AND DEVELOPMENT BUDGET

In most companies, control of research and development expense commences with the establishment of a specific annual appropriation. The magnitude of this appropriation or budget depends on management's appraisal of the sum which should be spent on the activity in the light of the desired goal or objective. Quite understandably, the upper limit of expenditures ordinarily will be either the company's ability to finance the program or its means of effectively utilizing the expected results through manufacture and sale. The minimum research expenditure will be that amount which management feels is absolutely necessary merely to continue in business as against competitive activity in the market place.

There are no entirely satisfactory means of determining just what the amount of the appropriation should be. Some "rules of thumb" do exist as guides in checking on the adequacy or reasonableness of the proposed budget. These include (1) per cent of the sales dollar and (2) per cent of net income. Such measures may be applied to the company for either a single year or an average of several years. The yardstick also may be against expenditures by the more aggressive or progressive competitors.

It is to be noted that these measures are unsatisfactory if applied as rigid guides, and particularly if so used against the expected sales or income of a single year. Greatly fluctuating appropriations do not provide the stability probably needed for the most effective research application. Rather, consistent application over several years would appear prudent in securing the best long-term return on the research dollar. Moreover, a decline in sales or income might signal an increase in research activity instead of a retrenchment.

ALLOCATING FUNDS AMONG PROJECTS

In any company with a balanced research program, usually there are more ideas available to exploit through research than there are funds which can be provided. Consequently, it becomes necessary to select projects. In evaluating projects or programs these observations should be made:

1. Development projects ordinarily should be given a high priority. These are the projects for which successful applications seem most assured. Therefore, in a competitive economy, funds should be initially allocated to such projects, with residual funds, if any, available for exploratory and fundamental research projects.
2. The amount to be invested in fundamental research should probably be based on the collective judgment of management and the research director.
3. Development projects should be "ranked" or evaluated relative to each other, giving consideration to:
   a. Operating expenses, capital investment, and return, in the light of the best available alternatives and financing
   b. Time of application, recognizing that the earlier a process or product is used, the greater its value, other things being equal, on a present worth basis
   c. Potential licensing income

The question also arises as to the optimum limit of funds for a particular project. On the general thesis that the ultimate profits from the product or process must (1) carry the cost of research, (2) recover plant investment and working capital, and (3) provide a fair return, the profit volume relationship formula may provide a guide. For example, assume that:

1. A 6% return on sales is desired.
2. Annual sales of the new product are expected to be $10,000,000.
3. Investment is to be recovered in 5 years.
4. The required investment is $2,000,000 in plant and $500,000 in working capital.

The applicable formula then may be stated as

$$R = 2 \ (YNS - P - W)$$

in which

$R =$ maximum research and development expense for the project
$Y =$ the desired recovery period in years
$N =$ minimum acceptable net profit expressed in relationship to sales (decimal)
$S =$ annual sales volume in monetary terms
$P =$ plant investment
$W =$ working capital investment

Substituting values, the allowable research and development expense would be \$1,000,000, calculated as follows:

$$\begin{aligned}
R &= 2 \ [(5 \times .06 \times \$10,000,000) - \$2,000,000 - \$500,000] \\
&= 2 \ (\$3,000,000 - \$2,500,000) \\
&= \$1,000,000
\end{aligned}$$

Such a formula is only a guide. It may be adjusted to state the limitation on expenditures as measured by return on capital, etc.

PRESENTING THE APPROPRIATION REQUEST

From the planning and control viewpoint, the preceding discussion relates to the over-all amount to be spent on the research and development function, and evaluation of particular development projects. The remaining question is how the principles may be applied in an individual company.

In these days of somewhat limited availability of technically trained research men, the planning process quite often begins with an assessment of personnel and facilities which the research director expects to have available. In other words, the particular projects as well as the scope of all projects probably will be determined by the personnel limitations as well as the financial capability of the company. There is little purpose in planning the financial requirements if projects simply cannot be accomplished because of lack of manpower. Once the limitations are known, the specific projects can be planned, perhaps department by department, and perhaps expense by expense. These project costs, together with the related research administrative expenses, are summarized to give the complete picture. One such summary is illustrated in Fig. 80. New manpower requirements and total costs are shown. Naturally, the summary should be by the categories considered most significant in the particular case, and should be accompanied by appropriate commentary by the director. The example reflects the general type of expense by function and product line. In other instances, a simple summary by departments may suffice.

The Hyde Petro-Chemical Company
RESEARCH AND DEVELOPMENT BUDGET
Fiscal 1963 Appropriation—Summary

Project Budgets	1963—Proposed			1962—Actual
	New Men Required	Total Man-Hours	Cost ($000)	Cost ($000)
DEVELOPMENT				
Naphthalenes	10	60,000	$ 800	$ 570
Oxy-alchohols	20	129,000	2,840	2,240
Polyethylenes	5	20,000	220	70
Polymers	6	16,000	330	40
Total	41	225,000	4,190	2,920
FUNDAMENTAL RESEARCH				
"A" projects	10	23,000	410	60
"B" projects	4	10,000	140	10
"S" projects	13	36,000	360	170
Total	27	69,000	910	240
Total Project Budgets	68	294,000	5,100	3,160
Pilot Plants			2,740	2,010
ADMINISTRATIVE				
General			450	460
Library			720	810
Patents			1,340	1,720
Grand Total—Amount			$10,350	$8,160
% Net Sales—5-year average			5.5	5.3
% Net Income—5-year average			1.1	1.0

Fig. 80—Summary Request for Research Budget.

Supporting the summary ordinarily will be the data on each project. The economies of each such project may be shown, as in Fig. 81. As an alternative, the budget request might confine itself to broader aspects, and approval would constitute approval in *principle* only. As each individual project is presented for authorization, the up-to-date economics might be reviewed at that time, and prior to specific approval.

BUDGET REPORTS

Once the appropriation is approved, and the research director sets the program in motion, then the controller has the job of (1) recording actual expenditures and (2) reporting to the responsible official, as well as to top management, how budget and actual performance compare. The recording of actual expenses is a simple job order costing problem.

A. R. No. _____

The X Y Z Company
APPROPRIATION REQUEST—RESEARCH AND DEVELOPMENT DIVISION

Product Type_____

Purpose and Description of Work and Expected Results:

Summary of Estimated Expenditures and Savings or Earnings:

Research and Development (Man-hours _____) $

Experimental Equipment

Production—Expense (Machine hours _____)

—Material

Total Estimated Cost $ _____

Estimated Product Sales

First Year $ _____

Second Year $ _____

Third Year $ _____

Estimated Annual Savings (Out-of-Pocket) or Earn-
ings—First Year $ _____

Estimated Facility and Working Capital Investment $ _____

Estimated Return on Investment (D.C.F.) $ _____

Date _____

Originator _____

Approvals:

Director of Research   _____

Controller   _____

Sales Manager   _____

Director of Manufacturing   _____

President   _____

Board of Directors, by   _____

Fig. 81—Appropriation Request for Research and Development Project.

Typical budgetary control reports are illustrated in Figs. 82 and 83. In Fig. 82 the research director is advised of the over-all financial performance of each of his departments. The same information is summarized by type of expense in Fig. 83. Supporting each of these statements is

| ACE MANUFACTURING COMPANY | | BUDGET REPORT | | | | | |

BUDGET REPORT

MONTH __October__

DEPT. HEAD __R.R. Jones__
DEPARTMENT __TECHNICAL DIVISION__   NO. _____

DESCRIPTION	CURRENT MONTH			YEAR TO DATE		
	BUDGET	ACTUAL	(OVER)/UNDER	BUDGET	ACTUAL	(OVER)/UNDER
SUMMARY OF TECHNICAL DIVISION EXPENSE BY DEPARTMENTS						
RESEARCH & DEVELOPMENT						
901 Aluminum	$ 5,327	$ 5,195	$ 132	$ 29,129	$ 28,073	$1,056
902 Plastic	1,959	1,752	207	11,165	10,583	583
903 Rubber	3,074	3,246	(172)	16,454	16,333	121
904 Other Metals	3,169	2,815	354	16,941	16,090	851
TECHNICAL SERVICE						
911 Automotive	870	757	113	4,800	4,510	290
913 Aircraft	1,285	1,162	123	7,196	6,718	478
914 Boats	1,120	1,257	(137)	6,870	6,675	195
917 Military	1,573	1,444	129	8,293	8,075	218
918 Appliances - Small	1,194	1,162	32	6,996	6,823	173
OTHER						
920 General	129	129	-	1,527	1,527	-
930 Pilot Plant	9,587	9,587	-	55,455	54,369	1,086
945 Patents	6,355	6,941	(586)	38,130	38,557	(427)
949 Chicago Project	21,424	20,716	708	72,198	69,621	2,577
950 Library	752	752	-	752	752	-
TOTAL DEPARTMENT PERFORMANCE	$ 57,818	$ 56,915	$ 903	$ 275,906	$ 268,706	$7,200
PER CENT (OVER)/UNDER BUDGET			1.6%			2.7%

ISSUED BY THE ACCOUNTING DEPT. __November 14__

Fig. 82—Summary of Actual and Budgeted Technical Division Expense
by Departments.

the detail of actual and budgeted expense for each department in a form similar to this last summary. Depending on the degree of refinement or type of control, a project budget control report, as in Fig. 84, may be prepared.

ACE MANUFACTURING COMPANY	BUDGET REPORT					
MONTH October	DEPT. HEAD R.R. Jones DEPARTMENT TECHNICAL DIVISION NO.					

DESCRIPTION	CURRENT MONTH			YEAR TO DATE		
	BUDGET	ACTUAL	(OVER)/UNDER	BUDGET	ACTUAL	(OVER)/UNDER
SUMMARY OF TECHNICAL DIVISION EXPENSE BY TYPE OF EXPENSE						
CONTROLLABLE EXPENSES						
01 Labor-Hourly-St. Time	$ 867	$ 767	$ 100	$ 2,854	$ 424	
" " Bonus	27	27	-	46	-	
" " O.T.Penalty	-	-	-	41	-	
Total Hourly Labor	$ 894	$ 794	$ 100	$ 2,941	$ 424	
03 Labor - Salary	22,854	22,905	(51)	132,027	(139)	
07 Retirement	12,391	12,391	-	12,391	-	
08 Vacation	35	32	3	118	15	
10 Fuel	27	26	1	103	59	
11 Power	381	381	-	3,261	-	
34 Cartons & Containers	-	-	-	105	95	
39 Repairs-Materials	937	634	303	3,758	721	
" Labor & Overhead	858	674	184	2,900	556	
40 Supplies	5,484	5,248	236	12,878	2,136	
42 Postage	30	8	22	96	89	
43 Patent Applications	225	799	(574)	2,416	(831)	
45 Library	60	118	(58)	316	44	
49 Auto Trips & Mail	24	6	18	114	99	
53 Overtime Meals	36	1	35	27	214	
54 Safety Work Supplies	5	-	5	52	(22)	
64 Traveling	1,565	918	647	7,826	1,473	
65 Convention	-	-	-	690	350	
66 Telephone & Telegraph	301	314	(13)	1,999	(82)	
67 Legal & Professional	5,900	5,800	100	52,064	661	
68 Dues & Subscriptions	155	73	82	535	205	
75 Miscellaneous	2,109	2,282	(173)	11,101	999	
76 Laundry	100	79	21	297	153	
94 Taxes-Sales & Use	25	13	12	66	84	
96 " Federal Trans.	10	7	3	13	47	
97 " Unemp. & O.A.B.	467	467	-	3,438	-	
98 Comp-Gp-Hosp Ins.	456	456	-	2,238	-	
Allowance for Fin. Mat'l	-	-	-	-	(150)	
TOTAL CONTROLLABLE EXPENSES	$ 55,329	$ 54,426	$ 903	$ 260,970	$ 253,770	$7,200
NON-CONTROLLABLE EXPENSES						
Depreciation, Taxes & Ins.	2,489	2,489	-	14,936	14,936	-
TOTAL DEPARTMENT PERFORMANCE	$ 57,818	$ 56,915	$ 903	$ 275,906	$ 268,706	$7,200
PER CENT (OVER)/UNDER BUDGET			1.6%			2.7%
COMMENTS:						

ISSUED BY THE ACCOUNTING DEPT. ___November 14___

Fig. 83—Summary of Actual and Budgeted Technical Division Expense by Type of Expense.

The Plastic Manufacturing Company

SUMMARY PROJECT STATUS REPORT

For the Month Ended October 31, 1962

| | | EXPENDITURES | | | | | | Purchase Order Commitments | Estimated Cost to Complete | | Indicated Total Cost | Project Budget | Indicated Cost (Over) or Under Budget |
| | | Month | | | | Cumulative to Date | | | | | | | |
Project No.	Project	Man-Hours	Salaries and Wages	Other Expense	Total	Man-Hours	Amount		Man-Hours	Amount			
1123	Waterproofing compound "R"	317	$ 702	$ 610	$ 1,312	892	$ 5,420	$ –	300	$ 1,300	$ 6,720	$ 6,800	$ 80
1124	Automobile wax	214	427	410	837	612	3,241	160	100	500	3,901	4,000	99
1125	Urea filler	926	2,980	2,119	5,099	2,107	12,342	920	800	5,200	18,462	18,000	(462)
1126	Silicone coating resin	173	350	722	1,072	173	1,072	–	5,000	22,000	23,072	23,000	(72)
1127	Wet strength resin	223	415	375	790	315	875	–	200	600	1,475	1,500	25
1128	Core binder resin	519	1,350	727	2,077	921	3,760	–	50	150	3,910	5,000	1,090
1129	Phenolic resin	173	375	10	385	185	397	–	–	–	397	1,000	603
1130	Natural molding compound	865	2,310	2,460	4,770	2,540	16,310	2,400	2,000	7,100	25,810	30,000	4,190
1152	Reclaim urea	1,223	3,790	2,319	6,109	3,994	32,110	1,519	500	1,200	34,829	34,500	(329)
1154	Filter salvage	173	385	475	860	346	1,634	222	–	–	1,856	1,900	44
1159	Alkyd blending process	812	3,420	820	4,240	1,042	6,321	8,301	400	1,200	15,822	16,000	178
1160	Filler "G"	76	232	120	352	76	352	–	350	1,000	1,352	1,500	148
	Total	5,694	$16,736	$11,167	$27,903	13,203	$83,834	$13,522	9,700	$40,250	$137,606	$143,200	$5,594

Fig. 8-4—Research and Development Project Budget Report.

The Novelty Manufacturing Company

WEEKLY STATUS REPORT—WEEK ENDED DECEMBER 21, 1962
Reclaim Project (No. 247)

Department and Expense	Amount Authorized	Expenditures This Week	Expenditures To Date	Purchase Commitments	Total Expenditures and Commitments	Balance Unexpended
RESEARCH						
Salaries and Wages	$ 4,000	$ 475	$ 2,890	$ —	$ 2,890	$ 1,110
Supplies	5,000	319	3,870	1,540	5,410	(410)
Power	500	90	220	—	220	280
Other	100	15	35	10	45	55
Total	9,600	899	7,015	1,550	8,565	1,035
DEVELOPMENT						
Salaries and Wages	10,000	1,220	1,325	—	1,325	8,675
Traveling	10,000	1,200	1,410	—	1,410	8,590
Other	2,000	310	320	—	320	1,680
Total	22,000	2,730	3,055	—	3,055	18,945
PATENT						
Legal	2,000	—	800	—	800	1,200
Patent Applications	500	—	20	—	20	480
Miscellaneous	500	—	10	—	10	490
Total	3,000	—	830	—	830	2,170
Administrative	4,000	250	1,250	—	1,250	2,750
Grand Total	$38,600	$3,879	$12,150	$1,550	$13,700	$24,900

Fig. 85—Weekly Project Status Report.

The mechanics of preparing these reports are apparent. If in accordance with company policy, budgeted expenses may be transferred between departments and months to reflect changes in the timing of expenditures or changes in projects.

PREVENTIVE CONTROL

As in any type of good management, it is desirable to plan expenditures before moneys are actually spent, so that the total research and development costs do not exceed the budget. It is simple to determine the number of personnel required, calculate the resulting salary and wage expense, and institute controls to see that no excess staff is acquired. Similarly, commitments for laboratory chemicals and supplies, together with actual expenses, can be tabulated by the accounting department, so that the research director is kept informed by periodic statements as to how total expenditures and commitments relate to the budget. This type of information assumes more importance near the end of the project or budget period. A simple example of such detail is illustrated in Fig. 85. If required, even more detailed information can be furnished—in this case, for illustration, a tabulated listing of each supply requisition or invoice. In short, some of the same techniques as used for preventive management in the production and sales fields can be applied to the effective control of research and development costs.

While it is important that research expenditures stay within the designated limits, it is perhaps of greater significance that the funds be wisely spent. Therefore, it is desirable that periodically each project be reviewed and that the wisdom of spending the full amount already allotted be reconsidered. Also, of course, the project should be reappraised as to the desirability of granting an additional allowance, or otherwise transferring budgeted amounts to other activities.

CONTROL BY PERFORMANCE STANDARDS

Necessary though budgetary control is, such performance cannot and should not be the sole criterion of research effectiveness. It is entirely possible to waste funds or to use them inefficiently and still remain within the limits imposed on expenditures. What is needed, therefore, is performance standards. It is true that research and development work is varied and sometimes difficult to predict. Yet in many instances performance standards have been used to good advantage. These standards do not serve as a substitute for the watchful eye and necessary guidance of the research supervisors, but they can be of assistance in evaluating the quantitative aspects of some phases of the work. Where the activities are numerous, the benefit of close personal supervision by the higher echelon is lost, but reports on performance can give some indication as to effectiveness.

Standards based on performance of other similar activities can be devised. The ingenuity and guidance of the research staff must be used in gathering the data and selecting bases for measurement and the functions to be measured. It is a joint project for both the accountant and the research technician.

Some applications of performance standards are:

1. Number of requisitions filled (laboratory supply room)
2. Cost per man-hour of supplies
3. Cost per man-hour of total research expense
4. Number of tests per month
5. Number of formulas developed per man-week
6. Number of pages of patent applications written per man-day
7. Estimated man-hours for function (over-all project or part thereof; similar to estimating maintenance or other job orders)
8. Cost per patent application
9. Pounds of production per man-hour (pilot plant)
10. Cost per operating hour

DOES RESEARCH PAY DIVIDENDS?

When all is said and done, the final measuring stick is whether the research "paid off." Is the company earning a good return, or does the cost of research and development exceed the return? This is the acid test. Some means must be discovered or used to compare expense and income on a particular project or projects. How can this be done? Generally speaking, research and development result in:

1. A cheaper manufacturing process, or
2. An improved product, or
3. A new product

The problem is to value these results and compare them with the cost. The approach can take one of two avenues: The research expense can be compared with the *total* estimated savings or profits, or the expense may be compared against a *standard allowance*, perhaps expressed as a percentage of net sales. Obviously, not every research project undertaken can be expected to show a profit, but over a period of time management might well expect a rather high batting average.

If the fruit of research and development is a new process, the calculation of savings is relatively easy. The cost of the new process is compared with the old, including amortization of obsolete equipment, for an arbitrary number of years or for the life of the process.

It might be mentioned that some firms have rules of thumb which, for example, stipulate that new equipment or other expenditures must pay for themselves in two years. If an "index of return" is used, then the measuring stick, which might be 3% of net sales, can be applied against the value of all sales for the year or years.

Where an improved product is developed, the worth of research and development is more difficult to measure. Basically, of course, the yardstick is the net profit on the sales secured because of the improvement as compared with the research cost. Or it may be the normally expected research expense—for example, 3% of net sales—on the sales resulting from the improved product as compared with actual expense. If the sales manager cannot estimate this volume realistically, then arbitrary decisions must be made, such as an equivalent of one year's sales. Finally, if a new product is developed, the measure may be the normal net profit over a period of years, or as an index, the normally expected research expense on this sales volume, expressed as a percentage of sales.

A comparative statement incorporating the above suggestions might appear as follows:

Product	Cost Savings or Net Profit (Three Years)	Standard Research Allowance (3% of Net Sales)	Actual Research Expense	Gain or (Loss)
New Soapsaver	$ 3,540	$1,420	$1,560	$ (140)
New Allergon Process	12,400	5,400	1,100	4,300
New Quickmold	8,590	2,140	1,020	1,120
Improved Paintsaver	6,400	840	2,800	(1,960)
Total	$30,930	$9,800	$6,480	$3,320

Another acceptable basis of measuring return on research related to new products would be the discounted cash flow method.[1]

As a general comment, a periodic follow-up comparison of expected savings or earnings as shown on the authorization request should be made with actual realization. Among other advantages, it offers the benefit of keeping estimated earnings more reasonable.

OTHER USES OF RESEARCH COST DATA

Emphasis has been placed on the use of cost information to keep research and development expense within the bounds of the appropriation. Applications in terms of research effectiveness and planning also have been reviewed. While these are the primary ways in which research and development data may be put to work, there are some other uses of which the controller should be aware. First, in setting selling prices, consideration should be given to research and development costs—not only the expected level of expenses applicable to the product line, but also the past costs. Again, research and development may be carried on for customers who use the products of the company; or for the government on a contract basis. Under these circumstances research is the product sold, and the revenue accounting procedures should be reviewed to assure proper costing.

[1] See pp. 457–59.

ACCOUNTING PROBLEMS

When research and development costs are incurred, the controller is faced with several accounting problems which must be resolved. These include:

1. Determination of the extent to which research and development costs should be deferred
2. Treatment of the expense in the statement of income and expense
3. Manner of allocating costs to projects and to products
4. Treatment of research costs incurred for special assistance to other departments

While it is beyond the scope of this book to cover the accounting aspects in detail, some general comments may be helpful. Practice varies in different industries and companies as to the deferment or capitalization of research and development costs. Even among the authorities there is considerable difference of opinion as to the test of capitalization. By and large, however, the best practice favors conservatism and the writing-off of all expenditures which cannot be shown clearly to benefit future operations. Thus, where the project did not materialize or was unsuccessful, or where it represents continuing effort to maintain the same relative position in the industry, practice is to charge such costs against current revenues.

Treatment varies, also, in the manner in which research and development expense is reflected in the statement of income and expense. It may be included in inventories and written off as part of the cost of goods sold. It may be included in administrative or selling expenses; or it may be set out as a separate item. Trade practice, the relative importance of the expense, and other factors influence the accounting treatment.

Accounting for research and development expense has been described earlier as a simple job order accounting problem. Quite naturally, some of the charges may be direct as to projects. Joint costs may be allocated to projects on the basis of either man-hours or total allocated salaries and wages plus direct costs. Man-hours usually are a relatively simple but sufficiently accurate method of distributing indirect charges. Some projects relate directly to certain products and may be charged as such. Those which are of a general nature can be allocated to all products on the basis of the direct research costs.

Costing of research work done for other departments, customers, etc., is not uniform. If a separate project is set up, the cost may be gathered as direct plus allocated actual expense. On the other hand, simplicity may permit the use of a standard rate. If such services are rare and of relatively small expense, perhaps company policy might be to make no charge. If they bulk large, then the research division should be relieved of the cost, and the proper charge made to the factory department and product.

18

Control of Administrative
and Financial Expense

THE ADMINISTRATIVE FUNCTION

The general administrative function has to do with over-all policy determination, planning, direction, and control. General administrative activity includes some functions which relate to all other activities but are not strictly administrative in nature. They are so closely allied, however, as to warrant inclusion in this group. The departments in a typical business organization which may be gathered together as administrative include:

General Executive Departments
Legal Department
Financial or Treasury Department
Accounting (and Statistical) Department
Purchasing Department
Personnel or Industrial Relations Department

Some expenses of the general executive departments, as well as the legal and treasury departments, deserve special comment because of special limitations or because of their very nature. This is done later in the chapter. Aside from these expenses which require individual comment, the others are very much alike, regardless of the department in which they fall. They are, therefore, considered as a group in terms of the general procedure or method of control.

Sometimes the purchasing department or personnel department is considered a part of the manufacturing division. The method of cost control for these departments does not differ in principle from that which can be effectively used in keeping manufacturing expenses or administrative expenses within proper bounds. Therefore, no detailed discussion is included here.

ADMINISTRATIVE FUNCTION IN RELATION TO PRODUCTION AND DISTRIBUTION

It has been suggested by several writers that manufacturing and distribution are the two main activities of a producing concern, and that administration is merely facilitative or auxiliary. Therefore, it is advocated that the manufacturing and distribution costs each include its applicable share of general administrative and financial expense. The opposing viewpoint is, of course, that administration is a separate and distinct function from either production or distribution and should be treated as such.

In determining product costs, as well as other operational or functional costs, there is much to be said in favor of relating the administrative costs to each of these other major functions. From the control standpoint, however, costs must be directly related to those responsible for incurrence, and little is gained by prorating costs to other responsibilities except in special studies. In addition, some of the administrative costs have no immediate and direct relationship to production or distribution costs. For these reasons, administrative costs are here treated separately.

ITEMS INCLUDED

Administrative and financial expenses may be said to include all items of expense of a general administrative and financial nature which it is not feasible to include as distribution, manufacturing, or research costs. The usual departmental costs of doing business will be found herein: salaries, wages, supplies, dues and subscriptions, telephone and telegraph, traveling expense, rent, postage, depreciation, etc. In addition to these ordinary expenses incident to the actual operation of the administrative departments are some not usually found elsewhere:

Executive incentive payments
Contributions
Interest expense
Income taxes
Legal and professional expense
Corporate expenses
Excess facility costs
Gain or loss on sale of capital assets
Bad debts
Cash discounts
Other income and expense

APPROACH TO CONTROL OF EXPENSES

The authors have found from experience that there is a certain laxness in control of administrative and financial expense. This results in part from the fact that a variety of expenses is involved—many seemingly unpredictable and incapable of standardization. It may result, also, from failure to assign the responsibility for control of particular costs to a specific executive, as well as inadequate accounting methods or lack of sufficient imagination on the part of the controller to do something about out-of-line conditions. There are some kinds of administrative expense which are difficult to determine in advance and which bear little relationship to production or distribution activities. But losses can result from excessive expenditures in this field quite as readily as in the manufacturing, distribution, or research fields. Therefore, administrative and financial expenses must be controlled.

Two prerequisites are essential to acceptable accounting control procedures: (1) an intelligent classification of accounts which sets forth the expenses in necessary detail, and (2) the definite assignment of control responsibility to one individual. The expenses should be separated into their fixed or variable elements, and the best units of variability determined. Some may be related to sales dollars, production man-hours, or net profit before taxes. Whatever the unit of variability, it can be applied in the manner described in the chapters on manufacturing costs. Administrative and financial expenses are likely to be more constant and less likely to respond to changes in sales or production. Some are determined by the board of directors and are fixed in nature. The task in such cases is to see that the expenditure is kept within the authorized limits. Other expenses may be determined by the executive committee or the company president. In these cases, too, the problem is to see that the facts are presented to arrive at a fair level of expense for the expected volume, and then kept within the limitation set. The same type of preventive management and control reports can be applied here as for other expenses.

FUNCTIONS OF THE CONTROLLER

What can the controller of the business do to keep administrative and financial expense within reasonable limits? Because of the nature of the expenses, the origin or source of the limitation in some cases, and difference in responsibility assignment of this group of expenses, his functions are not always the same as for other expense control assignments. Of course, he is the fact-finder; and for some of the expenses controlled by the line executives, the controller operates in the same manner as for manufacturing and distribution costs. Thus, he must assist in the budget preparation, make periodic reports on performance, and provide control information to permit those responsible to keep within budget limitations. He may, perhaps should, suggest to these executives means of reducing costs. Where costs are set by the board of directors, the controller has the responsibility of gathering together the facts for presentation to the board, through the chief executive, so that fair decisions may be reached. This may include the submission of his recommendations as well as facts and figures concerning his own company or the industry. Once an authorization is approved by the board, the controller must take steps to report on expenditures so that no excess spending results. In no event can he play the part of the passive bookkeeper. For certain of the administrative expenses, the controller will be directly responsible—not only for the accounting division expenses, but also for certain other costs assigned to him for control purposes: income taxes, other income and expense, contributions, or payroll taxes and insurance. For these he must take direct action to keep expenses within reasonable confines.

ACCOUNTING DIVISION BUDGETS

One of the tools which the controller must use is the budget. Here he has the opportunity of exercising ingenuity to stay within the budget allowance for the period. He is on the receiving end and must plan steps to avoid overruns.

Within the accounting division, if the company is large enough, will be found several departments whose managers can be held responsible for cost control. Budgets should be prepared in detail for each activity whose head is given the authority and responsibility to keep expenses within the budget limits. Some of the departments which may be logical budgetary control units are:

General Accounting	Insurance
Cost Accounting	Office Service
Auditing	Payroll
Tax	Tabulating
Budgets and Standards	Systems and Procedures

Each department head should be given a voice in setting his budget.

Practical experience will indicate that accounting costs are not all fixed, any more than are purchasing costs or industrial relations costs. However, a relatively larger portion may be fixed. Some simple variable factors should be found which will serve to indicate the expense justified at each level of activity. Thus, standard or actual labor hours in the factory may be used in the payroll department. At any given time, the total budget allowance would be the fixed expense plus an amount per standard labor hour. Other factors of variability might be dollar sales volume, units of sale, or number of transactions.

The controller or chief accountant should prepare the same reports on his activity as he does on that of others in order that management may be informed of his budget performance. An example of a plant controller's budget report is shown in Fig. 86. In this case a base allowance has been established to which is added a fluctuating allowance depending on factory productivity. For this month, the added allowance was based on 73.275 thousand standard man-hours. In the following month, the additional allowance might be restricted to only 68 units. Such a method of granting allowances does relate accounting costs to the income-producing factor—standard labor hours.

Figure 86 also illustrates a practice of assigning to a specific executive the responsibility for expense control of items other than his own departmental expenses. In this case, office supplies, postage, etc., were not departmentalized and the controller was assigned the task of keeping them in line.

AUTOMOTIVE PARTS CORPORATION

DEPARTMENT BUDGET REPORT

Dept. 9 Accounting Department
Dept. Head J.B. Mills

Month November
Units 73.275 Base 6

CLASSIFICATION	AMT. IN DOLLARS		(OVER) OR UNDER		% REALIZATION		
	ALLOWED	ACTUAL	CUR. MONTH	YR. TO DATE	CUR. MONTH	MOVING AVG. - CUR.	PREV.
SALARIES AND WAGES							
601 Supervisory Salaries		1950					
605 Other Salaries		1863					
606 Indirect Wages		5457					
607 Janitors and Sweepers							
608 Trainees Salaries and Wages							
609 Idle Time							
612 Vacations and Holidays		498					
614-16 Overtime Premium		106					
Sub-Total	10010	9874	136	2459	101.4		
OTHER DEPARTMENTALIZED EXP.							
618 Special Printed Forms		786					
619 Travel Expense		2					
621 Telephone		132					
622 Books, Periodicals & Inf. Ser.		5					
623 Memberships							
624 Consultants' Fees							
625 Operating Supplies		13					
626 Perishable Tools							
628 Misc. Dept. Expense							
Sub-Total	630	938	(308)	445	67.2		
TOTAL DEPARTMENTALIZED EXPENSE	10640	10812	(172)	2904	98.4		
DEPT. PERFORMANCE (D. L. & DEPT. EXP.)	10640	10812	(172)	2904	98.4	99.1	101.6
ASSIGNED EXPENSE							
656 Office Supplies	129	559	(430)	(733)	23.1		
657 Postage	288	678	(390)	(307)	42.5		
658 Telegraph	462	332	130	(262)	139.2		
664 Property Taxes	3650	*10385	(6735)	(11027)	35.1		
665 State Franchise Tax	569	567	2	(1605)	100.4		
668 Other Taxes	320	505	(185)	(2045)	63.4		
669 Property Insurance	620	* 1154	(534)	1594	53.7		
671 Other Insurance	841	931	(90)	(3006)	90.3		
672 Audit Fees & Expenses	400	350	50	2603	114.3		
674 Rent Tabulating	1400	437	963	820	320.4		
688 Depreciation	3410	3346	64	4340	101.9		
TOTAL ASSIGNED EXPENSE	12089	19244	(7155)	(9628)	62.8		
TOTAL EXPENSE	22729	30056	(7327)	(6724)	75.6		
OVER-ALL PERFORMANCE					92.2	92.8	95.6

November Postage Meter Reading - $1,374.
*To Adjust Accruals Fiscal Year to Date.

Issued by Acct. Dept. Date: 12/19/

Fig. 86—Administrative Department Budget Report.

CONTROL OF ACCOUNTING COSTS THROUGH THE USE OF STANDARDS

Budgetary control may be used to assist in keeping accounting expense, as well as all other expense, within the limits of business income. A second tool to be used in controlling accounting costs is standards of performance and cost. These standards can be applied to many office functions just as they have been applied to manufacturing and sales functions. They are not applicable to all accounting activities, nor can the same degree of accuracy be secured as in the factory. But in many offices, the possible cost savings for certain clerical activities are sufficient to justify the effort of establishing the standards.

While the general method of setting standards was discussed in Chapter 11, the application to the measurement of clerical work is outlined as follows:

1. *Preliminary Observation and Analysis.* This step is fundamental in securing the necessary over-all understanding of the problem, and in selecting those areas of activity which may lend themselves to standardization. Also, it assists in eliminating any obviously major weakness in routine.

2. *Selection of Functions on Which Standards Are To Be Set.* Standards should be set only on those activities which are in sufficient volume to justify standards.

3. *Determination of the Unit of Work.* A unit must be selected in which the standard may be expressed. This will depend on the degree of specialization and the volume of work.

4. *Determination of the Best Method and Setting of the Standard.* Time and motion study can be applied to office work, with sufficient allowance being given for fatigue and personal needs.

5. *Testing of the Standard.* After the standard has been set, it should be tested to see that it is practical.

6. *Final Application.* This involves using the standard, and preparing simple reports which the supervisor and the individual worker can see. It also requires a full explanation to the employee.

Illustrative accounting and clerical functions which lend themselves to standardization, and the units of work which may be used to measure performance are these:

Function	Unit of Standard Measurement
Order handling	Number of orders handled
Mail handling	Number of pieces handled
Billing	Number of invoice lines
Check writing	Number of checks written
Posting	Number of postings
Filing	Number of pieces filed
Punching—tabulating cards	Number of cards punched
Typing	Number of lines typed
Customer statements	Number of statements
Order writing	Number of order lines

In addition to performance standards, unit cost standards can be applied to measure an individual function or over-all activity. Thus, applying cost standards to credit and collection functions may involve these functions and units of measurement:

Functional Activity	Unit Cost Standard
Credit investigation and approval	Cost per sales order Cost per account sold Cost per credit sales transaction
Credit correspondence records and files	Cost per sales order Cost per letter Cost per account sold
Preparing invoices	Cost per invoice line Cost per item Cost per invoice Cost per order line Cost per order
Entire accounts receivable records, including posting of charges and credits and preparation of customers' statements	Cost per account Cost per sales order Cost per sales transaction
Posting charges	Cost per invoice Cost per shipment
Preparing customers' statements	Cost per statement Cost per account sold
Posting credits	Cost per remittance Cost per account sold
Calculating commissions on cash collected	Cost per remittance
Making street collections	Cost per customer Cost per dollar collected
Window collections	Cost per collection

OTHER MEANS OF COST CONTROL IN ACCOUNTING DIVISION

Emphasis has frequently been placed on the fact that *people,* not *reports,* control costs. Budgets and standards are only an aid in control. This is just as true with respect to the administrative and office costs as anywhere else. It is well to explore the other methods for cost control within the controller's own bailiwick—methods quite independent of budgets or standards. It is obvious that the function of providing management with facts must be done in an efficient and economical manner. Quite understandably, the controller should keep his own house in order if he is to be fully effective in assisting in the control of costs of other divisions. He should do an even better job in his own division because he is more familiar with the detailed activities. This is but another way of stating that much can be accomplished through day-to-day observations by the controller and his staff. There should be a constant search for easier and better ways of doing things.

The potential savings which may be realized through the reduction of administrative and office expense are probably not as great as in the factory or sales operations. This is natural because the major expenses of a business are concentrated in these two functions of production and distribution. Yet any company can realize significant savings over a period of time. Without a doubt, there will be occasions when the pressure for cost reductions is greater than others, particularly in periods of business decline. But suggestions on which the controller can take action as a line executive in his own division, and as a staff official elsewhere, are outlined below. Basically, a periodic or continuous review of procedures and costs must be made for the specific purpose of effecting cost reductions.

Illustrative areas or specific points by which administrative or office expense may be reduced through observation and analysis are:

1. Staff
    a. Reduction in staff when the present number of employees is needed only for peak work loads
    b. Elimination or control of overtime through specific approval in advance of occurrence
    c. Reduction of staff by avoiding replacement in cases of voluntary quits
    d. Introduction of incentives and/or standards
    e. Review of job classifications to see that each employee is doing work required by the job description and for which he is being paid
    f. Making of job studies to ascertain if lower-rated men can do some work currently done by more highly rated men—to release the latter for more constructive thinking
    g. Review of jobs to see what combinations can be made, and that each employee is doing a full day's work
    h. Office shutdown when factory is not working
    i. Improvement in working conditions with consequent increased efficiency

2. Systems and Procedures
    a. Utilization of up-to-date machines and equipment
    b. Reduction in reports and records through thorough review, including elimination of duplications
    c. Use of internal auditors—to suggest method improvements and reduce time spent by public accountants on the engagement
    d. Introduction of work simplification program

3. Expense Control
    a. Telephone and telegraph
        1) Reduction in unnecessary equipment—both telephones and teletype
        2) Increased use of mail and telegraph instead of toll calls
        3) Advance approval for all long-distance calls

b. Postage
   1) Emphasis on use of regular instead of air mail
   2) Use of postage permits to save labor
c. Printing
   1) Creation of own printing establishment
   2) Reduction in number of special forms
   3) Preparation of own special forms where possible
d. Supplies
   1) Institution of policy of charging on a requisition basis (usage instead of purchase)
   2) Careful check of quality and type, before purchase, with view to saving clerical time

Though some of these points may seem but feeble means of reducing costs, savings can be quite sizable in the aggregate. Aside from these specific examples, the approach should be that of inculcating in *each employee* the need and desire of finding better and cheaper ways of doing things.

We have reviewed the means of controlling the usual or ordinary operating expenses of the administrative function. Certain of the expenses, however, are of such a nature as to require special comment.

COMPENSATION OF CORPORATE OFFICIALS

Compensation of officers and directors includes the salaries, bonuses if any, and directors' fees. Since these costs are usually determined by the board of directors or executive committee, there is little problem of control. The controller must make certain that the payments are in accordance with the authorization. If bonuses are payable, provision should be made for an accrual throughout the year, based on the best information available, in order to avoid extra heavy charges in the last month of the year. He should be aware of all laws and regulations relative to disclosure of this information, such as in SEC reports, and take necessary steps to comply with them. A thorough knowledge of tax laws and other applicable regulations also will assist the controller in conceiving and recommending the most advantageous compensation arrangements to both company and official alike.

INCENTIVE COMPENSATION PLANS

Most human endeavor can be made more intensive and more fruitful if properly stimulated. This is just as true of the highest type of business executive as it is of the salesman or the laborer pushing a wheelbarrow. All three will respond to the proper type of incentive. It is largely in recognition of this fact that recent years have seen the growth and adoption of financial incentive plans to reward meritorious performance among the administrative and executive group. While it is beyond the scope of this book to discuss at length the many types of plans, it must be mentioned that these are or can be effective means of achieving or encouraging cost control and of increasing net profits. Financial rewards are not the only incentives; the satisfaction from a job well done, the gratification of being considered efficient by one's fellowman, the pleasure of beating past performance or some other standard—all these are worthwhile rewards in themselves. But financial remuneration, too, can be a very real and positive influence in controlling expense. Through the sharing of profits, it is hoped the executive will adopt a more proprietary interest and will be more alert to cost savings and the profitability of the business.

Every controller should become reasonably familiar with executive incentive bonus plans not only because they are an important control tool, but also because he should play a leading part in their installation.

Executives may be classified into two distinct groups for purposes of bonus payments: (1) those general executives who exert a substantial influence on the over-all operations and policies, and (2) those whose influence on business results is confined largely to the effect of their own department. A man in the former group could be paid a bonus related to net profit before taxes because he has a substantial influence on it. The latter group has little influence thereon, and any bonus should not be contingent upon the earning of a profit. Rather, certain factors within an individual department should be governing. It may be the reduction of expenses, or material losses, or increased output—whichever factors management feels are significant and important as a contribution toward over-all results. The principle, in any case, is to pay for superior results which can be attributed to the efforts of the supervisor, and not because of favorable results over which he has little or no control.

FACTORS IN EXECUTIVE PROFIT-SHARING PLANS

Over a period of time numerous profit-sharing plans have been conceived. No one plan is the best for all businesses; in fact, each plan must be tailored to suit the needs of the individual organization where it is to be used. There are several features distinguishing one plan from another which must be considered in developing the plan best suited to the company.

1. *Proportion of Profits Which Are Assigned to Management for Profit Sharing.* The amount set aside should be sufficient to serve as an incentive, but not so large as to invite criticism from either the stockholders, the public, or other employees (through their union or otherwise).

2. *Method of Determining Management's Share.* This may be a fixed percentage of the profits or a percentage on an ascending scale as profits increase. Another aspect is the defining of the base—

whether before or after federal income taxes; and whether the stockholders have a prior claim on the profits.

3. *Method of Allocating Management's Share of Profit to Each Individual.* What factors are to be considered? Is it to be on a salary basis? Is credit to be given for length of service? Is it subject to discretion of a committee, or is a regular formula established?
4. *Eligibility Requirements.* A decision must be made as to just how far down the ranks profits are to be shared. Is it to apply only to officers?
5. *Manner of Payment—Immediate or Deferred.* To gain tax advantages, the share, or a portion thereof, may be paid to recipients in later years when earnings presumably will not be as high.
6. *Effects of Termination of Employment.* Plans may differ as to the rights of the individual when he is terminated or resigns.
7. *Retirement and Other Benefits.* The plan may or may not provide for retirement benefits or disability benefits.
8. *Other.* Plans may differ as to the methods of administration, whether by a committee appointed by the board of directors or otherwise. Another feature which may differ is the right of the company to terminate or modify the plan.

It may be worthwhile to dwell for a moment on the right of executives to share in the profits of a business. Why shouldn't all the profits go to the stockholders? The answer, of course, is that the salary paid to executives can reasonably be expected to produce the usual or normal profits of the industry, as measured by invested capital, perhaps 6% or 8%. Better results can usually be attributed to the extra effort of the salaried group, and they should be rewarded accordingly. Such supernormal performance by the managerial group can increase manyfold the return to the stockholder; and a share of this profit rightfully should be considered as belonging to the management group.

Other means of rewarding executive performance include special retirement benefits, pension plans, and participation in stock allotment plans. The responsibility of the controller with respect to such compensation plans is substantially the same as it is with respect to salaries of corporate officials.

CONTRIBUTIONS, DUES, AND SUBSCRIPTIONS

Most companies are called upon to contribute to various charitable institutions, civic undertakings, and similar activities. All of these causes cannot be ignored because the business organization has a certain social responsibility for the welfare of the community. However, lack of adequate control can easily result in donations either beyond the means of the company or at least of an unreasonable amount. For that reason, centralized control has been found desirable, either in the board of directors, or the chief executive or plant manager, or a committee. First, a general policy must be set. Then a normal procedure might be to secure approval of an appropriation type, or fixed sum budget, based on a list of specific items. Once such approval is secured, the controller should take steps to see that no bills are paid which are not on the approved list. Some businesses set aside additional lump sums which must cover other requests which may be received and approved. In other instances each request received after the annual budget has been approved must run the entire gauntlet. One means of establishing a general limit for particularly large contributions, or even the entire amount to be donated, is to determine a reasonable contribution per employee. For example, the management might decide that three dollars per employee is a fair sum to donate annually to the Community Chest in those areas where company plants or offices are located. A specified share of estimated income or a per cent of sales could be other measuring sticks.

Because charitable demands usually reach a peak when business conditions are at their worst and the donors are least able to give, some corporations establish charitable foundations. Contributions are then accelerated during the more prosperous years and held in reserve by the foundation for future disbursement.

Dues and subscription expense sometimes shows a similar tendency to get out of line in the aggregate. For this reason, some sort of a clearing house is necessary. This may consist of a simple card record, by publication, in the accounting department or library, showing who subscribes to each magazine, paper, or service. When a requisition to purchase is received, this file is checked to see whether anyone else has subscribed, and if so, whether the publication can be routed to each interested party. Aside from this control, of course, is the budget which sets the maximum amount expendable for this kind of expense.

INTEREST EXPENSE, INCOME TAXES

Interest expense, being directly related to borrowed funds, is kept within limits through the control of business indebtedness. Control of interest-bearing obligations affects control of interest expense. When the financial budget of the company has been established, the amount of interest expense can be calculated on the basis of predicted borrowings, payments, and similar facts. For this expense, as for any other, responsibility for control should be placed in one executive, either the treasurer or controller. The reason for excess costs over budget should be explained. Aside from budgetary control, the primary problem is one of securing loans on the most advantageous terms.

There are very few control problems in connection with income taxes. The first requirement is to estimate monthly the amount due and to make the proper accruals. Another function of the controller is to review carefully methods and transactions, securing tax counsel where necessary, in order to comply with all technicalities and thus secure the greatest tax advantage. Other than this, his responsibilities relate to keeping the required records and substantiating data to support tax claims, advising on capital gain and loss transactions, and arranging the capital structure, as well as the investments, so as to secure the maximum benefits under the tax laws. Quite aside from the tax problems of the individual company, the chief accounting officer can actively promote equitable tax laws directly or through associations.

LEGAL AND PROFESSIONAL EXPENSE

Included in this classification are the fees and expenses of outside lawyers, accountants, engineers, and economists engaged by the general executives. Perhaps the simplest type of control involves the establishment of a budget for the known or recurring expense anticipated for the budget period, supplemented by budget adjustments for each additional project undertaken. This is merely a means of measuring actual expense against estimated. Beyond assisting in the establishment of the budget and reporting performance, the controller can do two things: (1) where audit or accounting fees are involved, he can direct his staff in preparing the necessary working papers, and otherwise urge the utmost cooperation with the auditors, so as to keep the fees at a minimum; (2) he can secure comparative cost data and check trends of expenses giving due consideration to the quality of service.

The principle of preventive management can be applied in large degree so that no expenses need be incurred without thorough review as to the requirements. Many times the company will be staffed with the necessary talent, and it is a question of transferring duties in order to free personnel for the special assignments.

CORPORATE EXPENSES

For businesses organized as corporations there are numerous corporate expenses which must be assigned to particular executives for control purposes; for example, state and federal capital stock taxes, franchise taxes, fees of fiscal agents, stock transfer taxes, and fidelity bonds and insurance. There is no particular problem of control. The controller can assist in estimating the expenses for budget purposes, prepare the necessary reports, and make the required accruals.

EXCESS FACILITY COSTS

Occasionally some companies find themselves in possession of distribution or production facilities which appear to be permanently excessive. Usually they were built or acquired without a sound analysis of the potential demand for the company's products, or because of other errors in executive judgment. Whatever the reason, it is unwise to burden the current manufacturing or distribution operations with the charge. The costs are often carried as a separate administrative expense until the property can be disposed of. The continuing expenses usually consist of only depreciation, taxes, insurance, and a certain minimum amount of maintenance. It is a relatively simple matter to estimate the cost and to establish a budget to cover it. Management generally should be alert either to dispose of the property on favorable terms or possibly to rent it.

BAD DEBT LOSSES

Another item of expense peculiar to the financial group is bad debt loss. Quite obviously this loss is not the sole criterion of the efficiency of the credit department. Any bad debt losses could be eliminated either by making only cash sales or by restricting credit sales to only the financially strongest firms. Such a policy would drive business to competitors who are willing to take reasonable credit risks. Any discussion of bad debt losses must therefore assume that a company is competitive from the standpoint of extending credit. Under such circumstances there are some measuring sticks to be applied to loss experience over a period of time. These include:

1. Percentage of bad debt losses to total sales. This is to be used where the cash sales are relatively insignificant. Such a basis avoids the necessity of segregating cash and credit sales if solely for this purpose.
2. Percentage of bad debt losses to total net credit sales.

If warranted, these bases can be refined through a segregation by different classes of customer, methods or terms of sale, or by different territories.

For the purpose of setting budgets, the applicable percentage can be applied against budgeted sales. Control of the expense, of course, rests upon effectively policing accounts receivable to discover evidence of slow pay.

CASH DISCOUNTS

The review of costs for cost reduction or cost control purposes must include cash discounts. Granting of cash discounts is an outmoded practice which is carried over from the early days when working capital was scarce, credit risks were greater, and collection expense was higher. There is an increasingly larger number of businessmen who feel that the practice should be discontinued. In fact, some of the companies which have eliminated or reduced the cash discount find little or no noticeable effect on sales.

OTHER INCOME AND EXPENSE

Most business firms have various items of income and expense which are of a non-operating nature. The income may include interest income, royalties, rental income, dividends received, and income from sales of scrap; the expenses include loss on sale of fixed assets and sales discounts. Based on past experience and knowledge as to projected changes, reasonable estimates of these elements of income and expense can be made. Otherwise, control of a limited nature is exercised through the judgment of the official to whom the accounts are assigned.

PART IV

Planning and Accounting Control of Assets, Obligations, and Equity Interests

19

Planning and Control of Cash

OBJECTIVES OF CASH ADMINISTRATION

One of the functions of a controller is to safeguard the assets of a business through the introduction of the necessary records and controls. By this means accountability may be established and the required reports to management are made possible. Cash is a particularly vulnerable type of property because it is easily concealed and readily negotiable. Once it is stolen, tracing becomes difficult. However, cash administration involves much more than preventing the misappropriation of funds. From an over-all viewpoint, it includes the following objectives:

1. Proper planning so that the requisite funds are on hand to meet the business needs—both short-term and long-range
2. Effective utilization at all times of the company funds
3. Establishment of accountability for cash receipts and sufficient safeguards until the moneys are placed in the depository
4. Establishment of controls to assure disbursements only for the legitimate liabilities of the company

DUTIES OF CONTROLLER VS. TREASURER

With respect to the planning and control of cash, a very close and cooperative relationship must exist between the controller and treasurer. Duties and responsibilities vary in different firms. However, in most industrial or commercial concerns the treasurer is the custodian of cash funds and exercises supervision over the receipts and disbursements. He may select the depository, subject to the approval of the president or other designated authority. Usually it is he who maintains the necessary relationships with banks and other financial agencies.

Because of the assumed close relationship between cash and cash records, the duties of the treasurer often extend to prescribing the methods of recording cash transactions. In practice, however, with the concurrence of the treasurer, the cash receipts and disbursements procedures are established and periodically reviewed by the controller. This ties in with his usual responsibility for maintaining the corporate, general, and cost accounting records of the company. The actual handling of the cash is done by a cashier on the treasurer's staff. In only the larger firms can the segregation of duties as between controller and treasurer be observed.

Determining the prospective cash position is an integral part of the business forecasting procedure, and usually rests with the controller. By the same token, however, there should be close liaison with the treasurer. In many companies, preparation of the long-range cash projections and the annual or quarterly cash forecasts are the responsibility of the controller. However, determination of the daily and/or weekly balances for the immediate near term very often lies with the treasurer.

THE CASH FORECAST

PURPOSE OF CASH FORECASTING

A cash forecast is a projection of the anticipated cash receipts and disbursements, and the resulting cash balance within a specified period. This is a necessary function in any well-managed plan of cash administration.

Obviously, the operation of any business must be planned within the limits of available funds; and conversely, the necessary funds must be provided to carry out the planned business operations.

In these days of increasing sales, and earnings, and taxes, business management is rediscovering that profits are not the same as cash in the bank. The company may show a small profit, or even a loss, and have a very sizable cash balance. Particularly in those industries requiring heavy capital investment, the cash generation by the operations, the "cash flow," may be very heavy and yet result in mediocre profits. For reasons such as these, cash forecasting is being recognized as a vital management tool.

The basic purpose behind the preparation of the cash budget is to plan so that the business will have the necessary cash—whether from the short-term or long-term viewpoint. Further, when excess cash is to be available, budget preparation offers a means of anticipating an opportunity for effective utilization. Aside from these general purposes, some specific uses to which a cash budget may be put are:

1. To point out peaks or seasonal fluctuations in business activity which make necessary larger investments in inventories and receivables
2. To indicate the time and extent of funds needed to meet maturing obligations, tax payments, and dividend or interest payments

3. To assist in planning for growth, including the required funds for plant expansion and working capital
4. To indicate well in advance of needs the extent and duration of funds required from outside sources and thus permit the securing of more advantageous loans
5. To assist in securing credit from banks, and improve the general credit position of the business
6. To determine the extent and probable duration of funds available for investment
7. To plan the reduction of bonded indebtedness or other loans
8. To coordinate the financial needs of the subsidiaries and divisions of the company
9. To permit the company to take advantage of cash discounts and forward purchasing, thereby increasing its earnings

CASH FORECASTING METHODS

At least three methods have been developed for constructing a cash forecast. While the end product is the estimated cash balance, the methods differ chiefly as to the starting point of the forecast and the detail made available. The three techniques are described as follows.

1. *Direct Estimate of Cash Receipts and Disbursements.* This is a detailed forecast of each cost element or function involving cash. It is essentially a projection of the cash records. Such a method is the one most commonly used in business and is quite essential to giving a complete picture of the swings or gyrations in both receipts and disbursements. It is particularly applicable to those concerns which are subject to wide variations in activity. Moreover, it is very useful for controlling cash flow by comparing actual and forecasted performance. A cash forecast prepared on this basis is shown in Fig. 87.

2. *Adjusted Net Income Method.* As the name implies, the starting point for this procedure is the estimated income and expense statement. This projected net income is adjusted for all non-cash transactions to arrive at the cash income or loss, and is further adjusted for cash transactions which arise because of non-operating balance sheet changes. A worksheet showing the general method is illustrated in Fig. 88. This is the "cash flow" approach.

It will be observed that since net income is used, the true extent of the gross cash receipts or disbursements is not known. Where a company must work on rather close cash margins, this method probably will not meet the needs. It is applicable chiefly where sales volume is relatively stable and the out-of-pocket costs are fairly constant in relation to sales.

3. *Working Capital Differentials.* By this method the net working capital at the beginning of each month is adjusted by estimated net income

Economy Company

STATEMENT OF ESTIMATED CASH RECEIPTS AND DISBURSEMENTS
For the Fiscal Year 1963
(000's Omitted)

Description	Jan.	Feb.	Mar.	April	May	June	July	Aug.	Sept.	Oct.	Nov.	Dec.	Total
CASH AT BEGINNING OF PERIOD	$1,330	$756	$842	$617	$701	$1,154	$1,182	$1,853	$2,819	$3,433	$3,132	$2,339	$1,330
CASH RECEIPTS													
Collection on Account	2,985	3,255	3,975	4,081	4,235	4,288	4,240	4,218	4,256	4,226	4,100	4,087	47,946
Dividends—Subsidiaries	—	—	—	—	437	436	873	436	—	—	—	—	2,182
Bond Interest—Subsidiaries					Via Intercompany Account								
Short-Term Notes	—	—	600	—	—	—	—	—	—	—	—	—	600
Miscellaneous	25	38	25	55	20	20	20	20	20	20	20	20	303
Total Cash Receipts	3,010	3,293	4,600	4,136	4,692	4,744	5,133	4,674	4,276	4,246	4,120	4,107	51,031
Total Cash Available	4,340	4,049	5,442	4,753	5,393	5,898	6,315	6,527	7,095	7,679	7,252	6,446	52,361
CASH DISBURSEMENTS													
Accounts Payable	1,972	2,117	2,200	2,254	1,846	2,003	2,059	1,926	1,906	2,004	1,937	1,865	24,089
Payrolls—Net	1,096	1,067	1,034	1,001	1,018	1,034	1,083	1,167	1,307	1,351	1,296	1,272	13,726
Subsidiaries	210	—	366	367	367	367	239	368	368	369	366	366	3,753
Dividends—Preferred Stock	—	—	—	238	—	—	236	—	—	234	—	—	708
Interest—Mortgage Bonds	—	—	—	—	238	—	—	—	—	—	238	—	476
Short-Term Notes	—	—	—	—	700	500	600	—	—	—	—	—	1,800
Taxes—Federal Income	18	—	389	—	—	389	—	—	—	97	—	—	893
" —Withholding and S.S.	167	—	360	157	—	352	158	162	—	400	177	—	1,933
" —Real Estate	—	—	—	—	—	—	—	—	—	20	20	55	95
Funded Debt	—	—	—	—	—	—	—	—	—	—	800	—	800
Pension Plan	—	—	456	—	—	—	—	—	—	—	—	—	456
Purchases—$5 Pfd. Stock	78	—	—	—	48	48	48	49	48	49	48	48	464
Other Accruals	43	23	20	35	22	23	39	36	33	23	31	44	372
Total Cash Disbursements	3,584	3,207	4,825	4,052	4,239	4,716	4,462	3,708	3,662	4,547	4,913	3,650	49,565
CASH AT END OF PERIOD	$756	$842	$617	$701	$1,154	$1,182	$1,853	$2,819	$3,433	$3,132	$2,339	$2,796	$2,796

Fig. 87—Illustrative Statement of Estimated Cash Receipts and Disbursements.

Statement of Estimated Cash Flow
For the Year 1963
(In Thousands of Dollars)

Description	January	February	March	Quarterly Total	December	Quarterly Total	Year 1963 Estimate	Year 1962 Actual
CASH GENERATION FROM OPERATIONS								
Pre-Tax Income	$ 4,260	$ 3,780	$ 4,620	$12,660	$ 4,980	$11,330	$ 56,800	$ 59,600
Add:								
Depreciation, depletion, and amortization	4,870	4,340	4,770	13,980	4,990	12,010	49,300	47,880
Other non-cash items (describe)								
Sale of assets	—	2,090	—	2,090	—	—	8,420	2,000
Cash Generated from Operations	9,130	10,210	9,390	28,730	9,970	23,340	114,520	109,480
ADD OR (DEDUCT) WORKING CAPITAL CHANGES (except cash)								
Inventories	—	500	—	500	(1,000)	(2,000)	(2,000)	2,000
Receivables	600	1,220	500	2,320	(2,000)	(1,000)	(1,000)	500
Federal Taxes	1,200	1,460	1,320	3,980	1,220	3,880	3,880	(1,000)
Total Changes in Working Capital	1,800	3,180	1,820	6,800	(1,780)	880	880	1,500
OTHER USES								
Capital Expenditures	5,700	6,320	10,860	22,880	7,770	18,060	79,930	92,100
Dividends—Common	1,690	—	—	1,690	—	1,710	6,020	6,370
Long-Term Investments	—	—	6,900	6,900	8,000	8,000	25,000	17,410
Total	7,390	6,320	17,760	31,470	15,770	27,770	110,950	115,880
Increase (Decrease) in Cash Position	3,540	7,070	(6,550)	4,060	(7,580)	(3,550)	4,450	(4,900)
CASH POSITION AT END OF PERIOD								
Cash	29,800	33,870	33,320		29,800		29,800	27,260
Securities (cash equivalents)	3,000	6,000	—		3,910		3,910	2,000
Total	$32,800	$39,870	$33,320		$33,710		$ 33,710	$ 29,260

Fig. 88—Statement of Estimated Cash Flow.

359

and other receipts and disbursements to arrive at the estimated working capital at the end of each month. From this are deducted the required working capital, excluding cash, and the standard cash balance, to arrive at the amount of cash available for deposit and investment.

Such an approach has been used when standard valuations required for receivables, inventories, and other working capital at various sales volumes have been determined; and when the major objective is the reinvestment of surplus funds.

ESTIMATING CASH RECEIPTS

The sources of cash receipts for the typical industrial or commercial firm are well-known: collections on account, cash sales, royalties, rent, dividends, sale of capital items, sale of investments, and new financing. These items can be predicted with reasonable accuracy. Usually the most important recurring sources are collections on account and cash sales. Experience and a knowledge of trends will indicate what share of total sales probably will be for cash. From the sales forecast, then, the total cash sales value can be determined. In a somewhat similar fashion, information can be gleaned from the records to enable the controller to make a careful estimate of collections. Once the experience has been analyzed, the results can be adjusted for trends and applied to the credit sales portrayed in the sales forecast.

An example will illustrate the technique. Assume that an analysis of collection experience for June sales revealed the following collection data:

Description	% of Total Credit Sales
Collected in June	2.1
July	85.3
August	8.9
September	2.8
October	.3
Cash discounts	.5
Bad debt losses	.1
Total	100.0

If next year's sales in June could be expected to fall into the same pattern, then application of the percentages to estimated June credit sales would determine the probable monthly distribution of collections. The same analysis applied to each month of the year would result in a reasonably reliable basis for collection forecasting. The worksheet (June column) for cash collections might look somewhat as follows:

	Description		
Month of Sale	% Total	Net Sales	June Collections
February	.4	$149,500	$ 598
March	1.9	160,300	3,045
April	7.7	290,100	22,338
May	88.3	305,400	269,668
June	2.1	320,000	6,720
Total Collections			302,369
Cash Discounts (May)	.5	305,400	(1,527)
Losses	.1		(320)
Total			$300,522

Anticipated discounts must be calculated since they enter into the profit and loss forecast.

These experience factors must be modified, not only by trends developed over a period of time, but also by the estimate of general business conditions as reflected in collections, as well as contemplated changes in terms of sale or other credit policies. Refinements in the approach can be made if experience varies widely between geographical territories, types of customers, or channels of distribution. Obviously, the analysis of collections need not be made every month; it is sufficient if the distribution is checked occasionally.

Figure 89 is an example of a typical statement of estimated cash receipts. In this instance receipts from particular contracts are set out, in addition to the usual sales.

ESTIMATING CASH DISBURSEMENTS

If a complete operating budget is available, the controller should have little difficulty in assembling the data into an estimate of cash disbursements. The usual cash disbursements in the typical industrial or commercial firm consist of salaried and hourly payrolls, materials, taxes, dividends, traveling expense, other operating expenses, interest, purchase of equipment, and retirement of stock.

From the labor budget, the manufacturing expense budget, and the commercial expense budget, the total anticipated expense for salaries and wages can be secured. Once this figure is available, the period of cash disbursement can be determined easily, for payrolls must be met on certain dates closely following the time when earned. Reference to a calendar will establish the pay dates. Separate consideration should be given to the tax deductions from the gross pay, since these are not payable at the same time the net payroll is disbursed—unless special bank accounts are established for the tax deductions.

Consolidated Electronics Corporation

STATEMENT OF ESTIMATED CASH RECEIPTS

For the Period January 1, 1963 Through March 31, 1963

Description	January	February	March	Total
ELECTRONICS				
Fixed Price Contracts				
U. S. Government				
Progress payments	$ 625,000	$ 820,000	$1,150,000	$2,595,000
Collections on delivery . .	333,500	470,200	695,000	1,498,700
Total	958,500	1,290,200	1,845,000	4,093,700
Foreign Governments				
Advances	21,500	—	10,000	31,500
Collections on delivery . .	32,500	21,000	8,500	62,000
Miscellaneous	8,000	6,000	5,200	19,200
Total	62,000	27,000	23,700	112,700
Total Receipts—FP Contracts.	1,020,500	1,317,200	1,868,700	4,206,400
Incentive—Commercial				
Refinery				
Advances from customers	20,000	—	—	20,000
Collections on account . .	35,900	39,500	28,000	103,400
Cash sales	4,300	4,000	4,500	12,800
Total	60,200	43,500	32,500	136,200
Automotive				
Advances from customers	890,000	410,000	300,000	1,600,000
Collections on delivery . .	245,000	390,000	250,000	885,000
Total	1,135,000	800,000	550,000	2,485,000
Total Collections—Electronics	2,215,700	2,160,700	2,451,200	6,827,600
HEAVY MACHINE TOOLS				
Petroleum				
Deposits	5,500	—	2,000	7,500
Collections on account	8,300	9,200	6,400	23,900
Cash sales	2,000	2,000	2,000	6,000
Total	15,800	11,200	10,400	37,400
Chemical				
Collections on account	12,500	11,300	8,100	31,900
Deposits	500	200	300	1,000
Cash sales	1,000	750	500	2,250
Total	14,000	12,250	8,900	35,150
Total Machine Tools Collections.	29,800	23,450	19,300	72,550
Miscellaneous	1,000	1,000	1,000	3,000
Total Cash Receipts	$2,246,500	$2,185,150	$2,471,500	$6,903,150

Fig. 89—Statement of Estimated Cash Receipts by Source.

The material budget will set out the material requirements each month. The more important elements probably should be treated individually— power units or engines, for example. Other items will be grouped together. Only in a few instances is material purchased for cash. However, reference to required inventories and to delivery dates as well as assistance from the purchasing department will establish the time allowed for payments. If thirty days are required, then usage of one month can be moved forward for the purpose of estimating cash payments. The effect of cash discounts should be considered in arriving at the estimated disbursements.

The various manufacturing and operating expenses should be considered individually because they are by no means all the same. Some are prepayments or accruals, paid annually, such as property taxes and insurance. Some are non-cash items, such as depreciation expense or bad debts. For a large number of individually small items, such as supplies, telephone and telegraph, and traveling expense, an average time lag may be used.

Cash requirements for capital additions should be determined from the plant budget or other known plans. No particular difficulty presents itself because the needs are relatively fixed and are established by the board of directors or other authority.

Usual practice requires the determination of cash receipts and disbursements exclusive of transactions involving voluntary debt retirements, purchase of treasury stock, or funds from bank loans. Decisions relative to these means of securing or disbursing cash are reached when the cash position is known and policy formulated accordingly. When branch plants are involved, all such outlying activities must be consolidated to get the over-all picture.

A typical cash disbursements budget is illustrated in Fig. 90. The treatment of payments on other than a monthly basis is shown.

RELATION OF CASH BUDGET TO OTHER BUDGETS

From the preceding discussion it is readily apparent that preparation of the cash budget is generally dependent on other budgets—the sales forecast, the statement of estimated income and expense, and the various operating budgets. It is in reality part of a coordinated program of sales and costs correlated with balance sheet changes and expected revenues and expenditures.

It can be appreciated, also, that the cash budget is a check on the entire budgetary program. If the operating budget goals are achieved, the results will be reflected in the cash position. Failure to achieve budgeted performance may result in seeking additional sources of cash.

Depending on the financial position of the company, the cash forecast may have a high priority. Many executives prefer to review the cash fore-

Consolidated Spacecraft Corporation
Statement of Estimated Cash Disbursements
For the Period January 1 Through December 31, 1963

Description	January	February	March	November	December	Total
INVENTORY ITEMS						
Raw Material and Purchased Parts						
Project 615						
Power units	$1,350,000	$1,325,000	$1,375,000	$1,300,000	$1,300,000	$15,840,000
Landing gears	325,000	325,000	320,000	325,000	415,000	3,900,000
Radios	115,000	117,500	117,500	115,000	115,000	1,380,000
Tires and tubes	120,000	110,000	110,000	110,000	122,500	1,320,000
Other	35,000	30,000	35,000	30,000	25,000	360,000
Total	1,945,000	1,907,500	1,957,500	1,880,000	1,977,500	22,800,000
Project 616						
Power units	80,000	76,000	84,000	160,000	168,000	1,200,000
Radios	10,000	10,000	12,000	24,000	30,000	132,000
Other	4,000	3,500	5,000	10,000	12,000	72,000
Total	94,000	89,500	101,000	194,000	210,000	1,404,000
Total Raw Materials and Purchased Parts	2,039,000	1,997,000	2,058,500	2,074,000	2,187,500	24,204,000
Subcontracted Production						
Project 615	420,000	510,000	480,000	105,000	120,000	3,600,000
Project 616	20,000	10,000	10,000	–	23,000	150,000
Total Subcontracted Production	440,000	520,000	490,000	105,000	143,000	3,750,000
Expenses						
Salaries and wages—direct	560,000	458,000	562,000	657,000	665,000	7,380,000
Salaries and wages—indirect	36,500	36,000	36,500	36,000	37,000	432,000
Total salaries and wages	596,500	494,000	598,500	693,000	702,000	7,812,000
Payroll taxes, etc.	35,900	31,300	37,800	24,900	18,400	373,000
Property taxes	–	–	122,000	–	–	122,000
Property insurance	–	72,500	–	–	–	72,500
Supplies	2,000	1,800	2,100	2,000	2,000	22,800
Other	11,000	11,000	11,000	11,000	11,000	132,000
Total Expenses	645,400	610,600	771,400	730,900	733,400	8,534,300
Total Inventory Items	3,124,400	3,127,600	3,319,900	2,909,900	3,063,900	36,488,300
OTHER CASH DISBURSEMENTS						
Administrative expense	12,000	12,000	17,000	15,500	12,000	168,000
Selling and advertising	17,000	12,000	45,000	11,500	22,500	310,000
Advances to vendors	20,500	–	–	–	–	20,500
Additions to fixed assets	101,000	51,000	19,500	3,000	17,000	397,500
Other	2,000	2,000	3,000	–	2,000	30,000
Total	152,500	77,000	84,500	30,000	53,500	926,000
Total Cash Disbursements	$3,276,900	$3,204,600	$3,404,400	$2,939,900	$3,117,400	$37,414,300

Fig. 90—Statement of Estimated Cash Disbursements.

cast ahead of other projected statements, and it may, therefore, take the number-one spot in the complete report on expected operations.

LENGTH OF CASH BUDGET PERIOD

The length of the budget period depends on several factors, including the purpose the budget is to serve, the financial condition of the company, and the opinion of the executives as to the practicality and accuracy of estimating. For illustration, a short-term forecast would be used in determining cash requirements—perhaps for one to three months in advance. But if the cash margin is low, an estimate of cash receipts and disbursements may be necessary on a weekly basis, or even daily. On the other hand, a firm with ample cash may develop a cash forecast, by months, for six months or a year in advance. For the determination of general financial policy a longer-term budget is necessary. Some companies feel that estimating beyond three months is inaccurate and restrict the cash budget to this period. Other companies maintain a running budget for three or more months in advance, always adding one month and dropping off the present month. A controller will have to adapt his forecasting to the conditions he finds. He may prepare a short-term cash budget for cash requirements purposes and also a long-term forecast for use in financial policy decisions.

PUTTING THE CASH BUDGET TO WORK

The controller can prepare the cash budget in the usual manner, indicating the extent of additional cash funds needed, if any, and the probable duration of such need. However, the responsibility for securing these funds on the most advantageous basis rests with the treasurer or chief financial officer. He, and not the chief accounting officer, would usually negotiate with banks for loans or invest surplus funds. Yet the part played by the controller is not always as routine as might appear. In times of adversity, he must be prepared to furnish extra information. Thus the treasurer may need to know the exact cash needs of the following week. This can be furnished by manually adding the bills payable at that time, as well as the payrolls. If the accounts payable are on tabulating cards, the requirements can be readily determined by tabulating the applicable due date file. The same procedure can be used in determining the funds, if any, to be transferred to each branch for the weekly period.

Cash requirements must be planned just as other operations are planned. It simply is not satisfactory to assume that a high volume of sales will automatically result in a sound financial position, or that with a satisfactory budgeted profit and loss statement finances will take care of themselves. The controller can be an effective voice in establishing the necessity for a well-developed financial program.

INVESTING SURPLUS CASH

One of the advantages of short-term cash forecasting is a determination of surplus cash available for short-term investment. While such investment is primarily the concern of the treasurer, the controller has an interest in seeing that temporary excess funds produce earnings.

Surplus cash is that cash in excess of current operating requirements, giving consideration to compensating balances required to reimburse the bank adequately for its services and to provide the lines of credit or borrowing. Cash may be surplus over several years, and sound long-range planning should take this availability into account. Temporary surplus cash may be invested for short periods; later it may be needed to pay regular obligations such as taxes, dividends, or accounts payable. The principal criteria which govern the selection of the proper medium—probably in order of importance—are (1) security of the company funds, (2) marketability of the investment, and (3) yield.

CASH COLLECTIONS

ADMINISTRATION OF CASH RECEIPTS

One of the primary objectives of financial management is the conservation and effective utilization of cash. From the cash collection viewpoint, there are two phases of control: (1) the acceleration of collections, and (2) proper internal control of collections.

ACCELERATION OF CASH RECEIPTS

Two methods are commonly used to speed up the collection of receivables. They are known as the lock-box system and area concentration banking.

The lock-box system involves the establishment of depository accounts in the various geographical areas of significant cash collections so that remittances from customers will take less time in transit—preferably not more than one day. Customers mail remittances to the company at a locked post office box in the region served by the bank. The bank collects the remittances, and deposits the proceeds to the account of the company. Funds in excess of those required to cover costs are periodically transferred to company headquarters. Supporting documents accompanying remittances are mailed by the bank to the company. Collections are thus accelerated through reduction in transit time with resultant lower credit exposure. Arrangements must be made, however, for proper control of credit information.

Under the system of area concentration banking, local company units collect remittances and deposit them in the local bank. From the local bank, usually by wire transfers, expeditious movement of funds is made to a few area or regional concentration banks. Funds in excess of compensating balances are automatically transferred by wire to the company's banking headquarters. By this technique in-transit time is reduced.

The controller is expected to be aware of these and other devices for accelerating collections, to assist the treasurer, should that be necessary.

INTERNAL CONTROL OF CASH RECEIPTS

In most business organizations the usual routine cash transactions are numerous. The following sources are typical: (1) mail receipts, (2) over-the-counter cash sales, (3) sales or collections made by salesmen, solicitors, etc., and (4) over-the-counter collections on account. Naturally, all businesses have other cash transactions of a less routine nature, such as receipts from sale of fixed assets, which may be handled by the officers or which require special procedures. Most of the cash problems will be found to center on the transactions listed above, because the more unusual or less voluminous cash receipts are readily susceptible to a simple check.

Regardless of the source of cash, the very basis for the prevention of errors or fraud is the principle of internal check. Such a system involves the separation of the actual handling of cash from the records relating to cash. It requires that the work of one employee be supplemented by the work of another. Certain results must always agree. For example, the daily cash deposit must be the same as the charge to the cash control account. This automatic checking of the work of one employee by another clearly discourages fraud and locates errors. Under such conditions, any peculations are generally restricted to cases of carelessness or collusion.

The system of internal control must be designed on the groundwork of the individual organization. However, there are some general suggestions which will be helpful to the controller in reveiwing the situation in his own company:

1. All receipts of cash through the mails should be recorded in advance of transfer to the cashier. Periodically these records should be traced to the deposit slip.
2. All receipts should be deposited intact daily. This procedure might also require a duplicate deposit slip to be sent by the bank or person making the deposit (other than the cashier) to an independent department—for use in subsequent check or audit.
3. Responsibility for the handling of cash should be clearly defined and definitely fixed.
4. Usually the functions of receiving cash and disbursing cash should be kept entirely separate (except in financial institutions).
5. The actual handling of cash should be entirely separate from the maintenance of records; and the cashiers should not have access to these records.

6. Tellers, agents, and field representatives should be required to give receipts, retaining a duplicate, of course.

7. Bank reconciliations should be made by those not handling cash or keeping the records. Similarly, the mailing of statements to customers, including the check-off against the ledger accounts, should be done by a third party. The summarizing of cash records also may be handled by a third party.

8. All employees handling cash or cash records should be required to take a periodic vacation, and someone else should handle the job during such absence. Also, at unannounced times, employees should be shifted in jobs in order to detect or prevent collusion.

9. All employees handling cash or cash records should be adequately bonded.

10. Mechanical and other protective devices should be used where applicable to give added means of check—cash registers, the tape being read by a third party; duplicate sales slips; daily cash blotters.

11. Where practical, cash sales should be verified by means of inventory records, and periodic physical inventories.

ILLUSTRATIVE CASH RECEIPTS PROCEDURE

A simple and effective cash receipts procedure can be executed which embodies some of the controls mentioned in the preceding section and which is adaptable by most industrial firms receiving cash by mail. All incoming mail not addressed to a specific individual is opened in the mail room. Any mail containing remittances is listed on a daily remittance sheet prepared in triplicate. The name, check number, date, and amount are detailed on the record (Fig. 91). One copy is forwarded, with the envelopes and remittance slips, to the cashier; a second to the auditor, treasurer, or controller; and the third copy is retained by the mail room. The cashier records the cash received via the mail room on his daily cash sheet (Fig. 92), indicating the nature of the receipt, along with any other receipts from other sources. This cash sheet is subsequently sent to the accounting department for posting, details as well as summary, after the cashier has made a summary entry in his records. The deposit slip is prepared in quadruplicate. The cashier retains one copy. Three copies go to the bank for receipting, one of which is retained by the bank; another is returned to the cashier as evidence the bank received the funds; and a third is sent to the auditing department or controller's office. This is then compared in total, and occasionally in detail, with the daily cash register. The remittance sheet is also test-checked against the deposit slip. The cashier, of course, does not have access to the accounts receivable records or general ledger; nor does he handle disbursements.

The Blank Company

MAIL ROOM REMITTANCE SHEET

Receipts of __July 19, 1963__

Check No., etc.	Source if Not Check	Sender	City and State	Amount
1602		The Rush Airplane Company	Scranton, Pa.	$ 126.12*
195692	P.M.O.	Rentaul Air Service	Stamford, Conn.	19.50
2402		Automatic Service Company	Los Angeles, Calif.	316.00
1613		Voe Parts Dealer	Toledo, Ohio	2.90
9865		Brush Electric Company	Chicago, Ill.	25.50
2915		Ajax Manufacturing Company	Cleveland, Ohio	1,002.60
8512		Apex Machine Tool Co.	New York City	18.60

Total.. $1,511.22

Prepared by __J. J. B.__

Date __7/19/63__

Original: Cashier

Fig. 91—Mail Room Remittance Sheet.

COMMON METHODS OF MISAPPROPRIATING CASH

An enumeration of some of the more common methods of misappropriating company funds may be a guide to the controller in recognizing points to guard against:

1. Mail Receipts
   a. Lapping—diverting cash and reporting it some time after it has been collected; usually funds received from one account are credited against another account from which cash has been diverted earlier
   b. Borrowing funds temporarily, without falsifying any records, or simply not recording all cash received
   c. Falsifying totals in the cashbook

DAILY CASH SHEET

Date   April 20, 1962

Check No.	Description	Debit Cash (101)	Trade Accounts Receivable (108)	CREDIT					
				Deposits (104)	Cash Sales (501)	Employees Accounts Receivable (106)	OTHER Account	Description	Amount
1242	Jones Chemical Co.	$ 622.50	$	$	$ 622.50	$			$
846	Witmer Candy Co.	9,875.00	9,875.00						
101	Prescott Molding Co.	4,322.50	4,322.50						
10	Rush Mfg. Co.	12,500.00		12,500.00					
322	Monsanto Cyanamid Co.	16,321.50	16,321.50						
464	Laughlin Stamping Co.	421.12			421.12				
422	Aero Company	3,820.00	3,820.00						
	Marjorie Jones	16.00				16.00			
	Adela Castle	1.20				1.20			
	Pierre's Restaurant	19.70					662	Vending Machine Income	19.70
	Total	$47,919.52	$34,339.00	$12,500.00	$1,043.62	$17.20			$19.70

Fig. 92—Daily Cash Sheet.

 d. Overstating discounts and allowances

 e. Charging off a customer's account as a bad debt and pocketing the cash

 f. Withholding of miscellaneous income, such as insurance refunds

2. Over-the-Counter Sales

 a. Failure to report all sales and pocketing the cash

 b. Underadding the sales slip, and pocketing the difference

 c. Falsely representing refunds or expenditures

 d. Registering a smaller amount than the true amount of sale

 e. Pocketing cash overages

3. Collections by Salesmen

 a. Conversion of checks made payable to "cash"

 b. Failure to report sales

 c. Overstating amount of trade-ins

Where adequate internal control is used, most of these practices cannot be carried on without collusion.

OTHER MEANS OF DETECTING FRAUD

In addition to the segregation of duties which has been described, certain other practices may be adopted to further deter any would-be peculator or embezzler. One of these tools is surprise audits by the internal auditor as well as the public accountants. Another is the prompt follow-up of past-due accounts. Proper instructions to customers as to where checks should be mailed, and a specific request that they be made payable to the company, and not to any individual, also will help. Bonding of all employees, with a detailed check of references, is a measure of protection. Special checking of unusual receipts of a miscellaneous nature will tend to discourage irregularities.

CASH DISBURSEMENTS

CONTROL OF CASH DISBURSEMENTS

In this area of cash administration, also, there are two aspects of control: (1) the timing of payments, and (2) the system of internal control.

Experience indicates the value of maintaining careful controls over the timing of disbursements to insure that bills are paid only as they are due, and not before. In such a manner, cash can be conserved for temporary investment.

Another consideration in payment scheduling is the conscious use of cash "float." By recognizing in-transit items and the fact that ordinarily bank balances are greater than book balances because of checks not cleared, book balances of cash may be planned at lower levels. The incoming float may be balanced against the outgoing payments.

IMPORTANCE OF INTERNAL CONTROL

Once the cash has been deposited in the bank, it would seem that the major problem of safeguarding the cash has been solved. Indeed, it is quite true that control of cash disbursements is a relatively simple matter—if a few rules are followed. After the vendor's invoice has been approved for payment, the next step usually is the preparation of the check for executive signature. If all disbursements are subject to this top review, how can any problem exist? Yet it is at precisely this point that the greatest danger is met. Any controller who has had to sign numerous checks knows that it is indeed an irksome task—the review to ascertain that receiving reports are attached; the checking of payee against the invoice; and the comparison of amounts. Because it is such a monotonous chore, it is often done in a most perfunctory manner. Yet this operation, carefully done, is essential to the control of disbursements. Where two signatures are required, both signatories need not make the detailed review, but certainly one should. The other can review on a spot-check basis only. There are too many instances where false documents and vouchers used a second time have been the means of securing executive signatures. Prevention of this practice demands careful review before signing checks, as well as other safeguards. It cannot be taken for granted that everything is all right. Those who sign the checks must adopt a questioning attitude on every transaction which appears doubtful or is not fully understood. Indeed, the review of documents attached to checks will often bring to light foolish expenditures and weaknesses in other procedures.

SOME PRINCIPLES OF INTERNAL CONTROL

The opportunities for improper or incorrect use of funds are so great that a controller cannot unduly emphasize the need for proper safeguards in the cash disbursement function. Vigilance and sound audit procedures are necessary. While the system of internal control must be tailored to fit the needs of the organization, some general suggestions may be helpful:

1. Except for petty cash transactions, all disbursements should be made by check
2. All checks should be prenumbered, and all numbers accounted for as either used or voided
3. All general disbursement checks should require two signatures
4. Responsibility for cash receipts should be divorced from responsibility for cash disbursements
5. All persons signing checks or approving disbursements should be adequately bonded
6. Bank reconciliations should be made by those who do not sign checks or approve payments

7. The keeping of cash records should be entirely separate from the handling of cash disbursements
8. Properly approved invoices and other required supporting documents should be a prerequisite to making every disbursement
9. Checks for reimbursement of imprest funds and payrolls should be made payable to the individual and not to the company or bearer
10. After payment has been made, all supporting documents should be perforated or otherwise mutilated or marked "paid" to prevent reuse
11. Mechanical devices should be used to the extent practical—check writers, safety paper, etc.
12. Annual vacations or shifts in jobs should be enforced for those handling disbursements
13. Approval of vouchers for payment usually should be done by those not responsible for disbursing
14. Special authorizations for interbank transfers should be required; and a clearing account, perhaps called Bank Transfers, should be maintained
15. All petty cash vouchers should be written in ink or typewritten

METHODS OF MISAPPROPRIATING FUNDS

The safeguards listed above are some of those developed on the basis of experience by many firms. Some common means of perpetrating fraud are these:

1. Preparing false vouchers or presenting vouchers twice for payment
2. "Kiting," or unauthorized borrowing through not recording the disbursement, while recording the deposit, in the case of bank transfers
3. Falsifying footing in cash records
4. Raising the amount on checks after they have been signed
5. Understating cash discounts
6. Cashing unclaimed payroll or dividend checks
7. Altering petty cash vouchers
8. Forging checks and destroying them when received from the bank—substituting other canceled checks or charge slips

BANK RECONCILIATIONS

An important phase of internal control is the reconciling of the balance per bank statement with the balance per books. This is particularly true wtih respect to general bank accounts as distinguished from accounts solely for disbursing paychecks. If properly done, the task is much more than a listing of outstanding checks, deposits in transit, and unrecorded bank charges. For example, the deposits and disbursements as shown on the bank statement should be reconciled with those on the books. A convenient form to handle this is illustrated in Fig. 93. Then, too, it is desirable to compare indorsements with the payee, and to check the payee against the record.

It has been mentioned previously that bank reconciliations should be handled by someone independent of any cash receipts or disbursements activities. The job can be handled by the internal auditor if one is available. Particular attention should be paid to outstanding checks of the preceding period and to deposits at the end of the month, in order to detect "kiting."

The Jones Company

BANK RECONCILIATION

Bank   National Trust Co.

Account   General

As of   December 31, 1962

	Balance 11/30/62	Receipts	Disburse-ments	Balance 12/31/6?
Per Bank................	$126,312.50	$92,420.00	$85,119.00	$133,613.50
Add: Deposits in Transit				
Date per Bank Per Book				
12/1 11/30	5,600.00	(5,600.00)		
1/2 12/31		12,500.00		12,500.00
Deduct: Outstanding Checks				
Nov................	4,320.00		(4,115.00)	205.00
(Per List Attached)				
Dec................			6,110.00	6,110.00
Other Items: Bank Charges Not Re-corded.............			(5.01)	5.01
Per Books..............	$127,592.50	$99,320.00	$87,108.99	$139,803.51

Prepared by   R. S.

Date   1/12/63

Fig. 93—Bank Reconciliation.

PETTY CASH FUNDS

Most businesses must make some small disbursements. To meet these needs, petty cash funds are established which operate on an imprest fund basis, i.e., the balances are fixed. At any time the cash plus the unreimbursed vouchers should equal the amount of the fund. Numerous funds of this type may be necessary in the branch offices or at each plant. A uniform receipt and uniform procedure should be provided, including limits on individual disbursements through this channel, proper approvals, etc. If it is practicable, the person handling cash receipts or disbursements should not handle petty cash. Other safeguards would include surprise cash counts, immediate cancellation of all petty cash slips after payment, and careful scrutiny of reimbursements. While the fund may be small, very considerable sums can be expended. The controller should not neglect checking this activity.

PAYROLLS

In most concerns payroll disbursements represent a very sizable proportion of all cash payments. Proper safeguards for this disbursement are particularly desirable. The use of a special payroll account is a very common procedure. A check in the exact amount of the total net payroll is deposited in the payroll account against which the individual checks are drawn. This has advantages from an internal control standpoint and it may facilitate the reconciling of bank accounts.

The preparation of the payroll, of course, should be separate from the actual handling of cash. Special payroll audits are advisable—by the internal audit staff—to review procedures, verify rates, check clerical accuracy, and witness the pay-off.

REPORTS ON CASH

CASH REPORTS

The cash reports used in most businesses are rather simple in nature but still provide important information.

Reports on estimated cash requirements and balances, or receipts or disbursements, have been illustrated in Figs. 88–90.

For information purposes, a simple daily cash report is prepared in most companies for the chief executive and treasurer. It merely summarizes the cash receipts and cash disbursements, as well as balances of major banks. An example is shown in Fig. 94. Such a report may be issued weekly or semimonthly, depending on needs. A detailed statement of cash receipts is illustrated in Fig. 95.

The Day Company

DAILY CASH REPORT

As of the Close of Business, June 16, 1963

Balance, June 15, 1963	$135,300
Receipts	10,200
Total	145,500
Disbursements	15,300
Balance, June 16, 1963	$130,200

Bank Balances, etc.

National City Bank—General	$ 65,900
Commerce National Bank—General	22,100
Ohio Trust Company—General	30,500
Total	118,500
Petty Cash and Payroll Funds	11,700
Total	$130,200

Fig. 94—Daily Cash Report.

The X Y Z Company

STATEMENT OF DAILY CASH RECEIPTS

Date_____

Account		Amount
No.	Name	
201–1	Accounts Receivable—Aircraft	$
201–2	Accounts Receivable—Parts	
201–3	Accounts Receivable—Employees	
201–5	Accounts Receivable—Intercompany	
201–6	Accounts Receivable—Miscellaneous	
303	Claims Receivable	
801	Deposits on Account	
1001–1	Cash Sales—Aircraft	
1001–2	Cash Sales—Parts	
1001–3	Cash Sales—Scrap	
1001–4	Cash Sales—Miscellaneous	
6001	Revenue—Vending Machines	
6005	Royalty Income	
6010	Miscellaneous Income and Expense	
Total	....	$

Fig. 95—Statement of Daily Cash Receipts.

From the control viewpoint, it is desirable to know how collections and disbursements compare with estimates. Such information is shown in Fig. 96, as well as the expected cash balance at month-end.

The Roth Company

Weekly Cash Report

For the Week Ended November 16, 1962

(In Thousands of Dollars)

Description	Actual Week Ended 11/16/62	Month to Date	
		Actual	Estimated
Beginning Cash Balance	$17,890	$ 32,511	$ 32,510
Cash Receipts			
Government	10,810	18,310	18,000
Wholesale	19,620	67,730	65,500
Retail	8,330	21,100	23,400
Total	38,760	107,140	106,900
Cash Disbursements			
Accounts Payable—Expenses	12,330	12,860	12,300
Payrolls	12,660	37,010	36,900
Material Purchases	1,890	19,340	14,300
Federal Taxes	2,790	8,640	8,920
Capital Expenditures	13,370	39,990	40,190
Other	1,060	2,030	2,000
Total	44,100	119,870	114,610
Ending Cash Balance	$12,550	$ 19,781	$ 24,800
Estimated Month-End Balance			$ 30,000

Fig. 96—Comparison of Actual and Estimated Cash Activity.

In addition to comparing actual and forecasted cash activity, it is also useful to compare periodically book balances with those required to meet service charges of the banks and compensating balances. Such a report compares the "objective" balance with actual book and actual bank balances. This type of report provides a periodic check on effective cash utilization by recording (1) the absence of excessive balances, and (2) progress in keeping bank balances adequate to fairly compensate the financial institution. Such an illustrative cash management report is shown in Fig. 97.

The Steven Company

QUARTERLY REPORT ON BANK BALANCES

As at June 30, 1963

(In Thousands of Dollars)

Bank	Actual per Books	Objective	(Over) Under Objective	Balance per Bank Statement
First National City	$ 19,870	$ 20,200	$ 330	$ 23,070
Chase Manhattan	17,440	17,800	360	19,120
Morgan Guaranty	16,850	16,500	(350)	17,180
Bank of America	14,310	15,700	1,390	15,810
Security First National	10,870	10,250	(620)	12,300
United California	6,430	5,900	(530)	7,110
American Trust	5,510	5,800	290	5,840
Anglo-American	4,380	4,500	120	4,760
National Bank of Commerce	2,890	3,000	110	3,020
Other Local	490	—	(490)	520
Total Cash in Banks—U. S.	99,040	99,650	610	108,730
Subsidiaries—Foreign	8,190	7,000	(1,190)	8,600
Cash Funds	760	750	(10)	
Total Cash	$107,990	$107,400	$ (590)	$117,330

Fig. 97—Actual and Objective Bank Balances.

There are any number of variations in cash reports, including some that are greatly detailed as to daily cash receipts, etc. The suggested reports are merely examples.

20

Control of Receivables

REQUIREMENTS OF RECEIVABLES CONTROL

Customers' accounts receivable are an important item in the balance sheets of most business concerns. Proper procedures and adequate safeguards on these accounts are essential not only to the continued success of the enterprise but also to satisfactory customer relationships. Receivables, of course, extend beyond customers' receivables to amounts due from employees, notes receivable, freight claims receivable, insurance claims receivable, balances due from creditors, amounts due from affiliated companies, etc. But customers' accounts receivable are usually the most important in aggregate value.

The planning function, of course, will take into account the amount to be invested in accounts receivable, and measure this against available capital as well as the acceptable relationship to sales, as discussed in this chapter.

Control of accounts receivable begins, in reality, before the agreement to ship the merchandise, continues through the preparation and issuance of the billing, and ends with the collection of all sums due. The procedure is closely related to cash receipts control on one hand, and to inventory control on the other. The receivable is the link between the two.

From the preventive management approach there are three general control areas—points at which action can be taken to realize control of accounts receivable. These are:

1. *Granting of Credit.* Credit policies and terms of sale must neither discourage sales to financially sound customers nor incur serious losses because of excessive bad debts.
2. *Making Collections.* Once credit is granted, every effort must be made to secure payment in accordance with the terms of sale and within a reasonable time.
3. *Installation and Maintenance of Proper Internal Control.* Even though credit and collection procedures are well administered or properly effected, this does not assure control of receivables. It does not guarantee, or even make reasonably certain, that all ship-

ments are invoiced, or properly invoiced, to customers and that the payment finds its way into the company's bank account. An adequate system of internal control must be in operation.

While reference is made primarily to accounts receivable from customers, the general principles are applicable to any receivables.

RESPONSIBILITIES OF THE CONTROLLER

The size of the firm, the type of organization, the capabilities of the controller—all these factors and others will determine the duties and responsibilities of the chief accounting officer in regard to accounts receivable. In many small and medium-sized firms the functions of the treasurer or controller are one and the same. In larger companies the credit and collection functions are usually under the control of the treasurer. But even where the controller is not directly responsible for accounts receivable, he has certain real responsibilities. These may be outlined as follows:

1. Maintenance of the accounts receivable records in a satisfactory condition to meet the needs of the treasurer, credit manager, and controller
2. Installation and maintenance of the necessary internal control safeguards
3. Preparation of the required reports for management, the credit department, and others as to the condition of the receivables and related matters
4. Proper valuation of receivables on the balance sheet, including establishment of the necessary reserves

In all these matters, the controller and the treasurer must work closely together.

FUNCTIONS OF THE CREDIT DEPARTMENT

Because the controller is sometimes responsible for credit approval and since, in any case, the relationship between the accounting and credit departments is close, the functions of the credit department ought to be defined. In a broad sense the credit manager should stimulate business through wise extension of credit and keep bad debt losses at a minimum. In another sense, he is to grant credit after due inquiry, if warranted, and collect the accounts receivable. A more detailed statement of the task is this:

1. *The Establishment of Credit Policies.* This involves such questions as: what class of risk shall be accepted, how rigidly shall credit terms be enforced, what adjustment policies shall be followed?

2. *Credit Investigation.* This requires a continuous procedure for securing and analyzing information concerning the responsibility of present and prospective customers.
3. *Credit Approval.* This requires a procedure by which the credit department definitely passes on new customers and the continuance of old ones.
4. *Establishment of Credit Limits.* Usually approval is limited to a certain amount and a plan must be designed to check the extension of credit at this point or, at least, to notify the proper authority when the limit is reached.
5. *Enforcement of Discount Terms.* Discounts offered for prompt payment are frequently taken by customers after the time allowed. A policy must be established and a procedure designed for the enforcement of the discount terms.
6. *Collection Methods.* Definite collection steps must be arranged for slow and delinquent accounts. This involves schedules of collection letters, follow-up procedure, and suspension of accounts from approved lists.
7. *Credit Adjustments.* This involves settlement of accounts, participation in creditors' committees, and representation in receivership and bankruptcy proceedings.
8. *Approval of Writing Off Bad Accounts.* Responsibility for writing off bad accounts must initiate with the credit department, although final approval may be required from the treasurer.
9. *Credit Records.* In the performance of the foregoing task, certain credit records must be maintained in addition to the general accounting records. These consist of files, reports, and ratings.

MEASUREMENT OF CREDIT DEPARTMENT EFFICIENCY

Every credit manager appreciates the need for, and use of, objective data in measuring the efficiency of his own department. One of the functions of the controller's staff is to provide such aids. Obviously such measuring sticks have a direct bearing on the control of receivables for they furnish the credit manager with tools to improve his performance.

One such device is standards to measure the cost of each function, which has been discussed in Chapter 18. In addition, other indexes or standards have found general use:

1. *Relationship of Credit Sales to Total Sales.* Over a period of time, such information can provide some indication as to the effect of credit policy on sales volume. The data are even more useful if comparable information for the industry or other similar firms can be obtained. Such data can be refined to provide information in different territories, channels of distribution, or by type of credit sale.

The Aircraft Corporation

SUMMARY OF PAST-DUE ACCOUNTS RECEIVABLE

As of March 31, 1963

Customer	Balance 3/31/63	Current	Past Due 30 Days	Past Due 60 Days	Past Due 90 Days and Over	No. of Items 90 Days and Over	Collection Efforts 60 Days Past Due and Over Remarks
TRADE:							
Aviation Service Co.	$ 13,300	$ 100	$ 500	$ 9,800	$ 2,900	3	Jones advised he will pay $3,400 on 4/25.
Clean Ridge Skyways	65,400	5,900	11,300	48,200	–	–	Fire claims now settled. Payment expected on 4/10.
Des Moines Flying Co.	19,800	–	–	8,100	11,700	5	
Eager Beaver Flyers	5,100	–	2,800	2,300	–	–	Collection letters #1 and #2 sent.
Flight, Incorporated	7,240	210	3,930	3,100	–	–	$3,100 received on 4/3/63.
Green Light, Inc.	900	–	–	320	580	4	Bankruptcy proceedings under way.
Mountain States Aircraft, Inc.	3,100	300	900	1,100	800	2	Will be deducted from commissions payable in April.
Cia Mexicana de Aero	72,400	15,800	15,800	20,800	20,000	12	Consists of aircraft delivered against letters of credit.
Others (under $500 each) past due	3,200	1,500	750	250	700	35	
Subtotal	190,440	23,810	35,980	93,970	36,680	61	
Other (current)	592,100	592,100	–	–	–	–	
Total	782,540	615,910	35,980	93,970	36,680	61	
CLAIMS RECEIVABLE	8,300	8,300	–	–	–	–	
ITEMS BILLABLE	500	500	–	–	–	–	
Employees	1,500	1,500	–	–	–	–	
Total	$792,840	$626,210	$35,980	$93,970	$36,680	61	

2. *Relationship of Bad Debt Losses to Credit Sales.* High losses may indicate too lax a credit policy.
3. *Collection Percentage.* This is the relationship of collections for a month to the receivables at the beginning of the period.
4. *Average Length of Time Receivables are Outstanding.*
5. *Delinquency Percentage.* This measures the number and amount of accounts which are past due.
6. *Rejection Percentage.* Such data, usually prepared by the credit department itself, show the proportion of credit applications declined.

LENGTH OF CREDIT PERIOD

One of the tests of the efficiency of the credit department is the average length of time accounts receivable are outstanding. This information is arrived at by the use of the formula:

$$\frac{\text{Average receivables}}{\text{Annual credit sales}} \times 365 = \begin{array}{l}\text{Average number of days accounts are}\\ \text{outstanding}\end{array}$$

Trends, of course, should be watched; but the really significant measure is the comparison of average number of days of outstandings as compared with the credit period as set by management. Although the nominal terms of sale may be 30 days net, the actual average credit period might be 40 to 60 days. The influence on costs of carrying accounts receivable is a subject every controller should consider if receivables are an important item in the balance sheet. One of the authors made a study of the effect of the credit period on the cost of carrying accounts receivable. Giving consideration to interest expense, bad debts, bookkeeping costs, and credit and collection department expense—all of which were influenced by the credit period—it was found that the cost ranged from 1.67% of net sales for nominal terms of 10 days (actual of 15) to 4.74% for an actual term of 120 days. This information is indicative of the value which an intelligently directed analysis of the subject may have—a job for the controller.

AGE ANALYSIS OF ACCOUNTS RECEIVABLE

Some of the most useful reports which the accounting department can issue in connection with the control of accounts receivable have to do with an age analysis. The reports may be in summary form, possibly by organizational segment (Division) responsible, which may be territory or product.

Such a summary may be supported by an analysis of the larger past-due accounts, including an explanation of steps being taken to collect the

SHEET 1 of 5

FORM DE-1-0376-1

GENERAL MANUFACTURING COMPANY

AGED TRIAL BALANCE

REPORT No. 3

DATE December 31

CUSTOMER NAME	CUSTOMER NO.	INVOICE DATE	INVOICE NO.	TOTAL	CURRENT	30 DAY	60 DAY	90 DAY
AMERICAN STEEL CO	1281	1123	11666	64031	90904	64031		
	1281	1230	12336	90904	90904	64031		
				154935 *				
APALACHIN LUMBER CO	2179	915	9852	46920	143930	25461		46920
	2179	1114	11609	25461	143930	25461		46920
	2179	1230	12335	143930				
				216311 *				
B J E SERVICE CORP	2283	1229	12332	147478	147478			
				147478 *	147478			
BARRETT MACHINE	3076	1125	11717	58715	61023	58715		
	3076	1231	12347	61023	61023	58715		
				119738 *				
CHENANGO RAILROAD CO	11975	1217	12262	31682	31682			
				31682 *	31682			
CHOLMAR FURNITURE CO	149910	1016	10628	151600	143432	7688	151600	
	149910	1128	11490	7688	143432	60095	151600	
	149910	1128	11750	60095		67783		
	149910	1231	12356	143432				
				362815				

Fig. 99—Aged Accounts Receivable Trial Balance.

The Hydrocarbons Company
Summary of Consolidated Accounts Receivable
As at September 30, 1963
(Dollars in Thousands)

Description	Total as at 9/30/63	Current	Past Due Total	Past Due 30 Days	Past Due 60 Days	Past Due 90 Days	No. of Days' Sales in Rec.	Control Objectives
EASTERN DIVISION								
Wholesale	$15,867	$12,249	$ 3,618	$1,412	$ 571	$1,635	28	25 days
%		77.2	22.8	8.9	3.6	10.3		75% current
Retail	3,771	2,466	1,305	539	196	570	18	15 days
%		65.4	34.6	14.3	5.2	15.1		80% current
Total	19,638	14,715	4,923	1,951	767	2,205		
SOUTHERN DIVISION								
Crude Oil	11,936	10,205	1,731	418	597	716	14	13 days
%		85.5	14.5	3.5	5.0	6.0		86% current
Gas Products	3,456	2,706	750	145	522	83	27	25 days
%		78.3	21.7	4.2	15.1	2.4		76% current
Petrochemicals	1,889	1,854	35	35	—	—	10	10 days
%		98.1	1.9	1.9				97% current
Total	17,281	14,765	2,516	598	1,119	799		
WESTERN DIVISION								
Crude Oil	234	171	63	33	8	22	27	25 days
%		73.2	26.8	14.1	3.6	9.1		76% current
Wholesale	14,891	12,250	2,641	1,671	582	388	37	35 days
%		82.3	17.7	11.2	3.9	2.6		84% current
Retail	10,852	8,302	2,550	1,573	380	597	25	20 days
%		71.5	23.5	14.5	3.5	5.5		78% current
Total	25,977	20,723	5,254	3,277	970	1,007		
Consolidated Total	$62,896	$50,203	$12,693	$5,826	$2,856	$4,011		

Fig. 100—Status of Accounts Receivable—Summarized.

account. This type of report is illustrated in Fig. 98. Of course, where the detail is not too voluminous, or where the records are on mechanical equipment, the story of each account may be furnished. A tabulated report is shown in Fig. 99. It is usually desirable to establish standards as to per cent currency, or number of days' sales in receivables. A summary report containing such comparisons is presented in Fig. 100.

Simple charts, such as Fig. 101, may also serve a useful purpose in highlighting the condition of the receivables.

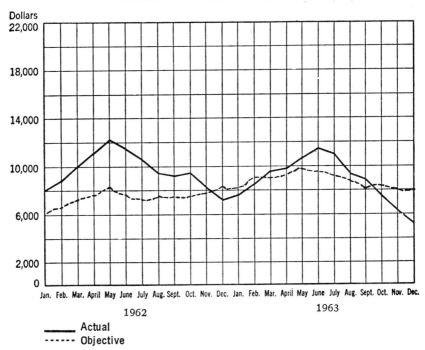

The Jones Company
AMOUNT OF PAST-DUE ACCOUNTS
For the Period 1/1/62 through 12/31/63

——— Actual
------ Objective

Fig. 101—Chart of Past-due Accounts.

OTHER REPORTS

In addition to the age analysis of accounts receivable, there are a great many reports which may be prepared on the activity in the receivables and on the credit and collection function. While some would normally be prepared by the accounting staff for the use of the credit manager and general executives, still others may be prepared by the credit department itself, or as a joint activity by the two departments. Some typical reports might cover this information:

1. Detail of accounts charged off, and reasons why
2. Per cent of bad debt losses to credit sales, by months, including comparison with similar periods in prior years
3. Historical summary, by months, of average number of days of outstandings, by classifications
4. Analysis of bad debt losses by classes of customers, terms of sale, size of account
5. Comparison of actual and budgeted collections
6. Detail of bad debts collected
7. Relationship of credit department costs to credit sales
8. Comparison of budgeted and actual credit and collection expense
9. Sales, collections, and percentage of collections to sales, for the month and year to date

ASSISTING CUSTOMERS

One indirect method of improving the accounts receivable picture, with a related reduction in investment and avoidance of collection problems—to say nothing of gaining customer goodwill—is by assisting these customers in obtaining financing elsewhere. Very often sales are made to companies with little financial know-how. Some firms, therefore, in an effort to assist the customer to meet its obligations, offer advice and aid by their own credit personnel. Such help may range from assisting in bank contacts, to suggesting a sound management reporting system, to partially guaranteeing indebtedness.

INTERNAL CONTROL REQUIREMENTS

The vast number of shipments to customers from most business concerns gives rise to an ever present danger that all such goods are not properly charged to customers' accounts receivable. Further, even though an invoice is prepared, the customer may be billed for an incorrect amount due to differences in quantity shipped, price, or extensions. Such happenings can be due to bookkeeping errors or fraud. Unfortunately, most customers do not complain about undercharges. Under the circumstances, the controller must assure himself that proper procedures are instituted to reduce such risks to a minimum.

Several practices have been found useful in combating discrepancies. Some of the more common are as follows:

1. Invoices to customers are compared to shipping memos by an independent party. This comparison includes both quantity and description of goods shipped.

2. All goods leaving the plant must have a shipping memo. Preferably these are prenumbered, and the independent party ascertains that all numbers are accounted for.

3. Prices appearing on invoices are independently checked against established price lists, and all extensions and footings are checked.

4. Periodically the detail of the accounts receivable is checked against the control and reconciled, preferably by an internal auditor or other independent party.

5. Surprise mailings of monthly statements and confirmation requests should be made by third parties.

6. All handling of cash should be segregated from the maintenance of receivable records.

7. All special adjustments for discounts, returns, or allowances should have special approval.

8. A special record should be kept of all bad debts written off; and a definite follow-up should be made on these items to minimize the danger of collections being received and not recorded.

9. On a test-check basis, remittance sheets can be compared with accounts receivable and shipping reports.

10. Invoices may be mailed to customers by a separate unit.

MISCELLANEOUS RECEIVABLES

There is a sizable number of receivable transactions other than regular sales which may cause losses for the company. Some common examples are freight claims, insurance claims, and sales to employees. It is amazing to find a number of concerns which have no well-devised plan for handling these transactions, or whose sole records are pieces of correspondence. One firm, for example, charged employee accommodation purchases to expense, crediting the expense account when payment was received. All such items should be charged formally into a receivable account so as to facilitate follow-up and payment.

ESTABLISHMENT OF RESERVE FOR BAD DEBTS

Two principal methods, or a combination, are used to establish an adequate reserve for bad debts. The first method is the application of a percentage against monthly sales to establish the provision. This percentage is based on past experience, and may be applied against total sales if most are on credit. Where cash sales are an important factor, then only credit sales should be used. This method may be refined by applying applicable percentages of differing amount to sales by territory, product, or class of customer.

Another means of establishing the requisite reserve is through the analysis or appraisal of each individual account. Such a technique is feasible when there are relatively few accounts. In practice it may be advisable to make provision throughout the year based on the monthly sales, and adjust the reserve at the year-end by reference to the account analysis. Proper weighting should be given to the past-due amounts reflected in the aging.

21

Planning and Control of Inventories

INVENTORY MANAGEMENT

In its broadest sense inventory management involves the dual function of planning and control of inventories. Included are the determination and maintenance of the proper composition and quantity of materials or products needed to best meet manufacturing requirements or customer orders. Still broadly speaking, it also encompasses the maintenance of a proper flow of the materials from the receiving dock to storage, into process, and through the factory to the customer. Inventory planning relates to determining what the composition should be—as to content, timing, and location—to meet the projected business needs. Inventory control is the regulation of the inventory within predetermined limits.

The objective of this chapter is primarily to identify the broad considerations involved in inventory management insofar as they relate to the financial function of the business, and especially to the functions of the controller.

IMPORTANCE OF INVENTORY MANAGEMENT

The emphasis on the importance of inventory planning and control is no mere academic platitude. Inventories are the largest single item among the current assets of many industrial firms, to say nothing of mercantile concerns. Within the experience of many controllers the importance of inventory control is vivid—whether because of sizable adjustments as a result of physical inventories, whether as a result of heavy losses from obsolescence or market declines, or merely because inventories were allowed to grow to unwieldy sizes with the risk of losses and excess costs. Inventories have frequently been the prime cause of business failure, and it is not without reason that they have been called "the graveyard of American business."

COST OF CARRYING INVENTORIES

Any controller should be interested in reducing costs; yet the possibilities of cost reduction through inventory control have frequently been overlooked. In fact, the cost of carrying inventories is quite often higher than management realizes. For manufacturing firms it is seldom less than 10% per year on the average inventory investment, and quite often it is as high as 25%. The U. S. Department of Commerce has made the following statement:

The average cost of carrying supply stocks is 25 per cent of their value, divided as follows: Storage facilities, ¼ of 1 per cent; insurance, ¼ of 1 per cent; taxes, ½ of 1 per cent; transportation, ½ of 1 per cent; handling and distribution, 2½ per cent; depreciation, 5 per cent; interest, 6 per cent; and obsolescence, 10 per cent. These figures represent average warehouse stocks and include the desirable active items.

Thus it can be seen that an inventory investment of $500,000 conservatively can cost $75,000 per year, figuring an average rate of 15%. A reduction of $100,000 in the average investment could produce annual savings of about $15,000. An improvement in turnover alone could help make this saving possible.

ADVANTAGES OF INVENTORY MANAGEMENT

The following benefits or advantages to be gained from proper inventory planning and control emphasize the value of the tool:

1. Keeps at a minimum the capital invested in inventories
2. Eliminates or reduces waste and cost resulting from excess handling, spoilage, storage, obsolescence, and taxes and insurance on inventories
3. Reduces risk from fraud or theft of inventories
4. Avoids production delays by having necessary materials on hand —with resulting longer runs and lower production costs
5. Permits more satisfactory service to customers by having the materials or goods on hand
6. May reduce investment in storage facilities and equipment
7. Permits the leveling-out of production through fluctuating inventories, and thus contributes to stability of employment
8. Avoids or reduces losses resulting from price declines
9. Reduces the cost of taking the annual physical inventory
10. Through proper control and the information available on the inventories, permits better purchasing and taking advantage of special prices and price movements
11. Reduces sales and related clerical costs through better customer service

Hence, it can be recognized that inventory management is an important phase of the business operations affecting every function: sales, production, purchasing, accounting, administration.

Mere reduction in size of inventories is not the primary objective. The composition must be correct, and policy changes or makeup changes should be made as conditions warrant. Proper inventory involves the planning and balancing of all factors, and not necessarily the maintenance of low inventories.

TECHNIQUES OF PLANNING AND CONTROLLING INVENTORIES

From the management viewpoint, planning must avoid the improper accumulation of inventories. The attack must be against the acquisition stage, and directed primarily toward two objectives: (1) planning and control of purchases so that only the necessary materials are accumulated, and (2) control of the authorization to manufacture in order that the proper quantity and type of goods may be produced.

It is necessary to know that proper plans exist, that such plans are modified as business conditions demand, and that their execution is in conformance with the plan. Preventive control in this latter area, before goods are received or manufactured, can be helpful.

Any other approach to control must be confined largely to corrective action after the fact. Excessive and unwanted finished stocks can be disposed of through intensive selling. But there are limits as to how much selling of this nature can be done; and in any event such a procedure can hardly be labeled as the most profitable utilization of manufacturing and selling efforts. Accounting control, or audit and analysis of inventories, permits a reporting on the success of the preventive control and highlights weak spots for corrective action. It should not be overlooked, however, that accounting control techniques also can be used as a tool of preventive management. The records are an integral part of any control action.

Some of the specific techniques or means of achieving inventory control, all of which are discussed below, are:

1. Establishment of and operation under minimum and maximum inventory points
2. Use of turnover rates
3. Executive judgment, particularly where speculation is an important factor
4. Budgetary control

In many concerns, one control may be used for some inventory items, while another is used for other inventories with different control needs. Supplies may be handled on a minimum-maximum basis, while finished inventories may be operated on a budgetary control basis. Again, if certain basic raw materials are critical or scarce, one or more of the executives may directly supervise such procurement.

The use of minimum-maximum points, or the related limitations of inventories to a given number of days' supply, as well as the establishment of turnover rates, are traditional or accepted control techniques in many businesses. In recent years, however, there has been a trend toward relating inventory levels to future requirements, and setting more accurate stock levels and economic purchasing quantities. The improved technology afforded by the use of computers and rapid data transmission, in conjunction with mathematical formulas, can be of assistance in meeting the company objective of maximizing return on investment.

CONDITIONS ESSENTIAL TO PROPER INVENTORY MANAGEMENT

The most effective inventory management doesn't just happen; it must be planned and directed. Experience has shown, moreover, that certain factors or conditions are prerequisite to the most successful management of inventories. Some of these are:

1. Clearly defined responsibility and authority in regard to inventories
2. Well-defined objectives and policies
3. Adequate storage and handling facilities
4. Proper classification and identification of inventories
5. Standardization and simplification of inventories
6. Adequate records and reports
7. Satisfactory personnel

RESPONSIBILITY FOR INVENTORY MANAGEMENT

In any business organization, in any undertaking, an essential element is the proper delegation of responsibility and authority. It is not a requirement only for inventory planning and control. Yet it is astounding to see the number of instances where no one is assigned such responsibility, or where the assignment is not clearly defined. Some managements become aware of the lack of responsibility for inventory control only when a major loss has been sustained or is imminent. Responsibility may be defined as the specific assignment of work and the obligation of the individual to perform to the best of his ability. With this responsibility must be the requisite authority—the right to make decisions and to demand or secure compliance with instructions related to the performance of the demand. Authority has often been called the right to command. To secure proper coordination, responsibility and authority must be defined for each phase of inventory management.

Who, then, should be responsible for inventories? No single rule can be laid down, for it depends on the size and type of organization, the industry, and the personalities of the executive group. Some general observations can be made, however.

Operating control of raw material and supply inventories generally rests with either the factory management or the purchasing department. Where supply factors or market conditions are predominant factors instead of production requirements, the purchasing department is likely to be governing. In other instances where production is for stock, then the production planning executive may be responsible. Regardless of who is responsible, there must be close coordination with sales so that raw materials and supplies are not purchased out of all proportion to estimated production needs as reflected in the sales forecast.

Work in process, of course, is strictly the responsibility of the production executive, as far as operating control is concerned.

Inventories of finished goods held for sale present a somewhat different problem. In some instances the responsibility rests with factory management. There is an increasing tendency, however, to place this inventory control function under the sales group, and with good reason:

1. The sales department is, or should be, in the best position to sense trends and to know the market demands. These are very important factors in inventory accumulation. If the sales executive is responsible for the inventory, he is given an added incentive to use the knowledge of markets to the fullest extent—much more so than if another individual were responsible for the inventory.

2. If the sales executives have the responsibility for finished inventory control, they are more likely to take a greater interest in keeping stock current. Otherwise, there may be a tendency for them to feel they are doing a clean-up job for someone else. The incentive to secure the maximum profits, when the problem is that of disposing of odd lots or older stock, is greater if the sales manager is responsible.

3. Responsibility for finished stocks is conducive to better estimating of requirements in projecting sales needs and demands on production.

There are those who may take exception on two counts with the statement that the sales organization should be responsible for finished inventories. They may contend: (1) that the primary job of the sales department is to *sell* and that any other function reduces the amount of time which can be devoted to sales effort; (2) that when the production executives are not responsible, there is a great tendency to place goods in finished inventory, which the sales organization does not want. The first argument may be countered with the statement that, while the job of the salesman is to sell, the objective of the sales executive is maximum *profit*. This can be accomplished by having proper inventories which reflect customer demand. The actual details of inventory control, of course, can be delegated by the sales manager to a non-selling staff member. The answer with respect to transfers to finished goods inventory, of course, is a proper method of release of goods and acceptance by the sales division.

The preceding discussion relates primarily to operating planning and control of inventories. It will bear mentioning that one of the weakest spots in many companies is the contact between the sales department and the production department. It is here that some coordinating authority is often found necessary to install and maintain required procedures and to keep the necessary flow of information. One means of accomplishing this is the establishment of an inventory committee composed of the representatives of all departments concerned, including the controller.

RESPONSIBILITY OF THE CONTROLLER

This raises the question as to the function of the chief accounting official with respect to inventory management. Being a staff executive he should not direct the day-to-day activities of operating control. That is the responsibility of the line executive. The controller, however, is in an excellent position to contribute a very real service on inventory planning and control. For, regardless of where responsibility for inventory management is placed, the problem is secondary to the main function, whether it be sales, production, or purchasing. So the controller must be the coordinator, analyzing the conflicting needs and preparing a solution. He coordinates, assists, and suggests answers to the various problems. A general outline of his more specific duties relating to inventories is as follows:

1. As a member of the inventory committee, or as a representative of the chief executive, assist in over-all inventory policy determination
2. As coordinator of the business plan, or forecast, or budget, ascertain that realistic inventory levels and investments are developed and changed as required; this function will include not only the over-all budget, but also related data such as:
   a. Turnover objective
   b. Economic lot size
   c. Purchase quantities
3. Maintain usable inventory records
4. Prepare and install required control procedures
5. Prepare and issue regular periodic control reports on inventory position for the guidance of line executives
6. Install necessary internal controls for the protection of property from fraud and theft

7. Supervise special audits or analyses as required
8. Supervise annual physical inventory
9. Determine the method of costing inventories and related material flow
10. Secure necessary compliance with instructions of regulatory bodies as regards the treatment of inventory and disclosure of valuations, etc.

INVENTORY OBJECTIVES AND POLICIES

Those who are responsible for carrying out the wishes of management in regard to inventories must clearly understand the rules of action by which they are to be guided. Nothing is quite so destructive of morale, and nothing creates so much confusion, as to be assigned a job and not know what is expected.

The general policies which will govern inventory accumulation, as well as the related functions in the various divisions of the business, should be made at the top-management level. Some of the matters to be covered are the following:

1. *Maximum Capital To Be Invested in Inventories.* What funds are available for investment in inventories? These limitations must be known.
2. *Extent of Speculative Purchasing Permissible.* To what extent can advantage be taken of forward buying? Should purchasing cover only the immediate needs of the production plans?
3. *Probable Changes in Models, Customer Service, or Selling Effort.* The time and extent of such changes, and their probable effect on sales, should be known. Are credit terms to be eased? What policy will be followed with respect to customer delivery, i.e., must goods be shipped within 24 hours? Are any plans afoot for new products which will change the demand for present goods?

ADEQUATE STORAGE AND HANDLING FACILITIES

A third essential factor in inventory control is adequate storage and handling facilities. No procedure, regardless of how well planned, can succeed in a disorganized or ill-equipped warehouse or storage area. Because items cannot be located, excess or really unnecessary materials will be purchased. Shipping memos calling for one lot of material will be filled with another—at the risk of customer ill-will—without proper reporting. Losses from obsolescence and damage will run high. Such conditions will make perpetual records meaningless. Under such a handicap, good inventory control is virtually impossible. On the other hand, the facilities should not be so elaborate as to incur unnecessary handling and storage costs.

PROPER CLASSIFICATION AND IDENTIFICATION OF INVENTORIES

The usual inventory of a manufacturing firm includes these classifications:

Raw materials
Supplies
Work in process
Finished goods

Each of these major categories may have several major subdivisions. Since the goods may be at several locations, another breakdown may be made by branch warehouse. In addition, there are often extraneous transactions, such as returnable containers, goods on loan, goods on consignment, or material in transit. For the purpose of budgetary control and proper accountability, these various classifications must be kept separate and transactions properly recorded.

Within each major classification, there are very often thousands of items which must be accurately identified if the movement of material is to be reported correctly. Improperly identified material can cause production delays or at least unnecessary effort if the wrong item is brought to the production line. On the other hand, accounting control becomes quite useless if one item is requisitioned but reported as another. Proper classification and identification of material are necessary to an effective inventory control system.

STANDARDIZATION AND SIMPLIFICATION OF INVENTORIES

Another important consideration in establishing sound inventory management is the standardization of materials and products and the simplification of the line. Simplification is merely the elimination of excess types and sizes. The elimination of those items which do not sell readily can contribute greatly to reducing the inventory which must be carried.

Standardization is a more general term having to do with the establishment of standards. In the application to inventories, it has reference to the reduction of a line to fixed types, sizes, and characteristics which are considered to be standard. The object is to reduce the number of items, to establish interchangeability of manufactured parts and products, and to establish standards of quality in materials. With a reduction in the possible number of inventory items to be carried, the control problem is facilitated.

ADEQUATE RECORDS AND REPORTS

Inventory planning and control presupposes a knowledge of the facts; and availability of the facts requires adequate inventory records and reports. Inventory records should contain the information to meet the needs of the purchasing, production, sales, and financial staffs. Typical information which may be required of any class of inventory is the following:

Quantity on hand
Location
Quantities on order
Quantities in transit
Amount set aside for particular customers or production orders
Past experience as to purchases, production, or sales
Unit cost
Minimum and maximum quantities
Standard ordering quantity
Reorder point

Every controller is interested in keeping clerical costs at a minimum, and the records and reports should be so designed. However, the objective is proper inventory management, and lack of control because of inadequate records has usually proved to be a foolish economy.

SATISFACTORY PERSONNEL

Inventory management is not attained through the establishment of procedures and the maintenance of records. It is secured through the action of people; and there is no substitute for human intelligence and judgment. The records may show an item to be slow-moving or may reveal an excess inventory; but the record can neither dispose of the item nor reduce the inventory. Someone must have enough interest and initiative to review the records and recommend or take corrective action. This intelligence cannot be only at top levels of management, but must reach down to those who are given the specific responsibility for inventory control. Indeed, it may pay dividends to have someone in the organization whose sole job is to review inventories and spot weaknesses. More than to any other factors, the lack of effective inventory control in many businesses can probably be attributed to inadequately trained and unqualified personnel and improper organization.

MAXIMUMS AND MINIMUMS

One of the means available for inventory control is the use of maximum and minimum stock quantities. A determination should be made as to the suitability of that type of control in a specific business. It might apply to one class of inventory but not another. For example, it may be applicable to the supply inventory but not to the raw materials or finished goods. As a general rule the use of maximums and minimums is practical where the rate of sale or use of the products is fairly stable, and not subject to wide fluctuations or sporadic movements, and where the order time is fairly short.

In establishing maximum and minimum inventory points, the following factors must be considered:

1. *The Rate of Usage or Shipment.* This can be secured from an analysis of past experience, although current production and sales plans must be considered. The rate of usage must recognize not merely the average rate but also the *range* of usage, i.e., the highest rate and lowest rate of consumption.

2. *The Time Requirement for Either Purchase or Manufacture.* This should be the time from the placing of the order until delivery, including a reasonable "safety" factor for delays. Past experience and a knowledge of current conditions are both important in making this determination.

3. *The Economical Quantities To Order.* Discount brackets, setup time in a machine shop, and similar considerations can be factors in determining the economical amount to purchase or manufacture.

4. *Storage Facilities Available.* The cost of outside storage and added handling may make this factor decisive.

5. *Working Capital Available.*

6. *Cost of Carrying the Inventory.* Rent, taxes, insurance, interest on investment, etc.

7. *Possibility of Deterioration or Obsolescence of Materials Stored.*

8. *General Market Conditions and Extent of Speculation.*

9. *Effect on Labor Turnover.* It may be desirable to fluctuate inventories to stabilize employment or retain basic personnel.

With this information the maximum and minimum stock points can be set. An explanation of the relationship of various quantities may be helpful. The minimum is the lower limit of the desirable inventory on a particular item. It represents a "cushion" or margin of safety to be used only in an emergency. Somewhat above the minimum point is the reorder point, which represents the minimum inventory plus the quantity required for use between the ordering and delivery period. The maximum is the upper limit of the desirable inventory, and usually is the minimum quantity plus the standard ordering quantity.

Once the minimums and maximums have been set, the inventory should be reviewed periodically by an inventory manager to detect any need for changes. Further, it should be a responsibility of the controller to have the inventory detail reviewed periodically to ascertain that the limits are being observed and that the limits are reasonable. As business conditions change, the upper and lower limits of the inventory will require adjustment.

CONTROL THROUGH TURNOVER

Another means by which some companies control inventories is through turnover rate. Standard turnover rates may be established for an entire inventory or for different sections. The executives responsible for the inventories must keep within the limits. A variation of the same principle is the establishment of a limit on the funds which may be invested in the inventory. Department stores operate on a turnover basis, and each buyer is expected to secure the required rate. Thus, if an inventory turnover of four times per year is required, and if anticipated sales (cost) are $2,800,000, then the average inventory cannot be greater than $700,000. Such a method is feasible under rather stable conditions, and when materials can be readily secured.

Turnover is obtained by dividing the usage factor by the average inventory. For example, the turnover of various inventories would be determined as follows:

> Finished goods — Cost of sales/Average inventory of finished goods
>
> Work in process — Cost of goods completed / Average inventory of work in process
>
> Raw materials — Materials placed into process / Average inventory of raw materials
>
> Supplies — Cost of supplies used / Average supply inventory

The result is the number of turns. Common practice is to express rate in number of turnovers per year, although average length of time per turnover is often used. A turnover rate of four times per year would be expressed as a three-month turnover.

Such standards can be used as a guide, but their usefulness should not be overstated. A slow turnover can be an indication of overinvestment in inventories. On the other hand, a very high turnover can be secured by keeping an unduly small inventory with resulting lost sales or higher costs through fractional buying due to incomplete stocks. The objective of business is profit, not just turnover. Turnover can be secured through increased sales or usage, which also brings profit, and not merely by reducing inventories.

Turnover rates have a definite place in judging efficiency, but improvement in turnover should not be sought as an end in itself. They should by no means be an automatic control, arbitrarily imposed. An intelligent appraisal of the situation is always necessary.

VALUE ANALYSIS

Proper inventory planning and control begin with an analysis of the individual elements of the inventory. Each class or type of material has its own characteristics which may determine the technique applicable. It has been found in manufacturing companies that inventories may be segregated into three categories based upon unit dollar value and usage: A, B, and C (also known as "ABC analysis" or proportional parts system). The experienced usage and cost relationship, based on a study of many companies, for each of the three groups is approximately as follows:

	Category			
	A	B	C	Total
Number of parts used	15%	35%	50%	100%
Annual dollar value	65	20	15	100

In other words, by carefully controlling only 15% of the parts, 65% of the inventory investment can be controlled. Further, when control is extended through the B parts, about 85% of the inventory value is covered.

The category of material may be the basis for establishing the inventory policy and procedure. Different policies are required for these three differing groups. The goal of this segregation or "fractionation" is to minimize the cost of inventory investment on high-usage-value items, to minimize the cost of running out of stock, and to reduce to a minimum the acquisition cost of the low-usage-value items.

Generally speaking, A items, or high-value items, are usually ordered, either externally or internally, on the basis of the more or less exact quantity needed to meet customer and manufacturing requirements. There may be a daily, weekly, or monthly review of requirements; and a consequent rather continuous scheduling of receipts. The budgetary control approach, discussed later, probably will be used. Changes in sales forecasts or trends must be quickly reflected in increases or decreases in quantities to be ordered and receipts to be scheduled. Because of the high-usage and high-value criteria, those fixed costs of order writing, follow-up, setup, record keeping, and material handling are a small proportion of the total cost.

B items, or middle-value items, very often are ordered in quantities which may vary from actual need for economic reasons. For example, they may be ordered a minimum of two times per year or a maximum of three times. By ordering a larger quantity currently needed, the unit cost per item may be reduced significantly. Size of facilities, setup cost, etc., will influence the amount purchased. These items may not be stocked in generally unlimited quantity by reason of carrying costs or the original cost of the item.

A mathematical formula has been devised which takes into account such things as usage, setup cost, carrying charges, and unit cost (material, labor, and overhead cost) of the item. The formula determines the economical order quantity for an item. For example, as setup cost rises, the quantity rises; and as carrying charges increase, the quantity declines. The formula is as follows:

$$Q = \sqrt{\frac{2 \times (\text{Annual usage}) \times (\text{Setup or order cost})}{(\% \text{ Carrying charge}) \times (\text{Unit cost})}}$$

C items, or low-value items, may be ordered also on the basis of economical order quantities, or by a method known as maximum-minimum control. This method is generally used for low-unit-cost items which are consumed in volume and at a steady rate. After a shipment of the item is received, stock is at its maximum. When stock gets to a predetermined level, another order is entered to replenish it. The stock is depleted further until the ordered item has been received, at which time there should be only a reserve amount of the stock left. In calculating the reorder point, the normal period usage, a reserve amount, and the time to receive stock after ordering are considered. Computers or tabulating machines may be used to calculate when the reorder point has arrived. The reorder point is recalculated periodically to take into account any changes that might have occurred in usage or lead time.

In applying the principle of value analysis, it is merely necessary to list each component in descending order of annual usage value, as in Fig. 102.

VALUE ANALYSIS OF INVENTORY

Part Number	Unit Cost	Estimated Annual Usage (Quantity)	Annual Usage Value	Cumulative Annual Usage	Sequence Number
4201	$2,000.00	200	$400,000.00	$ 400,000.00	1
9867	1.00	320,000	320,000.00	720,000.00	2
3026	312.00	1,000	312,000.00	1,032,000.00	3
5095	.10	2,600,000	260,000.00	1,292,000.00	4
8766	.25	1,000,000	250,000.00	1,542,000.00	5
3221	4.00	50,000	200,000.00	1,742,000.00	6
12415	190.00	1,000	190,000.00	1,932,000.00	7
3901	.05	200	10.00	9,999,997.00	8,762
8666	.03	100	3.00	10,000,000.00	8,763

Fig. 102—Sequential Listing for Use in Value Analysis of Inventory.

On such a basis, the controller can group the various items in accordance with the method of control which he proposes be used. The desired turnover, optimum quantity to be stocked, etc., may then be applied to each item or group as may be applicable.

BUDGETARY CONTROL

The techniques of control through minimum-maximum inventory points, turnover rates, or executive decisions regarding speculation can each be used alone, against all or some segments of the inventory. However, in some companies the inventories are tied in more closely, more formally, to expected operations. This is accomplished through budgetary control, of which inventory planning is a phase. After all, many of the same considerations necessary in establishing turnover rates or minimum or maximum inventories are required in budgeting the purchases and inventory. Usually budgetary control tends to get the inventories coordinated more closely with expected usage. This application is discussed in the next few sections.[1]

BUDGETING THE MATERIALS INVENTORY

There are basically two methods of developing the inventory budget of raw materials and supplies:

1. Budget each important item separately based upon the production program
2. Budget materials as a whole or classes of materials based upon selected production factors

Practically all concerns must employ both methods to some extent though one or the other predominates. The former method is always preferable to the extent that it is practicable.

BUDGETING INDIVIDUAL ITEMS OF MATERIAL

The following steps should be taken in budgeting the major individual items of materials and supplies:

1. Determine the physical units of material required for each item of goods which is to be produced during the budget period.
2. Accumulate these into total physical units of each material item required for the entire production program.
3. Determine for each item of material the quantity which should be on hand periodically to provide for the production program with a reasonable margin of safety.
4. Deduct material inventories, which it is expected will be on hand at the beginning of the budget period, to ascertain the total quantities to be purchased.
5. Develop a purchase program which will insure that the quantities will be on hand at the time they are needed. The purchase program must give effect to such factors as economically sized orders, economy of transportation, and margin of safety against delays.
6. Test the resulting budgeted inventories by standard turnover rates.
7. Translate the inventory and purchase requirements into dollars by applying the expected prices of materials to budgeted quantities.

In practice, many difficulties arise in executing the foregoing plan. In fact, it is practicable to apply it only to important items of material which

---

[1] Adapted from J. Brooks Heckert and James D. Willson, *Business Budgeting and Control,* 2d ed., New York: The Ronald Press Company, 1955, pp. 146–156.

are used regularly and in relatively large quantities. Most manufacturing concerns find that they must carry hundreds or even thousands of different items of materials and supplies to which this plan cannot be practically applied. Moreover, some concerns cannot express their production programs in units of specific products. This is true, for example, where goods are partially or entirely made to customers' specifications. In such cases it is necessary to look to past experience to ascertain the rate and the regularity of movement of individual material items and to determine maximum and minimum quantities between which the quantities must be held. This necessitates a program of continuous review of material records as a basis for purchasing, and frequent revision of maximum and minimum limits, to keep the quantities adjusted to current needs.

BUDGET BASED ON PRODUCTION FACTORS

For those items of materials and supplies which cannot be budgeted individually, the budget must be based on general factors of expected production activity, such as total budgeted labor hours, productive hours, standard allowed hours, cost of materials consumed, or cost of goods manufactured. To illustrate, assume that cost of materials consumed (other than basic materials which are budgeted individually) is budgeted at $1,000,000 and that past experience demonstrates that these materials and supplies should be held to a rate of turnover of five times per year; then an average inventory of $200,000 should be budgeted. This would mean that individual items of material could be held in stock approximately 73 days ($\frac{1}{5}$ of 365 days). This could probably be accomplished by instructing the executives in charge to keep on hand an average of 60 days' supply. While such a plan cannot be applied rigidly to each item, it serves as a useful guide in the control of individual items and prevents the accumulation of excessive inventories.

In the application of this plan, other factors must also be considered. The relationship between the inventory and the selected factor of production activity will vary with the degree of production activity. Thus, a turnover of five times may be satisfactory when materials consumed are at the $1,000,000 level but it may be necessary to reduce this to four times when the level goes to $750,000. Conversely, it may be desirable to hold it to six times when the level rises to $1,250,000. Moreover, some latitude may be necessitated by the seasonal factor, as it may be necessary to increase the quantities of materials and supplies in certain months in anticipation of seasonal demands. The ratio of inventory to selected production factors at various levels of production activity and in different seasons should be plotted and studied until standard relationships can be established. The entire process can be refined somewhat by establishing different standards for different sections of the materials and supplies inventory.

The plan, once in operation, must be closely checked by monthly comparisons of actual and standard ratios. When the rate of inventory movement falls below the standard, the records of individual items must be studied to detect the slow-moving items.

PURCHASING BUDGET ILLUSTRATED

Some of the problems and methods of determining the total amount of expected purchases may be better understood by illustration. Assume, for example, that this information is made available as to production requirements, after a review of the production budget:

| | Class | | | |
| | Units | | | Amount |
Period	W	X	Y	Z
January	400	500		
February	300	600		
March	500	400	*Unknown*	*Unknown*
Subtotal	1,200	1,500		
2d Quarter	1,500	1,200		
3rd Quarter	1,200	1,500		
4th Quarter	1,000	1,700		
Total	4,900	5,900	10,000	$20,000

Solely for illustrative purposes, the following four groups of products have been assumed:

Class W   Material of high unit value, for which a definite quantity and time program is established in advance—such as for stock items. Also, the material is controlled on a minimum-maximum inventory basis for budget purposes.

Class X   Similar to item W, except that, *for budget purposes,* minimum-maximum limits are not used.

Class Y   Material items for which definite quantities are established for the budget period, but for which no definite time program is established—such as special orders on hand.

Class Z   Miscellaneous material items which are grouped together and *budgeted* only in terms of total dollar purchases for the budget period.

In actual practice, of course, decisions as to production time must be made as to items using Y and Z classifications. However, the bases described later in this chapter are applicable in planning the production level.

Class W.   Where the items are budgeted on a minimum-maximum basis, it usually is necessary to determine the range within which purchases must fall, so as to (1) meet production needs, and (2) stay within inventory limits. A method of making such a calculation is shown below:

	Units	
	For Minimum Inventory	For Maximum Inventory
January production requirements	400	400
Inventory limit	50	400
Total	450	800
Beginning inventory	200	200
Limit of receipts (purchases)	250	600

Within these limits, the quantity to be purchased will be influenced by such factors as unit transportation and handling costs, price considerations, storage space, availability of material, capital requirements, etc.

A similar determination would be made for each month for each such raw material, and a schedule of receipts and inventory might then be prepared, somewhat in this fashion:

	Units					
Period	Beginning Inventory	Receipts	Usage	Ending Inventory	Unit Value	Purchases Budget
January	200	400	400	200	$200	$ 80,000
February	200	400	300	300		80,000
March	300	400	500	200		80,000
Subtotal		1,200	1,200			240,000
2d Quarter	200	1,350	1,500	50		270,000
3rd Quarter	50	1,200	1,200	50		240,000
4th Quarter	50	1,200	1,000	250		240,000
Total		4,950	4,900			$990,000

Class X. It is assumed that the class X materials can be purchased as needed. Since other controls are practical on this type of item, and as no other procurement problems exist, purchases are determined by the production requirements. A simple extension is all that is required to determine dollar value of expected purchases:

Period	Quantity	Unit Price	Total
January	500	$10	$ 5,000
February	600		6,000
March	400		4,000
Subtotal	1,500		15,000
2d Quarter	1,200		12,000
3rd Quarter	1,500		15,000
4th Quarter	1,700		17,000
Total	5,900		$59,000

Class Y. The breakdown of the class Y items may be assumed to be as follows:

Item	Quantity	Unit Price	Cost
Y-1	1,000	$1.00	$ 1,000
Y-2	2,000	1.10	2,200
Y-3	3,000	1.20	3,600
Y-4	4,000	1.30	5,200
Total	10,000		$12,000

A determination as to time of purchase must be made, even though no definite delivery schedules, etc., have been set by the customer. In this instance, the distribution of the cost, and units, might be made on the basis of past experience or budgeted production factors, such as budgeted machine hours. The allocation to periods could be made on past experience, as follows:

Period	Past Experience as to Similar Units Manufactured	Y-1	Y-2	Y-3	Y-4	Total	Values (Purchases Budget)
January	10%	100	200	300	400	1,000	$ 1,200
February	15	150	300	450	600	1,500	1,800
March	10	100	200	300	400	1,000	1,200
Subtotal .	35	350	700	1,050	1,400	3,500	4,200
2d Quarter	30	300	600	900	1,200	3,000	3,600
3rd Quarter	20	200	400	600	800	2,000	2,400
4th Quarter	15	150	300	450	600	1,500	1,800
Total ...	100%	1,000	2,000	3,000	4,000	10,000	$12,000

The breakdown of units is for the benefit of the purchasing department only, inasmuch as the percentages can be applied against the total cost, and need not apply to individual units. In practice, if the units are numerous as to types and of small value, the quantities of each might not be determined in connection with the forecast.

Class Z. Where the materials are grouped, past experience again may be the means of determining estimated expenditures by period of time. Based on production hours, the distribution of class Z items may be assumed to be as follows (cost of such materials assumed to be $2 per production hour):

Period	Productive Hours	Amount
January	870	$ 1,740
February	830	1,660
March	870	1,740
Subtotal	2,570	5,140
2d Quarter	2,600	5,200
3rd Quarter	2,230	4,460
4th Quarter	2,600	5,200
Total	10,000	$20,000

When all materials have been grouped, requirements determined, and translated to cost, the materials budget may be summarized, principally for the financial forecast, as follows:

The Blank Company
PURCHASES BUDGET
For the Year 196—

Period	Class				Total
	W	X	Y	Z	
January	$ 80,000	$ 5,000	$ 1,200	$ 1,740	$ 87,940
February	80,000	6,000	1,800	1,660	89,460
March	80,000	4,000	1,200	1,740	86,940
Subtotal	240,000	15,000	4,200	5,140	264,340
2d Quarter	270,000	12,000	3,600	5,200	290,800
3rd Quarter	240,000	15,000	2,400	4,460	261,860
4th Quarter	240,000	17,000	1,800	5,200	264,000
Total	$990,000	$59,000	$12,000	$20,000	$1,081,000

The above illustration relates to raw materials. A similar approach would be taken with respect to manufacturing supplies. A few major items might be budgeted as the class W or X items above, but the bulk probably would be handled as Z items.

Once the requirements as measured by delivery dates have been made firm, it is necessary for the financial department to translate such data into cash disbursement needs through average lag time, etc.

TABULATING OR COMPUTER APPLICATIONS

The many ways in which information must be presented for the most effective use by both the purchasing department and the financial division, and the numerous extensions necessary, make the determination of purchase requirements a suitable application for automatic tabulating or computer equipment. For example, the total material requirements for the budget periods may be presented in several ways, merely by a re-sorting of cards, etc.:

1. By type of raw material, in summary form as to total of each item
2. By type of raw material, segregated quantitatively as to finished product line
3. By product line, detailed by type of raw material

BUDGETING WORK IN PROCESS

The inventory of goods actually in process of production between stocking points can be best estimated by applying standard turnover rates to budgeted production. This may be expressed either in units of production or dollars and may be calculated for individual processes and departments or for the factory as a whole. The former is more accurate. To illustrate this procedure, assume the following inventory and production data for a particular process or department:

Process inventory estimated for January 1 .....   500 units (a)
Production budgeted for month of January ..... 1,200 units (b)
Standard rate of turnover (per month) ....   4 times (c)
Average value per unit of goods in this process . . $10

With a standard turnover rate of four times per month the average inventory should be 300 units $(1,200 \div 4)$. To produce an average inventory of 300 units, the ending inventory should be 100 units $\left(\dfrac{500 + 100}{2} = 300 \right)$. Using the symbol X to denote the quantity to be budgeted as ending inventory, the following formula can be applied:

$$X = \frac{2b}{c} - a = \frac{2\,(1,200)}{4} - 500 = 100 \text{ units}$$

Value of ending inventory is $1,000 (100 $\times$ $10).

Where the formula produces a minus quantity (as it will if beginning inventory is excessive), the case should be studied as an individual problem and a specific estimate made for the process or department in question.

Control over the work-in-process inventories can be exercised by a continuous check of turnover rates. Where the individual processes, departments, or plants are revealed to be excessive they should then be subjected to individual investigation.

The control of work-in-process inventories has been sorely neglected in many concerns. The time between which material enters the factory and emerges as finished product is frequently much longer than necessary for efficient production. An extensive study of the automobile tire industry revealed an amazing spread of time as between five leading manufacturers, one company having an inventory float six times that of another. This study indicated also, by an analysis of the causes of the float time, that substantial reductions could be made in all five of the companies without interference with production efficiency.

While it is desirable to reduce the investment in goods actually being processed to a minimum consistent with efficient production, it is frequently desirable to maintain substantial inventories of parts and partially finished goods as a means of reducing finished inventories.

Parts, partial assemblies, processed stock or any type of work in process which is stocked at certain points should be budgeted and controlled in the same manner as materials. That is, inventory quantities should be set for each individual item, based on the production program; or inventory limits should be set which will conform to standard rates of turnover. In the former case, control must be exercised through the enforcement of the production program; in the latter case, maximum and minimum quantities must be established and enforced for each individual item.

BUDGETING FINISHED GOODS

The budget of finished goods inventory (or merchandise in the case of trading concerns) must be based upon the sales budget. If, for example, it is expected that 500 units of item A will be sold during the budget period, it must be ascertained what number of units must be kept in stock to support such a sales program. It is seldom possible to predetermine the exact quantity which will be demanded by customers day by day. Some margin of safety must be maintained by means of the finished goods inventory so that satisfactory deliveries can be made. With this margin established, it is possible to develop a program of production or purchases whereby the stock will be replenished as needed.

BUDGETING FINISHED GOODS BY INDIVIDUAL ITEMS

Two general methods may be employed in budgeting the finished goods inventory. Under the first method, a budget is established for each item separately. This is done by studying the past sales record and the sales program of each item and determining the quantity which should be on hand at various dates (usually the close of each month) throughout the budget period. The detailed production or purchase program can then be developed to provide such quantities over and above current sales requirements. The total budget is merely the sum of the budgets of individual items. This total budget can then be tested by the rate of turnover desired as proof that a satisfactory relationship will be maintained between inventory and sales and that it harmonizes with the general financial program. If it fails in either respect, revision must be made in the program of sales, production, or finance until a proper coordination is effected.

Under this plan, control over the inventory is effected by means of enforcement of the sales and production programs. If either varies to any important degree from the budget, the other must be revised to a compensating degree and the inventory budget revised accordingly.

Where the sales and production programs can be enforced with reasonable certainty, this is the preferable method. It is particularly suitable for those concerns which manufacture a comparatively small number of items in large quantities. The application is similar in principle to that illustrated in connection with raw materials controlled budget-wise by minimums and maximums.

BUDGETING TOTAL FINISHED QUANTITIES AND VALUES

Where the sales of individual items fluctuate considerably and where such fluctuations must be watched for hundreds or even thousands of items, a second plan is preferable. Here basic policies are adopted relative to the relationship which must be maintained between finished inventory and sales. This may be done by establishing standard rates of turnover for the inventory as a whole or for different sections of the inventory. For example, it may be decided that a unit turnover rate of three times per year should be maintained for a certain class of goods, or that the dollar inventory of another class must not average more than one-fourth of the annual dollar cost of sales. The budget is then based upon such relationships, and the proper executives are charged with the responsibility of controlling the quantities of individual items in such manner that the resulting total inventories will conform to the basic standards of turnover.

With such standard turnover rates as basic guides, those in charge of inventory control must then examine each item in the inventory; collect information as to its past rate of movement, irregularity of demand, expected future demand, and economical production quantity; and establish maximum and minimum quantities, and quantities to order. Once the governing quantities are established, they must be closely watched and frequently revised if the inventory is to be properly controlled.

The establishment and use of maximum, minimum, and order quantities can never be resolved into a purely clerical routine if it is to be effective as an inventory control device. A certain element of executive judgment is necessary in the application of the plan. If, for example, the quantities are based on past sales, they must be revised as the current sales trend indicates a change in sales demand. Moreover, allowance must be made for seasonal demands. This is sometimes accomplished by setting different limits for different seasons.

The most frequent cause of the failure of such inventory control plans is the assignment of unqualified personnel to the task of operating the plan and the failure to maintain a continuous review of sales experience relative to individual items. The tendency in far too many cases is to resolve the matter into a purely clerical routine and assign to it clerks capable only of routine execution. The danger is particularly great in concerns carrying thousands of items in finished stock, with the result that many quantities are excessive and many obsolete and slow-moving items accumulate in stock. The successful execution of an inventory control plan requires continuous study and research, meticulous records of individual items and their movement, and a considerable amount of individual judgment.

The plan, once in operation, should be continually tested by comparing the actual rates of turnover with those prescribed by the general budget program. If this test is applied to individual sections of the finished inventory, it will reveal the particular divisions which fail to meet the prescribed rates of movement. The work of correction can then be localized to these divisions.

Whenever possible, the plan of finished inventory control should be exercised in terms of units. When this is not practicable, it must be based on dollar amounts.

AN ILLUSTRATIVE INVENTORY MANAGEMENT SYSTEM

From the preceding comments, it is evident that the inventory management procedure is part of a total *system*. Moreover, technological advances permit more sophisticated techniques. It will be helpful, therefore, to illustrate an approach using a computer. One such application has been developed by the Pease Woodwork Company,[2] which is in the highly seasonal prefabricated home business, where inventory control assumes even greater importance.

THE INVENTORY MANAGEMENT SYSTEM

The Pease management recognizes both the importance of customer service and the inherent cost of carrying the inventory to make this service possible. At the same time, experience shows that unless a constant balance is maintained between the supply and demand for each stock item, out-of-stock conditions continue to exist regardless of the total size of the overall inventory. Management has decided that in order to control its total service, total investment and total cost, it is necessary to control each of the 8,000 manufactured and 2,000 purchased stock items.

The IBM punched card equipment installed in 1955 reduced the clerical effort and increased the speed and accuracy of updating inventories and writing order confirmations, production orders and invoices. It was not until the IBM RAMAC® 305 System was installed in September of 1959, however, that Pease was able to:

1. *Forecast* the future requirements in two-week intervals for the 8,000 manufactured and 2,000 purchased stock items.
2. *Plan* the floating order and expedite points to implement the forecast for the current biweekly period.

[2] From "Pease Woodwork Company Inventory Management System," *IBM General Information Manual*, 1961, pp. 2–9.

3. *Control* the inventory level of each stock item as the materials are received and shipped.
4. *Procure* a balanced stock for each family of items in the most economic lot sizes.

The IBM 305 tells the buyers *when to order* and *how much to buy*. Order points and expedite points are automatically adjusted every two weeks to reflect the current rate of demand and seasonal fluctuations.

Previously, the buyers spent most of their time estimating requirements on the basis of on-hand and usage information which was from 15 to 45 days old. Now, their buying requirements are determined for them on the basis of seasonally adjusted information as current as the last order shipped or received. This permits the buyers to concentrate their efforts on studying new products and seeking more favorable prices, terms and conditions.

FORECASTING REQUIREMENTS

It was not an easy task to establish practical inventory management policies which would realistically forecast the demand requirements of this highly seasonal business. A sound forecasting system must take into consideration usage, trends, cycles and other factors. It must be responsive to periods of uncertainty and must incorporate provisions to permit management to raise or lower inventory levels as special situations develop.

Demand Pattern

Pease took several months to review, plot and study their sales records for the previous five years. They selected five curves as a foundation for their inventory management policies—first load homes, final load homes, total stock sales, material sales and sink front deliveries.

Forecast Policy

Because of the seasonal nature of the demand pattern, management decided to establish a biweekly forecast policy. The average sales for each two-week period were related to the average annual sales to provide the percentage of the annual sales for each of the 26 periods throughout the year. To forecast the annual sales at the current rate, the actual sales for each stock unit in the last six periods are divided by the accumulated predetermined percentages for the six periods involved. The biweekly forecast is then established by applying the predetermined percentages for the coming periods to the annual forecast.

FUTURE REQUIREMENTS FORECAST

Last Six Periods	Units Shipped	Percentage of Annual Usage
6	264	1.2
5	317	1.8
4	528	2.8
3	634	3.5
2	687	4.3
1	739	5.0

Current
Annual Rate = 3,169   18.6% = 17,036 Units

Current
Forecast   = 17,036   ×   5.6% =   954 Units

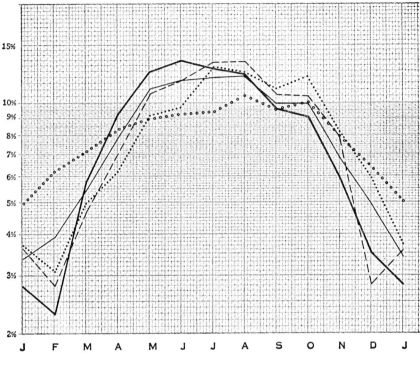

IST LOADS HOMES ━━━━━
FINAL LOADS HOMES ━ ━ ━ ━ ━
TOTAL STOCK SALES $ ━━━━━━
MATERIAL SALES $ o o o o o o o o o
636 SINK FRONT ••••••••••••••••••

PLANNING STOCK LEVELS

Pease employs a sophisticated approach to implement the inventory management policies necessary to plan their operations. As the forecast for each stock-keeping unit is determined, it is immediately incorporated into the current operating plan. This plan establishes the new order and expedite points for the next two-week period.

Variable Order Point Policy

Stock items are categorized into groups—variable order point and fixed order point. Twenty percent of the stock items represent ninety percent of the inventory investment. Variable order points are recalculated biweekly to control these items. The variable order point is equal to:

Lead Time Requirements + Safety Stock

where:

Lead Time Requirements	=	Predetermined % of Annual Shipments during Lead Time	×	Current Annual Rate

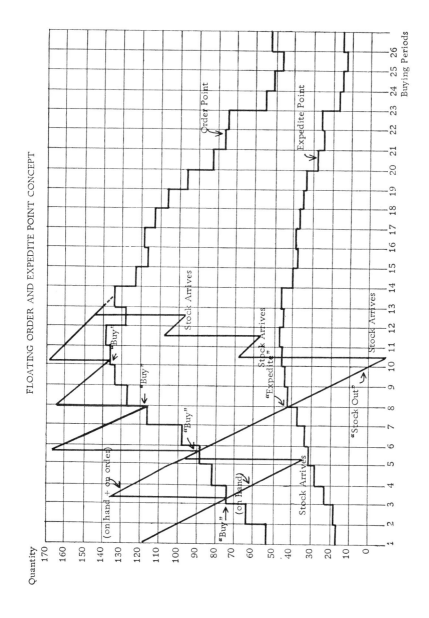

FLOATING ORDER AND EXPEDITE POINT CONCEPT

and:

$$\frac{\text{Safety}}{\text{Stock}} = \frac{\text{Level}}{\text{Factors}} \times \frac{\text{Item}}{\text{Factors}} \sqrt{\frac{\frac{\text{Lead Time}}{\text{Requirements}} \times \frac{\text{Avg. Demand}}{\text{Per Order}}}{\text{Lead Time (Periods)}}}$$

and:

$$\text{Level Factors} = \frac{\text{Business Trend}}{\text{Factor}} \times \frac{\text{Inventory Management}}{\text{Factor}}$$

and:

$$\frac{\text{Item}}{\text{Factors}} = \frac{\text{Order}}{\text{Frequency}} \times \text{Reliability} \times \frac{\text{Stock-Out}}{\text{Consequences}} \times \text{Adjuster}$$

To illustrate the application of the variable order point formulas, suppose:

5.6 = Predetermined % of Annual Shipments during Lead Time
17,036 = Current Annual Rate
14 = Lead Time (Days)
62 = Average Demand Per Order
1.1 = Business Trend Factor
.9 = Inventory Management Factor
1.2 = Order Frequency Factor
1.0 = Reliability Factor
1.2 = Stock-Out Consequences Factor
1.8 = Adjuster Factor

then:

Lead Time Requirements = $5.6\% \times 17,036 = \underline{954}$ Units

Level Factors = $1.1 \times .9 = \underline{.99}$

Item Factors = $1.2 \times 1.0 \times 1.2 \times 1.8 = \underline{2.592}$

Safety Stock = $.99 \times 2.592 \sqrt{\dfrac{954 \times 62}{1}} = \underline{624}$ Units

so the:

Variable Order Point = $954 + 624 = \underline{1578}$ Units

The precision built into the IBM RAMAC 305 programs to react not only to the external demand generated daily by a changing market but also to a flexible set of inventory management policies, merits a more detailed examination:

1. The *Order Frequency Factor* is based on the number of orders per year:

No. of Orders	Factors
1 or less	0.9
2	1.3
3	1.5
4	1.7
6	1.8
8	2.0
12	2.1
26	2.2
52 or more	2.3

2. The *Reliability Factor* is based on forecasted versus actual demand:

Degree of Reliability	Factor
Extremely Stable	0.8
Average	1.0
Fairly Erratic	1.2
Extremely Erratic	1.4

3. The *Stock-Out Consequence Factor* is determined by the buyer:

Consequence	Factor
Not Critical	0.8
Average	1.0
Critical	1.2
Extremely Critical	1.4

4. The *Adjuster Factor* is used to arbitrarily set the stock level to operating experience:

Adjuster	Factor
Initial Value	1.0
Maximum Value	3.0

5. The *Business Trend Factor* reflects management's evaluation of the current home building market:

Trend	Factor
Definite Unseasonal Slowdown	0.8
Slight Unseasonal Slowdown	0.9
Normal Seasonal Activity	1.0
Slight Unseasonal Buildup	1.1
Definite Unseasonal Buildup	1.2

6. The *Inventory Management Factor* reflects management's recognition of an abnormal situation:

Abnormal	Factor
Minimum	0.5
Maximum	6.0

Variable Expedite Point Policy

Expedite points for the high dollar volume items vary with the current usage forecast. The expedite times are expressed in working days and include the total elapsed time from the moment the IBM 305 signals that the expedite point has been reached to the time that the material is unloaded and ready for use. The expedite points are recalculated every two weeks using the following formula:

$$\text{Expedite Point} = \frac{\text{\% of Annual Usage During Expedite Time}}{} \times \text{Current Annual Usage Rate}$$

Fixed Order and Expedite Point Policy

The buyers set the fixed order and expedite points for the low dollar volume items. These items represent eighty percent of the total stock but only ten percent of the total inventory investment. Most of them are consumed in volume at a fairly steady rate. The order points, expedite points and standard order quantities are stored in the IBM 305 and are automatically checked as each stock withdrawal is made.

Stock Status Report

The IBM 305 computes and stores the variable order and expedite points. As it applies the formulas, it automatically prints a complete stock status report for the current period. This report shows the current stock status and usage (last three periods, year-to-date, current rate and last year) in addition to the values assigned to the management policy factors involved in each calculation.

STOCK STATUS

PERIOD 24 CODE	FAMILY 152		DESCRIPTION	FACTORS (Stock Status / Order Period / Reliability / Stock Out Consequence / Adjuster)	LEAD TIME	EXPEDITE TIME	ON HAND	EXPEDITE POINT	ON HAND + ON ORDER	ORDER POINT	22	23	24	YR. TO DATE	CURRENT RATE	19 LAST
060901	PC 2X4	6FT	COM	1 2 1 0 1 0 1 0	35	15	7914	477	7914	1578	634	687	739	17453	17036	1?
060902	PC 2X4	8FT	COM	1 7 1 0 1 0 1 0	35	15	3747	960	3747	2442	3150	420	987	31530	43642	1?
060903	PC 2X4	10FT	COM	1 5 1 0 1 2 1 0	35	15	2600	227	4600	655	600	200	200	12550	10362	1?
060904	PC 2X4	12FT	COM	2 1 1 0 1 2 1 0	35	15	7045	1332	7045	4051	2047	1698	1177	60425	60549	4?
060905	PC 2X4	14FT	COM	2 1 1 0 1 2 1 0	35	15	5400	1039	9700	3174	1361	1336	825	44774	47248	3?
060906	PC 2X4	16FT	COM	2 0 1 0 1 2 1 0	35	15	2600	814	4700	2441	1600	1000	400	37824	37005	2?
060907	PC 2X4	18FT	COM	5 1 7 1 0 1 2 1 0	35	15	0	55	0	174	0	0	300	3267	2507	?
060908	PC 2X4	20FT	COM	5 1 7 1 0 1 2 1 0	35	15	2-	26	498	94	0	0	0	1935	1202	?
060961	PC 2X4	6FT	CONST FIR	1 5 1 2 1 2 1 0	35	15	6005	328	6005	1034	200	1113	0	20759	14948	1?
060963	PC 2X4	10FT	CONST FIR	1 5 1 2 1 2 1 0	35	15	2400	341	3600	967	400	200	200	12704	15544	?
060965	PC 2X4	14FT	CONST FIR	1 8 1 2 1 2 1 0	35	15	1600	188	3200	694	100	600	0	10687	8549	1?
061672	PC 2X4	7- 0	CONST PATTERN 1	1			2940	1000	2940	2000	0	0	0	1613		
061767	PC 2X4	8- 0	CONST PATTERN 1	1			1050	500	1050	1000	0	0	0	835		
061768	PC 2X4	8- 0	CONST PATTERN 2	1			705	500	705	1000	0	0	0	1260		

CONTROLLING STOCK LEVELS

The determination of the variable order and expedite points establishes the current operating plan. The IBM 305 immediately puts this plan into action to control the inventory stock levels. As each item is received or shipped, the inventory in disk storage is updated and the current inventory is scanned. An IBM card is automatically punched to initiate order action. Buyer signal reports are printed to instantaneously point out expedite and out-of-stock conditions.

RAMAC ADD.	CODE	DESCRIPTION	FAMILY	ACTION CODE		ON HAND	EXPEDITE POINT	ON HAND + ON ORDER	ORDER POINT	ORDER AMT.	MAX. SALE LIMIT	ORDER NO.	BUYER SIGNAL REPORT
16012	228115	SET KD PARTS FOR 1270XX0	772G	339	E 4	54	55	204	100				

ACTION TAKEN:

RAMAC ADD.	CODE	DESCRIPTION	FAMILY	ACTION CODE		ON HAND	EXPEDITE POINT	ON HAND + ON ORDER	ORDER POINT	ORDER AMT.	MAX. SALE LIMIT	ORDER NO.	BU SIG REP
14440	189840	PC CORNICE 1 1/4X8 20FT SELECT	199	X 6		0	17	100	57				

ACTION TAKEN:

PROCURING ECONOMIC LOTS

Carload prices and freight rates are a substantial source of cost savings in the building materials industry. To take full advantage of these potential savings, carload orders are written whenever possible.

Frequently, the overall cost and inventory considerations will not justify the purchase of a carload lot of a single item. Even if it would, the total cost may be reduced even further by taking into consideration the future requirements of each item within the stock family. To enable the buyers to balance out each purchase, an order analysis report is automatically generated for each item to be procured.

ORDER ANALYSIS

	FAMILY 152			ACTION CODE	STOCK STATUS	CURRENT STATUS				ORDER REQUIREMENTS AT END OF PERIODS:					
DE		DESCRIPTION				ON HAND	EXPEDITE POINT	ON HAND + ON ORDER	ORDER POINT	25	26	1	2	3	4
901	PC 2X4	6FT	COM	B	2	7914	477	7914	1578	6794	6607	6386	5995	5467	4701
902	PC 2X4	8FT	COM	B	2	3747	960	3747	2442	913	433	134−	1137−	2489−	4452−
903	PC 2X4	10FT	COM	B	2	2600	227	4600	655	3852	3739	3605	3367	3046	2580
904	PC 2X4	12FT	COM	B	2	7045	1332	7045	4051	2450	1784	997	395−	2272−	4996−
905	PC 2X4	14FT	COM	B	2	5400	1039	9700	3174	6101	5582	4968	3882	2418	292
906	PC 2X4	16FT	COM	B	2	2600	814	4700	2441	1926	1519	1038	187	960−	2625−
907	PC 2X4	18FT	COM	B	6		55		174	196−	223−	255−	312−	389−	501−
908	PC 2X4	20FT	COM	B	6	2−	26	498	94	394	381	366	339	302	248
961	PC 2X4	6FT	CONST FIR	B	2	6005	328	6005	1034	4837	4673	4479	4136	3673	3001
963	PC 2X4	10FT	CONST FIR	B	2	2400	341	3600	967	2494	2324	2122	1765	1284	585
965	PC 2X4	14FT	CONST FIR	B	2	1600	188	3200	694	2430	2336	2225	2029	1764	1380
672	PC 2X4	7− 0	CONST PATTERN 1	B	2	2940	1000	2940	2000	4560	36480#				
767	PC 2X4	8− 0	CONST PATTERN 1	B	2	1050	500	1050	1000	1920	17472#				
768	PC 2X4	8− 0	CONST PATTERN 2	B	2	705	500	705	1000	2080−	18720#				
		LEAD TIME 35								23130	23737	25797	43035	105642	201952

The order analysis report shows the current status and future requirements for each item in the family. It provides a complete picture of the on-hand, on-order and projected stock positions for the next six periods. The last line indicates the accumulated weight of the items required. This report enables the buyers to balance out the purchase and the stock position for an entire family of items. It is a management tool for attaining the total service, total investment and total cost objectives.

EVALUATING THE FORECAST

Since the biweekly forecast and operating plan is tied directly to the predetermined percentages of the annual sales, a constant surveillance is maintained between actual and estimated sales.

The X's (in the graph) connected by the straight lines represent the estimated percentages. The O's are the actual percentages. This graph is printed on an IBM 407 Accounting Machine from cards produced by the IBM 305. Management determines whether the deviations are serious enough to warrant a change in the assigned percentages.

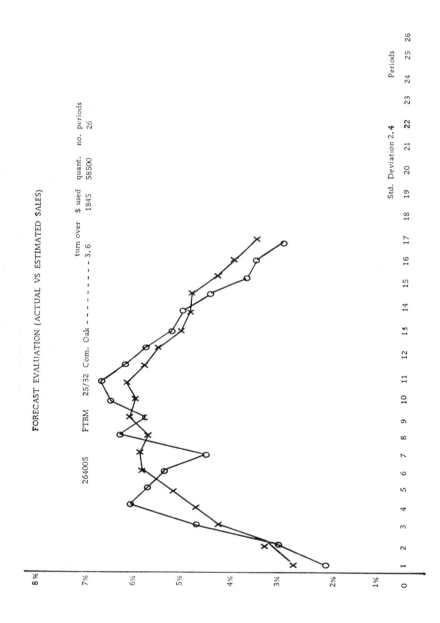

FORECAST EVALUATION (ACTUAL VS ESTIMATED SALES)

INTERNAL CONTROL AND INVENTORIES

Accounting control of inventories loses much of its effectiveness if the records on which such control is based are inaccurate to any degree. This is true whether control is exercised through minimum-maximum points, through turnover rates, or through budgetary control. There is little doubt that proper accounting for inventories is one of the most difficult problems of a controller. Yet it is one which requires close attention and a high degree of cooperation with plant personnel.

Any controller can understand that it takes more than general statements to explain a major inventory shortage at the year-end, or losses resulting from obsolete stocks. Such conditions are often but a manifestation of poor physical control of materials, insufficient coordination between the accounting department and the production or sales department, or a poor system of internal control.

Obviously, one way to assure physical control of the inventories, and consequently fewer losses, is to place all items under lock and key, and have the stores and stock rooms under custody of the controller. Since he appreciates the need for control perhaps more than the factory or sales personnel, it could be expected that procedures used by him would greatly reduce losses, or discrepancies between physical count and records. But practical considerations do not make this possible, and many departures must be made in the interest of efficient manufacturing operations. A large number of the inventory problems are conceived when strict control procedures are relaxed in order to facilitate efficient production. Internal control with respect to receipt of goods has already been reviewed in Chapter 19. It is often after this point that the greatest weaknesses develop, that is, from the withdrawal of raw materials for production until the goods are transferred to finished stock. It is a matter not only of inaccurate inventory records but also of unrecorded manufacturing inefficiencies through excess usage of material.

To the extent that poor physical control of the inventories, or a weak system of internal control, is responsible for the losses, the following general suggestions are made:

1. Keep all items of high unit value and small bulk under lock and key, and issue them only upon the presentation of a requisition duly authorized.
2. Permit no goods or materials to leave the plant without propeɪ passes—shipping memos, notice of material returned to vendor, material passes, etc.
3. Segregate duties so that those who keep the records are not responsible for the actual physical receipt or shipment, and so that the purchasing department is not in charge of stores.

4. Make a rotating physical count or frequent spot-checks of the inventory on hand. Occasionally trace a specific batch of material back to the records—a small-scale internal audit.

5. Review unusually good yields or performance for an indication of improper or erroneous paper work which might affect the inventories.

It is evident that successful inventory control requires continuous study and checking.

PHYSICAL INVENTORY

Engineers often assert that the accountant's inventory records are of no value, and that a physical inventory must be taken once a year to see that the recording is correct. While such a statement is not an indictment of records, but rather of lack of proper procedures, the fact remains that an annual count of all goods is highly desirable, particularly where close control cannot be exercised. This annual physical inventory should be under the supervision of the controller, although the counting may be done by the factory organization. This function, a part of the control system, is discussed in Chapter 39.

PERPETUAL INVENTORY RECORDS

The exact type of inventory records to be maintained is a decision to be made by the controller, giving consideration to the needs of the operating departments, the type of business, and equipment available. While it is not within the scope of this book to consider system design, a general observation can be made.

A problem faced by every controller is whether perpetual inventory records should be maintained. There can probably be little argument that perpetual control accounts should be kept on each major inventory classification. The question is whether detailed perpetual stock records are practical under the circumstances. It can be a voluminous job and often entails considerable clerical cost. Most controllers are aware of the need for keeping such costs as low as possible. But, as has been mentioned, the cheapest method is not necessarily the best, and the objective is inventory control.

Sometimes an attempt is made to keep memorandum perpetual records of quantities which are not tied into the financial records. Often this may fail because sufficient safeguards are not provided to see that all paper work is completed and that it is routed through the record clerk.

Proper maintenance of stock records gives current data on the stock. Review of such records is a means of obtaining current and up-to-date information on the condition of the stock. Every controller should weigh fully the considerable advantages of perpetual records before deciding against them.

A common type of perpetual card is shown in Fig. 103. It may be kept with or without values. Under a standard cost system some time and clerical cost can be avoided by keeping quantities only. It is a relatively simple matter to reconcile receipts with recorded liabilities.

Such records may be physically located in the warehouse or stock room itself. It is not necessary that they be in the central accounting department. Under ordinary circumstances the recording should be done by an accounting representative.

STOCK LEDGER CARD															

Item_____   Code No._____
Size or Type_____   Section No._____   Max._____
Unit_____   Bin_____   Min._____

ORDERED			RECEIVED					ISSUED					BALANCE		
Date	P. O. No.	Quan-tity	Date	P. O. No.	Quan-tity	Unit Cost	Total Cost	Date	Req. No.	Quan-tity	Unit Cost	Total Cost	Quantity	Unit Cost	Total Cost

Fig. 103—Stock Ledger Card.

INVENTORY REPORTS

The computer application on continuous inventory management used by the Pease Woodwork Company is illustrative of the up-to-date control techniques. Such methods can signal the need for action before losses are incurred. It is expected that the controller will be aware of systems which are most suitable under the circumstances.

Such technological progress will improve the speed and content of reports which the chief accounting officer is able to prepare for inventory planning and control.

By means of reports the controller is able to advise management of the effectiveness with which its plans on inventory control are being carried out. At the same time weak spots are pointed out for necessary action by the line staff, and this is of considerable assistance to them. Aside from the direct control purposes, inventory reports can stimulate ideas concerning standardization or simplification of materials, substitute materials, and improvements in material handling.

Meeting the inventory problems face-to-face will suggest practical reports which the controller can develop to aid and assist those charged with responsibility for control. The following are indicative of the great variety of reports that may be useful:

1. General summary of inventory by category.

2. Comparison of budgeted and actual inventory by classification.

3. Report on turnover (Fig. 104).

4. Summary of inventory activity, showing balances on hand and commitments, compared with requirements. Figure 105 is an illustration of such a report. An availability report is shown in Fig. 106.

5. Summary of inventory aging, indicating all slow-moving or obsolete material.

6. Report on overages or shortages (Fig. 107).

7. Comparison of actual and maximum inventories.

INVENTORY ANALYSIS

INV. CLASS	PART NUMBER	PART NAME	DATE OF LAST TRANSACTION MO.	DAY	YR.	NUMBER OF TRANSACTIONS	TWELVE MONTHS USAGE	AVERAGE INVENTORY	TURN-OVER
1 4 2		HARDWARE							
	3 2 9 8	SCREW	1 2	1 0		6 5	2 5 4 4 0	1 0 2 0	2 5
	3 7 8 6	SCREW	1 2	1 5		3 2	3 7 8 5 0	3 1 2 8	1 2
	4 3 2 5	WASHER	1 0	2 0		8 7 5	1 0 2 7 5 0	3 1 4 2 7	3
	4 3 2 6	WASHER	1 2	1 0		6 2 4	9 8 4 6 2 0 0	8 2 4 7 0 0	1 2
	1 0 1 1 1	NUT	1	1 5		1	1	3 1 0 0	
	1 1 1 2 1	BOLT	1 2	1 3		1 3 0	4 8 7 5 0	8 1 0 7	6
	1 2 0 3 2	COTTER PIN	4	1 1		6 4	6 5 4 7	2 1 8 2	3
	1 3 2 4 2	SCREW	1 1	2 8		7 7 0	1 2 5 4 7 0	1 0 4 5 5	1 2
	2 8 7 8 5	BOLT	1 0	2 7		7 0 0	9 5 6 2 2	9 5 6 7 5	1
	3 5 4 8 5	BOLT	1 2	3		5 0 0	4 2 8 7 2 0	9 0 7 5	4 8
	4 3 2 9 2	NUT	6	1 5		2 8	6 5 2 8 0	1 0 8 8 0	6
	4 7 8 5 6	WASHER	1 0	2 3		1 3 9	3 2 5 7 5 5	1 3 3 3 0	2 5
	4 9 2 2 1	PIN	1 2	7		2 7 0	9 5 4 7 0	8 2 4 7	1 2
	5 5 6 8 7	TAPER PIN	1 2	7		8 0 1	4 2 8 6 7 5	2 2 1 5 2 5	2
	6 5 4 9 3	LOCKWASHER	1 1	2 1		7 6 5	7 9 5 2 5 0	4 0 0 5 5 0	2
	6 5 4 9 4	LOCKWASHER	1 1	9		7 2 4	7 8 7 3 4 3	1 9 6 8 0 5	4
	6 5 4 9 5	LOCKWASHER	1 0	1 1		1 5 8	6 0 2 2 2	2 0 0 7 4	3
	7 2 1 8 7	STUD	7	1 4		1 0 3	3 0 4 8 0	3 8 1 0	8
	7 2 1 9 5	STUD	8	1 7		4 8	3 2 7 8 5	4 0 9 6	8
	7 5 1 4 8	SCREW	1 2	2		7 2 5	8 6 5 4 2 0	9 6 1 5 0	9
	9 0 1 8 5	BOLT	1 1	3 0		4 1 5	5 2 8 7 8 0	5 2 9 6 1	1 0

Fig. 104—Inventory Turnover Report.

RAW MATERIAL AND PURCHASED PARTS
INVENTORY AND OUTSTANDING COMMITMENTS

Class No.	Description	Balance 2/28/63	Receipts	Production	Disbursements Other	Disbursements Obsolete	Total	Balance 3/31/63	Outstanding Purchase Commitments 3/31/63	Total Commitments & Inventory 3/31/63	Unit Cost per Ship	Equiv. Ships Inventory	Equiv. Ships Purchase Commitments	Equiv. Ships Total
1	Raw Stock—Aluminum	$163,244	$15,835	$49,105	$602	$—	$49,707	$129,422	$9,341	$138,763	$253.00	511.5	36.9	548.4
2	Aluminum Forgings	5,967	3,335	3,420			3,420	5,882	1,210	7,092	21.58	272.5	56.1	328.6
3	Raw Stock—Steel	27,565	2,822	6,843	2		6,845	23,542	822	24,363	39.63	594.0	20.7	614.7
4	Steel Tubing	24,974	11,395	14,923	12		14,935	21,433	1,857	23,290	90.81	236.0	20.4	256.5
5	Wood	10,759	1,691	3,922	15		3,937	8,513	2,844	11,357	27.38	310.9	103.8	414.7
6	Fabrics	55,193	26,306	28,143	11,853		40,001	41,498	31,604	73,102	117.73	352.4	268.4	620.9
7	Plastics	3,101	7,390	4,253	3,297		7,550	2,942	873	3,815	18.99	154.9	45.9	200.8
8	Rubber	4,686	1,782	2,335			2,330	4,138	1,831	5,969	12.23	338.3	149.7	488.0
9	Paint	17,624	11,498	16,002			16,002	13,120	33,127	46,247	126.88	103.4	261.0	364.4
10	Standard Small Parts—Steel	63,591	7,792	18,203	233	18	18,454	52,929	6,299	59,228	84.43	626.8	74.6	701.5
11	Standard Small Parts—Aluminum	11,674	645	2,865			2,865	9,454	276	9,730	10.04	941.6	27.4	969.1
12	Standard Small Parts—Synthetic	8,958	2,739	4,106			4,106	7,591	650	8,241	18.66	406.8	34.8	441.6
15	Instruments and Controls	7,141	10,655	15,996		67	16,063	1,733	21,585	23,318	70.74	24.4	305.1	329.6
	(a) Special Equipment	10,963	6,495	10,129			10,129	7,329	24,492	31,821	—	—	—	—
16	Electrical Equipment	8,188	2,214	3,975		64	4,039	6,363	692	7,055	15.04	423.0	46.0	469.0
17	Landing Gear Equipment	12,858	24,658	25,153	799		25,952	11,564	35,938	47,502	110.19	104.9	326.1	431.0
19	Engine Parts	401	—	7			7	394		394	—	—	—	—
20	Propellers	1,020	6,894	7,814			7,814	100	10,600	10,700	32.06	3.1	330.6	333.7
	(a) Special Equipment	2,584	14,996	7,548			7,548	10,032	12,375	22,407	—	—	—	—
21	Batteries	439	3,351	3,166			3,166	624	9,211	9,835	18.11	34.4	508.6	543.0
22	Radio Equipment	8,592	3,533	6,819			6,819	5,306	40,233	45,539	84.40	62.8	476.6	539.5
25	Exhaust Stacks	6,789	1,155	5,957			5,957	1,987	12,540	14,527	33.10	60.0	378.8	438.8
26	Miscellaneous Trim Parts	8,827	4,487	3,811	763	399	4,973	8,341	975	9,316	20.97	397.7	46.4	444.2
27	Seat Cushions	4,012	2,348	2,232			2,232	4,128	4,125	8,253	14.57	283.3	283.1	566.4
28	Landing Gear Beams	1,771	8,117	6,890		48	6,938	2,949	6,782	9,731	24.07	122.5	281.7	404.2
29	Hardware	19,924	14,012	11,110		360	11,470	22,466	9,083	31,549	64.63	347.6	140.5	488.1
30	Fabric Parts	398	—	—			—	398		398	—	—	—	—
	Total	$491,243	$196,195	$264,727	$17,576	$956	$283,259	$404,177	$279,365	$683,542	$1,309.24	295.4	185.2	480.7
39	Engines	22,610	195,520	209,637	173		209,810	8,320	572,280	580,600	1,077.70	8.0	531.0	539.0
	Grand Total	$513,853	$391,715	$474,364	$17,749	$956	$493,069	$412,497	$851,645	$1,264,142	$2,386.94	165.5	341.3	506.8

RECAP OF TOTAL (LESS ENGINES)

Ships Released	4,667	Ships to Build	5,259
Spares Released	233	Spares to Build	263
Work in Process	288		5,522
Total	5,188	Less Comp. Prod.	5,188
		Net to Build	334

Inventory and Commitments (Less Special Equipment) 481
(Over) or Under Equivalent Ships .... (147)
Excessive Inventory or Commitments .... $(192,458)

DISTRIBUTION: R. D. Philips (2)   G. T. Tidmark (1)
J. A. Marse (1)   J. D. Hamilton (2)

Issued by the Accounting Department, April 3, 1963.

Fig. 105—Report on Inventory and Commitments Compared to Requirements.

STOCK STATUS SUMMARY

PERIOD ENDING _____

ITEM DESCRIPTION	ITEM CODE	ISSUES YEAR TO DATE	LAST ACTIVE MO	DAY	E.O.Q.	AVERAGE UNIT COST	PREVIOUS BALANCE	− ISSUES	+ RECEIPTS	= ON HAND	MINIMUM BALANCE	+ ON ORDER	− REQUIRED	= AVAILABLE	INACTIVITY	REORDER
SQ SHANK SWIVEL	11202	3825	6	10	250	8.50	250	75	100	275	100			275		
SQ SOCKET RIGID	16102	6775	6	18	300	2.05	1750	1500		250	500	1000		1250		
EXT SHANK WITH BRK	17203	2445	6	15	350	4.30	575	125		450	100	700	1138	12		*
ADJ ADAPTER SQUARE	23702	6518	6	20	375	18.68	1370	243		1127	200		170	957		*
SQ SOCKET SWIVEL	26302	6682	6	10	250	1.12	175	112	25	88	600		30	58	*	
FLAT TOP SWIVEL	33202	6725	5	20	200	1.04	4650			4650	300			4650		
FLAT TOP SWIVEL	33205	5924	6	05	375	1.06	2257	662	75	1670	100			1670		
CUSTOM BUILT	35105	6827	6	20	420	34.01	3652	300	420	3772	100	125	160	3737		
RND SPR RING STEM	44104	5525	5	10	300	.42	257			257	200			257	*	
RND SPR RING STEM	44106	4537	6	09	325	.50	1022	785	700	937	100			937		
SQ SHANK RIGID	51105	4357	6	19	300	1.50	1572	637	150	1085	200			1085		
FLAT TOP SWIVEL	53208	6498	6	25	150	2.75	2275	278		1997	150		400	1597	*	
FLAT TOP SWIVEL	53209	3752	4	15	200	2.50	1027			1027	50			1027	*	
ROUND SOCKET SWIVL	55706	5722	4	25	125	3.42	1975			1975	225	400		1975		
BOLT AND NUT SHANK	62110	7712	6	17	175	.30	4025	837		3188	150		500	2688		
CUSTOM BUILT	65112	5428	6	05	175	27.50	2172	250		1922	100			1922		

Fig. 106—Stock Status Summary and Availability Report.

REPORT ON INVENTORY DIFFERENCES
ROTATING INVENTORY

Page 5 of 5

Date _____

Description	Item No.	Unit	Physical Count	Stores Record Quantity	Physical Over (Short)	Unit Cost	Value Gain	Value Loss
Batteries......	41,213	ea.	324	324	–	$ –	$ –	$ –
Cable ig., wire —small.....	77,021	ft.	227	207	20	.20	4.00	–
Distributor— "C"........	26,110	ea.	116	120	(4)	4.00	–	16.00
Spark plug as-sembly......	8,510	ea.	42	42	–	–	–	–
Pulleys—½"...	91,306	doz.	5	4	1	3.00	3.00	–
Hub caps—2½	70,010	ea.	62	64	(2)	1.75	–	3.50
Page Total..							$7.00	$19.50

SUMMARY

	Units	%
Items Correct......................	410	90.7
Items Incorrect....................	42	9.3
Total Counted..................	452	100.0

Net Gain or (Loss)...............................$(305.10)

Fig. 107—Report on Physical Inventory Differences.

The controller should review the type of information most suitable to management and arrange for its preparation. In general, it is suggested the summary report recognize the principle of responsibility accounting as well as measurement against predetermined objectives. One such report, indicating both value and quantities compared to plan (budget) is shown in Fig. 108.

Graphic reports may be helpful. One application is shown in Fig. 109, wherein a permissible deviation is permitted, shown as a band (±12%). Corrective action is taken when the actual line moves outside of the limit.

TREATMENT OF SURPLUS STOCK

It is preferable, of course, that preventive management avoid any accumulation of surplus stock. However, once stocks are set out as obsolete or unnecessary, a disposal problem presents itself. Specific executives may

Roth Oil Company
INVENTORY SUMMARY—MARCH 31, 1963

	Values (M$)			Quantities (M bbls) at 3/31/63				
Description	March 31	Over/(Under) Plan	Chng from 12/31/62	Physical Stocks	Exchange Balance	Book Stocks	Over/(Under) Plan	Chng from 12/31/62
EASTERN DIVISION								
Gasolines	8,000	27	(2,000)	1,500	38	1,538	38	(336)
Middle distillates	11,000	385	(8,500)	2,500	222	2,722	722	(2,094)
Heavy fuel	500	42	(500)	700	(386)	314	14	(345)
Other	1,088	134	(300)	300	(109)	191	51	(19)
Total Refined Products	20,588	588	(11,300)	5,000	(235)	4,765	825	(2,794)
Crude oil	7,541	541	595	2,500	78	2,578	178	(9)
Total	28,129	1,129	(10,705)	7,500	(157)	7,343	1,003	(2,803)
SOUTHERN DIVISION								
Refined products	—	—	—	—	—	—	—	—
Crude oil	2,701	201	(236)	900	(12)	888	88	(77)
Total	2,701	201	(236)	900	(12)	888	88	(77)
WESTERN DIVISION								
Gasolines	15,000	1,000	2,000	2,800	68	2,868	368	761
Middle distillates	5,000	1,000	1,000	1,200	(74)	1,126	326	452
Heavy fuel	3,000	1,000	(3,000)	1,900	(23)	1,877	877	(1,461)
Other	756	756	272	300	29	329	129	25
Total Refined Products	23,756	3,756	272	6,200	—	6,200	1,700	(223)
Crude oil	7,543	543	(152)	2,900	23	2,923	223	135
Total	31,299	4,299	120	9,100	23	9,123	1,923	(88)

	813	13	(10)	45	—	45	5	(4)
PHILIPPINES	813							
Total: Refined Products	45,157	4,357	(11,048)	11,245	(235)	11,010	2,530	(3,021)
Crude oil	17,785	1,285	207	12,500	89	6,389	489	49
Total Petroleum	62,942	6,642	(10,841)	17,545	(146)	17,399	3,019	(2,972)
LIFO Reserve	(31,278)	—	(2,239)					
Total Book Value	31,664	6,642	(8,602)					
MATERIALS & SUPPLIES								
Eastern Division	4,839	839	(243)					
Southern Division	5,954	954	656					
Western Division	7,501	501	(171)					
Philippines	388	88	52					
Foreign Exploration & Production Division	389	(11)	13					
Other	193	43	(32)					
Total M & S Inventory	19,264	2,414	275					
TOTAL INVENTORIES AT BOOK VALUE	50,928	9,056	(8,327)					

Fig. 108—Inventory Summary—Comparison with Forecast.

Jones Refining Company

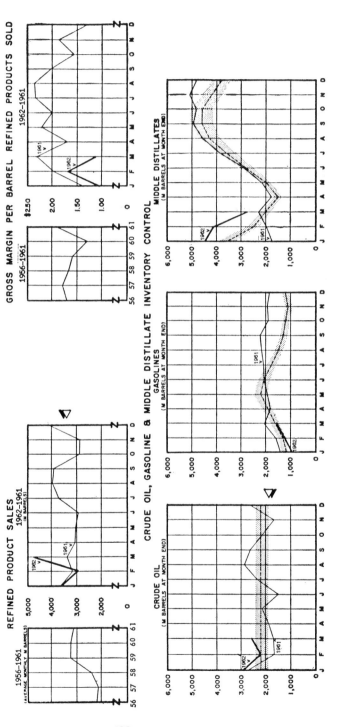

430

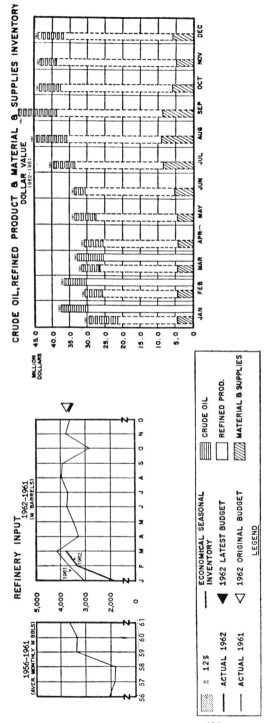

Fig. 109—Charts for Inventories and Operating Statistics.

be assigned the task of getting rid of the material, or the problem may be referred to an obsolescence committee. This committee should be composed of representatives of the sales, production, and accounting departments. Engineers may be called in to study possible uses for the material. If it cannot be utilized, then the committee might release it for salvage, or request the sales department to dispose of surplus finished products as second-class material.

If stocks are determined to be obsolete or slow-moving, the material should be written off or written down. Such action usually attracts sufficient attention to avoid further losses and keeps the key executives aware of inventory risks.

22

Valuation of Inventories

SIGNIFICANCE OF PROPER INVENTORY VALUATION

Problems of inventory valuation center about two phases: (1) the selection of that principle or method which will most satisfactorily reflect the earnings and financial condition of the particular business, and (2) the technique or procedures necessary to accomplish the objective. Since the inventories are usually the most significant item in the current assets, the method of valuing inventories is a very important factor in determining the results of operations and the financial condition.

One of the objectives of accounting for inventories, and this includes valuation, is to determine income properly by matching the applicable costs against the revenues of the firm. In the normal course of business, goods are sold and other merchandise is secured for additional sales. In this process of selling and either buying or making other goods for sale, it can be seen that the inventory is the residual value—the value remaining after costs have been applied to sales, the amount which is chargeable against future sales. A demonstration of the effect of inventory valuation is simple. For example, suppose a dealer purchased an airplane for $5,000 and sold it for $8,000. Suppose, further, that he then purchased another identical one for resale at a cost of $6,000. What is his profit? On one basis it is $3,000. But he has only $2,000 in cash as evidence; the other $1,000 is invested in the second plane—his inventory. By another basis of valuation, his actual profit is only $2,000. Which is correct? Clearly, the method of valuing inventories affects the statement of income and expense. The accountant has the responsibility for determining which basis of valuation more clearly reflects income.

Another objective of inventory valuation is to state correctly the financial position—the financial condition of a going concern, not one in liquidation. This purpose is perhaps somewhat less important than income determination because actual inventory worth cannot be determined until sales are made in the course of future operations. Further, there is a tendency to regard the earnings statement as of more importance than the balance sheet. Basically there should be no conflict between the two objectives.

The subject of inventory valuation includes not only a selection of the proper basis and method of valuation, but also a determination as to what is included in the cost. For example, should the expenses of the purchasing department or accounting department be included? Is freight-in to be considered an inventory cost? What about handling costs? Questions such as these can have great practical significance in valuing inventories.

CONTROLLER'S RESPONSIBILITY FOR INVENTORY VALUATION

The many alternatives open to the accountant in valuing inventories obviously mean that much study can be devoted to the subject. These many choices confuse the average businessman. It is probably safe to say that the typical business management is not aware of the effect of different valuation methods on profits. This is true in part because most likely no one has determined net profit for the business on several different bases. Under the circumstances the controller must take the initiative in all matters relating to inventory valuation. Some of the duties and responsibilities which he must assume are as follows:

1. Select the basis of valuation which will most satisfactorily reflect income. The board of directors or chief executive actually may approve or select the method. However, the controller should prepare the case and guide or influence the decision. He should be the member of the management team most familiar with the ramifications.

2. Where necessary or desirable, prepare supplementary data as to the effect on income of different bases, or changes in bases, of valuation, including standard cost changes.

3. Provide for a continuous review of procedures and records to assure that inventories are being properly valued. This will include procedures for notification when materials become unsalable, and for keeping abreast of market conditions. It will involve constant vigilance as to the effect of manufacturing developments on inventory balance and value.

4. Study the effect of tax legislation on inventory valuation and records; and act in the best interests of the company in dealing with the representatives of the Internal Revenue Service and other taxing authorities.

EMPHASIS ON THE COST BASIS

Most of the methods of valuing inventories involve "cost." Our entire system of accounting is based on cost, and this same concept is applied to inventories. As related to inventory, cost may be defined as the sum of all applicable expenditures and charges directly or indirectly incurred in bringing an article to its existing condition and location.[1] Just what are "applicable" expenditures and charges? The cost principle is easy to state but difficult to apply. Judgment must be exercised in determining what costs ought to be included, and a consistent policy must be followed. It is generally accepted practice to exclude from inventory costs that share of general and administrative expense not clearly related to production. However, exclusion of all overhead charges from inventory costs would not constitute acceptable accounting practice. Then, too, abnormal costs of various nature may be of such magnitude as to require omission. Some examples are excess spoilage, rehandling costs, and idle facility expense.

INVENTORY CHARACTERISTICS AND EFFECT OF VALUATION BASE

In a stable price economy fewer questions of inventory valuation policy normally arise. It is in periods of rapid price change that the valuation base selected may have a significant influence on income determination. Obviously, the effect of price changes is not uniform in every industry or in every company. Certain features or characteristics of the inventory determine the effect of price changes on an individual business concern. Among these are:

1. Degree of selling price responsiveness to cost changes
2. Relative share of investment in inventories
3. Possibility of price hedge
4. Rate of turnover

The heart of the problem, of course, is the responsiveness of selling price changes to costs. If prices bear little immediate relationship to costs, then the selling price to be realized upon disposition of the present inventory will not impair its value. There will be no problem of write-down.

Relative size or importance of the inventory is a factor, for the larger the inventory, the greater the risk and the more significant the write-down if values decline greatly. Certainly a firm whose major investment is in inventory is considerably more vulnerable to market changes than one which requires a heavy investment in plant and equipment in order to engage in business. Under these latter circumstances the effect of price changes may be considerably diluted.

The reduction in risk when hedging operations are possible is self-evident. Losses on the stock inventory are offset by gains on the futures. A similar hedge on finished goods inventory, of course, is accomplished by firm sales contracts.

[1] American Institute of Certified Public Accountants, "Restatement and Revision of Accounting Research Bulletins," *Accounting Research Bulletin* No. 43.

Finally, inventory turnover is important. If the turnover is rapid, a shorter time will lapse between sale of the goods and purchase of items for additional sales. Consequently in periods of upswing or downswing the fluctuations will not be as violent, even when a traditional method of inventory costing, such as first-in, first-out, is used.

SELECTION OF COST BASE

The primary objective in choosing a cost basis for valuing inventories is to select that method which, under the circumstances, will most satisfactorily reflect the income of the period. In many instances the units sold are not identifiable with the specific cost of the item, or at least such an application is impractical. For this reason, a variety of cost applications have been developed which recognize differences in the relationship of costs to selling prices under various conditions. For example, the last-in, first-out method may be applicable where sales prices are promptly affected by changes in reproduction costs. In another situation, the conventional first-in, first-out method may apply. Circumstances of the individual company or industry must govern; but uniform methods within the industry will permit useful comparisons.

A very brief description of the more common inventory valuation methods based on costs follows.

1. *Identified or Specific Costs.* Under this method, purchases are not commingled, but are kept separate. The issue or sale is priced at the exact cost of the specific item. Such a system is not widely adopted because it requires too much physical attention as well as accounting detail. It is sometimes used in costing perishable stock or non-standard units which have been purchased for a specific job.

2. *First-in, First-out (FIFO).* This means is often known as the original cost method. It assumes that items first received are first issued.

To illustrate the operation, assume an opening inventory of 50 units at $10 each; receipts on January 11 of 10 units at a cost of $15; and issues on January 3 and 12 of 40 each. The issue on January 3 would be costed at $10 per unit, leaving a balance of 10 units at $10 each. The issue of January 12 would be priced:

10 units at $10 each	$100
30 units at $15 each	450
Total	$550

The requisition must be priced on two bases since two different acquisitions were issued.

3. *Simple Arithmetic Average Cost.* The average is computed by dividing the total unit prices for the inventory on hand by the number of such

prices, without regard to the quantities to which the prices relate. It is mathematically unsound.

4. *Weighted Average Cost.* This procedure involves the determination after each receipt of the total quantity and value on hand. The total units are divided into the total value to secure an average unit cost. All issues are priced at this average cost until the next receipt, when the new average is computed. The unit price must be carried out to sufficient decimal places to retain accuracy.

Disadvantages of this method include the detail calculations necessary and the length of time taken to reflect recent purchases in the average. It has the advantage of stabilizing costs when prices fluctuate.

5. *Moving Average Cost.* This method uses an average price of a convenient period of time, such as three or six months. It is a variation of the weighted average method. The effect of price fluctuations is minimized.

6. *Monthly Average Cost.* The total beginning inventory and the receipts for the month are divided into the aggregate cost to determine an average. This average is then applied to the issues for the period. The method has the advantage of eliminating some clerical work. But the disadvantage is that the requisitions cannot be costed for the month until the new average cost is determined. Sometimes this disadvantage is avoided by using the previous monthly average.

The period of time over which the receipts are accumulated need not necessarily be a month, nor need the end of the period coincide with the monthly closing.

7. *Base or Normal Stock Method.* The assumption under this method is that a certain inventory must be carried at all times to meet the production or sales needs. In this sense, the base or normal stock is considered analogous to a fixed asset. This stock is carried at a long-run price, while the remaining inventory is valued on some other basis, usually the lower of cost or market. The base inventory, of course, is maintained over a period of several years.

The advocates of the base stock method feel it is particularly applicable in process inventories which have a relatively long period of processing, and where the principal share of the finished product cost is that of the basic raw material. Inventories are conservatively stated, sometimes grossly understated. The method is not recognized by the Internal Revenue Service, and may not be used for tax determination.

8. *Standard Cost.* As the name implies, a predetermined or standard cost is used. The price variance on raw materials may be recognized when the material is received or when it is issued into process.

Use of standard costs eliminates much clerical effort. No cost columns are needed on the ledger cards, and the repeated calculation of unit costs is avoided.

9. *Last-in, First-out Cost* (LIFO). The use of this method assumes that the last unit purchased is the first to be requisitioned. The mechanics used are very similar to the first-in, first-out method except that requisitions are priced at the cost of the most recent purchase. For example, assume that 100 units are purchased at $4 each, and that later 50 units are purchased at $6 each. A requisition for 75 units would be priced as follows:

50 units at $6	$300
25 units at $4	100
75 Total	$400

The purpose of the LIFO method is to state, as closely as possible, the cost of goods sold at the current market cost. This method reduces unrealized inventory profits to a minimum.

10. *Replacement Cost.* By this method, the inventory is priced at the cost which would be incurred to replace it at current prices and in its current condition.

It can be seen that the method is not the same as LIFO for the latter uses the latest price on the books, which is not necessarily replacement cost.

The method has many practical difficulties, and it is not approved by the Internal Revenue Service.

11. *Retail Inventory Method.* This method is used largely in department stores, where the inventories are marked item by item at selling price rather than cost. The average margin or markup is determined for the period, and this is applied against the ending inventory at retail in order to ascertain cost. It is a type of average costing.

For details on each of these costing methods, the reader is referred to the many excellent accounting texts on the subject.

DEPARTURE FROM THE COST BASE

Under ordinary circumstances inventories should be valued at cost. There are occasions, though, where cost is not a proper measure of the charge against the revenues of future periods. In such instances a departure from the cost basis is necessary if the utility of the goods disposed of in the ordinary course of business is less than cost. Loss in value can occur by reason of damage, deterioration, obsolescence, changes in the price level, and other causes. Such loss should be recognized as a charge against the period in which it occurs. In these instances the goods should be valued at "market," which will be lower than cost.

How, then, is "market" defined? As used in the phrase "lower of cost or market" the term signifies current replacement cost by either purchase or manufacture, whichever is applicable. However, there are definite limits to the application of this rule. Market should not exceed the estimated selling price less the costs of completion and disposal. On the other extreme, it should not be less than the estimated net realizable value minus an allowance for the normal profit margin.

The explanation of the phrase "lower of cost or market" may be stated as follows:

9. The rule "cost or market, whichever is lower" is intended to provide a means of measuring the residual usefulness of an inventory expenditure. The term "market" is therefore to be interpreted as indicating utility on the inventory date and may be thought of in terms of the equivalent expenditure which would have to be made in the ordinary course at that date to procure corresponding utility. As a general guide, utility is indicated primarily by the current cost of replacement of the goods as they would be obtained by purchase or reproduction. In applying the rule, however, judgment must always be exercised and no loss should be recognized unless the evidence indicates clearly that a loss has been sustained. There are therefore exceptions to such a standard. Replacement or reproduction prices would not be appropriate as a measure of utility when the estimated sales value, reduced by the costs of completion and disposal, is lower, in which case the realizable value so determined more appropriately measures utility. Furthermore, where the evidence indicates that cost will be recovered with an approximately normal profit upon sale in the ordinary course of business, no loss should be recognized even though replacement or reproduction costs are lower. This might be true, for example, in the case of production under firm sales contracts at fixed prices, or when a reasonable volume of future orders is assured at stable selling prices.

10. Because of the many variations of circumstances encountered in inventory pricing, Statement 6 [which is a definition of the phrase "lower of cost or market"] is intended as a guide rather than a literal rule. It should be applied realistically in the light of the objectives expressed in this bulletin and with due regard to the form, content and composition of the inventory. The committee considers, for example, that the retail inventory method, if adequate markdowns are currently taken, accomplishes the objectives herein. It also recognizes that, if a business is expected to lose money for a sustained period, the inventory should not be written down to offset a loss inherent in the subsequent operations.[2]

In applying the rule of cost or market, whichever is lower, the question arises as to whether the test should be applied directly to each item of the inventory or to the total inventory or major categories. Since the purpose is properly to reflect income of the period, that method which achieves this objective should be used. In practice, most companies apply the rule to each item in the inventory. There are instances, however, when application to the total inventory would have the greatest significance. Thus, one component may be less than cost, while another component to the same article may have a market value equally higher than cost. If a balanced inventory condition exists, no adjustment might be necessary.

[2] *Ibid.*, pp. 31–32.

There are other specialized exceptions to the cost basis of valuing inventories, instances where inventories may be valued above costs. Under certain conditions, for example, gold or silver may be so valued. Such facts should be fully disclosed in the statements.

CONSISTENCY IN VALUATION

Irrespective of the method of pricing the inventory, the essential requirement is consistency from period to period. Over the long run, the basis of valuing inventories will not affect the total gain or loss. However, from year to year the effect on profit can be very marked if the treatment is changed. If circumstances require change, the nature of the change and the effect on income, if significant, should be disclosed to management and other interested parties.

INCOME TAX CONSIDERATIONS IN VALUING INVENTORIES

Nothing has been said concerning the relationship of inventory valuation and determination of taxable income. By and large, it seems desirable and necessary to consider the general principles of inventory valuation from the standpoint of sound business practice. Quite often the acceptance of an idea or procedure for tax purposes may lag somewhat behind its acceptance as a good business practice.

Where the basis of valuation proposed for income determination is substantially different from that allowable for tax purposes, a serious distortion can exist between the relationship of income taxes to reported income before taxes. Further, such major differences may result in a substantial amount of added clerical work in calculating inventory values on two or more bases. With the high tax rates that appear certain to apply for some years in the future, it is probably advisable to conform to the tax laws and regulations for all inventory valuation purposes if the difference is not substantial.

The provisions of the federal tax law are relatively simple concerning valuation of inventories. Under Section 22(c) of the Internal Revenue Code, they must conform to the best accounting practice in the trade or business; and they must clearly reflect income. In applying this latter test, greater weight is to be given to consistency in inventory practice from year to year rather than to any particular method. However, the regulations go on to state that there are two common bases of inventory valuation, either one of which may be adopted: (1) cost, or (2) cost or market, whichever is lower.

Under Section 22(d) the taxpayer is permitted to use the last-in, first-out rule of valuing inventory provided it is consistently used and provided the election of the method is approved by the Commissioner. The basis on which this may be done is quoted from Section 22(d) of the Code as follows:

(1) A taxpayer may use the following method (whether or not such method has been prescribed under subsection (c) in inventorying goods) specified in the application required under paragraph (2):

(A) Inventory them at cost;

(B) Treat those remaining on hand at the close of the taxable year as being: First, those included in the opening inventory of the taxable year (in the order of acquisition) to the extent thereof, and second, those acquired in the taxable year; and

(C) Treat those included in the opening inventory of the taxable year in which such method is first used as having been acquired at the same time and determine their cost by the average cost method.

(2) The method described in paragraph (1) may be used—

(A) Only in inventorying goods (required under subsection (c) to be inventoried) specified in an application to use such method filed at such time and in such manner as the Commissioner may prescribe; and

(B) Only if the taxpayer establishes to the satisfaction of the Commissioner that the taxpayer has used no procedure other than that specified in subparagraphs (B) and (C) of paragraph (1) in inventorying such goods to ascertain the income, profit, or loss of the first taxable year for which the method described in paragraph (1) is to be used, for the purpose of a report or statement covering such taxable year (i) to shareholders, partners, or other proprietors, or to beneficiaries, or (ii) for credit purposes.

In complying with the Regulations, certain difficulties have sometimes been encountered when actual inventories fall below the previous year's balances. To make the method workable, certain reasonable grouping of inventory items is essential. For any further details, reference should be made to the literature on the subject.

INTERIM STATEMENTS AND OPERATING CONTROLS

The method of valuing inventories poses no particular problems in connection with the preparation of interim statements. Under certain conditions, however, adjustments may be required if the base stock or the LIFO method is used.

Application of the base stock method raises a question as to treatment of cost of sales under circumstances when the inventory drops below the normal stock level. The effect of costing any goods sold at the base stock value might seriously distort the gross margin. Companies operating under the method work on the fiction that the base stock is not used. The stock is costed at market, with the result that the inventory may be reduced substantially, since the remaining quantity has deducted from its value the difference between market and base stock price. When the stock is replenished, the inventory is charged at the market price with a result that the base value is reinstated. The same effect can be obtained by establishing a temporary reserve so that operations are charged with the market value of the goods sold.

A somewhat similar situation may arise when the LIFO valuation base is used. For tax purposes, and perhaps for management purposes also, the inventory quantities are of particular importance from a valuation standpoint only at the year-end, and not each month. From month to month the difference in value is not known because the year-end inventories are not determinable. It is customary, therefore, when inventories drop below the beginning of the year levels, to establish a reserve to cost sales at the current market price. If, at the close of the year, the inventory has not been replenished, the reserve may be closed to the profit and loss account.

For operating control reports stated in terms of units, the valuation factor has no significance. If the control reports contain costs, it may be desirable to use one basis for such reports and another for statement purposes, provided the two can be reconciled. Generally the controller must study the situation and determine the best practice under the circumstances.

OTHER INVENTORY VALUATION PROBLEMS

The inclusion or exclusion of certain costs in inventory is controversial. A wide-awake management may often seize upon these points for discussion with the controller. Some of these questions are outlined here.

Storage and Handling Costs. One debatable point is whether or not storage and handling charges should be included in raw material inventories. Many companies do not write up the raw materials to include such costs. Instead, they consider them part of the general manufacturing overhead and prorate the charges to work in process and finished goods.

Such a practice is satisfactory unless there is a great variation or irregularity between receipts and consumption of the material. Under such circumstances, it may be permissible to include normal storage and handling costs in the raw material valuation.

Purchasing Department Expense. A similar question is raised with respect to purchasing department overhead as well as the clerical costs of the accounting department which are related to raw materials. The costs of these departments generally would continue the same from one period to another regardless of receipts. Thus, they are more attributable to accounting period than to batches of material, and it is not desirable to increase raw material inventory value by these expenses. They may be treated more properly as manufacturing overhead.

Inbound Transportation Costs. Where the cost of getting the goods to the factory site is identifiable with particular material or lots, the cost may properly be added to the raw material. If such allocation is impractical, it may be considered part of the manufacturing overhead.

Cash Discounts. This item can be treated as a deduction from the cost of the material or as other income. Where unit actual costs are used, deduction of the discount may cause odd fractions. It is sometimes desirable to treat the item as other income rather than to refigure unit costs.

INVENTORY RESERVES

Inventory reserves and inventory valuation are closely related. Surplus reserves may be established to provide for anticipated losses. This type of contingency reserve is discussed in a later chapter. It may be well to emphasize here, however, that controllers should take every precaution to report income as it is, and not as management would like it to be. Therefore, extreme care should be exercised in creating any inventory reserves through charges against current operations, which are based upon rather uncertain assumptions as to future price levels and other contingencies, and which are not capable of verification by objective tests. Above all, reserve provisions which equalize profits between years must be avoided.

The reserves under consideration here are those for which the provision is charged against the operations, the reserve itself being deducted from the inventory in the balance sheet, in accordance with generally accepted accounting practice. Because of the possibility of losses, controllers may find it advisable to charge a monthly provision against the cost of sales to cover shortages and write-downs. If such a practice is followed, it is advisable to let management know from time to time what charges are made against the reserve. Otherwise, it is too easy to bury losses here without the knowledge or consent of the executive staff. In this connection, it would be desirable for the controller to require his personal approval before any charges are deducted from the reserve.

For valuation purposes, where it is not desired to change the detailed inventory cards, an over-all reserve can be made to accomplish the same result.

23

Control of Investments

CONTROLLER'S RESPONSIBILITY FOR INVESTMENTS

The authority to invest company funds in securities, or other types of investments, rests with the board of directors. Within the limits stipulated by the board, such authority is often conferred on the treasurer. He usually has custody of the securities and supervises the analysis, purchase, and sale of the investments. Sometimes a committee handles such matters, and the controller may be a member.

Under conditions where the controllership function is divorced from the treasurer, the controller is responsible for these activities:

1. Maintaining all necessary records as to securities or investments
2. Determining that all investments are properly valued
3. Ascertaining that the directives of the board are followed as to investment of funds
4. Reporting on investments, as may be required

The reporting function has two aspects, as usual:

1. The necessary reporting to permit the company to measure and evaluate investment performance by study of the gains and losses— the managerial accounting objective, and
2. The required reporting to other than the management, viz., taxing authorities, other governmental authorities such as the SEC, shareholders, etc.

The usual internal control function and other accounting duties also exist.

TAX LAWS AND INVESTMENTS

Because the provisions of the federal income tax regulations are constantly subject to change, no detailed review is being made here. However, the effect of the laws should be considered when establishing the records as well as considering the purchase or sale of securities or other investments. Thus the regulations do not permit the averaging of costs in determining

444

the loss or gain from sale of securities. If the individual units cannot be identified, then a first-in, first-out basis must be used. Again, it is foolish under ordinary circumstances to sell securities shortly before the six-month period expires, if the same price can be secured after such period—with considerable savings as a capital gain. Also, the loss on stock determined to be worthless must be taken in the year when such loss occurs if the tax deduction is to be secured. These matters, and other provisions of the law, must be appraised as to effect on tax liability when considering investment control.

RECORDS OF INVESTMENTS

The ordinary business may invest in several stock or bond issues. Although the problem is not the same as that of banks or other financial institutions which deal in securities, nevertheless a systematic manner of recording information relative to the purchase or sale of investments is required. Adequate and detailed records are necessary to provide the information management needs as well as to establish and support gain or loss for tax purposes.

The file of invoices or statements from the broker may be thought sufficient in some cases. Indeed, these documents are the source of much information. Generally, however, it is necessary to establish a control account or accounts for investments in securities and to support this with a securities ledger or register. Such a record may be a simple loose-leaf book, or a formal ledger as illustrated in Figs. 110 and 111.

The basic information to be included in the securities ledgers consists of the following:

For Stocks

Description of issue—name, type, par value, certificate numbers
Dividend dates
Record of purchase—date, number of shares, price, commission, tax, total cost, broker
Date and amount of dividends received
Record of sale or disposition—date, broker, number of shares, sale or call price, commission, and net proceeds
Dividends in arrears
Loss or gain

For Bonds

Description of issue—name, interest rate, maturity date, interest dates, serial numbers, tax position
Record of purchase—date, broker, price, accrued interest, commission, tax, total cost, maturity value
Date and amount of interest received
Amortization of premium or discount

BOUGHT / SOLD / BALANCE Ledger

Issued by ___United States Steel Corporation___

Class ___Common___   Par Value ___$100___

| | BOUGHT | | | | SOLD | | | Profit or Loss | BALANCE | | |
Date	No. of Shares	Price	*Cost	Date	No. of Shares	Price	*Total Received		No. of Shares	Average Price	Cost
19— Jan. 30	100	$30	$3,020	19— Sep. 30	25	$36	$890.00	$135.00	100 75	$30.20 30.20	$3,020 2,265
Oct. 3	50	35	1,770	Nov. 15	25	38	940.00	133.00	125 100	32.28 32.28	4,035 3,228

*Gives effect to commission and tax.

Fig. 110—Stock Ledger Sheet.

Name of Bond ___Asher Company,___ ___First Mortgage,___   ___Sinking Fund, 1965___

Purchased Through ___Marks and Co.___ Nominal Rate ___5%___   Actual Rate ___4.65%___

Description

Numbers	B1676, B1677	Price	107½	Face Amount
Denomination	$5,000			
Where Payable	First Trust Co., Detroit	Cost	$10,750.00	~~$10,000~~
Trustee	First Trust Co., Detroit			
Dated	Jan. 1, 1956	Accrued Interest 125.00		$5,000
When Due	Dec. 31, 1965			
Interest Payable	June 30-Dec. 31	Remarks:		
Redeemable	No			

Date	Pieces	Memo	Price	Debit	Credit	Balance	Profit or Loss	Due	Interest Amount	Paid
19— Apr. 1	2	Marks & Co.	107½	10,750.00		10,750.00		19— 6-30	250.00	19— 6-30
June 30		Premium			50.00	10,700.00		12-31	250.00	12-31
Dec. 31		Premium			100.00	10,600.00		19— 6-30	250.00	19— 6-30
19— June 30		Premium			100.00	10,500.00				
July 1	1	Cen.Natl. Bk.	107		5,250.00	5,250.00	100.00			

Fig. 111—Bond Ledger Sheet.

Record of disposition—date, broker, redemption or sale price, accrued interest, commission, net proceeds
Loss or gain

The ledger may be kept alphabetically by issuer.

Where a large number of transactions are involved, punched card equipment may be useful.

REPORTS ON INVESTMENTS

The activity in investments for most industrial firms normally will be quite limited and few reports need be prepared. Periodic reports to management to show the details of the investment would appear desirable. These may be simple reports containing the following information:

As to Each Security
Name of security
Cost
Market value
Effective yield (rate)
Dividend or interest received to date

For All Investments
Over-all rate of return
Cost and market value

Such a report is illustrated in Fig. 112.

The Illustrative Company
INVESTMENT POSITION AS OF JULY 31, 1963

	Security	Number of Shares	Market Value	Purchase Price	Rate of Return *	Total Dividends for Year to Date
1	Bristol-Myers	500	$ 37,000	$ 31,000	5.2%	$ 800
2	Eagle-Picher	100	2,400	2,400	6.3	75
3	Chesapeake & Ohio	1,000	30,000	31,000	6.5	1,000
4	Libbey-Owens-Ford Glass Co.	1,000	65,500	64,000	7.8	2,000
5	National Gypsum Co.	100	1,900	1,875	7.5	70
6	Owens Illinois Glass Co. ..	500	42,000	38,000	5.3	1,000
	Total or Average		$178,800	$168,275	6.5%	$4,945

* Based on payments for past twelve months, or current rate if believed more applicable.

Fig. 112—Report on Investment Position.

Where movement takes place, it is desirable to advise management of the purchase or sale together with the gain or loss in case of disposition.

If the treasurer prepares such a report the controller, as well as top management, should receive a copy.

24

Planning and Evaluation of Fixed Assets

NATURE OF THE PROBLEM

The statement, "Today's decisions determine tomorrow's profits," is pertinent to the planning and control of fixed assets.

An important criterion of business success is the ability to maintain a fair or satisfactory return on investment. Funds should not be committed without a proper test of profitability. It follows, therefore, that prudent business practice will not permit the purchase of plant or equipment unless there is a reasonable expectation of a normal return—either as a result of increased profits or, at the least, through the maintenance of the present level of earnings.

Investment in capital assets has other ramifications or possible consequences not found in the typical day-to-day expenditures of a business. First, once funds have been used for the purchase of plant and equipment, it may be a long time before they are recovered. Unwise expenditures of this nature are difficult to retrieve without serious loss to the investor. Needless to say, imprudent long-term commitments can result in bankruptcy or other financial embarrassment.

Second, a substantial increase in capital investment is likely to cause a much higher break-even point for the business. Large outlays for plant, machinery, and equipment carry with them higher depreciation charges, heavier insurance costs, greater property taxes, and possibly an expanded maintenance expense. All these tend to raise the sales volume at which the business will begin to earn a profit.

Again, increased competition and higher income taxes result in a decreased profit per dollar of net sales. This makes it proportionately more difficult to earn a satisfactory return on investment. This condition is aggravated, of course, as plant and equipment costs rise.

448

A considerable share of corporate earnings is going into capital expenditures, induced in part by the difficulty of securing new capital from other sources. Mass production requires heavy investment in equipment. The relative amount of capital invested in long-term assets varies by industry; but a particularly heavy share, sometimes as much as 85%, is so used in public utilities, transportation, steel, and mining enterprises.

These conditions make it imperative that wisdom and good judgment be exercised in making investments in capital assets. Too often decisions have been made on the basis of hunches. The application of analysis is necessary. This statement is not made to discourage investment, but rather to encourage an intelligent approach to the problem. For much of American progress has been due to the courage and wisdom of our industrial leaders in expanding facilities in accordance with the indicated future possibilities as revealed by thorough analysis.

THE CONTROLLER'S RESPONSIBILITY

What part should the controller play in the planning and control of capital commitments and expenditures? The board of directors, the chief executive, and other members of management often are under considerable pressure to approve expenditures. Perhaps the sales department is extolling the need for expansion to secure a vast increase in sales volume or the addition of a new line. Again, the manufacturing department may be emphasizing the tremendous savings possible through the purchase of new equipment —for many of the production staff like new machinery just as the ordinary man likes a new car. The talk about high profits and the thought of shining new buildings is appealing. The enthusiasm of these groups must be counteracted, and the proposal must be subjected to a most thorough analysis. Too many times, indeed, heavy losses have been incurred because of too optimistic an outlook. So the responsibility is placed on the controller and his staff for a completely objective appraisal of the potential savings or earnings. It is to him that management looks for an evaluation of the proposal. Inability or failure to do an adequate job can prove costly.

Once the moneys are spent, the controller must establish proper accountability, and institute reporting and recording procedures for control of the equipment.

A detailed statement of the controller's duties would include the following:

1. Preparation of financial forecasts—both short- and long-term— to indicate availability of funds, and required investment in plant and equipment to meet the sales and manufacturing programs
2. Establishment of a satisfactory over-all procedure for the effective administration of capital spending in both planning and control phases

3. Establishment of standards or guides as to what constitutes a satis-factory measure of return on capital
4. Review of alternatives to equipment acquisition, such as leasing, and the relative cost, for the purpose of making recommendations
5. Critical analysis of all requests for capital expenditures, including calculation of savings or potential earnings
6. Establishment of controls to keep expenditures within authoriza-tion limits
7. Design and maintenance of property records
8. Establishment of an adequate system of reporting, including:
   a. Comparison of actual and authorized costs
   b. Maintenance costs by types of equipment
   c. Idle hours of machinery
9. Development of a sound depreciation policy
10. Determination of the basis of accounting for fixed assets and the applicable reserves
11. Institution of auxiliary control procedures, including those related to:
    a. Identification of machinery and equipment
    b. Transfers
    c. Sales and retirements
12. Handling of matters related to taxes and insurance

OBJECTIVES OF FIXED ASSET PLANNING AND CONTROL

Plant and equipment expenditures may be made for new additions, re-placements, or the maintenance of existing equipment. Certain of these disbursements cannot be delayed if operations are to continue; others may be put off for a reasonable time; and some, which are desirable but not essential, need not be made until and unless management chooses. Within the range between the most urgent expenditure on the one hand, and the least essential on the other, lies a large area over which business judgment can be exercised. Planning relates to the intelligent commitment of funds for properties. Control over the expenditures for fixed assets has the objec-tive of authorizing acquisition only after considered judgment as to the necessity or desirability and in accordance with the planned availability of funds.

From the time commitments are made for fixed assets until final disposi-tion through retirement or sale, other phases of control must be exercised. The property must be accounted for, properly utilized, adequately insured, and otherwise handled as prescribed by management.

Included in the more specific objectives of fixed asset planning and con-trol are:

1. Determination of the probable rate of return on the proposed investment in fixed assets

2. Selection of those projects which offer the relatively greater return on investment

3. Ascertainment that the planned aggregate capital expenditures are within the financial capabilities of the company

4. Determination that the immediate-term program of capital expenditures fits within the long-term corporate plans

5. Planning the proper timing of capital expenditures

6. Determination that the company has the required facilities to carry out the production and sales program

7. Encouragement of study of the exact type of equipment best suited to the company's needs, and the most advantageous means of financing the acquisition

8. Critical review of facilities to determine whether cost savings would justify replacements

9. Restriction of capital expenditures to the authorization limits or actual needs of the company

10. Determination, on the basis of past and proposed capital expenditures, and perhaps replacement cost, that the related treatment of current depreciation and amortization charges results in a proper costing of products and functions

11. Establishment of proper accountability for plant and equipment

12. Promotion of a more effective utilization of existing equipment through elimination of unnecessary downtime

13. Correlating the planned expenditures to take maximum advantage of tax legislation

14. Establishment of procedures which provide for proper physical care of the properties

REQUISITES FOR SOUND ADMINISTRATION OF CAPITAL SPENDING

A primary purpose in this chapter is to consider some of the techniques for evaluating capital expenditures. Businessmen have been paying increasing attention to the use of the so-called "scientific" methods in making capital decisions, and an intelligent approach through economic and financial analysis is needed in this difficult area. In fact there are innumerable ways to invest funds uneconomically without knowing it! Yet, techniques to evaluate, let us say, an investment are not ends in themselves. Rather, one must look beyond such factors to the total procedure of originating, evaluating, executing, and auditing the expenditure proposals. In short, one must look at the entire administrative procedure or process.

In view of the long-term nature of the decision, and the relatively large sums invested in capital equipment, it is perhaps desirable to be somewhat repetitive in listing the basic factors or requisites which make for a completely well-rounded approach to wise capital investments.

The existence of the following plans and procedures are believed essential to a sound administration of capital spending.

Long-Range Corporate Plans and Objectives. Such a program, general in terms, will be for the next five to ten years. It may consist of general statements embracing the following:

1. Market—expected size and share the company should try to secure
2. Industry conditions expected to exist
3. Physical growth objectives of the company
4. Product lines, or fields, or geographical areas which the firm intends to penetrate
5. Any other long-range factors which could affect capital spending

Dissemination of such information will provide broad guidelines for capital expenditures, and will stimulate thinking as to capital projects at the several levels of management. The existence of such plans will tend to insure that expenditures fit with a pattern leading to the accomplishment of the company's objectives.

A Short-Range Corporate Plan. This plan includes the forecasted earnings, the expected cash generation or availability, and planned capital expenditures. It ordinarily covers a period of one year. Such a device facilitates coordination of the capital program with the operating plans and permits rather specific planning.

A Procedure for Determining the Sum that Should Be Spent on Capital Expenditures Annually (or Periodically). General guides or limitations are needed to avoid devoting either excessive or insufficient cash to capital projects.

A "Cost of Capital" Figure, Representing the Components of the Company's Invested Capital. The composite return or cost of capital should be known as one means of measuring the desirability of new projects. It should include the cost of long-term debt, preferred stock, if any, as well as common shareholder equity. A factor in further capital spending is whether the project return is higher or lower than the cost of capital presently employed in the company.

Means of Evaluating Individual Projects. Projects differ in time and amount. Some method must be used which puts all projects on a comparable basis, as far as possible, and recognizes the important factors to be considered in judging the economic worth of a proposed capital investment.

A Method or Procedure for Ranking Capital Projects. Proposed expenditures must be weighed against alternatives, and these alternatives must be given a priority or place in the program in relationship to all others.

A Procedure to Balance Executive Judgment Against the Mathematical Results. Once projects are rated relatively, the factor of judgment must be brought to bear on the figures in order to arrive at a balanced opinion. The intangibles must be weighed against the quantified factors.

The combined management intelligence of most of the functions should be focused on the proposed program.

An Approval Procedure to Authorize Individual Projects. The various management levels should be recognized as to limits of approval authority for the various projects. These are ordinarily dollar dividing lines. Such a procedure should outline the kind of data needed to support the specific proposal.

A Control Procedure. Means must be taken, once a project is approved, to see that commitments and expenditures are kept within the authorized limits, and that proper accounting is used.

A Program of Post-Audit. Periodically after completion of a project, a review or reviews should be made for the purpose of comparing actual and expected earnings or savings. This is a means of appraising the entire capital budgeting procedure.

The elements of this total system which need further elaboration will be reviewed in the following sections.

METHODS OF EVALUATING PROJECTS

In an effort to invest funds wisely in capital projects, companies have developed several techniques. It is these expenditures which provide the foundation for the firm's growth, efficiency, and competitive strength. Since most companies do not have sufficient funds to undertake all projects, some means must be found to evaluate the alternate courses of action. Such decisions are not merely the application of a formula. The evaluation of quantitative information must be blended with good judgment, and perhaps good fortune, to produce that aggregate wisdom in capital expenditures which will largely determine the company's future earning power.

The more important valuation methods in use, which are mathematical in nature, consist of the following or some variation thereof:

1. *Payout, or Payback, Method.* This is the simple calculation of the number of years required for the proceeds of the project to recoup the original investment.
2. *Rate of Return Methods.* Among them are:
   a. "Operators' Method," so called because it is often used to measure operating efficiency in a plant or division. It may be defined as the relationship of annual cash return plus depreciation to the original investment.
   b. "Accountants' Method," perhaps so named because the accounting concept of average book value and earnings (or book profit)

is employed. This method is merely the relationship of profit after depreciation to average annual outstanding investment.

   c. "Investors' Method," or Discounted Cash Flow Method. This rate of return concept recognizes the time value of money. It involves a calculation of the present worth of a flow of funds.

THE PAYOUT METHOD

Among companies which make some attempt to use quantitative measurements, the payout or payback method is probably most common.

Assume that project A calls for an investment of $1,000,000, and that the average annual income before depreciation is expected to be $300,000. Then the payout in years would be 3.3 years, calculated thus:

$$\text{Payout time in years} = \frac{\text{Investment}}{\text{Yearly net income} + \text{Depreciation}}$$

$$= \frac{\$1,000,000}{\$200,000 + \$100,000}$$

$$= 3.3 \text{ years}$$

In circumstances where the net income and depreciation are not approximately level each year, then the method may be refined to reflect cash flow each year to arrive at the payback time—instead of the *average* earnings.

Briefly stated, the payout method offers these advantages:

1. It may be useful in those instances where a business firm is on rather lean rations cash-wise, and must accept proposals which appear to promise a payout, for example, in two years or less.
2. Payout can be helpful in appraising very risky investments where the threat of expropriation or capital wastage is high and difficult to predict. It weighs near-year earnings heavily.
3. It is a simple manner of computation, and easily understood.
4. It may serve as a rough indicator of profitability to reject obviously undesirable proposals.

There are, however, some very basic disadvantages to the payout method:

1. *Failure to Consider the Earnings After the Initial Outlay Has Been Recouped.* Yet, the cash flow *after payback* is the real factor in determining profitability. In effect, the method confuses recovery of capital with profitability. In the above example, if the economic life of the project is only 3.3 years, there is zero profit. If on the other hand, the capital life is ten years, the rate of return will differ significantly from that produced by a four-year life.
2. *Undue Emphasis on Liquidity.* Restriction of fund investment to short payout may cause rejection of a highly profitable source of

earnings. Liquidity assumes importance only under conditions of tight money.

3. *Capital Obsolescence or Wastage Is Not Recognized.* The gradual loss of economic value is ignored—the economic life is not considered. This deficiency is closely related to item 1 above. Similarly, the usual (average) method of computation does not reflect irregularity in the earning pattern.

OPERATORS' METHOD

A manner of figuring return on investment, using the figures of the payout method, is as follows:

$$\text{Return on investment} = \frac{\text{Annual earnings} + \text{Depreciation}}{\text{Original investment}}$$

$$= \frac{\$200,000 + \$100,000}{\$1,000,000}$$

$$= 30\%$$

The technique may be varied to include total required investment, including working capital.

The Operators' Method has these advantages:

1. It is simple to understand and calculate
2. In contrast with the payout method, it gives some weight to length of life and over-all profitability
3. It facilitates comparison with other companies, or divisions, or projects

The basic disadvantage is that it does not recognize the time value of cash flow.

THE ACCOUNTANTS' METHOD

This technique relates earnings to the average outstanding investment rather than the initial investment or assets employed. It is based on the underlying premise that capital recovered as depreciation is therefore available for use in other projects and should not be considered a charge against the original project.

There are variations in this method, also, in that return may be figured before or after income tax, and differing depreciation bases may be employed.

The rate of return, using the Accountants' Method, and assuming a ten-year life and straight-line depreciation on project A is shown in Fig. 113.

RETURN ON INVESTMENT—THE ACCOUNTANTS' METHOD
AVERAGE BOOK INVESTMENT AND AVERAGE PROFIT

Project A

Year	Net Earnings Before Depreciation	Depreciation	Net Profit	Average Investment Outstanding
1	$ 300,000	$ 100,000	$ 200,000	$ 950,000
2	300,000	100,000	200,000	850,000
3	300,000	100,000	200,000	750,000
4	300,000	100,000	200,000	650,000
⋮	⋮	⋮	⋮	⋮
9	300,000	100,000	200,000	150,000
10	300,000	100,000	200,000	50,000
Total	$3,000,000	$1,000,000	$2,000,000	$5,000,000

$$\text{Rate of return} = \frac{\text{Profit after depreciation}}{\text{Average outstanding investment}}$$

$$= \frac{\$2,000,000}{\$5,000,000}$$

$$= 40\%$$

Fig. 113—Return on Investment—Accountants' Method.

RETURN ON INVESTMENT—THE ACCOUNTANTS' METHOD
DECREASING PROFIT

Project A

Year	Net Earnings Before Depreciation	Depreciation	Net Profit	Average Investment Outstanding
1	$ 400,000	$ 100,000	$ 300,000	$ 950,000
2	400,000	100,000	300,000	850,000
3	400,000	100,000	300,000	750,000
4	400,000	100,000	300,000	650,000
5	400,000	100,000	300,000	550,000
6	200,000	100,000	100,000	450,000
7	200,000	100,000	100,000	350,000
8	200,000	100,000	100,000	250,000
9	200,000	100,000	100,000	150,000
10	200,000	100,000	100,000	50,000
Total	$3,000,000	$1,000,000	$2,000,000	$5,000,000

$$\text{Rate of return} = \frac{\text{Profit after depreciation}}{\text{Average outstanding investment}}$$

$$= \frac{\$2,000,000}{\$5,000,000}$$

$$= 40\%$$

Fig. 114—Return on Investment—Decreasing Profit Condition.

456

This basic procedure has two chief shortcomings. First, it is heavily influenced by the depreciation basis used. Double declining balance depreciation will, of course, reduce the average investment outstanding and increase the rate of return. Secondly, it fails to reflect the time value of funds. In the example, if the average investment were the same, but income was accelerated in the early years and decelerated in later years (with no change in total amount) the rate of return would be identical. Such conditions are reflected in Fig. 114. By many measures, the cash flow shown in this illustration is more desirable than that reflected in Fig. 113, because a greater share of the profit is secured earlier in the project life, and is thus available for other investment.

Most projects do vary in income pattern, and the evaluation procedure probably should reflect this difference.

The Accountants' Method offers the advantage of simplicity over the discounted cash flow approach.

THE INVESTORS' METHOD—DISCOUNTED CASH FLOW

The limitation on the rate of return methods previously reviewed is an inability to evaluate properly the time value or pattern as to when the capital is spent and returned. The discounted cash flow method overcomes this objection. Technically, the rate of return on any project is that rate at which the sum of the stream of after-tax (cash) earnings, discounted yearly according to present worth, equals the cost of the project. Stating it another way, the rate of return is the maximum constant rate of return which a project could pay throughout the life of the outstanding investment and just break even.

The method may be simply described by an example. Assume that an investment of $1,000 may be made and, over a five-year period, cash flow of $250 may be secured. What is the rate of return? By a cut-and-try method, and the use of present value tables, we arrive at 8%. The application of the 8% factor to the cash flow results in a present value of approximately $1,000 is as follows:

Year	Annual Cash Flow (a)	8% Discount Factor (b)	Present Value (a) × (b)
1	$250	.926	$232
2	250	.857	214
3	250	.794	198
4	250	.735	184
5	250	.681	170
	Total present value		$998

The proof of the computation is the determination of an 8% annual charge with the balance applicable to principal:

Year	Cash Flow (a)	Return at 8% of Investment Outstanding at Beginning of Year (b)	Balance Applicable to Investment (c) = (a − b)	Outstanding Investment at Year-End (d)
0	$ —	$—	$ —	$1,000
1	250	80	170	830
2	250	66	184	646
3	250	52	198	448
4	250	36	214	234
5	250	19	231	3 *

* Due to rounding.

By trial and error, application of the proper discount factor can be explored until the proper one is found. Using a 10% discount factor and a 40% discount factor, the $1,000,000 assumed investment, discussed in connection with other evaluation methods, to be recouped over ten years, results in a 36% rate of return, as shown in Fig. 115.

DISCOUNTED CASH FLOW METHOD
PRESENT VALUE OF STREAM OF CASH

Years from Start of Operation	(Expenditure) or Income	10% Discount Rate		40% Discount Rate	
		Discount Factor	Amount—$M	Discount Factor	Amount—$M
0	$(1,000,000)		$(1,000.0)		$(1,000.0)
0 to 1	300,000	.953	285.9	.844	253.2
2	300,000	.866	259.8	.603	180.9
3	300,000	.788	236.4	.431	129.3
4	300,000	.716	214.8	.308	92.4
5	300,000	.651	195.3	.220	66.0
6	300,000	.592	177.6	.157	47.1
7	300,000	.538	161.4	.112	33.6
8	300,000	.489	146.7	.080	24.0
9	300,000	.444	133.2	.060	18.0
10	300,000	.404	121.2	.041	12.3
Total Cash Flow	$ 3,000,000				
Discounted Cash Flow			$ 1,932.3		$ 856.8

Discounted Rate of Return:

$$10\% + 30\% \left[\frac{1,932 - 1,000}{1,932 - 857} \right] = 36\%$$

Fig. 115—Trial and Error—Computation of Present Worth.

The steps in application of the method may be described as follows:

1. Determine the amount and year of the investment
2. Determine, by years, the cash flow after income taxes by reason of the investment
3. Extend such cash flow by two discount factors, to arrive at present worth
4. Apply various discount factors until one calculates close to the original investment, and interpolate, if necessary, to arrive at a more accurate figure

The disadvantages of the discounted cash flow method are:

1. It is somewhat more complex than other methods; this apparent handicap is minor in that those who must apply the technique grasp it rather readily after a couple of trials
2. It requires more time for calculation

These two rather small obstacles are more than offset by benefits which include:

1. Proper weighting is given to the time value of investments, cash flow, and salvage values
2. The use of cash flow minimizes the effect of arbitrary decisions as to capital vs. expenses, depreciation ratio, etc., or other accounting techniques
3. Provides the answer which is most comparable with the cost-of-capital concept discussed in the following section.

A STANDARD FOR PROJECT EVALUATION—COST OF CAPITAL

To know how to determine the project profitability or rate of return is a step in the right direction. In addition to knowing the rate of return, some benchmark or yardstick is required as a guide of acceptability. For example, suppose a given proposal is expected to yield 15%. Should such a project be rejected?

Two acceptable financial yardsticks are the company rate of return on long-term capital employed, or the cost of additional capital. This latter is applicable particularly in those instances where the cost of this additional capital may differ significantly from the company's rate of return on existing capital. Such a consideration is important when internally generated funds are insufficient to meet the planned capital needs.

A company's average long-run cost of capital may be considered a type of break-even point for additional capital investment. Why? Because projects earning a lower rate of return than cost of capital will tend to reduce the return on investment.[1] Therefore, proposals of this nature should

---

[1] See also Chapter 4.

be favorably considered only in the light of strong non-financial organizational or operational reasons. If a company is to grow, it is imperative that capital funds be proportioned to those projects producing a rate of return higher than the cost of capital.

Several bases are used to calculate cost of capital. Three may be expressed by these formulas:

1. $\dfrac{\text{Net income after income taxes}}{\text{Net worth}}$. This technique indicates the return on shareholder equity, and is not a true measure of cost of capital.

2. $\dfrac{\text{Net income after income taxes and before interest}}{\text{Net worth} + \text{Long-term debt}}$. This method is a measure of present capital cost based on the existing capital structure.

3. $\dfrac{\text{Net income after income taxes and before interest}}{\text{Net worth (weighted)} + \text{Long-term debt (weighted)}}$. This means of calculation, as will be seen, permits consideration of the sources of capital expected to be employed.

In using a weighted formula, recognition is given to the source and cost of each type of capital. *Long-term debt* presents no particular problem. By discussion with the company's investment bankers, or commercial bankers, the long-term cost is ascertainable. If the corporation has a good credit rating and earning power, interest cost may approximate 4½% in today's market. It may be assumed that the net after tax cost is approximately 2¼%.

Equity capital may be measured by the relationship of earnings to market price of the stock—either the company's or perhaps a competitor's of approximately the same general regard in the security market. In the case at hand, assume that earnings approximate $2.00 per share on an average market price of $36.00. To avoid diluting common shareholder earnings, a return of $2 ÷ $36 or 5.56% must be secured.

Assume further that over the longer period, funds are expected to be provided 30% from long-term debt and 70% from common shareholders (either equity capital invested or retained earnings).

The weighted cost of capital may then be calculated as follows:

$$\frac{30\% \ (2.25\%) + 70\% \ (5.56\%)}{100} = 4.57\%$$

This 4.57% may be regarded as a quantitative yardstick against which all new investments may be measured regardless of source. Over the longer term, all funds coming from the pool will have an average cost of 4.57%. Of course, where a major project is under review, to be financed by a special security issue, then comparison with this cost of capital may be used.

RANKING THE PROJECTS

In most companies, spending opportunities exceed the supply of funds. Therefore, it is illogical to approve projects in the order of chronological presentation. And this is true even if the proposal indicates a return higher than the cost of capital. To follow such a procedure would, for example, permit approval of, say, a project with a 12% rate of return and subsequent rejection of a proposal indicating a 30% rate of return.

The solution to the problem is to rank projects selected on the basis of economics in the order of descending rate of return. This will assure that ordinarily the more attractive projects will receive first consideration.

Under normal circumstances, the proposal which reflects the higher rate of return on a discounted cash flow basis will be the more desirable. However, this is based on the assumption that the company can *re-invest* the cash flow on about as profitable a basis as the present investment is returning. If, however, no good opportunities for use of the funds exist at the time, a slightly lower rate of return project may be more desirable because the funds are employed for a longer period of time at a satisfactory rate.

Such a situation exists when the pattern of earnings or cash flow between two projects differs significantly.

A check against the desirability of two projects is afforded by determining the present worth at the rate of return the company reasonably can be expected to earn on the future investment. This discounted present worth may be related to the investment and a "profitability index" established. As an example, assume the following for two competing projects:

	Project	
	A	B
Investment	$1,000,000	$1,000,000
Annual earnings	$1,200,000	$ 300,000
Expected life	1 year	5 years
Return on investment	20%	15%
Profitability at 10% rate	$1,090,900	$1,137,300
Profitability index	1.09	1.14

Thus, the use of the present worth concept applied to a stream of earnings at a predetermined rate is a valuable cross-check.

There will be situations wherein tangible factors or economics are not the sole criteria. Consequently, provision should be made in the budget for required projects which may not be justified solely on an easily measured economic basis. A suggested schedule of groupings is as follows:

1. Absolutely essential
   a. Necessary rebuilding or replacement of facilities which are physically exhausted
   b. Modifications, changes, or additions necessary to the safety and health of the employees
2. Necessary—quality improvement
3. Economically desirable
   a. Any changes or additions or improvements to effect cost savings
   b. Additions for new lines or new products
   c. Additions for increased capacity
4. Other
   a. General plant improvements desirable from an employee morale standpoint or for reasons of prestige

It is clearly apparent that the "absolutely necessary" items should have first call on available moneys. The facilities must be kept operating. Of only slightly less urgency are those changes essential to the safety and health of employees and the public. These also could impair the operations if in violation of state or local health and safety codes. Furthermore, every enlightened employer will attempt to take any and all really necessary steps to protect the health and safety of his employees, as well as of the community.

THE AMOUNT OF THE CAPITAL BUDGET

The making of capital commitments is basically a management decision. The procedure of deciding just what aggregate sum should be devoted to plant and facilities is not one ascertainable by a formula, however simple or complex. Some general yardsticks or factors to be taken into account should, however, be mentioned.

A great many influences are at work in determining the proper size of the capital budget. These include:

1. Amount of internally generated funds
2. Amount of annual depreciation—either unadjusted or adjusted for inflation
3. Growth status of the industry and company
4. Availability and cost of funds, from whatever source
5. Investment already in plant and equipment, as tested by standard or industry ratios [2]
6. A given percentage of earnings or cash flow
7. Competitive activity

[2] See Chapter 5.

8. Prospective ratios of return
9. Debt structure—or capitalization—of the company
10. Stage of the business cycle—for industry and/or business generally
11. Long-term plans of the company—as to timing and character of investment

It is not intended to discuss each of these factors. Rather, the reader would do well to consider how each of these elements should apply in his particular business.

A firm must keep its financial structure well balanced. For example, the proper relationship should be maintained between working capital and investment in plant and equipment. Generally a business concern should invest funds where they will yield the greatest return, risk considered. This may be in additional working capital instead of plant facilities.

The exact amount which should be invested in plant and equipment can never be known, but some ratios useful in a comparative sense are available. Their use can point out weaknesses or pitfalls to be avoided. A general pattern of investment in fixed assets is discernible in each industry. Particular attention should be paid to those concerns in the industry which are regarded as the most progressive, or have had a long and prosperous experience. Some ratios which may serve as a guide include:

1. *Ratio of Net Worth to Fixed Assets.* This is secured by dividing the net worth by the fixed assets less the reserves for depreciation. Such a ratio will give some indication of any tendency to overinvest in capital assets. The same information can be gained by checking the percentage of fixed assets to net worth.
2. *Ratio of Sales to Fixed Assets.* Such a ratio indicates the use being made of fixed assets. The markup factor is included in the sales figure, and may distort the relationship somewhat. However, the information to calculate the ratio of the industry is usually available from published reports.
3. *Ratio of Cost of Goods Manufactured to Fixed Assets.* Where available, the ratio gives a more accurate indication than item 2 above, although it serves the same general purpose.

Such relationships are only guides, and cannot take the place of good judgment. But if indications are present that a firm has too large a share of its investment in plant and equipment, then it would do well to strengthen its position before adding more facilities.

It seems appropriate to comment on the *reason for* or *character of* proposed capital expenditures as an influence in setting the amount of planned commitment.

Generally speaking, capital investments may be classified as for either *replacement* or *expansion.*

Replacement commitments or expenditures may, in turn, be grouped into three general categories:

1. *Replacements by Reason of Sheer Physical Exhaustion.* Under such circumstances, if the product or service is to be continued (for any number of reasons, including profitability) then the asset must be replaced.
2. *Replacements by Reason of Competitive Action, viz., Need to Improve Quality or Styling, etc.* Judgment plays an important role, and payout periods and rates of return perhaps assume a minor role if considered at all.
3. *Replacements by Reason of Economics—Cost Reduction or Profit Improvement.* In this category, a choice does exist of whether to replace or not. Funds to be made available for replacement of exhausted assets may be measured by the adjusted cost of the equipment being replaced. Moneys to be spent on replacement for quality control, styling, and similar items probably must be limited as a matter of judgment. Replacements by reason of cost reductions perhaps should be governed by the savings or profits made available. If return on investment is not applicable—and it should be in most instances—then rules of thumb such as payout may be considered.

Amounts to be committed for growth and expansion are to be considered in the light of profit goals established, return on investment, and the maintenance of a sound financial structure.

25

Planning and Control of Fixed Assets

THE SHORT-TERM BUDGET

The short-term plant and equipment budget generally extends over the same period as the financial budget, usually six months or a year. Most businesses can determine fairly accurately what their needs will be as to capital assets over this period, and also can estimate quite closely what the earnings and working capital requirements will be. The objective is to restrict these short-term plant and equipment expenditures to the available funds over this span. Usually the budget procedure commences by having the department heads submit their estimate of requirements. If all the projects cannot be undertaken, then priorities must be established, taking into account the long-term considerations.

Approval of this short-range plant and equipment budget usually does not constitute authority to incur obligations, or to undertake construction or purchase. This must await approval of the specific appropriation request. The short-term budget approval is merely a concurrence *in principle* with the projects, and permits the spending only up to the budget limits as and when the specific or individual requests for appropriations are approved.

A summary of the annual capital budget request, which usually will be supported by substantial detail, is shown in Fig. 116.

OTHER CONSIDERATIONS IN APPROVING PLANT INVESTMENT

Approval of either the budget or appropriation requests for plant or equipment, as may be applicable, must be founded on proper justification. The accountant can do much in effecting control in this area. Some basic factors to be considered are:

1. Common weaknesses in underlying data
2. Timing of expenditures

The Allan Company
ANNUAL CAPITAL BUDGET REQUEST—1963
(In Thousands of Dollars)

	Appropriations							Schedule of Capital Expenditures				
		New				Return on Investment (DCF)	Total Commitments					
Description	Prior Years	1st Quarter	2nd Quarter	Last Half	1963			1962 and Prior	1963	1964	Later Years	Total
EXPANSION AND GROWTH												
Naphthalene plant				$ 8,650	$ 8,650	22.3	$ 8,650		$ 2,130	$ 3,890	$2,630	$ 8,650
Butadiene recovery system				3,100	3,100	19.2	3,100		2,200	900		3,100
Hydrogen plant	$2,600					14.2	2,600	2,310	290			2,600
Sulfur recovery system	1,900					8.7	1,900	1,500	400			1,900
Alkylate plant			$12,300		12,300	17.6	12,300		6,000	6,300		12,300
Isocracker		$25,000			25,000	23.8	25,000		6,500	17,300	1,200	25,000
Total Expansion	4,500	25,000	12,300	11,750	49,050		53,550	3,810	17,520	28,390	3,830	53,550
REPLACEMENTS												
Absolutely Essential												
Fitzpatrick grinder	590						590	400	190			590
Pneumatic tube system		390			390		390		390			390
"R" Plant conveyor			800		800		800		400	400		800
Rosin crushers	210						210	190	20			210
"X" air pollution catcher				1,020	1,020		1,020		300	720		1,020
Other	20	10	10	30	50		70	15	55			70
	820	400	810	1,050	2,260		3,080	605	1,355	1,120		3,080
Competitively Necessary												
"L" Quality Control Lab.	300						300	200	100			300
Fine screening plant			670		670		670		240	430		670
Color retention process				2,300	2,300		2,300		870	1,430		2,300
Other	20	20	10	20	50		70	10	60			70
	320	20	680	2,320	3,020		3,340	210	1,270	1,860		3,340

Economics Basis												
Urea system		800			800	20.0	800		800			800
Drum dumpers			200		200	16.4	200		200			200
Lift trucks				100	100	12.3	100		100			100
		800	200	100	1,100		1,100		1,100			1,100
Other												
Roof—North plant			70		70		70		70			70
Toledo landscaping ...		5	10	15	15		15		15			15
Miscellaneous	40	5		10	25		65	35	30			65
	40		80	25	110		150	35	115			150
Total Replacement ...	1,180	1,225	1,770	3,495	6,490		7,670	850	3,840	2,980		7,670
CONTINGENCY	300	2,000	700		2,700		3,000	300	1,000	1,700		3,000
GRAND TOTAL	$5,980	$28,225	$14,770	$15,245	$58,240		$64,220	$4,960	$22,360	$33,070	$3,830	$64,220

Fig. 116—Annual Capital Budget Request.

3. Alternatives in meeting the problem
4. Type of cost analysis
5. Intangible factors

WEAKNESSES IN UNDERLYING DATA

Much of the information used to arrive at decisions on plant expansion or changes comes from those who would normally be expected to have an optimistic bias. The controller must act to see that data received as to sales volume and prices, distribution costs, and engineering and production costs are carefully analyzed and represent realistic estimates.

The sales department is usually the source of information as to the probable sales volume, the unit sales prices, and the changes in expense level which can be expected as a result of new product developments or capacity increases. Before these data are used to estimate sales income, they must be tested by the accountant to establish their reliability. Unfortunately, much expansion occurs near the peak of the business cycle. At such times, the estimate of sales volume is optimistic; the lower volumes of the less prosperous days seem to have been forgotten. Therefore, the controller's staff must use every means to establish the probable average sales volume level over the period of the business cycle. The return on an investment should not be related to a temporary maximum volume, although this is a consideration. References to historical records of sales volume or indexes may provide information as to probable rate of growth, as a basis for checking the sales estimate. Some check must be made of competitive activity, for one firm may not get all the planned or possible increase in sales. In the same manner, the sales prices should be reviewed. Comparisons can be made with competitors' price lists and published reports, taking into account probable changes in the price level. It may be desirable to project earnings at several assumed price levels in order to let management realize the effect of price changes on earnings as well as the break-even point. Before the results of these studies are presented to management, it is desirable to review the figures with the sales manager and secure his opinion as to whether or not the data are realistic.

A critical analysis of information submitted by the production or engineering groups is equally desirable. A failure to engineer a project thoroughly may cause errors of omission. Expansion of plant may require additional storage space, more power or steam capacity, more sewage disposal facilities. Again, new bottlenecks may be created which do not permit full realization of the objective. There are, indeed, technical phases which the accountant cannot check—phases requiring a chemical or mechanical engineering background, for example. But reference to past experience on labor costs, material usage, and manufacturing overhead will serve as a guide in the estimates. Certainly they can be a reference point in thoroughly questioning the engineers regarding the proposal. It is easy for either the engineer or the accountant to neglect some aspects, and a review on a cooperative basis is in the company's interest. The controller can stimulate much thought by a searching review of the engineering proposals. Here, too, the results of the analysis should be reviewed with the line executive before presentation to management.

TIMING OF EXPENDITURES

All expenditures for capital assets must await the availability of funds, and the time is best judged on the basis of the financial budget. Quite aside from this, however, are other factors to consider. For example, the introduction of new facilities bring problems of organization. A certain start-up time must be allowed. In some circumstances, it will be found desirable to begin operation of the equipment at that time least likely to interfere with other functions or when the product can be used immediately.

Beyond the immediate short-term problem is that related to the business cycle. Any expansion of plant facilities should, insofar as possible, be made during periods of depression when prices are low rather than in periods of intense activity when prices are high. To a considerable extent this rule applies also to major repairs and replacements. Some of the latter must be made currently as old equipment becomes useless but, with many items, there is several years' latitude in which the replacements may be made.

Far too often the opposite rule is followed, with the result that periods of depression are loaded with high fixed costs resulting from expanded facilities constructed at excessive costs during previous periods of prosperity. It must be admitted that considerable courage is required to replace and expand facilities when business is at a low ebb; and, likewise, that some executive willpower is necessary to resist the temptation of expansion when volume is easy to get; however, such a policy has been followed by some of the most successful concerns.

Long-term planning of plant requirements assists materially in timing the expenditures to the best advantage and strengthening the courage of management to follow such a course.

ALTERNATIVES IN MEETING THE PROBLEM

A truly analytical approach to the problem of plant expenditures requires consideration of all possible courses of action. This relates to (1) alternatives to making capital expenditures, (2) alternatives relating to the types of equipment or facilities, or the nature of the change, best suited to the needs of the company, or (3) the various methods of procuring the equipment. Most such problems have more than one solution.

Before any request for capital expenditure, or budget, is placed before management, a full exploration is necessary to determine whether new facili- ties or replacements are needed. Suggested questions to ask are:

1. Can another machine be used?
2. Can the process be changed?
3. Can the work be speeded up?
4. Can addition of another shift or a seven-day week eliminate the ne- cessity or desirability of capital expenditures?
5. Can some of the work be subcontracted in part in order to provide added capacity?
6. Can downtime be eliminated or reduced so as to provide more oper- ating hours?

Many times a large part of the projected savings may be realized through a much smaller plant investment than was originally anticipated. In any event, to paraphrase the question of World War II, the test is still: "Is this expenditure really necessary?" Much of the answer will depend on the *long-run* sales outlook.

How many times have companies purchased equipment only to find later that another type would have been preferable? Care must be taken in the selection of facilities, and the budgeting of plant expenditures gives the op- portunity to survey the field thoroughly. Usually alternative makes or models of equipment, or other processes, are available. Systematic plan- ning and study permit adequate consideration of each.

Plant and equipment can often be procured by purchase, construction, or lease. A review should be made of the economies of each, so that the best method may be selected.

COST FINDING FOR JUSTIFICATION

Good common sense should be the controller's main reliance in checking the justification of a capital asset expenditure. In many instances the tra- ditional accounting approach to cost finding is to be avoided. The regular accounting methods or practices generally are not applicable in auditing the possible benefits of fixed asset procurement. Different problems or situa- tions regarding acquisitions may have to be handled somewhat differently.

New equipment is purchased basically for one of two reasons—either to increase sales revenue or to reduce costs. An increase in sales revenue may be secured by (1) expanding the unit sales of existing products, (2) im- proving the value, and therefore the price, of existing products, or (3) add- ing new products. Any decline in sales volume may be offset by the latter two methods. Reduction in costs may be achieved through lowered operat- ing expenses resulting from more efficient equipment, or by reason of less downtime or reduced maintenance costs.

When facilities are being considered for the purpose of increasing sales volume, at least two factors should be kept in mind when calculating the applicable costs.

1. The "marginal" or "incremental" approach should be used in determining the true earning possibilities. General manufacturing overhead, as well as other overhead, should not be allocated in the customary way over the new sales or production. Or, to state the principle in other words, any reduction in overhead allocated to the present production should be considered a saving as a result of the proposed investment.

2. The effect of the increased volume on the level of selling and administrative expense, as well as working capital, should be viewed realistically. It is often assumed that new products, or a higher volume of existing goods, can be distributed without incurring additional selling or administrative expense. Rarely is this the case. Increased volume usually means increased billings to customers, an increase in other administrative services, a heavier work load on the supervisory staff with resulting increase in personnel or higher salaries, or an expanded advertising program to reach new markets. It cannot be concluded that such costs are entirely fixed. The added costs should be charged against the increased sales volume.

If contemplated capital asset expenditures are for the purpose of reducing manufacturing costs, then some additional chances of error exist. Careful analysis must be made of the proposal, and the advantages must be proved. Production men want new tools or machines which will perform faster or better than the old. Yet, the economics of the situation may not justify the new equipment. The older and slower machinery may more than meet the requirements. There may be strong non-cost factors which dictate the purchase of the new facilities, but the cost aspects should be clearly revealed.

Several comments applicable to the purchase of replacement equipment may be noted.

1. Estimates of costs should be based on the expected sales volume. Though the proposed equipment has added capacity over and above the facilities to be replaced, the present sales volume should be the basis of calculation unless there is a good reason to anticipate a permanently higher sales level.

2. Only the scrap or sales value of the old equipment should be considered in making cost comparisons. This is but a reflection that some share of the expenditure already made may be lost. If the undepreciated balance is much higher than the sales value, this may be evidence of obsolescence or too low a depreciation rate. The error in past costing should not burden present costs.

For the same reason, the undepreciated cost of present equipment should not be added to the proposed investment. It is a "sunk" cost and has no bearing on the savings or profits to be realized from new investments.

3. The effect of reduced direct costs in relation to manufacturing overhead should be carefully weighed. For example, assume a case where overhead is allocated on a direct labor-hours basis. It does not follow that because the labor-hours will be reduced the overhead will be lowered correspondingly. Application of a given overhead rate to a labor-hour base will probably result in an overstatement of the cost reduction. The manufacturing expense should be checked to ascertain the true effect. In many instances, it will be found practical to ignore any overhead savings.

4. Actual costs incident to the operation should be considered, regardless of the normal accounting treatment. In addition to the usual operating costs and the expenditure to be capitalized, there may be other non-recurring costs, incident to the removal of old equipment or to rearrangements. Such costs should be considered in computing cost savings.

5. Interest on investment should be included as part of the cost. The rate should depend on the return which would be earned, were the funds employed otherwise.

6. The estimated savings or profits should be calculated after income taxes. The high tax rates make it mandatory to determine the effect of the proposal after income taxes.

A calculation of net savings, based on the factors mentioned above, is illustrated on page 473. Assume, for example, that a new installation would cost $40,000, with an estimated useful life of ten years, and no salvage value. Further, assume the present equipment cost $20,000 with an undepreciated balance of $10,000, a remaining useful life of five years, and a scrap value of $4,000 in the market today.

Thus, over the next five years, the length of life of the present equipment, a net annual savings of $581, or 2.58% of average net investment, reasonably can be expected to be realized if related production and sales volume are as forecasted.

THE INTANGIBLE FACTORS

A book on controllership will naturally emphasize those factors which can be reduced to a mathematical basis. Yet measurable costs or savings are not the only considerations in judging the desirability of plant and equipment expenditures. Attention must also be given to the non-cost factors, the intangibles, which affect the decision; in fact, these influences may be the deciding ones where the cost results either are quite close or contain a possible wide margin of error.

The controller cannot be expected to have a complete knowledge and understanding of all intangible factors which have a bearing on the decision. However, it is well for him to make mention of them in his comments. And he should make every attempt to see that the person best qualified

INVESTMENT REQUIRED:

New equipment, delivered	$40,000
Removal of old machinery, and necessary rearrangements (expense)	5,000
Total cost	45,000
Less salvage value of old equipment	4,000
Net investment	41,000
Average net annual investment $\left(\dfrac{\$41,000 + \$4,100}{2}\right)$ *	$22,550

ANNUAL OPERATING COSTS:

Description	Present Installation	Proposed Installation
Direct labor	$12,600	$ 8,100
Payroll taxes and insurance	1,260	810
Power, repairs, and supplies	3,000	1,700
Other variable overhead	700	700
Total direct cost	17,560	11,310

Depreciation:

Present unit (1/5 times $4,000)	800	
Proposed unit (1/10 times $41,000)		4.100

Property taxes and insurance:

Present unit $\left(2\% \text{ of } \dfrac{\$4,000 + \$800}{2}\right)$ or (2% of $2,400)   48

Proposed unit $\left(2\% \text{ of } \dfrac{\$45,000 + \$4,500}{2}\right)$ or (2% of

$24,750)   495

Interest on investment:

Present (6% of $2,400)	144	
Proposed (6% of $24,750)		1,485
Total annual cost	$18,552	$17.390

Annual Savings:

Net annual savings before income taxes ($18,552 − $17,390)	1,162
Less applicable income taxes (50%)	581
Net savings	$ 581

* The average of a reducing balance is calculated as an average of the net value of the equipment at the beginning of the first and last years of estimated useful life.

to discuss the factors has an opportunity to present his views. While some of these subjects have been mentioned, the more important are:

1. Industrial relations
2. Public relations
3. Competitive reaction
4. Quality control
5. Competitive position in the industry

Recognized as an increasingly important factor is a company's relationship with its employees. Most progressive managements make every attempt to create and maintain good labor relations. An intangible consideration in plant expansion is the provision of good working conditions as a contribution toward those relationships.

Quite distinct from its relationship with employees is its relationship to the public. Provision of a modern and up-to-date plant may influence public opinion. This is not to imply that matters of pride or prestige should dominate executive thinking as to plant expansion; but they may be a factor.

Investment in plant and equipment, particularly for expansion purposes, always involves certain risks as to what competitive reaction may be. It already has been suggested that this feature be considered insofar as effect on sales volume and prices is concerned. But beyond this, newer and cheaper products might be on the verge of introduction. Then, too, integration may stimulate similar attempts at economies by competitors.

Sometimes plant and equipment changes are desired to improve the quality of the product. It may not be possible to show any savings, but quality improvement may be essential to continued long-term acceptance of the article.

Finally, capital asset expenditures may be considered desirable to keep a company ahead of competition. Savings may not be ascertainable in some projects; they may be purely experimental. Yet, certain risks of this nature are essential if new products and processes are to be developed. On occasion, too, expansion may be planned under very favorable conditions, although not capable of demonstration at the time as to immediate need.

THE APPROPRIATION REQUEST

The plant and equipment budget coordinates the allowable disbursements with the available funds. Submission of a budget request for capital assets may or may not be accompanied by a detailed analysis until it is determined that the necessary funds may be forthcoming. Usual practice requires approval of an appropriation request for each specific expenditure for plant or equipment. Such a procedure may be followed for items to be capitalized as well as major repairs or replacements.

The authority required for approval of each specific appropriation request usually depends on the relative amount of the request. In small firms, perhaps each one would require the approval of the president. Typically, however, a regular ascending scale of required approvals is provided:

Less than $5,000	Plant Manager
$5,000 to $10,000	General Manager
$10,000 to $50,000	President or Executive Vice-President
$50,000 to $100,000	Executive Committee
Over $100,000	Board of Directors

An illustrative form is shown in Fig. 117. This summary sheet contains the pertinent facts and approvals. Requests for large sums typically are supported by rather comprehensive facts and figures. It is to be noted that the format shown here provides for the return on investment, calculated on the discounted cash flow basis as well as the payout period. Space is provided for the comments of the controller, including a check against minimum standards established in the company.

Distribution of the approved request serves to initiate the project. If rejected, the originator is advised as to the reasons.

KEEPING EXPENDITURES WITHIN LIMITS

Once the request for appropriation has been approved, the next problem is that of keeping expenditures within the limits of the appropriation. In many cases this is not quite as easy as it sounds. One essential step is the establishment of procedures to accumulate actual costs for comparison at frequent intervals with the authorized amounts. But mere accumulation of actual costs is not enough, for commitments can be made far beyond the bounds of the appropriations. It is usually found necessary, therefore, to maintain a record of commitments and periodically report such information as the following:

Amount authorized	Unencumbered balance
Actual costs incurred	Estimated cost to complete
Commitments	Indicated overrun or underrun

Figure 118 is illustrative of this type of report. A commitment register is prepared on the basis of purchase orders issued.

In actual practice one of the problems is getting all commitments recorded. On occasion some enterprising young men incur obligations without the necessary paper work. Sometimes the estimated cost of the article or service is not stated on the purchase order. It requires some persuasion by the controller, and some diligent policing, to break such bad habits. Ordinarily a fair and reasonable solution can be found.

Authorization for Capital Expenditure

AFE No. 605

Date   6/27/62

Western   Los Angeles
Division   Plant

This request for authorization of a capital expenditure is made necessary by:

☐ Normal replacement   ☒ Cost reduction
☐ Change in manufacturing method   ☐ New business – product
☐ Change in quality control requirements ☐ Increased volume of business
☐ Change in styling

Title: Automatic Packaging Equipment

Description and Justification:

Bagomatic to be used in packaging "R" chemical at Smead
Avenue warehouse. Cost of container will be reduced by $.50.
Present usage 36,000 per year. See attached study on packag-
ing operation.   (Use added sheets if necessary)

Estimated Cost		Return on Investment	
Materials	$ 800.	(Discounted Cash Flow Method)	40.1%
Purchases	21,600.		
Labor	-	Pay-out period	2.61 yrs
Total	$22,400	Estimated useful life of equipment	6 yrs
Contingency 5%	1,100	Time to construct	
Total Cost	$23,500	Salvage value	$500

Controller's Comments and Recommendations: Accounting Dept.
                                                          No.   Amount

Cash flow appears realistic   Capital Account 19-790 $23,500
Return is above minimum of 16%   _____   _____
Approval recommended
                               Expense   _____   _____
                                                 _____   _____
                                                 _____   _____

Approvals and Authorization: Date
                             Approval Rejection   Reason for Rejection:

Requested by _____   _____ _____
Approved by _____   _____ _____

Department Head _____ _____ _____
Executive Committee_____ _____ _____
Board of Directors, per___ _____ _____

Fig. 117—Appropriation Request for Capital Expenditure.

Monroe Manufacturing Company
APPROPRIATION STATUS REPORT
As of August 31, 1963

Appropriation No.	Work Order No.	Description	Amount Appropriated	Actual Completion Date	Original Estimate	Outstanding Commitments	Actual Expenditures to Date	Estimated Cost to Complete	Indicated Total Cost	(Over) or Under Original Estimate
24		OTTAWA AVENUE PLANT	$ 750,000		$670,796.52	286,672.84	384,123.68	–	670,796.52	$ –
	241	Buildings and Equipment			13,552.86	–	13,552.86	–	13,552.86	–
	242	Site Clearance								
		Total Appropriation 24			684,349.38	286,672.84	397,676.54	–	684,349.38	–
25		MODIFICATIONS OF OVERHEAD CONVEYOR	35,000		28,353.00	14,533.05	236.39	13,583.56	28,353.00	–
	251	Installation Y Building			2,990.00	–	4,645.55	–	4,645.55	(1,655.55)
		Others Completed as of 7/31/63								
		Total Appropriation 25			31,343.00	14,533.05	4,881.94	13,583.56	32,998.55	(1,655.55)
26		MISCELLANEOUS IMPROVEMENTS	183,400							
	261	Magnesium Pilot Line		7/31	8,910.00	–	8,551.48	–	8,551.48	358.52
	262	Wrapping Equipment		2/28	16,900.00	6.50	14,122.52	–	14,129.02	2,770.98
	263	Roll Mill—Design and Install—A.C. Plant			11,680.00	8,944.00	154.00	2,582.00	11,680.00	–
	264	Intercommunication System		5/31	24,974.00	4,794.57	20,179.43	–	24,974.00	–
	265	Move Hydraulic Press and Install in Y Building			1,155.50	79.15	926.68	348.16	1,005.83	149.67
	266	Design and Install Air Conditioning Unit in Y Building		5/31	9,725.00	750.00	8,626.84	–	9,725.00	–
	267	Changes and Modifications in Paint Room			30,115.00	29.89	26,664.06	–	26,693.95	3,421.05
	268	Buggy Scales			11,275.00	212.20	10,158.39	904.41	11,275.00	–
	269	Tote Boxes—A.C. Plant		7/31	3,597.00	340.57	3,198.86	–	3,539.43	57.57
	270	Prepare Annealing Oven for Production Use			7,700.00	1,290.03	6,202.29	207.68	7,700.00	–
	271	Move Electric Furnaces to A.C. Plant			3,585.00	2,989.20		595.80	3,585.00	–
	272	Lift truck with Exide batteries and Battery Charger			30,486.00	21,670.19	2,737.83	6,077.98	30,486.00	–
	273	Purchase and Install 100 HP motor in Y Building		7/31	4,692.00	424.00	3,701.97	–	4,125.97	566.03
		Others Completed as of 7/31/63			3,701.00	–	2,482.18	–	2,482.18	1,218.82
		Total Appropriation 26			168,495.50	41,530.30	107,706.53	10,716.03	159,952.86	8,542.64
29		ALUMINUM EXPERIMENTAL UNIT	50,000		50,000.00	5,533.34	15,385.04	29,081.62	50,000.00	–
	291	Construction of Unit								
		Total Appropriation 29			50,000.00	5,533.34	15,385.04	29,081.62	50,000.00	–
		Grand Total	$1,018,400		$934,187.88	348,269.53	525,650.05	53,381.21	927,300.79	$ 6,887.09

Issued by Accounting Department—September 5, 1963.

Fig. 118—Report on Status of Capital Expenditures Under Appropriation.

477

The same principles and procedures applicable to capital asset expenditures may be used to control major repairs, etc.

AN ILLUSTRATIVE PROCEDURE

Outlined below is the procedure followed in a medium-sized company in securing capital asset replacements or additions. Quite obviously, the method of securing approvals and exercising control may vary in different firms.

1. *Origination of the Idea.* Anyone may create an idea—a factory hourly laborer, a foreman, an engineer, a time-study man. It may be submitted as part of a suggestion plan, or simply in an effort to improve methods. Preferably the matter should be put in writing, with sketches, etc., for this will encourage a more thoughtful approach.

2. *Preliminary Review.* The idea is forwarded to the industrial engineering department where it is given a preliminary review by a methods man. Rough estimates are made as to the apparent savings or other benefits offered. If the idea seems to have possibilities, it is reviewed more thoroughly, and outline drawings and specifications are prepared and forwarded to the plant engineering department.

3. *Determination of Cost.* The plant engineering department reviews the plans and specifications and prepares an estimate of cost. Bids may be secured.

4. *Budget Approval and Request for Appropriation.* The estimated costs of the asset, together with estimated savings, are forwarded to the works manager. If he approves, he uses the estimate as the basis for securing a budget approval, along with other projects, on a form similar to Fig. 117. At the same time a request for appropriation is prepared, with the exception of the part pertaining to annual savings, and is sent to the accounting department for review.

5. *Analysis by Accounting.* The controller's representative reviews the proposal and calculates the likely annual savings. In doing this, he makes a thorough review of estimated costs submitted by the industrial engineers. Typical points covered include:

   a. A review of the reasonableness of the manpower requirements by discussion with the engineers. This means "getting behind the figures."
   b. A review of the wage rates and probability of wage increases.
   c. A check into the operating requirements to review probability of overtime.
   d. A review of probable incentive earnings, if any.
   e. Calculation of all non-wage payments or benefits for the workers—vacations, health and accident insurance, Social Security taxes, etc.
   f. Review of maintenance problems and possible expense.

g. Review of every other overhead account to ascertain that all costs have been included, and that the amounts appear reasonable, based on comparative data, if available.

h. Review of material costs, with particular reference to
 1) Present prices and likelihood of increases
 2) Availability of materials, and cost of possible substitutes
 3) Expected scrap or off-grade losses, in comparison with present experience

i. Review of expected production per hour, and comparison with similar operations in the plant.

After such a detailed analysis, the section on annual savings can be calculated, observing the principles mentioned earlier.

6. *Approval of the Request for Appropriation.* If the review indicates the necessary savings, it is approved by the controller, forwarded to the works manager for his approval, and then forwarded to the general manager for the required approval. If the proposal does not warrant approval, it may be returned to the works manager without signature, and with reasons for non-approval. If all those concerned approve, the request for appropriation is forwarded to the controller for distribution. Copies are distributed for action as follows:

1. To general manager
2-3. To engineering department for authority to commence project
4. To purchasing department as authority to honor purchase requisitions against it
5. To cost accounting for setting up necessary records and accumulating costs
6. To general accounting in order to permit payment of invoices and to set up property record cards, when necessary

7. *Control over Expenditures.* Periodic reports are forwarded and actual expenditures and commitments compared with authorized amounts, as in Fig. 118. Indication of overruns is the signal to hold further commitments until a supplemental appropriation request is approved or a review made for possible modifications to reduce the cost.

8. *Close-out and Follow-up.* When the project is completed, the third copy of the approved request is forwarded to accounting as a signal to close out the work order. The final report indicates the project to be completed, with total actual costs shown. Sometime later the installation is checked and a report submitted on actual savings vs. the estimated.

UNUSED PLANT CAPACITY

Another phase of control over fixed assets relates to unused facilities, whether only of short duration or for more extended periods. In every business it can reasonably be expected that some loss will be sustained because of idle facilities and/or idle workers. The objective is to inform management of these losses and place responsibility in an attempt to eliminate the avoidable and unnecessary costs. But aside from stimulating action to eliminate the causes of short-term idleness, such information may be a guide in determining whether additional facilities are necessary. Also, such knowledge may encourage disposal of any permanently excess equipment, giving consideration to the medium-term plans.

Losses resulting from unused plant facilities are not limited to the fixed charges of depreciation, property taxes, and insurance. Very often idle equipment also results in lost labor, power, and light, as well as other continuing overhead expenses, to say nothing of start-up time and lost income from lost sales.

Causes of idle time may be threefold:

1. Those controllable by the production staff. These may result from:
   a. Poor planning by the foreman or other production department staff member
   b. Lack of material
   c. Lack of tools or other equipment
   d. Lack of power
   e. Machine breakdown
   f. Improper supervision or instructions, etc.
2. Those resulting from administrative decisions. For example, a decision to build an addition may force the temporary shutdown of other facilities. Again, management may decide to add equipment for later use. Here certain idle plant costs may be incurred until the expected demand develops.
3. Those arising from economic causes. Included are the causes beyond the control of management, such as cyclical or seasonal demand. In somewhat the same class is idle time resulting from excess capacity in the industry. The effect of such conditions may be partially offset by efficient sales planning and aggressive sales effort.

The cause of idle time is important in determining the proper accounting treatment. Where idle facilities result from economic causes, or are otherwise highly abnormal—such as a prolonged strike, it may be desirable for the controller to have such costs segregated and handled as a separate charge in the statement of income and expense. Such expenses should not be included in inventory or cost of sales.

Some companies isolate in the manufacturing expenses the cost of idle time which is controllable by the production staff. In other cases, a simple reporting of the hours is all that is necessary. Where it is desirable to charge the costs of idle time to a separate account the segregation is simple through a comparison of normal and actual hours, and the use of standard rates.

A typical report on idle time is illustrated in Fig. 150 on page 560.

A PERFORMANCE REVIEW OF CAPITAL EXPENDITURES

An essential ingredient to a sound capital management program is a post-completion audit or performance review of capital expenditure decisions. This is not simply a matter of determining if project assets were maintained within authorized limits. Rather, it seeks to check on the wisdom of the capital expenditures and the sufficiency of the procedures which resulted in approval.

Specifically, the following advantages may accrue from an intelligent post-audit:

1. Experience can focus attention on basic weaknesses in over-all plans, policies, or procedures as related to capital expenditures
2. Strengths or weaknesses in individual performance can be detected and corrected—such as a tendency to overoptimistic estimates
3. It may enable corrections in other current projects prior to completion of commitments or expenditures
4. It affords a training opportunity for the operating and planning staff through the review of entire capital budgeting procedure
5. Prior knowledge of the follow-up encourages reasonable caution in making projections or preparing the justification

The scope and post-completion period of the review will depend on circumstances. Some companies limit the audit only to major projects over $1,000,000 and only until the payout period is completed.

A simple form of graphic report quickly summarizing actual and expected performance is illustrated in Fig. 119.

LEASING EQUIPMENT

Closely allied to the planning and control of fixed assets is the matter of leasing equipment. In many circumstances, the leasing route may be used as a means of securing the use of capital equipment where absence of funds would not otherwise permit it.

Among the responsibilities of the controller is the review of this method of providing needed facilities. Under certain conditions, the lease provides cash flow advantages for those businesses which can use additional working capital to good advantage. It may be that the added expense is outweighed by the earnings from the capital thus made available. Low depreciation rates, inflation, and provisions of the tax laws may encourage leasing. The relative economies should be studied.

NEED FOR A STANDARD PRACTICE

From the foregoing comments it can be realized that there are many ramifications to the control of capital assets. Inasmuch as several departments are involved, the proper control and accounting can be facilitated by

Financial Supplement

CAPITAL EXPENDITURE PERFORMANCE REPORT

(Actual vs. Justification)

DEPARTMENT __Naphthalene__   TITLE __Install Turbo-Generator__

AUTHORIZATION NO. __12345__   DATE APPROVED __6/20/58__   AMOUNT __$1,200,000__   MONTH OPERATION BEGAN __April 1961__

REPORT OF STATUS AS OF __12/31/63__

(000's OMITTED)	Original Authorization Justification To Date	ACTUAL TO DATE	Actual over (+) or Under (-) Justification		
			DOLLARS	%	
Expenditures charged to Auth. A/C - Plant	$ 800	$ 900	$ +100	+13	(1)
Expense	350	200	-150	-43	(2)
Investment	50	75	+25	+50	(3)
Total	1,200	1,175	-25	-21	
Other Balance Sheet Charges - Inventory, Equipment, Etc.	100	225	+125	+125	(4)
TOTAL	1,300	1,400	+100	+8	
Net Cash Income (Before F.I.T.): For Year 1954	350	370	+20	+6	(5)
For all Prior Years	650	330	-320	-49	(6)
TOTAL	1,000	700	-300	-30	
Evaluation: Cumulative Cash Position	-300	-700	-400		
Cumulative Book Income	382	525	+143		
Rate of Return (Approved Method)	19%	22%			
Original Authorization Justification-Life of Project					
Rate of Return (Approved Method)	30%				

ANALYSIS OF DIFFERENCES BETWEEN ACTUAL AND JUSTIFICATION

(1) Price rise in materials and labor.

(2) Lower cost of site clearance.

(4) Increase in inventories.

(5) Higher sales price.

(6) Slower start-up of 9 months accounted for lower income of $125.

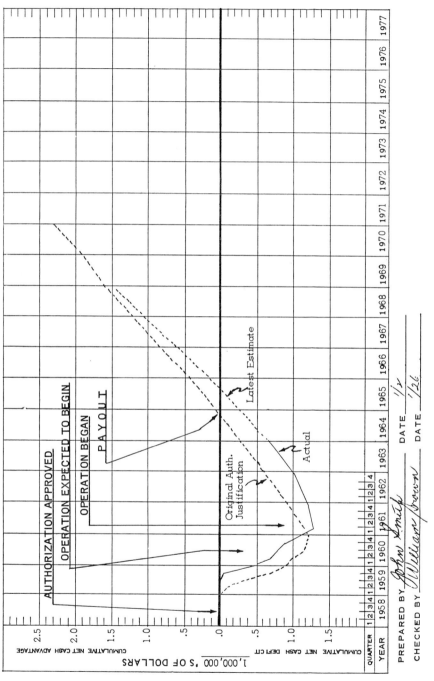

Fig. 119—Capital Expenditure Performance Report.

a written statement of policy and procedure—often known as a "standard practice." One or more procedures may be written, each dealing with a separate phase of control. The duties and responsibilities of each department affected should be outlined therein.[1]

INTERNAL CONTROL AND ACCOUNTING REQUIREMENTS

Once the property has been acquired, the matter of proper accounting and control arises. Usually such duties become the responsibility of the controller. The problem is essentially very simple, but a few suggestions may prove helpful:

1. All fixed assets should be identified, preferably at time of receipt; a serial number may be assigned, and should be affixed to the item. Use of metal tags or electrical engraving is a common method of marking the equipment.
2. Machinery and equipment assigned to a particular department should not be transferred without the written approval of the department head responsible for the physical control of the property. This procedure is essential to know the location for insurance purposes, and to correctly charge depreciation, etc.
3. No item of equipment should be permitted to leave the plant without a property pass signed by the proper authority.
4. Periodically a physical inventory should be taken of all fixed assets.
5. Detailed records should be maintained on each piece of equipment, or similar groups.
6. Purchase requisitions and requests for appropriations should be reviewed to assure that piecemeal acquisitions are not made to avoid the approval of higher authority. Thus, if all expenditures over $100 require the signature of the general manager, individual requisitions may be submitted for each table or each chair to avoid securing such approval.
7. Retirement of fixed assets by sale or scrapping should require certain approvals to guard against the disposal of equipment which could be used in other departments.
8. If possible, bids should be secured on any sizable acquisitions.
9. Provision should be made for proper insurance coverage during construction as well as upon completion.
10. Expenses should be carefully checked to decrease the possibility that portions of capital expenditures are treated as expenses to avoid budget or appropriation overruns.

PLANT AND EQUIPMENT RECORDS

Adequate plant and equipment records are a necessary adjunct to effective control. They provide a convenient source of information for planning

[1] See Chapter 37 on preparation of manuals.

and control purposes as well as for insurance and tax purposes. Some of the advantages may be enumerated as follows:

1. Provide necessary detailed information as to original cost (and depreciation reserves) of fixed assets by types of equipment or location
2. Make available comparative data for purchase of new equipment or replacements
3. Provide basic information to determine proper depreciation charges by department or cost center, and serve as basis for distribution of other fixed charges such as property taxes and insurance
4. Establish basis for property accountability
5. Provide detailed information on assets and depreciation for income tax purposes
6. Are a source of basic information in checking claims and supporting the company position relative to personal and real property tax returns
7. Serve as evidence and a source of information for insurance coverage and claims
8. Provide the basis for determining gain or loss on disposition of fixed assets
9. Provide basic data for control reports by individual units of equipment

Property records include, of course, the plant ledgers and detailed equipment cards. The ledgers will follow the basic property classifications of the company. Detailed cards must be designed to suit the individual needs of the company. A very common form of card is illustrated in Fig. 120. Some companies maintain a basic reference source, and supplement this with tabulation card records. Figure 121 illustrates a tabulating card on which the basic source data are typed or written. Figure 122 is the supplementary tabulating card used to provide the required working reports on cost by account classification, by type of equipment, etc., and related data on depreciation. Irrespective of the exact format, the following information may be found desirable on each item or group of similar items:

Description and identification (serial number, asset number, etc.)
Type of equipment (classification)
Date of acquisition
Original cost
Estimated life and rate of depreciation
Annual depreciation and cumulative depreciation to date
Record of changes in depreciation
Information on appraisals
Estimated scrap value
Record of repair costs

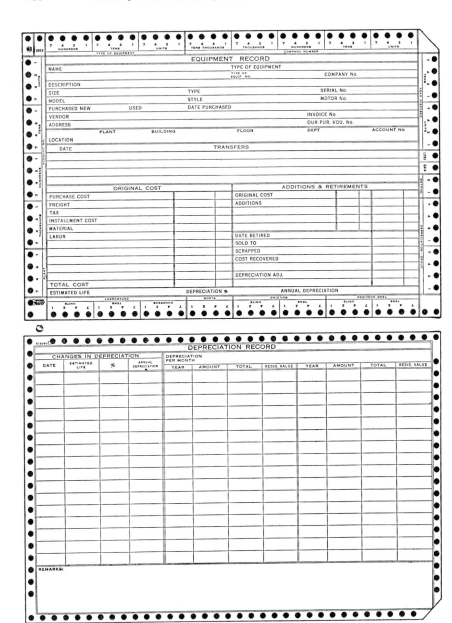

Fig. 120—Equipment Record Card.

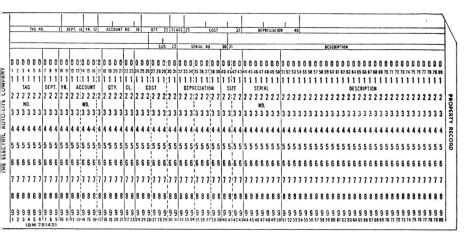

Fig. 121—Basic Property Record Card.

Fig. 122—Tabulating Card for Property Reporting Purposes.

REPORTS ON PLANT AND EQUIPMENT

Depending on the needs and desires of management, a substantial number of useful reports may be prepared. Typical are the following:

1. Comparison of expenditures and commitments with authorized amount (illustrated in Fig. 118)
2. Report on machine utilization—designed to show lost machine hours
3. Maintenance or repair costs by asset classifications or individual pieces of equipment (illustrated in Fig. 123)

4. Summaries of fixed asset investment, by type of equipment, cost center, etc.
5. Summary reports on acquisitions and retirements
6. Comparisons of estimated and realized savings or profit on capital asset expenditures (illustrated in Figs. 119 and 124)
7. Special studies on justification for expenditures

REPAIR COST ANALYSIS

MONTH OF _____   DEPT NO.   15

EQUIPMENT NUMBER	ORDER JOB OR ACCOUNT NUMBER	CURRENT MONTH			YEAR TO DATE	
		LABOR & BURDEN		MATERIAL	LABOR BURDEN	
		HOURS	AMOUNT		HOURS	& MATERIAL
2902	221	3 0 0	6 7 5	1 8 7 5		
	229	4 0 0	9 0 0	1 2 9 3 0		
	287	1 6 0 0	3 6 0 0	4 5 0		
		2 3 0 0	5 1 7 5	1 5 2 5 5	3 0 5 0 0	2 3 0 1 10
4911	647	8 0 0	1 8 0 0	5 2 5		
	843	1 0 0	2 2 5	7 5 0		
	827	1 0 0 0	2 2 5 0	1 1 0		
	987	5 4 0 0	1 2 1 5 0	4 6 2 0 0		
		7 3 0 0	1 6 4 2 5	4 7 5 8 5	2 6 5 0 0	1 8 0 6 00
8037	274	2 0 0	4 5 0			
	693	4 0 0	9 0 0	1 2 7 2		
		6 0 0	1 3 5 0	1 2 7 2	6 0 0	2 6 22

Fig. 123—Punched Card Analysis of Repair Cost by Equipment Item.

OTHER RESPONSIBILITIES OF THE CONTROLLER

The controller is directly concerned with more than just the control of fixed assets, and the records and reports necessary to effect it. He must be conversant with the possible application in his firm of various accounting and related techniques having to do with capital assets. These are briefly outlined in the following sections.

VALUATION OF FIXED ASSETS

For most businesses there is no continuous problem pertaining to the basis for recording and valuing fixed assets. Normally such accounting should be at cost, less the applicable allowance for depreciation, depletion, or amortization. There are instances, however, where the board of directors has directed and authorized valuation on a basis higher or lower than actual cost. Generally, experience with plant revaluation indicates that it is neither practical nor advisable to attempt to reflect current values. Except in the case of sale, current value has little significance. The true worth of fixed assets is measured by their earning power and not replacement cost or value.

In those instances where the owners have directed that appreciation must be reflected in the accounts, the controller must see that the facts are

The General Refining Corporation

SUMMARY OF CAPITAL EXPENDITURE PERFORMANCE

Completed Projects over $200,000 Only

(Dollars in Thousands)

Division and Function	Completion Date	Project Cost Performance				Return on Investment					
				(Over)/Under Estimate		Cumulative Cash Flow		(Over)/Under Estimate		Indicated Rate of Return	
		Actual	Estimated	Amount	%	Actual	Estimate	Amount	%	Original	Present View
EASTERN DIVISION											
Manufacturing											
Reformer	11/15/61	$ 2,500	$ 2,650	$ 150	5.7	$ 320	$ 310	$ (10)	(3.2)	8.6	8.6
Crude Unit	1/18/62	8,740	7,620	(1,120)	(14.7)	2,800	3,060	260	8.5	19.6	15.4
Isocracker	6/30/62	18,390	17,250	(1,140)	(6.6)	3,600	3,110	(490)	(15.7)	25.3	26.5
Naphthalene	12/20/61	4,300	3,870	(430)	(11.1)	1,770	2,430	660	27.2	20.6	14.5
Other		1,200	1,250	50	4.0	540	490	(50)	(10.2)	10.5	12.0
Subtotal		35,130	32,640	(2,490)	(7.6)	9,030	9,400	370	3.9	22.3	21.8
Marketing											
Bayonne Terminal	9/10/61	3,220	3,400	180	5.3	870	850	(20)	(2.4)	9.8	10.0
Boundbrook Packaging Plant	8/31/60	1,890	1,960	70	3.6	430	450	20	4.4	11.9	11.9
Team Distributorship	6/30/61	3,800	3,900	100	2.6	330	820	490	59.8	8.3	4.8
Other		260	240	(20)	(8.3)	90	90	0	0.0	5.1	5.0
Subtotal		9,170	9,500	330	3.5	1,720	2,210	490	22.2	9.0	9.0
Eastern Division Total		44,300	42,140	(2,160)	(5.1)	10,750	11,610	860	7.4	20.6	19.4
SOUTHERN DIVISION											
Transportation											
Buffalo Pipe Line	8/31/59	4,810	4,950	140	7.8	2,570	3,810	1,240	32.6	23.3	18.3
Delaware Loading Facility	7/31/58	2,800	2,650	(150)	(5.7)	1,990	1,470	(520)	(35.4)	25.2	28.7
"R" Tanker Fleet	5/31/60	7,760	7,940	180	2.3	2,860	2,420	(440)	(18.2)	17.7	20.5
Subtotal		15,370	15,540	170	1.1	7,420	7,700	280	3.6	18.4	18.6
GRAND TOTAL		$59,670	$57,680	$(1,990)	(3.5)	$18,170	$19,310	$1,140	5.9	20.0	19.3

Fig. 124—Summary Report on Capital Investment Performance.

489

correctly stated. It is suggested that reference be made to accounting literature on the subject, but three pertinent comments can be made:

1. The write-up of the property should *not* be credited to earned surplus. It may be credited to a reserve established for the purpose, to a special surplus account—surplus from appraisal of fixed assets, or perhaps to the capital surplus account.
2. Depreciation should be properly calculated and recorded. There is considerable difference of opinion among accountants as to how this should be done. Some believe income should be charged only with depreciation based on original cost; and others favor replacement cost. It is probably now accepted that a corporation may not use one basis for valuing its properties in the balance sheet, and another basis for amortizing the cost in its statement of income and expense.
3. The estimated present values of fixed assets may be revealed by explanatory notes in the balance sheet rather than through the formal entry of appraisals on the books of account.

DEPRECIATION ACCOUNTING

Depreciation has been variously defined. Bulletin "F" of the Internal Revenue Service defines allowable depreciation for purposes of computing net income as "a reasonable allowance for the exhaustion, wear and tear of property used in the trade or business, including a reasonable allowance for obsolescence." Perhaps the most acceptable definition is:

Depreciation accounting is a system of accounting which aims to distribute the cost or other basic value of tangible capital assets, less salvage (if any), over the estimated useful life of the unit (which may be a group of assets) in a systematic and rational manner. It is a process of allocation, not of valuation. *Depreciation for the year* is the portion of the total charge under such a system that is allocated to the year. Although the allocation may properly take into account occurrences during the year, it is not intended to be a measurement of the effect of all such occurrences.[2]

In arriving at the applicable charges for depreciation, there are at least three related objectives of proper accounting: (1) to state earnings correctly; (2) to protect the investment of owners and creditors by maintaining the integrity of the fixed capital accounts (a write-off of plant and equipment over the useful life, by charges against income, tends to avoid the payment of dividends out of capital); and (3) to secure useful costs through proper depreciation allocations to cost centers.

The accomplishment of these objectives must lie largely in the controller's hands. The determination of the useful life of the plant and equipment is largely an engineering problem. However, the ramifications and

[2] American Institute of Certified Public Accountants, *Accounting Research Bulletin* No. 22.

implications of depreciation policy—such matters as treatment of obsolescence, accounting for retirements, determination of allocation methods, and selection of individual or group rates—are best understood by the accountant. For these reasons, the controller should be the primary force in recommending to management, as may be necessary, the policies to be followed.

OBSOLESCENCE

Obsolescence, sometimes called functional depreciation as distinguished from physical depreciation, can be a highly significant factor in determining useful economic life. More often than not, the usefulness of facilities is likely to be limited by obsolescence, so that it may outweigh the depreciation factor. Such a condition can occur as a result of two causes. The product manufactured may be replaced by another, so that the need no longer exists for the facility. Or a new type of asset—one which produces at a much lower cost—may be developed to supersede present manufacturing equipment. Sometimes the need for expanded capacity has the effect of rendering obsolete or inadequate the existing asset.

Obsolescence may be of two kinds—normal or special. The former is the normal loss in value and can be anticipated in the same degree as other depreciation factors. It should be included in the estimate of useful life. Extraordinary or special obsolescence, on the other hand, can rarely be foreseen. The controller's responsibility generally should extend to a review of past experience and trends to determine whether obsolescence is an important consideration in his industry. If so, then it should be duly recognized in the useful life estimates.

In accounting for obsolescence, the question must be settled as to whether a distinction should be made in the accounts between charges for obsolescence and depreciation. In practice, the normal obsolescence will be combined with depreciation in both the provision and the reserve. A highly abnormal and significant obsolescence loss probably should be segregated in the income and expense statement. Aside from this, circumstances may indicate the desirability of segregating a reserve for obsolescence. It may not be possible to identify obsolescence with a particular asset, although experience will indicate the approximate amount. This can be handled as a general provision without regard to the individual piece of equipment.

FULLY DEPRECIATED ASSETS

In properly stating on the balance sheet the value of fixed assets, and in making the proper charge to manufacturing costs for the use of the plant and equipment, the question is raised as to the correct accounting treatment of fully depreciated assets. Obviously, if the facilities are no longer of use, they should be retired, and the amount removed from both the asset and the reserve.   If the item is fully depreciated but still in use, then the depreciation charge to the earnings statement must be discontinued—unless, of course, a composite useful life estimate or a composite depreciation rate is being used.   Some accountants advocate the continuance of the depreciation charge, as long as the asset is in use, to state manufacturing costs correctly.   They would credit a variance or adjustment account so as to report earnings properly.   The controller should exercise his discretion in determining whether such a practice should be followed.   For example, the lack of depreciation charges may in fact be offset by very heavy maintenance costs.   The objective should be to follow that policy which most clearly reflects actual operating conditions and which makes the resulting statements most useful to management.

A related problem is the treatment of fully amortized facilities which were secured under certificates of necessity.   Management is permitted to restate them at a fair value, not to exceed cost less normal depreciation.   However, an extremely conservative attitude should be taken in any such case before committing the company to additional future charges for depreciation or obsolescence.   Consideration ought to be given to the condition of the facilities, their probable length of use, and the extent to which competition permits the recovery of such costs through the selling prices.   For internal statement purposes, manufacturing costs may be adjusted to reflect normal depreciation charges through the use of a variance or adjustment account. By and large, however, any difference between charges for internal statement purposes and profit and loss purposes should be kept to a minimum, and made only as necessary to reflect actual operating conditions properly.

APPRAISALS AND APPRAISAL RECORDS

Management may request appraisals of property for any one of several reasons: for the purchase or sale of property, for reorganization or liquidations, for financing when the property is collateral, for insurance purposes, for taxation purposes, and for control purposes when the records do not indicate investment by process or cost center.

The basis of valuing fixed assets has already been reviewed, and the desirability of stating such property at original cost has been emphasized. However, occasions arise when management directs the valuation of property on another basis—perhaps to remove extremely high depreciation charges.   When appraisals are recorded, the original cost and depreciation on original cost should continue to be reflected in the detail records, along with the appraised value and depreciation thereon.

LOSS OR GAIN ON SALE OF FIXED ASSETS

The matter of accounting for the loss or gain on sale or other disposition of fixed assets is primarily one of accounting theory. Some have supported the proposition that losses resulting from premature retirement or technological advances are properly capitalized and charged against future operations. Most authorities do not concur in this view. The sound value, or asset value less accumulated depreciation, for all assets retired is a loss which should be charged off as incurred. It is in the nature of a correction of prior profits. Usual practice is to carry such gain or loss, if important, in the non-operating section of the statement of income and expense.

FUNDS FOR PLANT REPLACEMENT AND EXPANSION

Unfortunately, a great deal of confusion has arisen among laymen as to the distinction between a reserve and a fund. Some think that the creation of a depreciation reserve also establishes a fund to replace the property. Accountants know that a reserve may exist independent of a fund, and that a fund can exist without a reserve. The depreciation reserve does not represent a fund of cash or other assets which has been set aside. It only expresses the usage of the asset. If the operation has been profitable, and if dividends have not been paid in excess of net income after recognizing depreciation, then values of some sort are available to offset the charge for use of the plant and equipment.

Most companies do not establish funds for property expansion or replacement, but use the general funds instead. However, such funds can be created; and some exponents believe that public utilities and wasting asset industries, such as mining, should establish such funds. Such funds are not necessarily to be measured by the depreciation reserve because replacement costs may be quite different. The depreciation reserve is a measure of expired *past* value, not *future* requirements for replacement.

PLANT AND EQUIPMENT IN RELATION TO TAXES

Many local communities and states levy real and personal property taxes, or enforce payment of franchise taxes based on property values. Maintenance of adequate records can be a means of satisfying the taxing authorities on problems of valuation.

Plant and property values, through the resulting depreciation charges, are important from the federal income tax viewpoint. As mentioned previously, the depreciation allowance for tax purposes, if significantly different from depreciation for book purposes, can distort the profit before taxes and the tax charge. Where the estimate of useful life and the base for tax and book purposes are not greatly different, an effort should be made to bring the two in line. It may save the maintenance of a separate set of records.

In any event, the burden of proof as to the correctness of the depreciation claimed is placed on the taxpayer, who must keep the necessary records and other data to support his claim.

PLANT AND EQUIPMENT—SEC REQUIREMENTS

The increasing number of federal regulatory bodies gives added emphasis to the need for adequate records and reports. Many controllers are required to prepare data for filing under Regulation S–X of the Securities and Exchange Commission. The requirements of the Commission with respect to schedules on property, plant, and equipment, and the related reserves, should be reviewed in considering the types of records to be maintained.

26

Control of Liabilities

OBJECTIVES OF LIABILITY CONTROL

For a conservative layman the practical meaning of "liability control" might be the avoidance of debt or the protection of his credit standing. There are, of course, certain seeds of truth in this viewpoint. But to the controller of a business, the more specific objectives of satisfactory accounting control of liabilities include:

1. A proper recording and disclosure of all financial obligations of the company
2. The maintenance of a sound financial structure, through planning and controlling the proper relationship of borrowed and equity capital
3. Procurement of borrowed capital on the most advantageous basis
4. Restriction of commitments within well-defined limits, before they become actual liabilities.

RESPONSIBILITY OF THE CONTROLLER

With these rather broad objectives defined, the question is raised as to what part the controller should play in achieving them. Certainly it is within the functions of the board of directors or the chief executive officer to determine the means by which, the extent to which, and the time when a corporation may borrow funds. However, these decisions should be based upon sound analyses. Such studies may be prepared by the controller or the treasurer or perhaps jointly. In any event, the analytical ability of the chief accounting officer, coupled with his responsibilities in the planning or forecasting area, should enable him to contribute in this important field.

Although the bylaws of the company, the desires of the management, and the personal attributes of the controller may determine just what his duties are relative to accounting control of liabilities, the following outline is suggestive of the responsibilities which he should be assigned:

1. A proper recording of all liabilities. This includes the institution of procedures to assure that *all* actual liabilities are entered in the rec-

ords. This involves more than being satisfied that the invoice of XYZ Company is included in accounts payable. The records must be in useful form, the liabilities must be properly classified, and the amount of the liability must be correct.

2. The preparation, in correct form, of any required reports on the details of the liabilities. This involves the presentation of the data in a manner which will highlight the points which need to be emphasized.

3. Audit or review of practices to insure compliance with bylaws, instructions of the board of directors, the terms of indentures, etc. Where evidence of non-compliance is found, it must be reported for corrective action.

4. Report, as may be required, on significant trends and developments in financial matters affecting liabilities.

5. Determine, as part of the planning phases of business management, the budgeted cash requirements and so advise the necessary authority so that required loans can be negotiated.

6. Determine, as requested, the cost of financing on various alternative bases; or evaluate the recommendations of the treasurer.

APPLICATION OF SOUND ACCOUNTING PRINCIPLES

This chapter is not concerned primarily with all the accounting principles applicable in the recording of obligations. Reference is made to the many authoritative writings on the subject.[1] It is expected that the controller and his staff keep abreast of the many developments affecting adequate disclosure of liabilities, including proper classifications and presentation, income tax accounting, long-term lease obligations, etc. This chapter is directed toward some of those procedural and operational considerations which many accountants are prone to ignore.

INCOME TAX LIABILITY

The accrued or estimated income tax liability, with particular reference to the federal income tax, is a complicated affair. Under the circumstances it is common procedure at year-end to provide a conservative estimate of the amount due. The liability recorded should give recognition to probable results of the examination by the Internal Revenue Service.

The estimated liability for *interim statements* should, of course, give consideration to the latest information on probable liability, including likely changes in the tax laws.

A particularly difficult accounting problem arises when material or extraordinary differences exist between taxable income and book income.

[1] For example, see American Institute of Certified Public Accountants, "Restatement and Revision of Accounting Research Bulletins," *Accounting Research Bulletin* No. 43.

Such circumstances have given rise to the net-of-income tax accounting concept, with its effect on the treatment of the deferred income tax liability. Pertinent excerpts from *Accounting Research Bulletin* No. 43 of the American Institute of Certified Public Accountants are as follows:

1. This section deals with a number of accounting problems which arise in the reporting of income and excess-profits taxes (hereinafter referred to as income taxes) in financial statements. The problems arise largely where (a) material items entering into the computation of taxable income are not included in the income statement and where (b) material items included in the income statement do not enter into the computation of taxable income. The section does not apply where there is a presumption that particular differences between the tax return and the income statement will recur regularly over a comparatively long period of time.

2. Basic difficulties arise in connection with the accounting for income taxes where there are material and extraordinary differences between the taxable income upon which they are computed and the income for the period determined in accordance with generally accepted accounting principles. For example, provisions may be made in the income statement for possible losses not yet realized but requiring recognition under generally accepted accounting principles, such losses, however, being deductible for tax purposes only when they occur. On the other hand, deductions may be taken in the tax return which are not included in the income statement, such as charges against an estimated liability account created in a prior period. Likewise, gains subject to income tax may not be included in the income statement, as, for instance, a gain on the sale of property credited to surplus. Also, credits in the income statement may not be includible in taxable income, as when an unneeded past provision for an estimated liability is restored to income.

3. In some cases the transactions result in gains; in others they result in losses or net costs. If all the effects of the transactions (including their effect on income tax) were reflected in the income statement the income would, of course, be increased where the transactions result in a gain and reduced where they result in a loss or net cost. But where the effects are not all reflected in the income statement, and that statement indicates only the income tax actually payable, exactly the opposite effect is produced—where the special transactions result in a gain the net income is reduced; and where they result in a loss, or net cost, the net income is increased. Such results ordinarily detract from the significance or usefulness of the financial statements.

4. Financial statements are based on allocations of receipts, payments, accruals, and various other items. Many of the allocations are necessarily based on assumptions, but no one suggests that allocations based on imperfect criteria should be abandoned in respect of expenses other than income taxes, or even that the method of allocation should always be indicated. Income taxes are an expense that should be allocated, when necessary and practicable, to income and other accounts, as other expenses are allocated. What the income statement should reflect under this head, as under any other head, is the expense properly allocable to the income included in the income statement for the year.

5. In cases in which transactions included in the surplus statement but not in the income statement increase the income tax payable by an amount that is substantial and is determinable without difficulty, as in the case of a gain credited to surplus, an allocation of income tax between the two statements

would ordinarily be made. Objection to allocation in other cases, as where a loss is charged to surplus, has been made on the ground that the amount shown for income taxes in the income statement would be increased beyond the amount of the tax estimated to be actually payable. Further objection has been made on the ground that the amount attributable to accounts other than income is not reasonably determinable.

6. The committee sees no objection to an allocation which results in the division of a given item into two parts one of which is larger than the item itself and is offset by the smaller. The argument that the effect of the special transactions on the amount of tax is not identifiable is usually without substantial merit. The difficulties encountered in allocation of the tax are not greater than those met with in many other allocations of expenses. The allocation procedure recommended here does not, of course, contemplate a determination of the tax effect attributable to every separate transaction. In the committee's view, all that is necessary in making an allocation is to consider the effect on taxes of those special transactions which are not included in the income statement.

*   *   *

DEFERRED-CHARGE AND ESTIMATED LIABILITY ACCOUNTS

11. The principle of allocation applies also where an item resulting in a material reduction in income taxes is charged to or carried forward in a deferred-charge account or charged to an estimated liability account.

12. The deduction for tax purposes in a given year of an item which is carried to or remains in a deferred-charge account will involve a series of charges in future income statements for amortization of the deferred charge, and these charges will not be deductible for tax purposes. In the period in which the item is taken as a deduction for tax purposes a charge should be made in the income statement of an amount equal to the tax reduction, in the manner set forth above with respect to charges to surplus, with a corresponding credit in the deferred-charge account. Thereafter amortization of the deferred charge should be based on the amount as adjusted by such tax reduction.

13. Where an item resulting in a material reduction in income taxes is charged to an estimated liability account the principle of allocation may be applied in the income statement in any of three ways: (a) the current provision for income taxes may be shown as if the item in question were not deductible (the total amount of tax estimated to be due for the year being indicated), or (b) a charge may be included for a portion of such item equal to the tax reduction resulting therefrom, or (c) the item in question may be charged in the income statement and a credit made in the income statement representing a portion of the estimated liability account equal to the excess of such item over the related tax reduction.

SPECIAL TREATMENT

14. Where the treatments recommended above are considered to be not practicable, the amount of taxes estimated to be actually payable for the year may be shown in the income statement, provided that the pertinent facts, including the amount of the increase or decrease attributable to other accounts, are clearly disclosed either in a footnote or in the body of the income statement.

ESTIMATED LIABILITIES

Circumstances very often arise where an obligation is known, but the amount is uncertain. An example would be amounts due pursuant to warranty or guaranty agreements. Under such conditions it is considered proper to charge the appropriate expense account and credit an appropriate liability account for the estimated obligation of the company. Past experience may be a guide. Such a procedure permits the matching of costs with related revenues as well as recognition of the obligation that does exist.

These estimated liabilities may be classified properly as current liabilities if extinguishing the claim will require the use of current assets during the next operating cycle of one year or less. On the other hand, the recorded liability would be excluded from the current category if it is expected to be liquidated from funds not included in current assets or in a period longer than one year.

A principal concern of the controller is to ascertain that the recorded obligation is in fact proper.

DISCLOSURE OF CONTINGENCIES

In appraising the effect of prospective transactions, the controller is expected to be conversant with the effect upon the financial statements, and the need for disclosure. Many have had the experience of recommending against a proposal on the grounds that disclosure in the annual report would have a deleterious effect—quite aside from the merits of the case itself. One of the particularly troublesome areas is contingencies. The audit by independent accountants will cause the subject to be reviewed. However, the chief accounting officer should be knowledgeable on current practice in this area. *Accounting Research Bulletin* No. 50 on "Contingencies," issued by the Committee on Accounting Procedure of the American Institute of Certified Public Accountants, is authoritative:

1. In the preparation of financial statements presenting financial position or operating results, or both, it is necessary to give consideration to contingencies. In accounting a contingency is an existing condition, situation or set of circumstances, involving a considerable degree of uncertainty, which may, through a related future event, result in the acquisition or loss of an asset, or the incurrence or avoidance of a liability, usually with the concurrence of a gain or loss. A commitment which is not dependent upon some significant intervening factor or decision should not be described as a contingency.

DISCUSSION

2. The contingencies with which this bulletin is primarily concerned are those in which the outcome is not sufficiently predictable to permit recording in the accounts, but in which there is a reasonable possibility of an outcome which

might materially affect financial position or results of operations. Examples of contingencies which may result in the incurrence of liabilities, or in losses, are pending or threatened litigation, assessments or possible assessments of additional taxes, or other claims such as renegotiation refunds, that are being or would be contested, guarantees of indebtedness of others, and agreements to repurchase receivables which have been sold. Examples of contingencies which may result in the acquisition of assets, or in gains, are claims against others for patent infringement, price redetermination upward and claims for reimbursement under condemnation proceedings. Material contingencies of the types discussed in this paragraph should be disclosed.

3. Other contingencies may exist where the outcome is reasonably foreseeable, such as probable tax assessments which will not be contested, or anticipated losses from uncollectible receivables. Contingencies of this type which are expected to result in losses should be reflected in the accounts. However, contingencies which might result in gains usually are not reflected in the accounts since to do so might be to recognize revenue prior to its realization; [2] but there should be adequate disclosure.

4. There are also general risk contingencies that are inherent in business operations and which affect many if not all companies, such as the possibility of war, strike, losses from catastrophes not ordinarily insured against, or a business recession. Contingencies of this type need not be reflected in financial statements either by incorporation in the accounts or by other disclosure.[3]

DISCLOSURE

5. Disclosure of contingencies referred to in paragraph 2 should be made in financial statements or in notes thereto. The disclosure should be based as to its extent on judgment in the light of the specific circumstances and should indicate the nature of the contingency, and should give an appraisal of the outlook. If a monetary estimate of the amount involved is not feasible, disclosure should be made in general terms describing the contingency and explaining that no estimated amount is determinable. When amounts are not otherwise determinable, it may be appropriate to indicate the opinion of management or counsel as to the amount which may be involved. In some cases, such as a law suit involving a substantial amount, management may reasonably expect to settle the matter without incurrence of any significant liability; however, consideration should be given to disclosing the existence of the litigation and the opinion of management or counsel with respect thereto. Although disclosures discussed here should be made with respect to those contingencies which may result in material gains or assets as well as with respect to those which may result in material losses or liabilities, care should be exercised in the case of gains or assets to avoid misleading implications as to the likelihood of realization. The discussion in this bulletin does not deal with the question as to whether the existence of any of the contingencies discussed above is such as to require a qualified opinion or a disclaimer of an opinion by the independent certified public accountant.

[2] See Chapter 1, *Accounting Research Bulletin* No. 43, "Restatement and Revision of Accounting Research Bulletins."

[3] For the committee's position with respect to contingency reserves, see Chapter 6 of *Accounting Research Bulletin* No. 43.

6. Certain other situations requiring disclosures have sometimes inappropriately been described as though they were contingencies, even though they are of a nature not possessing the degree of uncertainty usually associated with the concept of a contingency. Examples are unused letters of credit, long-term leases, assets pledged as security for loans, pension plans, the existence of cumulative preferred stock dividends in arrears, and commitments such as those for plant acquisition or an obligation to reduce debts, maintain working capital, or restrict dividends. While some of these situations may develop into contingencies, they should not be described as contingencies prior to such eventuality.

THE ECONOMICS OF DIRECT BORROWING

In making studies of alternate methods of financing, an overriding consideration, of course, is the maintenance of a proper relationship of debt to equity. However, the tax deductibility of interest payments may produce a significant leverage effect on the return to the common shareholders. If, therefore, the earning capacity of a company is sufficiently stable so that even under rather depressed circumstances the profits are conservatively estimated to cover the debt servicing, then financing plans should weigh the desirability of debt incurrence.

It may be helpful to consider an example of the effect of differing sources of capital on the return to the common shareholders.

Assume the following for Company Y:

1. Present assets and sources of capital:

Total Assets	$ 500,000
Sources of Capital	
Non-Cost (creditor supplied, non-interest)	50,000
Long-Term Debt	150,000
Preferred Shareholders	100,000
Common Equity—Residual	200,000
Total	$ 500,000

2. Present earnings:

Net Sales		$1,000,000
Costs and Expenses		
Salaries and Wages	$450,000	
Materials	306,000	
Depreciation	30,000	
Interest Expense	6,000	
Federal Income Tax	108,000	900,000
Net Income		100,000
Less: Dividends for Preferred Shareholders		5,000
Net Income Available for Common Shareholders		$ 95,000

3. It has been decided to expand for competitive reasons, and it is estimated that:
   a. The annual pre-tax earnings will be $232,000
   b. Additional capital required for the expansion will be $150,000

4. The capital investment may be available either through additional common shareholder investment (Plan A), or through securing a long-term loan of $100,000 at 4% and an additional preferred stock issue of $50,000 at 5% (Plan B).

The controller is requested to determine the earnings under each plan, and the rate of return on each for the common shareholders.

Based on available information, Plan A earnings would be as follows:

Net Sales		$1,100,000
Costs and Expenses		
Salaries and Wages, etc.	$480,400	
Materials	336,600	
Depreciation	45,000	
Interest Expense	6,000	
Federal Income Tax	120,640	988,640
Net Income		111,360
Less: Preferred Dividends		5,000
Net Income Available for Common Shareholders		$ 106,360

The income statement and earnings available to common shareholders under Plan B would aggregate $101,940, determined in this manner:

Net Sales		$1,100,000
Costs and Expenses		
Salaries and Wages	$480,400	
Materials	336,600	
Depreciation	45,000	
Interest Expense	10,000	
Federal Income Tax	118,560	990,560
Net Income		109,440
Less: Preferred Dividends		7,500
Net Income Available for Common Shareholders		$ 101,940

The comparative rates of return are:

	Plan A	Plan B
Return on total capital employed (net income plus interest expense)		
117,360 ÷ 650,000	18.05%	
119,440 ÷ 650,000		18.38%
Return on common shareholder equity		
106,360 ÷ 350,000	30.39	
101,940 ÷ 200,000		50.97

Therefore, it can be seen from this example that the leverage under Plan A is 12.34 percentage points and under Plan B is 32.59 percentage points.

The return to common shareholders on the additional $150,000 such ownership could invest may be determined in this manner:

Return on $350,000 investment $106,360
Return on $200,000 investment 95,000

Return on additional $150,000 .... $ 11,360

This represents a 7.57% rate of return ($11,360 ÷ $150,000). The present rate of return before the planned expansion is 47.5% ($95,000 ÷ $200,000). In view of the *relatively* low rate of return on the new investment, and the high leverage for the common shareholders in using 4% or 5% funds, consideration should be given to Plan B.

While this illustration is a highly simplified example, it may indicate an approach to studying the effect of alternate financing plans.

LONG-TERM LEASE FINANCING

A consideration of the control of liabilities must naturally include long-term lease obligations. Most companies are short of capital; many have restrictions as to direct debt; and, therefore, some secure needed facilities by means of leases.

It is difficult to generalize on the question of the relative desirability of leasing vs. direct financing. Each company must make its own decision in the light of its own financial status, the characteristics of the lease, the type of asset involved, and the state of the money market. However, some general observations may be made:

1. Lease financing is normally (at the present time) recorded off the balance sheet or in footnotes. In contrast, both direct debt and equity financing are clearly displayed. Perhaps the trend of thinking is such that at some time in the near future long-term lease financing may be formally classified as debt by the financial community and as an accepted accounting practice. Until that time, the controller might be well advised to consider lease financing as part of capital in weighing alternative capital sources.
2. Long-term lease financing is a form of debt obligation for the lessee. From the banker's viewpoint, debt service and lease rental obligations are strikingly similar. Since rentals are as effective a claim on cash throw-off as debt service, some financing institutions are interested in cash generation before both debt service and lease financing in judging the margin of safety.
3. Usually lease financing carries a higher interest rate than direct debt because it is not a direct obligation, because it is more complicated

SHEET 1 OF 2 GENERAL MANUFACTURING COMPANY REPORT No. 102

CASH REQUIREMENTS STATEMENT DATE December 31

FORM DE-1-0372-2

ENTRY DATE MO.	ENTRY DATE DAY 4	INVOICE DATE MO.	INVOICE DATE DAY 8	VENDOR ABBREVIATION 19	VENDOR NUMBER 24	VENDOR'S INVOICE No. 30	OUR INVOICE NUMBER 35	ENTRY 37	ACCOUNT No. GEN. LEDGER 40	ACCOUNT No. SUB. LEDGER 43	DEPT. CHGD. 3	JOB ORDER NUMBER 8	DUE DATE MO.	DUE DATE DAY 12	DATE PAID MO.	DATE PAID DAY 16	ITEM OR INVOICE AMOUNT 24	DISCOUNT 32	AMOUNT TO PAY / AMOUNT PAID 42
12	22	12	21	ABBOT BRASS	1179	AB2576	12121	30	211				12	31			98 13	1 96	96 17
12	22	12	18	ABBOT BRASS	1179	AB2531	12120	30	211				12	31			158 78	3 18	155 60
12	31	12	28	ABBOT BRASS	1179	CM0085	12905	39	211				12	31			25 00 CR	50 CR	24 50 CR
12	24	12	21	ABRAMS COAL	1180	1486	12138	30	211				12	31			277 35	8 31	269 04
12	28	12	24	ABRAMS COAL	1180	1573	12147	30	211				12	31			300 00	10 50	289 50
12	10	12	10	ACE INS CO	1181		12068	35	211				12	31			18 50		18 50
12	15	12	10	ACE INS CO	1181		12088	30	211				12	31			118 02		118 02
12	4	11	27	WATERS FND	79234	460	12031	30	211				12	31			9003 00	270 09	8732 91
12	7	12	4	WATERS FND	79234	485	12039	30	211				12	31			8720 08	174 40	8545 68
12	8	12	4	WATERS FND	79234	499	12048	30	211				12	31			6748 20	134 96	6613 24

Fig. 125—Cash Requirements Statement.

as to procedure and documentation, and because it has a narrower money supply market.

4. Lease financing may involve the loss of valuable residual equities. In times of inflation this may be an important consideration.

There are times, of course, when lease financing is necessary or desirable. Some possible circumstances are these:

1. It may be the only means of acquiring use of an asset—the owner simply may not desire to sell.
2. Tax advantages may be realized; for example, where non-depreciable land is a high percentage of the asset cost.
3. Special service factors may exist. A lease contract, for example, may provide desired maintenance or other lower operating costs.
4. Joint ventures or similar arrangements may dictate the use of leases as a means of bringing several parties together into an economically sized unit.
5. It may be the only source of capital open to some companies by reason of debt restrictions.
6. Lease financing sources may provide capital, albeit at high rates, which is simply not available from traditional sources.

There are other reasons which make lease financing desirable. The objective in this brief review is to make the controller aware of some of the factors to be weighed in considering alternative financing proposals.

INTERNAL CONTROL

The accounts payable procedure is closely related to the procedures for cash disbursements and payroll. But a fundamentally sound routine for the recording of liabilities is basic to a well-founded disbursements procedure. The essence of the problem is to make certain that no improper liabilities are placed in line for payment. Routines must be instituted to see that all liabilities are properly certified or approved by designated authority. The proper comparison of receiving reports, purchase orders, and invoices by those handling the detail disbursement procedure eliminates many duties by the officers; but the liabilities not covered by these channels must have the necessary review. The controller or treasurer, for example, must approve the payrolls before payment. The chief purchasing agent, or chief engineer, treasurer, or some official must approve invoices for services, because no receiving report is issued. Certain special transactions may require the approval of the president. Again, invoices for such items should be checked against the voucher file for duplicate payments. In summary, the controller should consider the system of recording payables somewhat independently of the disbursements procedure to give added assurance that the necessary controls exist.

ACCOUNTING REPORTS ON LIABILITIES

Reports for the planning or control of liabilities are less frequent and less widely distributed than other reports. This condition may be due in part to the indication of the liability status in the monthly statement of financial condition.

Some suggested periodic reports useful to the chief executive and chief financial officer might include:

1. The projection of debt incurrence and repayment over several years —perhaps as part of the forecasting procedure. Such debt structure should be related also to the equity outstanding.
2. Periodic determination of outstanding obligation due under long-term lease arrangements.
3. Summarization of outstanding commitments under purchase orders, etc.
4. In periods of tight cash position, frequent runs of cash requirements by due dates to facilitate timely borrowings, etc. (see Fig. 125).
5. Reports on cash discounts earned or cash discounts lost.
6. Comparison of actual and budgeted obligations.
7. Detailed statement of liabilities by source, for credit purposes.

27

Control of Capital, Retained Earnings, and Reserves

CAPITAL AND RETAINED EARNINGS AS RELATED TO LIABILITIES

Control of liabilities was discussed in the preceding chapter. Such control is closely associated with control of capital and retained earnings, for both are related to the securing or retention of funds. Capital for expansion or improvements may be generated within the business, or derived from outside sources. Additional funds may be secured within the business from:

1. The net income of the business, after providing for all depreciation charges, interest, etc., and all dividend payments to stockholders, or
2. The excess of depreciation charges over and above the necessary replacements of existing facilities, or
3. Contraction of working capital through such means as reduced inventory levels resulting from better control, or reduced accounts receivable because of better collections, or
4. Sale of investments or fixed assets which are not essential to the operations.

When these sources are unable to meet the demand for capital, or whenever it is deemed unwise to use such means, then funds must be procured from new areas outside the business. Capital can be obtained by incurring short-term or long-term indebtedness, or by issuing capital stock—either common or preferred.

The maintenance of a sound financial structure, including the proper relationship of borrowed and equity capital, is an objective common to the control of both liabilities and capital.

DUTIES OF THE CONTROLLER

Planning and control of capital, retained earnings, and reserves do not require the same day-to-day vigilance which is desirable in the control of revenue, expenses, or cash, inventory, and other assets. This stems from the fact that the movement or activity in the net worth section is less frequent. On the other hand, the extent of changes in the equity section of the financial statement must be known so that the assets represented thereby may be most effectively used. The duties of financial planning and financial policy determination call for the exercise of sound judgment and a broad point of view.

The normal responsibilities of the controller with respect to equity include such functions as:

1. Application of sound accounting principles in properly recording and disclosing the facts as to capital, retained earnings, and appropriation of retained earnings
2. Forecasting and planning the capital requirements
3. Determination, in cooperation with the treasurer, of comparative costs of financing on various alternative bases
4. Establishment of the records which will provide the necessary information on a convenient and economical basis
5. Audit of accounts or transactions to determine compliance or noncompliance with instructions of the board of directors or other authority; e.g., the payment of dividends
6. Establishment of necessary internal control procedures
7. Preparation of necessary reports on capital, surplus, and reserves
8. General counseling on matters of financial policy

Some of these topics have been reviewed in other sections of this book; others are beyond its scope. The areas for applications of professional know-how have been listed so that the controller may be aware of what often can and should be done.

Aside from the specific duties and responsibilities listed above, it is highly desirable for the chief accounting officer to have a good working knowledge of equities and equity financing for use in possible acquisitions and mergers or other business combination problems with which he must deal. For this reason, a few of the fundamentals are briefly reviewed in the sections that follow.

CAPITAL STOCK

CLASSES OF CAPITAL STOCK

The capital stock of a corporation can be defined as the ownership interest. Such interest is divided into shares, and the ownership is evidenced by stock certificates. The more important basic rights of stockholders are:

1. To vote at the meetings of stockholders, thus participating in management
2. To participate in profits, in the form of dividends, as declared by the directors
3. To share in the distribution of assets in the event of dissolution
4. To subscribe to new issues of stock so as to protect their proportionate rights in the surplus and in the control of the corporation; this is known as the preemptive right

These rights are inherent in all shares of stock, but some classes of shareholders may give up certain rights and accept a subordinate position in respect to some matters. This gives rise to various classes of stock—principally common and preferred. The preferred stock may have preference as to (1) dividends, which may be cumulative or non-cumulative, or participating or non-participating; (2) assets in the event of liquidation; or (3) voting rights.

The controller should be familiar with the general features of different classes of capital stock, and, of course, be fully informed as to the specific provisions of each class of stock issued by his company. This would seem to be prerequisite to the maintenance of adequate records and to the fulfillment of his audit function as to compliance with the contract terms. He will have available the advice of counsel for all matters of a legal nature, but a general knowledge of the stock rights is necessary in judging when to seek assistance.

CAPITAL STOCK RECORDS

The primary concern of the controller in regard to capital stock is, quite naturally, the maintenance of the necessary records.

In the larger companies the stock ledgers and transfer records are kept by the transfer agent. The information relative to payment of dividends on outstanding shares, for example, is secured from this source. Under these circumstances a ledger control account for each class of stock is all that is necessary.

If a corporation conducts its own transfer department, then a separate ledger account must be maintained for each stockholder as to each class of stock. An illustrative form is show in Fig. 126. The ledger should contain the following information:

1. Name and address of holder with provision for address changes
2. Date of changes in holdings
3. Certificate numbers issued and surrendered
4. Number of shares in each transaction
5. Total number of shares held

Optional information might include a record of dividend payments.

| Name and Address | | | | | | | |
| Common | | John C. Doe
4161 Maxwell St.
Toledo 12, Ohio | | | | | |

Old Balance	Date	Page	Certificate No.		No. of Shares		New Balance
			Dr.	Cr.	Dr.	Cr.	
	Dec. 12, 1961	20		C 122		100	100
100	Jan. 16, 1962	31		C 196		50	150
150	Nov. 17, 1962	110	C 321		100		50

Fig. 126—Capital Stock Ledger Sheet.

The stock ledgers should be supported by registration and transfer records which give the details of each transaction. Transfer journals are not required in all states.

RETAINED EARNINGS, DIVIDENDS, AND APPROPRIATIONS OF RETAINED EARNINGS

NATURE OF THE PROBLEM

Proper treatment of capital stock presents no particular difficulties to the controller. His problems relating to the corporate net worth arise primarily in connection with retained earnings.

Management of the equity portion of the balance sheet outside of the capital stock account may be regarded as consisting of two major and related phases: (1) dividend policies and payments, and (2) appropriations or reserves. The problems associated with these subjects are complicated by the temptations of some managements to manipulate income through the use of reserves, and the necessity of complying with certain legislative requirements. While the controller does have certain duties in connection with the net worth, it remains, nevertheless, the ultimate responsibility of the board of directors to manage surplus so that the owners receive a fair return on their investment and the corporation has sufficient resources for its needs.

DIVIDEND POLICIES AND PAYMENTS

Generally the right to declare dividends rests with the board of directors. The directors must decide whether a dividend may be *legally* declared, and whether such action would be prudent from the *financial* point of view.

When a question as to the legality of a dividend declaration arises, the matter is one for the lawyers to settle; and the statute of the state of incorporation is the chief governing factor. As a generalization, however, dividends for a going business may be paid only out of accumulated earnings or profits; and such payments may not impair capital.

From the standpoint of financial policy, decisions must be reached with respect to at least three matters:

1. What should constitute the long-term dividend policy?
2. What policy should be followed with respect to current declarations?
3. What are the tax consequences of any given action?

The decision as to general dividend policy will be influenced by several factors, including the earnings history, dividend history, business outlook, working capital needs, fixed capital needs, nature of the stockholders, and effect of policy on the company's credit rating. The policy may be one of paying no dividends, or of paying regular cash dividends, regular and extra dividends, regular stock dividends, or only irregular dividends. Some basis exists for each of these policies. The short-term policy may be governed largely by the immediate availability of funds. For all of the problems which arise, the controller should marshal the available facts.

The actual payment of dividends creates no particular problem. In many companies this is handled by the transfer agent. It is well to retain a complete listing of the dividend payment made to each stockholder for each declaration. If dividends are unclaimed, the liability should remain recorded until the limitation period prescribed by law has passed. Then such unclaimed amounts should be either paid to the state under the escheat law, if applicable, or returned to retained earnings. The controller should assure himself that the dividend payment is made in accordance with the instructions of the board of directors.

RETAINED EARNINGS

The other phase of equity control, which is closely related to dividend policy, is the desirability of earmarking retained earnings for a particular purpose. It may be appropriated by the board of directors in accordance with the terms of a bond indenture or other contract, or simply as a conservative measure. The practical effect of the appropriation is to make a share of accumulated earnings unavailable for immediate dividend payments with the consequent retention of cash (or other assets). The amount of cash or other distributable assets is the principal factor in limiting the amount to be paid as dividends. However, some boards are of the opinion that the financial statements should show the extent to which accumulated earnings are not available for distribution by reason of specific reservations.

IMPROPER ACCUMULATION OF RETAINED EARNINGS

A matter of concern to the controller should be avoidance of any violation of Section 102 of the Internal Revenue Code. This section imposes a surtax or additional income tax, as a penalty, upon any corporation "formed or availed of for the purpose of preventing the imposition of the surtax upon its shareholders or the shareholders of any other corporation through the medium of permitting gains and profits to accumulate instead of being divided or distributed." The tax is measured by "undistributed section 102 net income." This may be defined as the corporate net income less the following items:

1. Corporate income taxes (excluding the surtax on improper accumulation of surplus)
2. Charitable contributions which are in excess of that allowed as a deduction from gross income
3. Disallowed capital losses

The basic question is whether earnings have been permitted to accumulate beyond the reasonable needs of the company. While the regulation is a cause of alarm to some, the evidence indicates that to date, at least, the law has been administered with a considerable degree of tolerance. It should not be the cause, therefore, of dividend declarations by companies with a bona fide need for retaining funds for expansion. If funds are retained for expansion purposes, a basic test would appear to be the existence of a definite and bona fide program for such purposes. It probably cannot be only a general idea or intent.

Another consideration is the liquidity of the business. There has been some evidence that the courts have relied on the *amount* of retained earnings as a measure of improper accumulation. In one case [1] the dissenting opinion points out that liquidity should be the essential test to determine whether a company is retaining profits beyond the reasonable needs of its business. It would appear that the makeup of the assets of the corporation should be considered, among other things. Whether the courts will do this is another matter.

Corporate management will want to review the matter with its counsel if there is any question about violation of Section 102. However, the controller may wish to keep in mind that a corporation paying some dividends may be in a much better position defense-wise than a company paying none. Also, he may suggest that the minutes of the board contain at least a general

---

[1] World Publishing Company v. U.S., 169 F.2d 186 (C.A. 10th 1948), *affirming* 72 F. Supp. 886 (N.D. Okla. 1947).

statement as to its thinking if the profits are to be retained and not distributed. It is the responsibility of the controller to keep his management and board informed on this subject.

RETAINED EARNINGS—TAX BASIS

In the face of the tremendous impact of income taxes on a company and on individuals, another problem for the controller is the proper treatment of earnings from the tax viewpoint. Just the reverse of the improper accumulation of earnings is the danger of dividend payments which in fact constitute a return of capital. This does not reveal itself in ordinary accounting because the official records reflect retained earnings. However, because of differing treatment of transactions for tax purposes and book purposes, a deficit might exist, and the dividends would be tax-free in whole or in part. Therefore, it is desirable that a "tax balance sheet" be maintained so that the tax status of retained earnings is fully known, and dividends are properly handled—from the tax viewpoint of the shareholders.

EMPLOYMENT OF RESERVES TO EQUALIZE INCOME

The management team is made up of human beings. As such, it may want to show improvement and progress, and may wish to resort to book-keeping changes to accomplish this. The controller may find that management may be tempted to equalize income through the use of reserves. The creation of surplus reserves by a charge to surplus and an ultimate transfer back to surplus—with the actual loss appearing in the income and expense statement when it is definite—is not subject to question here. It is book-keeping manipulations affecting the income account which are the topic of this discussion.

Such practices bring discredit upon the controller and the accounting profession in several ways. The controller would be issuing a statement which would not reflect the facts—the true earnings—and third parties could be injured thereby. Aside from this, such action would reduce the value of the income statement generally. Further, public confidence in financial statements would be undermined even more than it is now. It is therefore incumbent upon the controller to resist pressure for any such action.

The chief accounting official may run abreast of the problem in at least two ways. First, there can be the request that normal operating reserves be adjusted from month to month, depending upon the profits. The reserve for inventory adjustments, for example, might be the object of heavy provision in a month of high profits and reversals or low provision in a month of low profits or losses. Again, at the year-end, unwarranted reserves may be created by charges against the income account.

Improper accounting as to reserves can show itself in at least three ways:

1. Reserve provisions for future contingencies, created largely at the whim of the management, may be charged to current income
2. Reserves created out of income in one year may be used to absorb charges of another year, thus creating a second distortion of income
3. Reserves may be credited directly to income, and may be later used to absorb losses; or may be transferred directly to surplus

The use of such reserves to equalize income is a practice condemned by all reputable accountants. This is not to state that any known losses should not be recognized and unknown losses provided for. The importance attached, correctly or incorrectly, to the "net income per share" is such that the controller should see that it is significant as to his company.

ACCOUNTING TREATMENT OF RESERVES

The use of reserves to equalize income involves the matter of intent. Quite separate from the tendency of some managements to attempt this practice is the much broader problem of the proper accounting treatment of reserves. The basic accounting consideration is whether such reserves may be used to increase net income in some other accounting period. It is acceptable accounting practice to provide, by charges against current income, for all foreseeable costs and losses applicable against current revenue, to the extent that they can be measured and allocated to fiscal periods with reasonable approximation. The test for accepted accounting practice is then twofold: (1) Is the charge proper against current income? (2) Is the cost measurable?

For some purposes, reserves may be divided into two classes—those which are provided in accordance with accepted accounting practice as above defined, and those additional reserves created in the discretion of management as a matter of conservative business policy. The question arises as to how certain reserves fit into this category, and how they are to be treated. One group is general contingency reserves.

Accounting Research Bulletin No. 43 issued by the Committee on Accounting Procedure of the American Institute of Certified Public Accountants well states the prevailing view on Contingency Reserves:

1. The purpose of this chapter is to consider problems which arise in the accounting treatment of two types of reserves whose misuse may be the means of either arbitrarily reducing income or shifting income from one period to another:
   (a) General contingency reserves whose purposes are not specific;
   (b) Reserves designed to set aside a part of current profits to absorb losses feared or expected in connection with inventories on hand or future purchases of inventory.

2. Charges to provide, either directly or by use of a reserve, for losses due to obsolescence or deterioration of inventory or for reducing an inventory to market, or for reducing an inventory to a recognized basis such as last-in first-out or its equivalent in accordance with an announced change in policy to be consistently followed thereafter, are not under consideration here.

3. If a provision for a reserve, made against income, is not properly chargeable to current revenues, net income for the period is understated by the amount of the provision. If a reserve so created is used to relieve the income of subsequent periods of charges that would otherwise be made against it, the income of such subsequent periods is thereby overstated. By use of the reserve in this manner, profit for a given period may be significantly increased or decreased by mere whim. As a result of this practice the integrity of financial statements is impaired, and the statements tend to be misleading.

4. The committee recognizes the character of the income statement as a tentative installment in the record of long-time financial results, and is aware of the tendency to exaggerate the significance of the net income for a single year. Nevertheless, there still exist the responsibility for determining net income as fairly as possible by sound methods consistently applied and the duty to show it clearly. In accomplishing these objectives, it is deemed desirable to provide, by charges in the current income statement, properly classified, for all foreseeable costs and losses applicable against current revenues, to the extent that they can be measured and allocated to fiscal periods with reasonable approximation.

5. Accordingly, inventories on hand or contracted for should be priced in accordance with principles stated elsewhere by the committee. When inventories which have been priced in accordance with those principles are further written down by a charge to income, either directly or through the use of a reserve, current revenues are not properly matched with applicable costs, and charges to future operations are correspondingly reduced. This process results in the shifting of profits from one period to another in violation of the principle that reserves should not be used for the purpose of equalizing reported income.

6. It has been argued with respect to inventories that losses which will have to be taken in periods of receding price levels have their origins in periods of rising prices, and that therefore reserves to provide for future price declines should be created in periods of rising prices by charges against the operations of those periods. Reserves of this kind involve assumptions as to what future price levels will be, what inventory quantities will be on hand if and when a major price decline takes place, and finally whether loss to the business will be measured by the amount of the decline in prices. The bases for such assumptions are so uncertain that any conclusions drawn from them would generally seem to be speculative guesses rather than informed judgments. When estimates of this character are included in current costs, amounts representing mere conjecture are combined with others representing reasonable approximations.

7. The committee is therefore of the opinion that reserves such as those created:

    (a) for general undetermined contingencies, or

    (b) for any indefinite possible future losses, such as, for example, losses on inventories not on hand or contracted for, or

    (c) for the purpose of reducing inventories other than to a basis which is in accordance with generally accepted accounting principles, or

(d) without regard to any specific loss reasonably related to the operations of the current period, or

(e) in amounts not determined on the basis of any reasonable estimates of costs or losses

are of such a nature that charges or credits relating to such reserves should not enter into the determination of net income.

8. Accordingly, it is the opinion of the committee that if a reserve of the type described in paragraph 7 is set up:

(a) it should be created by a segregation or appropriation of earned surplus,

(b) no costs or losses should be charged to it and no part of it should be transferred to income or in any way used to affect the determination of net income for any year,

(c) it should be restored to earned surplus directly when such a reserve or any part thereof is no longer considered necessary, and

(d) it should preferably be classified in the balance sheet as a part of shareholders' equity.

RESERVES AND THE TAX LAWS

Under the federal tax law, certain deductions are allowable as "ordinary and necessary expenses paid or incurred" or as reductions in gross income. The fundamental purpose of the law is to tax a taxpayer on his actual income. Devices which arbitrarily or otherwise change this "actual" income are not permitted. In general, this means that accounting reserves are not recognized, except:

1. By specific permission in the statute, such as a "reasonable addition to the reserve for bad debts," or

2. Where all the transactions used in determining the reserve have been consummated during the year, or

3. Where the reserve method would be implicit in the practice allowed, such as the valuation of inventories.

The general rule with respect to reserves, other than the three exceptions mentioned, is that the expenses or losses may be deducted only in the accounting period when they actually accrue and are chargeable to the reserve.

As a word of caution, the controller should make a careful distinction between permissible reserves and denied reserves under the tax law. The reserves should be kept "pure," for the inclusion of non-allowable items in a permissible reserve might lead to a denial of all credits to the reserve.

REPORTS ON OWNERSHIP INTEREST

There appears to be little need for additional periodic reports on the net worth section of the statement of financial condition beyond the preparation of the basic financial statement itself and the related analysis of retained earnings, etc. Such reports as are prepared probably will be special in nature and rather infrequent.

Suggestive of useful information for management are the following:

1. Comparative data showing industry and principal competitors' trends as to
   a. Return on net worth
   b. Per share earnings
   c. Per share cash flow
   d. Percentage growth in net worth or book value
   e. Market price and price earnings ratio per share
2. Stock purchases in relationship to sinking fund requirement or other objective, including number of shares, average price, and treasury shares available
3. Trend of return on shareholder equity
4. Projection of equity financing and status in five-year forecast, etc.
5. Effect on shareholder interests of proposed mergers, acquisitions, or other financing

PART V

Accounting Reports – Principles and Applications

28

Internal Managerial Reports

MAKING THE INFORMATION EFFECTIVE

Perhaps it may seem unnecessary to discuss at any length the importance of statement or report presentation. Yet costs will not be controlled, sales effort will not be directed into the proper channels, and profit planning will not be effective unless the facts are presented to executives and supervisors in such a manner that they can understand them, and will act upon them. Merely to present the facts is not enough. These facts must be understood; their significance must be realized by the management team. Yes, the management must be motivated.

It is in this field, perhaps, that the accountant has performed less successfully than in others. A great deal of the reporting done by him has been unsatisfactory. Facts have been poorly presented. There has been a tendency to submit mere tabulations or schedules. Little or no attempt has been made to summarize, to digest, or to interpret the data. The information must be refined and highlighted to provide the basis for executive action. If this is not done, the loss is double. The cost of preparing the data is a total waste; and the corrective action is not taken for lack of necessary information.

Too often the controller may feel that the department managers should come to him if they want information. He would be superhuman if he could anticipate all needs. But he should take the initiative, to the extent practicable, in providing information which he feels is pertinent. Very often, he will be able to suggest a report better in scope and content than those requesting the data might have in mind. Certainly he should possess this capability since reporting techniques is one of his specialties. The successful controller cannot sit in his office and wait for others to ask for information. He cannot consider his work done when the figures are recorded in the books and the statements are issued. This is only the beginning.

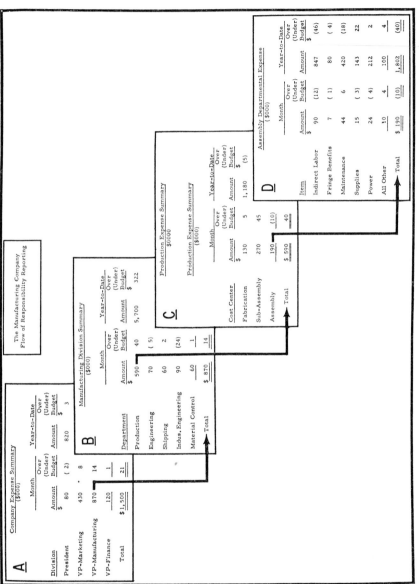

Fig. 127—Responsibility Reporting—Flow of Information.

FIVE BASIC PRINCIPLES OF REPORT PREPARATION

In preparing effective reports for internal management purposes, there are certain general principles which the controller should observe. Some of these principles are basic to sound management reporting; others may be regarded as subsidiary or supplemental. These basic and overriding guidelines are five in number.

1. The "Responsibility" Concept Should Be Employed. Under responsibility reporting, the dissemination of facts and figures concerning revenues and costs relates to the segment of the organization being reported upon. The communication concerns costs and/or revenues which can be controlled by the person being reported upon, or which are attributable to his efforts. Such a system avoids allocation of costs for *control* purposes to any organizational unit which does not control them and cannot be held accountable for them.

The principle is illustrated in Fig. 127 relative to a simplified *expense* structure wherein the reporting follows the organizational chart. Since the president is accountable for the *entire* business, he would receive an expense summary segregated by the functions incurring such expenses, and assignable to the individual whom he holds responsible—item A in the illustration. In this case, his own departmental expenses are compared with budget, as are those of each vice-president who reports to him.

The vice-president for manufacturing receives a summary of expense performance for each organizational segment reporting to him—shown as item B in Fig. 127. In turn, the production superintendent receives a summary on the three cost centers—item C—for which he is accountable. Finally, the departmental foreman is informed on his cost performance in detail by type of expense as reflected in item D on Fig. 127.

Each manager may secure such further detailed reports as he desires on each area for which he is assigned responsibility, authority, or accountability.

2. The "Exception" Principle Should Be Applied As Much As Possible. Generally speaking, for control purposes, the out-of-the-ordinary operations should be emphasized. As the scope of a function expands, the responsible executive cannot oversee, check, or follow up on every detail. Therefore, the reporting must distinguish between those things that are progressing satisfactorily and those that need attention—the "exceptions." On such a basis, normal or routine situations do not receive prominence, and the executive need not waste time plowing through the detail of operations which are "on-course." As an example, perhaps performance which exceeds budget by more than 5% should be reported upon, and not every deviation.

3. In General, Figures Should Be Comparative. Actual performance data alone usually are of little significance. Rather, actual must be compared with a target or reasonable yardstick. Comparison with budget, standards, or past performance is necessary.

As a corollary, significant trends and relationships should be revealed. Signals as to what should be done or what requires attention are desirable. For example, it is one thing to report that warehouse labor costs were $10,000 for the month, and quite another to indicate that such total labor cost has steadily increased despite a decline in physical volume handled.

4. To the Extent Practical, Data Should Be Increasingly in Summary Form for Each Successively Higher Level of Management. It is perhaps obvious that the kind of information needed by a salesman differs from that to be furnished the sales manager. With a broad area of responsibility, the sales manager cannot look at every detail on each territory. As a general rule, reports should tend to a minimum of information rather than a maximum. Further, the communication should be long enough to get the story across—and no longer. As a matter of fact, it might be advantageous to commence each report with a summary, and allow the remainder to be supporting detail which need not be read in its entirety.

5. Reports Generally Should Include Interpretative Commentary or Be Self-Explanatory. The primary purpose of a report is to *communicate* ideas. Anyone in the accounting profession soon learns the significance of the figures; but this is not true for many other functions. Consequently, it is usually desirable that commentary direct the attention of the reader to the important happenings and help him understand the data presented. Interpretative remarks explain the "why" of the situation, and very often indicate action taken or to be taken to correct an out-of-line condition.

SOME SUPPLEMENTARY CONSIDERATIONS

The above five principles are, in the opinion of the authors, rather fundamental to a good financial reporting system. In addition, there are some other factors which will assist in getting an improved reception from the reader. These include the points described below.

1. Reports Should Be Timely. The frequency of issuance should be determined with care, and once a decision is reached, the reporting should be prompt. A late report is almost as useless as no report at all. Regular reports should be presented on a definite schedule. Often it will be found desirable to issue "flash" reports rather than wait for the final and exact figures. Controllers should perhaps consider first the preparation of the control reports, and then the completion of the accounting process.

2. Reports Should Be Simple and Clear. They should be so designed that the reader will be able to secure all the essential facts with a minimum of effort. Technical accounting language should be avoided. Complicated statements should be omitted. Simplicity and clarity are requisites of all useful reports.

3. Reports Should Be Expressed in Language and Terms Familiar to the Executive Who Will Use Them. For example, tons, man-hours, and machine operating hours are likely to be more expressive terms to production executives than dollar costs of manufacturing. A statement that raw materials remain in the storerooms on an average of 90 days after time of receipt is likely to be more expressive than a turnover figure.

4. Information Should Be Presented in Logical Sequence. Just as displays attempt to show articles in natural surroundings or in use, so also a logical pattern should be followed in report presentation. Perhaps the sequence of operations should be followed in a labor report. Again, a statement of changes in financial position should indicate, first, what the significant changes are, and, next, the cause.

5. Reports Must Be Accurate. The information must be dependable and sufficiently accurate to satisfy the purpose of the report. Errors on reports result in a lack of confidence in them—and in the accounting department.

6. The Form of Presentation Should Be Suited to the Executive Who Will Use It. Statistical, graphical, or narrative form, or a combination of these, may be used, depending on the desires and aptitudes of the men who will use the report.

7. Reports Should Be Standardized Wherever Possible. To the extent consistent with the other rules of reporting, the style, design, and size of the report should be standardized. It is desirable, for example, that all plants of a company use a similar labor report. Further, when a report has been standardized, it is desirable to make changes only infrequently. The operating people become accustomed to a certain style, and a change may cause confusion for a time.

8. The Report Design Should Reflect the Viewpoint of the Executive. This requirement is quite inclusive. To begin with, the extent of responsibility and level of supervision must be considered. Those supervisors far away from the scene of operations may require quite different information from those on the spot. The general executives are interested in general movements; the departmental executives, in the departmental performance; and the lower echelon of supervision, in the performance of individuals.

In all cases the information should be presented through the eyes of the executive, and not the accountant.

9. Reports Must Be Useful. That a report should be useful to the executive for whom it is prepared may seem self-evident. Yet, there is a tendency in some quarters to insist on "accepted form and in accordance with accepted accounting practice." For external reports, for final audited statements for creditors, stockholders, and governmental divisions this is desirable. But there should be no hesitancy in disregarding such methods in the preparation of periodic reports for managerial purposes when it is apparent that other means will provide more useful managerial data.

10. The Cost of Report Preparation Should Be Considered. Under ordinary circumstances the preparation of reports should be a natural process or step in the regular accounting and statistical work. But the cost of special reports should not be overlooked. Where such reports are interesting but have no particular value, the cost of preparation should be weighed in relation to the benefit. Again, when simple sketches will do the trick equally effectively, expensive artwork is to be avoided.

11. The Care Taken in Preparing a Report Should Be Commensurate with Its Use. While *all* reports should be accurate and dependable, the more important a report, the greater the degree of care that should be exercised. Reports going to top executives should be double-checked, as important policy decisions may be made on the basis of information contained therein.

TYPES OF INTERNAL MANAGEMENT REPORTS

It may be well to consider the types of internal management reports which a controller may be called upon to prepare, before discussing some of the detailed phases of report preparation. Although reports can be grouped in any one of several classifications, a very practical basis is according to their function or purpose. From experience, every controller knows that reports may fall into three groups: (1) planning reports, (2) control reports, and (3) informational reports. Planning reports deal with anticipated programs as to future operations or financial condition. As the name implies, control reports are intended to assist in the control of operations or the business by indicating areas which need corrective action. Informational reports are of a broader scope and use in that they are intended to present and interpret facts for management to use in planning and policy determination.

The distinction among these three kinds of reports is not a mere academic nicety. By recognizing the difference in purpose, the controller can plan a better system of reports. Differences in purpose result in differences in content, timing, and design. Stated more positively, the controller must know the purpose of the report before preparing it. One purpose may require one kind of cost, for example, out-of-pocket costs; another purpose may need another type of cost. It is difficult for one trained in accounting to realize how easy it is for some executives with other backgrounds to draw unwarranted or incorrect conclusions from a very routine accounting statement. By recognizing the differences in planning, control, and informational reports, the controller will be more careful in his interpretations and in limiting the use to which reports will be put—to the extent that he can.

A brief outline of possible subdivisions of this threefold report classification follows.

Planning Reports

1. *Short-range Corporate-wide or Division-wide Forecasts.* Such reports deal with relatively broad sections of the company, either the entire operation, or a major segment, and project results and conditions for a relatively short period of time—usually one year or less. Examples of such short-range planning reports are:
   a. Statement of Estimated Income and Expense
   b. Statement of Estimated Cash Flow
   c. Statement of Budgeted Capital Expenditures
   d. Statement of Estimated Financial Condition
   These projections or programs would be prepared on a regular time schedule.

2. *Special Short-range Planning Studies of Particular Segments of the Business.* This grouping is intended to include those special studies of particularly troublesome or substandard segments on which planning attention must be focused to arrive at a suitable program. It encompasses all special studies which deal with only limited functions or geographical areas of the business. Such analyses as these might fit into this category:
   a. Product distribution in Y territory
   b. Compensation of salesmen
   c. Warehouse handling expense—Cleveland, Ohio
   d. Expansion in the naphthalene market
   e. Computer applications for credit cards
   f. Plant location study for Los Angeles

3. *Long-range Forecasts.* Such studies must be rather general or "broad brush" in nature. They would include five or even ten or more years' projections of the company's activities over-all or in particular areas or fields. Such studies very often are the result of joint effort with either the company's sales department or economic research groups. The controller's department would be involved in forecasting the effect of proposed plans on future capital investment, cash availability, operating results. For the company or

major divisions, or even smaller segments, the reports while less detailed would be somewhat similar in nature to those included in the short-range planning reports.

Control Reports

1. *Summary Control Reports.* These reports summarize the performance over a period of time, usually a month, and serve at least two useful functions: they inform higher management of the general effectiveness of performance, and they act as a check against the current control reports. Generally speaking, the current control reports should be reconciled with the summary control reports which "tie into" the financial statements. Since timeliness is a factor, some small differences are expected. Examples of summary control reports include:

   a. Statement of actual and budgeted income and expense
   b. Statement of income and expense by products
   c. Comparison of actual and budgeted sales by territory
   d. Divisional or departmental summary cost reports
   e. Summary of excess manufacturing costs by responsibility
   f. Monthly statement of inventories
   g. Monthly aging of accounts receivable

2. *Current Control Reports.* These are reports, issued hourly, daily, or weekly, which point out deviations from planned or standard performance. The objective is prompt corrective action before large losses develop. Examples of this type of report include:

   a. Daily or weekly reports on sales by product, compared to quota or forecast
   b. Daily or weekly reports on scrap or excess material usage
   c. Hourly, daily, or weekly labor reports comparing actual and standard man-hours
   d. Monthly (or semimonthly) departmental expense statements of actual and budgeted expenses
   e. Weekly reports on cash receipts, disbursements, and balances compared to objective

Informational Reports

1 *Trend Reports.* These reports compare the results of an activity or a condition over a period of months or years to point out changes in growth or composition. They may be expressed as ratios, as in Chapter 5, or in units. Trend reports cover a wide area, and may relate to any income or cost items as well as assets, liabilities, and net worth in the balance sheet; or they may present relationships over a period of time, such as percentage of selling expense to net sales.

2. *Analytical Reports.* For want of a better term, the other broad category of informational presentations is referred to as analytical reports. Essentially, analytical reports deal, not especially with successive periods of time as do trend reports, but more particularly with a limited time period and with reference to the composition or makeup of an item. Some illustrations of analytical reports include:

a. Analysis of changes in gross profit
b. Analysis of sales by customer or product
c. Analysis of excess manufacturing costs
d. Analysis of changes in financial condition
e. Determination of break-even points
f. Determination of marginal income by products

Other classifications of reports can be made, but the most important distinction for a controller to make is between reports for control purposes and those for policy and planning purposes. Quite often both types will be used in arriving at decisions.

CONTENT OF REPORTS

The contents of an accounting report obviously will depend upon the needs of the situation. It may be a routine weekly report, or it may be a special report dealing with a particular phase of the business. The purpose of the report, the personalities of those who receive it, the subject—all these factors permit a great deal of latitude in content. While a statement of principles may be somewhat repetitious, it would seem that the content should:

1. Be restricted to the essential facts
2. Indicate comparisons, or trends and relationships
3. Indicate areas where improvements or changes should be made

A primary requirement, of course, is to report matters that need reporting. A vast amount of information is accumulated in the accounting records. The clerk in the corner of the factory, for example, may be busily recording facts which show the company is grossly overstocked with a certain kind of paint; or that certain items in the inventory are slow-moving. While this information is in the records, if it doesn't get into an effective report, it might as well never have been recorded. Reports must bring to the attention of management conditions which need correction.

FREQUENCY OF REPORTS

The frequency with which reports should be issued also depends on the needs of the occasion. If the situation is particularly critical or unsatisfactory, then reports would be issued more frequently than otherwise. The level of responsibility of the executive is a factor, too. Major executives,

The Airconditioning Company
OPERATING RESULTS

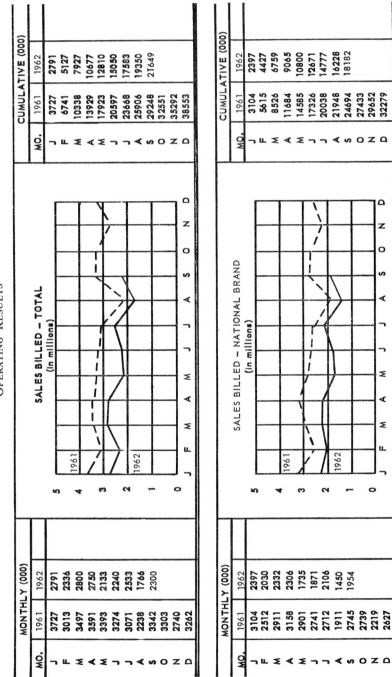

SALES BILLED – TOTAL (In millions)

MONTHLY (000)

MO.	1961	1962
J	3727	2791
F	3013	2336
M	3497	2800
A	3591	2750
M	3393	2133
J	3274	2240
J	3071	2533
A	2238	1766
S	3342	2300
O	3303	
N	2740	
D	3262	

CUMULATIVE (000)

MO.	1961	1962
J	3727	2791
F	6741	5127
M	10338	7927
A	13929	10677
M	17923	12810
J	20597	15050
J	23668	17583
A	25906	19350
S	29248	21649
O	32551	
N	35292	
D	38553	

SALES BILLED – NATIONAL BRAND (In millions)

MONTHLY (000)

MO.	1961	1962
J	3104	2397
F	2512	2030
M	2911	2332
A	3158	2306
M	2901	1735
J	2741	1871
J	2712	2106
A	1911	1450
S	2745	1954
O	2739	
N	2219	
D	2627	

CUMULATIVE (000)

MO.	1961	1962
J	3104	2397
F	5615	4427
M	8526	6759
A	11684	9065
M	14585	10800
J	17326	12671
J	20038	14777
A	21948	16228
S	24694	18182
O	27433	
N	29652	
D	32279	

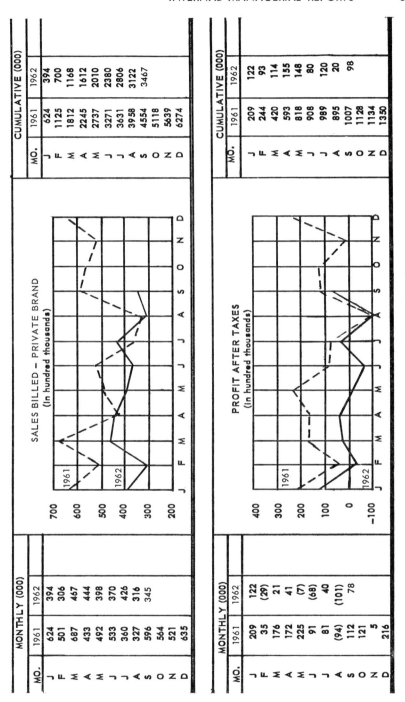

Fig. 128—Graphs Supported by Related Statistics.

SALES BILLED — PRIVATE BRAND
(In hundred thousands)

MONTHLY (000)		
MO.	1961	1962
J	624	394
F	501	306
M	687	467
A	433	444
M	492	398
J	533	370
J	360	426
A	327	316
S	596	345
O	564	
N	521	
D	635	

CUMULATIVE (000)		
MO.	1961	1962
J	624	394
F	1125	700
M	1812	1168
A	2245	1612
M	2737	2010
J	3271	2380
J	3631	2806
A	3958	3122
S	4554	3467
O	5118	
N	5639	
D	6274	

PROFIT AFTER TAXES
(In hundred thousands)

MONTHLY (000)		
MO.	1961	1962
J	209	122
F	35	(29)
M	176	21
A	172	41
M	225	(7)
J	91	(68)
J	81	40
A	(94)	(101)
S	112	78
O	121	
N	5	
D	216	

CUMULATIVE (000)		
MO.	1961	1962
J	209	122
F	244	93
M	420	114
A	593	155
M	818	148
J	908	80
J	989	120
A	895	20
S	1007	98
O	1128	
N	1134	
D	1350	

on the one hand, require monthly reports, with quarterly and yearly summaries. Some minor executives, on the other hand, such as foremen, may require daily reports of the performance of their men. In general, the higher the level of responsibility, the less frequently the report is required.

FORM OF ACCOUNTING REPORTS

The form of the accounting report is to some extent determined by the content. Aside from this, a primary consideration is the preference of the executives who use them. Some prefer more statistical detail than others; some prefer graphic presentation. In many cases the controller may have to experiment with the best method.

The chief accounting official, and all of the financial-accounting management for that matter, have available a rather wide selection of communication media in presenting the financial facts and figures of the business. The following summary outline indicates the principal forms that accounting reports might take:

1. *Written*
   a. Tabular
      1) Formal accounting statements
      2) Statistical
   b. Expository or narrative
   c. Pictorial—graphic
   d. A combination of all or some of the above

2. *Oral*
   a. Formal group presentations; these may include the use of visual aids
   b. Individual conferences

Before reviewing reporting principles or examples for each of the various levels of management, some remarks on the non-tabular techniques which are perhaps in less than optimum use, may be helpful.

GRAPHIC PRESENTATION

The employment of graphs is becoming more widespread in presenting financial information. The principal advantage of graphic presentation for numerical data is the ease with which trends and relationships between figures may be more readily visualized. Charts and similar devices minimize the time which management must spend to grasp significant relationships or trouble spots. On the other hand, graphs do not readily permit the determination of a precise amount. Where the exact figure is desired, therefore, it is often desirable to accompany the charts with the related statistical tables. This technique is illustrated in Fig. 128.

COST AND EXPENSES AS PER CENT OF SALES

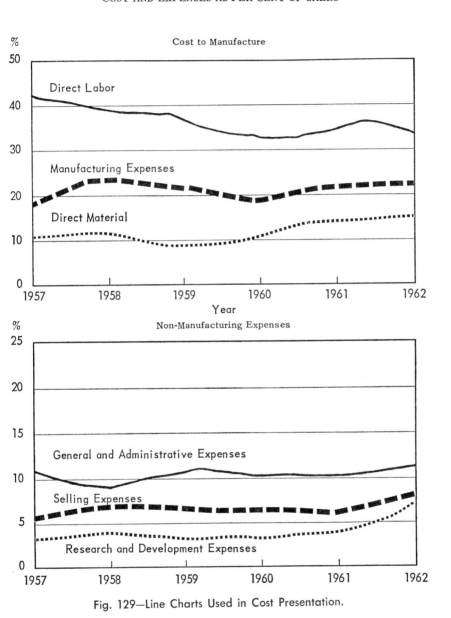

Fig. 129—Line Charts Used in Cost Presentation.

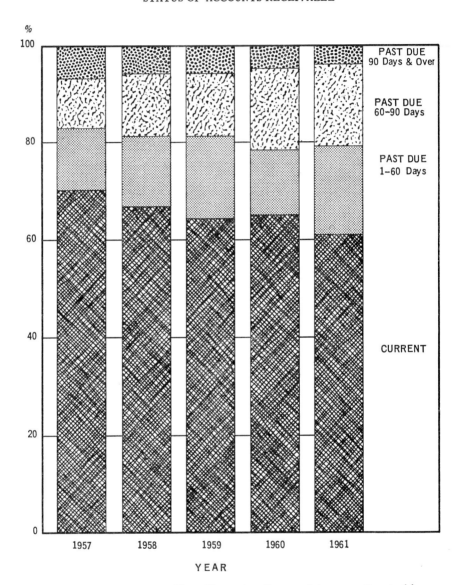

Fig. 130—Percentage Bar Chart Illustrating Status of Accounts Receivable.

There are any number of methods for presenting statistical data in visual form, and the reader is referred to the many excellent texts on the subject. In summary, however, graphs may be divided into the following groups:

1. *Line or Curve Charts.* Variations in the data are indicated by means of a line or curve. The scale may be arithmetic, semilogarithmic or logarithmic ruling. Straight lines (as in Fig. 129) or bands (as in Fig. 142) may be employed.

2. *Bar Charts.* The absolute bar charts contrast quantities by comparison of bars of varying length but uniform width. Simple percentage bar charts are constructed in a similar fashion, except that the length of the bar represents a percentage. Component bar charts may be used, wherein the bars are of the same width and length representing 100%, and the size of each segment indicates the per cent of the total figure (as in Fig. 130).

3. *Area Diagrams.* This technique contrasts quantities by comparing figures with varying areas. The most popular type is the pie chart, illustrated in Fig. 131.

4. *Solid Diagrams.* These diagrams consist of geometric forms (cubes, spheres, cylinders, etc.) used to illustrate comparison of magnitudes through a comparison of volumes of the figures—and not the height or length of the figures. Accurate comparisons are therefore difficult to make.

5. *Map Graphs.* This method presents in pictorial form the facts in a geographic distribution.

The most simple and common types of graphic presentation for use with financial data are the line and bar charts. Figure 129 readily indicates the trend of the selected cost elements in relationship to sales. A component bar chart is used in Fig. 132 to reveal the trend of sales, costs, and income. The relative composition of accounts receivable is well illustrated by the use of a percentage bar chart in Fig. 130.

Charts will be found effective as an aid in oral presentation.

Some companies follow a plan wherein a book of charts is maintained for either the entire top-management echelon or for each executive in the group. A more common practice, perhaps, is the condition wherein each individual executive maintains those particular charts which he finds most useful.

"FLASH" REPORTS

Timeliness is often very important in the usefulness of financial figures. It is, therefore, found desirable in many instances to provide information which is largely, but not entirely, complete so that appropriate action may be taken. The dissemination of such data may mean a sacrificing of accuracy, and the use of estimates instead of actual results, where such estimates will not impair the utility of the data. Such reports often are called "flash"

GROSS PROFIT

BY PRODUCT LINE

For the Twelve Months Ended November 30, 1962

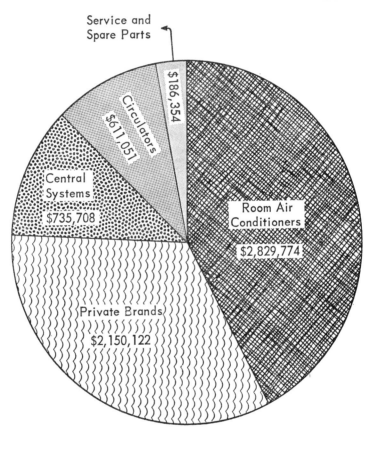

Product	% of Total
Room Air Conditioners	43.7
Private Brand	33.2
Central Systems	11.4
Air Circulators	9.4
Service and Spare Parts	2.9
	100.0

Fig. 131—Pie Chart Illustrating Analysis of Gross Profit.

reports and may be employed in a variety of circumstances. The monthly operating results in summary form—when sales volume, standard costs, and perhaps major variances are known—is an example of a quick report to meet the needs of top management. A handwritten report, in lieu of a type-written one, may suffice. A "flash" income statement indicating the *reason* for the results is illustrated in Fig. 133.

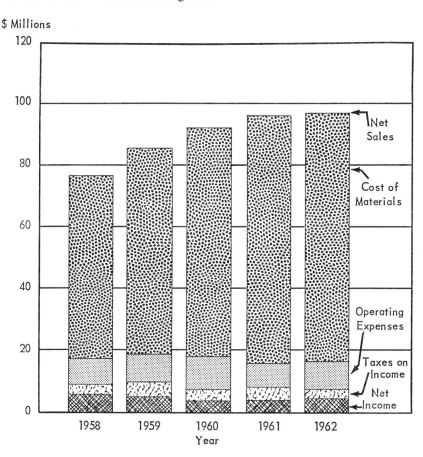

Fig. 132—Vertical Bar Chart Used to Depict Operating Results.

ORAL REPORTS

Oral communication is a very important phase of the reporting function. It can be appreciated that such personal contact permits a great saving of management time by the opportunity afforded to point out significant trends and relationships. Moreover, very often it assures proper interpretation of the numerical data.

GENERAL OIL COMPANY

FLASH REPORT - CONSOLIDATED NET INCOME

H. O. Corp. Acctg.   *October, 1962*   Confidential

November 4, 1962

(Thousands of Dollars)	Prior Month	Current Month Actual	Better/(Worse) Than Forecast	Better/(Worse) Than Last Year	Year-to-Date Actual 1962	Better/(Worse) Than 1961
1. Western Division	(2,475)	(2,200)	(1,748)	(1,012)	(9,048)	402
2. Southern Division	2,938	3,100	(100)	88	35,860	2,833
European Division	1,548	1,700	(247)	(333)	11,728	(12,272)
Arabian Oil Company	17	10	(83)	33	(881)	(724)
French African Division	(22)	(15)	(15)	(15)	(166)	(166)
3. Total European Operations	1,543	1,695	(345)	(315)	10,681	(13,172)
4. Foreign Expl. & Prod. Div.	(1,143)	(246)	119	131	(4,354)	(746)
5. Tanker Operations	(170)	(516)	(278)	(118)	(2,594)	(279)
6. Export Operations	82	146	(26)	(12)	1,331	(100)
7. Home Office	(982)	(1,039)	(42)	(284)	(10,257)	(2,994)
8. Other Subsidiaries	38	21	211	(90)	1,109	(589)
9. Consolidated Net Income	(769)	967	(2,209)	(1,612)	22,728	(14,635)
10. Preferred Dividend	311	309		(72)	3,444	(792)
11. Consol. Net Income applicable to Common	(480)	658	(2,209)	(1,684)	19,284	(15,427)
Per Share	$(.40)	$ .05	$ (.16)	$ (.11)	$ 1.41	$ (.99)

Consolidated Net Income - October - $967,000 - equal to $.05 per share after preferred dividend. October results below current forecasted income by $2,209,000. Net income - 10 months' operations - $22,728,000 - equal to $1.41 per common share.

Western Division - October loss - $2,200,000 - result of crude unit shutdown and further weakening of gasoline prices to a new low for the year.

Southern Division - income for October - $3,100,000 - under estimate by $100,000. Producing days in Texas were 8 (forecast - 9) with resulting lower crude and liquids production.

European Division Income - $1,700,000 - up slightly over prior month - below forecast by $247,000 - increased book depreciation charges due to revision of reserves.

Tanker Operations - loss for October - $516,000 - above forecasted loss by $278,000 - due primarily to revised schedule for deliveries.

Fig. 133—"Flash" Report of Consolidated Net Income.

Typical occasions for the use of oral reports by the controller, including visual aids, are the review of monthly operating results; or annual review of the forecast for the next year. Members of the controller's staff also may discuss monthly cost and profit results at various departmental meetings or may be present at such conferences to answer questions concerning costs.

Aside from group conferences, a discussion between the controller and individual executives should prove beneficial to a better understanding of the facts and figures. And in the field of oral communications, mere *availability* of the chief accounting official and his staff is an important consideration in the effective exercise of the controllership function.

29

Applications of Internal Managerial Reports

REPORTS FOR THE BOARD OF DIRECTORS

Now that the generalizations or basic considerations in report preparation have largely been covered, some applications to the various executive levels may prove helpful.

There is a great deal of variation between companies as to information presented to the board of directors. This may stem in large part from (1) differences in composition of the board, or (2) differences in management philosophy, or (3) differences in sophistication or experience in report preparation by the controller or in report reading by the recipients. If the board membership consists largely of successful businessmen who must manage their own companies, and who have no significant financial interest in the corporation, then the tendency is for less detailed reports. Moreover, some managements desire little assistance in the nature of direction of the company's affairs, and less data may be made available. At the other extreme is the board consisting largely of those with heavy investments in the business, and a professional management which wishes to keep its board informed to a high degree so as to secure a maximum of assistance. Under such circumstances, a great deal of financial-operating data is furnished.

Generally speaking, the board of directors is interested in broad policy matters, general trends of sales and earnings, competitive performance, and plans for the immediate and longer term. Under such circumstances, the reports of a financial nature to the board, by either the president, chief financial officer, or controller (but usually prepared by the latter), should include and interpret such matters as:

1. Company-wide and major divisions monthly (or quarterly) and year-to-date operating results
2. Statement of financial condition or pertinent excerpts therefrom

3. Statement of cash flow
4. Quarterly and annual forecasts by significant breakdown
5. Status of capital expenditures
6. Significant trends and relationships—special studies

The Appliance Corporation
REPORT TO BOARD OF DIRECTORS
March, 1961 and Fiscal Year-to-Date

Item	This Year	Forecast	% of Forecast
OPERATIONS			
Net Sales			
Month	$ 3,044,907	$ 2,554,197	119.2
Year-to-Date	29,217,348	32,443,942	90.1
Income Before Taxes			
Month	401,852	221,987	181.0
Year-to-Date	3,412,776	3,236,330	105.5
% of Sales	11.7%	10.0%	
Net Income			
Month	193,713	97,746	198.2
Year-to-Date	1,746,623 [1]	1,387,958	125.8
Earnings Per Share of Common			
Month	.136	.069	198.2
Year-to-Date	1.233 [1]	.980	125.8
OTHER SELECTED DATA			
Cash	$ 2,447,777	$ 1,415,695	
Receivables (Net)	5,351,463	3,904,747	
Inventories	6,866,954	6,314,933	
Other Current Assets	252,903	381,500	
Total Current Assets	14,919,097	12,016,875	
Current Liabilities	4,929,618	4,506,056	
Working Capital	$ 9,989,479	$ 7,510,819	
Current Ratio	3.0 to 1	2.7 to 1	
Capital Expenditures	$ 465,717	$ 1,696,933	
Return on Capital Employed	9.0%	7.2%	
Return on Stockholders' Equity	11.2%	9.6%	
Book Value Per Common Share	$13.78	$12.38	

[1] Note: All extraordinary gains on subsidiary dissolution have been excluded.

Fig. 134—Summarized Report to Board of Directors.

The Appliance Corporation
SUMMARY OF DIVISION PERFORMANCE
March, 1961 and Fiscal Year-to-Date

Item	This Year	Forecast	% of Forecast
NET SALES			
Western Division			
Month	$ 1,676,566	$ 1,354,138	123.8
Year-to-Date	16,223,374	18,844,877	86.1
Eastern Division			
Month	947,390	788,377	120.2
Year-to-Date	9,398,478	9,918,521	94.8
South Central Division			
Month	271,818	295,483	92.0
Year-to-Date	2,672,630	2,330,649	114.7
Canadian Operations			
Month	175,073	53,389	327.9
Year-to-Date	1,103,441	745,034	148.1
General Electronics, Inc.			
Month	—	67,865	—
Year-to-Date	—	692,775	—
Consolidated			
Month	3,044,907	2,554,197	119.2
Year-to-Date	$29,217,348	$32,443,942	90.1

INCOME BEFORE TAXES—% OF SALES	Mo.	Y/D
Western Division	12.7	10.8
Eastern Division	13.0	14.4
South Central Division	28.7	27.1
Canadian Operations	(8.4)	(34.2)

Item	This Year	Forecast	% of Forecast
NET INCOME (OR LOSS)			
Western Division			
Month	$ 102,541	$ 79,696	128.7
Year-to-Date	855,430	962,341	88.9
Eastern Division			
Month	59,230	(7,533)	—
Year-to-Date	766,963	289,810	264.6
South Central Division			
Month	37,401	41,469	90.2
Year-to-Date	349,642	244,538	143.0
Canadian Operations			
Month	(7,103)	(8,118)	—
Year-to-Date	(181,093)	(36,661)	—·
General Electronics, Inc.			
Month	—	1,571	—
Year-to-Date	—	19,643	—
Consolidated			
Month	193,713	97,746	198.2
Year-to-Date	$ 1,746,623	$ 1,387,958	125.8

Fig. 135—Report to Board of Directors—by Responsibility.

The Appliance Corporation and Subsidiaries
Consolidated Statement of Income and Expense
For the Month, and _____ Months Ended _____

	Month		Year-to-Date	
	Amount	% Net Sales	Amount	% Net Sales
Net Sales—Regular— This Year Forecast Last Year				
Less: Cost of Sales (excluding overhead)				
Gross Profit— This Year Forecast Last Year				
Less Expenses:				
Operating Manufacturing Selling and Advertising Administrative				
Total Expense— This Year Budget Last Year				
Operating Profit (Loss)				
Other Income				
Other Expense				
Less: Contribution to Pension Fund: Net Income before Federal and State Taxes on Income—This Year Objective Last Year				
Federal and State Taxes on Income (estimated)				
Net Income before Amortization of Goodwill				
Less: Amortization of Goodwill				
Net Income—This Year Objective Last Year				
Amount applicable to Minority Interest in Gain or (Loss) of Subsidiaries				
Controlling Interest in Consolidated Net Income				
Provision for Contingencies—Current Year				

Fig. 136—Comparative Income Statement—for Top Management.

An example of a simple two-page report which contains all vital financial information for board discussion purposes is shown in Figs. 134 and 135. This concise report is accompanied by written remarks and usually by further oral comments of the chief executive officer and chief financial officer relating to important underlying causes, trends, etc.

An example of a somewhat more detailed income statement which includes comparison with forecast as well as with the prior year is illustrated in Fig. 136. Such a report may be prepared for each division and for the entire company. Comparable financial data, indicating both the forecasted position and the actual condition at the end of the previous year, may be presented for financial position.

REPORTS FOR OTHER MAJOR EXECUTIVES

The interests of the major executives encompass the entire business enterprise. Even those executives in charge of a division are concerned with the over-all or composite picture. The vice-president in charge of sales, for example, is interested in production efficiency and volume, the research program, general business conditions, the price level, and a host of other matters. His major concern is slanted toward his special function, but nevertheless his interest is widespread. In developing reports for this class of executives, the controller must keep in mind their interests in such matters as:

1. The over-all return on the investment
2. The operating efficiency of every division of the business
3. The maintenance of a proper balance or coordination among the various divisions
4. The position of the firm in relation to the industry

Under the circumstances, the regular reports for the general executives usually present such information as the following:

1. Summary statement of financial condition
2. Analysis of significant changes in financial condition
3. Statement of cash position
4. Condensed statement of income and expense
5. Statement of income and expense by product lines or divisions of the business
6. Statement accounting for changes in net profit
7. Summary of sales by geographical area
8. Summary of orders received, unfilled orders, sales, and production
9. Financial and operating ratios, relationships, and trends
10. General measurements of operating efficiency, by major division
11. Comparison of actual operations with the program
12. Comparison of operations with general indexes of business conditions
13. Forecast of the following period

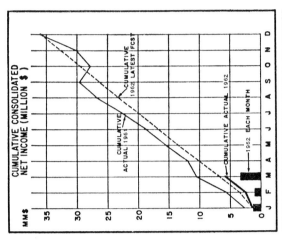

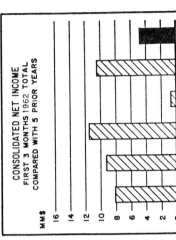

Los Angeles, California
April 13, 1962

Report on Operations and Financial Condition
March 31, 1962

OPERATIONS — GENERAL SUMMARY

Consolidated net income for the first quarter of 1962 was $5,932,000, the equivalent of $.38 per common share after provision for preferred dividend. This is a decrease of $4,531,000 from the 1961 first quarter earnings of $10,463,000, or $.70 per share. In comparing profit performance with this prior year period, it will be seen that all divisions and the subsidiaries, collectively, except the Eastern, produced $2,493,000 more profit. Income (loss) of the Eastern Division, reflecting severe price weakness and the catalytic cracker shutdown in January, was $7,024,000 less favorable (more loss) than in the corresponding '61 period.

Some of the price problems and excess costs were anticipated, in that the $5,932,000 net income represents a 95.8% achievement of the annual forecast first quarter earnings of $6,193,000. In this important comparison of actual performance with objectives, we find better than expected performance in the Southern and Foreign Divisions as well as the subsidiaries; but Western Division missed target by $1,256,000 (21.3%), and Eastern Division failed to meet the goal by $917,000 (15.8%). The better than forecast performance in the two divisions and subsidiaries, and a favorable LIFO inventory adjustment of $900,000 almost offset the Eastern-Western deficiency, and brought overall performance close to forecast.

Operating results were somewhat close to forecast because such projections, being realistic, did not assume standard performance. The review of the consolidated income statement for the first quarter reveals unfavorable sales price deviations from standard to the extent of $6,496,000, and controllable costs and expenses over standard aggregating $7,331,000. These are areas either of potential profit improvement or factors to be considered in long term planning.

FINANCIAL CONDITION

Consolidated working capital of $77,366,000, while adequate, has declined $12,341,000 since the first of the year as a consequence of recording liability for the offshore acreage award of $14,907,000 during the first quarter 1962.

Cash and equivalents of $39,683,000 is $1,600,000 lower than anticipated, entirely due to the decrease in earnings from that forecast. Despite this decrease in cash availability, the company has been able to absorb the payment in April of the aforementioned offshore acreage purchase ($14.9 million) with only a short term borrowing of $8 million. High cash generation during the month of April enabled us to repay one-half of this temporary borrowing on April 29.

Such information is usually presented monthly to the general executives with suitable comparisons and explanatory comment and, while general, is in more detail than for the board of directors. The above reports are only suggested examples, and may be varied as circumstances warrant. For example, an aging of the accounts receivables or a report on inventory activity may be included. In any event, at this executive level the emphasis is on the *summary* or *over-all* aspects and not departmental performance or other details.

While the general content of such reports is probably known to the reader, some illustrative material may be useful.

Figure 137 represents a page from the general summary comments on operations and financial condition, together with related graphs of comparative performance. This interpretation is supported by a company-wide income statement, shown in Fig. 138, which compares actual performance with plan or forecast, and with standard. The "block" technique is used to identify the more important areas of variance from plan or standard. The over-all company statement is supported with a summary by division—the responsibility reporting principle. The condensed statement of financial condition (Fig. 139) compares results with forecast and the preceding year-end.

Results of performance in relationship to budget or standard for each major executive may be summarized graphically as in Fig. 140. This same type of presentation can be made with the bars indicating variances only, and not the total costs or expenses, as shown in Fig. 141.[1]

Again, for the use of the major executives, the graph in Fig. 142 gives a clear indication of the trend in costs and net profit.

A three-way comparison of current year's sales, budgeted sales, and past year's sales is graphically presented in Fig. 143. For the information of the general executive as well as the sales executive, sales performance by geographic area or by product lines may be summarized on a responsibility basis.

A summary of over-all performance of the manufacturing division of a company is illustrated in Fig. 144. An over-all summary of the excess costs for all divisions, by responsibility, is illustrated in Fig. 145.

A simple statement accounting for change in operating profit is illustrated in Fig. 146.

The chief executives are interested very often in simple, highly condensed reports which indicate daily performance or condition. An example of a daily financial report for the president of a medium-sized corporation which provides information on the critical areas—sales, manufacturing efficiency,

[1] Used by permission of Frank A. Wallace, Principal, McKinsey & Company.

Description	Month of March 1962	Month of March Better or (Worse) than Forecast	3 Months, Year-to-Date 1962	3 Months Better or (Worse) than Current Views	3 Months Better or (Worse) than Original Forecast
REVENUES					
Gross revenues at standard	55,880	2,027	150,024	(1,872)	(400)
Sales price variance - (favorable) or unfavorable	3,113	(722)	6,496	(2,106)	(3,893)
Total revenues	52,767	1,305	143,528	(3,978)	(4,293)
CONTROLLABLE ITEMS					
Less:					
Controllable standard cost of goods sold (incl. raw material, purch. products and production costs)	26,383	(39)	70,512		
Over or (under) standard	1,511	(1,144)	3,265	(445)	(291)
Gross margin before expenses	24,873	(122)	69,751	(1,326)	(2,635)
Less:					
Controllable standard manufacturing costs	4,162	(483)	12,061	1,241	(550)
Over or (under) standard	497	266	2,462	(420)	1,129
Controllable margin before mktg. and prod. transp. costs	20,214	(339)	55,228	(505)	(2,056)
Less:					
Controllable standard product transportation costs	1,330	157	3,868	94	(50)
Controllable standard marketing costs	4,549	(47)	12,701	(327)	327
Standard advertising expense	382	19	1,162	58	(47)
Mktg., transp. and adv. over or (under) standard	403	(6)	1,456	(1,077)	(152)
Less:					
Controllable exploration costs	1,055	153	3,090	183	168
Over or (under) standard	-	-		43	58
Less:					
Controllable standard General & Administrative costs	987	49	3,123	79	160
Over or (under) standard	54	16	148	48	69
Dividends and miscellaneous (income)	150	5	172	15	15
Margin before non-controllable costs	11,599	7	29,852	(1,389)	(1,508)
NON-CONTROLLABLE COSTS					
Depreciation, taxes and insurance	6,546	79	20,038	464	1,175
Interest expense	1,015	23	3,046	57	57
Other non-controllable costs	80	1	200	15	15
Total non-controllable costs	7,641	103	23,284	536	1,247
Income before taxes based on income	3,958	110	6,568	(853)	(261)
Taxes based on income	451	-	636	-	-
CONSOLIDATED NET INCOME	3,507	110	5,932	(853)	(261)
Preferred dividends accrued	241	-	734	-	-
Consolidated net income applicable to common shares	3,266	110	5,198	(853)	(261)
Per share	$ 0.24	($ 0.01)	$ 0.38	($0.06)	($0.02)

Fig. 138—Consolidated Income Statement for Major Executives.

and working capital elements (for a company rather short in cash)—is that in Fig. 147. The use of estimates is to be noted. Some companies extend the use of estimates to preparing a daily income statement.

Daily reports would, of course, apply to each major function as well as to the over-all operation. Figure 148 pictures a daily statistical report on manufacturing costs. A graph of daily production as related to standard is illustrated in Fig. 149.

General Oil Company
CONSOLIDATED STATEMENT OF FINANCIAL POSITION AT JUNE 30, 1962

(in M$)

Description	Actual June 30, 1962	Better/(Worse) than Original 1962 Forecast	Better or (Worse) than	
			Actual 12/31/61	Actual 6/30/61
CURRENT ASSETS				
Cash and equivalents	$ 39,683	$(1,617)	$ 3,110	$(9,828)
Receivables	72,900	2,800	(1,660)	9,571
Inventories	53,370	(430)	(8,248)	(3,011)
Other current assets	13,946	3,846	3,991	2,678
Total Current Assets	179,899	4,599	(2,807)	(590)
CURRENT LIABILITIES				
Current portion of long-term debt .	26,077	23	(104)	(15,029)
Accounts payable	76,456	(5,756)	(9,430)	(15,522)
Total Current Liabilities	102,533	(5,733)	(9,534)	(30,551)
NET WORKING CAPITAL	77,366	(1,134)	(12,341)	(31,141)
INVESTMENTS AND ADVANCES				
Property and equipment	14,944	(56)	(532)	754
At original cost	1,197,014	(1,886)	22,365	82,502
Less accumulated depreciation ..	(524,293)	707	(7,875)	(35,372)
LONG-TERM DEBT	281,945	55	2,806	7,376
Total Net Worth	483,086	(2,314)	4,423	24,119
NET WORTH				
Preferred stock outstanding at par .	60,768	32	(845)	(1,625)
Common stock outstanding at par .	138,529	(29)	—	7,631
Reinvested earnings & capital in excess of par value	283,789	2,311	5,268	18,113
Total Net Worth	483,086	2,314	4,423	24,119
Book Value of Common Shares	$30.49	$(0.06)	$ .38	$ 1.86

Fig. 139—Comparative Statement of Financial Position for Major Executives.

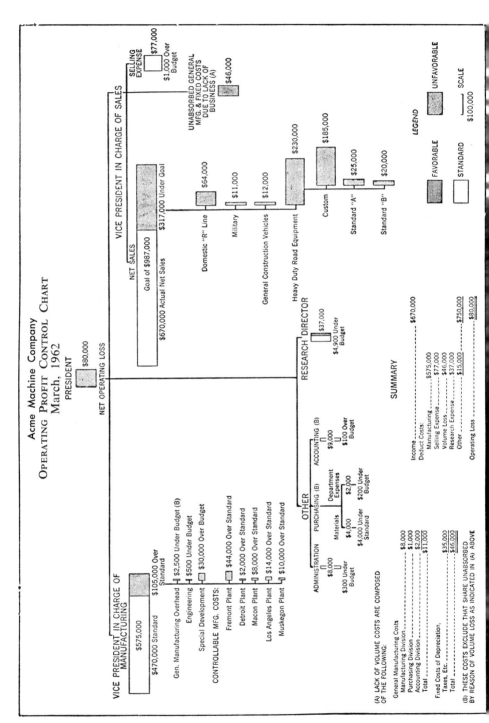

Acme Machine Company
OPERATING PROFIT CONTROL CHART
March, 1962

PRESIDENT

$80,000

NET OPERATING LOSS

VICE PRESIDENT IN CHARGE OF MANUFACTURING

$575,000

$470,000 Standard $105,000 Over Standard

Gen. Manufacturing Overhead $2,500 Under Budget (B)

Engineering $500 Under Budget

Special Development $30,000 Over Budget

CONTROLLABLE MFG. COSTS:

Fremont Plant $44,000 Over Standard
Detroit Plant $2,000 Over Standard
Macon Plant $8,000 Over Standard
Los Angeles Plant $14,000 Over Standard
Muskegon Plant $10,000 Over Standard

OTHER

ADMINISTRATION   PURCHASING (B)   ACCOUNTING (B)

$8,000   Materials   Department Expenses $9,000
$300 Under Budget $4,000 $2,000 $100 Over Budget
    $4,000 Under Standard $200 Under Budget

VICE PRESIDENT IN CHARGE OF SALES

SELLING EXPENSE

$77,000

$1,000 Over Budget

UNABSORBED GENERAL MFG. & FIXED COSTS DUE TO LACK OF BUSINESS (A)

$46,000

NET SALES

Goal of $987,000

$317,000 Under Goal

$670,000 Actual Net Sales

Domestic "R" Line $64,000
Military $11,000
General Construction Vehicles $12,000
Heavy Duty Road Equipment $230,000
Custom $185,000
Standard "A" $25,000
Standard "B" $20,000

RESEARCH DIRECTOR

$37,000

$4,900 Under Budget

LEGEND

FAVORABLE   UNFAVORABLE

STANDARD

SCALE

$100,000

SUMMARY

Income	$670,000
Deduct Costs:	
Manufacturing	$575,000
Selling Expense	$77,000
Volume Loss	$46,000
Research Expense	$37,000
Other	$15,000 $750,000
Operating Loss	$80,000

(A) LACK OF VOLUME COSTS ARE COMPOSED OF THE FOLLOWING:

General Manufacturing Costs
Manufacturing Division $8,000
Purchasing Division $1,000
Accounting Division $2,000
Total $11,000

Fixed Costs of Depreciation,
Taxes, Etc. $35,000
Total $46,000

(B) THESE COSTS EXCLUDE THAT SHARE UNABSORBED BY REASON OF VOLUME LOSS AS INDICATED IN (A) ABOVE

548

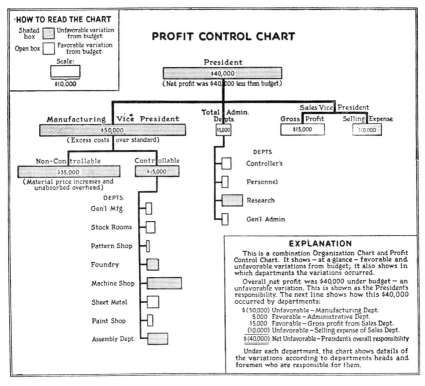

HOW TO READ THE CHART

Shaded box — Unfavorable variation from budget

Open box — Favorable variation from budget

Scale: $10,000

PROFIT CONTROL CHART

President
$40,000
(Net profit was $40,000 less than budget)

Manufacturing Vice President
$50,000
(Excess costs over standard)

Total Admin. Depts.
$5,000

Sales Vice President
Gross Profit $15,000
Selling Expense $10,000

Non-Controllable
$35,000
(Material price increases and unabsorbed overhead)

Controllable
$15,000

DEPTS.
Controller's
Personnel
Research
Gen'l Admin

DEPTS.
Gen'l Mfg.
Stock Rooms
Pattern Shop
Foundry
Machine Shop
Sheet Metal
Paint Shop
Assembly Dept.

EXPLANATION

This is a combination Organization Chart and Profit Control Chart. It shows — at a glance — favorable and unfavorable variations from budget; it also shows in which departments the variations occurred.

Overall net profit was $40,000 under budget — an unfavorable variation. This is shown as the President's responsibility. The next line shows how this $40,000 occurred by departments:

$(50,000) Unfavorable – Manufacturing Dept.
   5,000 Favorable – Administrative Dept.
  15,000 Favorable – Gross profit from Sales Dept.
 (10,000) Unfavorable – Selling expense of Sales Dept.
$(40,000) Net Unfavorable – President's overall responsibility

Under each department, the chart shows details of the variations according to departments heads and foremen who are responsible for them.

Fig. 141—Profit Control Chart.

It will be observed that some of the reports listed or illustrated are of the control type. Timeliness is important in their issuance. Where the reports are of an informational nature, for policy making and planning, the time factor is not quite as dominant. Nevertheless, a definite schedule should be prepared and adhered to, indicating the day or even the hour when the executive report is to be presented.

The controller should exercise care in the design of the form and physical characteristics of these regular executive reports. They should be neatly prepared, easy to read, and insofar as possible, self-explanatory. They could be attractively bound in appropriate covers bearing the name of the executive to whom they are given. If preferred, the executives may be given loose-leaf report books, with dividing tabs for months or subjects. in which the reports may be filed as received.

The Jones Company
TRENDS IN FUNCTIONAL COSTS AND PROFITS

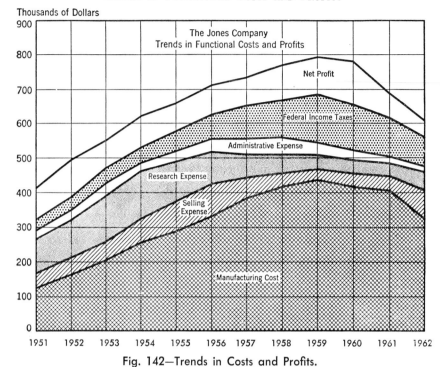

Thousands of Dollars

The Jones Company
Trends in Functional Costs and Profits

Net Profit

Federal Income Taxes

Administrative Expense

Research Expense

Selling Expense

Manufacturing Cost

Fig. 142—Trends in Costs and Profits.

The Ball Manufacturing Company
COMPARATIVE SALES
This Year, Last Year, and Budget

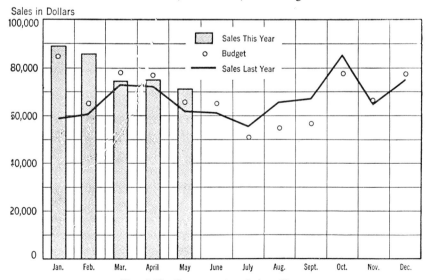

Sales in Dollars

☐ Sales This Year
○ Budget
— Sales Last Year

Fig. 143—Comparative Sales Chart.

CLEVELAND STEEL AND
CHEMICAL CO.

BUDGET REPORT

MONTH __February__

DEPT HEAD __J.A. Jones__
DEPARTMENT __Manufacturing Division__ NO ____
SUMMARY

DESCRIPTION	CURRENT MONTH			YEAR TO DATE		
	BUDGET	ACTUAL	(OVER)/UNDER	BUDGET	ACTUAL	(OVER)/UNDER
PLANTS						
Lorain Ave. Steel	$ 384,909	$ 396,433	$(11,524)	$ 684,639	$ 794,232	$(109,593)
Coke Works	44,631	44,579	52	91,735	96,293	(4,558)
Sharon Recovery	75,839	78,265	(2,426)	147,230	154,067	(6,837)
Stout Chemical	322,699	336,196	(13,497)	613,955	644,565	(30,610)
Bainbridge Chemical	227,354	239,805	(12,451)	491,422	522,480	(31,058)
GENERAL MANUFACTURING OVERHEAD						
Works Administration	5,237	5,499	(262)	11,814	13,231	(1,417)
Product Engineering	8,030	7,363	667	22,069	20,967	1,102
Engineering	5,515	4,689	826	10,703	9,709	994
Personnel	9,390	9,703	(313)	19,544	19,235	309
Purchasing	2,755	2,798	(43)	5,520	5,719	(199)
Stores	1,351	1,437	(86)	2,649	2,473	176
Traffic	1,166	1,103	63	2,367	2,161	206
Small Lot System	4,476	4,698	(222)	9,284	10,415	(1,131)
Pilot Development Line	4,164	4,164	-	6,218	6,218	-
Heat Treat Pilot Plant	2,470	2,470	-	4,716	4,716	-
Industrial Engineering	1,950	1,991	(41)	1,950	1,991	(41)
Operations Administration	1,743	1,597	146	1,743	1,597	146
Process Water	3,488	4,502	(1,014)	6,896	7,763	(867)
Boiler -G	16,077	17,719	(1,642)	31,358	32,780	(1,422)
" -S	5,327	5,494	(167)	11,007	11,404	(397)
Maintenance	28,158	31,422	(3,264)	54,681	61,458	(6,777)
Yard	2,683	2,742	(59)	5,744	5,297	447
OTHER						
Material Price	3,695	-	3,695	26,278	-	26,278
Material Freight	79	-	79	2,489	-	2,489
Lost Hrs.-Mat'l Shortages	(5,863)	-	(5,863)	(5,863)	-	(5,863)
TOTAL DEPARTMENT PERFORMANCE	$1,157,323	$1,204,669	$(47,346)	$2,260,148	$2,428,771	$(168,623)
PER CENT (OVER)/UNDER BUDGET			(4.09%)			(7.46%)

This is the initial report summarizing the performance of the operations division.
For detail, refer to monthly budget reports, the summary of excess costs by
responsibility and the Profit and Loss Statement.

ISSUED BY THE ACCOUNTING DEPT. __March 19__

Fig. 144—Summary of Manufacturing Division Budget Performance.

SUMMARY OF MANUFACTURING COSTS OVER OR (UNDER) STANDARD
BY RESPONSIBILITY

Month of February, 1962

| | | PLANT | | |
Description	Total All Products	Refrig-erators	Stoves	Small Appli-ances
CONTROLLABLE COSTS				
Manufacturing Division—				
Plant Superintendent's Level				
Direct Labor—Per Budget Report.	$17,277	$ 8,540	$ 6,322	$2,415
Direct Material—Per Budget Report......................	9,795	7,980	1,310	505
Variable Manufacturing Expense— Per Budget Report..........	7,883	4,395	2,478	1,010
Total Plant Superintendent's Responsibility...............	34,955	20,915	10,110	3,930
General Manufacturing Expense Over or (Under) Budget..........	5,260	3,110	2,070	80
Total Manufacturing Division..	40,215	24,025	12,180	4,010
Purchasing Division—				
Prices Paid for Raw Materials......	1,020	2,390	(910)	(460)
Sales Division—				
Idle Time—No orders (5-day cap.)..	12,307	9,100	3,207	–
Special Handling.................	2,190	870	1,320	–
Total Sales Division..........	14,497	9,970	4,527	–
Financial Division—				
Cost Department Over or (Under) Budget........................	160	110	40	10
Payroll Department Over or (Under) Budget........................	(70)	(30)	(30)	(10)
Total Financial Division.......	90	80	10	–
TOTAL CONTROLLABLE COSTS...........	55,822	36,465	15,807	3,550
NONCONTROLLABLE COSTS AND STANDARD APPLICATIONS, ETC.				
Fixed Expenses—Depreciation, Taxes, Insurance......................	7,900	4,390	2,760	750
Fixed Expenses—General Manufacturing, etc.........................	4,640	3,110	890	640
Standard Applications..............	935	125	770	40
Interplant Transfers................	1,020	670	340	10
Total Noncontrollable Costs and Standard Applications, etc....................	14,495	8,295	4,760	1,440
Total Excess Costs per Income and Expense Statement...................	$70,317	$44,760	$20,567	$4,990

Issued by Accounting Department—March 5, 1962.

Fig. 145—Summary of Manufacturing Costs Over (or Under) Standard, by Responsibility.

The Ajax Corporation
STATEMENT ACCOUNTING FOR CHANGE IN OPERATING PROFIT
February, 1962

OPERATING PROFIT

February, 1962	$198,500
January, 1962	67,300
Increase—February over January	131,200

Accounted for as follows:

Factors of Increase

Higher sales volume	76,312
Reduced manufacturing expenses over standard	44,800
Reduced excess material usage	26,110
Reduced development expense	12,916
Total elements causing increase in operating profit	160,138

Factors of Decrease

Lower average profit margin	$ 8,602	
Increased selling expenses	12,420	
Higher raw material prices	4,125	
Increased extraordinary deductions	3,791	
Total elements causing decrease in operating profit		28,938
Net Change in Operating Profit, as above		$131,200

Fig. 146—Statement Accounting for Change in Operating Profit.

SPECIAL REPORTS TO TOP MANAGEMENT

In every business, special circumstances arise which require separate analysis and study. For example, continuing decline in the profitability of a territory may warrant special investigation. The possibility of acquiring a new plant in potentially profitable areas would need a review. Some such studies may be initiated by the controller. In many cases, they will be made at the request of the board of directors, the executive committee, or the chief executive. The method of presentation can be varied, for the field is broad. Certainly the narrative portion of such reports is extremely important. An illustrative special report to the Executive Committee is presented on page 557. (The data are purely hypothetical and are used for illustrative purposes only.)

The Appliance Corporation, Inc.
and Wholly Owned Subsidiaries

DAILY CONDITIONS REPORT

Date: January 29, 1963

Working Days This Month _____ 22

Worked to Date _____ 20

SALES

	Today	Month to Date	Last Month to Date	Forecast to Date	Same Period Last Year
Parent	$ 173,401	$7,009,835	$ 866,716	$ 7,576,148	$4,968,717
Subsidiary	6,781	308,603	234,887	1,007,900	194,022
Consolidated Net	$ 180,182	$7,318,438	$1,101,603	$ 8,584,048	$5,162,739

PRODUCTION

Through 8:00 A.M.

Standard Hours	119,018
Actual Hours	130,203
% Efficiency	90.7%

WORKING CAPITAL

CASH

	Beg. Balance	Additions	Deductions	Ending Bal.
Fourth Nat'l Bank—Los Angeles	$ 645,898	$ 466	$ 151,025	$ 495,339
First Nat'l Bank—Chicago	234,142	—	—	234,142
Other Accounts	88,307	—	—	88,307
Total Cash	968,347	466	151,025	817,788

					Past Due
ACCOUNTS RECEIVABLE					
Current—House Brand	1,125,162	(1,078)	(35,657)	1,159,741	$ 580,925
Private Brands	1,271,114	91,884	—	1,362,998	57,387
Deferred—House Brand	2,929,366	85,046	—	3,014,412	—
Subsidiary Distributing Co.	1,597,427	7,156	—	1,604,583	509,296
Total Receivables	6,923,069	183,008	(35,657)	7,141,734	1,147,608
INVENTORIES					
Raw Material & WIP	4,395,714	215,000	156,821	4,453,893	
Finished Goods	5,406,720	151,821	149,004	5,409,537	
Total Inventories	9,802,434	366,821	305,825	9,863,430	
OTHER CURRENT ASSETS	359,956	—	—	359,956	
Total Current Assets	18,053,806	550,295	421,193	18,182,908	
CURRENT LIABILITIES					
Notes Payable	7,350,000	—	—	7,350,000	
Accounts Payable	2,772,969	170,344	115,368	2,827,945	
Payrolls—Estimate	175,213	50,000	—	225,213	
Other Accruals—Estimate	1,578,396	6,108	—	1,584,504	
Total Current Liabilities	11,876,578	226,452	115,368	11,987,662	
WORKING CAPITAL	$ 6,177,228	$ 323,843	$ 305,825	$ 6,195,246	

Fig. 147—Daily Conditions Report for Major Executives.

GENERAL
MANUFACTURING CORPORATION
DAILY PLANT REPORT

Owosso ___ Plant ___   Date February 13 __ 19 .

	TODAY					MONTH TO DATE					VARIABLE RATE	
	TOTAL BURDEN	DEDUCT FIXED	ACTUAL VARIABLE	STANDARD VARIABLE	SAVINGS	TOTAL BURDEN	DEDUCT FIXED	ACTUAL VARIABLE	STANDARD VARIABLE	SAVINGS	ACTUAL	STANDARD
INDIRECT LABOR	1,820	65	1,755	2,241	486	56,805	1,365	55,440	49,062	6,378	45.2	40.0
O.T. PREMIUM AND N.S. BONUS	730	–	730	810	80	13,124	–	13,124	12,265	859	10.7	10.0
OPERATING SUPPLIES	94	23	71	982	911	17,041	483	16,558	14,718	1,840	13.5	12.0
TOOLS	105	–	105	810	705	14,842	–	14,842	12,265	2,577	12.1	10.0
POWER	90	5	85	324	239	5,870	105	5,765	4,906	859	4.7	4.0
MAINTENANCE	1,002	–	1,002	2,661	1,659	26,739	–	26,739	25,144	1,595	21.8	20.5
LOSSES	188	–	188	446	258	8,218	–	8,218	6,746	1,472	6.7	5.5
DEPRECIATION	812	135	677	810	133	15,959	2,835	13,124	12,265	859	10.7	10.0
INSURANCE AND TAXES	483	77	406	810	404	14,987	1,617	13,370	12,265	1,105	10.9	10.0
OTHER OVER-HEAD EXPENSES	921	–	921	1,044	123	16,801	–	16,801	15,947	854	13.7	13.0
CREDITS	–	–	–	–	–	–	–	–	–	–	–	–
TOTALS	6,245	305	5,940	10,938	4,998	190,386	6,405	183,981	165,583	18,398	150.0	135.0

	TODAY	MONTH TO DATE	YEAR TO DATE		TODAY	MONTH TO DATE
ACTUAL PROD. LABOR	7,648	122,155	1,853,243	SCHEDULED SHIPMENTS	87,600	1,767,500
STANDARD PROD. LABOR	8,102	122,654	1,843,570	ACTUAL SHIPMENTS	84,260	1,927,634
SAVINGS LABOR	454	499	(10,327)	OVER/(UNDER) SCHEDULE	(3,340)	160,134
SAVINGS BURDEN	4,998	38,477	10,425	RETURNS & CREDITS		6,119
TOTAL SAVINGS	5,452	38,976	98			

REMARKS:

DISTRIBUTION:

DATE ISSUED: 2-14-

_____ DIVISION CONTROLLER

(REVERSE SIDE FOR ADDITIONAL REMARKS)

Thousands of Pounds

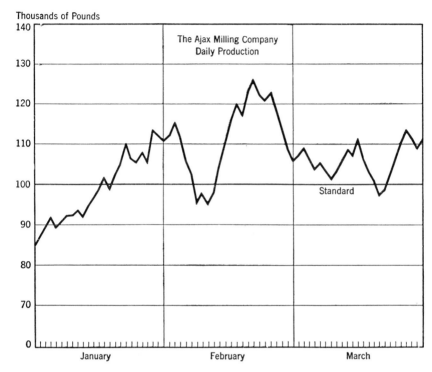

Fig. 149—Graphic Trend of Daily Production.

Special Report to Executive Committee

December 29, 1962

BOARD OF DIRECTORS

The following confidential report briefly summarizes our operations for the past six years, indicating certain significant trends, and sets forth an estimate of what our Net Loss will be during the first three months of 1963. It also sets forth a general estimate of our Net Loss for the entire year of 1963. This will naturally be subject to revision from month to month and I shall make this revision in special reports from month to month.

To save you time in reading a long report I have summarized the significant facts of this report in the first few pages and you need not refer to the remaining pages except as you wish additional information.

Throughout this report the figures for 1962 have been taken as a full year. To do this it has been necessary to estimate the results for the last two weeks of December; however any error in such estimate will be so small as to have no effect on the general situation.

SUMMARY

On January 1, 1957, we had Assets of $4,241,000, Debts of $572,000, and a Net Worth of $3,669,000. In the six years to December 31, 1962, we have operated at a Net Loss of $63,000 and during this time we have paid out in Dividends, $1,198,750; hence our Net Worth has been reduced during the six years by $1,261,750. This has greatly weakened our financial condition until now it appears as follows:

Assets	$3,316,000
Debts	909,000
Net Worth	$2,407,000

Our creditors now have an equity of 27.4% of the business which is entirely too much for a concern of this type in which the indebtedness is all current. The banks would be entirely justified in calling loans against such a condition.

The conclusion naturally is that we do not dare suffer any further inroads on our financial strength by either dividends or losses unless new capital is to be called into the business. Our operations from January 1, 1963, must carry themselves or we shall have to secure new capital elsewhere.

For the year 1962 we shall have Net Sales of $3,119,000 and our Net Loss for the year will be $260,000.

It is impossible, of course, to accurately predict our volume for 1963 but there are very serious reasons to question whether it will equal the volume for 1962. These reasons are:

1. Business in the early months of 1963 will certainly be at a lower level than in the early months of 1962. That is, we shall start the year from a much lower level. December volume a year ago was $386,057; this year it will be $210,000.
2. Statistical services generally speaking do not see any improvement in the early months of 1963.
3. Our level of prices will average lower in 1963 than 1962.
4. Our special-order volume may be smaller in 1963 than 1962.
5. The industries which constitute our main customers will be forced to curtail expenditures.

There are, of course, offsetting factors; we have two additional men in the sales division; the decline in business generally has leveled-out somewhat since July and there appear to be prospects of some special business which we did not get in 1962.

It appears, however, that we cannot count on a volume of more than $3,000,000 to $3,250,000 for 1963.

Our Cost of Goods Sold has run quite uniform. It will average about 62% of the Sales. This leaves us 38% to cover the Cost of Doing Business. This Cost of Doing Business is more or less a fixed cost except as it is arbitrarily changed by the management. Just now it amounts to $120,000 per month and consists of the following items:

Selling Cost	$ 62,600
Receiving and Shipping	6,150
Office	8,100
Administrative, Legal, and General	43,300
	$120,150

If our sales amount to $3,000,000 or an average of $250,000 per month, we shall lose $25,000 a month.

To carry our present overhead of $120,000 a month, without loss, would require sales of $315,700 per month or a total of $3,788,000 for the year.

To operate without a loss on the basis of sales of $250,000 per month will require that the overhead be cut from $120,000 to $95,000 per month, a cut of 20.8%.

It is recommended that we review every item of overhead expense in detail and make reductions effective at once which will reduce the overhead to a figure not to exceed $100,000 per month, and further that this amount be budgeted in detail to the various departments with responsibility for holding the figures to their respective allowances.

Barring such immediate reductions, I would estimate the operating results of the next three months to be as follows:

ESTIMATED NET LOSS FOR FIRST THREE MONTHS OF 1963

	January	February	March
Sales	$272,250	$228,250	$316,250
Gross Profit	106,200	89,000	123,000
Cost of Doing Business	120,000	120,000	130,000
Net Loss	$ 13,800	$ 31,000	$ 7,000

The foregoing figures are based on an expected $3,000,000 sales volume. The sales of these particular months give effect to the usual seasonal variations.

A preliminary estimate for the year 1963 follows, on the assumption that overhead is not to be changed.

ESTIMATED NET LOSS FOR 1963

With estimated sales for the year of $3,000,000 our operations should result as follows:

Sales		$3,000,000
Cost of Goods Sold		1,840,600
Gross Profit		1,159,400
Cost of Doing Business		
Selling Expense	$751,200	
Receiving and Shipping	73,800	
Office Expense	97,200	
Administrative, Legal, and General Expense	517,800	
Total		1,440,000
Net Loss		$ 280,600

CONTROLLER

The Chicago Chemical Company
SUMMARY OF IDLE MACHINE HOURS
For Week Ended October 19, 1962

Department	Available Hours	Operating Hours	Lost Hours	% Available Hours Utilized	REASON FOR LOST HOURS				COST OF IDLE TIME			
					Lack of Material	Lack of Orders	Operating Down Time	Other Unacct. For	Out of Pocket	Total Dept. Cost	Lost Pounds	Lost Profit
PHENOLIC SYSTEM												
51 Mixing	304	304	—	100.0	—	—	—	—	$ —	$ —	—	$ —
52 Milling	456	456	—	100.0	—	—	—	—	—	—	—	—
53 Grinding	1,872	1,870	2	99.9	—	—	2	—	5	12	624	115
54 Granulating—1	48	45	3	93.7	—	—	3	—	16	43	1,437	376
55 Screening	864	864	—	100.0	—	—	—	—	—	—	—	—
56 Granulating—2	144	144	—	100.0	—	—	—	—	—	—	—	—
Total or Average	3,688	3,683	5	99.9	—	—	5	—	$ 21	$ 55		$ 491
MELAMINE RESIN SYSTEM												
21 Mixing	240	120	120	50.0	—	120	—	—	$ —	$ 738	135,451	12,466
22 Milling—5	120	46	74	38.3	—	—	—	74	548	1,907	191,257	16,352
23 Milling—7	240	164	76	68.3	—	—	—	76	293	521	53,387	4,565
24 Grinding	120	115	5	95.8	—	—	—	5	19	45	5,647	523
27 Granulating—3	120	96	24	80.0	—	—	—	24	56	118	6,228	532
31 Granulating—4	120	118	2	98.3	—	—	2	—	35	100	2,381	204
Total or Average	960	659	301	68.6	—	120	2	179	$ 951	$3,429		$34,642
INDUSTRIAL RESINS SYSTEM												
106 Drying	120	111	9	92.5	—	—	9	—	$ 72	$ 257	6,390	353
111 Blending	240	111	129	46.3	—	129	—	—	260	1,486	124,227	6,870
112 Liquid Resins	120	119	1	99.2	—	—	1	—	2	12	766	14
114 "200" Series	120	111	9	92.5	—	9	—	—	55	118	3,402	154
Total or Average	600	452	148	75.3	—	138	10	—	$ 389	$1,873		$ 7,391
Grand Total	5,248	4,794	454	91.3	—	258	17	179	$1,361	$5,357		$42,524

Issued by Accounting Department—October 22, 1962.

Fig. 150—Summary of Idle Machine Hours.

560

REPORTS FOR DEPARTMENT MANAGERS AND SUPERINTENDENTS

The duties and responsibilities of department managers and superintendents are more restricted than those of the general executives, and are related to particular departments and cost centers. These executives have two major functions: (1) the supervision of the minor executives responsible to them, and (2) the coordination of the departments over which they have authority, so as to have a unified operation. Consequently, this echelon of executives should have reports on departmental performance. Although trend or planning reports are of use, the major emphasis is on current control.

A typical executive at the departmental level is the superintendent of a group of assembly departments. He needs to keep the material flowing to the cost center; he must keep the production of parts in balance within his groups; and he must keep expenses within budget. Since he has foremen responsible for the cost centers or sections, his interest lies in the performance of the cost centers as units, and not the individual workmen.

An outline of reports which would be useful to such an executive includes:

1. Daily report of labor performance by cost center [2]
2. Weekly report on labor performance by cost center
3. Weekly report on material losses over standard (Fig. 77)
4. Weekly report on idle machine time (Fig. 150)
5. Monthly report on expenses by cost center
6. Monthly summary of performance (Fig. 151)

Graphic presentation of performance can be effective at this level. Typical applications are the average per cent of standard efficiency in Fig. 152, and trend of material usage in Fig. 153.

Each major division within the business has executives at this same level. The district sales manager might be at a comparable supervisory level. His chief concern would be the sales and expense performance by branch. A typical report is shown in Fig. 154, summarizing the sales and selling expense performance.

REPORTS FOR MINOR SUPERVISORS

The executives at the lowest echelon of supervision are the men on the firing line. They deal with the individual performer—the salesman, the operator or mechanic, the clerk, the laboratory technician. This is where controls commence, where the money is really spent, and where savings can be made. These supervisors are constantly engaged in suggesting how sales of particular products may be increased; how material losses can be reduced; how the operation should be performed: how the machine should be

[2] See p. 285.

The General Manufacturing Corporation
Wayne Avenue Plant
MONTHLY COST SUMMARY—SMALL PARTS SECTION

For the Month Ended January 31, 1962

General Foreman _____ R. Jones

Cost Center	DIRECT LABOR			DIRECT MATERIAL			MANUFACTURING EXPENSE			TOTAL			
	Budget	Actual	(Over) or Under Budget	Budget	Actual	(Over) or Under Budget	Budget	Actual	(Over) or Under Budget	Budget	Actual	(Over) or Under Budget	Per Cent (Over) or Under Budget
Fabrication..........	$17,755	$17,732	$ 23	$ 27,340	$ 29,983	$(2,643)	$ 4,376	$ 4,799	$(423)	$ 49,471	$ 52,514	$(3,043)	(6.15)
Subassembly.........	11,603	11,091	512	16,803	17,083	(280)	6,310	6,873	(563)	34,716	35,047	(331)	(.95)
Processing..........	14,199	14,572	(373)	12,911	12,431	480	4,523	4,312	211	31,633	31,315	318	1.01
Machine Shop........	6,631	6,709	(78)	6,430	6,479	(49)	1,432	1,471	(39)	14,493	14,659	(166)	(1.15)
Paint...............	9,080	8,078	1,002	29,310	29,987	(677)	3,684	3,627	57	42,074	41,692	382	.91
Final Assembly......	10,646	10,874	(228)	49,691	50,312	(621)	6,397	6,214	183	66,734	67,400	(666)	(1.00)
Total..............	$69,914	$69,056	$ 858	$142,485	$146,275	$(3,790)	$26,722	$27,296	$(574)	$239,121	$242,627	$(3,506)	(1.47)
Per Cent (Over) or Under Budget...........			1.23			(2.66)			(2.15)				1.47

Issued by Cost Department—February 6, 1962.

Fig. 151—Summary of Monthly Performance by Department.

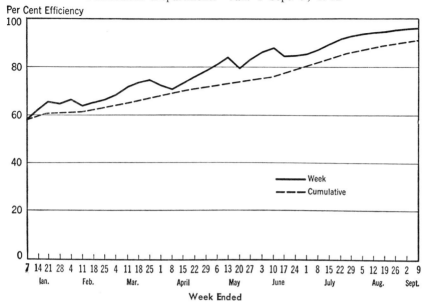

The Ritter Manufacturing Co., Inc.

DIRECT LABOR EFFICIENCY—PER CENT OF STANDARD

Fabrication Departments—Jan. 1–Sept. 9, 1962

Per Cent Efficiency

—— Week
- - - Cumulative

Week Ended

Fig. 152—Trend of Direct Labor Efficiency.

The Milling Company

PROGRESS CHART ON MATERIAL USAGE

Milling Department—Jan.–May, 1961: Costs per Cwt. Over or Under Standard

Dollars Per CWT.

Over Standard

Under Standard

Week Ended

Fig. 153—Trend of Material Usage.

563

The Illustrative Company
DISTRICT SALES REPORT
For the Month of June, 1962

District ___ Michigan   Manager ___ Cummerow

Branch	SALES Actual	SALES Budget	SALES Over or (Under) Budget	DIRECT SELLING EXPENSES Actual	Budget	(Over) or Under Budget	% of Net Sales Actual	Budget	Remarks
SUBSTANDARD SALES PERFORMANCE:									
Ypsilanti	$ 14,610	$ 21,000	$(6,390)	$ 2,050	$ 2,100	$ 50	14.0	10.0	Account lost to competition
Ann Arbor	29,520	30,000	(480)	2,990	3,000	10	10.1	10.0	
Wayne	13,810	17,000	(3,190)	1,470	1,700	230	10.6	10.0	Plant closing down
Muskegon	6,400	12,000	(5,600)	640	1,200	560	10.0	10.0	Strike at X factory
Total	64,340	80,000	(15,660)	7,150	8,000	850	11.1	10.0	
STANDARD OR BETTER SALES PERFORMANCE:									
Detroit	241,620	215,000	26,620	15,870	16,000	130	6.6	7.4	5 new accounts
Monroe	74,100	73,000	1,100	6,020	6,000	(20)	8.1	8.2	
Pontiac	30,100	29,000	1,100	3,000	2,900	(100)	10.0	10.0	
Flint	12,090	12,000	90	1,270	1,200	(70)	10.5	10.0	
Green Bay	5,670	5,000	670	580	500	(80)	10.2	10.0	
Grand Rapids	47,770	46,000	1,770	3,470	3,500	30	7.3	7.6	
Lansing	25,050	25,000	50	2,000	2,000	–	8.0	8.0	
Total	436,400	405,000	31,400	32,210	32,100	(110)	7.4	7.9	
Grand Total	$500,740	$485,000	$ 15,740	$39,360	$40,100	$ 740	7.9	8.3	

Fig. 154—Report on Sales District Performance.

THE ELECTRIC COMPANY

DAILY LABOR REPORT

DAY ENDED___5.P.M.___11/27/___

CLOCK NO.	PART NO.	OPERATION NO.	QUANTITY	SHIFT	DEPT.	ACTUAL HRS.	STD. HRS.	ACTUAL HRS. VS. STD. HRS.	
								UNDER	OVER
615	A51935	449	225	2	2	5	6		1
			225			5	6		1
1069	A51935	455	270	1	2	32	31	1	
1162	A51935	455	288	2	2	38	31	7	
280	A51935	455	171	3	2	22	31		9
1069	A51935	455	27	1	2	2	31		29
1162	A51935	455	234	2	2	38	31	7	
1162	A51935	455	225	2	2	31	31		
280	A51935	455	180	3	2	30	31		1
			1395			193	217	15	39
807	A51935	459	300	2	2	20	10	10	
615	A51935	459	90	2	2	3	10		7
692	A51935	459	130	1	2	5	10		5
807	A51935	459	200	2	2	10	10		
692	A51935	459	200	1	2	10	10		
615	A51935	459	225	2	2	5	10		5
			1145			53	60	10	17
567	A51935	501	293	2	2	54	54		
			293			54	54		
331	A52338	302	1575	1	2	7	25		18
331	A52338	302	7735	1	2	25	25		
331	A52338	302	9675	1	2	30	25	5	
			18985			62	75	5	18
			113736			1677	1271	1907	1501

Fig. 155—Daily Labor Report—Tabulating.

used. These supervisors finally carry out the policies of the company. They are the ones who build morale among the workers, who pass on or create spirit and enthusiasm among the individual performers.

In some companies the major executives believe that this lower level of supervision does not need reports. They feel that any good foreman, for example, should be able to see what is happening, observe when performance is not satisfactory, and know exactly what steps should be taken to increase efficiency, lower costs, or improve quality. Whether reports are needed depends on the organization—the process, the concept of supervision at this level, the personality and training of the man. In general, a good answer to the question is that, even with the best supervision, and keen and experienced observation, reports are of assistance in permitting review and comparison with past performance, standards, or budgets. The reports facilitate a review of progress and also record efficiency or inefficiency. They are a record of the degree to which the supervisory responsibility is being carried out. Moreover, the reports can contribute to the building of morale by showing who are the best performers. Again, they can be helpful in showing why a man failed to earn the maximum bonus or what he can do to earn even more.

Since the minor supervisors are concerned with the performance of the individual workman, salesman, etc., the reports should show individual performance. While cost may be used, the emphasis should be on units of output and not necessarily on dollars. Some illustrative reports for the foreman are shown in Figs. 155 through 157. Figure 155 is a daily report

The Manufacturing Company
WEEKLY SPOILAGE REPORT
Week Ended November 30, 1962

Cost Center___Polishing___   Foreman___R. Jones___

Operator	Total Production	Passed	Spoiled	Per Cent of Spoilage	Cost of Spoilage
1	356	324	32	8.99	$ 161.92
2	259	255	4	1.54	20.24
3	324	300	24	.74	121.44
4	292	281	11	3.77	55.66
5	302	276	26	8.61	131.56
6	313	298	15	4.79	75.90
7	290	267	23	7.93	116.38
8	327	302	25	7.65	126.50
9	184	164	20	10.87	101.20
10	288	277	11	3.82	55.66
11	318	296	22	6.92	111.32
12	299	278	21	7.02	106.26
Total.....	3,552	3,318	234	6.59	$1,184.04

Remarks:

Fig. 156—Weekly Spoilage Report.

prepared on a tabulating machine showing actual hours by man, and the standard hours earned on each type of item produced. In Fig. 156 the weekly spoilage of the men is summarized. Figure 157 presents the actual labor cost, the standard allowance, and the reason for off-standard conditions. For the branch sales manager, or his equivalent, reports on the activity of the individual salesmen are helpful. Figure 158 illustrates a weekly sales summary. Another weekly report giving information on the gross profit, direct expense, and number of calls is shown in Fig. 159. A monthly report summarizing sales performance similar to Fig. 160 is used extensively. A summary of budget performance of the individual salesmen, as in Fig. 161, can be supported by a more detailed report given to the man himself.

The Assembly Corporation

DAILY LABOR REPORT

Date November 19, 1962

Cost Center Polishing
Foreman Smith

| Operators | | Labor Cost | | Over or (Under) | Reasons for Off-Standard Costs |
No.	Name	Actual	Standard	Standard	
OFF STANDARD					
1620	Smith	$ 14.81	$ 9.10	$ 5.71	Operator inefficiency
1697	Jones	13.98	12.00	1.98	Faulty tools
1722	Loy	12.14	11.72	.42	Fatigue
1732	Carl	15.62	12.99	2.63	Operator inefficiency
1781	Black	16.21	10.84	5.37	Nonstandard material
1798	Symanski	13.87	12.07	1.80	Lack of materials
1801	Deal	19.87	14.77	5.10	Machine breakdown—overtime ($3.10)
	Total	106.50	83.49	23.01	
ON STANDARD		822.04	824.19	(2.15)	
	Total	$928.54	$907.68	$ 20.86	
Average Per Cent of Standard				102.3%	
Average Per Cent of Standard—Last Week				103.4%	

Fig. 157—Daily Labor Report—Exception Reporting.

The Sales Corporation

WEEKLY SALES SUMMARY

For Week Ended November 30, 1962

Branch _____   Branch Manager _____

Salesman	Pounds Sold		Sales by Product Line				
	Last Week	This Week	3100	3200	3300	Odd Lot	Other
Abrams	16,100	21,500	10,100	3,000	8,300	–	100
Black	8,400	16,700	4,000	–	12,700	–	–
Coldwell	9,100	9,100	–	6,100	3,000	–	–
Ernst	42,000	29,800	800	–	20,000	9,000	–
Gould	11,300	7,200	2,000	2,200	3,000	–	–
Horvath	1,900	1,300	–	–	1,300	–	–
Jones	8,100	10,500	–	–	5,500	–	5,000
Keeler	3,400	2,200	–	200	2,000	–	–
Vaach	8,000	13,800	6,800	2,000	5,000	–	–
Total	108,300	112,100	23,700	13,500	60,800	9,000	5,100

Standard Gross Margin............ $10,800

Remarks:

Special promotion on 3300

Fig. 158—Weekly Branch Sales Summary Report.

The Jones Company

WEEKLY SALES REPORT

DETROIT DISTRICT

Week Ended November 30, 1962

Salesman	Net Sales	Gross Profit		Direct Expense		Margin After Direct Expense	No. of Calls Made	New Customers
		Amount	%	Amount	% of Net Sales			
Walker.........	$ 3,600	$1,656	46.0	$125	3.47	$1,531	23	1
Smead.........	3,100	982	31.7	110	3.55	872	21	1
Piceu.........	3,061	1,184	38.7	134	4.38	1,050	29	—
Taylor.........	2,640	789	29.9	155	5.87	634	17	—
Brown.........	2,200	972	44.2	105	4.77	867	20	3
Joll.........	1,650	790	47.9	125	7.58	665	12	2
Total or Average..	$16,251	$6,373	39.2	$754	4.64	$5,619	20.3	7

Fig. 159—Weekly Report on Sales District Performance.

Wayne Lathe Corporation
SALES INCENTIVE PLAN
ACTUAL vs. QUOTA SALES

Salesman or Agent	For the Month of March, 1962				For the Period October, 1961, Through March, 1962			
	Quota	Actual	Over or (Under) Quota	% of Quota Attained	Quota	Actual	Over or (Under) Quota	% of Quota Attained
NEW UNITS								
Burdinhaw, R. W.	$ 180,000	$ 353,905	$ 173,905	196.6	$1,080,000	$1,603,226	$ 523,226	148.4
Farth, C. J.	155,000	122,747	(32,253)	(79.2)	930,000	550,252	(379,748)	(59.2)
Raymore, H. A., Jr.	—	54,951	54,951	—	—	257,170	257,170	—
Walker, C. E.	145,000	121,833	(23,167)	(84.0)	870,000	839,779	(30,221)	(96.5)
Saryan, H. J.	190,000	260,830	70,830	137.3	1,140,000	962,294	(177,706)	(84.4)
Sho, D. M.	180,000	201,685	21,685	112.0	1,080,000	1,069,694	(10,306)	(99.0)
Salesman Total	850,000	1,115,951	265,951	131.3	5,100,000	5,282,415	182,415	103.6
General Sales Corp.	300,000	403,800	103,800	134.6	1,800,000	3,106,700	1,306,700	172.6
Agents and Export	33,600	4,150	(29,450)	(12.4)	201,600	20,241	(181,359)	(10.0)
Total Sales	1,183,600	1,523,901	340,301	128.8	7,101,600	8,409,356	1,307,756	118.4
REPLACEMENT PARTS								
Burdinhaw, R. W.	30,000	—	(30,000)	—	180,000	12,000	(168,000)	(6.7)
Farth, C. J.	25,000	40,080	15,080	160.3	150,000	161,967	11,967	108.0
Raymore, H. A., Jr.	150,000	57,184	(92,816)	(38.1)	900,000	528,786	(371,214)	(58.8)
Walker, C. E.	25,000	1,854	(23,146)	(7.4)	150,000	43,372	(106,628)	(28.9)
Saryan, H. J.	25,000	—	(25,000)	—	150,000	11,288	(138,712)	(7.5)
Sho, D. M.	25,000	—	(25,000)	—	150,000	17,360	(132,640)	(11.6)
Salesman Total	$ 280,000	$ 99,118	$(180,882)	(35.4)	$1,680,000	$ 774,773	$(905,227)	(46.1)

NOTE: ( ) indicates unfavorable.

Issued by Accounting Department—April 12, 1962.

Fig. 160—Report on Quota Sales Performance.

BUDGET REPORT

MONTH __March__

DEPT. HEAD _____
DEPARTMENT __New York Office__ NO. _____
Selling Expense

DESCRIPTION	CURRENT MONTH			YEAR TO DATE		
	BUDGET	ACTUAL	(OVER) UNDER	BUDGET	ACTUAL	(OVER) UNDER
SALESMAN						
Abbott	$1,234	$ 1,128	$ 106	$ 3,448	$ 3,628	$ (180)
Carrol	906	1,066	(160)	2,812	3,024	(212)
Higgins	1,489	1,230	259	3,678	3,855	(177)
Jones	1,189	1,625	(436)	3,720	4,200	(480)
Lambert	1,066	1,008	58	3,132	3,258	(126)
Orin	1,076	1,136	(60)	3,152	3,192	(40)
Prescott	1,770	1,719	60	4,790	5,100	(310)
Welsh	1,006	1,166	(160)	3,000	2,700	300
Total	$9,736	$10,069	$(333)	$27,732	$28,957	$(1,225)
TOTAL DEPARTMENT PERFORMANCE						
% of Net Sales	2.4	2.6		2.5	2.7	

ISSUED BY THE ACCOUNTING DEPT. __4/12/.__

Fig. 161—Branch Report on Actual and Budgeted Selling Expense.

A BALANCED REPORT STRUCTURE

As a business firm becomes increasingly cost-conscious or profit-conscious, there is likely to be a growing and continued demand for accounting and statistical reports. More and more information is developed for the use of the executives. Coupled with this tendency is the dynamic character of most businesses with their ever changing needs. Under such circumstances it is relatively easy, over a period of time, to continue the issuance of a mass of reports which do not necessarily serve a useful purpose. Old reports are continued because no one suggests that they be stopped, and new ones are added.

With such possibilities in mind, it is highly desirable that the controller attempt to keep the report program or structure in balance with the needs of the organization. When a request is received for a new report, he may find it advisable to inquire into the reason for the request and the purpose the information is designed to meet. Quite often another report already being prepared can be modified slightly and fill the requirement. Such a review also prevents a special or one-time report from becoming a routine report.

Besides this audit of report requests, the controller might profitably conduct a periodic survey of the report situation as follows:

1. Review with each executive the reports being issued to ascertain if the need still exists, if the information is in the desired form, and if other data are needed but are not being secured.
2. Analyze the reports and objectives in an attempt to suggest new and better ways of presenting the information.
3. Review the operations to find what monthly data can be conveniently summarized for useful informational reports; and to see if any weak spots are developing which need emphasis for a time.
4. Cross-reference and reconcile all reports to make sure that the information is correct within the practical needs of the situation. Such a review will serve as a check on current control reports and may reveal any erroneous or otherwise unauthorized changes in the method of compiling the data.

Some companies have a report committee which passes on the need for additional reports, and periodically reviews existing reports as to necessity. In any event the objective is to provide the management team with sufficient and useful information without a duplicity of reporting. After all, reports cost money.

A suggested report which the controller might add to the list is an annual internal report for the top executives. It might consist of two sections: one including the comments and exhibits by each operating executive relating to his own division or function; the other, a section where the controller puts together financial facts and figures in an over-all analysis.

A CONTROLLER'S CONTRIBUTION

The mere issuance of a report does not complete the controller's job by any means. He must know his company, its policies, and its methods. Through continuous contact with the functional and divisional executives he must learn to see through the eyes of these executives. He must know their difficulties and be sympathetic with their problems. In some respects he is the contact man between central management and operating executives right down the line. He must not assume the role of chief executive but he should attempt to interpret the policies and program of the company as the chief executive would like them to be known and followed. Conversely, he is in a position to present to central management many of the problems of the men at the front. The controller who can intelligently represent management in developing and enforcing the company program and who is accepted by operating heads as a welcome counselor will reach an extremely high level of usefulness to his company. This is but an expression of the fact that the controller, although objective in the approach to problems, cannot be an automaton, as financial people are so often pictured. He must be a human engineer who bridges the gap between a mass of meaningless figures and their translation into purposeful activity. Intelligent relations with employees are just as essential in the controller's department as they are elsewhere.

In all these matters, reports are but an aid to management, and not a substitute for it.

30

Reports to Shareholders

OBJECTIVES OF THE ANNUAL REPORT

NATURE OF THE PROBLEM

The reporting problems of the controller, indeed of corporate management itself, do not relate solely to internal managerial reports. In the past few years an increasing amount of information has been made available to interests other than the management group. These interests are many—the shareholders, employees, general public, customers, stock exchanges, governmental agencies, and creditors. Reporting to each group poses separate problems.

The more intensive efforts by corporate management to improve reports, particularly those to the shareholders, employees, and the public, have been stimulated by two forces. One is related to the widespread ownership of corporate securities and the consequent attempt by business, as well as regulatory bodies such as the Securities and Exchange Commission, to assist in making such public financing as healthy and as intelligent as practicable. Another relates to the various social and political forces which to an increasing degree are influencing the regulation or conduct of business. Both movements have quickened a realization that external reports have not had the desired result—namely, acquainting the reader with the *facts* about the business. Such inability to tell adequately the story of the business has evidenced itself in an increasing amount of criticism voiced in the public press and elsewhere.

But it is not merely an isolated business enterprise that has been the object of criticism. In reality it has been, and still is, free independent enterprise—the American system—that is subjected to a critical review. Such a development is not surprising. The early 1930's witnessed a vast amount of economic distress suffered by a large share of the population. It is indeed quite natural that some doubt should have arisen as to the adequacy or efficiency of American business as it was then known. These doubts were never completely dispelled, and circumstances in recent years have encouraged distortions about our American economy. The enemies, or at least the seeming enemies, of free business have been loud enough in their criticism to confuse the public because the public doesn't have the facts. Such developments have impressed upon business management the need for bringing about a better understanding of the private enterprise system, and the part played by each unit of business in the competitive economy.

Much of the misunderstanding has arisen from a review of the financial statements themselves. The basic problem, then, is to present these statements, and factual interpretations of them, in a form that the reader will understand. It is principally a matter of preparing statements, not for the accountant, but for the ordinary citizen who has had no specialized accounting training—statements of fact, based on generally accepted accounting principles which are simple enough to be understood by the layman. The need is for a presentation that will convey to the interested parties the story of the individual company, and that will adequately inform the American people so as to combat those groups which would abolish private enterprise or place all industry under rigid government control. The annual report to the shareholders is scarcely the place for an airing of the controversy. But each company which convinces its owners of its place in the economic order is contributing to the continuance of the free enterprise system everywhere.

FOR WHOM THE ANNUAL REPORT?

The annual report is one of the most important mediums for telling the business story. There are perhaps five major groups toward which the corporate report may be directed: the shareholders, employees, security analysts, customers, and general public. Certainly these groups have definite claims, in varying degree, upon the management for information about the company. Depending on the audience to be reached, there may be different techniques for each.

Quite obviously the information given to any one group is not mutually exclusive of the others. Sharp lines of demarcation cannot be drawn between them. Many shareholders also may be employees or customers. It does seem evident, however, that those who write or edit reports can do a much better job if they know generally what audience is to be stressed. A review of present-day annual reports indicates some lack of decision when comparing the content and the addresses. The majority of the corporate reports are addressed to shareholders, but some are beamed to shareholders and employees, or to shareholders, employees, and customers. It might seem desirable to prepare either separate reports for each of the groups indicated, or one annual report available to all, with perhaps supplementary data, where needed, for the natural interests of each class.

The annual report under discussion in this chapter is primarily the one to the shareholders, and the emphasis is consequently on this phase. Practice as well as argumentation might favor separate reports to each of the interests mentioned. However, this development in many instances might well have to be a gradual process. A further consideration is whether the added expense of such reports is justified by the better communication. It is certainly logical that a better job could be done by preparing data for a specific group. Of course, were this line of action taken, the cry might be raised that different information is being given to different groups, with an implied difference in alleged facts or the implied concealment of information. This could be avoided by making all reports public.

PURPOSE OF ANNUAL REPORT TO SHAREHOLDERS

The annual report to shareholders may serve several purposes, but it is primarily an accounting of stewardship to the owners. It is a report by the management explaining the results of operations and the financial position of the company. It is, or should be, a means of permitting a discerning reader to analyze the operations and form a considered opinion of the worth or potential worth of the securities. An important related purpose of the annual report is to secure and hold venture capital. It is a selling device in attracting this capital from prospective shareholders.

Although the report preferably should be directed solely to the shareholders, current general practice is still to make one report serve several groups. Under such circumstances, there are other incidental or supplementary purposes of the annual report. It may be prepared for the present or prospective employee and thus serve as a tool in the maintenance of good personnel and industrial relations. Or it may be prepared to create and retain customers, particularly where shareholders can be an important segment of the market. Finally, the report may be directed toward the general public and may constitute a means of building goodwill and influencing legislation.

THE CONTROLLER AND THE ANNUAL REPORT

Preparation of the annual report calls for the cooperation of several executives or departments. The financial staff must furnish the financial information and supervise its use. Those handling public relations or advertising must see that the report is attractive, understandable, and consistent with published utterances. The industrial relations department may contribute data regarding labor matters. Legal counsel should check it for legal aspects. The chief executive and top management will give it a general review and make certain policy decisions. Each of these groups, and others, can and should make a contribution to the corporate annual report.

However, the foundation of the annual report is the financial statements and the interpretation thereof. This basic information must come from the controller's office—from the accounting and statistical records of the business. For this reason, and because its managerial and accounting aspects are too important or too technical to be satisfactorily handled by others, the report should be the product of the controller's office in close cooperation with the operating and management staff. It should not be turned over to the advertising or public relations department. While capable advertising men can do an outstanding job in many ways, there is often a tendency for them to make the annual report a somewhat blatant and obvious sales or advertising tool. As a result, its real purpose as a report of stewardship is somewhat obscured. Under the circumstances, it is believed the talents of these departments should be put to work for the controller, and not the controller put to work for them.

Another question arises as to the responsibility and liability of the controller to the shareholders, the directors, and the public. While such matters have not always been clearly defined, there has developed an increased sense of responsibility by controllers for the published reports of their company. As a member of management the controller cannot escape a share of responsibility for those actions which come within his sphere of activity. Quite naturally, final responsibility for adequate disclosure must rest with the directors and officers of the company. But it is nevertheless the duty of the controller to make the facts known to management and to press for sufficient disclosure of information. If he finds that the wishes of the management are substantially adverse to his sense of professional ethics, and the subject is material, then he might have occasion to resign.

TECHNICAL ASPECTS OF THE SHAREHOLDERS' REPORTS

GENERAL CONTENT OF ANNUAL REPORT

In considering the content and form of annual reports, it should be understood that there is no one answer applicable to all companies and all conditions. The kind and amount of information to be given will depend upon the type of industry and the specific company. A corporation producing consumer materials might find the most suitable approach much different from one supplying principally industrial materials. Then, too, while the intent may be to give shareholders all salient facts concerning their investment, there are many intangibles which cannot be discussed. For example, in the final analysis the quality of management is an important but difficult aspect of risk to measure or talk about. But within these limits, the first and basic question to be answered is whether the management officials honestly desire to inform the shareholders and provide a full understanding of the business. Much depends on this, for if the management does so desire, then the most appropriate means must be considered. If the management does not wish to so inform the owners, then discussion of improved techniques would serve little purpose. It is understandable that the shareholders' interest might center on two things: (1) the dividends paid, and (2) the market price of the security. One objective of the report is to convey to the shareholder a realization that the dividends paid are reasonable in relation to the earnings. Yet the contents of the report should not be restricted to this phase and the related market price of the stock. The opportunity to create a broader and more fundamental understanding of the company should be carefully considered. In this connection, management should not assume the owners are ignorant; the report should be prepared in non-technical language for a reasonably intelligent person.

A number of methods are available for determining the content of the annual report. Some companies have a committee composed principally of financial and public relations personnel who make recommendations on the general theme and content. The operating departments are contacted, and all suitable ideas, after screening, are submitted to top management for final decision. When final revisions have been completed, test readings may be made by supervisory personnel or shareholders.

A well-balanced annual report perhaps should seek to provide meaningful information for the shareholder and yet sufficient facts and figures to meet the needs of the professional reader. One means of accomplishing this objective is to prepare the front part of the report in an attractive and easy-to-understand manner for the relatively untrained reader. The back part of the annual report may be organized more particularly for the professional financial group—investment advisers, brokers, security analysts, etc.—who are more inclined to analyze data by means of ratios, etc., and formulate an investment opinion. For more information that might be included in the report to shareholders, a statistical supplement might be issued.[1]

An outline of some of the more basic contents of an effective, easy-to-read annual report follows:

1. *Basic.*
   a. *Highlights or summary page.* This presents fundamental and comparative data on financial results and condition as well as operating information. Particularly desirable are:
      Per-share earnings
      Per-share dividends
      Book value
   b. *President's comments.* Such a section, under the signature of either the chairman of the board or president, or both, is most

[1] See p. 599.

effective as a one- or two-page bird's-eye view stressing the over-all outlook and problems likely to affect the company's future. It generally avoids facts and figures presented elsewhere.

   c. *Narrative section.* This segment of the annual report provides the explanation and detailed story of the business. Through the use of commentary, charts, and photographs, it describes the activities of the various departments and/or areas of significance to the company.

   d. *Financial statements.* Comparative financial statements, including appropriate footnotes and the opinion of independent auditors, provide the basic information on the results of stewardship.

   e. *Historical statistical summary.* Such a section provides a long-term—usually ten or more years—picture of relevant operating and financial statistics.

2. *Supplemental—But Desirable.* By experience, other features found helpful in best presenting the corporate story include:

   a. *Table of Contents.* Permits quick reference in a multipage booklet.

   b. *Attractive cover design.* An appropriate photograph or drawing implying the nature of the business, or products, or industry has been found a helpful communication device.

   c. *Directory.* This portion indicates the names of officers and directors, and perhaps other key management personnel, as well as counsel, independent auditors, transfer agents, registrars, etc. At present, also, the tendency is to show the affiliation of directors who are not corporate officers.

Some pertinent comments on the sections which are of particular interest to the controller are made in the following paragraphs. The chief accounting officer is, however, encouraged to review annual reports of his industry, and of leading companies in other industries, in a continual search for improved techniques and an awareness of trends in reporting.

HIGHLIGHTS OR SUMMARY PAGE

In presenting information to the shareholders, as well as to professional readers, it has been found helpful to permit a quick review of operations before proceeding to a detailed discussion. A suitable device for this purpose is the highlights page.

An effective presentation is the "Facts in Brief" from the Sperry Rand Corporation report to shareholders for the year ended March 31, 1961, as shown in Fig. 162. The data contained in the summary are representative of the more effective annual reports.

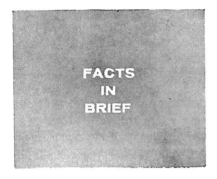

	1961	1960
For the Years Ended March 31:		
Net Sales of Products and Services . . .	$1,176,999,343	$1,173,050,913
Net Income	$ 27,815,655	$ 37,235,823
Per Common Share*	95¢	$1.30
Percentage of Sales	2.4%	3.2%
Cash Dividends		
Preferred ($4.50 Per Share)	$ 460,184	$ 460,184
Common	$ 16,974,718	$ 22,624,977
Total Cash Dividends	$ 17,434,902	$ 23,085,161
Per Common Share	60¢	80¢
Stock Dividend on Common Stock . . .	2%	—
Wages, Salaries and Employee Benefits . .	$ 571,877,737	$ 528,743,347
At March 31:		
Number of Common Shares Outstanding . .	28,883,615	28,284,691
Number of Common Stockholders	170,230	174,135
Stockholders' Equity	$ 370,788,629	$ 360,057,234
Per Common Share*	$12.48	$12.37
Working Capital	$ 278,747,965	$ 300,115,666
Net Investment in Property, Plants, Equipment, and Rental Machines	$ 288,919,273	$ 254,272,965
Number of Employees	105,265	108,421

* Based on the number of shares outstanding at the end of each year.

Fig. 162—Highlights Page from Annual Report to Shareholders.
(By permission Sperry Rand Corporation.)

The highlights page may also include:

1. Total cash flow (net earnings plus depreciation)
2. Cash flow per share of common stock
3. Capital expenditures for the year
4. Income taxes paid or accrued, in total and per share of common stock
5. Depreciation and depletion

The use of comparative information and presentation of per-share data and significant ratios are to be encouraged.

FINANCIAL STATEMENTS IN THE ANNUAL REPORT

Much progress has been made during the past decade in the presentation of financial data. Current techniques reflect an evolution in the art. While the section on financial statements may be either expanded or contracted to fit certain needs (stock exchange requirements, etc.), typical annual reports contain the following:

1. Statement of Income and Expenses, or
2. Statement of Income and Retained Earnings
3. Statement of Retained Earnings
4. Statement of Financial Condition
5. Source and Use of Funds
6. Accountants' Opinion

Although the first five statements mentioned above usually are comparative with the preceding year, the longer-term comparisons may be included in a financial section, or preferably, may be located at the back part of the report for ready analysis by those who are interested.

An informative ten-year summary as contained in the 1960 annual report of Parke, Davis & Company is illustrated in Fig. 163. The provision of significant per common share information as well as data on costs and earnings in relationship to the sales dollar is noteworthy.

The use of explicit and more "modern" terminology in the financial statements is strongly advocated. As examples, the term "surplus," which has unfortunate connotations, is to be discontinued in favor of a more descriptive phrase, such as "shareholder equity." Again, the term "income" or "income and expense" statement is increasing in usage as compared with the somewhat self-contradictory words "profit and loss" statement. As a last example, "reserve for depreciation" is giving way to the alternate usage "accumulated depreciation." The reader will recognize this terminology as being preferred by the American Institute of Certified Public Accountants. Perhaps the controller would do well to encourage trends to such less technical words in all reporting.

10 YEAR FINANCIAL SUMMARY

		1960
Net sales by major trading area:		
United States and Canada		$136,929
Other Western Hemisphere		21,342
Other World Trade		41,732
	TOTAL	$200,003
Cost of products sold		$ 63,914
Research and product development expenses		12,693
Selling, administrative, and general expenses		67,130
Currency exchange *revenue* or expense—net		85
Royalties and other *revenue* less interest expense—net		2,843
Earnings before taxes on income and minority interest		59,023
Taxes on income		28,350
Net earnings applicable to minority interest		203
Net earnings		30,470
Expenses included above:		
Depreciation of plant and equipment		5,134
Cost of employee pension program		3,369
Salaries and wages		55,201
Dividends declared		20,789
Current assets		135,197
Current liabilities		59,733
Working capital		75,464
Total assets		217,979
Land, buildings, and equipment acquired		16,439
Stockholders' investment		150,293
Per $100 of net sales:		
Cost of products sold		$ 31.96
Research and product development expenses		6.35
Selling, administrative, and general expenses		33.56
Net earnings		15.24
Per share of Capital Stock: (5)		
Earnings before taxes on income		$ 3.96
Taxes on income		1.91
Net earnings		2.05
Dividends declared		1.40
Stockholders' investment		10.12
Number of stockholders at year end		40,300
Number of employees at year end		11,803

In Thousands of Dollars

(1) Taxes on income include United States excess-profits taxes for the years 1951 and 1952.
(2) The year 1957 is the first to include a charge for annual bonuses awarded under the plan approved by the stockholders in that year.

Fig. 163—A Ten-Year Financial Summary for an

PARKE, DAVIS & COMPANY and Subsidiaries, Years Ended December 31

1959	1958	1957	1956	1955	1954	1953	1952	1951
$132,767	$120,856	$113,434	$ 91,492	$ 78,473	$ 67,566	$ 66,825	$ 80,311	$ 93,427
19,983	18,450	18,142	15,404	18,260	15,654	18,675	19,725	19,080
38,777	33,277	30,712	27,197	26,380	26,716	24,352	26,277	25,629
$191,527	$172,583	$162,288	$134,093	$123,113	$109,936	$109,852	$126,313	$138,136
$ 60,971	$ 58,156	$ 54,981	$ 52,631	$ 50,275	$ 50,797	$ 52,002	$ 53,310	$ 55,792
9,481	8,388	6,585	5,408	4,662	4,514	4,656	4,314	3,312
60,682	53,780	49,828	43,112	39,993	36,755	36,091	37,272	31,960
1,438	1,101	248	51	1,655	817	662	200	66
2,795	3,683	3,488	2,453	2,194	2,041	1,303	1,089	716
61,750	54,841	54,630	35,446	28,722	19,094	17,744	32,706	47,854
30,650	26,800	26,700	17,800	14,400	8,600	8,400	16,450(1)	28,800(1)
139	—	—	—	—	—	—	—	—
30,961	28,041	27,930	17,646	14,322	10,494	9,344	16,256	19,054
4,181	3,380	3,054	3,218	2,860	2,525	2,126	1,934	1,298
2,604	2,334	2,261	2,074	1,988	1,476	2,013	1,811	1,773
50,911	45,981	42,138(2)	37,683	36,200	36,128(3)	33,880(4)	34,104	30,300
20,760	15,540	14,269	8,838	7,596	6,853	7,342	9,300	9,298
134,355	124,583	116,597	98,998	84,041	72,610	72,365	81,538	88,069
56,847	51,178	48,767	36,354	30,472	24,052	24,560	33,546	42,596
77,508	73,405	67,830	62,644	53,569	48,558	47,805	47,992	45,473
204,273	187,665	170,859	139,262	124,251	110,874	108,284	114,704	116,782
17,445	13,198	6,055	3,594	4,424	5,063	5,118	6,497	6,835
140,326	129,800	116,925	102,909	93,778	86,822	83,163	81,158	74,186
$ 31.83	$ 33.70	$ 33.88	$ 39.25	$ 40.84	$ 46.21	$ 47.34	$ 42.20	$ 40.39
4.95	4.86	4.06	4.03	3.79	4.11	4.24	3.42	2.40
31.68	31.16	30.70	32.15	32.48	33.43	32.86	29.51	23.14
16.17	16.25	17.21	13.16	11.63	9.55	8.51	12.87	13.79
$ 4.16	$ 3.70	$ 3.70	$ 2.41	$ 1.95	$ 1.30	$ 1.21	$ 2.23	$ 3.26
2.07	1.81	1.81	1.21	.98	.59	.57	1.12	1.96
2.09	1.89	1.89	1.20	.97	.71	.64	1.11	1.30
1.40	1.05	.97	.60	.52	.47	.50	.63	.63
9.46	8.77	7.92	6.98	6.38	5.91	5.66	5.53	5.05
38,912	29,175	25,025	25,457	25,711	24,846	24,226	23,366	22,473
11,275	10,617	10,354	9,849	9,941	9,584	9,707	9,861	9,348

(3) The year 1954 is the first in which the accrual for vacations, approximately $1,350,000, was charged to the year in which earned.
(4) The year 1953 reflects the effect of a work stoppage for approximately 7 weeks.
(5) Adjusted for the 3-for-1 stock split on November 12, 1958.

Annual Report. (By permission Parke, Davis & Company.)

THE STATEMENT OF INCOME AND EXPENSE—SIMPLIFIED

The progress in the use of simplified income statements and improved terminology has been great; and there is need for only a brief discussion of this phase of annual reports. The 1960 issue of *Accounting Trends and Techniques* [2] in corporate annual reports, as published by the American Institute of Certified Public Accountants, for example, reflects that the "single-step" form of income statement—that is, an income grouping over a single

TIDEWATER OIL COMPANY

Consolidated Statement Of Income

For the Year

	1961	1960
SALES, OTHER REVENUE AND EXCISE TAXES.................	$751,811,000	$705,505,000
Less—Excise Taxes..	128,707,000	122,355,000
NET SALES AND OTHER REVENUE............................	623,104,000	583,150,000
COSTS, EXPENSES AND TAXES		
Crude oil, products, materials and services.........................	419,929,000	379,102,000
Salaries, wages and employee benefits	77,734,000	71,887,000
Depreciation, depletion, amortization and dry hole losses..........	63,255,000	60,598,000
Tanker cancellation costs..	—	2,805,000
Interest...	13,075,000	12,900,000
Taxes, other than income taxes.....................................	19,287,000	19,067,000
Income taxes..	2,002,000	1,728,000
Total Costs, Expenses and Taxes............................	595,282,000	548,087,000
NET INCOME...	$ 27,822,000	$ 35,063,000

Fig. 164—Illustrative Condensed Comparative Income Statement.
(By permission Tidewater Oil Company.)

total, and an expense group over a second total—has exceeded in numerical application the multiple-step format. This latter type contains the conventional groupings with intermediate balances. Such a format, together with the use of non-accounting language to the extent possible, facilitates understanding by the layman.

A simplified comparative income statement of the Tidewater Oil Company is illustrated in Fig. 164. Another form, which combines the income statement and analysis of retained earnings is shown in Fig. 165.

[2] It is suggested that controllers review this annual publication.

Brown Shoe Company Inc.
and Subsidiaries
Year Ended October 31, 1960

STATEMENTS OF CONSOLIDATED EARNINGS, ADDITIONAL
CAPITAL AND RETAINED EARNINGS

CONSOLIDATED EARNINGS

Net Sales..		$295,802,246
Sundry income—net.................................		376,354
		$296,178,600
Deduct:		
Cost of goods sold, selling, and administrative expenses— Note E..	$268,000,046	
Depreciation and amortization charges................	3,827,641	
Interest expense....................................	933,269	
Federal and state taxes on income—estimated..........	12,347,000	285,107,956
Net earnings for the year		$ 11,070,644

ADDITIONAL CAPITAL

Balance at November 1, 1959..........................	$ 9,036,143
Add excess of option price over par value of 26,985 shares of Common Stock issued under stock option plan........	553,320
Balance at October 31, 1960	$ 9,589,463

RETAINED EARNINGS

Balance at November 1, 1959..........................	$ 39,377,941
Add net earnings for the year..........................	11,070,644
	$ 50,448,585
Deduct cash dividends of $2.65 a share.................	4,895,845
Balance at October 31, 1960—Notes A and C	$ 45,552,740

See Notes to Financial Statements

Fig. 165—Statements of Consolidated Earnings, Additional Capital, and Retained Earnings. (By permission Brown Shoe Company, Inc.)

An example of rather complete absence of accounting terms, and summary explanation of the year's operating results, including significant percentage relationships, is the "Summary of operations, 1961 . . ." taken from the Parke, Davis & Company annual report as illustrated in Fig. 166. This same company provided, as an insert or supplement with the annual report, as part of "Financial Data 1961 Parke-Davis," a single-step consolidated statement of net earnings as shown in Fig. 167.

SUMMARY OF OPERATIONS, 1961

		PER CENT OF RECEIPTS	
WE RECEIVED	**Year 1961**	**1961**	**1960**
From sale of products.	$184,304,365	98.3	98.4
From royalties, interest earned, etc.	3,184,214	1.7	1.6
TOTAL RECEIPTS	$187,488,579	100.0	100.0

WE PAID OUT OR PROVIDED			
For wages and salaries, including employee benefit plans and payroll taxes.	$ 61,916,879	33.0	30.4
For materials, services, supplies, and other expenses.	78,214,599	41.7	36.2
For depreciation and obsolescence.	5,954,330	3.2	2.5
For taxes other than payroll taxes.	18,804,819	10.0	15.8
For minority interest in subsidiaries.	271,625	.2	.1
TOTAL COSTS	$165,162,252	88.1	85.0

WE HAD LEFT			
In net earnings.	$ 22,326,327	11.9	15.0

WHICH WAS USED			
For dividends to stockholders.	$ 17,089,409	9.1	10.2
For continuing needs of the business.	5,236,918	2.8	4.8
	$ 22,326,327	11.9	15.0

Fig. 166—Simplified Income Statement. (By permission Parke, Davis & Company.)

OTHER CONSIDERATIONS IN PRESENTING OPERATING DATA

The matter of how much information should be included in a report to shareholders is a subject for management decision. In the opinion of the authors, the annual report should bring to the owners' attention any significant trends or developments which affect their equities—whether taxes, labor problems, sales trends, or other factors. Again, a primary objective is to state the facts so clearly that the chance of misconceptions is reduced to

Parke, Davis & Company
and Subsidiaries

CONSOLIDATED
STATEMENT OF
NET EARNINGS

Years ended December 31, 1961, and December 31, 1960

	1961	1960
REVENUES:		
Net sales...	$184,304,365	$200,002,706
Royalties, interest, and other revenues........................	3,184,214	3,153,227
	$187,488,579	$203,155,933
COSTS AND EXPENSES:		
Cost of products sold......................................	$ 68,611,324	$ 63,913,560
Research and product development............................	12,976,921	12,692,525
Selling, administrative, and general..........................	64,481,254	63,112,205
Cost of employee pension program............................	2,442,097	3,369,361
Awards under Bonus Plan...................................	356,440	648,800
Interest...	322,947	309,775
Currency exchange adjustments (in 1961, principally devaluations in Brazil and Canada).....................................	649,644	86,080
Taxes on income—United States and other countries............	15,050,000	28,350,000
Net earnings applicable to minority interest in subsidiaries........	271,625	203,163
	$165,162,252	$172,685,469
NET EARNINGS	$ 22,326,327	$ 30,470,464

Depreciation of plant and equipment charged to costs and expenses amounted to $5,954,330 in 1961 and $5,134,003 in 1960.

See notes to financial statements.

Fig. 167—Illustrative Single-Step Income Statement. (By permission Parke, Davis & Company.)

PARENT COMPANY AND ALL SUBSIDIARIES

SALES BY PRODUCT GROUPS

	1961 %	1960 %	1956 %
Chemical Fibers	25.2	23.6	16.2
Plastics, Synthetic Resins and Surface Coatings	21.0	21.7	23.5
Phosphate Products and Detergents	12.2	12.0	15.1
Intermediates and Plasticizers	10.7	11.2	11.3
Rubber and Oil Chemicals	7.7	8.3	9.7
Agricultural Chemicals	7.2	6.3	6.3
Petroleum Products—Net of purchases	6.7	6.6	6.8
Pharmaceuticals, Flavors and Condiments	3.6	3.6	4.2
Textile and Paper Chemicals	2.8	3.5	2.3
Heavy Chemicals	2.6	2.9	4.1
Other	.3	.3	.5
	100.0	100.0	100.0

PARENT COMPANY

SALES TO PUBLIC AND CONSUMING INDUSTRIES

	1961 Position	1961 % of Total	1960 Position	1960 % of Total	1959 Position	1959 % of Total
Agriculture	1	13.16	2	11.85	2	11.46
Soap and Detergent	2	12.56	1	12.03	1	12.75
Petroleum	3	11.16	3	10.91	4	9.88
Plastics and Resins	4	9.37	4	9.57	3	10.03
Rubber	5	7.90	5	8.81	5	8.94
Paper and Printing	6	5.73	8	5.57	9	4.96
Textile	7	5.06	7	5.62	6	6.54
Stone, Glass and Vitreous Product	8	4.90	9	5.32	8	6.00
Metal	9	4.82	6	5.63	7	6.07
Public-Service Station Sales, etc.	10	4.67	10	4.58	10	4.35
Paint, Varnish and Printing Ink	11	3.45	11	4.20	11	4.01
Pharmaceutical	12	3.37	12	3.03	12	2.72
Food	13	3.01	13	2.61	13	2.50
Lumber and Timber	14	2.06	14	2.09	14	2.31
Iron, Steel and Related Product	15	1.68	15	1.59	17	1.28
Color and Dyestuff	16	1.26	17	1.28	15	1.58
Transportation Equipment	17	1.15	16	1.30	16	1.32
Non-ferrous Metal	18	.71	18	.74	18	.56
Other		3.98		3.27		2.74
		100.00		100.00		100.00

Fig. 168—Monsanto Chemical Company Sales Analysis for Annual Report. (By permission Monsanto Chemical Company.)

a minimum. Some general suggestions, indicating present-day practices, are outlined as follows:

1. *Income and Expense Data Should Be Comparative To Be Most Useful.* Some companies present comparative data for the preceding year. Others include statements covering a period of perhaps ten or more years.

2. *A Sales Analysis May Be Helpful and Informative to Stockholders.* Some companies include in the annual report an analysis of sales on one or more of these bases:
   a. By chief customers or industries, as in Fig. 168
   b. By types of product or commodity groups, also as in Fig. 168
   c. By territories or divisions
   d. As between governmental and private business
   e. By quarters, to indicate seasonal fluctuations
   Such analyses should be supplemented by explanatory comments.

3. *Wage Data Are of Interest to Shareholders.* The owners may be interested in the share of income distributed as wages. Graphic presentations of the amount of salaries and wages, as in Fig. 169, can be included in the report.

The Jones Company
EMPLOYMENT AND PAYROLLS

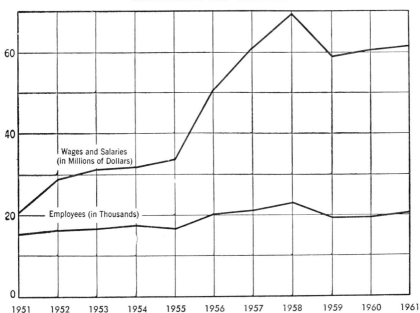

Fig. 169—Wage and Employee Information for an Annual Report.

November 30,	1960	1959
Current assets:		
Cash	$ 10,977,856	$ 9,191,805
United States Government securities, at cost	656,371	760,000
Receivables—trade and sundry, less allowance for cash discounts and doubtful accounts	53,598,067	52,417,711
Inventories (note 2)	83,384,701	80,198,399
Prepaid insurance premiums, taxes, and sundry	781,026	679,909
Total current assets	149,398,021	143,247,824
Less—current liabilities:		
Notes payable to banks	720,000	11,144,950
Current maturities of long-term debt	1,755,250	1,755,250
Accounts payable and accrued expenses	19,114,335	20,723,392
Employees' balances and tax withholdings	1,339,615	1,467,594
Federal and Canadian taxes on income	6,599,914	7,830,113
Total current liabilities	29,529,114	42,921,299
Net working capital	119,868,907	100,326,525
Physical properties—based on appraisal April 30, 1925, plus subsequent additions at cost, less accumulated depreciation (note 3)	40,538,083	38,587,982
Customers' secured loans, deferred maturities	6,688,409	7,409,966
Excess of investment over equity in subsidiaries, net	1,304,580	1,153,940
Employees' notes receivable for stock, secured by 54,851 shares (58,544 shares in 1959) of parent company's common stock	1,117,250	1,294,296
Sundry investments and deferred charges	1,228,545	946,944
	170,745,774	149,719,653
Deduct:		
Long-term debt, less current maturities (note 4)	58,585,250	40,350,500
Minority interests in subsidiaries..............................	1,394,571	1,452,897
	59,979,821	41,803,397
STOCKHOLDERS' EQUITY	$110,765,953	$107,916,256
Represented by:		
Common stock without nominal or par value: Authorized 4,000,000 shares; issued 3,400,000 shares	51,000,000	51,000,000
Capital in excess of stated amount; (the decrease in 1960 arose through a transaction in treasury stock)	1,023,957	1,037,123
Retained earnings (note 5)	58,814,897	56,060,400
	110,838,854	108,097,523
Less common stock in treasury, 1,978 shares (4,778 shares in 1959), at cost	72,901	181,267
Stockholders' equity applicable to common stock outstanding, 3,398,022 shares (3,395,222 shares in 1959)	$110,765,953	$107,916,256

See accompanying notes to financial statements.

Fig. 170—Illustrative Statement of Consolidated Financial Position.
(By permission International Shoe Company.)

4. *Taxes Are of Interest to the Owners.* Shareholders usually want to know what share of the income or earnings over the years is paid for taxes, with particular reference to income and excess profits taxes.

5. *Profits Need a Great Deal of Explanation.* Profits are the most misunderstood of many items in the statement; and it may be found desirable to restate and discuss the importance and nature of profits, and reasons for the change in profits. Net income data may include:

   a. Profits as a percentage of the sales dollar, as a percentage of wages, or as a percentage of capital employed in the business
   b. Earnings per share of stock
   c. Trend over a period of years
   d. Effect of volume on profits
   e. Distribution as between dividends and the amount retained for use in the business

6. *Non-recurring Items Should Be Clearly Set Forth.* This is important in evaluating the year's performance.

HOW WE STAND on December 31, 1961

	December 31, 1961	INVESTMENT PER EMPLOYEE	
		1961	1960
WHAT WE OWN			
Cash and marketable securities needed for prompt payment of current obligations and to provide for future expansion programs	$ 46,988,449	$ 3,986	$ 4,578
Receivables due from customers for merchandise delivered	32,803,979	2,783	2,720
Claims for recoverable excise taxes	490,041	42	53
Inventories and supplies for servicing customer needs	40,703,985	3,453	3,743
Taxes, insurance, and other expenses paid in advance	4,231,959	359	360
Investment in affiliated companies	1,944,507	165	163
Land, buildings, and equipment which originally cost $125,479,285 and against which depreciation in the amount of $41,781,840 has been charged to operations	83,697,445	7,100	6,328
Sundry other assets	871,359	74	83
Deferred pension plan costs	4,248,537	360	440
	$215,980,261	$18,322	$18,468
WHAT WE OWE			
Obligations to employees for wages, salaries, and commissions; to manufacturers for materials purchased; to various governments for taxes other than taxes on income; and to stockholders for dividends	$ 28,287,814	$ 2,400	$ 2,893
Taxes on income to United States and other countries	23,434,223	1,988	2,461
Money borrowed to provide for current requirements in other countries	7,770,503	659	328
Minority interest in subsidiaries	799,697	68	53
	$ 60,292,237	$ 5,115	$ 5,735
STOCKHOLDERS' INVESTMENT AND SAVINGS			
Amounts owned less amounts owed, representing the value of the original investment made by stockholders plus accumulated savings	$155,688,024	$13,207	$12,733

Fig. 171—Simplified Statement of Financial Position.
(By permission Parke, Davis and Company.)

Parke, Davis & Company
and Subsidiaries

CONSOLIDATED

ASSETS

	1961	1960
CURRENT ASSETS:		
Cash...	$ 40,380,660	$ 31,406,250
Marketable securities—at lower of cost or market plus accrued interest..........	6,607,789	22,633,535
Trade accounts receivable, less allowance of $766,000 at December 31, 1961, for doubtful accounts..	32,803,979	32,103,238
Recoverable excise taxes..	490,041	625,775
Inventories—at lower of cost (first-in, first-out method) or market:		
Finished products..	$ 16,239,509	$ 18,100,058
Work in process...	12,760,333	14,146,789
Raw materials and supplies..	11,704,143	11,929,779
	$ 40,703,985	$ 44,176,626
Prepaid taxes, insurance, and other expenses...............................	4,231,959	4,251,755
TOTAL CURRENT ASSETS	$125,218,413	$135,197,179
INVESTMENTS AND OTHER ASSETS:		
Investment in affiliates—at cost...	$ 1,944,507	$ 1,919,346
Other assets...	871,358	980,019
TOTAL INVESTMENTS AND OTHER ASSETS	$ 2,815,865	$ 2,899,365
PROPERTY, PLANT, AND EQUIPMENT --at cost, less accumulated depreciation:		
Land..	$ 5,308,381	$ 4,833,539
Buildings and improvements...	53,833,535	44,553,369
Machinery and equipment...	48,122,173	40,832,029
Office furniture and fixtures...	8,992,135	8,261,380
Construction in process..	9,223,061	12,774,703
	$125,479,285	$111,255,020
Less accumulated depreciation...	41,781,840	36,561,972
TOTAL PROPERTY, PLANT, AND EQUIPMENT	$ 83,697,445	$ 74,693,048
FORMULAE, PROCESSES, PATENTS, AND COPYRIGHTS......................	1	1
DEFERRED PENSION PLAN COSTS (Note B)...............................	4,248,537	5,189,048
	$215,980,261	$217,978,641

Fig. 172—Condensed Balance Sheet. (By

BALANCE SHEET

December 31, 1961

and

December 31, 1960

LIABILITIES AND STOCKHOLDERS' INVESTMENT

	1961	1960
CURRENT LIABILITIES:		
Loans in other countries for current requirements of subsidiaries and branches....	$ 7,770,503	$ 3,870,099
Accounts payable and accrued expenses:		
Trade accounts..	12,463,156	13,410,864
Salaries, wages, and commissions..................................	5,339,942	6,212,240
Property, pay roll, excise, and miscellaneous taxes.......................	4,233,106	4,442,451
Dividend payable in January...	5,944,610	9,656,735
Taxes on income—United States and other countries........................	15,514,223	22,141,213
TOTAL CURRENT LIABILITIES	$ 51,265,540	$ 59,733,602
DEFERRED LIABILITIES:		
Awards under Bonus Plan, less related reduction in future income taxes..........	$ 307,000	$ 423,000
United States income taxes on undistributed earnings of subsidiaries in other countries..	7,920,000	6,900,000
TOTAL DEFERRED LIABILITIES	$ 8,227,000	$ 7,323,000
MINORITY INTEREST IN SUBSIDIARIES.....................................	799,697	628,872
STOCKHOLDERS' INVESTMENT:		
Capital Stock, no-par value (Note C):		
Authorized 20,000,000 shares		
Issued 14,860,713 shares at December 31, 1961—at stated capital amount, including $65,282 added in 1961 from exercise of stock options.........	$ 14,994,843	$ 14,929,561
Additional paid-in capital, including $92,657 added in 1961 with respect to stock options...	1,299,532	1,206,875
	$ 16,294,375	$ 16,136,436
Earnings retained for use in the business:		
Balance at beginning of year..	$134,156,731	$124,475,581
Net earnings for the year...	22,326,327	30,470,464
	$156,483,058	$154,946,045
Less cash dividends declared (1961—$1.15 a share; 1960—$1.40 a share).....	17,089,409	20,789,314
Balance at end of year...	$139,393,649	$134,156,731
TOTAL STOCKHOLDERS' INVESTMENT	$155,688,024	$150,293,167
	$215,980,261	$217,978,641

See notes to financial statements.

permission Parke, Davis & Company.)

STATEMENT OF FINANCIAL CONDITION

Just as the traditional income statement has confused many laymen, so also the conventional "balance sheet" has often failed to present data clearly. It has been said that although it should show the maximum information in a minimum of space, the results indicate a minimum of information and a maximum of confusion. Consequently, simplified forms for reflecting the financial condition of a company have been developed. In one such form, the asset and liability sides have been eliminated, and a single column has been utilized to arrive at the owner's capital. Also, that confusing term "surplus" has been avoided in favor of the description "retained earnings." An example of this modified form, the consolidated financial position of the International Shoe Company, is shown in Fig. 170.

Parke-Davis has effectively explained the financial position of the corporation in language readily understood by most shareholders, as illustrated in Fig. 171. This statement also is accompanied by a consolidated balance sheet, as an insert, in progressive financial terms and eliminating controversial terminology, as presented in Fig. 172.

Some topics which deal with items in the statement of financial condition and which are suggested for inclusion in the narrative comment are as follows:

1. *Cash.* The cause of any important changes may be explained.
2. *Investments.* Some corporations give a detail of their holdings.
3. *Receivables.* A comment on the collection of past-due accounts, if significant, may be made. The number of days of average sales these receivables represent can be mentioned.
4. *Inventories.* Subjects such as the basis of valuation or effect of price changes on value may be discussed.
5. *Fixed Assets.* An analysis of the properties may be made. The investment per employee can be shown (as in Fig. 171). At least one railroad company has translated the value into the number of locomotives, boxcars, etc., that the company owns. The effect of new acquisitions on company earnings would appear to be a timely subject.
6. *Surplus.* The word may be eliminated and replaced by a more descriptive term.

SOURCE AND USE OF FUNDS STATEMENT

One of the financial statements of growing use and importance is the "cash flow" statement, or what is sometimes called the source and application of funds. It is found particularly valuable by security analysts in industries of heavy capital investment and consequent large depreciation charges, and where depreciation policies differ widely from company to company. An example of a comparative statement, taken from the 1960 annual report of the Aluminum Company of America, is illustrated in Fig. 173.

Source and Application of Funds during 1960 and 1959

Source of Funds:	1960	1959	Application of Funds:	1960	1959
Net income	$ 40,044,105	$ 55,570,854	Additions to properties, plants and equipment, less net retirements of $10,169,140 in 1960 and $10,425,064 in 1959	$ 70,172,161	$ 44,235,928
Depreciation and depletion	80,194,803	73,060,312			
Reduction in reserve for future taxes on income	(3,148,280)	(1,855,964)	Payments on long-term debt....	27,143,147	35,782,341
Other	406,422	1,622,123	Dividends declared:		
Total from operations	$117,497,050	$128,397,325	Preferred stock	2,474,688	2,474,688
			Common stock	25,649,928	25,241,943
Proceeds from sale of common stock	954,673	1,203,549	Increase in investments, net	5,869,177	2,624,562
			Increase in receivables and advances—noncurrent, net....	8,512,906	4,537,356
Working capital of acquired subsidiaries at dates of acquisitions	6,837,067	11,815,827	Other	915,882	256,471
				$140,737,889	$115,153,289
			(Decrease) Increase in working capital	(15,449,099)	26,263,412
Total	$125,288,790	$141,416,701	Total	$125,288,790	$141,416,701

Fig. 173—Statement of Source and Application of Funds.
(By permission Aluminum Company of America.)

The data which such a statement reveals include:

1. Share of funds provided from operations
2. Amount of funds provided from outside sources—by source
3. Disposition of funds, including impact on working capital
4. Proportion of funds applied to plant, and each other important factor
5. Indication of impact of sources and application upon the future dividend paying probabilities
6. By comparison with other companies in the industry, a better comparison of financial strength not distorted by differences in accounting

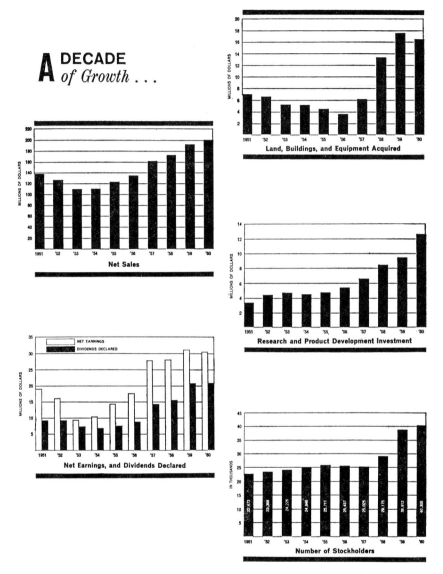

Fig. 174—Graphic Presentation of Trends—Use in an Annual Report.

UTILIZATION OF CHARTS AND GRAPHS

In reports to shareholders, as in management reports, charts and graphs may be employed as effective communicating devices. The same principles reviewed in Chapter 28 [3] are applicable in telling the corporate story to its

[3] See pp. 521 to 538.

owners. The selection of pertinent data, which highlight the growth of a company, is illustrated in the graphic presentation of the 1960 Parke, Davis & Company annual report shown in Fig. 174.

FORM OF ANNUAL REPORT

What is included in the annual report is certainly important, but *how* it is presented has much to do with getting the message understood. Summarized below are some comments on various aspects of the physical form of the report which, if heeded, may assist in getting the document read:

1. *Language.* Short sentences and a simple and brief conversational style have been found most effective.
2. *Arrangement.* A summary presented at the beginning is helpful. Distinctive headings and subtitles make reading easier. A division of the report into technical and non-technical sections can be helpful.
3. *Illustrations.* An increasing use of photography or illustrations is being made to get and hold attention. These devices relieve the monotony of a page; and they may be excellent for illustrating the use of the product.
4. *Graphs.* Graphs can be important timesavers and are an easy means of illustrating trends. Supporting tables are desirable.
5. *Cover.* The cover preferably should identify the company, and indicate the contents to be the annual report. The name of the corporation should be easily readable and perhaps placed against an effectively colored background. Application or uses of the company's product may be effectively illustrated. The inside cover may be used for listings of offices, plants, directors, etc.
6. *Size of Pages.* The size may be influenced by the use of photographs. A common size is $8\frac{1}{2}'' \times 11''$.
7. *Number of Pages.* The report should be sufficiently complete to give the idea of thoroughness, but not so long as to be too bulky. The common range is perhaps 16 to 36 pages.
8. *Paper.* A good quality paper should be used, but not such as to give the impression of being unduly expensive.
9. *Typography.* Different sizes of type headings are desirable. The main objective is to make the report easily readable. The advertising department can be helpful in this respect.

STANDARDIZATION IN ANNUAL REPORTS

From what has been said, it is probably evident that the annual report should be clearly identified with the company and its products. This requires individualism, and the trend is toward even more individuality. There are, however, certain areas where standardization can and should be practiced. The accounting organizations, including the American Institute of Certified Public Accountants, Financial Executives Institute, and

National Association of Accountants, emphasize the need for financial accounting standards. Among those areas in which standardization should be considered are:

1. The terminology used to describe individual items in the financial statements
2. The arrangement of items in the statements
3. Practice of giving comparative statements
4. Adequate disclosure of elements of income and expense
5. Disclosure of nature and disposition of reserves
6. Treatment of charges or credits to the surplus or income accounts—the accounting for extraordinary items, for example

Standardization in the financial statements will tend to promote a better understanding of the financial data. For it is indeed easy to appreciate why a layman is confused, with such differences in accounting treatment.

OTHER REPORTS TO SHAREHOLDERS

Providing the owners of the business with adequate information requires some consideration of frequency. The annual report issued only once a year, and perhaps several months after the fiscal period has ended, can

JEWEL TEA CO., INC.

Consolidated Income Account

	12 WEEKS ENDED		40 WEEKS ENDED	
	OCTOBER 7, 1961	OCTOBER 8, 1960	OCTOBER 7, 1961	OCTOBER 8, 1960
Retail sales	$120,165,080	$114,146,394	$403,272,000	$381,887,864
Earnings before federal income taxes	3,974,934	3,762,304	13,307,445	13,393,352
Provision for federal income taxes	2,052,000	1,959,000	6,761,000	6,961,000
Net earnings for the period	1,922,934	1,803,304	6,546,445	6,432,352
Less preferred dividend requirements ..	49,239	49,647	163,762	165,481
Earnings applicable to common stock ..	$ 1,873,695	$ 1,753,657	$ 6,382,683	$ 6,266,871
Earnings per share of common stock ..	$.54	$.51	$1.85	$1.85

The operations of Osco Drug, Inc., which was acquired by exchange of stock on February 16, 1961, have been included in the periods above. Shares issued in exchange have been considered as outstanding throughout these periods in computing earnings per share. Results for the current year are subject to the usual year-end review by independent public accountants.

Fig. 175—An Interim Earnings Report. (By permission Jewel Tea Co., Inc.)

hardly be said to inform the shareholders on current operations. Because of this great lag and the need for more contacts with the owners, the practice of publishing interim reports has grown. More and more firms issue quarterly statements. In fact, a corporation making application for listing on the New York Stock Exchange agrees, except in very unusual circumstances, to publish quarterly statements of earnings on the basis of the same degree of consolidation as in the annual report; and such statements must show net profits before and after federal taxes, and, further, must disclose any substantial items of unusual or non-recurring nature. These quarterly releases are usually quite simple in nature, and not as elaborate as the annual reports. There is, however, considerable variation. Some firms issue highly condensed statements, whereas others give quite detailed statements and narratives. Figure 175 illustrates some of the financial and operating information from a quarterly report. Because of possible seasonal influences or other abnormal transactions, care must be exercised that such interim reports will not mislead.

There are other means of contact with the shareholders. Some of the more commonly used devices include:

1. A letter of welcome to new shareholders
2. Minutes of the annual shareholders' meeting
3. Periodic letters, etc., perhaps included with the dividend check
4. Special anniversary booklets
5. Special letters on matters of immediate interest
6. Advertising in the financial or other sections of the public press
7. Shareholders' data book
8. Reprints of speeches by executives

INFORMATION FOR SECURITY ANALYSTS AND INVESTMENT ADVISORS

Much of the preceding commentary has related to, or emphasized, simplified reporting to the owners of the business. Yet the fact remains that it must usually serve also as a contact document with the security analysts and investment advisors. And ordinarily such professionals desire a great deal more information than the shareholder either wishes or is capable of understanding. One means of solving the problem is to provide, upon request, a financial and statistical supplement for this group. It could contain more analyses of the type requested by them.

Whether the information be included in or with the annual report, or in a supplement mailed only to the professional group, the following is indicative of analytical information which, if management chooses, the controller may make available:

1. Sales analyses—perhaps for several years to show trend
   a. By product
   b. By division

2. Income analyses
   a. By product
   b. By division
3. Expense analyses
   a. By type in relationship to sales
   b. Identified types of expense, viz., employee benefits, pension costs, advertising, research and development, etc.
   c. Industry comparisons
4. Selected ratios (many of which can be calculated from available data in annual report)
   a. Return on capital employed
   b. Return on common shareholder equity
   c. Profit margin, before and after taxes, as a per cent of sales
   d. Per cent of net income paid in dividends and retained in business
   e. Current ratio
   f. Turnover of working capital
   g. Turnover of receivables
   h. Turnover of inventories
   i. Special statistics applicable to an individual industry

31

Reports to Employees and to the General Public

REPORTS TO EMPLOYEES

THE EMPLOYEE AND BUSINESS

In reviewing the subject of reports to shareholders, the problem centered, first of all, around the basic attitude of management toward the owners. Does management really want informed shareholders? So, also, in considering reports to employees, it is a matter of understanding the true interest of employees in the business and of deciding whether information should be shared with employees.

On the surface, the major attention of the average employee seems to be on higher wages, shorter hours, and better working conditions. Yet, whether he realizes it or not—and perhaps it is partly management's fault if he does not—the employee has a much greater concern in the business than these day-to-day objectives. For example, consider him in relation to the shareholders or bondholders. They make investments of money; but the investments can be sold and the money recovered. However, the employee also has made an investment—the fifteen, or twenty-five, or forty years of his life. At the age of fifty he is not the same man as he was at twenty-five. During those years the business wanted his skill, his talents, his help in expanding and developing a profitable venture. Now, with his gray hair and stooped shoulders, the employee has lost youth, flexibility, and salability; they may have gone largely into the business. Does he have an interest in the company? To induce employees to contribute whole-heartedly to the success of the enterprise, the day-to-day wage, even including certain pension benefits, is not enough. The need is beyond any mere contractual limitations. For the highest degree of success, there are two other indispensable ingredients: (1) a recognition by management of its obligation to those who spend many years of life as wage-earners in the business, including the obligation to manage wisely, and (2) the encouraging of the wage-earners to demand or recognize a competent management as the best form of social security. The sharing of information with the employees can assist in this understanding and in creating a mutuality of interests.

OBJECTIVES OF REPORTS TO EMPLOYEES

By and large it is recognized that the employee is entitled to information about the company's operations. His job and his wages ultimately depend upon earnings, just as much as do the shareholders' dividends. The fact that an employee has not been interested in the operations may be due in part to his failure to recognize his stake in the progress of the company. Such understanding can be enhanced by providing the necessary facts.

The problem with which management is faced appears to have three aspects:

1. To convey to the employees and the general public an appreciation of the relationship among the shareholders, employees, management, and the customers
2. To bring about a clear understanding of the company's progress during the year, including its income and its expenses, and its outlook for the coming year or years
3. To outline some of the economic problems that shareholders, employees, and management must face together in the future

Giving information to employees in order to meet these objectives does not mean giving them a mass of figures which would confuse; but it does mean giving facts that their natural interests would comprehend. It does imply giving facts which will take them beyond the machines and daily routine to a better understanding of the business. Moreover, business management should be realistic in recognizing that the existence of the free enterprise system is doomed unless the employees understand the relationship and interdependence between their own work, those who furnish the tools of production, and those who manage them. The employee must be given the facts, which will enable him to judge for himself whether the American system offers ultimately more and better living for the individual than does any other economic order.

SPECIAL REPORTS TO EMPLOYEES?

Reports to employees may be of an infinite variety. However, this discussion is concerned principally with whether an annual report or other reports on operations should be prepared especially for the employees. It was pointed out in the preceding chapter that logic would favor a special report, but that the circumstances of each case must govern. In defense of a special report to employees, it can be said that employees are usually interested in subjects that are of little or no interest to shareholders. Moreover, even as to items of mutual interest, the viewpoint is different. The wage-earner looks at wages, job security, and other employee benefits quite differently from the shareholder. Whenever the feeling might be prevalent among the employees that facts are distorted or withheld, a compromise solution is the preparation of special reports which emphasize the interests of each group; both reports should then be available to shareholders and employees.

Ten or twelve years ago an annual report exclusively to employees was issued by only a few pioneering companies. But considering an employee's natural interest and curiosity in the company from which he gains his livelihood, the report to employees should be recognized as a significant opportunity for employee communications.

Some companies consider that the little added costs make worthwhile a special annual report to employees. Others devote an issue or section of the house magazine to the year's financial results. Still others issue to the employees a condensed version of the annual report to shareholders with an invitation to request the latter. Such an approach was used by the General Motors Corporation for 1961. The excerpt published in "Facts at your finger tips . . . ," highlights of the General Motors annual report for 1961, is illustrated in Fig. 176.

INFORMATION PRESENTED TO EMPLOYEES

Generally speaking, the job of a daily wage-earner is an important influence in his life. When he reads about company operations, he relates the facts and figures to his own job. And he is interested in a great many things. He is interested in how much income the company received and what happened to it, the past history of the company and its prospects for the future, the use and importance of the products manufactured, the wage rate for his job as compared with the wage rate for like jobs in other companies, and the benefits the employees of other companies receive. There are any number of questions of this nature which the employee raises. If management's reports are to be useful to the employee, if he is to read them, then they must provide many of the answers.

No single list of topics will serve all companies in terms of what information should be given to employees. Current trends also are an influence. What one company may find desirable, another will consider inadvisable. Furthermore, the more detailed the listing, the greater the area of disagreement. For example, many will agree that the employee should be provided with financial information about the operations. Yet, one firm would in-

HIGHLIGHTS OF THE YEAR

	1961	1960	1959
DOLLAR SALES OF ALL PRODUCTS			
Civilian	$ 11,037,426,000	$ 12,389,388,000	$10,842,060,000
Defense	358,491,000	346,612,000	390,997,000
Total	$ 11,395,917,000	$ 12,736,000,000	$11,233,057,000
FACTORY SALES OF CARS AND TRUCKS			
Manufactured in U. S. plants	3,150,000	3,682,000	2,960,000
Manufactured in Canadian plants	197,000	208,000	180,000
Manufactured in Overseas plants	690,000	771,000	711,000
Total	4,037,000	4,661,000	3,851,000
NET INCOME	$ 892,821,000	$ 959,042,000	$ 873,100,000
As a percent of sales	7.8%	7.5%	7.8%
Earned per share of common stock	$3.11	$3.35	$3.06
Dividends per share of common stock	$2.50	$2.00	$2.00
TAXES			
Provision for U. S. and foreign income taxes	$ 875,200,000	$ 1,078,500,000	$ 919,100,000
Other tax provisions (including state, local and GM's share of social security taxes)	372,200,000	370,400,000	331,000,000
Total	$ 1,247,400,000	$ 1,448,900,000	$ 1,250,100,000
Total taxes per share of common stock	$4.41	$5.14	$4.45
Total taxes per dollar of net income	$1.40	$1.51	$1.43
Total taxes per dollar of dividends	$1.73	$2.51	$2.18
WORLD-WIDE EMPLOYMENT			
Average number of employes	553,000	595,000	557,000
Total payrolls	$ 3,238,818,000	$ 3,487,093,000	$ 3,083,760,000
U. S. HOURLY-RATE EMPLOYMENT			
Average number of hourly-rate employes	300,000	337,000	312,000
Total hourly-rate payrolls	$ 1,894,059,000	$ 2,151,361,000	$ 1,882,711,000
Average weekly pay of hourly-rate employes	$121.22	$122.74	$116.04
SHAREHOLDERS AS OF DECEMBER 31			
Common	841,000	805,000	761,000
Preferred	26,000	26,000	26,000
Total	867,000	831,000	787,000
INVESTMENT AS OF DECEMBER 31			
Net working capital	$ 3,058,577,000	$ 2,799,316,000	$ 2,566,157,000
Net real estate, plants, and equipment	3,028,866,000	3,010,422,000	2,837,545,000
Shareholders' net investment	6,025,655,000	5,814,661,000	5,371,011,000

Fig. 176—Excerpts from an Annual Report.

What Happened to the Money GM Received During 1961

GM received in 1961	Millions	
From sale of its products and other income (net) _ _ _ _ _	$11,513	100%
These receipts went		
To suppliers for materials, services, etc. _ _ _ _ _ _	5,465	47½
To employes for payrolls, employe benefit plans, etc. _ _ _ _ _ _	3,499	30½
For Federal, state and local taxes _ _ _ _ _ _	1,247	10¾
To provide for depreciation and obsolescence of plants and equipment _ _ _ _ _ _	409	3½
To GM shareholders _ _ _ _ _ _	720	6¼
For use in the business to provide facilities and working capital _ _ _ _ _ _	173	1½

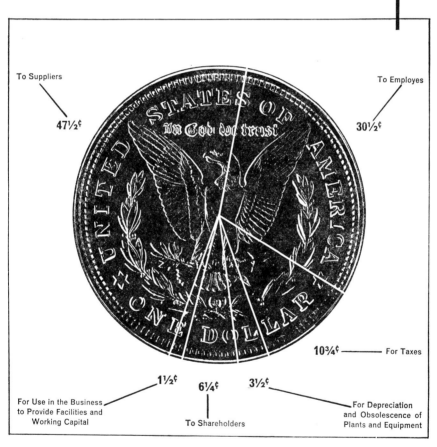

To Suppliers
47½¢

To Employes
30½¢

10¾¢ ———— For Taxes

1½¢   6¼¢   3½¢

For Use in the Business to Provide Facilities and Working Capital

To Shareholders

For Depreciation and Obsolescence of Plants and Equipment

(By permission General Motors Corporation.)

clude information on executive salaries while another would not. Some topics on which there is general agreement, however, include:

Company finances, including understandable financial statements
Company personnel and organization
Company history
Employment and payrolls
Labor policies
Company position in its own industry, and competitive activity

Productivity
Company products and their uses
Expansion plans
Sales and order prospects
Research and development activities
Industry outlook
Taxation
Educational activities

Many of these are proper subjects for discussion in the annual report.

The emphasis here relates more particularly to the financial aspects of the reports, where a great many topics can be used to bring about a better understanding of the company and the economy. Basically, the employee is interested in his share of the total reward, and the financial statements should set this out in clearly understandable language. If every corporation would make certain that its employees have a full knowledge of the earnings and the disposition of these earnings, employee relations would be greatly improved. As has been mentioned, the employee should understand the relationship between those who provide the tools and those who use them. What the Standard Oil Company (N. J.) said in one issue of the company magazine, *The Lamp,* is illustrative of a point which should be understood: "The management has stated that the company's chief asset is its personnel. But the employees, unaided by capital, could not produce a barrel of crude nor deliver a gallon of gasoline. Back of them must be money, i.e. stockholders, management and goodwill. How much capital is required, and what do labor and the management cost?"

A more specific indication of financial subjects which may be covered in employee reports is suggested in the following outline:

1. Investment
   a. Explanation of statement of financial condition
   b. Nature of properties
   c. Source of capital
   d. Need for stockholders
   e. Investment per employee

2. Operations
   a. Total income (gross) and disposition
      1) Relative share for wages, material, etc.
   b. Comparative or analytical profit information
      1) With other years

   2) Profit per employee
   3) Profit per dollar invested
   4) Profit per dollar of sales
   5) Profit per unit of product sold
 c. Salaries and wages
   1) Total
   2) Salaries of executives
   3) Average weekly or hourly wage
   4) Comparisons with other industries, cost of living, etc.
 d. Taxes
   1) Per employee
   2) In relation to wages
   3) Per share of stock
   4) In relation to dividends
   5) In relation to net profit
 e. Dividends
   1) Total amount
   2) In relation to wages
   3) Per stockholder and per employee
   4) As a per cent of investment
 f. Depreciation
   1) Total amount
   2) Nature and value to employee
 g. General
   1) Nature and importance of the break-even point
   2) Trends in industry
   3) Effect of expansion on job opportunities, etc.
   4) Appraisal of future outlook
   5) Discussion of achievements in production, sales, or safety
   6) Explanation of how the company benefits the community and the nation
   7) Explanation of changes in pension, welfare, or other such plans or policies

FINANCIAL STATEMENTS FOR EMPLOYEES

There is no consistent pattern as to the practice of giving financial statements to employees. Some managements give the same statements to both employees and shareholders, while others restate the data in what is considered to be a more understandable form. Other managements do not make financial statements generally available to employees, but rather present extracts from statements, together with explanatory comments. Still other companies feel it desirable to avoid statements in any form and use other devices to get the picture of company operations across to the employees. The authors are of the opinion that it is desirable to place understandable statements in the hands of employees without any attempt to "write down" to employees. If statements are to be made available, there is general agreement that such statements should be in simple, non-technical language. The same general principles applicable to simplified statements for shareholders, as discussed in the preceding chapter, can be applied to employee statements. Such an approach may develop along any one of three lines, or a combination. Employees may be given:

1. The modified or "single-step" earnings statement, and modified statement of owner capital given to shareholders, as discussed in Chapter 30. There is, of course, a certain value in presenting the same type of statement to employees as to shareholders, or

2. A simplified type of statement, which is characterized by departures from conventional accounting form and terminology, or

3. A "per-employee" statement or statements which translate the financial data into terms of a single employee.

MODIFIED SHAREHOLDER-EMPLOYEE STATEMENTS

The modified statements, such as those issued by Parke, Davis & Company,[1] are believed to be one form quite suitable for employees as well as shareholders. They are understandable by the ordinary reader. By and large the average employee is no less intelligent than the average shareholder. What is suitable for one is generally the type suitable for the other.

SIMPLIFIED STATEMENTS

Another possibility for employee statement presentation is a somewhat more simplified statement. Perhaps the only difference between this classification and the modified shareholder-employee statements is the degree to which conventional accounting terminology has been abandoned.

Since the emphasis in an employees' report is directed more toward the salaries and wages, the shareholder-employee operating statement may be rearranged to a "first-cost" statement. Basically, this merely involves deducting all costs and expenses from income to arrive at the balance distributed to employees and shareholders, or retained in the business. An example of such a presentation, together with the inclusion of "per-employee" data, is illustrated in Fig. 177. No particular additional comments are necessary regarding this attack on the problem except to point out the desirability of showing all other employee benefit expenditures in addition to salaries and wages; and to suggest that there may be good reason for

[1] See pp. 586 and 591.

The Parent Company
STATEMENT OF INCOME AND EXPENSE
For the Year Ended December 31, 1962

	Total Amount	Amount per Employee	Cents per Dollar of Receipts
The Company Received:			
From customers for goods and services purchased...................	$12,490,500	$11,783	97.8
Dividends from subsidiaries.............	265,000	250	2.1
Interest on receivables, miscellaneous income, etc.....................	12,300	12	.1
Total Company Received.............	12,767,800	12,045	100.0
The Company's Expenses Were:			
For materials, supplies, and other expenses...	7,392,450	6,974	57.9
For wear and tear on buildings, machinery, and equipment (depreciation)............	267,800	253	2.1
For taxes—federal, state, and local, but excluding social security.................	248,900	235	1.9
Making a total of..................	7,909,150	7,462	61.9
Which left for wages, salaries, dividends, and reinvestment in the business.............	4,858,650	4,583	38.1
This Was Divided as Follows:			
Paid to employees (excluding officers) as wages and salaries........................	3,621,430	3,416	28.4
Paid for employee benefits, including social security taxes, contributions to pension fund, group life insurance, etc...........	365,400	345	2.9
Total............................	3,986,830	3,761	31.3
Paid to officers as compensation...........	119,800	113	.9
Paid to stockholders as dividends for the use of buildings, machinery, and equipment and working capital provided by their investment..................................	405,300	382	3.2
Reinvested in the business to cover the growing needs of the company...............	346,720	327	2.7
Total division......................	$ 4,858,650	$ 4,583	38.1

Fig. 177—Illustrative Statement of Income and Expense for Employees.

1960 Report to Employees---How TRW Available Income Was Divided

FROM OUR CUSTOMERS
for all goods and services we received

$420,421,158

This record income came from sales of TRW products and services in five major areas: (1) Missile and Space sales amounted to $121,579,499. (2) Automotive sales were $112,157,385. (3) Aircraft sales were $104,794,163. (4) Electronics sales were $73,464,370. (5) Sales of unclassified products and services totaled $8,425,741.

THESE BILLS HAD TO BE PAID...

EVER-MOUNTING TAXES TOOK

$21,447,536

Taxes, which amounted to $820 per TRW employee, came first, and this huge sum went to help pay the increasing cost of government. TRW pays more than 150 kinds of local, state and federal taxes.

WE BOUGHT MATERIALS AND SUPPLIES WORTH

$131,297,587

After payrolls, this was the second biggest expense. More than 131 million dollars went for steel, aluminum, cast iron, oil, tools and supplies. This amounted to more than $5,000 per TRW employee.

FOR DEPRECIATION
—useful life taken out of our equipment

$12,493,631

This is the amount we set aside in 1960 to replace worn-out and obsolete equipment and machines. At today's higher prices it is not sufficient to do the job, and in addition we must draw upon profit.

BILLS for other necessary expenses CAME TO

$57,318,724

Hundreds of items make up this cost, including heat, light, power, telephone, telegraph, postage, price catalogs, advertising and other bills essential to running a business.

That Left Us $197,863,680 To Split Between:

❶ EMPLOYEES (Payrolls)
❷ STOCKHOLDERS (Dividends)
❸ REINVESTMENT in the Business (Plowback)

❶
EMPLOYEES WERE PAID $187,687,125 OR 94.9%

Payrolls were the biggest single item of expense during 1960. This amounted to 94.9 percent of all the money left to be divided. In other words, nearly 95 cents of every available income dollar went back to TRW's approximately 26,000 employees.

❷*
Stockholders—for use of their money—Received in Dividends
$4,723,100
or 2.4% of available income

Stockholders, who risked their savings in our business, received only 2.4 percent of the available income dollar, as compared with 94.9 percent paid to employees.

❸
To insure a growing future we reinvested
$5,453,455
or 2.7% of available income

To build for the future and make jobs, we re-invested 2.7 percent of the available income. This is what we call "plowback"; it helps insure growth.

* Profit for the year was $10,176,555, the sum of dividends paid to stockholders (Box 2) and money reinvested in the business (Box 3). **Profit was only 2.4 percent of sales.**

setting out executive compensation to reveal the relative cost as compared to the payments to other employees. Such information is usually available to shareholders, so why not give it to the employees?

An informal presentation of operating results can be achieved by means of graphs and brief explanatory comment. Figure 178 is illustrative of this type of treatment, as presented by Thompson-Ramo-Wooldridge. Another effective financial statement is illustrated in Fig. 179.

THE "PER-EMPLOYEE" STATEMENT

"Per-employee" figures are determined by dividing the dollar value of each item in the statement by the number of employees in an effort to indicate the relationship of each such item to the individual employee. It is an attempt to convey to the employee what the investment of the shareholder, as well as the items of expense, mean to each one individually. There are at least three general methods of presenting the "per-employee" statement:

1. *Use of the Modified Statement.* Accounting terminology is discarded, and ordinary language is used to itemize the elements (see Fig. 177). While total figures as well as per-employee figures are usually included, some companies present only individualized data.
2. *Use of Parallel Columns.* In one column appear the data employed in the statement to stockholders, usually with a detailed explanation of the item. In the other column is presented the "per-employee" information with further explanation.
3. *Use of Conventional Statements.* This method presents both the total amount and "per employee" amount in usual accounting form. The description, however, is followed by an explanation of each item in everyday language.

The limitations of the "per employee" data should be recognized. Accompanying explanations should attempt to clarify as much as possible. Thus, it is not to be implied that a lower tax expense per employee would result in higher pay. Moreover, the investment per employee should not be construed as the *value* of the company. It may be more or less than this sum. Be that as it may, if it is correctly used, the per employee data can serve a useful purpose in explaining facts to company personnel.

SOME FUNDAMENTAL ECONOMICS

The emphasis to this point has been on understandable and readable reports to employees. Where the management has done a good job in employee communications—where the employees have been educated to the basic facts of business—then it is easier to secure an understanding of the problems faced by the business. A good illustration of a candid discussion

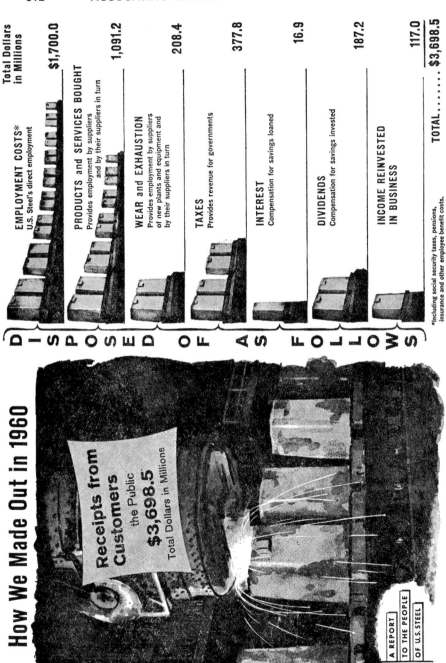

How We Made Out in 1960

Receipts from Customers the Public $3,698.5 Total Dollars in Millions

A REPORT TO THE PEOPLE OF U.S. STEEL
1960 1961

	Total Dollars in Millions
EMPLOYMENT COSTS* U.S. Steel's direct employment	$1,700.0
PRODUCTS and SERVICES BOUGHT Provides employment by suppliers and by their suppliers in turn	1,091.2
WEAR and EXHAUSTION Provides employment by suppliers of new plants and equipment and by their suppliers in turn	208.4
TAXES Provides revenue for governments	377.8
INTEREST Compensation for savings loaned	16.9
DIVIDENDS Compensation for savings invested	187.2
INCOME REINVESTED IN BUSINESS	117.0
TOTAL.......	$3,698.5

DISPOSED OF AS FOLLOWS

*Including social security taxes, pensions, insurance and other employee benefit costs.

Fig. 170. Simplified Income and Retained Earnings Statement. (By permission U. S. Steel Corporation.)

of return on investment is the "Special Report to Employees," the pertinent excerpts of which are shown in Fig. 180, taken from the house organ of Continental Oil Company.

FORMAT OF REPORTS

Whether the employee reads the reports will depend greatly on the form. The same comments made on page 597 as to shareholders' reports are applicable here, and need not be repeated. Simple, frank statements, the effective use of graphs, charts, or illustrations, and employment of color will assist in telling the business story. Moreover, the report should have a certain dignity. It may be found desirable to mail it to the employee's home.

CRITICISMS OF EMPLOYEE REPORTS

With a trend toward special communications to employees concerning the financial results and condition of the company, criticism naturally has appeared. For appropriate consideration, a summary of present-day (limited) adverse comments is as follows without any attempt at evaluation by the authors:

1. Those reports which attempt to appeal to both shareholder and employee usually fail to "get through" to the employee
2. Reports tend to be too skimpy, including only bare essentials
3. Many needlessly extol the free enterprise system without adequately telling the story of the company itself—that is, how it fared
4. Some reports are burdened with special gimmicks in an attempt to secure attention, thus burying the story of the company's progress

With a knowledge of the risks and dangers, ways can be found to present the company story intelligently.

This chapter has been concerned with the provision of information by company management to employees as a communication device. It has not been concerned with the desire of organized labor for further information for purposes of collective bargaining.[2]

OTHER AVAILABLE MEDIA

Several other channels, in addition to the special or separate annual report, are available for getting information to the employee, be it financial or otherwise. These means, with brief comments, are outlined as follows:

1. *House Organ.* This means, which may be addressed to customers as well as employees, is often used as a device to present the salient parts of the annual report or periodic financial information. It is a

[2] On this aspect, see Wilbur F. Pillsbury, "Organized Labor's Views of Corporate Financial Information," *Journal of Accountancy,* June, 1958, pp. 46–55.

Special Report To Employees

How We Did Last Year

OPERATING

Production: UP some . . . 3.9% . . . to 185,675 b/d.

This is Conoco's domestic production plus its share of oil produced by its domestic and foreign affiliates. Domestic production alone was up 0.6%. The industry average domestic production dipped below 1959.

Exploration: Conoco drilled 94 net exploratory wells and had a 20.2% success ratio. The industry's success ratio was 13.5%.

Net Expl. Completions

	1959	1960
oil wells	12	13
gas wells	4	6
dry holes	60	75

Manufacturing: UP. a little . . . 0.6% . . . to 181,927 b/d.

Refinery runs were up slightly less than the average for the industry, which was up 1.0%.

Marketing: UP a little . . . 0.3% . . . to 221,-856 b/d.

Conoco again in 1960 sold more products than it produced and refined by buying the extra barrels from other refiners.

The company's total gasoline sales increased 0.9% during 1960.

FINANCIAL

Gross Income: UP a little . . . 1.6% . . . to $799.1 million.

This is the money we receive from sales of crude oil, refined products, petrochemicals, and the excise taxes we collect for the government.

Gross income doesn't reflect true success, but can be used to show company's relative size.

Costs, Expenses, and Taxes: UP a little . . . 1.6% . . . to $737.9 million.

Costs continued to rise at a faster rate than net income.

Salaries, wages, and benefits were UP 4.7% to $83.7 million in 1960. A 5% general wage increase went into effect Dec. 16, 1960.

Net Income: UP a little . . . 0.6% . . . to $61.2 million.

While net income rose 0.6%, Conoco's capital expenditures were 22.1% greater than in 1959.

This means that it is taking a lot more investment money to earn just a little more in net income. Net income is used to pay dividends and to re-invest for growth.

Investments Are Rising

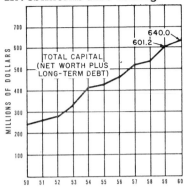

CONOCO IS GROWING. Each year our company invests more and more in our business. This chart illustrates the upward trend of invested capital over past decade.

Rate of Return Is Skidding

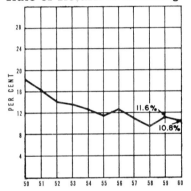

WHILE INVESTMENT in our business goes up, the rate of return slides down. The line on this chart shows that in 1950 the return was 18.6% and in 1960 it was 10.8%.

Costs Are the Reason

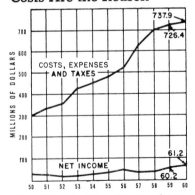

HERE IS WHY earnings have not kept pace with investment. Conoco's costs, expenses and taxes have climbed steadily and kept the net income line fairly even.

Fig. 180—Explanatory Report to Employees—Return on

Investing Earns, Spending Does Not

THE record shows that Conoco's net income for 1960 was the highest we ever have recorded. We also were able to report that we produced more crude oil and sold more refined products last year than ever before.

Naturally, we have every right to be proud of our performance in these respects; it indicates that we continue to be a growing and aggressive company. However, the fact that we keep on "setting records" must not encourage us to become complacent, and to assume that all we need to remain prosperous is to take more and more oil from the ground, and sell more and more products.

Actually, the key to our ability to remain successful is the rate of return on our investment . . . and here the record offers us much less reason for cheering. While it is true that we can describe our 1960 net income as a "record high", each year the amount of money we must invest and spend to earn a dollar becomes greater and greater. While our earnings become larger, the dollars we earn in relation to the dollars we have invested become fewer and fewer.

Elsewhere on these pages, I understand you can look at some simple charts which show graphically how, over the past 10 years, our income has increased annually . . . while the rate of return on our investment has declined steadily. The result, which also is illustrated, is that while our net earnings — the money available to repay stockholders for the use of their funds, and to reinvest in our business — have grown, they are growing very slowly indeed.

I call your attention to these charts particularly because they show also very clearly the reason for our declining rate of return on investment, and the very slow growth of our net earnings. The reason is contained in a five-letter word with which all of us are abundantly familiar — costs. You will notice on the charts that the curve showing what has happened to our costs over the last 10 years rises steadily and steeply, year after year.

Somehow we must slow the rise of that curve if we are to go on being the sort of company that offers good opportunity and a high degree of security to the people who work in it.

Costs are the one factor which we can control toward the goal of increasing our earnings. If we are to grow, to expand, to gain a step on our competitors, we simply can't stop investing money in prospects that can return a profit to us. But we can control expense items.

Now let me say this . . . the expression, "cost control", sometimes becomes badly twisted through its interpretation. It is never my intention, nor that of any other responsible manager in Conoco, to suggest that we become a company of "penny pinchers", nor that we run anything but a first-class operation in all of our affairs.

I am interested — as a matter of fact I insist upon it — in Conoco being a company where conservation of dollars is foremost in the minds of everyone. In my definition, conserving dollars means using them wisely to produce the greatest benefit to the Company, for its stockholders and for you as an employee. Conserving money does not mean "nickel nursing" . . . it does mean constantly seeking more economical ways to do things, and stopping up any loopholes of waste of our dollars.

As I write this, it looks as if 1961 can be a good year for Conoco, even in the heat of the fiercest competition I ever have witnessed in the oil business. We have many interesting plans about which you will be hearing.

Some of these plans and projects will require us to invest very large sums of money. Some of this money will come from past earnings; a larger portion must be borrowed, and repaid out of our future earnings.

Right there is the important difference between conserving dollars and cost control . . . which is the difference between investing and spending.

When we invest money, we do so with the expectation of getting that money back through efficient operation, plus some more money as earnings on our investment.

However, when we spend money, that money is gone, and we cannot get it back, much less hope for any earnings from it. It is as simple as that . . . money invested earns more money . . . money spent in costs earns nothing.

About two-thirds of you are stockholders in our company . . . you men and women certainly should be in the front ranks when it comes to conserving our dollars, for this is one way to increase the value of your investment.

But when you come right down to it, every employee of this company profits through our growth . . . in opportunities for advancement . . . a more secure future . . . and continued good salaries, wages and benefits.

I have said many times how proud I am that there is a degree of cooperation among Conoco people that I simply do not find in other companies.

This cooperation helped us report a good year in 1960 . . . it has got us off to a good start in 1961. I am confident that it will be a main factor in helping all of us work toward improving our rate of earnings, so that together we will grow still stronger, more secure and more prosperous.

L. F. McCollum

Investment. (By permission Continental Oil Company.)

means of building esprit de corps, and presenting timely subjects in the employee's language.

2. *Letters or Leaflets* (*Direct Mail*). Such means usually generate interest at home, and can be effective in that area.
3. *Bulletin Boards.* This is a useful means for getting a brief message to all employees.
4. *Payroll Inserts.* Generally this method should be used only for items directly affecting an employee's pay.
5. *Advertisements.* This medium reaches the employees and the public at the same time.
6. *Handbook.* This method is useful primarily to acquaint new employees with company policies, etc.
7. *Personal Contact.* This means is one of the best, and the employee's supervisor should be an important cog. Other means of personal contact include employee mass meetings or civic group meetings where facts can be presented.
8. *Films.* This means has been developed more recently as a means of getting visual and auditory contact with employees.

REPORTS TO THE GENERAL PUBLIC

THE OBJECTIVE

Unfortunately there is a great public misconception regarding American business. A large number of people think that business makes unwarranted profits; that corporations are owned by a few wealthy individuals; that large companies are not to be trusted; that business is responsible for rising prices on the one hand and depressions on the other; and that business always profiteers out of any war or defense effort. To answer those who spread such misinformation, it is not enough to reply with broad unsupported generalities. The public needs to know the *facts* about business, since it is they who ultimately will determine the kind of economic order that will predominate. The basic objective is to convey to the general public facts about business in a way it will comprehend. The individual business wants to create a "good impression" concerning itself, and business generally needs to explain the advantages and gains of the free enterprise system to the community at large.

THE CONTROLLER'S PART

Although the problem may be attacked from several avenues, the fact remains that accounting information must play a major role. It is largely from a misunderstanding by the public of the financial statements, or misunderstanding by those who "tell" the public, that many of the misconceptions have arisen. Clear, simple, and understandable financial statements are among the best tools available to correct these distortions and half-truths.

Since the proper interpretation of the financial operations is a main support in the solution of the problem, a certain responsibility must fall on the accountant—and that means the controller. Of course, he will require the active help and support of those who are experts in persuasion—the public relations director, the advertising manager, etc. However, as the chief problem is the proper presentation and interpretation of accounting data, he must assume a major responsibility. Whether the public continues to believe the distortions of those who for selfish reasons do not provide all the facts; whether, indeed, private enterprise will be strengthened, and the public will realize the tangible benefits of this system, depends in no small part on the accounting profession. The presentation of complete, unbiased, and clearly interpreted financial information can contribute much to the confidence of the general public in the American system.

WEAKNESSES IN PRESENT-DAY REPORTS

With reference particularly to the financial statements and annual reports, there are certain definite weaknesses which have prevented business from getting its story understood by the public. Though some of these were reviewed in the preceding sections, they may be summarized as follows.

Common Everyday Words Are Used in a Special Technical Sense. The most commonly misunderstood term, perhaps, is "surplus," which to the ordinary citizen means excess. Another such term is "reserve." While the word has several connotations to an accountant, to the layman it is something set aside for future use. Such terms as these must be eliminated when presenting information to the public if there is to be a clear understanding.

The Form and Designation of Financial Statements Are Misleading. "Balance sheets" with the assets on the left and liabilities and net worth on the right appear to be more for the convenience of the bookkeeper than anything else. To the layman, the question is raised that if assets are equal to the liabilities, how can a company prosper? Again, the many types of "profit" in a statement of income and expense are confusing. Moreover, how can a statement be one of profit and loss? It is either one or the other. Here, too, accounting tradition must give way to more realistic terms.

Inadequate Information Is Given. In many instances only partial information is given. For example, sales data may be withheld; yet such figures can be used to good advantage in demonstrating to the public the relationship between sales volume and operating profit. Perhaps nothing breeds distrust as much as half-truths, or a feeling that information is being withheld. Facts should be supplied that will solve a problem but will not give vital information to competition, or otherwise injure the company.

Presentations Aid Misinterpretation. Some attempts to lead to misinterpretation are deliberate and fall into the propaganda classification, but in many instances the misunderstanding results from a poor presentation. Examples of what may be described as poor judgment in report presentation include: (1) a comment on return on investment, calculated on total capital invested under circumstances when shareholder equity might have been more appropriate; (2) an attempt at conveying the impression that the employees received most of the sales dollar when this is not borne out by the facts; (3) emphasis on the high level of taxes, with the implication that this condition prevented higher wages, when such may not be the case.

PRESENTING FIGURE-FACTS TO THE PUBLIC

Generally, the same principles discussed in previous chapters are applicable in presenting financial information to the general public. The report should contain all the pertinent facts on the subject, presented in an understandable manner. The mass of information should be ignored and the really vital aspects covered. Moreover, in many cases it will be advisable to give figures for several years. Then, too, the use of clear, simple language, color, photography, and charts can be effective.

It is desirable that the subject matter be directed to the audience. Items of particular interest or concern to the public should be emphasized. Some suggested topics, which may be a part of an annual report or of data released at the same or other times, include:

1. The place of free, private enterprise in our economy
2. Unsound legislation
3. Unsound governmental policy
4. Taxation
5. Interrelationship of industries; of labor, agriculture, and industry
6. Cooperation between government and industry
7. The relationship of the industry to the community
8. The extent of research
9. The creation of new markets
10. Financial data of many sorts:
    a. Relationship of sales volume and profits
    b. Profit as a percentage of net sales
    c. Reasons for increased profit
    d. Comparison of profits with other periods
    e. The cost of management
    f. The distribution of corporate ownership
    g. Reasons for price increases
    h. Distribution of the sales dollar
11. Relationship with labor
12. The outlook

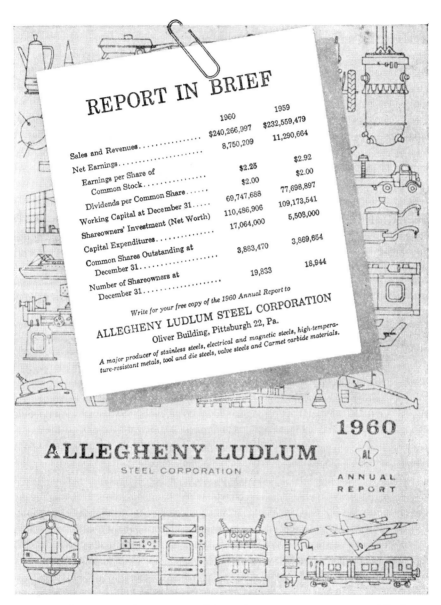

REPORT IN BRIEF

	1960	1959
Sales and Revenues...............	$240,266,997	$232,559,479
Net Earnings....................	8,750,209	11,290,664
Earnings per Share of Common Stock..............	$2.25	$2.92
Dividends per Common Share......	$2.00	$2.00
Working Capital at December 31.....	69,747,688	77,698,897
Shareowners' Investment (Net Worth)	110,486,906	109,173,541
Capital Expenditures..............	17,064,000	5,503,000
Common Shares Outstanding at December 31..................	3,883,470	3,869,654
Number of Shareowners at December 31.................	19,833	18,944

Write for your free copy of the 1960 Annual Report to

ALLEGHENY LUDLUM STEEL CORPORATION
Oliver Building, Pittsburgh 22, Pa.

A major producer of stainless steels, electrical and magnetic steels, high-temperature-resistant metals, tool and die steels, valve steels and Carmet carbide materials.

1960

ALLEGHENY LUDLUM
STEEL CORPORATION

ANNUAL REPORT

Fig. 181—Illustrative Advertisement of Annual Report. (By permission Allegheny Ludlum Steel Corporation.)

It is to be observed that the consumer, employee, and shareholder also will have an interest in many of these subjects.

FORM OF STATEMENTS FOR THE PUBLIC

A question arises as to the necessity of preparing any special form of financial statements for the public. As has been previously mentioned, the public as well as the shareholders and employees do not understand the conventional statements. However, the simplified forms or summary data are as well suited to the needs of the public as to the owners or employees. No special construction is considered necessary. An illustration of an effective advertisement of financial facts which Allegheny Ludlum Steel Corporation published in newspapers of the various communities in which their plants are located, as well as in certain financial papers, is shown in Fig. 181.

METHODS OF REPORTING TO THE PUBLIC

Several media are available to convey the business story to the public:

1. *Shareholders' Reports.* Many companies make a wide distribution of the annual report to the general public. A related practice is to make such reports available to certain special groups that may be interested.
2. *Institutional Advertising.* Some of the corporations purchase newspaper or magazine space to summarize the results of operations, to present the company's position on some particular topic, or to explain why certain action was taken. Perhaps it might be regarded as a duty of a particular company, rather than merely a right, to inform the public how it serves.
3. *Press Releases.* Information may be released to the press on specific points, such as earnings, employee benefits, and new products.
4. *Radio and Television Broadcasts.* This medium can be used effectively to explain particular subjects—financial or otherwise.
5. *Special Letters, Booklets, and Pamphlets.* Reprints from magazines can be made available to visitors, or to the public as requested.

Each medium has its particular purpose and can be used to present the facts about business. Several media may be employed to get the proper coverage.

32

Reports to Governmental Divisions and Stock Exchanges

GOVERNMENTAL CONTROL

Of all the leading countries in the world, only in the United States and Canada can private enterprise be said to dominate the economic system. Even in these two nations the trend unmistakably has been toward more and more governmental regulation and control.

The phase of governmental control which is under immediate discussion is the reporting to governmental divisions. As most controllers are well aware, a mass of reports must be filed. And in times of national emergency these reports increase manyfold: inventory reports, reports relative to price control, statistics on production and sales, information on number of employees, on wage rates and average earnings—the number and variety seem endless. These reports or forms are of concern to the accountant. But the requirements are set out, in a more or less clear manner, on the reporting forms, and no particular comments need be made. Consequently, this chapter deals principally with reporting of an over-all financial nature to both governmental agencies and stock exchanges.

GOVERNMENTAL REGULATORY AGENCIES

Governmental regulation can be effected by means of statutory direct control, by charter, by franchise, or by other methods. In recent years, however, legislators have begun to effect regulation largely by creating administrative agencies and delegating to them certain powers and duties. It is with these governmental regulatory agencies, and their reporting requirements, that the accountant or controller is chiefly concerned.

Some of the more important federal bodies are commented upon briefly.[1]

[1] Adapted in part from the *United States Government Organization Manual, 1961–62.*

Securities and Exchange Commission. The Securities Exchange Act of 1934 created the Securities and Exchange Commission and assigned to it the administration of the Act, along with other subsequent enactments.

The general objective of the statutes administered by the Commission is to protect the interests of the public and investors against malpractices in the securities and financial markets. Thus the laws provide for public disclosure of pertinent facts concerning new security offerings to the public and securities listed on exchanges; regulation of trading in securities on the exchanges and in over-the-counter markets; enforcement of sanctions against companies and persons guilty of securities frauds, manipulations, and other violations; integration and simplification of holding company systems of electric and gas utilities; supervision of the purchase and sale of securities, utility properties, and other assets of such holding companies or their subsidiaries, and approval of their reorganizations, mergers, and consolidations; improved protective provisions in mortgage indentures under which debt securities are sold to the public; supervision of the activities of investment companies engaged in the purchase and sale of securities; regulation of the activities of investment advisers who render securities advisory service to others; and performance by the Commission of advisory services to courts in reorganization proceedings for bankrupt corporations.

It is evident that the SEC activities are not restricted to new security issues.

Federal Trade Commission. The Federal Trade Commission was organized as an independent administrative agency by the Federal Trade Commission Act of 1914.

The general purposes of the Federal Trade Commission Act are threefold: (1) to promote free and fair competition in interstate trade in the interest of the public through prevention of price-fixing agreements, boycotts, combinations in restraint of trade, unlawful price discriminations, and other unfair methods of competition and unfair or deceptive acts and practices, including false advertising; (2) to safeguard the life and health of the consuming public by preventing the dissemination of false advertisements of food, drugs, cosmetics, etc.; and (3) to make available to the President, the Congress, and the public, factual data concerning economic and business conditions as a basis for remedial legislation where needed, and for the guidance and protection of the public. This Act has since been amended by other legislation which has broadened the jurisdiction of the Commission.

Of particular interest to accountants is the relation of the Commission to the administration of the Robinson-Patman Act.

Section 6 of the Federal Trade Commission Act empowers the Commission to ascertain the facts with respect to the organization, business, conduct, practices, and management of any corporation subject to its jurisdiction, and the relations of any such corporation to other corporations, partnerships, etc. Moreover, this section gives the Commission the power to require such corporations to file with it annual or special, or both, reports or answers in writing to specific questions, as may be required by the Commission in respect to matters within its jurisdiction.

Interstate Commerce Commission. The Interstate Commerce Commission was created in 1887 by what is now known as the Interstate Commerce Act. Here also, subsequent legislation has broadened the scope of the Commission's jurisdiction.

The general purpose of creating the Commission was to provide a body empowered to regulate, in the public interest, common carriers subject to the Act engaged in transportation in interstate commerce. The provisions of the Act are to be so administered that all modes of transportation subject to its provisions are to be so regulated as to recognize and preserve the inherent advantages of each; to promote safe, economical service; to encourage the establishment and maintenance of reasonable charges for transportation services, without unjust discrimination or unfair competitive practices; and to encourage fair wages and equitable working conditions— all to the end of developing, coordinating, and preserving a national transportation system adequate to meet the needs of commerce, the postal service, and the national defense of the United States.

The Commission prescribes the forms of the accounts and records to be kept by the carriers subject to the Act. Further, it requires those under its jurisdiction to file annual reports and such intermediate reports as it deems necessary. Present regulations require certain monthly operating reports from certain carriers, quarterly reports as to certain matters, in addition to the annual report or other special reports.[2]

Regulations or codes detail the accounts to be used, the nature of the charges and credits, and similar points.

Federal Power Commission. The Federal Power Commission was organized as an independent commission in its present form in 1940, although originally created by the Federal Water Power Act of 1920.

Broadly, the Commission is to carry out the policies of Congress providing for the development and improvement of navigation and the development, transmission, and utilization of power on streams subject to federal jurisdiction.

---

[2] See the Code of Federal Regulations for details.

The Commission has prescribed uniform systems of accounts for public utilities subject to its jurisdiction. Moreover, it requires certain reports, such as:

1. Annual reports, rendered by every electric utility, setting forth complete financial and statistical data as to assets, liabilities, revenues, generating capacity, number of consumers, and similar information
2. Power system reports rendered by every electric utility system, setting forth information with respect to generating capacity and transmission facilities, loads and load characteristics, and similar information
3. Monthly and annual reports containing such information as production of electricity for public use, fuel consumed, and stocks of fuel on hand
4. Reports from electric utilities and industrial corporations with respect to their electric power requirements and supply

In addition, special reports are prescribed from time to time, such as reports on the areas served by each electric utility.

Federal Communications Commission. The Federal Communications Commission was created by the Communications Act of 1934. This Act was passed for the purpose of regulating interstate and foreign commerce in communication by wire and radio so as "to make available to all the people of the United States a rapid, efficient, nation-wide, and world-wide wire and radio communication service with adequate facilities at reasonable charges. . . ."

The Commission has not prescribed any uniform chart of accounts, but has certain reporting requirements. Thus, Section 43.21 of Title 47 of the Code of Federal Regulations provides that all communication common carriers, and persons immediately controlling any such carriers, must file in duplicate annual reports. Provision is made for filing verified copies of any statements, such as Form 10–K, filed with the Securities and Exchange Commission. Moreover, each carrier having annual operating revenues in excess of $250,000 must prepare, on forms adopted and furnished or approved by the Commission, monthly reports of revenues, expenses, and other data as designated on such forms. Again, the regulation provides for a filing of changes in depreciation rates, for the filing of copies of pension plans, and other data. It is to be noted, also, that carriers subject to the Commission's accounting rules and regulations must file with it a certified statement indicating (1) the name and title of the accounting officer who is responsible for compliance with the Commission's accounting regulations, (2) the source of such assignment or authority (bylaws, etc.), and (3) the name of the individual or group to whom such accounting officer is responsible.

The foregoing comments indicate the accounting and reporting requirements of several of the governmental regulatory bodies. Other federal agencies as well as many state commissions have reporting requirements for particular types of business in which the public is deemed to have a special interest. Although not entirely discernible from brief statements made herein, it is to be observed that the prescribed records and reports vary greatly in nature and extent. The range includes:

1. A complete and detailed uniform system of accounts which sets forth the data to be maintained in each account, and the accounting principles and theories to be applied thereto
2. Extensive instructions on form and content of reports and records, short of the prescription of a complete chart of accounts, to be maintained, as illustrated by the SEC requirements relative to records to be maintained by traders in securities
3. Very limited record requirements having little effect on the form, and referring to information that probably would be retained despite legislative requirements

ACTIVITIES OF THE SECURITIES AND EXCHANGE COMMISSION

As the principal accounting officers of industrial corporations, many controllers are likely to be directly involved in complying with requirements of the Securities and Exchange Commission. The statutes relating to the activities of the Commission which are of direct concern to most controllers are the Securities Act of 1933, the Securities Exchange Act of 1934, and the Trust Indenture Act of 1939. The first is designed, among other things, to compel disclosure of material facts concerning securities publicly offered and sold through the mails or in interstate commerce. Such a disclosure is effected by filing a registration statement with the Commission, which registration statement must include a prospectus containing in summarized form the pertinent information concerning the issue. The Securities Exchange Act complements the Securities Act by requiring comparable disclosure, though in briefer form, by companies whose securities are traded in on a national securities exchange. The Trust Indenture Act requires, in substance, that a company offering a bond, note, or debenture issue of more than $1,000,000 shall issue such securities pursuant to an indenture containing various provisions designed to protect the purchaser.

The effect of the various Acts is to give the Commission extensive powers with respect to financial statements filed with it. The statutes do not give any authority to interfere with the actual operations or internal management of operating businesses, except as to certain financial matters relating to public utility holding companies and companies emerging from reorganization. Moreover, the Acts do not authorize the Commission to pass on the investment merits of securities.

THE SEC AND ACCOUNTING PRACTICES

The Securities Exchange Act of 1934 has established a governmental body which can settle accounting problems authoritatively as to a large field of accounting activity. The powers of the SEC are exercised through several means:

1. *Regulation S–X.* The Securities Act and Securities Exchange Act granted broad power as to accounting matters, but left the prescribing of detailed accounting requirements as an administrative matter for the Commission. Pursuant to such authority, Regulation S–X was promulgated in 1940, and governs the form and content of most of the financial statements filed with the SEC under the Acts of 1933, 1934, and 1940. Prior to such issuance, the accounting requirements were set forth in the particular form filed. Moreover, new forms were originated and differences arose. Regulation S–X was designed to integrate these different requirements into a single and more simple regulation.

2. *Formal Decisions.* Formal decisions are rendered as to accounting matters. Publication of such findings constitutes an important means by which its conclusions are made known.

3. *Accounting Series Releases.* Starting in 1937, these releases were issued to contribute to the development of uniform standards and practices on major accounting questions. Some deal with specialized types of problems, but amendments to Regulation S–X and formal decisions also are included.

Decisions, rules, or policies of the SEC may be said to relate to three main phases of accounting activity:

1. *Matters of Accounting Principles or Practice.* These pertain to the recording of financial transactions and the presentation of financial statements.

2. *Matters of Auditing.* Such comments relate to the procedures by which accountants review and report on financial statements prepared by corporate management.

3. *Matters of Professional Conduct.* These relate to the standards of professional conduct of those public accountants who certify financial statements, such as the matter of independence of auditors.

The financial statements required in the Commission forms prescribed under the Acts (including the Public Utility Holding Company Act of 1935 and the Investment Company Act of 1940) are the conventional balance sheet, income and surplus statements, and certain supporting schedules. Registration forms for new issues ordinarily require three-year income and surplus statements as well as a summary of earnings for an appropriate period, usually not less than five years.

A comment is in order as to the procedure of the SEC. After financial statements have been filed, they are reviewed by the staff. If such statements have not been prepared in accordance with generally accepted accounting principles, or if they otherwise fail to meet the requirements of the SEC in any significant respect, a so-called deficiency letter or letter of comment is prepared and sent to the registrant. These letters serve as the basis of correspondence or conferences with the corporations whereby accounting questions usually are expeditiously resolved without time-consuming and expensive formal hearings. Of course, if the matters are not satisfactorily resolved, or if the company fails to modify the statements as requested, then proceedings are instituted to determine whether the statements are in fact materially inadequate or misleading. The SEC has the authority to issue stop orders whereby the securities may not be offered to the public.

NATURE OF DEFICIENCIES REPORTED BY SEC

The controller should be aware of the types of deficiencies which have been found prevalent, as an aid in avoiding them. With respect to deficiencies in financial statements other than those of broker-dealers, a majority of the deficient items are the result of failure to comply with specific rules, contained, for the most part, in Regulation S–X.

While each several years may raise accounting problems peculiar to that span of time, a few of the specific types of items which have been the subject of deficiencies are outlined: [3]

1. *Reserves for Inventory Losses.* Reserves for future inventory losses have been created out of income which improperly reduces current profits and improperly increases profits of subsequent periods. The SEC permits provisions for inventory losses only to the extent that the losses actually have taken place but have not been realized by use or sale of the materials involved.

2. *Contingency Reserves.* In a footnote relating to the reserve, the Commission has required a positive statement to the effect that the account will not be used in such a manner as to relieve the income account for any future period of a charge that properly should be made thereagainst.

3. *Premium on Preferred Stock.* The question was whether a premium paid on the redemption of preferred stock, in excess of the amount paid in thereon, may properly be charged against paid-in surplus contributed by another class of shareholders; or whether, when earned surplus is present, the excess premium should be charged thereagainst to the extent available. The Commission, in *Account-*

---

[3] From Earle C. King, "What the SEC Requires in Financial Statements Filed with the Commission," *Journal of Accountancy,* November, 1947, pp. 377–84.

ing Series Release No. 45, indicated that the amount paid in redemption of preferred stock in excess of the amount originally paid in thereon should be charged to earned surplus.

4. *Qualified Certificate on Depreciation.* From time to time the accountants' certificates which accompany financial statements of public utility companies filed with the Commission contain the following, or a similar, qualification: "—subject to the adequacy of the provision and the reserve for depreciation, as to which we are not in a position to express an opinion—the accompanying balance sheet presents fairly. . . ." In recent years when depreciation accounting generally has displaced the retirement reserve or other methods of providing for the exhaustion of the useful life of utility property, the accountants have had an opportunity to familiarize themselves with property accounts and depreciation problems. Under the circumstances, the SEC is of the opinion that if the depreciation reserve is inadequate, the accountants should so state in the certificate; and there is little justification for their avoidance of full responsibility for the adequacy of depreciation provisions or reserves of such companies, except in very unusual situations.

These are examples of some common subjects of deficiency statements.[4] Many controllers will recognize the subject matter as generally covered by the Accounting Research Bulletins of the American Institute of Certified Public Accountants.

A review of problem areas perhaps would lead to the conclusion that some companies prefer a lesser degree of disclosure than that desired by the Commission.[5] Additional information often must be requested as to

1. Methods of pricing inventories
2. Classification of plant assets
3. Methods followed in measuring depreciation, depletion, and amortization
4. Accounting treatment relative to maintenance and repairs, and disposition of assets
5. An elaboration in notes relating to pension plans, stock options, income taxes, and restrictions on retained earnings

Under Regulation A relating to filings for small companies, common deficiencies in the content of financial statements include such items as

1. Improper accounting for deferred charges
2. Use of written-up values of assets

---

[4] See the Annual Report of the SEC for the nature of deficiencies each year.

[5] Some of the information adapted in part from Andrew Barr, "Comments on Financial Statements Filed With the SEC," *New York Certified Public Accountant,* October, 1957, pp. 686–94.

3. Improper classifications of items which usually result in an over-statement of working capital
4. Failure to disclose the pledging of assets
5. An inadequate description of securities of the issuer
6. Failure to make appropriate accruals, especially in interim period statements
7. Failure to disclose the basis of valuation of inventories or fixed assets

Another recent problem has related to the independence of the accountant. Thus, Rule 2–01 of Regulation S–X prohibits the accountant from having *any* interest in the registrant or its affiliates, although the American Institute of Certified Public Accountants merely requires disclosure of a *substantial* interest of the accountant if he renders an opinion on the financial statements.

The matter of ambiguous opinions of the accountants has been a subject of discussions. An opinion containing the words "subject to . . ." is rarely acceptable. The Commission desires that the exception be clearly stated. This is certainly a reasonable position.

Another example of accounting matters reviewed by the Commission is the treatment of deferred income taxes.[6] The Securities Act Release No. 4010 prescribes the statement of administrative policy regarding the balance sheet treatment of the credit equivalent to the reduction of income taxes—a subject of increasing importance.

This statement said in pertinent part "any financial statement filed with this Commission which designates as earned surplus (or its equivalent) or in any manner as a part of equity capital (even though accompanied by words of limitation such as 'restricted' or 'appropriated') the accumulated credit arising from accounting for reductions in income taxes resulting from deducting costs for income tax purposes at a more rapid rate than for financial statement purposes will be presumed by the Commission to be misleading or inaccurate despite disclosure contained in the certificate of the accountant or in footnotes to the statements, provided the amounts involved are material."

The need for the controller to keep current on SEC matters regarding accounting practice is evident.

REPORTING FORMS TO THE SEC

The SEC has created registration and reporting forms of several types. Detailed instructions as to use are available from the Commission, but the following listing and comments are made to apprise the reader of the extent of reporting currently in effect, but subject to change:

[6] 1960 Annual Report of the SEC, p. 212.

Commission's Statement or Form Designation	Description
	For Registration Statements Under the Securities Act of 1933
C–2	For certain types of certificates of interest in securities
C–3	For American certificates against foreign issues and for the underlying securities
D–1	For certificates of deposit
D–1A	For certificates of deposit issued by issuer of securities
F–1	For voting trust certificates
S–1	General form for commercial or industrial companies—used when no other form is authorized
S–2	For securities of non-successor commercial and industrial corporations without subsidiaries and still in the development stage
S–3	For shares of mining corporations in the promotional stage
S–4	For closed-end management investment companies registered on Form N–8B–1
S–5	For open-end management investment companies registered on Form N–8B–1
S–6	For unit investment trusts registered on Form N–8B–2
S–8	For certain types of employees' stock purchase and savings plans
S–9	For registration of high-grade debt securities
S–10	For oil or gas interests or rights
S–11	For securities of certain real estate companies
S–12	For American Depositary Receipts issued against outstanding foreign securities
S–14	For securities acquired in mergers and consolidations
	Forms Pertaining to Exemptions
1–G	Report of sale of oil or gas right
2–G	Report of sale of oil or gas right
	Regulation A Notification and Consents
1–A	Notification under Regulation A
2–A	Report pursuant to Rule 260 of Regulation A
3–A	Irrevocable appointment by individual or agent for service of process
4–A	Irrevocable appointment by corporation of agent for service of process
5–A	Certificate of resolution authorizing irrevocable appointment by corporation of agent for service of process
6–A	Irrevocable appointment by partnership of agent for service of process
	Regulation E Notification
1–E	Notification under Regulation E
2–E	Report pursuant to Rule 609 of Regulation E
	Proposed Regulation F Notification
1–F	Notification under Regulation F
	Forms for Registration and Exemption of Securities Exchanges
1	Application for registration or exemption from registration as a national securities exchange

Commission's Statement or Form Designation	Description
1–A	Amendment to an application for registration or exemption from registration as a national securities exchange

Registration of Securities Pursuant to Section 12(b) and (c)

10	General form of application for registration of securities on a national securities exchange
14	Application for registration of certificates of deposit issued by a committee
16	Application for registration of voting trust certificates and underlying securities
18	Application for registration of securities of foreign governments and political subdivisions thereof
19	Application for registration of American certificates against foreign issues and for the underlying securities
20	Application for registration of securities other than bonds of foreign private issuers
21	Application for registration of bonds of foreign private issuers

Amendment to Application or Report

8	Amendment to application for registration or report filed pursuant to Section 12, 13, or 15(d)

Registration of Additional Securities

8–A	Application for registration of additional classes or series of securities on a national securities exchange

Successor to Issuer of Registered Securities

8–B	Application for registration of securities issued in certain cases upon the registrant's succession to an issuer or issuers of previously registered securities

Registration on Additional Exchange

8–C	Application for registration on an additional exchange

Removal of Securities from Listing and Registration

25	Notification of the removal from listing and registration of matured, redeemed, or retired securities

Admission to Trading of Substituted or Additional Securities

26	Notification of the admission to trading of a substituted or additional class of security under Rule X–12A–5

Unlisted Trading Privileges

27	Notification of changes in securities admitted to unlisted trading privileges
28	Notification of the termination or suspension of unlisted trading privileges

Current Reports of Issuers of Securities Registered on Exchanges and of Certain Issuers of Securities Registered Under Securities Act of 1933

8–K	Current reports

Commission's Statement or Form Designation	Description

Annual Reports of Issuers of Securities Registered on Exchanges

9–K	Semi-annual report
10–K	General form of annual report
14–K	Annual report for certificates of deposit issued by a committee
16–K	Annual report for voting trust certificates and underlying securities
18–K	Annual report for foreign governments and political subdivisions thereof
19–K	Annual report for American certificates against foreign issues and for the underlying securities
20–K	Annual report for securities, other than bonds, of foreign private issuers
21–K	Annual report for bonds of foreign private issuers

Registration of Brokers and Dealers

BD	Application for registration as a broker and dealer or to amend such an application
7–M	Irrevocable appointment of agent by individual non-resident broker or dealer
8–M	Irrevocable appointment of agent by corporation non-resident broker or dealer
9–M	Irrevocable appointment of agent by partnership non-resident broker or dealer
10–M	Irrevocable appointment of agent by non-resident general partner of broker or dealer

Annual Reports Required of Certain Issuers of Securities Registered Under Securities Act of 1933

10–K	General form of annual report
2–MD	Investment trusts having securities registered on Form C–1
3–MD	Voting trust certificates
4–MD	Certificates of deposit issued by committee

Registration of National Securities Associations or Affiliated Securities Associations

X–15AA–1	Application for registration as a national securities association or affiliated securities association
X–15AJ–1	Amendatory and/or supplementary statement to registration statement
X–15AJ–2	Annual consolidated supplement

Reports Required of Officers, Directors, and Principal Stockholders Pursuant to Section 16

3	Initial statement of beneficial ownership of securities
4	Statement of changes in beneficial ownership of securities
4	Change in ownership of equity securities during last calendar month
5	Ownership of equity securities where registration of an equity security of same issuer has become effective during past calendar month
6	Ownership of equity securities upon becoming a director, officer, or holder of more than 10% of any class of equity securities

Commission's Statement or Form Designation	Description

Reports of Stabilizing Activities

X–17A–1	Report pursuant to Rule X–17A–2

Annual Reports of Certain Brokers, Dealers, and Exchange Members Pursuant to Rule X–17A–5

X–17A–5	Report of financial condition

Official Forms Issued by the Securities and Exchange Commission Under the Public Utility Holding Company Act of 1935

U–A	Facing sheet for amendments to applications, declarations, reports, and statements
U–1	Application or declaration that includes an issue or sale of securities, acquisition or sale of assets, change of rights, guaranty or assumption of liability, or transaction subject to rules under Section 12(b) or 12(c) of Act
U–3A–2	Statement by holding company claiming exemption under Rule U–3A–2 from provisions of Act
U–3A3–1	Twelve-month statement by bank claiming exemption under rules of the Commission pursuant to Section 3(a)
U5A	Notification of registration filed under Section 5(a) of Act
U5B	Registration statement filed pursuant to Section 5 of Act
U5S	Annual report
U–6B–2	Certificate of notification
U–12(I)–A	Statement pursuant to Section 12(i) of Act by person employed or retained by a registered holding company or a subsidiary thereof
U–12(I)–B	Annual statement—Statement pursuant to Section 12(i) of Act by person regularly employed or retained by a registered holding company or a subsidiary thereof
U–13–1	Application for approval of mutual service company pursuant to Rule U–13–22 or declaration with respect to organization and conduct of business of subsidiary service company pursuant to Rule U–13–22
U–13–60	Annual report for mutual and subsidiary service companies
U–13E–1	Report to be filed pursuant to Rule U–13E–1 by an affiliate service company or a company principally engaged in the performance of services
U–17–1	Form to be filed by officers and directors of registered holding companies following registration of such companies or following appointment or election as officer or director of such company
U–17–2	Statement to be filed if there have been any changes during last calendar month in ownership of officer or director of registered holding company, with respect to securities of such company or any subsidiary company thereof
U–R–1	Declarations as to solicitations pursuant to Rule U–62

Forms Issued by the Securities and Exchange Commission Under the Investment Company Act of 1940

N–8A	Notification of registration
N–8B–1	Registration statement of management investment companies
N–8B–2	Registration statement of unit investment trusts which are currently issuing securities

Commission's Statement or Form Designation	Description
N–8B–3	Registration statement of unincorporated management investment companies currently issuing periodic payment plan certificates
N–8B–4	Registration statement of face-amount certificate companies
N–5	Registration statement of small business investment company under the Securities Act of 1933 and the Investment Company Act of 1940
N–5R	Annual reports of small business investment companies
N–23C–1	Statement by registered closed-end investment company with respect to purchases of its own securities pursuant to Rule N–23C–1 during the last calendar month
N–30A–1	Annual report of management investment company
N–30A–2	Annual report of unit investment trusts which are currently issuing securities registered under the Investment Company Act of 1940
N–30A–3	Annual report of unincorporated management investment companies currently issuing periodic payment plan certificates, registered under the Investment Company Act of 1940
N–30B–1	Quarterly report of management investment company
N–30F–1	Initial statement of beneficial ownership of outstanding securities of closed-end investment companies registered under the Investment Company Act of 1940
N–30F–2	Statement with respect to changes during the last calender month in beneficial ownership of any outstanding securities issued by closed-end investment companies registered under the Investment Company Act of 1940

Forms Issued by the Securities and Exchange Commission Under the Investment Advisers Act of 1940

ADV	Form of application for registration as investment adviser or to amend or supplement such an application
4–R	Service of process on individual non-resident investment adviser
5–R	Service of process on corporation non-resident investment adviser
6–R	Service of process on partnership non-resident investment adviser
7–R	Service of process on non-resident general partner of investment adviser

Forms Adopted Under the Trust Indenture Act of 1939

T–1	Statement of eligibility and qualification of corporations designated to act as trustees under trust indentures
T–2	Statement of eligibility and qualification of individuals designated to act as trustees under trust indentures
T–3	Application for qualification of indentures pursuant to Section 307
T–4	Application for exemption

OBTAINING SPECIFIED FORMS

The particular forms to be used in particular circumstances are available in any regional office of the Securities and Exchange Commission or from the Publications Unit.

THE SECURITIES EXCHANGES

The Securities Exchange Act of 1934 was passed by Congress to regulate the various stock markets. Most of the control was delegated to the newly created Securities and Exchange Commission, although some power was conferred upon the Federal Reserve Board. The Commission was given considerable latitude for the exercise of administrative discretion; and, in turn, has adopted a policy of securing voluntary cooperation of the exchanges, including the encouragement of adoption of adequate self-regulations or exchange rules.

The foundation of federal regulation is the requirement that all national securities exchanges must register unless specifically exempted by the SEC by reason of limited volume, among other things. Any exchange may be registered by filing a statement of agreement to comply with and enforce on members any rules and regulations made under the Act, and by filing also certain other data, including a copy of its constitution, bylaws, and rules of procedure.

At the close of the 1960 fiscal year, the following fourteen exchanges were registered under the Exchange Act as national securities exchanges:

American Stock Exchange
Boston Stock Exchange
Chicago Board of Trade
Cincinnati Stock Exchange
Detroit Stock Exchange
Midwest Stock Exchange
New York Stock Exchange
Pacific Coast Stock Exchange

Philadelphia-Baltimore Stock Exchange
Pittsburgh Stock Exchange
Salt Lake Stock Exchange
San Francisco Mining Exchange
San Francisco Stock Exchange
Spokane Stock Exchange

At the same time four exchanges exempted from registration were:

Colorado Springs Stock Exchange
Honolulu Stock Exchange

Richmond Stock Exchange
Wheeling Stock Exchange

LISTING REQUIREMENTS—NEW YORK STOCK EXCHANGE

The listing and reporting requirements of the national securities exchanges undoubtedly have been influenced by the 1934 Act. So that the reader may have an indication of the extent of such requirements, the procedure of the New York Stock Exchange, in respect to some of these pertinent matters, is reviewed.

Before securities may be admitted to trading on the exchange, they must be approved for listing by the exchange and also must be registered under the Securities Exchange Act of 1934. Listing is effected by the submission to, and approval by, the exchange of an application prepared and signed by the issuer in conformity with the rules of the exchange. Registration under the Securities Exchange Act requires filing with both the exchange and the SEC of a registration statement conforming to the rules of the Commission. Moreover, the exchange must certify to the Commission that it has received what purports to be a registration statement and has approved the particular securities for listing and registration. Ordinarily, registration becomes effective automatically thirty days after receipt by the Commission of the exchange's certification, but may become effective within a shorter period by order of the Commission.

The listing application serves two purposes: (1) it places before the exchange the information essential to a determination of the suitability of the security for public trading on the exchange, and (2) it provides the investing public (through the printing of about 800 copies) with such information as it might reasonably be presumed to require as an aid in judging the merits of the security. No prepared or blank forms are available for the application itself. The data are set forth in narrative style and supplemented by financial statements. It provides a comprehensive description of the applicant corporation and the security. Naturally, the form is quite standard. The listing application may, at the option of the applicant, incorporate a prospectus relating to the securities applied for, which has been issued in accordance with the Securities Act of 1933, provided the application is filed within one month following the date of the prospectus.

REPORTING REQUIREMENTS OF THE NEW YORK STOCK EXCHANGE

When stocks are listed on the New York Stock Exchange, such listing application contains an agreement relative to the publishing of certain annual reports and periodic interim statements. In this connection it is of interest that the financial statements contained in the annual reports of the corporation to its shareholders must be in the same form as the statements contained in the listing application.

The current form of listing agreement with the New York Stock Exchange, which indicates the several reporting requirements, compliance with which usually is the responsibility of the controller, is reproduced below. Its objectives include:

1. Timely disclosure, to the public and to the exchange, of information which may affect security values or influence investment decisions, and in which stockholders, the public, and the exchange have a warrantable interest
2. Frequent, regular, and timely publication of financial reports prepared in accordance with accepted accounting practice, and in adequate (but not burdensome) detail

3. Providing the exchange with timely information to enable it to perform, efficiently and expeditiously, its function of maintaining an orderly market for the company's securities and to enable it to maintain its necessary records

4. Preclusion of certain practices not generally considered sound

5. Allowing the exchange opportunity to make representations as to certain matters before they become accomplished facts

Current Form of Listing Agreement

Nothing in the following Agreement shall be so construed as to require the Issuer to do any acts in contravention of law or in violation of any rule or regulation of any public authority exercising jurisdiction over the Issuer.

.... (hereinafter called the "Corporation"), in consideration of the listing of the securities covered by this application, hereby agrees with the New York Stock Exchange (hereinafter called the "Exchange"), as follows:

I

1. The Corporation will promptly notify the Exchange of any change in the general character or nature of its business.

2. The Corporation will promptly notify the Exchange of any changes of officers or directors.

3. The Corporation will promptly notify the Exchange in the event that it or any company controlled by it shall dispose of any property or of any stock interest in any of its subsidiary or controlled companies, if such disposal will materially affect the financial position of the Corporation or the nature or extent of its operations.

4. The Corporation will promptly notify the Exchange of any change in, or removal of, collateral deposited under any mortgage or trust indenture, under which securities of the Corporation listed on the Exchange have been issued.

5. The Corporation will:

a. File with the Exchange four copies of all material mailed by the Corporation to its stockholders with respect to any amendment or proposed amendment to its Certificate of Incorporation.

b. File with the Exchange a copy of any amendment to its Certificate of Incorporation, or resolution of Directors in the nature of an amendment, certified by the Secretary of the state of incorporation, as soon as such amendment or resolution shall have been filed in the appropriate state office.

c. File with the Exchange a copy of any amendment to its By-Laws, certified by a duly authorized officer of the Corporation, as soon as such amendment shall have become effective.

6. The Corporation will disclose in its annual report to shareholders, for the year covered by the report, (1) the number of shares of its stock issuable under outstanding options at the beginning of the year; separate totals of changes in the number of shares of its stock under option resulting from issuance, exercise, expiration or cancellation of options; and the number of shares issuable under outstanding options at the close of the year, (2) the number of unoptioned shares available at the beginning and at the close of the year for the granting of options under an option plan, and (3) any changes in the exercise price of

outstanding options, through cancellation and reissuance or otherwise, except price changes resulting from the normal operation of anti-dilution provisions of the options.

7. The Corporation will report to the Exchange, within ten days after the close of a fiscal quarter, in the event any previously issued shares of any stock of the Corporation listed on the Exchange have been reacquired or disposed of, directly or indirectly, for the account of the Corporation during such fiscal quarter, such report showing separate totals for acquisitions and dispositions and the number of shares of such stock so held by it at the end of such quarter.

8. The Corporation will promptly notify the Exchange of all facts relating to the purchase, direct or indirect, of any of its securities listed on the Exchange at a price in excess of the market price of such security prevailing on the Exchange at the time of such purchase.

9. The Corporation will not select any of its securities listed on the Exchange for redemption otherwise than by lot or pro rata, and will not set a redemption date earlier than fifteen days after the date corporate action is taken to authorize the redemption.

10. The Corporation will promptly notify the Exchange of any corporate action which will result in the redemption, cancellation or retirement, in whole or in part, of any of its securities listed on the Exchange, and will notify the Exchange as soon as the Corporation has notice of any other action which will result in any such redemption, cancellation or retirement.

11. The Corporation will promptly notify the Exchange of action taken to fix a stockholders' record date, or to close the transfer books, for any purpose, and will take such action at such time as will permit giving the Exchange at least ten days' notice in advance of such record date or closing of the books.

12. In case the securities to be listed are in temporary form, the Corporation agrees to order permanent engraved securities within thirty days after the date of listing.

13. The Corporation will furnish to the Exchange on demand such information concerning the Corporation as the Exchange may reasonably require.

14. The Corporation will not make any change in the form or nature of any of its securities listed on the Exchange, nor in the rights or privileges of the holders thereof, without having given twenty days' prior notice to the Exchange of the proposed change, and having made application for the listing of the securities as changed if the Exchange shall so require.

15. The Corporation will make available to the Exchange, upon request, the names of member firms of the Exchange which are registered owners of stock of the Corporation listed on the Exchange if at any time the need for such stock for loaning purposes on the Exchange should develop, and in addition, if found necessary, will use its best efforts with any known large holders to make reasonable amounts of such stock available for such purposes in accordance with the rules of the Exchange.

16. The Corporation will promptly notify the Exchange of any diminution in the supply of stock available for the market occasioned by deposit of stock under voting trust agreements or other deposit agreements, if knowledge of any such actual or proposed deposits should come to the official attention of the officers or directors of the Corporation.

17. The Corporation will make application to the Exchange for the listing of additional amounts of securities listed on the Exchange sufficiently prior to the issuance thereof to permit action in due course upon such application.

II

1. The Corporation will publish at least once a year and submit to its stockholders at least fifteen days in advance of the annual meeting of such stockholders and not later than three months after the close of the last preceding fiscal year of the Corporation a balance sheet as of the end of such fiscal year, and a surplus and income statement for such fiscal year of the Corporation as a separate corporate entity and of each corporation in which it holds directly or indirectly a majority of the equity stock; or in lieu thereof, eliminating all intercompany transactions, a consolidated balance sheet of the Corporation and its subsidiaries as of the end of its last previous fiscal year, and a consolidated surplus statement and a consolidated income statement of the Corporation and its subsidiaries for such fiscal year. If any such consolidated statement shall exclude corporations a majority of whose equity stock is owned directly or indirectly by the Corporation: (a) the caption of, or a note to, such statement will show the degree of consolidation; (b) the consolidated income account will reflect, either in a footnote or otherwise, the parent company's proportion of the sum of, or difference between, current earnings or losses and the dividends of such unconsolidated subsidiaries for the period of the report; and (c) the consolidated balance sheet will reflect, either in a footnote or otherwise, the extent to which the equity of the parent company in such subsidiaries has been increased or diminished since the date of acquisition as a result of profits, losses and distributions.

Appropriate reserves, in accordance with good accounting practice, will be made against profits arising out of all transactions with unconsolidated subsidiaries in either parent company statements or consolidated statements.

Such statements will reflect the existence of any default in interest, cumulative dividend requirements, sinking fund or redemption fund requirements of the Corporation and of any controlled corporation, whether consolidated or unconsolidated.

2. All financial statements contained in annual reports of the Corporation to its stockholders will be audited by independent public accountants qualified under the laws of some state or country, and will be accompanied by a copy of the certificate made by them with respect to their audit of such statements showing the scope of such audit and the qualifications, if any, with respect thereto.

The Corporation will promptly notify the Exchange if it changes its independent public accountants regularly auditing the books and accounts of the Corporation.

3. All financial statements contained in annual reports of the Corporation to its stockholders shall be in the same form as the corresponding statements contained in the listing application in connection with which this Listing Agreement is made, and shall disclose any substantial items of unusual or non-recurrent nature.

4. The Corporation will publish quarterly statements of earnings on the basis of the same degree of consolidation as in the annual report. Such statements will disclose any substantial items of unusual or non-recurrent nature and will show either net income before and after federal income taxes or net income and the amount of federal income taxes.

5. The Corporation will not make, nor will it permit any subsidiary directly or indirectly controlled by it to make, any substantial charges against capital

surplus, without notifying the Exchange. If so requested by the Exchange, the Corporation will submit such charges to stockholders for approval or ratification.

6. The Corporation will not make any substantial change, nor will it permit any subsidiary directly or indirectly controlled by it to make any substantial change, in accounting methods, in policies as to depreciation and depletion or in bases of valuation of inventories or other assets, without notifying the Exchange and disclosing the effect of any such change in its next succeeding interim and annual report to its stockholders.

III

1. The Corporation will maintain in the Borough of Manhattan, City of New York, in accordance with the requirements of the Exchange:

a. An office or agency where the principal of and interest on all bonds of the Corporation listed on the Exchange shall be payable and where any such bonds which are registerable as to principal or interest may be registered.

b. An office or agency where

(1) All stock of the Corporation listed on the Exchange shall be transferrable.

(2) Checks for dividends and other payments with respect to stock listed on the Exchange may be presented for immediate payment.

(3) Scrip issued to holders of a security listed on the Exchange and representing a fractional interest in a security listed on the Exchange will, during the period provided for consolidation thereof, be accepted for such purpose.

(4) A security listed on the Exchange which is convertible will be accepted for conversion.

If at any time the transfer office or agency for a security listed on the Exchange shall be located north of Chambers Street, the Corporation will arrange, at its own cost and expense, that its registrar's office, or some other suitable office satisfactory to the Exchange and south of Chambers Street, will receive and redeliver all securities there tendered for the purpose of transfer.

If the transfer books for a security of the Corporation listed on the Exchange should be closed permanently, the Corporation will continue to split up certificates for such security into certificates of smaller denominations in the same name so long as such security continues to be dealt in on the Exchange.

If checks for dividends or other payments with respect to stock listed on the Exchange are drawn on a bank located outside the City of New York, the Corporation will also make arrangements for payment of such checks at a bank, trust company or other agency located in the Borough of Manhattan, City of New York.

c. A registrar where stock of the Corporation listed on the Exchange shall be registerable. Such registrar shall be a bank or trust company not acting as transfer agent for the same security.

2. The Corporation will not appoint a transfer agent, registrar or fiscal agent of, nor a trustee under a mortgage or other instrument relating to, any security of the Corporation listed on the Exchange without prior notice to the Exchange, and the Corporation will not appoint a registrar for its stock listed on the Exchange unless such registrar, at the time of its appointment becoming effective, is qualified with the Exchange as a registrar for securities listed on the Exchange; nor will the Corporation select an officer or director of the Corporation as a

trustee under a mortgage or other instrument relating to a security of the Corporation listed on the Exchange.

3. The Corporation will have on hand at all times a sufficient supply of certificates to meet the demands for transfer. If at any time the stock certificates of the Corporation do not recite the preferences of all classes of its stock, it will furnish to its stockholders, upon request and without charge, a printed copy of preferences of all classes of such stock.

4. The Corporation will publish immediately to the holders of any of its securities listed on the Exchange any action taken by the Corporation with respect to dividends or to the allotment of rights to subscribe or to any rights or benefits pertaining to the ownership of its securities listed on the Exchange; and will give prompt notice to the Exchange of any such action; and will afford the holders of its securities listed on the Exchange a proper period within which to record their interests and to exercise their rights; and will issue all such rights or benefits in form approved by the Exchange and will make the same transferable, exercisable, payable and deliverable in the Borough of Manhattan in the City of New York.

5. The Corporation will solicit proxies for all meetings of stockholders.

6. The Corporation will issue new certificates for securities listed on the Exchange replacing lost ones forthwith upon notification of loss and receipt of proper indemnity. In the event of the issuance of any duplicate bond to replace a bond which has been alleged to be lost, stolen or destroyed and the subsequent appearance of the original bond in the hands of an innocent bondholder, either the original or the duplicate bond will be taken up and cancelled and the Corporation will deliver to such holder another bond theretofore issued and outstanding.

. . . .

By . . . .

Date . . . .

SIMPLIFIED REPORTING AND THE SEC

In discussing the matter of reports to shareholders, employees, and the public, the authors have stressed the need of simplified financial statements which would *inform* the readers. While the conventional statements have their uses, the non-accountant can better understand the version devoid of some of the technical accounting language. Much the same problem presents itself as to the requirements of the SEC, for some of the data are given to the investor.

Generally speaking, the registration statement required under the Securities Act of 1933 is composed of two parts: (1) a prospectus which should set forth all significant facts about the company, and (2) an appendix which contains more detailed information. The prospectus must be given to each buyer in the course of sale. Thus, under the law it is a primary means of giving the investor information about the newly issued security.

This prospectus, in turn, is made up of two major sections: (1) the textual or narrative portion which discusses the business, the management, the securities, and other non-financial information, and (2) the financial statements in conventional form. The prospectuses can be said to contain much information, but whether ample informing is accomplished is quite another matter. The question is raised as to whether further simplification is desirable and would aid.

The SEC has made much progress in securing disclosure. Generally, it has attempted to get timely information to the investor; and it has tried to make the prospectuses more readable and understandable. Some of the legal verbiage has been eliminated, and the important facts have been highlighted. But the forms of financial statements have remained the traditional or conventional ones. It would appear that the arguments for simplifying statements to stockholders are just as applicable to the prospectuses as to the annual reports. This is not to say that the regular statements should be omitted from the registration statement. They may be shifted to the appendix; or, as a matter of compromise, they might be relegated to a spot in the prospectus. But understandable statements appear to have a place in the prospectus going to the prospective investor. The intent of the Act is to make available financial statements which will be most useful to the investor. The matter cannot be resolved solely by encouraging investors to learn accounting principles.

33

Reports to Creditors

CREDITORS' REPORTS AND THE CONTROLLER

Reports made to commercial banks, investment bankers, trade creditors, or bondholders for the securing of borrowed capital make up another group of reports necessary in our economy. Preparation of these statements ordinarily falls to the controller. Usually it is his responsibility to ascertain that the statements show the true financial condition or results of operations and that the form is suitable for the purposes intended.

Another phase of creditors' reports relates to the review of prospective customers' financial statements in considering an extension of credit. Very often this function is handled by the credit manager or treasurer, but the controller is frequently consulted and called upon to review the reports and make recommendations or comments.

THE USE OF FINANCIAL STATEMENTS FOR CREDIT

The proper understanding and interpretation of financial statements are essential to the successful operation of the business from both the credit-granting and borrowing viewpoints as well as the internal management aspects. But even for credit purposes, financial statements are only one of the requisites to sound decisions. The financial information is not the only type of information needed, whether to judge a credit risk or to secure a satisfactory line of credit. The data needed for the extension of credit may be classified somewhat arbitrarily into these three categories:

1. Financial information
2. Antecedent information
3. Investigational facts

Financial information relates to all available financial facts. These may be extremely detailed financial statements with supporting data, on the one hand, or mere rumors concerning financial strength, on the other. Oral statements from salesmen, creditors, or lawyers may be the sole source.

Antecedent information includes the following pertinent data about the

STATEMENT MADE TO

STATEMENT FORM C

Dun & Bradstreet, Inc.

Credit -
MAN'S CONFIDENCE
IN MAN . . . . .

For the use of Subscribers as a Basis for Credit and Insurance

NOTE: Transmittal of financial statements on this particular form is optional. Financial statements on your own stationery or on that of your accountant will be equally useful. The full report of your accountant is preferred.

Business Name
Used for Buying...Street Address...

Other Name or
Style Used, if any..City.............................Zone...........State................

Business...County....................

| FINANCIAL CONDITION AS OF...19...... | IS THIS FISCAL ☐ OR INTERIM? ☐ |

ASSETS		LIABILITIES	
CASH...$		DUE BANKS	$
GOVERNMENT SECURITIES................		Unsecured ....$	
MARKETABLE SECURITIES..................		Secured	
NOTES RECEIVABLE (Customers)............		ACCOUNTS PAYABLE	
ACCOUNTS RECEIVABLE (Customers)		Not Due.............................$	
Not Due...............$		Past Due..............................	
Past Due..........................		NOTES PAYABLE-TRADE ACCEPTANCES	
Less Reserves..............		Merchandise ....$	
INVENTORY		Machinery & Equip't.........	
Finished Goods...............$		Other	
In Process........................		DUE RELATED CONCERNS	
Raw Materials..................		Loans & Advances.............$	
		Merchandise	
OTHER CURRENT ASSETS		LOANS & ADVANCES	
.............................$		From Officers...................$	
		Others	
TOTAL CURRENT ASSETS.........		TAXES	
FIXED ASSETS		Federal Income..............$	
Land ....$		Other	
Buildings		ACCRUALS	
Machinery and Equip't.......		Salaries & Wages............$	
Furniture and Fixtures..........		Other	
Less Depreciation...........		MORTGAGES—DUE WITHIN 1 YEAR	
INVESTMENTS—RELATED CONCERNS		Real Estate.....................$	
Stocks & Bonds..................$			
Loans & Advances.............			
Accounts Receivable..............			
INVESTMENTS—OTHER		TOTAL CURRENT LIABILITIES.........	
.............................$		DEFERRED DEBTS—DUE AFTER 1 YEAR	
		Due Banks.....................$	
MISCELLANEOUS RECEIVABLES		Real Estate Mtg.................	
Officers & Employees...........$			
Other			
PREPAID—DEFERRED.............			
DEPOSITS............................		PREFERRED STOCK........................	
SUPPLIES............................		COMMON STOCK...........................	
		CAPITAL—PAID IN SURPLUS...............	
		EARNED SURPLUS—RETAINED EARNINGS......	
		NET WORTH (Proprietor or Partners)......	
TOTAL ASSETS...............$		TOTAL LIABILITIES AND CAPITAL....$	

SUMMARY STATEMENT OF INCOME

ABOVE FIGURES
PREPARED BY_____

NET SALES $————————FROM————TO————

Name   Independent Accountant Yes ☐ No ☐

FINAL NET INCOME (LOSS) $————

DIVIDENDS OR WITHDRAWALS $————

BUSINESS NAME————————

BASIS OF INVENTORY VALUATION————

SIGNED BY————————

RECEIVABLES PLEDGED OR DISCOUNTED   YES ☐   NO ☐

TITLE————————DATE————

CONTINGENT LIABILITIES $————————————(SEE OVER)
5G-10 (32198)   *(Use the reverse side of this form for submitting important supplementary details)*

Fig. 182—Dun & Bradstreet

<table>
<tr><td colspan="2">STATEMENT OF INCOME</td><td colspan="2">SURPLUS OR NET WORTH RECONCILIATION</td></tr>
</table>

STATEMENT OF INCOME

From_____, 19__ TO_____, 19__

NET SALES...$

COST OF GOODS SOLD.................................

GROSS PROFIT (LOSS) ON SALES.....................

EXPENSES

   Selling ....$

   General ....

   Administrative ....

   ....

   ....

NET INCOME (LOSS) ON SALES.........................

OTHER INCOME

   ....$

   ....

   ....

OTHER EXPENSES

   ....$

   ....

   ....

NET INCOME (LOSS) BEFORE TAXES

   Federal Income Tax............$

   Other Taxes on Income.........

FINAL NET INCOME (LOSS) ....___..........$

SURPLUS OR NET WORTH RECONCILIATION

SURPLUS OR NET WORTH AT START.................$

ADDITIONS

   Final Net Income.............$

   ....

   ....

DEDUCTIONS

   Final Net Loss.................$

   Dividends ....

   Withdrawals ....

   ....

   ....

SURPLUS OR NET WORTH AT END.................$

When financial statements prepared or certified to by independent accountants are transcribed to this form, indicate whether the statements transcribed are identical with the accountant's statement(s) Yes ☐ No ☐. If No, please describe adjustments. Attach copy of accountant's certificate.

THE FOREGOING STATEMENTS, IF CONSOLIDATED, INCLUDE THE FIGURES OF WHAT OTHER CONCERNS?.....................................

ANNUAL RENT $.......................... LEASE EXPIRES............................ 19........ FIRE INSURANCE ON: Merchandise $............................... Machinery & Equipment $.......................... Furniture & Fixtures $........................... Bldgs. $........................... ARE OFFICERS AND EMPLOYEES BONDED?..........................

IS BUSINESS INTERRUPTION INSURANCE CARRIED?.......................... IS BODILY INJURY AND/OR PROPERTY DAMAGE INSURANCE CARRIED?..........................

BASIS OF VALUATION OF: Fixed Assets..Marketable Securities—Investments..........................

ARE LIABILITIES SECURED IN ANY MANNER? Yes ☐ No ☐ If Yes, describe the security and the manner of payment..........................

STATE AMOUNT OF EACH CONTINGENT LIABILITY: (Describe)..........................

REAL ESTATE—LOCATION	Title—In Name Of	Value Mkt. ☐ Cost ☐	Mortgage	Due Date	Net Income—R. E.
		$	$		$

BRANCH LOCATIONS:..........................

NOTE: Comments will be appreciated on any phase of your operations, including developments since the statement date.

Full Names of all Officers, Directors, Partners or Proprietor. If Partners, state if General, Special or Limited				
FULL NAMES AND TITLES	% of Ownership	Year of Birth	Marital Status	Life Insurance Carried for the Benefit of the Business
A.				
B.				
C.				
D.				
E.				

Form of Financial Statement.

men who manage or own the business, whichever is applicable: their experience and ability; their record of failures, or fires; previous employment and position; married or single status. It is intended to shed light on the *character* of the men comprising management.

Investigational facts include the following data secured from banks, trade creditors, and insurance companies, which aid in appraising the financial information: payment habits, i.e., whether discounting, prompt, or slow; size of bank balances; borrowings and nature of collateral.

It can thus be seen that the information provided in the financial statements is only a part of the whole data that creditors attempt to secure and analyze in judging the soundness of a credit risk.

TRADE CREDIT INFORMATION

Credit information must be made available to the trade or mercantile creditor. There are many sources which may provide such data to the business needing it. Among them are the following:

1. The mercantile agencies—both general and special
2. The credit risk (i.e., the company seeking credit)
3. Credit bureaus, which exchange ledger experience
4. Other creditors, through direct exchange of experience
5. Other general sources, such as trade and financial publications and corporation manuals
6. Special representatives who are familiar with the credit risk: banks, attorneys, salesmen of the creditor

In the usual circumstances, where the company is furnishing financial information to creditors, a copy of the annual report to shareholders, or the interim published statement, may suffice. As to the mercantile agencies, which are perhaps the most important source of credit data, a special report may be required. Mercantile agencies, fundamentally, are companies organized primarily for the purpose of gathering credit information on businesses and making such data available to their subscribers. The best-known general mercantile agency, and the only one at present, is Dun & Bradstreet, Inc., known to the trade as the Mercantile Agency. There are, in addition, special agencies which serve only a single trade, or area, or line of business. Some examples are the National Credit Office, Inc., the Iron and Steel Board of Trade, Lyons, and local credit bureaus.

These agencies generally have their own standard forms for the reporting of financial data. Thus, Dun & Bradstreet, Inc., contacts the larger business houses by mail every January and attempts to secure a financial statement on the form illustrated in Fig. 182. A form used by the National Credit Office, Inc., which may be supplemented by a statement from the independent accountants, is illustrated in Fig. 183.

FEDERAL SECURITIES REGULATIONS AND THE BONDHOLDER

Another class of creditor for whom reports may be required is the bondholders. The Securities Act of 1933 and the Securities Exchange Act of 1934 refer to "securities" offered for sale in interstate commerce, and this coverage includes bonds as well as stocks. These Acts offer the same protection to bondholders as to shareholders, and the comments of the previous chapter, as to these Acts, are largely applicable.

However, most bonds are handled through trustees acting as agents for the bondholders. Various investigations as to the operations of trustees led to the conclusion that in a great many cases they were either unwilling or unable to take the necessary steps to protect their principals; and further that in a great number of instances the trustee appeared more eager to look after the interests of the debtor corporation than those of the bondholder. Consequently, another step in the extension of government control over securities was taken by the Trust Indenture Act of 1939. This Act requires that bonds, notes, debentures, and similar securities publicly offered for sale, sold, or delivered after sale through the mails or in interstate commerce (except as specifically exempted by the Act) be issued under an indenture which meets the requirements of the Act and which has been qualified by the SEC. The Act contains certain stipulations as to trustee, and further requires such trustee to make annual and periodic reports to bondholders. This legislation is integrated with the Securities Act of 1933 so that the registration procedure under both Acts is substantially similar.

A copy of a prospectus on a bond issue may be secured from any investment banking house. For illustrative purposes, the contents of a typical prospectus of a public utility company for which a registration statement was filed with the SEC are outlined as follows.

1. *Introductory Statement.* Includes statement that a Registration Statement has been filed with the SEC under the Securities Act of 1933, as amended. Further explains nature of the company and history of recent consolidations.

2. *Use of Proceeds.* States purpose to which proceeds will be applied and source of payment for, and amount of, estimated expenses in connection with the sale of the bonds.

3. *Summary of Earnings.* Presents the summary of income and expense for each of the past five years.

4. *Redemption Provisions.* States the general redemption provisions of the issue, and presents in tabular form the redemption prices for each successive year until maturity.

5. *Funded Debt and Capitalization of the Company and Its Subsidiaries.* Details the long-term and short-term debt, and stock capitalization of the parent and subsidiaries. Also details other

FINANCIAL STATEMENT SUBMITTED TO **NATIONAL CREDIT OFFICE, INC.**

Name...Business...

Street and No...City...Zone.;.........State.........................

STATEMENT OF (DATE)   19

ASSETS		
CASH IN BANK...........$_____		
ON HAND.....$_____	$_____	
U. S. GOVERNMENT SECURITIÉS.............		
RECEIVABLES for Mdse. Sold to Customers (Age at Foot of Page)		
ACCOUNTS ....$_____		
Less Res. for Discounts ....$_____		
Less Res. for Doubtful ....$_____		
NOTES & TRADE ACCEPTANCES (Less $_____ discounted)		
DUE from FACTOR or FINANCE CO.	_____	
PHYSICAL INVENTORY OF MDSE. (Valued at lower of Cost or Market)		
Raw Materials........$_____		
In Process...............$_____		
Finished Mdse........$ _____	_____	
....	_____	
CURRENT ASSETS		
Due from Partners, Officers, or Employees	_____	
Due from Affiliated or Assoc. Companies	_____	
LAND & BUILDINGS $_____		
Less Depreciation..$_____		
MCHY., EQUIP., FURN., & FIXT........$_____		
Less Depreciation..$_____		
INVESTMENTS (Describe on opp. page)	_____	
PREPAID & DEFERRED.............................	_____	
....	_____	
....	_____	
TOTAL ASSETS		

LIABILITIES	
ACCOUNTS PAYABLE...............................	$_____
DUE CONTRACTORS (without offset)	_____
UNSECURED LOANS PAYABLE	
To Banks.......................................	_____
To Partners or Officers......................	_____
To Others......................................	_____
SECURED LOANS PAYABLE	
Owing to..	_____
ACCRUED WAGES & EXPENSES...............	_____
TAXES—Accrued and Payable: a. Withholding & Payroll.......................	_____
b. Federal & State Income......................	_____
c. All Other.....................................	_____
RESERVE for Income Taxes since last closing	_____
MORTGAGE—DEFERRED DEBT— Due within 12 mos.....................	_____
CURRENT LIABILITIES	
MORTGAGE—DEFERRED DEBT— Due after 12 mos.....................	_____
LOANS Subordinated until...........(date)	_____
....	_____
TOTAL LIABILITIES	_____
IF CORPORATION	
Capital Stock Pfd. $_____	
Capital Stock Common ....$_____	
Capital Surplus......$_____	
Earned Surplus......$_____	
Deficit (red).......$_____	
CORPORATE, PARTNERSHIP, or INDIVIDUAL..............**NET WORTH**	
TOTAL LIABILITIES & CAPITAL	

ACCOUNTANT—Was above statement prepared by an outside accountant? Yes ☐ No ☐ Is he C.P.A.? ☐ Registered? ☐ Licensed? ☐

Accountant's Name...

Address ....

On what date are your books closed?.................................

MERCHANDISE—If not valued at Lower of Cost or Market, state

basis used...

Is original inventory record retained by you ☐ or outside auditor ☐

Is any merchandise pledged as security for any debt? _____

If so, state amount so pledged. $_____

INSURANCE—Fire: Mdse. $_____, Bldg. & Fixt. $_____

Use & Occup. $_____; Burglary $_____; Life, Benefit

Business $_____ on...

61

RECEIVABLES

For goods shipped during months of:

a.. $_____

b.. $_____

c.. $_____

d. Prior Months................................ $_____

Do these include any consigned goods, uncredited returns, or unshipped merchandise? Yes ☐ No ☐

Have all bad accounts been charged off or reserved? Yes ☐ No ☐

During the past year have you sold, pledged, or assigned any receivables? Yes ☐ No ☐. If so, name financing concern and describe transaction:...

....

Fig. 183—National Credit Office Format for Financial

PLEASE LIST SUPPLIERS AND BANKS ON REVERSE SIDE

PROFIT AND LOSS STATEMENT

FOR PERIOD FROM......................19........ TO.....................19......

GROSS SALES................................... $_____

  Less RETURNS......$_____

  Less DISCOUNTS $_____ $_____

NET INCOME FROM SALES.................... $_____

  Inventory—begin'g $_____

  Purchases—Net ....$_____

  Labor ....$_____

  Factory Overhead ......$_____

           Total $_____

  Inventory at end........$_____

Cost of Goods Sold.......................... $_____

GROSS PROFIT ON SALES...................... $_____

  Selling & Ship. Exp. $_____

  Salaries—Officers
    or Principals ....$_____

  Adm. & Gen. Exp......$_____

  Bad Debts ....$_____

  Depreciation ....$_____ $_____

INCOME or (LOSS) ON SALES............... $_____

Other Income (exclude discount earned).. $_____

           Total $_____

  Deductions from Income............................ $_____

NET PROFIT or (LOSS) before Income
  Taxes .... $_____

Provision for Fed. & State Income Taxes.. $_____

NET PROFIT or (LOSS)............................. $_____

RECONCILIATION OF SURPLUS OR NET WORTH

Beginning (date) .... $_____

ADD: Profit for
    Period ....$_____

Other Crecits
  to Surplus..........$_____ $_____

           Total $_____

DEDUCT: Loss........$_____

  Div. & Withdr'ls..$_____

  Other Charges......$_____ $_____

NET WORTH or SURPLUS at end.......... $_____

INVESTMENTS—Describe (If subsidiary or affiliated state % owned)

a.. $_____

b. .... $_____

LIABILITIES—Merchandise received or charged to you but not included in Assets or Liabilities $_____

Amount of Contingent Liabilities............. $_____

Are any liabilities secured in any way?........................ If so, state

amount, creditor, and nature of security.................................

....

Annual Rent $_____ Lease Expires...........................

NET WORTH—Has this been decreased since statement date by
withdrawal, retirement of capital, payment of dividends, bonuses,
or personal Income Taxes?...

If so, by what amount? $_____

TAXES—Have all Federal, State, and Local tax assessments been
paid or shown accrued on statement?......................................

Tax Closing date?.. Date of latest return
examined by Internal Revenue Service?...................................

OWNER—PARTNERS—OFFICERS AND DIRECTORS

Name	Title	% Ownership	In charge of

TO **NATIONAL CREDIT OFFICE, INC.** The undersigned warrants that the foregoing figures and answers are true and accurate in every respect and orders this statement mailed to you with the intention that it shall be relied upon in the extension of credit or insurance by such concerns, including factors or agents, who may subscribe to your service now or hereafter. My (Our) accountants are authorized to supply you with any supplementary information that may be required.

Dated at.................this.................day of.....................19........

Signed in the presence of

....
(Name of Corporation, Partnership or Proprietorship)

Name..

By..

Address...

....
(Signature of Officer, Partner or Owner)   (Title)

INDEPENDENT ACCOUNTANT'S OPINION   (Please use your own Letterhead if additional space is necessary)

Signature..Address..Date...............................

Statement. (By permission National Credit Office, Inc.)

major construction projects which require further financing of an undetermined nature.

6. *Business of the Company and Its Subsidiaries.* Explains in considerable detail the nature of operations and locations, including quantitative data as to sales and revenue for each of five successive years; discusses electricity and gas rates, regulation by state and federal agencies, and employee relations, including pertinent details of union contracts and the retirement plan.

7. *Properties of the Company and Its Subsidiaries.* Details the name, location, age, capacity, and past year's kilowatt-hour generation, and gas generation of each unit.

8. *Franchises.* Summarizes the pertinent terms of the franchises under which the company operates.

9. *Management of the Company.* Presents the name, address, and position of the trustees and executive officers of the company, the nature of the experience of each for the past five years, the remuneration to certain officers and the trustees and officers as a group, and the equity ownership of the company by such group.

10. *Description of the Bond Issue.* Describes in a general manner the bonds to be issued, and details relating to date, interest, payment and redemption, security and priority, release and substitution of property, method of modifying mortgage, statement as to trustee, default provisions, means of discharging the mortgage, and evidence to be furnished the trustee as to compliance.

11. *Employment of Experts.* Comments on legal and accounting services.

12. *Financial Statements.* Presents opinion of independent public accountants and the consolidated balance sheet as of the close of the past year, the consolidated income statements for the past three years, and the statements of consolidated surplus as of the close of business for the past three years.

13. *Purchasers.* Lists the underwriters of the issue, and principal amount of bonds to be purchased by each.

14. *Terms of Offering.* States the basis on which the underwriters will offer the bonds for sale.

15. *Purchase Contract.* Outlines the pertinent provisions of the agreement between the issuing company and the underwriters.

Aside from the reporting requirements of the Acts or the exchanges, the trust indenture usually contains stipulations as to reports which must be made.

REPORTING AND COMMERCIAL BANKING PRACTICES

Quite often the controller may be called upon to furnish annual reports to creditor banks, and very frequently must supply interim statements and forecasts. By and large, the banks maintain their own staffs to analyze the statements, prepare comparative data, and check trends and relationships. While the annual statement certified by the independent accountant may fit the needs in some cases, in other cases a standardized form may be used. Figure 184 illustrates the long form of financial statement suggested by one of the Federal Reserve Banks.

NATURE OF FINANCIAL STATEMENTS FOR BANKS

In considering reports to banks, the basic questions relate to the type of information wanted and the form in which desired. The amount of information a banker needs varies with the situation. The size and term of the loan are important. Naturally, a small loan does not require the information that a large loan does; the risk to the bank is not as great, and the need for a detailed analysis is correspondingly less. If a longer-term loan is under consideration, the important factor is future income. The risks are correspondingly greater as to economic developments, i.e., the business cycle and general economic conditions; and the management factor, i.e., the chances for losses by reason of unsound management decisions. In sharp contrast is a short-term loan, where normally the liquidation of current assets is the primary consideration.

The size of the borrower very frequently is a matter which affects the form of reporting. Strange as it may seem, a large well-managed enterprise may be required to furnish less details than a smaller company with mediocre management. A large firm may be viewed in general, while the opportunity for management errors in the smaller company may require more frequent and detailed reporting.

The approach of credit men, including bankers, might be described as one of proportions. Statements often are analyzed in terms of relationships.[1] The ratios on which emphasis is placed depend, among other things, on the type of loan. For a short-term loan, the working capital and liquidity are of greater importance than the fixed assets.

Typical of the ratios in which a bank might be particularly interested are these:

1. *Current Assets to Current Liabilities.* The short-term lender is concerned with liquidity as measured by this current ratio. In many cases, the financing institution will want to see the projected improvement.
2. *Average Number of Days' Sales Outstanding.* Comparison with industry average, or specific competitors, might be made to determine if receivable turnover is adequate.
3. *Number of Inventory Turns per Year.* If investments in inventory are relatively large, an inability to operate on a conservatively low

[1] See Chapter 5.

CORPORATION STATEMENT

TO THE..BANK OF... ....

Name of Corporation...--..

Business ....

Location ....

For the purpose of obtaining and establishing credit with you from time to time, we furnish the following as being a fair and accurate statement of our financial condition on...192......

ASSETS						LIABILITIES					
Cash on Hand and in Bank........................						Notes Payable for Merchandise.:..............					
Government Securities						Notes Payable to Bank............................					
Notes Receivable, good, due from customers..						Notes Payable to Others..........................					
Accounts Receivable, good, due from customers						Open Accounts payable, due....................					
Merchandise, finished ... (How Valued...........)						Open Accounts payable, not due...............					
Merchandise, unfinished (" " ....)						Dividends Unpaid...................................					
Raw Material.............. (" " ....)						Deposits of Money with us.......................					
....						Interest on Bonded Debt.........................					
....						CURRENT					
LIQUID						Bonded Debt (due...........................) ..					
Real Estate..						Mortgages or Liens on Real Estate...........					
Plant or Factory..						Other Deferred Liabilities........................					
Machinery						....					
Stocks and Bonds......................................						....					
Other Assets						TOTAL					
....						Capital Stock..					
....						Surplus and Undivided Profits...................					
TOTAL						TOTAL					

Contingent Liability - - { Accommodation Endorsements...

{ Endorsed Notes Receivable Outstanding..

Are any of above Assets Pledged as Collateral?...

Number of Bank Accounts and where kept? ....

Amount of Annual Business $.........................Amount of Annual Expenses $.........................Annual Profits $...........................

Insurance carried on Merchandise $..On Real Estate $..

Do you carry Employers Liability Insurance?...........................

(Over)

Fig. 184—Corporation Financial

STATEMENT OF...
(Name of Corporation)

CAPITAL

Authorized $.. Subscribed $.. Paid in $..

How Paid in: Cash, $..Other Property.. ....

Description of other property and how valued...

....

Incorporated in what State and under what General Law or Special Act ....

Date of Charter...Commenced Business...

Regular times of Balancing Books ....

Regular times of Taking Inventory..

Give basis of statement, whether actual inventory, by whom ⎧ ....
taken and date, or if estimate, by whom made and date. ⎨ ....
⎩

What amount, if any, of Accounts and Notes Receivable are past due, extended or renewed? $....................................

OFFICERS

	Name in Full	Address
President	....	....
Vice-President	....	....
Secretary	....	....
Treasurer	....	....
	....	....
	....	....

DIRECTORS

Name in Full	Number Shares Held	Address
....	....	....
....	....	....
....	....	....
....	....	....
....	....	....
....	....	....

(Please sign here)...

SEAL OF CORPORATION	By ....
	Date signed...192....

Statement—Federal Reserve System.

stock-to-sales ratio might cause detailed questioning on this phase of the business.

4. *Fixed Asset Turnover.* A low ratio of sales to fixed assets could raise questions as to the prospects of increasing sales to a point where facility utilization is adequate.

5. *Ratio of Equity Capital to Total Debt.* As the tendency to rather higher borrowings grows, this ratio is being used to check the required margin of safety.

6. *Number of Times Debt Service and Long-Term Rental Obligations Are Earned.* This ratio measures the margin which earnings before debt service and lease obligation bear to such annual call on cash. As a rule of thumb, some banks want a coverage of two times.

7. *Per Cent Return on Total Capital Employed, or on Shareholder Equity.* Lenders are interested in the leverage through the use of borrowed funds as well as comparative earning power.

PRESENT FINANCIAL CONDITION AND OPERATING RESULTS

As a general statement, the creditor bank wants assurances that the assets and liabilities as well as the income and expense are properly stated. The certificate of independent public accountants is relied upon in this respect. It will bear mentioning, however, that experience with differing ability of accountants has led many banks to request the long form of auditor's report as some added assurance of an examination of sufficient scope.

To generalize, the matters in which a bank usually is particularly interested are essentially the same as those with which an effective management is concerned, and include the following (especially for small businesses and new accounts).

Accounting Methods. Any change in accounting methods should be indicated, and the effect on the current statement made known.

Cash. The amount of cash on hand, if material, should be segregated from cash in banks. Often, the amount of cash in each depository must be identified. Funds which are in any way restricted or earmarked for any specific purpose should be designated.

Accounts and Notes Receivable. Accounts receivable should be segregated from notes receivable. Receivables should be aged to permit an appraisal of the *quality,* and comparison with standard sales terms, as well as a determination of the adequacy of the reserve for doubtful accounts.

Trends in collections and bad debt losses should be made known. The relationship of bad debts to sales for several years should be indicated.

Receivables from other than trade customers should be segregated if material—such as loans to officers, etc.

Any marked concentration of receivables in a relatively few customers together with their financial ratings might be a useful disclosure.

Inventories. Inventories, when appropriate, should be segregated by stage of manufacture. The basis of valuation should be indicated. Aside from the over-all inventory, if any one major item is excessive, it might be advisable to list the quantities on hand and indicate, based on present plans, the number of weeks of sales or manufacturing represented. Comment should also be made as to accounting treatment of any obsolete stock, as well as the date of the last physical inventory and per cent of loss or shrinkage normally experienced.

Cash Surrender Value of Life Insurance. The beneficiary, amount, names, and positions of the insureds, and cash surrender value of each policy should be disclosed. Also, policies assigned to secure indebtedness should be identified.

Property, Plant, and Equipment. Schedules similar to those used for 10K purposes would ordinarily meet any information needs of bankers.

For each major classification of property, and its related reserve, data as to (1) beginning balance, (2) additions during the period, (3) reductions during the period, and (4) ending balance are desirable.

The basis of valuation and depreciation methods will be helpful in appraising the adequacy of allowances for depreciation and depletion. Any liens or encumbrances should be designated.

Current Liabilities. Liabilities should be segregated between current (due within one year) and long-term. Notes payable should be identified as between those due to banks, principal suppliers, owners, affiliates, and others. Endorsed or guaranteed obligations, or those on a secured basis, should be disclosed.

It may be helpful to segregate and describe any accounts payable to other than trade creditors. Trade accounts payable should be summarized by date of origin, and related to customary trade terms. The names of important suppliers and the annual purchases from them should be identified, as the bank may wish to contact them. A reasonable detail of all other current accruals, etc., should be given.

Income Tax Liability. A full disclosure of the status of this tax liability should be made, including the most recent date through which federal income returns have been examined. Disclosure should be made of any significant findings, or assessments, etc., and the company position in regard to the expected liability.

Long-Term Liabilities. Such information as this is desirable: a schedule showing the repayment due dates and amounts; the matter of compliance with the indenture or other agreements, and pertinent credit features of such agreements—rates of interest, maturity acceleration, collateral security, etc.

Lease Obligations. The extent of any major long-term lease obligations should be indicated. Usually the bank desires a schedule of the annual lease rental obligations. The terms, including penalties for early termination, preferably should be summarized.

Contingent Liabilities. Any significant current or future commitment ought to be explained as to purpose, nature, and amount. Included in this category would be purchase and sales contracts, pending lawsuits, repurchase agreements, and unsettled claims. *Favorable* sales contracts should be disclosed.

Equity Interests. Disclosure in this area would include the analysis of changes in the capital accounts, and such information as:

1. Identification of the principal owners
2. Summary of rights for each class of stock
3. Dividend (or other) payments made to shareholders in recent years, including share of earnings paid out
4. Explanation of any adjustments to retained earnings

Insurance Coverage. A summary schedule of insurance coverage, and related book value and market value, as applicable.

Income and Expenses. The analysis of significant trends and relationships is suggested, including:

1. Trend of sales by major product line over past several years
2. Identification of changes in sales levels due to volume, prices, and abnormal situations, including strikes or "windfalls"
3. Either profit by product line, or contribution [2] to fixed costs and profit by product line
4. Identification of trends in each significant cost category of labor, material, and expense in relationship to sales (by type of cost and not by responsibility or department)
5. Comparative costs, if available, as related to industry or competitors; very often the banks have such data
6. Disclosure of special or non-recurring income or expense

Other. Any other conditions or developments which a prudent management would consider significant, such as

1. The planning and control system
2. The system of internal accounting control
3. The management team

[2] See pp. 224–226.

In this latter case, the lender will be most interested in the ability and experience of all major management and not merely the chief executive and financial officer. Very often the loan officer will evaluate the management, giving consideration to company size, industry, etc., on a score sheet somewhat as follows: [3]

Good Av'ge Bad

☐ ☐ ☐ Organization, including depth of management.

☐ ☐ ☐ Training and development programs.

☐ ☐ ☐ Knowledge of industry and competitors.

☐ ☐ ☐ Familiarity with markets, distribution channels, sales methods.

☐ ☐ ☐ Planning for the future.

☐ ☐ ☐ Personnel policies, employee relations.

☐ ☐ ☐ Knowledge of costs, cost control.

☐ ☐ ☐ Use of financial and other controls.

☐ ☐ ☐ Efficiency and attitude of labor force.

☐ ☐ ☐ Housekeeping.

☐ ☐ ☐ Plant layout.

Good Av'ge Bad

☐ ☐ ☐ Condition of buildings and equipment.

☐ ☐ ☐ Condition of inventory; inventory control.

☐ ☐ ☐ Efficiency of credit and collection operations.

☐ ☐ ☐ Quantity and quality of advertising and sales promotion.

☐ ☐ ☐ Customer service; handling of complaints, claims.

☐ ☐ ☐ Supplier relations (prompt payment, proper claims, etc.).

☐ ☐ ☐ Management balance among sales, production, finance, etc.

☐ ☐ ☐ Community relations.

☐ ☐ ☐ Alertness to new ideas, procedures, techniques.

It can be seen that the key point in the above discussion is *disclosure,* and the preparation of financial statements in accordance with generally accepted accounting principles consistently applied. Moreover, much of the information outlined above is that included in the "long-form" audit report of the knowledgeable independent public accountant—particularly when he is informed the statement will be provided to banks, and may be used for credit purposes.

BUDGETS AND FORECASTS

Preceding comments have related primarily to the historical financial statements. Yet, most lenders are concerned with the primary question, "Will the loan be repaid at maturity?" Emphasis is on the *future.* Hence, in negotiating or securing a loan, prudent company officials give particular attention to prospects. The business plans, instead of being in someone's head, will be translated into financial statements.

It is believed the request for short-term or long-term loans should be supported by *realistic* and *conservative* estimates of the future. Almost

[3] From Research Institute of America, Inc., Report to Management, File 31, "Your Business Through a Lender's Eyes," October 29, 1958.

anyone can prepare optimistic projections which never materialize, and never were based on sound business judgment—which ultimately work against the best interests of the company. It is suggested that, with appropriate commentary, the future plans of the company be supported by

1. A statement of estimated income and expense, for the current forecast period—usually one year
2. A statement of estimated cash flow for the short term, indicating source and disposition of funds
3. The statement of estimated financial position at the end of the forecast period
4. The projected income and expense statement, and cash flow, to the end of loan period

As a general word of caution, experience indicates the wisdom of *periodically* reviewing financial prospects with the company's principal bankers. Keeping these financial institutions informed, irrespective of the immediacy of the need for a loan, will do much to maintain sound banking relationships and tend to insure that necessary funds will be made available when needed.

SUMMARY

In preparing statements for creditors the controller should insist on full disclosure of pertinent facts and the application of sound accounting principles. For example, he should see that liabilities are properly segregated into current and long-term classifications; that receivables from affiliates and officers and employees are clearly identified from customer receivables; that assigned accounts receivable are indicated. Moreover, he can assist in promoting uniformity of reporting to facilitate the study of trends and comparisons with other companies. By the preparation of soundly conceived forecasts, he can help maintain the proper climate for loans.

The more the controller understands the problems and objectives of the bank and other creditors, the greater will be the progress toward intelligent credit granting.

PART VI

Administration of the Controller's Department— Some Technical Aspects

34

Office Management and Related Problems

THE CONTROLLER AND OFFICE MANAGEMENT

There are several reasons for the controller's interest in office management. In the first place, the function of office management usually falls within the controller's responsibility. Second, the costs incident to the maintenance of the clerical staff are high, and the chief accounting executive must consider means of keeping such expenditures at reasonable levels. Finally, the controller has a *functional* responsibility over much of the record keeping and related procedures of his company and must be acquainted with the nature of the problems and their solution.

It is not the intent here to deal at length with office management. However, there are certain administrative or control features directly related to the record-keeping function which are often overlooked by controllers; and it is felt desirable to review briefly these limited aspects of the subject.

FUNCTIONS OF THE OFFICE MANAGER

As a general statement the chief objective of the office manager is to operate the office with the optimum efficiency. This includes direct responsibility for the efficient functioning and coordinating of the units which usually make up the office organization: mailing, filing, office methods and routine, telephone and telegraph, general service, office maintenance, and procurement of office equipment. A chart illustrating the duties for which the officer manager is responsible in a number of companies is shown in Fig. 185.

In the larger companies the office manager is looked upon as a service executive. In smaller companies, however, no particular distinction may be made between the chief accountant and office manager; both functions may be combined. Where the office service functions do not require the

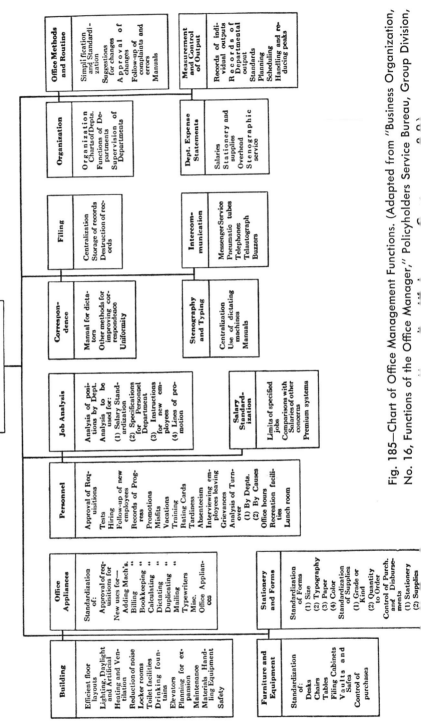

OFFICE MANAGEMENT FUNCTIONS

Building	Office Appliances	Personnel	Job Analysis	Correspondence	Filing	Organization	Office Methods and Routine
Efficient floor layouts Lighting, Daylight and Artificial Heating and Ventilation Reduction of noise Locker rooms Toilet facilities Drinking fountains Elevators Planning for expansion Maintenance Materials Handling Equipment Safety	Standardization of: Approval of requisitions for New uses for— Adding Mach's. Billing " Bookkeeping " Calculating " Dictating " Duplicating " Mailing " Typewriters Misc. Office Appliances	Approval of Requisitions Tests Hiring Follow-up of new employees Records of Progress Promotions Misfits Vacations Training Rating Cards Tardiness Absenteeism Interviewing employees leaving Grievances Analysis of Turnover (1) By Depts. (2) By Causes Office hours Recreation facilities Lunch room	Analysis of positions by Dept. Analysis to be used for: (1) Salary Standardization (2) Specifications for Personnel Department (3) Instructions for new employees (4) Lines of promotion	Manual for dictators Other methods for improving correspondence Uniformity	Centralization Storage of records Destruction of records	Organization Charts of Depts. Functions of Departments Supervision of Departments	Simplification and Standardization Suggestions for changes Approval of changes Follow-up of complaints and errors Manuals

Furniture and Equipment	Stationery and Forms	Salary Standardization	Stenography and Typing	Intercommunication	Dept. Expense Statements	Measurement and Control of Output
Standardization of: Desks Chairs Tables Filing Cabinets Vaults and Safes Control of purchases	Standardization of Forms (1) Size (2) Typography (3) Paper (4) Color Standardization of Supplies (1) Grade or Kind (2) Quantity to Order Control of Purch. and Disbursements (1) Stationery (2) Supplies	Limits of specified jobs Comparisons with Salaries of other concerns Premium systems	Centralization Use of dictating machines Manuals	MessengerService Pneumatic tubes Telephones Telautograph Buzzers	Salaries Stationery and supplies Overhead Stenographic service	Records of individual outputs Records of Departmental output Standards Planning Scheduling Handling and reducing peaks

Fig. 185—Chart of Office Management Functions. (Adapted from "Business Organization, No. 16, Functions of the Office Manager," Policyholders Service Bureau, Group Division,

full time of a supervisor, it is usually a simple matter to add other duties. Thus, tabulating might be regarded as a service department and included in this group. There is perhaps no other supervisory position in a business where the variety of responsibilities is so great.

ORGANIZATION STRUCTURE AND THE OFFICE MANAGER

The same principles of organization apply to office management as to any other functions. The office manager should be given definite and clear responsibilities and the necessary authority to carry out his job. He should have a clear understanding of his position in the organization, and his relationship to other executives or supervisors in the company.

Though the functions of the office manager are important, he is not considered one of the major executives. In most instances, however, he does report directly to an officer of the company. Usually one official has other duties or interests which cause him to be more concerned with the office than the other executives; and this is often the controller. Under such circumstances the office manager should report to this official.

PHYSICAL OFFICE FACILITIES

Good working conditions are an important factor in maintaining employee morale and securing a more efficient level of performance. Hence, the need of a clean, pleasant, healthy, and safe place in which to work should not be underestimated.

The following important physical factors deserve brief comment:

1. *Heating, Ventilation, and Air Conditioning.* The primary objective, of course, is to provide adequate comfort for the staff. Excessive heat induces mental sluggishness, and insufficient warmth results in "time out" to get warm.

2. *Lighting.* Here, the objective is to provide adequate and comfortable lighting conditions which are at the same time practical and economical to operate and maintain. The office manager often may request the services of the engineers or the staff of the local power company to check the adequacy of lighting conditions. Consideration must be given to brightness, glare, contrast, and size and type of lighting, with respect to both natural and artificial lighting.

3. *Noise.* More attention is being given to the problem of noise abatement. Noise from the factory, the outside, and other office machinery interferes with the efficiency of the worker. It makes concentration more difficult and increases tension.

4. *Safety.* The company should be interested in the physical wellbeing of its office staff just as much as it is in the well-being of factory or sales forces. While office work is relatively safe as compared to some factory jobs, the safety factor should not be over-

looked. The office should be included in the safety program. Consideration should be given to the condition of floors and stairways and to outlets and extension cords, edges on equipment, blind corners, inadequate railings, etc., so as to reduce accidents.

5. *Sanitation.* The objective is the preservation or restoration of health, and the elimination of conditions that facilitate the spread of disease. Thought should be given to adequate toilet facilities, clean and sanitary drinking fountains, other necessary restroom equipment and facilities, and first-aid equipment.

6. *Office Layout.* The layout affects the utilization of office space and the flow of work. These suggestions are made:

   a. Arrange the furniture and equipment so that work flows in a straight line, as an assembly line, and avoid as much as possible any criss-crossing or backtracking.

   b. Place related departments or work centers near each other.

   c. Develop work centers so that all related work is done in one area and is treated as a unit.

   d. Set up service centers, such as stenographic or reproduction, which are convenient to the work centers.

   e. Lay out the office so as to have short moves of material.

   f. Provide adequate transportation facilities within the office.

   g. Locate noisy departments away from other groups, or properly insulate the area.

   h. Keep private offices to a minimum. Only those executives and supervisors who require quiet and freedom from interruptions, or who have confidential interviews, should be given private offices.

NEED FOR FORM CONTROL

In most of our larger business organizations, standardization has been attempted through the design of forms for repetitive reporting conditions. Unfortunately, the design and control are often done in a somewhat haphazard manner. However, a very large part of clerical work consists of filling out information on forms or transferring information to other forms. It is, therefore, readily apparent that the preparation, control, and use of forms are important. The application of good judgment and procedure in the preparation and control of forms can be a means of considerable savings, both directly and indirectly.

Lack of adequate form control and poor design may be revealed in many ways. Some of the sources of waste include:

1. Poor physical control
   a. Depletion of stock, with long delays in securing refills
   b. Difficulty in locating the stock, even when forms are available

    c. Lost clerical time in locating a supply
    d. Uneconomical ordering of large quantities

2. Improperly designed forms
    a. Lost clerical and executive time due to misinterpretation, difficulty of typing or writing additional information on the form, and simple lack of sufficient information on the form
    b. Continuation of these same difficulties in reordering because of failure to make the necessary changes
    c. Higher printing and paper costs as a result of using non-standard sizes, with higher cutting waste, or use of wrong grade of paper
    d. Lost time in reordering as a result of non-identification of using department
    e. High cost of files and binders, because of lack of standardization

Thus, proper control and design can result in higher productivity per clerical employee as well as lower printing and paper costs.

FACILITATING ADEQUATE FORM CONTROL

The following simple suggestions will assist in form control:

1. Place all forms in an office stockroom, from which they may be requisitioned only on proper written authority. In this connection, clerical time may be saved by having certain limited hours, except in emergencies, when stock may be requisitioned.
2. Maintain perpetual inventory records or other checks on forms to permit reordering at the proper time, the rate of usage being considered.
3. Institute an adequate numbering system to identify forms. Several systems may be used, including a straight numbering plan. Another scheme includes the department code, the number of the departmental form, the quantity last printed, and the date printed. Thus, AC 7-4M-362 indicates form number seven of the accounting department, of which four thousand were printed in March, 1962.
4. Establish a master file of sample forms. A binder, or binders, should be prepared in which is kept a sample of every form used by the business. Letterheads, envelopes, and accounting department forms should be included—none should be overlooked.
5. Require a thorough analysis before new forms are added.
6. Make a periodic and systematic review of all forms. Questionnaires may be used to determine whether the form is needed. As changes appear necessary, notations should be made in the form file so that the modification is not overlooked.

FORM DESIGN

The design of forms should be approached on a scientific or analytical basis. The purpose of the form should be determined, and a decision made as to whether a form is really necessary. Moreover, perhaps minor modifications of other forms will satisfy more than one requirement. With the purpose and manner of use in mind, the following suggestions as to procedure are made:

1. List all information which the form should contain; eliminate all unnecessary information
2. Determine the relative importance of each type of information and the amount of space each will require
3. Select the style and size of sheet or card which will be most convenient, economical, and practical; or, in case mechanical equipment is used, the size and style of form suited to the equipment
4. Arrange the positions of the information in the manner most convenient for recording and for subsequent reference and use
5. If the form is for machine use, make sure that it will work efficiently in the machine for which it is designed
6. Omit horizontal lines from machine forms
7. Note carefully preceding forms from which information is taken and succeeding forms to which it is transferred so that convenient arrangement of data and multiple copies can be used to eliminate any unnecessary steps
8. Select colors which will be useful in identification and are readily legible
9. Place necessary instructions on forms to insure their proper use
10. Check carefully motions of clerks or machine operators in the use of the form to eliminate lost motion through imperfect arrangement
11. Carefully test all important forms by actual use before large quantities are printed
12. Secure the criticism of clerks and operators as the result of tests

CONTROL OF OFFICE COSTS

The principles and applications of cost control discussed in Part III are applicable to the office. In summary, there are several control tools and aids available in keeping office costs within reasonable limits:

1. Personal observation and supervision of the staff
2. Use of operational standards for measuring efficiency
3. Budgetary control over sectional or departmental costs
4. Financial incentives that are tied in with standards and/or budgets

Aggressive and intelligent supervision will usually find ways and means of keeping office efficiency high and costs relatively low. The use of standards, based on time and motion study, can be helpful. There are a great number of office activities which permit a ready approach to measurement of output. These include:

Comptometer operation	Filing
Accounts payable ledger posting	Key-punching (tabulating)
Accounts receivable ledger posting	Mailing department functions
	Inventory ledger posting
Typing	Timekeeping
Duplicating	Payroll work

If financial incentives are added, progress made in elimination of conditions which retard output may be astounding.

The controller can exercise line authority over his own department and accomplish much. However, he should not overlook his functional responsibility over office costs of other activities in his company. The same effort should be made, through the division head, to reduce such costs by means of standard applications, sufficiently "tight" budgets, and incentives. As a general comment, most production, sales, and research executives will welcome assistance in reducing office costs. Reduced clerical costs may permit somewhat higher expenditures in the directly productive functions of the business. Moreover, and perhaps more important, as the efficiency of the office staff is increased through better methods and procedures, the time demands for clerical supervision become less; and these supervisors may devote more hours to their primary function.

FACTORS IN SELECTING MECHANICAL OFFICE EQUIPMENT

In organizing his department, in planning or approving basic accounting and statistical procedures and methods, the controller has a wide variety of equipment from which to choose. To make a wise selection, he must know the equipment and devices available for the particular task and the relative cost. The selection of procedures and equipment may be mutually dependent jobs.

Controllers recognize that accounting and statistical matter should be gathered and reported upon when it is apparent that its value to management will exceed the cost. Of course, the cost of accumulation will depend upon the methods and equipment available to perform the task. Most accounting and statistical work can be done by hand, but this may make the cost excessive.

In considering whether mechanical or manual methods are to be used, the following factors should be considered:

1. The volume of work to be done—perhaps the amount is not enough to justify machine application
2. The operating cost with and without the machine

3. The initial cost of the equipment
4. The additional useful analyses which can be made available through machine methods
5. The effect of each method on internal control procedures
6. New routines or short cuts which may be available
7. The relative speed and accuracy of each method
8. The requirements as to specially trained personnel, and the effect of absenteeism on the operations
9. The degree of flexibility required

As a general statement, the advantages of using mechanical equipment include:

1. *Speed.* Very often the machine method is much faster than the manual; and in the case of peak loads and deadlines this is important.
2. *Flexibility.* The machine can frequently be put to various uses; moreover, new and useful analyses may be made available.
3. *Economy.* When the volume justifies machine methods, such means can usually be shown to be more economical. Also, it is much cheaper to have idle machines than idle payroll.
4. *Accuracy.* Human errors often occur as a result of fatigue, and use of mechanical equipment may reduce such fatigue and the resulting mistakes. Also, some machines have balancing features which reduce the amount of checking and rechecking.
5. *Internal Control.* The use of machine methods may add to the effectiveness of internal control.
6. *Appearance.* Machine-prepared records are usually neater than manually prepared ones; and this may be important if the data are to be seen by customers.

The application of the tests described above to the particular task to be done will indicate instances where mechanical equipment can be put into operation to great advantage. In other instances, the nature and type of the work to be done will not warrant the purchase of machines. In any event, the controller should expect the office manager to have up-to-date information on possible applications; to review the application with the several different manufacturers' representatives before making a decision; and to learn to justify most acquisitions on the basis of economies.

PUNCHED CARD EQUIPMENT

Electric tabulating and accounting methods deserve special comment in view of the many control and accounting uses to which they may be applied, particularly in medium-sized companies. Two types are available, usually on a rented basis, although one company now offers the equipment for sale.

There are three basic machine operations:

1. Punching—creating the card, which is the tool for all successive operations
2. Sorting—the arranging, on a machine, of the cards in the sequence desired for further use
3. Tabulating—the printing of the finished report

The basis of all such accounting is the tabulating card. Figure 186 illustrates a card printed to designate the fields. Each application may have, but does not need, printed cards, which indicate what each column represents.

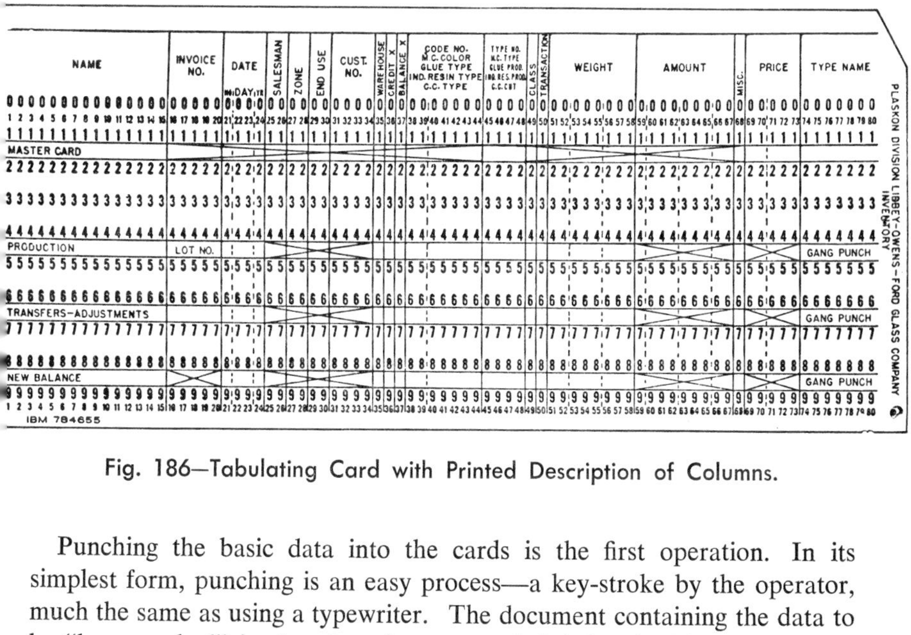

Fig. 186—Tabulating Card with Printed Description of Columns.

Punching the basic data into the cards is the first operation. In its simplest form, punching is an easy process—a key-stroke by the operator, much the same as using a typewriter. The document containing the data to be "key-punched" is placed at the operator's left hand. Then, the cards, especially designed to provide for easy progressive reading of the information to be punched, are fed automatically into punching position and are automatically ejected. The latest development, "mark-sensing," permits automatic punching from pencil marks on the cards, so that no manual punching is necessary. The punched cards may be "verified" or checked for accuracy of manual punching, and are then ready for the subsequent steps.

When the cards have been punched, they are usually in a miscellaneous order. The next step, before the information may be used, is to arrange them by some desired classification. This is done on an electric sorting machine. The automatic sort is made one column at a time, based on electrical impulses, if that type of machine is used. Thus, to arrange information according to data in three columns would require passing the group through the sorting machine three times.

Once the cards have been sorted into the desired sequence, the third step is the automatic compilation of the punched data into printed reports. The machines are so designed as to provide considerable flexibility in the arrangement of the printed data on the report forms. Summary cards also can be punched automatically and simultaneously with the printing of the report. The ability to sort and tabulate in various ways permits great flexibility in presenting information. Application of tabulating equipment for control reports has been illustrated throughout Parts III and IV of this book. To summarize, where basic information may be used in several different ways, that is, in several different arrangements, and where there are a large number of transactions, the punched card system may be warranted.

Computers are coming into prominence in the larger companies, and are discussed in Chapter 40.

35

Internal Auditing— A Management Tool

NATURE OF INTERNAL AUDITING

The concept of internal auditing has changed radically during the past decade. Formerly it was considered to be a mechanical review of arithmetical accuracy and a sort of police action, the main objective of which was to keep everyone honest. Now, however, to an increasing degree internal auditing is viewed as a more positive and dynamic influence in business—as an arm of management. This development is a product of the modern business environment. The larger and more complex the business organization, the greater is the gap between administrator or executive and the individual operator. Consequently, a sort of liaison is necessary. Further, top management needs a check quite independent of the line organization. Moreover, reviews are necessary to keep the business machine functioning smoothly. It is in this area or void that the internal audit is proving to be of value.

In summary, internal auditing may be described [1] as the independent appraisal activity within a business organization, established for the review of the accounting, financial, and other operations as a basis for protective and constructive service to management. It is a type of control which functions by measuring and evaluating the effectiveness of other types of control. While it deals primarily with accounting and financial matters, it may also deal with matters of an operating nature.

Satisfactory profits are depending more and more on effective management and efficient operations. Therefore, management must carefully analyze and check those activities for which it is responsible. The controller cannot afford to overlook the possibilities which the internal auditing tool offers.

---

[1] As defined by the Institute of Internal Auditors.

THE FUNCTIONS OF INTERNAL AUDITING

The broad objective of internal auditing is to assist management in achieving the most efficient operation and administration of the business enterprise. In so doing, the functions or services it can render may be grouped as follows: [2]

1. *Appraisal of Procedures and Related Matters.* This activity may involve several related phases, including:
    a. Expressing an opinion as to the efficiency or adequacy of existing procedures
    b. Developing new or improved procedures
    c. Appraising personnel
    d. Interchanging ideas as between plants, and perhaps standardizing on the best method

2. *Verification and Analysis of Data.* Here, also, this function may be subdivided into two or more parts, such as:
    a. The review of data produced by the accounting system to ascertain that the reports are valid
    b. The making of further analyses, as required, to support given conclusions

3. *Activities Verifying the Extent of Compliance.* This may involve determining that:
    a. Accounting procedures or other policies are being followed
    b. Operating procedures are being followed
    c. Governmental regulations are being complied with
    d. Other contractual obligations are being observed

4. *Functions of a Protective Nature.* This would include at least three subdivisions:
    a. Prevention and detection of fraud or dishonesty
    b. Review of care taken of company properties
    c. Check of transactions with outside parties, e.g., determining that all shipments are billed to customers

5. *Training and Other Aids to Company Personnel.* This is particularly applicable to accounting personnel.

6. *Miscellaneous Services.* Included are special investigations, and assistance to outside contacts such as the public accountant.

While these general activities may be overlapping to some extent, they do indicate the various phases of the services of internal auditing.

[2] See Victor Z. Brink and James A. Cashin, *Internal Auditing,* Second Edition (New York: The Ronald Press Company, 1958).

IS AN INTERNAL AUDITING DEPARTMENT NECESSARY?

The functions of internal auditing are carried on to some degree in every business, though often under another name. They *should* be performed, for they are essential to managerial control. Very often the line executives, controller, public accountants, or others find it necessary to perform these investigative and appraisal duties in the discharge of their normal responsibilities.

However, as the organization becomes larger, each company may well give consideration to the need for creating an internal auditing department or at least employing an internal auditor as such. There are several factors to be weighed; and while the particular circumstances must govern, the following points are indicative of conditions under which this function should be segregated:

1. If the company is relatively large, so that extensive use is being, or should be, made of accounting or statistical controls.
2. If operations take place at more than one location. This has reference to manufacturing or distribution operations other than a one-man sales office.
3. If the system of internal control is not being, or cannot be, made fully effective.
4. If the auditor can perform functions otherwise performed by the public accountant with a resulting reduction in the audit fee. The independent auditors should be consulted on such possibilities, for their long-term interests certainly must include the keeping of audit fees within reasonable limits.
5. If the owners or management desire or request such a tool as a means of keeping informed about certain aspects of the business.

ORGANIZATION OF THE INTERNAL AUDITING DEPARTMENT

The initial organization of the internal auditing department requires, in addition to the selection of adequate personnel, a consideration of (1) the place of the department in the general company organization, and (2) the general manner of departmental organization itself. As a broad statement, the function, whenever practical, should be divorced from any other activity. Experience indicates that if the service is not kept separate, the tendency is to let other duties come first; and the auditing activity is consequently neglected.

In deciding on the place of the department in the organization, it is axiomatic that it should be independent of the groups which it appraises or reviews. Conversely, of course, internal auditing is a staff function and should have no authority over any other departments. The chief auditor should report to a major executive so that any findings of importance will reach top management. Logically, also, the activity must be directly subject to management's guidance and supervision if it is to serve that group most effectively. Accordingly, current practice is to have the chief auditor report to the controller or chief financial officer, preferably the former, because much of the activity centers on accounting records and procedures. Moreover, the controller should be by nature objective in his appraisal of any controls, procedures, or other matters. Since subordinates of the controller, and not he personally, directly supervise the accounting system and procedures, the necessary independence of appraisal and action can usually be achieved.

The departmental organization structure will depend on many factors: the size of the company, the extent of its properties, the nature of the accounting system, the degree of internal control, the expected functions of the department, and the company organization structure. The unit may be built on any one of several bases by company division, e.g., by factory and retail division; or by physical location, e.g., home office, domestic branches, and foreign branches; or by nature of assignments, e.g., general manufacturing audits, general retail audits, or special surveys. No ideal organization structure can be suggested, for the particular circumstances must govern. However, an illustrative chart for a very large manufacturing company is shown in Fig. 187. In many instances the business will not be large enough to support the separate units and the functions must be combined.

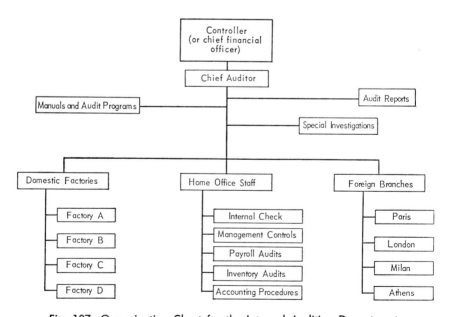

Fig. 187—Organization Chart for the Internal Auditing Department.

INTERNAL AUDIT PROGRAMS

In the supervision and direction of the internal auditing activity, another question to be settled is the need for an auditing program—written, detailed audit procedures. Although these are not absolutely essential, they are considered highly desirable. Audit programs are a means of securing uniform audit procedures where they are considered applicable. Moreover, such programs assist in getting more efficient and effective audits. The preparation of an internal auditing manual, which would normally include detailed audit procedures, should provide the advantages of any manual, as outlined in Chapter 37.

The development of the audit program and the organization of the department are perhaps interdependent, for both must recognize the limits of available funds. Within these confines the detailed procedures may be worked out, giving consideration to the nature of the auditing job to be done and the means by which it is to be accomplished. Assistance in extending the scope of audit may be secured by requiring that each department to be audited prepare basic information—in the nature of a standard practice manual—showing the routines followed, flow of work, job descriptions, etc.

ILLUSTRATIVE INTERNAL AUDIT PROGRAM

Audit programs may relate to any number of subjects to be examined; and they are usually very detailed in nature. A section of a typical audit program is illustrated by the following outline for the review of the inventories: [3]

PERPETUAL INVENTORY RECORDS

1. Examine records for the period to see that they are properly and well kept.
2. Test-check mathematics.
3. Take trial balance at audit date and compare with control.
   Trace any differences and obtain necessary explanations.
4. Vouch entries with receiving and inspection tickets, purchase invoices, completed requisitions, billing and shipping records, as well as other internal records, to check quantities and prices of receipts, transfers and credits to perpetual records (other than write-offs). Test postings as necessary.
5. Audit data used for vouching. See that they are properly authorized and approved. Check mathematics and pricing. Use collateral data where necessary. Investigate all erasures and changes.
6. Make test counts of stock and compare with balances. Investigate all differences carefully; determine cause. Adjust records after obtaining proper approvals.

[3] George A. Bricault and Cecil O. Marshall, "Inventories and the Internal Auditors," *NACA Bulletin*, November 15, 1946, pp. 387–89.

7. Obtain previous monthly trial balance records to see whether accounts are balanced regularly. Compare totals of some with related control account. Check individual balances with accounts. Investigate all differences.

8. In connection with all important discrepancies developed during the audit, determine whether accounts have been properly adjusted in accordance with company policies within a reasonable time, and whether all corrections have been approved by the appropriate executive. (In some instances shortages will be charged against employees personally. If so, determine what funds were collected.) See what measures have been taken to prevent recurrence of similar mistakes. Recurrent discrepancies in the current and previous periods should be forcefully brought to management's attention.

9. Compare quantities on hand with

   a) Authorized maximum stock level.
   b) Current consumption rate.
   c) Anticipated requirements (budgeted).

   Obtain data regarding discontinued lines and products, changes in materials, and supplies used. From this information compile list of excess, obsolete, or slow-moving stock. Compare list with duplicate advices to management relating to these situations. Find reason why these were not reported and include list of items of which management was not previously informed in audit report. Valuation of obsolete and slow-moving goods should be investigated.

10. Scan records to see what measures have been taken with regard to previously reported excess, obsolete, and slow-moving stock, and their effectiveness.

11. Investigate all write-offs and write-downs as well as unusual credits in inventory accounts. See that all are approved.

12. Confirm the following stocks located on outside premises:

    a) At warehouse.
    b) On consignment out.
    c) Materials and supplies out for subcontracting.
    d) At sales agents.

13. Confirm consignments in.

14. Correlate cut-off of sales, sales returns, purchases, and purchase returns with related records.

15. Examine shipping records for unrecorded or unauthorized shipments.

16. Examine receiving records for goods received for which liabilities have not been recorded or accounted for by consignments in.

17. If goods in transit records are kept test-check these as necessary.

18. Compare inventory values with insurance coverage to determine whether company is adequately protected.

PURCHASE JOURNAL

The auditing procedures and techniques are summarized below:

1. Vouch purchase journal entries with invoices.

2. Examine invoices used in vouching.

   a) Establish receipt of goods by comparison of receiving and inspection tickets, especially as to quantities, quality, sizes, and condition of goods. Investigate any erasures and changes in tickets. See evidence that quantities have been charged into perpetual records.

b) Compare purchase orders with invoices as to price, quality, size, quantity, payment, terms, freight charges.

c) If any errors are noted, care should be taken to see that adjustment was taken into consideration in paying the bill. The routine for charging or crediting back customers should be systematic and should provide for infallible addition or deduction from invoices.

d) Note whether all available discounts have been taken.

e) Compare some receiving slips with department records.

It is to be observed that this audit program for inventories goes beyond the accounting records and extends to all directly related functions. This approach is characteristic of an internal audit in that the entire phase of a subject is usually reviewed. Such an examination can very readily be adapted, if need be, to serve as a type of management audit.

THE AUDIT REPORT

When the audit is completed, it remains to present the results to management. Much skillful and constructive auditing has been ineffective as a result of poor reporting or poor presentation; and it behooves the accountant to give careful thought to this phase.

Before writing the formal report, the auditor should review with the divisional or departmental executive—the auditee—the scope of audit, the findings, and the proposed recommendations. Such a procedure has several advantages:

1. It permits the departmental supervisor to take immediate corrective action—and this is the ultimate objective.
2. It permits inclusion in the audit reports of a statement of corrective action taken or to be taken. Hence top management need not spend time and energy ascertaining what action is to be undertaken.
3. It tends to eliminate any unsound or impractical recommendations from the audit report. The auditee will point out such weaknesses.
4. It eliminates areas of disagreement or controversy from the report, or at least permits a concise statement as to the exact points of dispute.

Careful writing of the audit report is important, for it serves as a means of judging the efficiency of the operation, the audit, and the auditor. Further, it may be the basis of executive action. Finally, it is also a record of the audit. Under the circumstances the report should state the facts or opinions clearly, concisely, and accurately. It is a sales tool, so that inflammatory or denunciatory comments are to be avoided. Over the long run it must be an instrument in creating goodwill. The same principles of report preparation discussed in Chapters 28 and 29 are applicable in this case.

The form of the audit report varies. It may be in the nature of a brief letter, in questionnaire style, a formal narrative report, or a combination of these. The top executives are interested in a short report which concisely outlines the scope of audit, the findings, and the recommendations. Departmental supervisors are often interested in more details. Either two reports may be prepared, or a single document may highlight the points of emphasis with details available, if desired, in another section of the report.

FOLLOW-UP ON FINDINGS

An essential phase of internal audit administration is the follow-up where corrective action is to be taken. This may be handled by correspondence or even personal visits for just such a purpose. In other instances a re-examination of this aspect is made when the next audit is undertaken.

EXTENT OF INTERNAL AUDITING ACTIVITIES

Aside from problems relating to technical phases of manufacturing, selling, or research, the scope of activities of an internal auditing department is limited only by the ingenuity and resourcefulness of both the controller and chief auditor. Though by no means complete, a checklist of certain functions to be performed by the internal auditor may be suggestive. Some are to be found in most internal audit programs; others are less frequently used. The listing is as follows:

1. *Cash and Securities*
   a. Count petty cash to determine that funds are intact, that policy is followed regarding cashing of checks, etc.
   b. Review petty cash disbursements for proper approvals
   c. Test-check disbursements for accuracy of account distribution, approvals on vouchers, comparison with purchase order and receiving report
   d. Trace detail of deposits to accounts receivable postings, etc.
   e. Assist public accountants in security counts
   f. Reconcile bank accounts

2. *Accounts Receivable*
   a. Circularize accounts receivable
   b. Age accounts receivable
   c. Periodically mail statements to customers
   d. Check credit approval procedure
   e. Check procedure for write-off of uncollectible accounts

3. *Inventories*
   a. Observe physical counts during annual inventory and supplement work of public accountants
   b. Make physical counts during the year for comparison with books
   c. Review purchasing procedure
   d. Review minimum and maximum quantities and evaluate
   e. Compare commitments and quantities on hand with expected orders
   f. Follow-up changes in production schedules with action taken regarding inventories—e.g., cutbacks
   g. Check safeguards used in accounting for scrap or waste
   h. Review procedure for approval of inventory adjustments

4. *Fixed Assets*
   a. Check accuracy of accounting re capital items
   b. Check adequacy of depreciation rates
   c. Review acquisition procedure as to approvals
   d. Check scrapping procedure
   e. Take physical inventory of equipment
   f. Check authorization procedure for acquisitions

5. *Payrolls*
   a. Witness the pay-off at irregular intervals
   b. Check accuracy of cost distribution
   c. Reconcile bank accounts
   d. Check procedure for authorizing changes in rates
   e. Review control over unclaimed wages

6. *Cost Systems*
   a. Review development of cost standards
   b. Check on standard revisions
   c. Check adequacy of records on standards

7. *Reporting Systems*
   a. Review suitability of report forms
   b. Check accuracy of reports
   c. Check degree to which reports are used by line organization
   d. Review over-all reporting system as to need, duplication, and tie-in
   e. Review reporting procedure from standpoint of approvals required and reviews made prior to issuance

8. *Month-End Closings*
   a. Review entries for completeness and accuracy
   b. Check approvals and reviews of journal entries
   c. Review procedure for possible shortcuts

9. *Other*
    a. Review assignment of duties and responsibilities in accounting department and departmental organization structure
    b. Check adequacy of manuals, charts of accounts, etc.
    c. Check apparent degree of cooperation between line and staff departments

COORDINATION WITH THE PUBLIC ACCOUNTANTS

Coordination between the internal auditor and public accountant deserves special comment. As previously stated, one function of internal auditing is to realize economies through reduced audit fees.

The public accountant undertakes an examination, among other reasons, to express an independent opinion as to whether the representations of management in the financial statements present fairly the financial position of the company in accordance with accepted accounting principles applied on a consistent basis. To do this he must rely on test checks and the internal control of the company. Internal auditing is an important cog in the system of internal control—a factor which the independent accountant must consider in developing his audit program. Herein lies the basic reason for the coordination of the two groups, so that the work of each is combined to provide the most complete over-all audit.

The contribution which the internal auditor can make to the annual audit is through these means:

1. *Reduction in the Extent of Detailed Checks or Test Checks.*
2. *Provision of Information to the Independent Accountants.* Use should be made by the independent auditor of the audit working papers and reports of the internal audit staff to learn the weaknesses encountered, unusual transactions, and other useful information.
3. *Elimination of Examination at Selected Branch Plants.* If an effective internal audit is made at some branches, the public accountant may avoid an audit at such a location and may rely on the internal audit report. While all plants and warehouses may be examined over a period of years, visits to every location every year need not be made.
4. *Direct Assistance to the Public Accounting Staff.* Working papers may be prepared for the outside accountant under his direction; assistance in physical inventory counts may be given; and other information may be provided.

36

The Closing Procedure and Related Problems

GENERAL STATEMENT

Quite aside from the daily and weekly control reports, members of management want certain summarized information for the operating periods and for the year. The program of current and future executive action is based largely on past performance and a survey of present and expected conditions. The more up-to-date the information, the better are the chances for a sound plan of action. Past experience indicates that executives are interested primarily in four phases of the business at the end of the operating period:

1. The sales volume, perhaps in relation to the budget or quota
2. The net profit or loss, or operating profit or loss in total and by divisions, and in comparison with the budget
3. The summary of excessive manufacturing or other costs
4. The financial condition

This chapter deals with the ways and means of getting the information quickly. Questions which the controller should consider in connection with the periodic summarizing and closing procedures are:

1. On what date should the fiscal year end?
2. Into what periods should the fiscal year be divided, and how?
3. What steps can be taken to prepare the periodic reports quickly so as to be of maximum use to management?

CONSIDERATIONS IN SELECTING THE FISCAL YEAR

While the controller is not faced with the selection of a fiscal year very often, he should consider whether the present basis used is the most suitable. A choice may be made between the calendar year and the natural business year. The natural business year of an enterprise is the period of twelve consecutive months which ends when the business activities of the company have reached the lowest point in their annual cycle. Generally at this time the inventories which were depleted as a result of the active selling season have not been replenished. When the peak volume of sales has passed, the receivables either are at the minimum or are declining. For the same reason the bank loans or other liabilities needed in a period of high activity have reached a minimum or are being reduced.

Each business usually has a natural business year; and as a rule it does not coincide with the calendar year. From a practical standpoint, the selection of a fiscal year ending other than December 31 has certain definite advantages. This is evidenced in part by the substantial number of companies that have changed. For example, the largest meat packing houses close their books either on October 31 or on the last Saturday in October. Most department stores complete their fiscal year on January 31, and many farm equipment manufacturers have adopted the natural business year ending October 31. The advantages of adopting the natural business year lie in facilitating certain operations essential to the conduct of the business. These include the following:

1. *Inventory Taking.* Physical inventories can be taken at a lower cost and with fewer interruptions in the normal activities. Smaller stocks mean that the count can be taken, checked, and summarized more easily. The smaller scope of the job perhaps signifies also a smaller margin of error in valuing the inventory. Further, with other activities at a lower ebb, regular employees are available to assist in the inventory taking. (Of course, physical inventories need not be taken at the end of the fiscal year, but they must be taken near that time. The public accountants review all inventory transactions between the date of the annual physical inventory and the date of the statements being certified.)

2. *Preparation of More Accurate Financial Statements.* Financial statements are always a combination of facts and opinions. With smaller inventories and receivables, there are fewer estimates or arbitrary provisions. Valuation reserves are lower because of such lower values.

3. *Preparation of More Informative Statements for Planning and Control Purposes.* New policies are very often introduced at the beginning of the natural business year. Financial statements prepared at the end of such a period, reflecting as they do a complete annual cycle of operations, provide management with a better check on the effectiveness of these new policies.

4. *Formulation of Policies.* Closely related to the above is the general consideration of policies. When business is slack, the executives have more time to consider the statements and develop new pro-

grams and policies. Not only is the information available, but the time is more likely to be propitious.

5. *Securing Credit.* Bankers or other creditors prefer statements at the end of a natural year because they may better appraise the business. The statements contain more facts and fewer estimates; and a more accurate opinion may be formed as to liquidity. It is usually to the advantage of the company if the financial statements show its most liquid condition.

6. *Annual Audit.* If the work of public accountants were spread more evenly throughout the year, they could, in greater degree, give personal attention to the individual needs of each client. Furthermore, the audit work would interfere less with the normal activities.

DETERMINING THE NATURAL BUSINESS YEAR

It is a relatively simple matter to determine the natural business year. The controller is probably already familiar with the peaks and valleys of the business. However, one approach is to tabulate the monthly data to determine what month has the lowest activity or minimum investment in such matters as:

Value of production
Inventories
    Raw materials
    Work in process
    Finished goods
Sales
Accounts receivable
Accounts payable

This may be done by listing the dollar values for each item for each month of the year, and in total. Conversion of the amounts to percentage of the total for each factor may more clearly indicate the fluctuation. The more important factors should be considered; and the trend over several years should be checked.

As a result of surveys conducted by Dun & Bradstreet, Inc., in cooperation with the Natural Business Year Council and other groups, a list of recommended fiscal closing dates for various industries has been prepared and is available.[1]

[1] See American Institute of Certified Public Accountants, *The Natural Business Year.*

ADOPTING THE NATURAL BUSINESS YEAR

Once the natural business year is known, the question arises as to how it should be adopted. Some businesses, convinced of the advantages, have hesitated to make the change because of possible complications in connection with the tax laws. However, procedures involved in adopting the natural business year are few and simple.[2]

In establishing a new corporation, the desired fiscal year is simply written in the by-laws. For existing corporations whose fiscal year has been the calendar year, one of the first and most important requirements is to request from the Commissioner of Internal Revenue at Washington—using form 1128—permission to effect the desired change. Requests for such permission, when based upon sound reasons, are generally approved without further inquiry. Similar permission must be secured from state authorities in states which require corporations to file income-tax returns. It is usually granted upon notification that Federal authorities have approved the change.

A separate Federal tax return must be filed for the interim period between the end of the calendar year and the beginning of the new natural fiscal year. This interim return is identical in form with the annual return. A corresponding state income-tax return, for the interim period, must be filed in states which require annual returns of corporations. It is also necessary, if the company is subject to the jurisdiction of the Securities and Exchange Commission, to prepare an interim report for that body when the period between the end of the calendar year and the beginning of the natural fiscal year is three months or longer.

SELECTING THE OPERATING PERIOD

Most concerns use the calendar month as a basis for summarizing and reporting operating results within the fiscal year. There are certain advantages to this plan. Executives frequently think in terms of calendar months, statistics relative to business generally are usually expressed in such terms, many charges are based on the calendar month, salaries and wages are frequently set on a monthly basis, billings to customers may be made monthly, and relations with customers and vendors are likely to involve the calendar month as a basis of calculation.

There are, however, certain objections to the use of a calendar month as an accounting period, principally from the standpoint of comparability. Because the calendar month seldom contains the same number of respective days of the week as did the same month in the preceding year, or as did the preceding month, the sales or expense statements for the month are never comparable with these preceding periods. Yet comparison is a common practice; consequently, at least mental adjustments must be made for the total number of days in the month and also for the number of working days in the month.

[2] *Ibid.,* pp. 6–7.

Where such variations adversely affect the value of comparisons, several alternatives are possible. The following periods may be used:

1. A thirteen-month fixed calendar
2. A thirteen-period year, using the present Gregorian calendar
3. A World Calendar of twelve months, and equal quarters
4. A twenty-one workday month

Brief comments follow on each of the suggested periods. It should be realized, of course, that the choice of an accounting period has no direct connection with the selection of the fiscal year. Each is a separate problem.

THIRTEEN-MONTH FIXED CALENDAR

The thirteen-month calendar consists of thirteen months of twenty-eight days each, which accounts for 364 days. The extra day, called "year-day," is not in any month; and "leap day" is similarly treated. Each month within a year would start on the same day of the week, and each would so close. For example, the first day of every month might begin on Sunday and end on Saturday. The campaign to adopt this calendar has been going on for more than thirty years and there is no particular indication that it will be successful in the foreseeable future.

THE THIRTEEN-PERIOD YEAR

A plan adopted by a sizable number of firms is to split the present calendar into thirteen periods, each with twenty-eight days. The extra day, or two in leap year, may be treated in one of three ways:

1. Accumulate the extra day, and insert a week every five or six years. An advantage is that every period would begin on the same day of the week. The longer period, of course, would not be strictly comparable with the others.
2. Include the extra day or days in the thirteenth period. Most of the periods would be comparable.
3. Exclude January 1, which is a holiday, from the calendar. The leap day only is added.

The thirteen-period calendar gives the advantage of comparability, with the resulting greater usefulness of the data for control purposes. In some instances, because of the avoidance of partial week payrolls, clerical costs may be reduced. Also, the lapsed time between summary periods is shorter. However, there are several disadvantages or weaknesses:

1. It corrects only a part of the problem. While adjustment is made for the *total* days in a period, it does not adjust for legal holidays or plant-wide vacation periods.

2. It is adaptable for internal accounting purposes only. When monthly or period statements are prepared for stockholders or the government, adjustments must be made to conform to the calendar periods.
3. It results in one added closing. Instead of twelve there are thirteen; however, reduced clerical expense or effort may offset this.
4. Fixed charges may create a problem. Where contracts require payments on a calendar basis, or where salaries are paid monthly, some periods could receive an extra charge. This objection can be overcome, however, by revised contracts, depreciation calculations, and other adjustments.

THE WORLD CALENDAR

A movement has been under way to adopt a World Calendar. Until and if it is adopted rather widely, each business may need to use another alternative. This calendar is illustrated in Fig. 188. The basic idea recognizes that the cause of most of the calendar problems is the length of the solar year.

The unique features are as follows:

1. The first month of each quarter will have 31 days, and the other two months will have 30 days each. Hence, each quarter is of equal length.
2. Each month will have 26 weekdays.
3. Each year will begin on a Sunday, and each working year will begin on a Monday.
4. Each quarter begins on Sunday and ends on Saturday.
5. Each year is the same length, and perpetual.

The stabilization results in ending each year with a 365th day following December 30 called Worldsday and dated "W," or 31 December—a year-end world holiday. Leap year day is similarly added at the end of the second quarter, called Leap Year Day and dated "W."

This repetitive year approach offers business advantages in transportation, marketing, etc., in that holidays are constant.

A TWENTY-ONE WORKDAY ACCOUNTING MONTH [3]

Another approach, pending possible national adoption of a modified calendar, which seems based on good common sense, and which combines some of the advantages without the disadvantages of the thirteen-period plan, is a twenty-one workday accounting month. On such a basis, eleven of the periods are comparable, and the twelfth is not, but would not be anyway, by reason of the plant-wide vacation shutdown. Moreover, the

[3] Adapted from Lawrence P. Jennings, "Thirty Days Hath September," *NACA Bulletin,* March, 1951, pp. 802–7.

accounting months coincide with the calendar months sufficiently as to avoid adjustments for external purposes.

The cutoff days each month are established annually, and all plants are provided with a schedule. The procedure is as follows:

1. Starting with January 2, count off twenty-one working days. This establishes the first accounting period. (Saturdays, Sundays, and six holidays do not constitute workdays.)
2. Repeat the procedure until the last complete twenty-one workday period immediately prior to the vacation month is reached.
3. Follow the same procedure, working backward from December 31 until the first complete period immediately following the vacation month.
4. The period between the dates noted in steps 2 and 3 above constitutes the accounting month of the vacation period.

FIRST QUARTER

JANUARY							FEBRUARY							MARCH						
S	M	T	W	T	F	S	S	M	T	W	T	F	S	S	M	T	W	T	F	S
1	2	3	4	5	6	7				1	2	3	4						1	2
8	9	10	11	12	13	14	5	6	7	8	9	10	11	3	4	5	6	7	8	9
15	16	17	18	19	20	21	12	13	14	15	16	17	18	10	11	12	13	14	15	16
22	23	24	25	26	27	28	19	20	21	22	23	24	25	17	18	19	20	21	22	23
29	30	31					26	27	28	29	30			24	25	26	27	28	29	30

SECOND QUARTER

APRIL							MAY							JUNE						
S	M	T	W	T	F	S	S	M	T	W	T	F	S	S	M	T	W	T	F	S
1	2	3	4	5	6	7				1	2	3	4						1	2
8	9	10	11	12	13	14	5	6	7	8	9	10	11	3	4	5	6	7	8	9
15	16	17	18	19	20	21	12	13	14	15	16	17	18	10	11	12	13	14	15	16
22	23	24	25	26	27	28	19	20	21	22	23	24	25	17	18	19	20	21	22	23
29	30	31					26	27	28	29	30			24	25	26	27	28	29	30 W

THIRD QUARTER

JULY							AUGUST							SEPTEMBER						
S	M	T	W	T	F	S	S	M	T	W	T	F	S	S	M	T	W	T	F	S
1	2	3	4	5	6	7				1	2	3	4						1	2
8	9	10	11	12	13	14	5	6	7	8	9	10	11	3	4	5	6	7	8	9
15	16	17	18	19	20	21	12	13	14	15	16	17	18	10	11	12	13	14	15	16
22	23	24	25	26	27	28	19	20	21	22	23	24	25	17	18	19	20	21	22	23
29	30	31					26	27	28	29	30			24	25	26	27	28	29	30

FOURTH QUARTER

OCTOBER							NOVEMBER							DECEMBER						
S	M	T	W	T	F	S	S	M	T	W	T	F	S	S	M	T	W	T	F	S
1	2	3	4	5	6	7				1	2	3	4						1	2
8	9	10	11	12	13	14	5	6	7	8	9	10	11	3	4	5	6	7	8	9
15	16	17	18	19	20	21	12	13	14	15	16	17	18	10	11	12	13	14	15	16
22	23	24	25	26	27	28	19	20	21	22	23	24	25	17	18	19	20	21	22	23
29	30	31					26	27	28	29	30			24	25	26	27	28	29	30 W

W (Worldsday, a World Holiday) equals 31 December (365th day) and follows 30 December every year.
W (Leapyear Day, another World Holiday) equals 31 June and follows 30 June in leap years.

Fig. 188—The World Calendar.

Using this procedure for an August vacation period, the monthly cutoff date, and related data, for illustrative purposes, would be as follows:

| Month | Cut-off Date | Number of | |
		Working Days	Calendar Days
January	January 30	21	30
February	February 28	21	29
March	March 29	21	29
April	April 27	21	29
May	May 28	21	31
June	June 27	21	30
July	July 27	21	30
August	August 30	14 (Vac.)	34
September	October 1	21	32
October	October 30	21	29
November	November 29	21	30
December	December 31	21	32
Total		245	365

THE ADVANTAGES OF PROMPT REPORTING

No subject deserves more emphasis from the viewpoint of effective controllership than that of reporting information promptly. The reports of the controller more and more are becoming an impelling force in the guidance of business policy and in cost and revenue control. A careful analysis of the facts is expected from the accounting department, but, as stated previously, the data are valueless unless they are timely. If reports are tardy, not only is management left without the facts it needs, but the clerical cost is wasted.

Much information can be reported promptly without a monthly closing, and much is. The daily labor report, the daily report on excess material requisitioned, weekly reports on labor costs, supplies, scrap, sales, or inventory are examples of reports quite independent of the monthly closing procedure. Moreover, even certain facts covering the entire month need not await the completion of the periodic closing. For example, the gross sales in units and value usually can be quickly summarized and checked as a part of the closing procedure, and the information can be reported.

Other information which is primarily of a profit nature ordinarily is determined only after the closing is completed. Yet, possibly the accounting philosophy should be: first, preparation of the reports and *then* completion of the formal closing. Perhaps the flow of information should be such that reports in and of themselves serve as the basis for the formal accounting.

The final test of an efficient accounting department is getting the financial data promptly into the hands of management, with a follow-up as to interpretation, if necessary.

In addition to carrying out his accounting function properly, the controller will find these incidental advantages accruing from a program by which results are reported promptly:

1. Managements become aware of the need for accounting information, and tend to depend more on accounting guidance
2. The operating divisions become more cost- or profit-conscious when information is received promptly
3. Usually accounting economies result because it forces up-to-date and efficient procedures
4. The morale of the accounting personnel is higher, for they feel they are a part of the organization and not mere "bookkeepers"
5. Improved over-all control is made possible with more prompt information; this can be applied to costs, inventories, sales direction, or almost any other phase of accounting control
6. Billings and monthly statements to customers are frequently advanced, with a favorable effect on collections

A PROGRAM FOR PROMPT CLOSING AND REPORTING

The important question is *how* facts can be reported on a timely basis. Many controllers now place the monthly reports in the hands of executives during the first four or five days of the month. Reports presented later than this are of doubtful value for control purposes, and may be of lesser value for planning and policy determination. How, then, should the controller proceed to get out prompt statements? Frankly, the need is an objective analysis of every step in the closing procedure to (1) "spot" and eliminate bottlenecks, (2) determine whether the record system being used is the best means of accumulating the data, and (3) consider what functional activities can be transferred to earlier periods or what shortcuts can be taken. If the accounting staff is convinced of the need for early closings, then each supervisor and his staff should be able to suggest ways and means of speeding up the operations. Many of the suggestions must come from the "grass roots" of the organization—those who do the work.

In formulating a program for an early closing, some useful suggestions may be found in the following checklist:

1. Develop a practical and uniform chart of accounts. This should include (a) the proper grouping of accounts, and (b) compact control accounts which may be quickly summarized in statement form. Too many control accounts make the summarizing job more difficult.
2. Prepare many of the forms and schedules before the end of the month. Headings, descriptions, or account names, and comparative figures can be completed in advance, leaving only the current figures to be inserted.

3. Use standard or duplicated forms to avoid the manual setting-up of certain routine data.

4. Install procedures so that the daily records are kept up-to-date through most of the month. Schedules should be prepared and adhered to. This applies not merely within the accounting organization, but to all sales, production, or other company sources from which data are secured. Persuade the group of the need and benefits of such a system.

5. Eliminate the checking of small inaccuracies until after the closing. All differences should be checked out, but this may be done as a post-closing function. For example, small differences in intradivisional accounts may be held in inventory until resolved.

6. To the extent practical, install a system of self-balancing checks. For example, extension of individual elements of standard costs should be balanced against the over-all extensions.

7. Record all data on final reports, as far as possible, to eliminate further copying and duplication.

8. Use flexible crews to pass from section to section as the peak load progresses, or to assist in trouble spots.

9. Develop certain needed factors before the end of the month. It is possible to prepare distribution bases in advance, including shop factors, power factors, etc.

10. Estimate and accrue important cost items instead of delaying the closing of accounts payable. Thus, the power bill, the gas bill, or rental costs may be accrued and reversed or corrected in the following month. Usually accurate information may be secured by phone from the vendor, if necessary.

11. Secure branch reports within one or two days of the end of the month, and secure any essential information by wire. Use of air mail scheduled to take-off time should not be overlooked for early receipt of a branch trial balance.

12. Install efficient and up-to-date accounting equipment with particular reference to computers in the larger companies.

13. Make a proper split of records to facilitate the closing. For example, a loose-leaf journal system may be used in combination with a standard journal system. Thus, Journal No. 2 is always the summary of accounts payable; Journal No. 6 is always cash disbursements. In this manner the work can be divided among accountants on the basis of these journal vouchers. Such preparation by one does not "tie up" the general ledger or other journals.

14. Make provision for balancing certain records before the end of the month. In this way, all differences to date may be resolved. Thus the accounts receivable charges may be balanced against the sales summary to within two or three days of the month-end. Any differences which develop for the last days may be quickly checked.

15. During the closing, defer as much of the current work as is practical.

16. Prepare certain entries on a standard basis, and adjust only quarterly or annually. This can be done with respect to depreciation, some insurance costs, and similar items.
17. Introduce the thirteen-period or twenty-one workday calendar, if feasible.
18. As an administrative policy, check the system frequently to see that procedures are being followed. Look for new "bottlenecks."
19. Train an efficient staff, and educate them as to the need for speed and accuracy.
20. Issue preliminary figures, with a reasonable amount of cross-checking, for any vital aspects of the operation. For example, when the manufacturing variances have been summarized and checked, issue a summary report. The chances are that the closing will not be complete at this time, but the manufacturing portion may be; and this early information may provide useful data for the manufacturing group to act upon. Little extra effort is required.
21. Finally, prepare a schedule for the closing period and enforce it. This schedule should (a) fix responsibility for each movement of data, and (b) indicate the day and hour each task should be completed.

Basically, the program for a quick closing requires a well-coordinated organization as well as the intent to accomplish the job. Furthermore, some overtime is to be expected. Any accounting department which can prepare early statements without some overtime is probably overstaffed.

37

Preparation and
Maintenance of Manuals

NATURE OF MANUALS

A manual is nothing more than an orderly collection and presentation of directives, or instructions, or facts pertaining to a particular activity—a business, a major function, a job or procedure. While several classifications of manuals can be given, the following is useful for immediate purposes:

1. Policy
2. Organization
3. Procedures
4. Employees' Handbook

A policy manual is a compilation of company policy directives, which may be (1) basic, as established by the board of directors, or (2) general, as set forth by the administrative or management group of the company, or (3) departmental, as formulated by the division heads, e.g., policies applicable specifically to the sales department as promulgated by the sales manager. A policy manual may be divided into the three sections mentioned, viz., basic, general, and departmental.

The organization manual is intended to define the duties and functions of the various departments or sections, and the relationship of one with another. Such a manual would normally include an organization chart indicating the lines of authority, the names and location of departments and units, and the title and duties of the department head and of the managers of subdivisions.

A procedures manual may be a collection and presentation either of departmental or functional procedures or of detailed performance instructions. To illustrate, the basic procedures manual may consist of standard practice instructions which cover all procedures affecting two or more departments or there may be a detailed procedures manual for the use of one or more departments, such as an accounting manual. Within each section or unit of the accounting department, a manual may be used, viz., a tax manual or an insurance manual. Not only may these manuals contain the general explanations of the subject, but the manual, or a supplement, may include step-by-step procedures on *how* to perform a function. Thus the detailed procedure required to balance a subsidiary ledger with the control account may be included.

Finally, the employees' handbook contains information of both a general and specific nature which is of interest to all employees—such matters as vacation allowances, pay practices, employee seniority, grievance procedures, hours, and retirement benefits.

Very often it will be found that the manual does not conform to a single category described above. Thus the procedures manual may contain a section on organization, or another on policy. It is therefore possible to have one manual of general application, and other manuals relating to strictly intradepartmental matters.

For the purpose of this book, interest is centered principally on the procedures manual which often falls within the controller's orbit of responsibility. The policy manual may be in large part the work of the president's staff; the organization manual also may be prepared by the president's staff, although this can be assigned to the controller; and the employees' handbook is largely the responsibility of the personnel department.

NEED AND USE OF PROCEDURES MANUALS

It costs money to prepare manuals; hence the question should be raised as to whether they are really necessary. Most companies which have successfully introduced procedures manuals have found them highly useful. Some of the advantages of a procedures manual are:

General

1. Serves as a means of defining and clarifying matters. When a method or procedure must be reduced to writing, numerous uncertainties come to the surface and must be settled.
2. Promotes standardization and simplification. Preparation of the procedures manual usually brings up a consideration of several methods, and the one selected is presumably the best.

Specific Uses or Benefits

1. Assists in the training of employees on new jobs. Experience shows that employees may be trained better and faster through the use of manuals. This can apply to new employees or to older employees transferred to new positions. Standard practice instructions tell how the job should be done.

2. Permits better utilization of supervision. Use of manuals can save the time of the supervisors in giving explanations or instructions.
3. Provides a reference source when questions of procedure, jurisdiction, or responsibility arise.
4. Serves as another control tool, through the use of review or audit, to determine whether a function is being carried out in the standard manner.
5. Serves to get the procedure on record rather than "in the head" of employees who may leave at any time.
6. Assists in coordinating and synchronizing effort, in avoiding duplication of effort, and in promoting interdepartmental harmony.
7. Permits greater flexibility in job assignments.
8. Generally permits the faster introduction of new procedures.

Wherever a group of people are working together, wherever responsibility and authority are delegated, wherever the personal supervision of top management cannot extend to all functions, there is probably a need for a written procedure—short and simple though it may be. Under these circumstances, whether admitted or not, supervisory talent and time can be reduced by the use of manuals.

THE ORGANIZATION FOR PROCEDURES WORK

Procedures manuals should be written by those who are best qualified to do the job. There are two general approaches. One would assign the task of writing the procedures to each department primarily concerned; the other would assign the responsibility for all procedures to a departmental unit organized primarily for such a purpose. The latter arrangement is believed to be preferable, although the cooperation of the entire organization is necessary and must be secured by means discussed in the next section. In smaller companies the "procedures section" may consist of one man under the supervision of the controller. This one man devotes all or part of his time to such matters.

In some companies the procedure writing is a function of the industrial engineering department. While this can well be entirely satisfactory, the authors are of the opinion that a more desirable plan is to establish a manuals and procedures section as a staff function of the controller's organization. There are several reasons for such preference: (1) internal control is an important consideration in developing procedures, and accounting-trained men, working for the controller, are likely to be more aware of requirements of this nature; (2) many interdepartmental procedures involve paper work, the flow of which is of immediate concern to the accounting department; (3) an over-all rather than a departmental approach to the problem is necessary, and since the controller's function necessarily cuts across departmental lines already, it would seem sound to place the responsibility in this division; (4) many of the procedures are strictly of accounting concern, such as the accounts payable, accounts receivable, cash disbursements, and fixed asset procedure; and (5) engineering talent may be more fully utilized on manufacturing methods and not on paper-work procedures.

Under such a plan the manuals and procedures section would administer the manuals program for the company standard practices (involving more than one department), the various standard practices of the accounting department, the standard instructions relating to office procedure of any department, and such other practices for which assistance is requested. It would be responsible for coordinating and organizing manual material which it may originate, or which may be requested or originated by others, or in collaboration with others. Moreover, it would have the duty of verifying the fact that all manuals conform to company practice and policy; and would be responsible for keeping the manual and distribution lists up to date.

STEPS IN PREPARING A MANUAL

To be of value a manual must be used by those for whom it is primarily intended. If those who are to use it have a voice in its preparation, the chances are much greater that its use will be encouraged. The manual should be regarded as the result of the cooperative effort of the operating department and the procedures unit. Cooperation, then, is the keynote.

A suggested procedure for developing and preparing manuals, based on this cooperation, is as follows:

1. Determine by general meeting with those who will use the manual its general nature and content, the method in which it is to be used, and its objectives.
2. Prepare a general outline of the manual.
3. Perform the necessary research and investigation as to the basic data. This should be done in close cooperation with personnel of the operating department.
4. Prepare a rough draft of each proposed procedure.
5. Have all interested departments review the draft of the suggested procedure, and secure their comments.
6. Prepare the revised draft, or as many drafts as necessary, to reconcile conflicting viewpoints, and incorporate the suggestions to the extent practicable.
7. Prepare the final draft for executive approval.
8. Determine the distribution list.
9. Prepare and distribute the manual.

In preparing the drafts, the following points should be given consideration:

1. Procedures should be as brief and concise as possible.
2. Headings should be descriptive of the subject matter.
3. Extensive use of the outline form is desirable.
4. Titles should be used in lieu of personal names.
5. Drafts should be double-spaced to facilitate changes.
6. Space should be provided in the draft specifically for the necessary approvals, perhaps in this fashion:

Approved

Chief Engineer	Works Manager
Director of Purchases	Controller
Sales Manager	Research Director

Generally speaking, approvals of the drafts should be somewhat as follows:

President or Executive Vice-President	All procedures covering basic policies
Works Manager	All procedures relating to production, such as receiving, planning, and scheduling, etc.
Chief Engineer	All procedures relating to engineering
Controller	All procedures relating to accounting activities, including auditing, cash, payroll, cost, and office functions All procedures involving any interdepartmental cost transfers
Director of Industrial Relations	All procedures relating to personnel, plant protection, sanitation, and safety
Purchasing Agent	All procedures relating to purchases

In summary, all basic procedures, i.e., those relating to policy, must be approved by the chief executive; and those relating to divisions or functions must be approved by those in charge of such functions. However, some companies require the chief executive, or plant executive in a particular plant, to approve every standard practice affecting more than one divisional activity.

7. Where reference is made to forms, copies of such forms should be attached and their use illustrated if feasible.

FORMAT

The physical form of the manual will depend on its use, the type, the probable frequency of revision, and other factors. Decisions will have to be made as to several points:

1. *Form.* Bound or loose-leaf. A loose-leaf form facilitates revision.
2. *Size.* A pocket size may be convenient for the employees' handbook, but inadequate for those which are voluminous and are to be kept on desks.
3. *Method of Duplicating.* Printing is expensive and often unnecessary. The ditto or stencil reproduction method may be economical and practical.
4. *System of Numbering.* Some companies use numbers, while others may use letters to designate the function and division, with numbers to indicate the consecutive instruction number. Thus, F–2 might indicate standard practice two of the financial section.
5. *Extent of Indexing.* This may greatly help or hinder use of the manual. Cross-indexing is very useful.

CONTENT OF ACCOUNTING MANUAL

An accounting manual should set out all necessary instructions pertaining to the accounting and statistical procedures. While the content and arrangement of such a manual must vary somewhat according to the nature and size of the business and its operations, the following outline is illustrative:

1. Purpose and use of manual
2. Methods of initiating and approving changes
3. Organization of the accounting department
4. Classification and manual of accounts, including a general description of the classifications
5. Detailed instructions for individual procedures
6. Methods of analyzing operating accounts
7. Summarizing procedure and closing schedule
8. Report schedules, including departments responsible for preparation, due date, and distribution list
9. Cost determination under government contracts
10. Foreign exchange
11. Miscellaneous instructions, including:
    Material classifications
    Standard form letters
    Conversion tables
    Tables of equivalents
    SEC reporting requirements
    Other governmental requirements as to records and reports

REVISION OF THE PROCEDURES MANUAL

Once interest has been kindled in a procedures manual, the easiest way to let it die is to fail to keep it up to date. A manual which is not current, or which covers only a part of the subject, is worse than none at all because all errors or conflict may be blamed on the inadequate procedure. This phase of the manual program, therefore, cannot be overemphasized. Responsibility for revision should be definitely placed with the manuals and procedure unit. And even here a boy should not be assigned to do a man's job.

Revision of the manual generally follows the same steps as the writing of a new standard practice, including the securing of approvals of the rewrites.

The following suggestions are made as to revision procedure:

1. Revisions should be handled on a systematic basis. A schedule or standard procedure should be followed in checking the need for revisions.
2. When rough drafts of revisions are sent out, either the form or the transmittal letter should indicate the nature of the changes. This may avoid a complete recheck of the procedure and save time.
3. The standard practice, when revised, should carry the date of the revision and indicate that it is a revision. Recipients should be advised as to disposal of the superseded forms.

DISTRIBUTION OF THE MANUAL

The procedures section should maintain an up-to-date master distribution list. Each manual may have a separate list. By and large, each manual should be distributed only to those who can use it.

In instances where the manual contains restricted or confidential information, it may be assigned to a specific individual, with a requirement that it be returned before receipt of the final paycheck—as part of the termination procedure. Some concerns forward copies of the manual to the department head and he becomes responsible for distribution of the revisions.

A periodic audit or review of the manuals is helpful in seeing that they are kept up-to-date and that distribution lists are current.

ILLUSTRATIVE MANUALS

The exact form of the procedures manuals may vary from company to company depending on individual circumstances. Some excerpts are helpful in checking style. An illustration of a detailed procedure from an organization controlling many concessions is as follows:

Function	*Performed By*
XIV. ADVANCES TO CONCESSIONAIRES	
1. Upon request of concessionaire for an advance prior to close of settlement week, request Concessions Accounting Section to prepare T 704 (Estimated Statement of Concessionaire's Account) in duplicate, entering the following information thereon:	Director of Revenue Control
a) Date	
b) Concessionaire's name and contract number	
c) Amount of advance requested	
d) By reference to previous week's settlement statement, enter the amount of previous week's deposit credit less charges in detail, including participation, and amount of payment to concessionaire.	
e) By reference to current week's Revenue Control and Deposit Ledger-control sheet (T 289) enter the total amount deposited during the current week.	
f) By reference to current settlement statement enter the amount of charges, in detail, accrued during the current week, and on the basis of previous charges, estimate and enter all other charges, including participation.	
g) Deduct total accrued and estimated charges from deposit credit, balance equalling estimated amount due concessionaire.	
2. Forward original copy of T 704 to Director of Revenue Control for recommendation of amount to be advanced to concessionaire; retain duplicate for file.	Chief Concessions Accountant
3. If advance is recommended for approval, forward T 704 to Financial Director for approval and transmittal to Director of Banking and Cashiering.	Director of Revenue Control
4. Upon receipt of T 704, properly approved, draw check in triplicate, on special bank account and forward original and triplicate copies of check to Chief Concessions Accountant, duplicate to Receipts and Disbursements Cashier.	Office of Director of Banking and Cashiering
5. From duplicate copy of check make following entry on cash disbursements book: Debit Account 5824—Settlement Ledger Control (by settlement groups) Credit Account 11—Special Deposit Account	Receipts and Disbursements Cashier
6. Upon receipt of original and triplicate copies of check, forward original to concessionaire and from triplicate copy post to appropriate Concessionaire's Settlement Ledger and Statement, as provided in Article XV.	Chief Concessions Accountant

A representative description of an asset account and operating account, taken from the accounting manual of a large aircraft corporation, follows:

ACCOUNT 210—INTERDIVISION CLEARING ACCOUNT

This account is authorized for use as a clearing account for recording charges which are to be subsequently transferred to the General Office or to another Division.

It is to be debited with charges which are to be transferred on Interdivision Invoices (I.D.I.'s) as follows:

a) Charges which for some reason cannot be transferred immediately.

b) Charges after the 25th of a month.

c) Any other charges which can be more easily transferred through the use of this account.

It is to be credited with all such charges as they are transferred on I.D.I.'s. The corresponding debits to such credits are:

On Division books—Account 310, General Office Account
On General Office books—Division Accounts (801–822)

Every effort should be made to clear items from this account during the current month and except in unusual circumstances the balance at the month-end should be only those charges accumulated after the 25th of that month.

For further information on the handling of interdivision transfers refer to Accounting Direction 6.05, Interdivision Charges.

ACCOUNT 1104—DOMESTIC SALES—COMMERCIAL

This account is authorized for recording the sale of all commercial type aircraft within the United States and its territorial possessions, except sales to the U.S. Air Force, Army, and Navy.

It is to be credited with the net amount of each sale.

It is to be debited with sales returns and with allowances except those which are properly chargeable to Account 92, Service and Warranty Expense.

At the end of the year the balance in this account is to be closed out to Account 310, General Office Account.

Subsidiary records shall be maintained by models and contracts. Subaccounts shall be maintained as follows:

11—Airplane Sales
12—Airplane Returns
13—Airplane Allowances

21—Spares Sales
22—Spares Returns
23—Spares Allowances

31—Service Sales
32—Service Returns

A representative page from the standard practice instructions of another corporation is shown in Fig. 189.

	NUMBER_____
	ISSUE_____2_____
SUBJECT:	PAGE__1__OF__1__
DIVISION STANDARD PRACTICES	EFFECTIVE 11-25-

I - PURPOSE

To establish a Division Standard Practice system for establishing and recording operating policies and procedures at this Division.

II - PROCEDURE

1. This Division shall maintain a system of serially numbered Division Standard Practices (D.S.P.) to establish and record operating policies and practices to be followed by the Division departments. Division Standard Practice Supplements (D.S.P.S.) provide each department affected with such additional detailed instructions as are necessary.

2. Division Standard Practices shall be used only for the following:

   a. The application and extension of policies and practices established by Corporation Standard Practice (refer to Corporation Standard Practice in the introduction to this manual), to the activities of this Division.

   b. Policies and practices established by the General Manager affecting the Division as a whole, or two or more departments. This includes departmental functional organizations.

3. Division Standard Practices shall <u>not</u> be used for recording detailed routines or procedures of a single department or activity.

4. The preparation and issue of Division Standard Practices shall be controlled by the Accounting Department, which shall prepare them upon request of any department head; obtain the signatures of all department heads involved; and submit them to the General Manager for approval before issue.

5. The Accounting Department will make periodic reviews of issued D. S. P.'s to determine whether they are being followed by all concerned, or whether improvements can be made to them and shall submit findings to the General Manager for recommended action.

6. Two copies of each issued D.S.P. revision, or supplement, shall be submitted to the Controller's office.

AUTHORIZED BY_____*Lowdright Jr.*_____ DATE *11/24/*
GENERAL MANAGER

Fig. 189—Illustrative Sheet from Division Standard Practice Manual.

UNIFORM ACCOUNTING MANUALS

The accounting manual of a company has as one of its objectives the establishment of uniform accounting principles and procedures throughout the company. It serves as a guide in the preparation of financial and cost statements of the various plants and distribution points. However, there may be a wide diversity of accounting practices between the members of any single industry. To provide some uniformity, and to attempt to make comparative financial statements more significant, some trade associations have endeavored to secure the introduction of uniform accounting manuals. A great many have been successful, and any controller may wish to adapt the manual of his own company to coordinate with the industry manual.

SUMMARY

The effective use of procedures manuals depends on the following factors:

1. The cooperation of the procedures staff and the personnel of the operating division
2. A well-qualified staff that has the ability to write adequate procedures and tactfully reconcile conflicting viewpoints
3. Effective follow-up in seeing that
   a. Revisions are up to date
   b. Procedures are being observed, through a departmental audit

PART VII

Other Problems of Controllership

38

Maintenance and Destruction of Records

NATURE OF THE PROBLEM

A special aspect of record keeping has to do with the retention and disposition of inactive records. Records are the memory, the history, the story of the company and its transactions. The increasing size and complexity of the business unit, as well as the growth of government regulation, have resulted in a need for keeping more records and for retaining these records over a greater span of time.

Establishment of intelligent policies and procedures for the retention and destruction of inactive and obsolete records has considerable long-term significance to a business. On the one hand, a policy of retaining all, or almost all, documents for any extended period of time would become very expensive. However, the unthinking and arbitrary destruction of records would deprive the company of needed information. Thus, premature destruction of records may result in the loss of information essential to the effective defense or prosecution of lawsuits, the settlement of federal income tax matters, or the favorable disposition of many problems requiring documentary proof. Weighed against such disadvantages is the cost of maintaining old records: storage rental, or the use of storage space for other purposes; investment in equipment and facilities necessary to store the documents; insurance expense; the cost of transportation to storage; and other clerical costs incident to handling and indexing the material.

The problem is by no means simple. It involves the balancing of storage space and costs against a possible need for such records at some unforeseen future time. The task of assessing the future value of any particular record is difficult; judgment is needed. In any event, a reasonable solution to the problem requires procedures with a sound and systematic approach. There are three basic problems: (1) *What* must be kept? (2) *How long* must it be kept? and (3) *How* should it be kept?

RESPONSIBILITY FOR RECORD RETENTION AND DISPOSITION

One of the first prerequisites in meeting the problem of record disposition is the definite assignment of responsibility and authority for the function. This can be handled in any one of three ways:

1. Through the establishment of a committee
2. Through the assignment of the task to an individual executive
3. By charging each division head with the responsibility for such matters as relate to his own activity

Whoever tackles the job should have an over-all viewpoint as to the value of the records.

There is some weight of opinion that a committee type of organization is preferable because no exact or scientific determination can be made in many cases, and thoughts as to period of retention or destruction vary widely. Usually such a committee—whether it be called a "Retention of Records Committee" or some other name—is restricted to division heads who are more or less directly concerned with the company records. Invariably the membership includes both the accounting and legal executives.

Where the authority and responsibility for disposition of records have been assigned to a single individual, this executive has usually been the controller. Since he is the official "keeper of the records," this assignment is not surprising. He is responsible for creating many of the documents and should have a voice in their disposition—truly a "cradle-to-grave" affair. Whether he is selected because of his knowledge of the records or for other reasons, his responsibility is great. An error in judgment may quickly bring forth comment that authority should have been vested elsewhere, although these same critics probably would have been reluctant to assume full responsibility themselves. Indeed, there is some feeling that the responsibility should *not* be placed in the hands of any single individual, but rather should be shared. In the event of a lawsuit, with all records destroyed, there might be certain solace in having had the concurrence of others in the destruction of the data. Solicitation of the opinion of others as to disposition of the records is certainly desirable.

If an individual executive is to be responsible for the retention of records, a question may be raised as to the desirability of assigning the task to legal talent. It is certainly desirable to consider the legality of the disposition. There are, however, three general reasons for assigning the task to the controller in preference to the lawyer: (1) the lawyer is inclined to be conservative, and is likely to recommend retention as long as it is possible for a suit to be instituted, regardless of probability; (2) the controller, being more familiar with the records, is likely to be a better judge of their individual value, and to make a more intelligent selection; and (3) other related problems as to how and where the records are to be stored can probably be better handled by the controller.

The third possible assignment of responsibility is to the division or department heads. However, experience has indicated that some division executives "play it safe" by preserving every file and document for which there is the remotest possibility of use. At the opposite extreme are those who do not realize the importance of essential records in their own department and are prone to discard everything. Some companies have secured a degree of uniformity within the organization by placing responsibility with the controller or with a committee, but requiring approval of the department head before destruction of the documents.

In summary, then, the controller, either alone or jointly with certain other company officers, is usually charged with responsibility for determining the retention period of records and for authorizing their destruction.

A STANDARD PROCEDURE

Once the organization has been created and responsibility placed as to record retention, the next logical step is the establishment of policies and the institution of standard procedures to carry out such policies. A complete program of inactive record disposition should include:

1. The preparation, insofar as possible, of a schedule of retention and destruction for all records
2. Provision for determining the retention period for all items not covered by the retention schedule
3. Provision for periodic review and revision of the record retention schedule
4. Provision for a properly equipped depository
5. A procedure relative to transferring inactive records to the storage areas at periodic intervals
6. Maintenance of a follow-up system on transfers and destruction
7. Procedures as to actual destruction of the obsolete documents
8. Maintenance of adequate records of the materials destroyed

These procedures can be incorporated in the standard practice instructions of the company.

FACTORS AFFECTING THE RETENTION OF RECORDS

Even though there may be considerable divergence between companies as to retention periods and procedures, there are several fundamental considerations in determining which records must be preserved. These include:

1. Nature of the record itself
2. Statutes of limitation
3. Nature of the business
4. Governmental or statutory requirements

Quite obviously, the type of record is an important factor in determining whether it shall be kept. For example, the certificate of incorporation is in a category quite different from the triplicate copy of a vendor's invoice. Features which influence the value of the record include:

1. The worth of the document in terms of future company operations; thus, a franchise or lease may be vital to the company's existence
2. The availability of identical copies in other files
3. The extent to which the data are summarized on other available documents, or conversely, are a summary of other detailed information
4. The extent to which the record is the original evidence of certain transactions, i.e., is a basic document

In such instances as when the records are in the nature of contracts, notes or other evidence of indebtedness, or court judgments, the statutes of limitation may govern the retention period. Because these statutes fix or limit the period of court action, such documents may be retained until the right of action has passed. This period varies in different states and for various types of action; moreover, the statutes are subject to revision by legislative change.

The nature of the business also may be a factor in record retention. Thus, if a product must be aged several years before sale or use, the lot sheets attending the manufacture would probably be retained much longer than the records incident to the fabrication of a piston. Then, too, the nature of the business may determine the type of governmental regulation applicable.

Finally, of increasing importance are the governmental and regulatory requirements. Under various laws, both federal and state bureaus or agencies have promulgated record retention requirements which affect a large share of the records of the ordinary business. Among such organizations are the Internal Revenue Service, Interstate Commerce Commission, Securities and Exchange Commission, Federal Trade Commission, and various control agencies in times of war. Among the statutes requiring the preservation of certain records for a stipulated number of years, which apply to almost every concern, may be mentioned the Fair Labor Standards Act, the Walsh-Healey Act, the Federal Insurance Contributions Act, and the Contract Settlement Act.

CLASSIFYING RECORDS FOR RETENTION

One of the first steps in the development of the records procedure is the classification of records according to those to be retained permanently; those to be retained for a period of time, perhaps microfilmed, and then destroyed; and those to be preserved for some time and then destroyed.

Each type of record should be considered with respect to such probable future reference needs as the following:

Supports title to property
Supports payments made to others
Supports claims against outside parties
Is required by regulatory commission or other public law
Provides protection against future tax claims
Provides essential operating statistics

There are several means of classifying records, but a simple one is suggested which recognizes five groups: (1) vital or essential, (2) valuable, (3) important, (4) useful, and (5) non-essential.

Essential records are irreplaceable, or are not replaceable immediately, and are needed for the company's continuance in operation. This group would include:

Certificates of incorporation
Charters or franchises
Capital stock records
Constitution, bylaws, and amend-
ments
Deeds and leases
Directors' minutes books
Stockholders' lists and proxies

Powers of attorney
Copyrights, patents, and trademark
authorizations
Formulas and product analyses
Blueprints, drawings, and sketches
General journals
General ledgers

Valuable records are those necessary to prevent financial loss or to recover money or property. Some examples are:

Accounts receivable ledgers
Fixed asset ledgers
Securities
Claims files
Inventory records

Insurance policies
Contracts
Tax reports
Audit reports

Important records are administrative tools which might be obtained after considerable effort or delay, and which would not adversely affect essential operations to any serious degree. The great bulk of cost studies and summary accounting records would fit into this category. Some examples are:

Cost and profitability studies
Credit reports
Price records
Operating data
Customer data records

Personnel and payroll records
(other than those required by law)
Manuals and policy directives
Canceled checks
Government reports
Shipping documents

Useful records are those which are not needed for current operations, but are helpful for reference and similar purposes. Such records ordinarily would be destroyed when current usefulness ceases.

The non-essential records are those which are available for destruction relatively soon and which have no long-term value.

It is to be observed that such a classification would be useful in considering the necessity for record duplication for protection against losses resulting from fire, war, or other catastrophe, quite distinct from the matter of record retention.

A classification of records on the above suggested basis, when considered also in the light of governmental or other legal requirements, permits those who review the records to determine which documents are essential and must be preserved.

THE JONES COMPANY

RECORD RETENTION DETAIL

No. _____ 6 _____

Date _____ 6/30/ _____

Page _____ 7 _____

Department _____ Cost _____

Item or Form No. _____ Weekly Labor Reports _____

Description and Purpose _____ Comparison of departmental actual and standard labor _____

Classification (✓)   ☐ Vital   ☐ Valuable   ☑ Important   ☐ Useful

Origin _____ Labor section _____

Reason for Retention _____ For comparative labor costs by department _____

How Filed _____ Chronologically _____

Location · Active File _____ Cost Dept. _____

Location · Inactive File _____ Bldg. 7, File 603 _____

Retention Period _____ Four Years _____

Approvals	JOE			Dept. Mgr.	Div. Head

Fig. 190—Record Retention Detail.

THE RETENTION SCHEDULE

One of the most important phases of record maintenance is the preparation of the retention schedule. In preparing such a schedule, a form similar to Fig. 190 may be used. Each department manager should be given an ample supply to cover his needs. In this manner, the opinion of the department manager is secured. Use of such forms should be preceded or accompanied by a letter explaining the program, defining the classification, etc.

Those assigned the task of determining the retention period must give careful study to the actual and contingent worth of all records. Each individual record must be considered in the light of the needs of the particular business. Though this is true, a practical retention schedule as recommended by the National Fire Protection Association should serve as a helpful guide for the successful operation of an efficient record preservation program. This schedule is given on pages 713–717.

In evaluating the worth of any particular record, an objective approach is suggested. Simple mathematics may assist in revealing that retention of certain records is not worth the cost. An advantage must be shown in value and not mere personal satisfaction. When certain records are subjected to such a test, those who would retain them often change their opinions.

GOVERNMENTAL REQUIREMENTS

In considering record retention and maintenance, the varied requirements of the many governments and governmental agencies under which a given business enterprise must operate are, of course, of primary importance.

What complicates the problem is ambiguities or complete silence on the subject.

Some of the regulations promulgated by agencies of the federal government are very detailed, and others merely stipulate the retention period and the general class of records to be maintained. An example of the former are the regulations prescribed by the Interstate Commerce Commission governing the destruction of records of railroads. Detailed retention schedules by individual record are provided, together with the form of cremation certificate. On the other hand, the regulations issued by the Office of Price Stabilization provide merely that records supporting the calculations for ceiling prices be retained for a two-year period following the expiration of the Defense Production Act of 1950.

Perhaps the best guides on government requirements for the retention of records are the three volumes entitled *Corporate Records Retention,* published by the Controllership Foundation (the research arm of the Financial Executives Institute) in 1958–1960. Volume 1 deals with U. S.

federal requirements; volume 2 relates to Canadian federal and provincial requirements; and volume 3 is a guide to requirements of the state governments of the U. S. This publication, with which all controllers should be familiar, is a reference to record retention. It is not intended to provide legal interpretation of the statutes or regulations referred to.

The chief accounting official in each company may find it desirable to review the particular governmental regulations applicable under the circumstances, and consult with appropriate counsel. For illustrative purposes *only, some* of the requirements of three laws of general application are outlined.

Internal Revenue Code. It is ordinarily advisable to preserve for at least five years after the filing of a federal income tax return the related books and records that establish gross income, deductions, credits, and other pertinent matters. Documents supporting a long-term capital gain or loss may be advantageously retained longer than the five-year period.

Fair Labor Standards Act. Under regulations issued pursuant to this Act, each employer is required to preserve for at least four years:

1. Certain specified payroll records, the retention period commencing with the date of the last entry, and
2. Certificates, union agreements, and notices from their last effective date

Under Section 516.2, each employer subject to certain provisions must preserve the following payroll data:

1. Employee's name in full
2. Employee's home address
3. Date of birth, if under nineteen years of age
4. Occupation in which employed
5. Time and date on which employee's workweek begins
6. Regular hourly rate of pay and basis on which wages are paid
7. Hours worked each workday and total hours worked each workweek
8. Total daily or weekly straight-time earnings or wages
9. Total weekly overtime excess compensation
10. Total additions to, or deductions from, wages for each pay period
11. Total wages paid each pay period
12. Date of payment and pay period covered by payment

Other sections of the regulation have other provisions relative to certain supplementary records.

Description of Record	*Retention Period*
GENERAL AND FINANCIAL	
a) CAPITAL STOCK RECORDS	
Capital stock ledgers	Permanently
Records (or stubs) of capital stock certificates	Permanently
Stock transfer registers	Permanently
Canceled stock certificates	Optional, but clear record should be made. See note at end of schedule.
b) BOND RECORDS	
Registered bond ledgers	Permanently
Record (or stubs) of bonds	Permanently
Record of interest coupons, paid and unpaid	7 years
Canceled bonds and paid interest coupons	Optional, but clear record should be made. See note at end of schedule.
c) PROXIES AND VOTING LISTS	
Proxies of holders of voting securities	2 years
Lists of holders of voting securities presented at meetings	7 years
Minute books of stockholders, directors, and executive committee and other meetings	Permanently
d) CODES	
General codes and cipher books (Official Copies)	Permanently
e) TITLES AND MORTGAGES	
Deeds and other title papers and mortgages	Permanently
f) CONTRACTS AND AGREEMENTS	
In general	7 years
With employees for purchase of securities and memorandums, etc., pertinent thereto	7 years after expiration or cancellation
Records of contracts, leases, and agreements made, etc.	7 years after expiration or cancellation
g) RETIRED SECURITIES	
Canceled stock certificates, bonds, notes, interest coupons, receiver's certificates, and temporary certificates	Optional, but clear record should be made. See note at end of schedule
h) LEDGERS	
General ledgers and those auxiliary and indexes thereto	Permanently
Balance sheets of general ledgers	Permanently
Trial balances of general and auxiliary ledgers	Permanently
Accounts receivable ledgers, including branch office	7 years
Trial balances of accounts receivable ledgers	3 years
i) RECORDS OF SECURITIES OWNED IN TREASURY, OR WITH CUSTODIANS	Permanently
j) JOURNALS—GENERAL AND AUXILIARY	Permanently
k) CASH BOOKS	
Treasurer's and auditors' general cash books and auxiliary cash books subsidiary to general cash books	Permanently
Other auxiliary cash books and cash books at branch offices	Permanently
l) JOURNAL ENTRIES	
Journal entries and interdepartmental bills and supporting papers	Permanently

Description of Record	*Retention Period*

GENERAL AND FINANCIAL (*Continued*)

m) ACCOUNTS RECEIVABLE RECORDS

Records or register of accounts receivable (except ledgers previously mentioned) and indexes thereto, and summaries of distribution of credits through bills for entries in general books	Permanently
Accounting department copies of bills issued and supporting papers which do not accompany original bills, if the details have been summarized in registers, etc., so as to preserve a complete record of transactions	7 years

n) FIDELITY BONDS

Records and files of fidelity bonds of employees	3 years after expiration

o) INSURANCE RECORDS

Schedules of fire and other insurance; also records relating to premiums and amounts recovered and papers substantiating claims	7 years
Fire, liability, automobile, and other policies	Optional
Record of policies in force and notices of changes in and cancellation of such policies	3 years after expiration
Inspectors' reports and records of condition of property	Permanently

p) TAX RECORDS

Copies of schedule and returns to authorities for tax purposes and records of appeals	Permanently

q) RECORDS OF PLANT, FIXTURES, AND EQUIPMENT

Records of cost and inventory value of plant, fixtures, and equipment; records of retirement and replacement, contracts and agreements relating to construction, purchase or sale, and all papers actually supporting charges and credits to plant, fixtures, and equipment accounts	Permanently
Reports and papers pertaining to detail of charges and credits to plant, fixtures and equipment, which have been completely summarized in records previously mentioned herein	3 years

r) ENGINEERING RECORDS

Maps, plans, and specifications, etc., of work executed in whole or in part	Permanently
Maps, plans, and specifications, etc., of work abandoned	7 years

s) ACCOUNTANTS' AND AUDITORS' REPORTS	Permanently

TREASURY

a) STATEMENTS OF FUNDS AND DEPOSITS

Statements and summaries of balances with depositaries	Permanently
Authorities for and statements of transfers from one depositary to another, and periodical statements of working balances; statements of managers' and agents' deposits, grouped by depositaries	1 year
Requisitions and receipts for funds furnished by managers, agents, etc.	Optional after funds are accounted for
Estimates of working funds required	Optional

b) RECORDS OF DEPOSITS WITH BANKS AND OTHERS

Statements from depositaries, refunds received, disbursed, and transferred; bank reconcilement papers; statements

Description of Record	*Retention Period*
TREASURY (*Continued*)	
of interest due on daily balances and copies of bank deposit slips	1 year
Deposit books and stubs, records of checks	7 years
Advice of deposits made when information is shown on retained records	Optional
Correspondence and memoranda relating to stop-payment orders and issue of duplicate checks	Permanently
c) RECORDS OF RECEIPTS AND DISBURSEMENTS	
Records of outstanding checks, drafts, etc., issued and not presented	7 years
Periodical statements of receipts and disbursements; remittance slips or report of managers and agents and summaries thereof	3 years
d) MANAGERS' AND AGENTS' BALANCES	
Records of managers' and agents' accounts showing working fund debits and credits	3 years
e) FIELD CASHIERS' BALANCES	
Reports of working fund balances in hands of field cashiers	3 years
f) RECORDS PERTAINING TO VERIFICATION OF TREASURER'S CASH OR SECURITIES	3 years
EXPENDITURES	
a) VOUCHERS	
Register of audited vouchers and indexes thereto and summaries of distribution of charges through vouchers for entry in general books	Permanently
Paid and canceled vouchers, analysis sheets showing detailed distribution of charges on individual vouchers, etc.	Permanently
Paid drafts, checks, and receipts for cash paid out	Permanently
Authorities for payment of specific vouchers	3 years
Index of vouchers, lists of unaudited bills, of vouchers transmitted, etc.	Optional
b) PAYROLL RECORDS	
Payrolls and summaries, authorities for payroll changes, etc.	Permanently
Receipted pay checks, receipted time tickets, discharge tickets, and other evidence of payments for service	Permanently
Comparative or analytical statements of payrolls	3 years
Applications for payroll changes not authorized, records pertaining to payroll deductions, etc.	Optional
c) DISTRIBUTION OF EXPENDITURES FOR MATERIALS	
Journals, ledgers, and other records showing detailed distribution	Permanently
Material disbursement tickets and other papers if transcribed in detail to above	7 years
d) ASSIGNMENTS, ATTACHMENTS, AND GARNISHMENTS	
Record of and files of assignments, garnishments, etc., of employees' salaries, notices of suits and releases and related correspondence	3 years
Minors' salary releases	Optional

Description of Record	*Retention Period*
EXPENDITURES (*Continued*)	
e) AUTHORIZED EXPENSES	
Records, statements, etc., of authorized expenses by divisions, districts, departments, etc., which form basis of charges to accounts	Permanently
Requests and authorities for expenditures for incidental expenses, etc., not used in charging accounts	Optional
f) CLAIMS	
Registers and other records relating to damage, injury and overcharges (except as provided under "Adjustments with Customers")	Permanently
All papers substantiating claims (except those necessary for completion of vouchers)	7 years after settlement or rejection
g) RECORDS OF ACCIDENTS, DAMAGES, AND INJURIES	
Reports and statements regarding accidents, damage to property of company or others, statements of witnesses, and reports and statements of personal injuries, when not necessary to support vouchers	Optional
PURCHASES AND STORES	
a) MATERIAL LEDGERS	
Records of materials and supplies on hand	Permanently
Balance sheets of material and supplies received, issued and on hand at branch supply department	3 years
b) PURCHASING, ETC.	
Copies of purchase orders and authorities for sale of scrap	3 years
Bids and offers for sale or purchase of materials and supplies	7 years
Invoices for material purchased, records of such invoices, and freight bills covering charges on materials	Permanently
Price records of purchase (file copy)	Permanently
Contracts for purchase or sale of materials	Permanently
Advices or requisitions from storekeeper and others for purchase of materials	3 years
Summaries and distribution sheets and credit memoranda of materials sold or returned to supply house for credit	Permanently
Advices acknowledging receipt of orders for material, shipment notices, packing lists, copies of bills of lading	Optional
Records of invoices transmitted to or from storekeeper, copies of shipping instructions, records and reports used for checking and tracing materials, etc.	Optional
c) MERCHANDISE, MATERIALS, AND SUPPLIES RECEIVED AND ISSUED	
Records of materials received and issued	Permanently
Price records of material issued (file copy)	Optional
Records of materials transferred from one storeroom, department or division to another	3 years
Records of materials recovered and returned to stock if detailed on retained records and records of inspection and test of materials	3 years
Minor records pertaining to materials and supplies not involving cost or disposition	Optional

Description of Record	*Retention Period*
PURCHASES AND STORES (*Continued*)	
d) INVENTORIES OF MERCHANDISE, MATERIALS, AND SUPPLIES	
General inventories, with record of adjustments	7 years
e) CORRESPONDENCE	
Correspondence and records thereof relating to subjects listed therein	For period prescribed for item to which it relates
Stenographers' notebooks and mechanical device records; extra copies of letters if original is retained	Optional
SALES	
a) SUMMARIES OF SALES	
Records of sales (by classes) for entry in general books	7 years
Reports from managers, agents, etc., showing debits and credits to accounts, and summaries of such reports	7 years
b) COLLECTIONS, RATINGS, ETC.	
Itemized lists and summaries of agents' collections, branch offices, etc.	7 years
Ratings, credit classifications, and investigation of customers	3 years
Reports regarding status of customers' accounts	Optional
c) ADJUSTMENTS OF ACCOUNTS WITH AGENTS, MANAGERS, CUSTOMERS, ETC.	
Results of which appear in sales summaries	3 years
Records pertaining to settlement of sales, etc., with allied and subsidiary companies or firms	7 years
d) UNCOLLECTIBLE ACCOUNTS	
Records and reports regarding uncollectible accounts, including authorizations for writing off	7 years
e) CONTRACTS WITH CUSTOMERS	
Contracts and records thereof	7 years after expiration

NOTE: The record of destruction referred to under Capital Stock Records, Bond Records, and Retired Securities, should be a complete Certificate of Destruction, giving full descriptive reference to the documents destroyed, and should be made by the persons authorized to destroy such bonds and stock certificates. When the documents to be destroyed represent debt secured by mortgage, the Certificates of Destruction should also be authenticated by representatives of the Trustees acting in conjunction with those destroying the papers, or it should have the Trustees' acceptance thereon.

Walsh-Healey Act. Regulations issued by the Secretary of Labor, relative to records of contractors doing business with the United States Government, provide that any person subject to the provisions of the Act shall keep on file for at least four years from their last date of entry the following records of employment:

1. The name, address, sex, and occupation of each employee covered by the contract stipulations
2. Date of birth of each employee under nineteen years of age

3. Wage and hour records for each such employee, including the rate of wages and the amount paid each day, the hours worked each day and each week, and the period during which each such employee was engaged on a government contract, together with the number of such contract

TRANSFERRING THE RECORDS

A brief comment is in order regarding the transfer of records to inactive storage. Some concerns transfer their files once a year and set up the new files for the current year. The tendency is to send all the records to the storage vault, hoping to find time to dispose of useless ones later. However, the proper time to prepare the records is when they are current. Much material of a temporary nature gets into the files which should not have been filed in the first place. Examples are letters of transmittal, temporary reports or forms, etc. Some companies have installed a very practical procedure which indicates the destruction dates on papers as they go into the file. Some have temporary use, and may be placed in a 30-day or 60-day file and then destroyed. If the records are commingled with permanent papers, the pulling and destruction may be done a little each day after the regular filing has been completed. As another suggestion, where several copies of reports are prepared, it may be advisable to consider one as permanent and to set a short retention period for the others. Often the originating department keeps the permanent copy.

THE STORAGE AREA

A complete discussion of the details as to the selecting and equipping of a permanent storage area is outside the scope of this book. However, based on the authors' practical experience, the following suggestions may prove helpful:

1. The area preferably should be of fireproof construction
2. Ample provision should be made for future requirements
3. The aisles in the storage area should be lettered or numbered to permit quick identification if the location is of any considerable size; also, each container must be numbered or lettered to facilitate further identification
4. Each drawer should be labeled clearly to indicate the contents: name of record, period covered, department, etc.
5. Confidential records may need lock-equipped facilities
6. Responsibility for custody of the material should be definitely assigned, and material should be procurable only with a properly approved requisition
7. Enclosed containers are preferable; open bins and shelving ordinarily are not satisfactory

An ideal depository, of course, is one which is conveniently located, is fireproof and floodproof, and is equipped to fumigate the records before filing. The danger from rodents and vermin can present a serious problem.

INDEX OF INACTIVE RECORDS

Merely to store inactive records in a suitable manner is not enough. When these records are needed, they must be located quickly and easily. To facilitate this location of documents, a simple index, standard card size or otherwise, is recommended. This index may serve a twofold function: (1) a record as to location in the storage area, and (2) a record showing the date of destruction. Generally the following information will be found useful if placed on the card:

Description of record	Destruction date
Location	Cross-reference
Retention period	Other pertinent remarks

Cards of different colors may be used for the records of different divisions.

FINAL DESTRUCTION OF THE RECORDS

The index file for inactive records may be used as a tickler file for the removal of records scheduled for destruction, in addition to being a record of destruction dates for material already disposed of. In many instances it will be found practical to destroy records once a year.

By use of a schedule of retention, it seems rather a well-established procedure in many companies to destroy records more or less automatically after the retention period has expired. Of course, such a practice obviates the need for a periodic review and repeated authorizations for destruction. However, some companies prepare and execute a form similar to that shown in Fig. 191 for authorization to destroy records. This permits a recheck of the decision to destroy, even if on the retention schedule. This might be necessary if the retention periods are changed by law or other circumstances arise.

Each record scheduled for destruction should be checked, because it is far too easy to destroy vital records through erroneous filing. In no event should a drawer of records be destroyed on the basis of the label; the contents should be reviewed.

Although some records may be shredded and sold as waste paper, cremation is often preferred. Some companies are required by federal statute to execute cremation certificates. Even without such requirement, it may be desirable. A suggested form of cremation certificate is incorporated in the authorization for destruction of records (Fig. 191).

**AUTHORIZATION FOR DESTRUCTION OF RECORDS
AND CREMATION CERTIFICATE**

No. __38__

Date__3-10-62__

To: (Controller)

Authority is requested for destruction of the following records:

Form Number	Filing Schedule Number	Description of Records	Date of Records		Recommended Retention Period	Minimum Age	
			From	To		Yr.	Mo.
F-6	324	Trial Balances of Accounts Receivable	1-31-57	12-31-58	3 years	3	2

Destruction Recommended by_____

Destruction Approved by_____

Date_____

I hereby certify that I have this day destroyed, by cremation, the accounts, records, and memoranda listed above, and further that no accounts, records, or memoranda other than those named were destroyed herewith.

(witness)	(signed)
(location)	(position)

Fig. 191—Authorization Form for Destruction of Records, and
Cremation Certificate.

PROTECTING RECORDS IN WARTIME

A subject closely related to the normal preservation of valuable records is the protection of records from possible direct enemy attack. If the program is carried out over a long period of time, it brings several advantages: there is less disruption of everyday operations; it will be cheaper and better planned; and it will mesh well with the other program for retention and destruction of records.

Generally speaking, the planning and classification of records are the same for wartime as for normal purposes. The difference is chiefly in the *means* taken to preserve the records. There are three basic methods to be used:

1. Duplication
2. Dispersion
3. Vaulting

Duplication can be treated in several ways. In some instances carbon copies may be made, but the principal objection is the space required to protect the copies. Also, when any large volume is entailed, this method is not the cheapest. Another method is photocopying—either photostat, Ozalid, blueprint, or microfilm.

Not only must duplicate records be prepared, but they must be stored in separate areas if protection is to be secured. The depositories should be far enough away from the site of the original records to prevent simultaneous loss. Rural communities may be preferable to urban. During World War II, English companies found that a planned program of interchange of records was helpful.

A third phase of record protection in wartime is the use of well-constructed vaults. Experience with even atomic explosions indicates that most well-built vaults will withstand such blasts. The principal problem is one of fire or water damage; but precautions can be taken against these.

MICROFILMING

Microfilming is becoming an increasingly popular means of reproducing records. It is a process of duplicating records on small-scale (16-mm and 35-mm) cellulose acetate film somewhat similar to that used for motion pictures. The advantages claimed for the method include:

1. Requires a minimum of storage space. The duplicated image is only about 1% of the size of the original. About 5,000 sheets of paper 8½" x 11" can be duplicated on about 75 feet of film.
2. Is rapid and relatively inexpensive where used in large volume.
3. The copy is an exact image; there is no chance of typographical error.
4. It may be used to eliminate procedures, e.g., postings of accounts receivable have been eliminated in some department stores through the use of this method.
5. Is relatively permanent. Microfilm approved by the National Bureau of Standards has been tested to last five hundred years under proper conditions—40–50% relative humidity and 60–80° Fahrenheit.

To facilitate the use of this filming process, the devices used to enlarge and read film have been improved.

This method of duplicating also has its disadvantages:

1. It is expensive unless the program is well-organized and involves a large volume of records
2. Full-sized reproductions, if necessary, are expensive to make
3. Special equipment must be maintained to use the film
4. The film is more likely to be damaged by fire than are carbon copies or positive reproductions

It should be remembered that microfilming is no magic word which places disorderly or disorganized records in first-class shape. The records must be put in order, or in the sequence desired, before the filming is done.

Frequently records are microfilmed and the originals are then destroyed. Before such destruction, it may be well to request the lawyers to check the rules of evidence in states where business is transacted. It has been suggested that with each batch of reproductions an identifying document be prepared and filed. This document would record the procedures and methods of copying, and give the name of the person who ordered the copying done; and it may be microfilmed on the reel.

39

Physical Inventory Procedure

NEED FOR PHYSICAL INVENTORY

One of the basic responsibilities of the controller is the preparation of accurate reports on the results of operations and the financial condition of the company. Of all the elements affecting these statements, none is generally more significant than the inventory. Moreover, it is usually a relatively more important influence on the income and expense statement than on the balance sheet. For example, an error of 3% in the inventory might double or halve the profit, while making no significant change in the current assets. It is evident that the accuracy of the financial statements depends on the value placed on the inventories; and this relates to two factors: (1) the quantities on hand, and (2) the valuation placed on the reported quantities.

The value of the company's inventory may be determined by two methods, either a physical inventory or a perpetual book inventory. A physical inventory is defined as the periodic counting, weighing, measuring, and valuing of the goods owned. Even though perpetual records may be maintained, it is usually necessary that such records be periodically checked to establish or verify their accuracy. Several conditions would give added reason for making a physical inventory:

1. Where management specifically requires it as a matter of policy
2. Where periodic reviews have shown the perpetual records to be inaccurate
3. Where the inventory control procedures are not operating satisfactorily
4. Where materials are subject to shrinkage or loss while in storage
5. Where, for practical purposes, the units of receipt are different from units of disbursement, i.e., receipts may be in pounds and issues in gallons

6. Where the nature of the operation or process makes it difficult to check against usage or production, because of differences in moisture content or inadequate facilities

These conditions are not necessarily mutually exclusive.

There are also circumstances where physical inventories are not necessary, although such situations appear to be in the minority. Thus, where items are slow-moving and the internal control is foolproof, a physical count would seem of less value.

PLANNING THE INVENTORY PROCEDURE

Most effort is more productive if intelligently planned, and this is certainly applicable to inventory taking. In fact, the need for planning is particularly acute if the count is to be of any value. To begin with, the time available to take the inventory is short. Usually it must be accomplished over a weekend, or requires a plant shutdown with the consequent loss in production. Second, the inventories must be accurate, for carelessness and an incorrect inventory may be worse than none at all. Again, because of time limitations, the employees used are generally untrained in inventory taking, and a maximum of planning is needed to overcome this handicap. Furthermore, simple though physical inventories may sound, there are many possible sources of error. In addition, inventory taking and valuation impose one more burden on the accounting staff. Proper planning for the physical inventory can reduce the time as well as the cost, and greatly increase the accuracy of the job.

The amount of planning and advance preparation may vary from business to business because it is influenced by a number of factors, such as size and type of inventory; condition in which stocks and stores are normally maintained; experience of staff in inventory taking; number of stages in, and type of, operation or process; and quality of the material control system and records.

Planning for the physical inventory has two distinct phases: (1) that dealing with the physical count, and (2) that relating to the *accounting* aspects of summarizing and tabulating. It is not sufficient to consider only the phase relating to the physical count, for errors in summarizing can offset an accurate count. Planning of this work should be completed perhaps six weeks in advance of the count date. Matters to be covered include:

1. The organization, including the duties and responsibilities of each member
2. Detailed instructions for the staff
3. Preparation and distribution of forms and supplies

ORGANIZING FOR THE INVENTORY

A first step in planning the physical inventory procedure is the creation of an organization. Inventory planning and taking is not a full-time job, but nevertheless the duties, authority, and responsibility must be clearly established. It is usually the controller who is charged with responsibility for the physical inventory as a whole, although some companies have vested such matters in an inventory committee or other staff member.

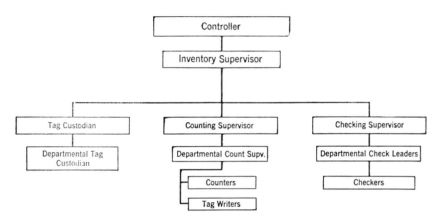

Fig. 192—Organization Chart for Annual Physical Inventory.

A typical organization chart for a medium-sized or large company is illustrated in Fig. 192. In this instance, duties have been split along functional lines, and are outlined for some of the supervisory positions as follows:

Controller: Responsible to the president for the complete planning and execution of the physical inventory program

Inventory Supervisor: Responsible to the controller (or plant controller) for the direction of the inventory program and the selection and training of personnel

Tag Custodian: Responsible to the inventory supervisor for the selection and training of all departmental and section tag custodians, for the issuance of inventory tags and supplies to subordinate tag custodians or writers, and for accounting for all tags issued

Counting Supervisor: Responsible to the inventory supervisor for the selection and training of departmental count leaders and counters, for the proper identification and counting of all materials to be inventoried, and for the preparation of all inventory tags

Checking Supervisor: Responsible to the inventory supervisor for selection and training of the checking staff, for the re-counting of all items inventoried to verify accuracy of original count, for the checking of all inventory tags as to completeness and accuracy of information thereon

Other plans of organization might be along departmental lines rather than functional lines, with the division supervisor responsible for all functions carried on in certain areas.

In building the organization, there are some other suggestions to be kept in mind:

1. No one individual should be placed in sole charge of an inventory who is normally responsible for such inventory as his regularly assigned duty—to recognize a principle of internal control
2. Where the organization is large, it may be helpful to prepare and post an inventory organization chart on the bulletin board
3. It may be desirable to establish a mobile squad in a large organization for duty wherever trouble spots appear—where counts are getting behind schedule, where improper counts are being made, etc.

INVENTORY INSTRUCTIONS

If the physical inventory is a major undertaking, the instructions should be prepared in writing so that the procedures may be more readily enforced. Since the physical custody and control of inventories are under an operating head, and not under the controller, the cooperation of both groups is necessary. Both have a stake in the accuracy of the physical inventory, and the two should work together. As an aid in accomplishing this, the inventory instructions should be prepared in draft form and routed to the supervisory staff of both the production and accounting groups for their criticism and approval. The instructions should be written in simple, clear language. Also, where circumstances require very detailed and lengthy procedures, it is preferable that they be prepared by sections so that each participant gets only the data relating to his responsibility, rather than a long dissertation. Charts and sample forms are useful and may be incorporated in the manual.

The detailed physical inventory instructions should cover the following points:

1. Date and places of physical inventory
2. Categories of inventories to be covered
3. Detail of the duties of each person assisting in the inventory
4. Special instructions in case of unforeseen trouble, difficulties, or problems
5. Explanation of method of control and distribution of tags and other forms

6. Method of completing tags
7. Method of identifying materials
8. Required preparatory work in nature of clean-up, records, etc.
9. Listing and examples of items not to be counted
10. Detail of counting method—use of scales, estimates, etc.
11. Description of checking methods
12. Special instructions as to confirmation of warehouse stocks, goods in hands of customers, customers' property in company possession
13. Instructions as to treatment of obsolete, spoiled, or slow-moving goods
14. Instructions on method of accounting for all tag numbers
15. Instructions on pricing and valuation methods
16. Procedure to be followed in cutoff—stamping paper work "after inventory," etc.
17. Instructions relating to comparison with perpetual records
18. Instructions on listing, extension, and summarizing methods
19. Instructions as to restrictions on movement of goods between plants and departments
20. Cooperation with the independent auditors and other observers

AN ILLUSTRATIVE MANUAL

Each controller must necessarily adapt the instructions to the particular problems in his company. However, an example of a short set of instructions used by a chemical manufacturer is illustrative of the type in common use:

Instructions on Annual Physical Inventory

1. *General*

The annual physical inventory will be taken on December 1, 1962; and on December 2, 1962 if the job cannot be completed in one day. A count is to be made of all raw materials, chemicals, pigments, work in process, or finished materials (whether approved or unapproved), and shipping containers. This count should be made on all *company* materials in (city), whether they be on the production floor, in warehouses, stock rooms, hoppers, tanks, or other storage areas. (*No count* is to be made of machinery and equipment used in processing.)

In order to determine the results of operations for the year, it is extremely important that the physical inventory be taken carefully and accurately.

2. *Preparation*

An accurate inventory requires an orderly arrangement of materials. Therefore, during the few days preceding the physical count, the material should be arranged in an orderly fashion so as to facilitate the counting of stock. Unusable material should be disposed of, and the stock piles, etc., put in as reasonable a condition as is practical.

3. *Inventory Tags*

Each Plant Superintendent will be assigned a certain series of pre-numbered tags. All such numbers shall be accounted for—either (1) returned as part of the count of stock, (2) voided and returned to Accounting, or (3) not used and returned to Accounting. It is suggested that each of the Plant Superintendents assign certain blocks of numbers to his staff directing the count and that they in turn be responsible for all prenumbered tags.

4. *Procedure*

A. On December 1 and 2, plant personnel will place tags on all piles, stacks, bins, etc. A physical count of the material will be made at the time the tag is placed thereon. However, if time permits, on November 30, the tags may be placed on the stocks of material on which there will be no movement for the remainder of the day. At this time the description can also be completed, although the *count* should be made only on December 1 and 2.

B. The following information must be written legibly on all tags (where applicable):

(1) Description of material.
Name and code number of chemicals, pigments, containers, or raw materials; type of process inventory; color or charge number, etc.

(2) Lot number or batch number.

(3) Number of pieces.

(4) Weight.
Where containers are of unequal weights, individual weights should be shown.

(5) Location.
Bag or bin, etc.

(6) Description of drum.
Either code number or size. This is applicable to work in process (material not yet finished and approved) only. For example, empty drums on the production floor would be inventoried in this manner. It would *not* apply to raw material or approved finished goods containers.

(7) Name of man counting.

C. The inventory tag is composed of two sections. When the material is counted, the entire tag will be taped or otherwise placed on the container or sacks, etc. Not more than one type of material is to be listed on any one tag. Each pile must contain a tag.

D. Where the weight or count cannot be secured for practical reasons, such as powder in the hoppers, it is permissible to make an estimate of the quantity. The tag should be marked "Estimate" or "E."

E. If the material appears to be old, slow-moving, or otherwise unusable, this fact should be noted on the front or reverse side of the large section of the tag.

F. It probably will be practical for employees taking the inventory to work in teams, one man preparing the tags, the other man counting the inventory.

G. After all materials in a plant, or a particular section of a plant, have been tagged and counted, the lower section of the inventory tag will be collected. A representative of the Accounting Department will accompany the collector. This team will ascertain that all items are tagged and shall satisfy themselves as to the accuracy of the count by making a substantial number of recounts. If any substantial number of errors are found, it will be the responsibility of the Accounting representative to advise the factory supervisor and request a recount on all items originally counted by the team responsible for the numerous errors.

The Accounting Department representative will

(1) Examine every tag to see that the required information is thereon.

(2) Ascertain that no tags are missed during the collecting.

(3) See that all piles, containers, or quantities, etc. are included in the count.

H. When all tags are gathered, they shall be placed in numerical order by the collecting team. When all numbers are accounted for, they shall be turned over to the Accounting Department representative together with any unused or voided tags.

5. *Public Accountants*

Representatives of ——, the independent auditors, will be present to observe the inventory-taking procedure. If they desire any recounts, factory personnel should be instructed to make such recounts and to cooperate in every reasonable way with the public accountants.

6. *Central Stores, Etc.*

No inventory need be taken of central stores or surplus stock in area "P."

7. *Check-off Against Records*

Perpetual unit inventory records or their equivalent are maintained for most raw materials, most work in process, and all finished material. When the physical count of each such grouping is completed, the count should be *immediately* compared with the record of quantity on hand. This will serve two purposes: (1) it may indicate an error in the count, or (2) it serves as a check of the accuracy of the records, and is an opportunity to make the necessary adjustments. An Accounting representative should assist the Production or Sales representative in making this comparison. Everyone probably realizes that *delay* in making this review of physical count with the records often creates a problem in later trying to reconcile the two figures.

8. *Other*

Mr. —— will act as coordinator in the preparation and taking of the inventories, and any production personnel having questions as to procedures, etc. will contact him.

Questions by accounting personnel as to accounting requirements will be directed to Mr. ——. Questions from production personnel on this same matter will be handled through Mr. ——.

The accounting personnel involved will be instructed separately on receiving and shipping cutoff, etc.

Your cooperation in securing an accurate inventory is requested.

CONTROLLER

CLASSIFICATION OF INVENTORIES

The various categories of items counted must be grouped so as to permit identification with the proper inventory account. Separate classes should be used, such as:

1. Raw materials
2. Work in process
3. Finished parts
4. Finished goods
5. Operating supplies
6. Perishable tools
7. Returnable containers
8. Goods out on consignment
9. Miscellaneous; e.g., property of others in our possession

To avoid improper grouping, it may be helpful to use differently colored tags for each classification. In other instances the proper category must be checked on the inventory tag.

FORMS USED IN TAKING PHYSICAL INVENTORY

The two chief forms prepared in a physical inventory procedure are inventory tags and inventory sheets. Usually the count is taken by using a tag to be affixed to each lot. The tags are numbered serially in advance; and since a portion of the tag is left on the stock, it serves as a means of assuring that all piles are counted. In the event of suspected errors, the remaining portion can be used for rechecking.

A form of illustrative tag is shown in Fig. 193. Space is provided on the reverse side for noting movements, so that slow-moving items may be counted in advance of the regular count. This is a two-part tag, the lower section being collected for summarization. Where further precaution is considered necessary, a three-section tag can be utilized, in which the third section duplicates the second. A count is made and the third section is removed; then another count is taken and recorded on the second section. This second section is then removed and compared with the previous count. Instead of a perforated card, a cardboard back with attached paper forms may be used.

A list of representative information usually required on an inventory tag is:

1. Part or assembly number
2. Description and size of item
3. General classification of item, viz., raw material, finished part, incomplete assembly, returnable container, etc.
4. Last operation completed
5. Quantity on hand
6. Unit of measure (pieces, pounds, feet, etc.)
7. Location of item
8. Names or employee numbers and initials of counters and checkers, etc.

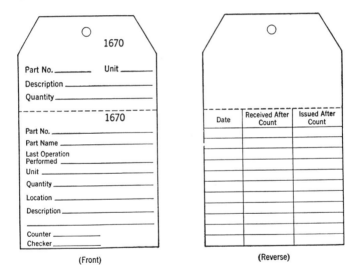

Fig. 193—Inventory Tag.

When the count is completed, all tags are gathered and all numbers are accounted for, perhaps with the use of check-off lists. The data are then listed on an inventory sheet. A standard printed form is illustrated in Fig. 194. It may be found, however, that the many reconciling factors to be considered will make a worksheet more desirable, as in Fig. 195. In this instance it was not practical to make an inventory count on the last business day of the month, so that adjustments were made to carry the physical count to the end of the period on which the books of account were kept.

| Inventory Listing | | | | | | | | Sheet No. ___8___ | |

Department ___Final Assembly___

Written By ___R. Jones___   Priced By ___C. Comes___   Checked By ___L. Austin___

Reference	Description	Unit	Quantity	Cost		Market		Lower of Cost or Market	
				Unit	Value	Unit	Value	Value	Remarks
1820	Batteries – 10 CL	ea.	24	$10.12	$242.88	$10.00	$240.00	$240.00	
1821	Lead clamps	doz.	3	1.80	5.40	1.80	5.40	5.40	
1822	Plastic caps	doz.	8	.25	2.00	.28	2.24	2.00	

Fig. 194—Worksheet for Pricing of Physical Inventory.

PROCEDURE FOR PHYSICAL COUNT

The detailed procedure for securing an accurate physical count is evident from a review of the standard instructions in a preceding section. The importance of securing an accurate count should be emphasized. The quantity and necessary descriptive data for each pile, bin, or batch should be recorded on the inventory tag and attached to the bin or bag by tape, wire, or otherwise. As the count proceeds, it should be ascertained that all lots are properly tagged. If items are not to be counted, sometimes a "Do Not Count" tag is placed thereon in advance.

Usually the count is done by stocktakers working in pairs, one man listing and one man counting. It may be advantageous to use an accounting department member for listing, and a production department member for counting. Those who list can from time to time make test checks of the count. When the counting has been completed, another group should remove the section of the tag, make test checks of the count, and verify that all lots have been tagged.

Usually physical inventories are attended by the independent public auditors as well as the company's own internal auditors. These representatives make test counts, observe the procedure generally, and subsequently trace the counts to the inventory summary. Their presence is another incentive for accurate counts.

Where inventories are located in warehouses, arrangements may be made to make counts or secure confirmation from the outside agencies as to quantities on hand. In any event, no inventory should be overlooked.

The Illustrative Company

ANNUAL PHYSICAL INVENTORY, OCTOBER 28, 1962

Inventory Summary

| Description | Unit | Physical Inventory 10/28/62 | ADJUSTMENTS | | | | Adjusted Physical Inventory | SUBSEQUENT TRANSACTIONS | | | Adjusted Inventory 10/31/62 | Unit Price | Value |
			Unrecorded Liabilities	Process Back to Raw*	Other	Total		Production	Usage & Shipments	Other			
CHEMICALS:													
Glycerine U.S.P.	lbs.	10,000	—	—	—	—	10,000	−1,000	+5,000	—	14,000	$.25	$3,500
Castor oil	lbs.	44,600	−4,600	+2,000	—	−2,600	42,000	−5,000	+1,000	—	38,000	.33	12,540
Linseed oil	lbs.	13,900	−2,400	—	—	−2,400	11,500	—	—	—	11,500	.28	3,220
Phenol	lbs.	6,800	—	—	—	—	6,800	—	—	—	6,800	.26	1,768

* Unrecorded process batch sheets.

Fig. 195—Worksheet for Physical Inventory Summary.

733

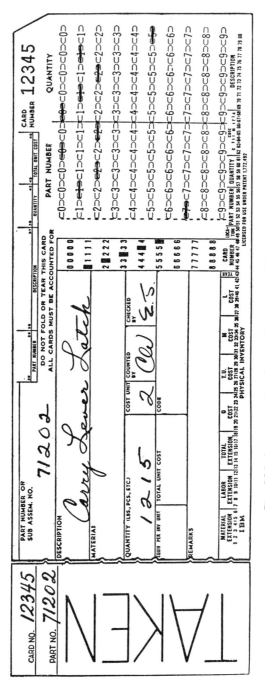

Fig. 196—Inventory Tag for Application of "Mark-Sensing."

ELECTRICAL TABULATING METHODS—COMPUTERS

Electrical tabulating methods may be readily applied to the physical inventory procedure and such methods may materially shorten the time within which the final results can be made available. Under this plan, a tabulating card with a stub may be used to record the inventory count, one card for each item of stock. The cards are serially numbered on the card itself, and on the detachable stub. The serial number may be prepunched at the card factory. The card form provides for information, in both written and punched form, covering a description of the item, its quantity, unit price, and total price. The identifying information and unit price may be written and punched prior to the inventory taking, in order to reduce the time required later for listing the inventory and punching the cards. After the count, the cards are detached from the stubs and the stubs affixed to the articles or bins as a visual indication that the items have been inventoried. The cards are then sorted by serial number and machine-listed to detect any missing cards. After all have been accounted for, it remains only for the quantity, or quantity and extension, to be punched. (The extension of individual items may frequently be omitted where only total values by departments are desired.) The cards are then tabulated to obtain the required accounting totals. Following this, a listing is made by stock number, which serves as a support for the accounting totals and as a cross-reference with the previous listing by tag numbers. Any special inventory analyses which are desired may be provided for by including the proper punching when the cards are originally prepared. Figure 196 illustrates an inventory tag designed as a tabulating card, using the "mark-sensing" principle.

The tabulating technique of "mark-sensing" may be used advantageously in valuing inventories from perpetual records because it avoids manual key punching. It may be used in connection with physical inventories, but studies should be made to determine whether it is to be preferred over manual punching in the particular application.

In the larger companies which make use of computers,[1] appropriate procedures must be established to take advantage of the machines' capabilities.

THE INVENTORY CUTOFF

Even if the counting is accurate and the summarizing and pricing are done with care, the inventory can be grossly misstated if the proper coordination is not secured between the physical count and the books of account. Thus, the inclusion in the inventory of a single carload of merchandise, if the liability is not recorded, may be the cause of more difference than all the

---

[1] See Chapter 21.

errors in counting. The controller should be quite certain that this aspect of physical inventory taking is handled properly.

To reduce errors from this source to an absolute minimum the following precautions should be considered:

1. Generally all receipts or shipments of goods should cease during the count.
2. Goods received or shipped after inventory should be so indicated on the receiving and shipping records as "Shipped After Inventory" or "Received After Inventory." Rubber stamps may be used.
3. Goods on the receiving and shipping docks at time of count may have stamped on the appropriate documents "Counted" or "Before Inventory."
4. The files of receiving reports should be checked for papers not yet matched with vendor invoices, to account for unrecorded liabilities.

COMPARISON WITH PERPETUAL INVENTORY RECORDS

Perpetual unit records may be maintained for material control or other purposes. When a physical inventory is taken, the results should be checked immediately against such information. The advantages are two-fold: (1) it serves as a check against the physical count and may suggest items to be re-counted, and (2) it permits quick adjustment of plant records so that up-to-date data are available when operations resume.

Any substantial differences between book records and the physical inventory should be investigated. This review can be accomplished in a number of ways, but could include these steps:

1. Review inventory tags for possible errors in pricing or descriptions
2. Compare present and previous inventory to locate seemingly un-warranted changes
3. Review all large quantity or value items for errors in extensions and footings
4. Where detail and control accounts are available, check the transactions for the period to reveal errors on purchases or usage
5. Check similar materials for corresponding but opposite overages or shortages, indicating wrong postings and similar errors
6. Have production men review the inventory to spot errors or secure explanations of shortages

PRICING AND SUMMARIZING THE INVENTORY

The object of the physical inventory is a summary of the individual items in a form or classification to compare with the financial records of the company. This involves the pricing of the units, the extension of the quantities and unit prices, the listing on schedules, and the addition of the listings. Here, also, it is clear that care must be exercised in preparing the summary.

The following points should assist in a speedy and accurate summarization:

1. Management should decide on the method of pricing before the work commences. This facilitates preparation of proper worksheets.
2. All tags should be accounted for before the listing. Normally this is done at the time of collection, when the count is completed. Under such circumstances, careful control should be exercised over the tags until the sorting and listing commences.
3. The tags should be sorted in the order of the desired listing.
4. The listing should preferably show all data pertinent to a complete review: tag number, part number and description, quantity, unit price, etc. Where several tags are combined for one item, this should be indicated; and the tags may be stapled together.
5. The summary should be extended and added, and then cross-checked.
6. The accuracy of the listing may be test-checked by some third party. This may involve tracing high-value items from the listing back to the inventory tags.
7. The listing should be reviewed for reasonableness. Thus, where thread inventory is a small item, a high value would indicate errors.

INVENTORY VARIANCES

When the counts are completed and all discrepancies are reviewed, the records should be brought into agreement with the resulting physical inventory. As to the perpetual inventory cards, this is done by marking "Physical Inventory," the date, and the correct balance; even though no adjustment is necessary, this should be done to indicate the time of the physical check. Differences may be summarized on a report for management similar to Fig. 107 (page 427). This type of report or a similar worksheet may also serve as support for adjustment of the inventory control accounts.

The physical inventory procedure may produce adjustments for at least three reasons:

1. Differences in physical quantities by reason of unaccounted-for differences or losses
2. Write-offs or write-downs of obsolete or slow-moving items
3. Differences resulting from changes in book valuation—the lower of cost or market, for example

In summarizing the results of the physical inventory, the controller should distinguish among the three causes of differences to avoid unwarranted conclusions and to make proper charges or credits, often to different accounts. Moreover, no adjustment of the records should be permitted without the proper approvals.

RETENTION OF PHYSICAL INVENTORY RECORDS

The physical inventory tags and summaries support adjustments used for tax purposes and otherwise. When the independent auditors have completed their examination, the records should be filed away in an orderly fashion which will permit ready reference and ultimate transfer to permanent storage for the retention period.

INTERNAL AUDIT OF THE INVENTORIES

When a company is large enough to support an internal auditor, he not only should observe and check the annual physical inventory, but may perform a very useful function in making periodic checks of the records to (1) determine the correctness of the records, (2) evaluate the system of internal control, and (3) check as to compliance with established procedures. While this is in part a phase of inventory control, it is directly related to physical inventory problems. The results of his examinations may be used to good advantage in planning the yearly inventory.

To secure the best use of the internal auditor's services, it is preferable that an internal audit program for the inventories be established.

ADVANTAGES OF CONTINUOUS PHYSICAL INVENTORIES

The physical inventory procedures just discussed have related mainly to a complete annual count of inventory. Such a practice is now quite common. However, the annual physical inventory may be *supplemented by* a rotational or "staggered" system of physical checks. Moreover, in some instances this one major cutoff each year has been eliminated and *replaced by* these periodic counts throughout the twelve-month period. As another alternative, some companies have found it desirable to make rotational counts of sections of the inventory. This permits the exclusion from the annual physical count of those areas of less value which cause greater difficulty in counting. A well-conducted rotational inventory in conjunction with the necessary unit records can produce a book inventory sufficiently accurate to be accepted by the independent accountants.

The many advantages of a rotating or cycle inventory system are not to be overlooked, including the possible ultimate objective of eliminating the annual physical count. A continuous inventory has the advantage of not requiring a complete, or at least partial, shutdown of operations which may cause the loss of needed production or which may interrupt customer service. Then, too, it may reveal shortages or errors more quickly after occurrence so that tracing of the causes may be facilitated. Moreover, these routine checks may disclose shortages, damaged or substandard materials, or mixed stock in time to avoid production delays. The procedure also probably stimulates more accurate daily performance if counts are known to be frequent. Finally, such checks tend to avoid serious year-end adjustments and consequently make the interim statements more reliable.

METHODS OF SECURING A CONTINUOUS PHYSICAL INVENTORY

Several methods may be used in securing these periodic counts. In some companies the physical check is made when the purchase requisition is prepared on 'he basis that at such a time the quantity is presumably low. Others have coordinated the receiving procedure and counting requirement whereby a check is made at the time of each receipt of additional stock. Provision is made on the receiving report for a recording of the bin count, and this information is passed on to the clerks who maintain the perpetual inventory records.

In still other instances what is equivalent to "a little physical inventory" is taken each week or at other regular intervals. Under such a cycle system, the various items in the inventory are grouped into categories which relate to the frequency of count. In determining the classification, consideration must be given to the value of each item, the rate of turnover, the ease of replacement, loss experience, and any other factors which should influence the interval between physical checks. Some categories perhaps need to be counted only once a year while others should be reviewed every three months. By way of procedure, the count may be recorded on a bin inventory tag as well as a physical inventory count tag. A cutoff date, perhaps the end of a week, is set; and all receipts and disbursements between the time of count and cutoff are recorded on the bin tag. At the cutoff date, the adjusted balance, representing the physical count plus all receipts and less all disbursements, also is recorded on the physical count tag and forwarded to the accounting department for comparison with perpetual records. This procedure lends itself to the use of prepunched tabulating cards.

The same degree of care is needed in a rotating or continuous system of inventory as in a complete annual physical count. Duplicate counts and overlooked items are to be avoided. Checklists are valuable in determining that no items are omitted. Usually perpetual inventory records are a necessity in making these continuous counts. The reconciliation of the perpetual unit records (which may be posted from receiving reports, and not from invoices) to the recorded liabilities is important; and provision to facilitate this is sometimes made on the inventory record by showing both receiving report number and invoice number.

40

A Broad Look at Electronic Data Processing —Some Implications

ELECTRONIC DATA PROCESSING AND MANAGEMENT

Relatively speaking, electronic data processing in business is a youngster. It was only in 1951 that the Bureau of Census first used an electronic computer in the solution of a business data processing problem. Recent years have seen substantial evolution in technology and in practices. The use of the computer in the data processing field is perhaps going through a transitional stage from initial acceptance—albeit on routine applications—to an intensive exploitation by business. Broader concepts in its use are gaining strength; and it is passing from primarily a mass clerical processing device to the more profitable tool applicable to the solution of management problems.

In general, some of the reasons given for making a "feasibility" study for the installation of electronic data processing equipment include such expectations as these:

1. Improved control over the business by reason of faster and better reports
2. Reduction in working capital requirements through reduced inventories and receivables
3. Improvement in speed and accuracy of clerical and accounting paper work
4. Significant savings in clerical costs
5. More effective planning through the study of alternatives not practical without the electronic computer
6. Competitive advantages through faster or better service or lowered costs

By and large, management is coming to accept the advantages to be gained through the application of scientific-mathematical techniques to business. In view of the rapidly evolving technology and related management problems, only some of the broad aspects are discussed in this chapter.

EDP IN RELATIONSHIP TO CONTROLLER

The controller is personally concerned with electronic data processing (EDP) for two principal reasons. To begin with, the accounting department in most instances, and at the present time, is the primary data processor. The chief accounting officer is therefore expected to be familiar in a general way with the latest and most economical techniques, and to build an organization to meet the needs of the company.

But aside from the supervisory aspects of staff data processing activities, experience indicates that the controller, and sometimes other principal officers of the company, must give personal attention to the subject. This is in rather direct contrast to usual practice wherein the task is delegated perhaps to the systems and procedure supervisor.

The reasons for top-level study of electronic data processing are several:

1. The investment in data processing can be substantial. It may range from hundreds of thousands to millions of dollars.
2. The method of planning and control may be vitally affected. New techniques may make economically feasible the providing of data not otherwise practical.
3. Basic changes in organizational structure often may be needed. As information flow is changed, duties and responsibilities might need corresponding modification.
4. Policies and procedures throughout the company may require alteration. These changes often will cut across many organizational lines, and therefore require top-management consideration.
5. Proper utilization of the equipment often is achieved only by intervention and support of a high level of management. As is understandable, frequently there is a reluctance to change. Active participation by top management encourages support among the middle-management echelon for a study of the best application of electronic data processing.

The extent to which technique can influence the controllership function is not to be overlooked. For, though computers are utilized rather extensively in large corporations, it is becoming more difficult to find medium-sized and smaller companies which either do not have modest installations of their own or do not use computer service bureaus.

PROBABLE TREND IN EDP APPLICATION

In the next several years, it is expected that more companies will use computers, and also that applications will grow in complexity as well as diversity. The search for sound uses well may be along four major lines: [1]

1. *Accounting Data Processing.*

   Although accounting data processing was the mainstay of early computer installations, the potential in this field is by no means exhausted. There are opportunities to bring other accounting tasks into the accounting fold. There are perhaps far larger opportunities to integrate separate accounting tasks so that more useful things are done with a single piece of information.

2. *Process Control.*

   Computers, usually highly specialized, are now used to position machine tools and to control certain industrial processes. These uses will grow substantially in number and importance as sensing and actuating devices become more generally available, and particularly as technicians and managers are able to establish decision rules to guide the computers.

3. *Decision Models.*

   Mathematical formulations for solving difficult one-time problems and for simulating complex events will be much more frequently employed by managers. Several such models already exist, particularly in production and physical distribution operations. These will multiply and to them will be added models for making decisions on marketing, financial, facilities, and other strategic questions.

4. *Management Data Processing.*

   By far the most extensive and important advances will take place in the development of integrated management-information systems for decision making and control. Such business intelligence systems will go far beyond the limits of classical accounting information to process and analyze a broad range of data—nonfinancial and financial—that are needed by top management to run the business. The ultimate achievement would be a system that not only encompassed all information-handling requirements but processed each piece of information instantaneously. The ultimate is certain to prove unattainable, of course, for every advance will undoubtedly reveal still greater opportunities. There will, however, be giant strides forward in providing up-to-the-minute information for better control of marketing, production, and distribution, and in providing incisive analysis for longer term tactical and strategic decisions. As computerized accounting and finance systems are tied in more closely with simulation and mathematical models, management judgment will become increasingly fact-founded across the whole spectrum of corporate decisions.

[1] From *EDP—The First Ten Years* (New York: McKinsey & Company, Inc., 1961), pp. 10–11.

EVALUATION OF PROJECTS

Generally speaking, and in view of possible large sums involved, business management applies the same criteria in evaluating an electronic data processing application as in any other expenditure of funds, such as for capital assets or research and development projects. There are, of course, some intangible factors to be weighed such as the benefits from faster management information. Suggestive of the principal points to be covered in the feasibility study or review are these:

1. Cost of the project, including equipment and staff, for programming and operation
2. Expected benefits or savings
3. Period of investment recoupment (payback)
4. Return on investment
5. Comparison with alternative methods
6. Experience of other companies in the application

Management necessarily relies heavily on the recommendations of its own staff. However, the counsel and advice of equipment manufacturers as well as outside consultants can be helpful if properly used.

PLACE IN ORGANIZATION FOR EDP

For the first computer installations in industrial companies, supervision was often placed under the controller or chief financial officer. Such an organizational decision was understandable for at least two reasons. First, the early applications were viewed merely as the more rapid processing of data conventionally handled by the tabulating equipment. Moreover, the justifications in many instances were achieved through a comparison of expenses of the new machines vs. the clerical cost reductions. The savings usually were in the controller's field of responsibility.

Through experience, this concept of computers is changing: computer applications are going beyond the purely accounting systems. Secondly, the problem is no longer being viewed as a piecemeal substitution in particular departments of the company. Rather, the "total system" concept is growing—the view that computers are part of an integrated system; that a single system should be used to process most information which would be used for several purposes—scientific, accounting, and managerial (if a distinction is to be made between the latter two).

These enlarging concepts are causing reconsideration of the location of computer departments. With the increasing importance of these electronic devices there is a corresponding rise in the status of computer services in the financial organization. In more and more cases, it is becoming a key group near the top of the financial organizational structure, and not a mere appendage of the systems department.

In some instances, corporation managements have decided that the task of designing and operating the business information system deserves a place outside of the financial organization. This department is sometimes known as the Department of Management Information Services.

Such a transfer or change in responsibility of the controller (or chief financial officer) would, indeed, be unfortunate for the controllership function. Yet, a primary cause for a change of this nature might be the inflexible attitude of many accountants who look to traditional accounting concepts and practices, and not to the management oriented approach adopted in this volume.

THE MANAGEMENT REPORTING SYSTEM AND EDP

Throughout this book the authors have stressed the *management service* function of the controller as contrasted to merely the *traditional* accounting concepts. A primary objective in systems design is, or should be, the preparation of management information. The integrated reporting system should accomplish at least two objectives:

1. The provision of necessary information for management planning and control
2. The fulfillment of legal and governmental reporting requirements

Controllers are expected to be flexible in meeting the need for management information. This requirement demands a break from the orthodox accounting tabulations so prevalent in many companies to these concepts:

Exception reporting
Responsibility reporting for control purposes
Comparative reporting for both planning and control
Analysis of trends and relationships for planning
Summarized reporting tailored to the management echelon being reported to
Interpretative reporting, so that the significance of the figures is understood

These principles require an intelligent and analytical approach to the needs of management. And the needs of management are not necessarily those furnished by the present reporting system. Electronic data processing permits the economical securing of other kinds of information. Such technological advances necessitate a continual re-examination by the controller of the information required for both policy guidance and day-to-day operations. Moreover, the availability of more data does not mean that additional facts should be given to management. Rather, *better* information should be furnished.

It is not unreasonable for the controller to

1. Provide the operating results of the preceding month on the first day of the following month
2. Provide economically—and rather continuously, such as each day or each week—a sound estimate of operating results
3. Secure monthly the expected income for the following month or year—on alternative bases using various assumptions

Yes, emphasis is on planning and control. With the tremendous knowledge possessed by the financial group, with perhaps a better understanding of the cost-volume-profit interrelationship than any other function, it would be disappointing if the controller by default lost the responsibility for the management reporting system.

41

Tax Records and Procedure

THE CONTROLLER AND TAXES

The reporting requirements of governmental agencies, already reviewed, influence record keeping. Furthermore, the very nature of the tax laws requires audit procedures as a means of enforcement. As a result, business records must now be planned to meet the requirements of a widely diverse pattern of federal and local laws. The most important of these relates to federal and state income taxes; but the payroll tax laws and other state tax laws must also be considered.

Some companies follow a practice of referring federal tax matters to the public accountants or tax attorneys. There are, of course, times when such assistance is desirable and necessary. However, the tendency to place such responsibility in hands outside the home organization is dangerous, and carries with it certain disadvantages. Knowledge of tax laws does not in itself assure the best answer. Such information must be applied in such a manner as to benefit the company to the greatest possible extent. This requires an intimate knowledge of the business and its transactions—something the external tax man cannot gain through an occasional or annual visit. More than this, the application of the tax laws must be considered in many of the day-to-day operating decisions. In addition, the controller has as a primary function the determination of the periodic and annual earnings; and federal taxes are an important factor in such a determination. Under the circumstances, it is felt that the controller has a fundamental responsibility to be fully informed on tax matters, particularly federal income taxes. A controller has not properly carried out his duties if he has not taken every possible step to avoid excess taxes. It is his responsibility to see that federal tax problems are handled competently.

In summary, the controller should be able to check the more important tax computations. He should have a general understanding of the tax laws.

He should be sufficiently aware of tax implications to inquire into, and secure an answer as to, the probable tax results of any given transaction. Finally, he should be able to arrive at intelligent conclusions regarding the management policies which will result in the most beneficial tax results.

THE TAX ORGANIZATION

The responsibility for the tax activities may rest with the controller, treasurer, or other official. Because of the close relationship to the accounts and the cost implications, it is believed to be more properly the controller's function.

Because of the increasing importance of taxes as a cost factor and the tremendous number and types of taxes to which a business is subject, the administration of tax matters cannot be regarded as an incidental phase of some executive's job. Businesses are finding it necessary and desirable to give more formal recognition to the tax function in the plan of organization. Tax problems are delegated to a specialist in taxes—a tax manager who may be also an assistant controller. A special tax department is being established in the larger firms. Depending on the complexity and size of the tax problems, the tax department may be departmentalized along lines of even more specialized knowledge, viz.:

1. Federal income taxes
2. Property taxes
3. Payroll taxes
4. State income taxes and sales taxes
5. Foreign taxes

An organizational chart of a home office tax department is illustrated in Fig. 197.

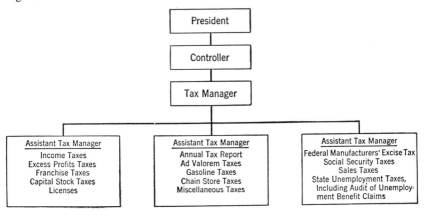

Fig. 197—Organization Chart for the Tax Department.

A basic question to be decided when a company has several plants, branches, or locations is the degree of centralization to be adopted in the administration of tax matters.

A CENTRALIZED TAX DEPARTMENT

A centralized tax organization may be defined as one which exercises direct control over all tax policies and procedures, quite irrespective of where the actual tax operations may be conducted. Under such a scheme, the tax manager is responsible for all tax policies, methods, and procedures within the company. Moreover, he exercises line control over his immediate organization, and functional control over the field organization. Where a company has several locations, some degree of centralization is ordinarily found. Almost all such companies, however, handle certain tax matters through local personnel to maintain good relationships with the local taxing authorities.

The degree to which actual tax return preparation is handled by the central tax department depends on the circumstances. The responsibility for tax report preparation may be placed in the field office, subject to the review of the head office. Also, each field office may be required to maintain records as stipulated by the central tax department, and to use certain prescribed forms. There are numerous variations in procedure. Centralized control does not necessarily imply physical centralization of all records.

Centralized tax control has the possible disadvantage of lack of contact with local taxing authorities unless accompanied by a special provision to secure this. In some instances, also, decentralization is said to be more economical. However, centralization, if properly carried out, appears to offer the following advantages:

1. Permits a higher degree of specialization not possible at various locations
2. Reduces the cost of various tax reporting services, since only one office need have them
3. Promotes uniformity
4. May add flexibility and distribute tax work more evenly

Another phase of centralization relates to the treatment of various types of taxes. Some companies, for example, may feel that the payroll department should handle payroll taxes; the billing department, sales taxes; the accounts payable department, the sales or use taxes on purchases. Such matters may be handled entirely by the tax department; or the various departments may prepare the reports and forms in accordance with the instructions of, and subject to the review of, the central tax department.

FUNCTIONS OF THE TAX MANAGER [1]

The functions of the tax manager will vary with the organization. However, the following listing is indicative of the extent of authority exercised or responsibility assumed in some of the larger companies:

1. *Organization of Tax Activity.*
    a. Organization of central tax department
        1) Selection of personnel
        2) Assignment of duties
        3) Supervision and control of activities
    b. Planning of local or branch office tax functions
        1) Decision regarding the employment of local full-time tax personnel and the partial utilization on tax work of employees primarily engaged in other functions
        2) Definition of the scope of the duties of local employees
    c. Provision for centralized supervision and control of tax activities

2. *Tax Procedure.*
    a. Responsibility for maintenance of adequate tax records
    b. Preparation of forms and designation of files and working papers to be prepared
    c. Designation of offices or locations at which tax records and procedures will be maintained
    d. Preparation of tax manual which crystallizes procedures and responsibilities
    e. Custody of licenses (except automobile), tax receipts, and other documents tendered by taxing authorities

3. *Tax Technique.* Studies of tax legislation, rulings, and decisions and of their effect on the company.

4. *Control Over Tax Expenditures.*
    a. Audit of tax bills, and approval for payment
    b. Designation of tax items that are reserved for personal scrutiny and approval by the tax manager
    c. Designation of tax items to be audited and approved for payment by personnel in the central tax department
    d. Prescription of limitations within which local or branch tax personnel may approve tax bills for payment
    e. Outline of method to be followed in checking tax bills

5. *Disputes and Litigation.* Conduct of negotiations with taxing authorities, including disputes, claims, etc.; and coordination in respect to audits or examinations by federal, state, and local agents.

---

[1] Adapted in part from Policyholders Service Bureau, Group Division, Metropolitan Life Insurance Company, *Centralized Control of Tax Work in Business Organizations,* pp. 9–11.

6. *Use of Outside Services.* Initiative regarding the use of legal counsel, public accountants, and tax consultants on such matters as:
   a. Formulation of tax policies
   b. Applicability of new types of taxes
   c. Questions regarding the propriety of individual assessments
   d. Verification or review of tax reports
   e. Acceptance or rejection of results of audits by revenue agents

7. *Interdepartmental Relations.*
   a. Issue of instructions and information regarding new and existing tax laws
   b. Designation of data required of accounting department and other divisions for compiling tax returns
   c. Decisions regarding special matters of tax policy and procedure raised by other company executives
   d. Cooperation with transportation, sales, and other departments regarding licenses, excise taxes, and other matters affecting their respective jurisdictions
   e. Utilization of traveling auditors on local tax problems

RELATIONS WITH OTHER DEPARTMENTS

The tax department activities, like most of the controller's functions, may reach into every department. As a matter of fact, when an organization becomes truly "tax-conscious," the tax department is consulted about any transactions which may have direct tax implications—for example, the tax problems of doing business in another state, the tax benefits of securing a certificate of necessity for additional facilities, or the savings, after taxes, of a given expansion. However, most of the contacts are with the accounting department because the tax returns are based in large part on the accounting records. Because each department head reports to the controller, coordination is easily achieved. To generalize, it might be said that the accounting supervisor is responsible for the mathematical correctness of the figures, while the tax manager is responsible for the method of utilizing them. The legal department also may have frequent contact with the tax manager in that the latter may often require opinions and legal interpretations of new tax matters.

TAX RECORDS IN GENERAL

The tax laws are so complex, so great in number, and of such differing nature that it is not practical to keep in mind all the provisions of the laws and all of the facts of the business which have direct bearing on taxability. Consequently, the company must have the necessary records if the desirable tax planning is to be consummated, if management is to have a clear view of the tax situation, or if any degree of administrative control is to be successful. The penalties for oversight or incompetence can be heavy. The nature of the records will be governed by the relative complexity of the tax problem. Broadly speaking, however, certain records are needed for administrative control purposes, to support the tax returns, and to meet the specific requirements of the law. Tax records may be grouped into four major classifications:

1. Call-up records
2. Information records
3. Working paper files
4. Supporting ledgers

While these will be reviewed briefly, it should be understood that in the final analysis, their suitability and timeliness depend on an alert staff. Records cannot be suggested which will meet all needs for all times. Flexibility must be provided in the organization. Thus, if sales are made in a new state, requiring the collection of a sales tax, the tax staff must take the initiative to get the necessary sales analysis by states, or the necessary accounts established. There is no substitute for such initiative.

CALL-UP RECORDS

An administrative tool needed in most concerns is the call-up record. It is merely a tickler file which serves to remind those responsible on such pertinent subjects as dates of filing tax returns, preparation of various reports, payment of tax bills, or preparation for hearings. These records may take any one of several forms:

1. *Index Card File.* The most popular method is the use of 3″ x 5″ or 5″ x 8″ cards. A separate card may be used for each tax, and multicolored clips may be attached to the months for filing returns or making payments. As one matter is attended to, the card is placed in order for the next follow-up subject. A sample form is shown in Fig. 198. This tickler card also can be designed to serve as a tax payment record as well.

2. *Loose-Leaf File.* This is principally a matter of using loose-leaf sheets instead of cards, and may take two forms: (1) a sheet for each day of the month, or (2) a sheet for each month with space for notations. Basically, it is a form of tax diary, and is suitable where tax operations are not too extensive.

3. *Combination Records.* Separate records may be kept of payments, for example, indicating the due date for all payments, and the date of actual payment. A similar record might be kept of assessment dates.

Such records may be perpetual records, with revisions made as changes occur in the law. Another practice is to prepare the file or calendar in December of each year for the following year.

Jan.	Feb.	Mar.	April	May	June	July	Aug.	Sept.	Oct.	Nov.	Dec.

Description of Tax
Apply for Forms
Assessment Date
Date of Return
Form No.
Date of Valuation
Last Date to File
Payment Date (s)
Discount Date
Tax Manual Ref.
File No.
Notes

Revision Date _____

Fig. 198—Tax Tickler File Card.

Regardless of the exact form, the important point is the need to provide a systematic and dependable means of bringing the subject to proper attention in sufficient time to take action. The advantages of call-up records are clear:

1. They allow sufficient preparation time so that proper consideration can be given to any problems that arise
2. They avoid penalties for late returns or failure to file a return

TAX INFORMATION RECORDS

Another basic type of record may be called a tax information record, and represents a summary of the tax law and related matters as they affect the business. Such a record is used as a reference when preparing the tax return, etc. The information may be compiled on cards, on loose-leaf sheets, or as part of the tax manual.

Suggestive of the information to be available as to each tax are the following:

1. Name of tax
2. Description of tax
3. Basis
4. Rate or rates of tax

5. Exemptions from tax
6. Time of filing return
7. Return form number and name
8. Approximate time required for preparation
9. To whom return is sent, and when
10. Source of data for return preparation
11. Why company is subject
12. The tax accounting
13. Procedure, including any special instructions
14. Penalties for non-payment

An illustrative page from a tax information record is shown in Fig. 199.

Where such data are part of a tax manual, it may be helpful to include other information, such as exhibits of the forms, perhaps a simple form of tax calendar, and general comments and procedure. If the manual is sufficiently large, a table of contents is desirable. Because of constant changes in the tax laws, it is necessary to review the manual frequently and keep it up-to-date. For the same reason, loose-leaf forms are to be preferred.

TAX WORKING FILES

The two types of records discussed are of a reference nature. The remaining records may be considered as the working files and contain the figures and facts incident to the year-to-year returns. These operating files are of an infinite variety, and are perhaps comparable to the permanent files and working paper files in connection with an audit. The central theme is a complete and orderly record of how the amount of tax was determined each year, the payment dates, etc. These files may include such information as:

1. Record of payments
2. Record of assessments
3. Reconciliations of tax data to the records
4. Copies of the return
5. Refund record, including basis
6. Correspondence on the tax

Such files must be prepared on the basis of the judgment of the tax manager or controller.

THE INTERNAL REVENUE CODE AND RECORD REQUIREMENTS

Under any tax law, the problem is to set up records which will provide the necessary data with the minimum of cost and effort. In considering record-keeping requirements under federal tax laws, the principal source of data is the Internal Revenue Code. The law is very general in regard to records; and Congress has specifically granted to the Commissioner of Internal Rev-

---

TAX INFORMATION RECORD

CLASSIFICATION. Sales and Use Tax

Name of Return: City of New York, Sales and Compensating Use Tax Return

Form Number: 12 SUX

Due Dates: Quarterly—April 20, July 20, October 20, January 20

Rate of Tax: 3% of taxable sales and purchases

Approximate Amount of Tax: $400 each quarter

Average Time Required for Preparation: 1 hour

Compendium: Every vendor engaged in the sale or rental of tangible personal property or rendering service in the city of New York, and all purchasers from whom the seller has failed to collect the Sales Tax or Compensating Use Tax must file, and must remit tax of 3% on such sales and purchases. In taxable sales 3% tax must be collected and subsequently remitted by vendor. Certificate of registration must be filed with the Treasurer of the City of New York to obtain certificate of authority to collect tax or to provide resale certificates. (Pages 15007–8—Vol. 3—CCH N. Y. Corp. Tax Ser.)

Why Company is Subject to Tax and Must File: Subject because of sales to customers in New York City (Section N41). Most sales are, however, for the purpose of resale, and allowable deductions if and when resale certificates obtained from such customers have been received and are on file (Par. 130–215 —Sec. N41–2.0). Tax on sales to ultimate consumers must be collected and remitted. Also, purchases of supplies, etc., by New York City office upon which vendor has not collected tax must be reported and 3% tax paid (Par. 131–003—Sec. N41–2.0 and Par. 140–003 etc.—Sec. M44).

Information Needed and Source: New York City sales for resale and New York City sales to ultimate consumers are separately listed and totaled quarterly by the tabulating section, from New York City invoices especially coded for this purpose.

A list of purchases by the New York City office, upon which the vendor collected no New York City Sales Tax, is prepared and supplied each quarter by the New York City office.

Comments: The sum of the New York City sales, as reported on the four quarterly Form 12 SUX reports, must agree with the amount reported in the annual Gross Receipts Tax return.

Fig. 199—Tax Information Record. (From Herman C. Weber, "A Personalized Tax Manual for Your Corporation," NACA *Bulletin*, June 14, 1947, p. 1282.)

enue the power to prescribe records which are necessary to determine liability to tax, or which will properly reflect the income of the business. The sections of the Internal Revenue Code dealing with accounting requirements for income tax purposes are contained principally in Sections 41, 42, 43, and 54, except as to certain very specific applications, which are beyond the scope of this book. The general nature of the regulations is evidenced by the Code provisions regarding net income (Section 41):

> The net income shall be computed upon the basis of the taxpayer's annual accounting period (fiscal year or calendar year, as the case may be) in accordance with the method of accounting regularly employed in keeping the books of such taxpayer; but if no such method of accounting has been so employed, or if the method employed does not clearly reflect the income, the computation shall be made in accordance with such method as in the opinion of the Commissioner does clearly reflect the income. If the taxpayer's annual accounting period is other than a fiscal year as defined in Section 48 or if the taxpayer has no annual accounting period or does not keep books, the net income shall be computed on the basis of the calendar year.

Section 54 indicates the authority of the Commissioner of Internal Revenue in regard to record keeping:

> Every person liable to any tax imposed by this chapter or for the collection thereof, shall keep such records, render under oath such statements, make such returns, and comply with such rules and regulations as the Commissioner with the approval of the Secretary, may from time to time prescribe.
>
> Whenever in the judgment of the Commissioner necessary, he may require any person, by notice served upon him, to make and retain, render under oath such statements, or keep such records, as the Commissioner deems sufficient to show whether or not such person is liable to tax under this chapter.

It is evident that adequate accounting records are required under the law, and further that they may be good insurance against unwarranted tax assessments.

DIFFERENCES BETWEEN INCOME TAX ACCOUNTING AND BOOK ACCOUNTING

The principal source of information required for federal income tax returns is, of course, the regular accounting records of the company. And though tax accounting and book accounting are generally the same, there are three important respects in which these two differ. These are:

1. Income and expenses specifically excluded for tax purposes. Examples include the tax-exempt income from government bonds, or contributions in excess of the allowable maximum.
2. Differences resulting from the recognition of the *time* when losses or income may be recognized. The reserve provisions and related charge-offs are included in this group.

3. Differences in cost bases. This general category would include differences in depreciation rates and bases, treatment of maintenance and repair costs, and inventory valuation.

An important schedule for the controller's review is the reconciliation of net income and surplus, contained in the federal income tax return. This schedule reveals the major points of difference between tax and book accounting.

TREATMENT OF THESE DIFFERENCES IN THE RECORDS

The controller and tax manager are faced with the problem of how these differences should be treated in the records. It is obviously necessary to maintain a running record of these differences, and to reconcile book and tax figures if a company is to secure full tax benefits. Maintenance of such records is essential to insure that the company will not overlook a tax deduction to which it could properly be entitled in a subsequent year. However, it does not follow that a completely independent set of books need be maintained for tax purposes.

Some useful generalizations can be made, based on the three groups of differences listed in the preceding section. The first group of items presents no problem of carry-over from year to year. Based on specific provisions of the Code, they are excluded from income or expense. They appear on the reconciliation; and that usually ends the matter. Where such items are numerous it may be found helpful to establish separate accounts, or groups of accounts, for such income or expenses.

The second group represents those items taken into the accounts earlier or later than is required or permitted under the statute or regulations. Thus, while a reserve for furnace repairs may be set up on the records of a steel company, for tax purposes, only actual costs may constitute allowable deductions. An analysis of the accounts, which would probably be prepared for the public auditors anyway, will provide the necessary data for tax purposes. Supplementary worksheets generally are sufficient for this group, and separate ledgers need not be maintained.

The major problems arise when different cost bases are used. In any business an analysis is necessary to determine whether a separate series of supplementary accounts need be maintained. Where substantially different depreciation bases and rates are used, then separate ledgers may be required. Again, for a securities broker, where different cost bases are in use, separate ledgers may be needed.

A special word is in order regarding depreciation claimed. The burden of proof as to the correctness of the depreciation charges is clearly on the taxpayer and he must keep the necessary records in support of the deduction. While no particular form of record is required, a form somewhat

SCHEDULE SUPPORTING DEPRECIATION CLAIMED

Name _____   Taxable Year Ended _____   Exhibit _____

Account(s) Classification _____   Original Estimated Useful Life ___ Years   Adjusted Life ___Years

(1)	(2)	(3)	(4)	(5)	(6)	(7)	(8)	(9)
Year Acquired	Original Cost and Subsequent Additions, by Years, Including Current Year	Deductions for Sales and Other Disposition in Prior Years	Adjusted Cost Beginning of Year	Reserve for Depreciation Beginning of Year	Remaining Balance (Col. 4 Less Col. 5)	Estimated Remaining Life (Years)	Depreciation Claimed for Current Year	Net Depreciation Reserve at End of Current Year

I hereby certify that all costs reported in Column 2 represent actual cash disbursement by taxpayer.

_____
Signed

Fig. 200—Tax Depreciation Schedule.

similar to Fig. 200 was suggested in 1934. The instructions with respect to depreciation deductions, issued at that time, contain the following comments:

Treasury Decision 4422, approved February 28, 1934, provides that taxpayers claiming deductions from gross income for depreciation must furnish full and complete information regarding (1) the cost or other basis of assets for which depreciation is claimed, (2) the age, condition and remaining useful life of the assets, (3) the portion of the cost or other basis which has been recovered through depreciation allowances for prior taxable years and (4) such other information as may be required to establish the correctness of the deduction claimed or to determine the amount of deduction properly allowable.

DEPRECIATION SCHEDULE

The accompanying form of schedule has been prepared for use in compiling the information required, and while it is believed applicable to most cases, any form that will clearly set forth the information required may be used in order to substantiate the cost or other basis of the property and the depreciation claimed. With respect to property acquired prior to March 1, 1913, property acquired by gift or transfer in trust, property transmitted at death, property acquired upon an exchange, property acquired in a reorganization after December 31, 1917, property acquired after December 31, 1920, by a corporation in exchange for its stock where immediately after the transfer the transferor of the property is in control of the corporation, property acquired by an involuntary conversion, and property acquired during affiliation, and certain other special cases, the statutes prescribe certain limitations with which compliance must be made. If in any case, therefore, depreciable assets have been included in the property account on any basis other than the actual cost of property acquired for cash, the taxpayer must furnish the information and evidence necessary to establish definitely the correctness of the basis claimed.

In preparing the schedules the original cost or other basis of the property and gross additions by years must be set forth separately. The schedule for each class of assets must likewise clearly reflect all adjustments to the property accounts which have been or should have been made in prior years as a result of the elimination of assets fully depreciated, the sale, abandonment or retirement of assets, or for any other reason. The adjusted property account as shown in the schedule should be reconciled with the property account as reflected on the books of the taxpayer.

If the segregation of property accounts in the past has not been sufficiently detailed to afford a reasonable basis for the determination of the depreciation deduction, the cost or other basis should be segregated into groups of accounts containing similar assets having approximately the same average lives, to serve as a basis for depreciation deductions for current and future years. If, however, a taxpayer for its own purpose keeps a record of each individual item or classifies its accounts into a large number of different groups, the data required by this mimeograph should be summarized in such form as will present an accurate statement of each distinctly different class of depreciable assets and of the reserve that has been accrued against each class to date for income tax purposes. The examining officer should verify the correctness of those summarized schedules from the taxpayer's records, but the inclusion in the schedule of a voluminous mass of detail is not ordinarily necessary.

In computing the reserve for depreciation, credits to the reserve on account of depreciation shall be in the amount allowable for each year except for such closed years for which a greater amount has been allowed, in which case the total amount allowed shall be credited to the reserve. If for income tax accounting other credits such as salvage value have been added to the reserve, these should be set forth separately with an explanation of such credits. Charges to the reserve that have not been recovered as expense or otherwise in closing prior income tax returns should be set up separately in the schedule. These charges, in addition to the cost of property retired, may be such items as repairs, renewals, fully depreciated assets, etc., all of which should be identified with an explanation respecting any unusual charges.

A PROPER CLASSIFICATION OF ACCOUNTS

It might indeed be a sorry day for private enterprise if the primary consideration in designing the accounting records were the preparation of tax returns. This factor must be weighed, however; and there are certain modifications or provisions which can be made to facilitate tax work and perhaps more fully protect the interests of the taxpayer. The following suggestions are noted:

1. It is desirable to maintain a record of original costs, whether for excess profits tax purposes or otherwise. For example, the write-off of goodwill may be accomplished by means of a reserve account rather than by a credit directly against the asset. On such a basis, such costs are less likely to be forgotten; and there will be no dependence on someone's recollection.
2. Where practical, non-taxable income or non-allowable deductions should be segregated in the accounts. Such a procedure may save costly analyses and make less likely the oversight of income not to be included as taxable.
3. Where conflicting or overlapping statutes affect taxability, columnar analyses may be incorporated in the general or subsidiary ledgers. If tabulating methods are in use, codes may be employed to make the necessary segregation or analysis.

PAYROLL TAXES AND RECORDS

The enactment of the Federal Insurance Contributions Act and Federal Unemployment Tax Act, together with the related state and city laws, has imposed additional requirements in payroll records and taxes. Generally most of the medium- and larger-sized businesses now must pay three types of payroll taxes and must file three sets of reports. Three general types of records must be prepared:

1. The basic payroll record, consisting of a listing of the employees' names, wages, and similar data, for each payroll period
2. A record of the individual earnings of each wage-earner for each pay period
3. A statement of earnings to be given to each employee at stated intervals

Generally no detailed or special method of record keeping is prescribed, but the tax manager should ascertain that the procedures in use will: (1) enable determination of the tax liability, (2) permit quick preparation of the reports, and (3) conform to the general law requirements.

In connection with payroll taxes it is to be mentioned that many states have merit-rating systems designed to reduce tax payments if labor turnover is low. Such tax advantages should not be overlooked.

OTHER TAXES

In addition to the federal income tax and the payroll taxes, there are a host of other taxes to which most businesses are subject in varying degree:

Excess profits taxes
State income and franchise
   taxes
Real property taxes
Personal property taxes

Gasoline taxes
Excise taxes
Sales and use taxes
Stamp taxes
City income taxes

The tax manager must be alert in suggesting procedures to gather the required data in an economical and convenient manner, and in keeping abreast of changes in the statutes. Provision for refunds should not be overlooked, however small they may seem at first blush. Refunds from gasoline taxes, for example, can greatly exceed the cost of effort in securing them.

INCOME TAXES AND BUSINESS PLANNING

A basic question which business management must consider is whether it should so conduct its affairs within the law as to minimize the tax consequences of its operating decisions. One phase of the problem is the *direct* tax costs. Through adequate knowledge of basic tax laws, regulations, judicial decisions, and current trends, the tax specialist can assist the business in minimizing the tax expense.

A much broader question is whether the large element of tax expense, particularly income taxes, should receive recognition in policy decisions. There are two theories concerning the payment of taxes and use of company funds. One school considers a basic objective to be the securing of a satisfactory return for the owners. As taxes increase, therefore, greater profits must be achieved through expense reduction and improvements in gross income to the end that *after* taxes an adequate margin or return is available for the owners. It is recognized that greater effort must be put forth to secure the comparable net profit. Moreover, this school assumes that high taxes will continue indefinitely.

In contrast to this conservative viewpoint is the expansionist approach. Implicit in this thinking is the assumption that high income tax rates are temporary; and that for such short periods of time full advantage should be taken of the "cheap" dollars. It is a time to experiment, to undertake research projects which might not otherwise be done, for the net cost to the owners is small. It is a time to exploit a public relations program to improve the organization. In short, it is a time to put the house in order for competition when the cheaper dollars are no longer available. Business management certainly should consider the tax outlook when faced with broad policy decisions of an expansionist nature.

SPECIAL TAX REPORTS

Generally speaking, the great majority of people, and this includes the employees of business, are not fully aware of the tremendous burden placed on business in the form of taxes. The controller or tax manager can put the information on tax costs to good use. After all, the data are of little value if retained in a file in the tax department.

It might prove useful if the tax manager would prepare an annual report to the controller, with copies for the chief executive, to indicate the total taxes paid by the concern. Some of this information would be useful in the annual report to shareholders.[2] Suggested data for this annual tax report follow:

1. Total taxes of various types paid or accrued during the year.
2. Comparison of such expense with prior years.
3. Relationship of taxes to other factors, such as
   a. Salaries and wages
   b. Net sales
   c. Total investment
   d. Dividends
   This information may be expressed in dollars and percentages, or may indicate the taxes per employee or per man-hour.
4. Explanation of any significant changes which have already occurred, as well as expected changes.

[2] See Chapter 30.

42

Insurance Records and Procedure

RESPONSIBILITY FOR INSURANCE RECORDS AND PROCEDURE

Good business judgment requires that a company adopt a sound and well-planned insurance program. Some insurance is compulsory, such as workmen's compensation; some may be required for contractual reasons, such as fire insurance under a bank loan agreement; and some is carried because of the risks which are inherent in the business. Also, shareholders and creditors expect a company to obtain protection against losses which prudent judgment dictates should be covered by insurance.

Responsibility for an insurance program sometimes is placed in an insurance committee, but usually it is under a financial officer, such as the treasurer or controller. A considerable amount of the information needed for insurance purposes is in the controller's field, so it is logical that he should eventually be directed to supervise or carry out the program. Even though the primary responsibility may be placed in other hands, the controller should be well informed on insurance matters.

If the insurance responsibility is assigned to the controller and the organization is of sufficient size, the handling of the program should be delegated to a qualified insurance manager who will carefully analyze all the hazards in connection with operations; see that state or federal requirements regarding insurance are complied with; deal with agents, brokers, advisers, and insurance company representatives; recommend when insurance is advisable; maintain records of insurance in force, premiums, and losses; supervise, if necessary, a loss prevention program; and keep abreast of changes in the company operations and activities as well as changes taking place in the field of insurance. Of course, when it is not possible to delegate this responsibility, the controller must exercise much personal supervision over these matters. His efforts can be made more effective in many cases by the securing of competent professional aid.

762

THE INSURANCE PROCEDURE

To protect adequately the properties and financial position of a business, it is mandatory that a well-planned insurance procedure or program be developed covering all vital points. Whether starting anew or reviewing the existing insurance coverage, the following procedure outlines the points that must be considered:

1. Determine the insurable hazards of the company through a *complete* review of the properties and operations. This would include a review not only of physical properties and processes but also of contractual obligations, leasehold requirements, and governmental requirements.
2. Determine the extent of the exposure or risk so as to ascertain the amount of coverage which is necessary.
3. Select desirable underwriters and brokers.
4. Determine the types of policies and bases or valuations to be used.
5. Establish proper reporting procedures and the necessary records, including an insurance manual.
6. Introduce a program for control or reduction of hazards and rates.
7. Make provision for a periodic audit or review of coverage.

This outline covers the essential phases of an insurance program. However, the actions need not follow in that order. Perhaps selection of a broker or underwriter, for example, will precede other steps.

SELECTING THE INSURABLE HAZARDS TO BE COVERED

The groundwork for a sound insurance program lies in an intelligent analysis of the company properties and operations to determine the extent and types of exposure. This phase should not be a superficial review; it is preferable that worksheets or schedules be prepared showing the details. These same schedules will assist in determining the extent of required insurance coverage. There are three separate matters to be covered in the review:

1. *Buildings and Equipment.* The type of construction, the location, and the hazards to which exposed should be listed. Provision should be made for a determination of replacement cost and extent of physical wear and tear. In this phase, the assistance of the engineers is desirable.
2. *Other Assets.* Since the purpose of the program is to protect all the properties of the company, a review should be made of all other assets—cash, negotiable securities, inventories, and receivables. Exposure to loss, whether by fire, flood, theft, or otherwise, should be considered. Moreover, losses resulting from business interruption (use and occupancy) should not be overlooked.

3. *Liability to Other Parties.* Finally, possible loss or damage to other parties, and to their properties, by reason of company products, operations, or acts of employees should be reviewed. This analysis should include a review of all contracts, including sales orders and purchase orders, and all applicable state laws, to determine what commitments have been undertaken and what exposure exists.

Such an approach will indicate the general nature and possibly the extent of hazards faced by the company. The next step is to get the facts and make decisions regarding the following questions:

1. Is insurance coverage available, and in what form, for each type of hazard? The broker or insurance consultant can assist in this. Generally speaking, most losses are insurable.
2. What is the extent of exposure? Much of this information will be available from the analysis sheets. It involves a consideration of the probability of loss and the degree and frequency. For example, what is the greatest amount of cash to be transported to the bank daily? Or what are the likely maximum inventories at particular locations?
3. What is the cost of insurance protection against the hazard?
4. Should the company operate on a self-insurance basis?

The determination of whether to insure against a risk is a matter of weighing the probability of loss against the premium cost. If the exposure is slight or if the premium appears greater than probable loss, it may not be economical to insure. Thus, if the records indicate average monthly repair costs of $1,000 resulting from auto collisions, and premium costs are $1,500, this phase of automobile coverage might not be insured—unless changed conditions are expected to alter this relationship.

SELECTING THE BROKER AND UNDERWRITER

A business firm may, of course, contact the insurance company directly. Usually, however, this is done through a broker who, because of his knowledge of the underwriters and other insurance matters, is in a position to render help and advice to the company. In selecting an insurance company, and to a lesser extent a broker, the following factors should be given consideration:

1. Comparative insurance rates—not all companies are the same.
2. Type of coverage—policies vary.
3. Financial strength of the insurer.
4. Reputation and facilities for service—the engineering staff, supervision of safety programs, and inspection service, which may be provided without direct charge.
5. Convenience—are local representatives or means available for quick consultation?

There are several types of insurance companies and the net insurance cost may vary considerably among them. Each may serve well, but the point to be made is the desirability of investigation before placing of contracts. These several types include:

1. *Mutuals.* Each policyholder is an owner, and earnings are distributed as dividends. If net losses result, policyholders may be subject to a levy of extra assessments in some instances. In other cases, non-assessable policies are issued.

2. *Stock Companies.* Such corporations are similar to other corporations in that dividends are distributed to stockholders and not to policyholders as such.

3. *Lloyds of London.* This underwriter operates under special authority of the English Parliament, and will be found to write insurance coverage of a nature which other companies will not handle. Lloyds also provides the usual types of coverage.

4. *Reciprocal Organizations.* These are associations of insureds operated by a manager. Advance deposits are made against which are charged the proportionate cost of operations.

TYPES OF INSURANCE

A discussion of the great variety of types of insurance coverage is beyond the scope of this book; it is suggested that an insurance broker or handbook be consulted. As a generalization, however, most industrial firms require the following common types of insurance coverage:

Fire and extended coverage
Comprehensive crime
General liability insurance
Workmen's compensation
Business interruption (use and occupancy)
Auto—comprehensive and public liability
Boiler insurance (where high-pressure boilers are in use)
Group life, health, and accident

A few words to controllers are in order with respect to use and occupancy insurance and blanket fidelity bonds. Many businessmen are of the opinion that business interruption, or use and occupancy insurance, is something quite mysterious. It is merely insurance protection to insure a company against loss of profits and all continuing expenses during the time the business may be wholly or partially shut down for repair or replacement of buildings, machinery, or stock as the result of a specified hazard. If properly written, it is intended to place the insured in the same position after the loss or damage has occurred that it would have been had the loss not occurred. Certain hazards can be very costly if business must be suspended for any length of time. These must be analyzed as to each individual business. Thus, destruction or damage of physical properties, boiler explosions, loss or damage of raw materials at outside locations, or accidents involving the properties of suppliers are conditions which require consideration.

The purpose of fidelity bonds is to indemnify the business for loss of money or other property resulting from dishonest acts of bonded employees. The acts insured against include larceny, embezzlement, forgery, misappropriation, wrongful abstraction, theft, or other dishonest acts. There are many types of fidelity bonds—individual bonds, name schedule bonds, position schedule bonds, blanket position bonds, and discovery bonds, to mention a few. The insurance manager should review the various types so as to understand their value and determine that the company is properly covered.

INSURANCE RECORDS—GENERAL

Insurance records are of two broad types: those which serve as administrative or procedural tools, and those which furnish the figures necessary for adequate insurance coverage or policy determination. The exact type of records will be influenced by the kind of insurance coverage, the size and nature of operation, and the policy reporting requirements. In summary, the following basic data should be provided by a well-designed system of insurance records:

1. *Insurance Coverage Information.* This type of record serves as a reference source, and includes such data regarding each policy as:
   a. Type of insurance coverage
   b. Insurer
   c. Effective dates or term of policy
   d. Policy number
   e. Broker
   f. Abstract of coverage
   g. Reporting requirements
   h. Rates, premiums, and refunds

2. *Working Files Regarding Exposure.* There are several types of records which may comprise this group:
   a. Binder records—to indicate coverage pending formal issuance of policy
   b. Location records—outlining the insurable values at various plant or branch locations
   c. Value report files—a summary of the insurable values at *all* locations, where a reporting form of policy is used
   d. Transportation logs—showing the location of vehicles, or miles driven, or hours flown for aircraft

---

INSURANCE INFORMATION RECORD

Policy No. ___6287B___

Type ___Boiler___

Description of Insurance:	Boiler Insurance—Stinson Plant
Type of Coverage:	Personal liability and property damage
Amount of Coverage:	$100,000 P L and $200,000 P D
Rate:	Adjusted annually $_____ per $100
Insurer:	United States Fidelity and Guaranty Co. of Baltimore, Md.
Broker:	Marsh and McLennan, San Diego, Cal.
Reporting Requirements:	Annual
Accounting Charges:	Account 131–12
Special Notes:	Check annual reporting values against F 306

Fig. 201—Insurance Information Record.

3. *Call-up Records.* This is a tickler file or files—usually a card system—to signal these events:
   a. Expiration dates of policies
   b. Reporting dates
   c. Premium payment dates
   d. Notices of hearings, settlements, or rebates
   e. Special accounting adjustments necessary
   f. Binder follow-up for policies
   g. Any other matters requiring follow-up

4. *Expense Distribution Records.* Such records may consist of the registers and worksheets indicating the periodic write-off or accrual, the bases of premium allocation, and the amounts to be allocated.

5. *Records of Losses, Settlements, and Premiums.* These records indicate the premium costs, compared to losses, to be used, among other things, for determining the desirability of insurance coverage.

6. *Claims Files.* These files indicate the status of each claim, and contain support for each claim filed, correspondence, etc.

7. *Insurance Manual.* This record may contain the basic coverage data outlined in item 1 of this list. In addition, it should contain

detailed procedures, instructions as to reporting forms, explanation of means to reduce losses, etc. A loose-leaf arrangement is usually desirable. A sample page is illustrated in Fig. 201. Separate manuals may be found necessary for certain general groups of insurance, e.g., group life, health and accident, property insurance.

PROPERTY RECORDS FOR FIRE LOSSES

The general practice of carrying fire insurance on the one hand, and the experience as to records and settlements on the other hand, seem to warrant some general comments. It is to be noted that the standard fire policy contains two clauses which must be considered in planning the records for insurance purposes. One stipulates it is the actual *cash value* of the property at time of loss that is insured. The other states that the insured must furnish a complete inventory of the destroyed, damaged, and undamaged property, showing in detail quantities, costs, actual cash value, and amount of loss claimed. Thus, *actual cash value* must be known. Such value (1) is not restricted to actual capitalized value, and (2) is not limited by original costs. Instead, actual cash value is defined as the cost of reproduction new, less depreciation. As to capitalized value, there may be expenditures for property in use which were not capitalized on the books. Examples include piping, wiring, tools, jigs, and dies. These items should be recorded properly and documented for insurance purposes.

The other problem, that of determining reproduction costs, may be more difficult of solution. Two general methods may be used to determine present worth: (1) have an appraisal made, either as such or by checking with contractors for estimates, or (2) adjust original costs by means of a price index. Either a general index or a specific index applying to each element of cost may be used. For example, one index may be applied to brick, another to steel, etc. A vast difference in the answer may result, depending on the method; and the controller must exercise caution. When the specific index method is to be used, the costs of construction must be segregated properly by classes which have the same price trend.

Three other considerations or requirements regarding the property records for insurance purposes are worth mentioning. First, the records should properly segregate the "excluded portion" of fire policies—the underground foundations, piping, etc. An estimate may be used. Second, quite often the risk or exposure differs considerably by building or area, and costs must be grouped properly. Finally, the records should be kept reasonably up-to-date.

The obligation to prove the loss rests with the insured. Records which are complete and which reflect proper values can be of substantial assistance in securing a fair settlement in the event of loss.

CLAIMS PROCEDURES AND PROBLEMS

Though the insurance coverage is adequate, a company may still suffer unnecessary, though perhaps hidden, losses if proper attention is not given to procedures to be followed in the event of a disaster or other major loss. From an organizational viewpoint, responsibility must be assigned for the carrying-out of certain functions. From the somewhat more limited standpoint of the controller's specific job, the losses must be reported promptly, and steps must be taken to substantiate the losses. The losses should include not only the direct losses of a fire, for example, but costs incidental to such losses, including clean-up.

Should a property loss occur, provision should be made for such matters as:

1. Segregation of damaged material from undamaged—until the property is checked by the adjusters. Damaged material might be segregated into salvageable and unsalvageable.
2. Preparation of detailed lists of all losses. This may require estimates, or perhaps a book cutoff to determine inventory values.
3. Accumulation of the incidental losses through proper coding of purchase orders and time cards:
   a. Fire fighting and property protection costs, if any
   b. Clean-up costs
   c. Expense of identifying property
   d. Repair costs, if any
   e. Other costs incident to resumption of production
   f. Expenses of preparing claims

Provision should be made for recording the claim to assure proper follow-up. The charges should be to a claims receivable account, for example, to avoid forgetting the claim because it is buried in some correspondence file.

INSURANCE AUDITS AND REVIEWS

Follow-up on insurance coverage is fundamentally the same as in other business activities. Once the insurance program has been established it must be kept up-to-date. As business needs change, the insurance coverage should be balanced or adjusted. Changes in the types of insurance protection are an added reason for reviews. Such examination may be made, perhaps yearly, by company executives who are familiar with insurance. However, there are insurance consultants who do not sell insurance, but who, for a fee, will make such reviews and furnish a continuing supervisory service. A review by such a concern may include: a detailed study of the business and its present need and coverage, the control aspects of insurance expenditures, the financial stability of the underwriters, and the problems of preparing claims.

ANNUAL INSURANCE REPORT

To keep the top-management group fully advised on general insurance matters, it may be found desirable to prepare an annual insurance report. Suggestions for the contents of such a report are:

1. Cost of insurance this year vs. prior years
2. Insurance coverage and hazards not covered
3. Significant changes in rates during the year
4. Comments on efforts to reduce exposure and risks
5. Annual losses and recoveries—perhaps a comparison with premiums paid
6. Anticipated major or significant changes in the insurance program
7. Condition of insurance reserves when hazards are self-insured

43

Procedures for Ownership and Long-Term Debt Interests

GENERAL STATEMENT

This chapter contains comments on administrative matters incident to the corporate form of organization—doing business in another state, minutes of meetings, capital stock and dividend records and procedures—and the subject of bond and interest payment records and procedures. These are topics about which the controller should be informed, and concerning which he may have a responsibility for audit and procedure writing. The tasks, however, usually are a matter for the corporate secretary, treasurer, or legal counsel.

DOING BUSINESS IN OTHER STATES

From a review of reports and records, and from the many and frequent contacts by the accounting staff with the operating departments, the controller can learn of the company activities in other states. This is important from the standpoint of legal requirements for doing business in these other states. While the problem is primarily legal, the controller has a responsibility in protecting company property and rights.

When a state charters a corporation, it may authorize it to do business in all the states of the United States and in foreign countries. However, the corporation is permitted to do business in other states and foreign countries only upon meeting the requirements imposed in these states and countries.

In relation to the state of its creation, a corporation is considered a domestic corporation; and in relation to all other states, it is a foreign corporation. A state is not obliged, except as a matter of courtesy, to permit a foreign corporation to do business within its boundaries. Further, it may impose on such corporations such terms and conditions as it deems fit. In exercising such powers, however, it may not interfere with interstate commerce. The imposition of taxes, for example, may be done only when a foreign corporation has been found to be doing business in the state. This is a legal question and many elements are involved. Thus the storage of materials, the making of local contracts, or the maintenance of an office may or may not constitute doing business. Each case depends upon the particular circumstances and the statutes and court decisions of the individual state.

But unless a corporation doing business in a particular state has been authorized by that state to transact business within the meaning of the laws of such state, it may suffer severe penalties. Among the penalties imposed by states upon a corporation which does business within the state without proper license is the denial of the right to maintain an action in the courts of that state. This has the effect of rendering the corporation contracts and accounts receivable in that state legally unenforceable. Other penalties include the removal of the statute of limitations, the imposition of fines on the corporation or its officers, the rendering void of title to property in the state, and even the imprisonment of officers. Hence, the performing of acts in other states where the company is not authorized to transact business must be given careful consideration.

CORPORATE MINUTES

The bylaws of most corporations provide that the secretary shall attend all meetings of the stockholders, the board of directors, and the standing committees of the board, and shall keep the minutes thereof. Such approved resolutions as are contained in the minutes constitute a medium through which stockholders exercise their controlling powers or through which the directors guide the corporate activities. It is therefore important that the minutes record accurately the proceedings, and further that the resolutions be properly and legally phrased. Improper wordings or failure to provide for contingencies may subject the company and officers to losses or litigation.

While the controller may sometimes act as secretary, his chief concern with the minutes is to ascertain that the wishes of the stockholders or directors, as evidenced therein, are carried out. Important financial matters should be recorded: salaries of officers, dividend declarations, authority for major capital expenditures, approval of the yearly operating budget, etc.

PROCEDURE IN STOCK ISSUANCE

For most of the middle-sized and larger companies, the original issuance of capital stock, or the issuance of a new stock authorization, must be preceded by certain definite acts or arrangements. The following steps are involved:

1. *Authorization by the Board of Directors.* A resolution, specifying the terms of the issue, must be passed by the board of directors.
2. *Consent by the Present Stockholders.* If a company already has stockholders, and an increase in the authorized capital stock is contemplated, the stockholders much adopt a resolution authorizing the action.
3. *Compliance with SEC Requirements.* If the issue is subject to the Securities Acts, then a registration statement and prospectus must be prepared.
4. *Completion of Listing Arrangements with the Exchange.* If a stock is to be listed on a stock exchange, arrangements must be made and requirements met.
5. *Making of Arrangements for the Sale of the Stock.* A company may sell its stock directly to the public, but in most instances the issue is underwritten by investment bankers.
6. *Providing for a Transfer Agent and Registrar.* If the company is small, with little or no trading in its securities, then a transfer agent is not necessary. Even in larger companies, it may be decided to create a transfer department. Usually, however, the larger and medium-sized companies engage a transfer agent. When the stocks are listed on the New York Stock Exchange, a transfer agent and registrar must be located in the financial district of New York City. Under such conditions, sometimes a co-transfer agent and a co-registrar are appointed in the New York City area, with another in the city of the company's principal activities. Most large and medium-sized companies must have a registrar; they may not function in such a capacity themselves. The function of a registrar is principally to prevent an overissue of stock.
7. *Designing a Stock Certificate.* Consideration must be given to (a) the method of production—engraving, printing, or lithographing (the stock exchanges have certain requirements); (b) the type or grade of paper; and (c) the design of the certificate—color, size, etc.
8. *Arranging for Issuance of the Certificate.* Details must be arranged by the company or transfer agent. In this connection, consideration must be given to the pre-emptive rights of stockholders and the use of subscription rights.

ADMINISTRATIVE CONSIDERATIONS REGARDING STOCK TRANSFERS

The corporate secretary is usually charged with responsibility for matters relating to stock transfers, although in some instances the treasurer may handle them. As the corporate ownership changes, arrangements must be made to record properly the transfer of the shares between owners. At least three factors have a bearing on such transactions:

1. *Statutory Requirements.* All states have adopted either the Uniform Stock Transfer Act or Uniform Commercial Codes.
2. *Stock Exchange Regulations.* If stocks are to be listed on one of the exchanges, the regulations of the exchange must be followed. Thus, most exchanges require that both a transfer agent and registrar be appointed. Usually the registrar must be an independent agent; although the company may act as its own transfer agent.
3. *Rights of Stockholders.* Stockholders have certain basic rights, which generally include the right to vote, to receive dividends, and to subscribe to additional stock. It is obviously necessary to maintain adequate records of ownership so as to avoid denying a stockholder his legal rights. The corporation and the officers can be held liable for damages to anyone injured through the wrongful transfer of stock.

A decision must be made as to whether the company will perform its own transfer work or use an independent agent. The majority of large companies employ a bank or trust company as a transfer agent or co-transfer agent; but some have found it economical to do their own work. Likewise some small companies have found it less expensive to handle all transfer work themselves.

It is largely a matter of analysis of the costs and other factors in deciding whether a corporation should establish its own transfer department. Certainly the following points are pertinent in any such decision:

1. Comparative costs. This includes consideration of the usual operating costs of salaries, supplies, rent or occupancy costs, depreciation, taxes, and insurance. The schedule of bank or trust company charges, or actual bills, should be compared with these costs.
2. Possible recapitalization or other problems which may present considerable difficulty.
3. Availability of office space.
4. Available capital for purchase of equipment.
5. Available staff.
6. Location requirements in connection with the stock exchange rules.
7. Legal opinion as to desirability.

The transfer function basically involves merely an orderly recording of canceled shares and the issuance of new certificates. Extreme care and protective procedures must be instituted. Controllers should be able to design satisfactory procedures covering all functions from the receipt and sorting of canceled certificates to the mailing of the new certificates. Provision must be made for "stop transfer orders" when such instructions are given in the event of loss or death. Another problem involves the location of missing stockholders.

THE DIVIDEND DISBURSING PROCEDURE

The quarterly payment of dividends is a fairly standard practice among the larger corporations. While the company may write its own dividend checks, in most instances a dividend disbursing agent is used. The transfer agent is the natural selection for the job because he has the necessary records to make payments.

Basically the procedure for paying dividends is as follows:

1. The board of directors adopts a resolution declaring a dividend. Usually a date of record and date of payment are specified. Also, certain legal requirements must be met; for example, generally the payment may be made only out of accumulated earnings. Moreover, the financial condition must be such that the payment will not make the corporation insolvent; nor can it be insolvent and legally declare a dividend.

2. The corporate secretary presents to the dividend disbursing agent a certified copy of the resolution declaring the dividend and also notifies the treasurer.

3. The required publication of the dividend declaration is made.

4. The treasurer transmits to the disbursing agent a check covering the required funds a few days prior to payment of the dividend.

5. The agent prepares and mails the dividend checks, together with any literature or enclosures the corporation wants distributed.

6. The dividend bank account is reconciled.

If the company prepares the dividend checks itself, much the same procedure is followed. The usual controls are instituted as in writing the payroll, for example.

CAPITAL STOCK AND DIVIDEND RECORDS

In situations where the capital stock and dividends are handled by a transfer agent, only control accounts for each class of stock and for the dividends payable need be maintained by the company. If the company itself keeps the records, then those of a nature discussed in Chapter 27 are needed. Fundamentally, there must be a permanent record of each stockholder's account and of all transfers.

When a transfer agent is employed, these basic records are kept by him. In such a case, a transfer sheet similar to Fig. 202 is sent daily to the secretary of the corporation, and to the registrar and co-transfer agent. Review of these sheets will indicate significant changes in ownership.

THE NATIONAL BANK OF _____ TRANSFER DEPARTMENT The Following Described Securities have been Transferred Today as Shown Below						
Date _____ Name of Corporation _____ Issue _____						
Transferor	Certificate Number	Shares	Transferee and Address	Certificate Number	Shares	Receipt Number
1 John Jones	TO-165	100	1 J. J. Herrip, 4124 Rushland Toledo, Ohio	TO-986	100	2157
2			2			
3			3			
4			4			
5			5			

Fig. 202—Stock Transfer Sheet.

One other phase of corporate ownership deserves special comment, and that relates to the cost of servicing small stockholders. It is desirable, of course, for large corporations with listed stocks to have widespread stock distribution. Such a condition encourages public interest in both the company and the free enterprise system. However, the cost of servicing a small stockholder—i.e., writing dividend checks and mailing stockholders' reports —is just as much as servicing a large one. Under the circumstances it well may be that there should be a minimum number of shares or size of holdings which any company will encourage. The problem resolves itself into balancing the costs of servicing with the benefits received.

BONDS AND INTEREST—RECORDS AND PROCEDURE

The method of recording bonds issued and interest payments largely depends on the nature of the bonds, the number of transactions, the size of the issue, and whether outside agencies are used. Very often the bond indenture requires a trustee as well as a registrar and interest-paying agent. Frequently, one party serves in all capacities, and this may be a bank or trust company. Under such conditions, any needed reports relative to bonds outstanding and coupons paid may be secured from the agent.

Records of non-registered bonds generally should show by denomination: the number of pieces outstanding, their serial numbers, principal amount, total coupons unpaid as of interest dates, and all issue and cancellation transactions with date and reference to source of information.

Records of registered bonds should indicate by denomination: the number of pieces outstanding; their serial numbers; registered holder; principal amount by holder and in total; coupons unpaid by serial number and in total; and a complete record of all issues, cancellations, and transfers with date and reference to source of data.

If an outside agent maintains the registration and transfer record, the issuing company may make entries in the control accounts on the basis of summary reports prepared by the agent.

44

The Controller's Contribution to Industrial Relations

BASIC INDUSTRIAL RELATIONS PROBLEMS

The modern concept of industrial relations embodies the principle that labor is not a commodity to be bought and sold in a free market. Rather, the workers are viewed as people, useful members of society, who make a contribution to the welfare of the community. On such a basis, they are entitled to a fair share of the fruits of production.

There was an era when the tough and greedy employer, with little social conscience, was in the driver's seat. This was followed by an era of powerful union leaders, some of whom were ruthless in their quest to have labor paid more and more for less and less production. Legislative means have been attempted to bring these forces into balance. However, any hope for a more or less permanent solution must depend far more upon a widely understood and accepted philosophy of social justice than upon legislation. There can be no one-way street if the American system is to survive. Labor relations must be a two-way street, with each party recognizing the rights of the other, and both recognizing that the true function of business is to serve human needs or wants.

USING FACTS

Whether it be the result of a growing realization that labor, capital, and management are partners, or because labor and management forces are getting into balance, or because each of these groups is becoming more mature, there is a trend in labor negotiations toward a search for facts rather than fights. Labor relations are entering a period where accurate financial data are playing, and will play, a more important role in bargaining. Once the theory of the social contribution of labor is accepted, there remain these questions:

1. What are the total fruits to be distributed—the income?
2. To what share is each partner entitled, i.e., management, labor, and capital?

The measurement of income is essentially an accounting problem, although some of the traditional concepts may need changing. The share to which labor is entitled is determined largely by collective bargaining. This share can be changed by at least three means: (1) by adjustment of the basic wage rate, (2) through the introduction of incentive bonuses, or (3) through the distribution on some accepted basis of the excess after each partner has received a stipulated share. In these problems, also, accounting can be useful.

Intelligent collective bargaining can be achieved only when each party has the facts. One would be naïve indeed to believe that mere presentation of the facts will solve the labor problem. But much can be gained through their intelligent use.

THE CONTROLLER'S FUNCTION IN LABOR RELATIONS

As financial facts and figures become more significant in labor negotiations, it is evident that the expert in handling them assumes greater importance as part of the bargaining group. Nevertheless, he does not negotiate —that is the function of the personnel manager or the attorney handling the case. The controller, however, should be at their right side, providing facts and figures required, analyzing the costs of the union demands, and checking any figures submitted by the union. This is a newer phase of the role played by the accounting executive. As a general responsibility, he, like any other official, is interested also in the development of good labor relations which generally mean lower over-all manufacturing costs.

Aside from these general statements, the following checklist indicates more specific ways in which the controller may function. It is to be understood, of course, that from company to company these duties differ.

1. *Directly in Labor Negotiation Matters*
   a. Develops and supervises the maintenance of company records which will provide essential data for labor negotiations
   b. Analyzes the union contracts and suggests changes which may be desirable from a cost or operating viewpoint
   c. In collaboration with the personnel manager, anticipates the data needed in negotiations, and takes steps to make them available
   d. Serves as a member of the policy committee on collective bargaining

e. Determines the cost—perhaps in the aggregate—per unit of product
f. Supervises the gathering of outside financial data on pertinent matters
g. As requested by the negotiator, presents figure-facts and interprets them during the negotiations
h. Analyzes the probable effect on the operations of decisions reached in labor negotiations; and makes plans so that the policies and operations may be adapted to best meet the competitive economic conditions
i. Prepares financial data to secure public support, where necessary, in connection with negotiations

2. *Other Industrial Relations Matters*
a. Renders the usual services related to payroll matters—prompt and timely preparation of paychecks, maintenance of necessary records required by law, handling of payroll deductions, etc.
b. Cooperates with the industrial relations department in interpretation of the contract provisions regarding wage payments as applied to the everyday problems which arise
c. Assists in the development and installation of wage incentive systems
d. Assists the union in accounting matters, including statement preparation relative to union business
e. Supervises or gives advice relative to credit unions, insurance plans, and similar matters

A great many factors will influence the degree to which the controller participates in some of the above matters: the size of the company, type of accounting system, personality of the controller and of the personnel manager, type of bargaining, physical location of the offices, and relative rank of both executives.

RELATIONS WITH THE PERSONNEL MANAGER

The benefit a business concern may secure from its accounting department in labor matters depends greatly on the relationship existing between the controller and the personnel manager. Though a competent accounting staff may be available to analyze and interpret figures, and though the basic data may be in the records, it will serve for nought unless the lines of communication are kept open between the two departments. Fundamental, of course, is a clear understanding of the responsibilities of each. The personnel manager should be willing to rely on the controller's specialized knowledge for analyzing the significance of cost factors on the company's operations. Further, he should be aware of what kind of information the controller can furnish. Complete cooperation is essential.

One means of encouraging cooperation is through a collective bargaining policy committee which might consist of the personnel manager, the legal representative, the controller, and the operating officials. Functions of such a committee, advisory in nature, might include:

1. Review of union contract for suggestions as to change
2. Consideration of long-term effects of various contract clauses
3. Consideration of company proposals

If the controller participates in such a committee, he should be in a better position to furnish more useful data.

Another means of securing cooperation between the personnel and accounting departments is interchange of staff for training.

RECORDS FOR LABOR RELATIONS INFORMATION

Of those who have conducted negotiations with labor unions, few will deny the importance of adequate records. As a matter of fact, without some records it would be well nigh impossible to determine the reasonableness of union demands, or what position the company should take on particular issues. Further, many labor unions have seized the initiative in using and securing facts and figures on the company operations. At the very minimum, then, the company must secure facts and figures to meet or combat the union arguments.

Responsibility for the maintenance of records depends on several circumstances, including the size and type of organization, the record-keeping system, the degree of centralization and mechanization, and the information wanted. Generally, the controller's department is responsible for payroll and insurance records, and other cost data; and the personnel department is responsible for such matters as seniority and grievances. The individual circumstances must govern. If, for example, a punched card system is installed, a great degree of flexibility may be obtained and the accounting department may provide other data in a form useful to the personnel department. Information may be quickly summarized, such as reports on employees by age groups, marital status, or sex.

Certain basic payroll information is or should be available from the earnings records and individual employee records as maintained by most companies. This includes:

1. *Aggregate Earnings Records*
    a. Analysis of hours, i.e., regular, overtime, incentive, vacation, etc.
    b. Analysis of pay—regular, overtime, shift differential, etc.— by job classification

c. Summary of deductions—federal withholding tax, social security taxes, insurance, etc.

2. *Individual Employee Records*
   a. Name, Social Security number, telephone, address, education, sex, age
   b. Length of service
   c. Seniority status, military status, etc.
   d. Starting rate and subsequent rate adjustments

Certain information often found desirable in labor negotiations is equally often not available. In designing the record system, consideration should be given to securing information in the following areas: [1]

Marital status
Dependents
Incidence of illness and the causes
  a) Among married men and women
  b) Among single men and women
  c) By age groups
Sickness figures by:
  a) Departments
  b) Causes
  c) Length of absences
Percentage of married men and women on payroll
Turnover by:
  a) Age groups
  b) Sex
  c) Occupation
  d) Length of service
Percentage of single men and women
Percentage of men and women living alone
Percentage of men and women living with families
How many full-time employees have been laid off over the years
  a) By occupation
  b) By length of service
  c) By length of layoff
Cost of strike per day
Cost of employee sickness to company
Sickness payments made to employees
Absentee rates by:
  a) Age groups
  b) Sex
  c) Before and after holidays
  d) Departments

Number of employees by months over the years of service
Layoffs by months
  a) Male and female
  b) By occupation
Cost of absenteeism
Cost of work stoppages
Cost of time spent on grievances
Anticipated age distribution of new employees
Distribution of present employees by age
Cost of accidents to company over the years
Employee earnings over the years
Real wages vs. take-home pay
Starting rates of pay
Mortality of employees before and after retirement
Rate at which employees will withdraw from service
Cost of funding process, if initial accrued liability for pensions is funded
Rate at which employees are expected to retire upon reaching the age of 65
Rate at which employees are expected to become permanently and totally disabled
Distribution of life insurance by age
Allocation of costs as between different types of insurance

[1] *Providing Facts and Figures for Collective Bargaining* (New York: Controllership Foundation Inc., 1950), pp. 41–42.

FACTS NEEDED FOR COLLECTIVE BARGAINING

Just as a lawyer must plan his case, so also in successful collective bargaining thorough preparation is essential. Such preparatory work is not to be treated as an emergency matter; rather it is a continuing process throughout the entire year. It involves anticipating the demands and securing the facts in proper form. Merely providing the system to gather basic payroll data hardly touches the surface of the real need.

Several sources may provide clues as to what information should be secured. These include:

1. Prior-year negotiations
2. Agreements reached between other companies and their unions
3. Discussions with union leaders regarding present contract
4. Comments of labor-management services
5. Union literature and speeches
6. Comments of trade associations
7. The grapevine

From these several sources may be gleaned indications and ideas as to the type of facts and figures to be gathered. In addition, of course, are the opinions of an aggressive management team based on its own plan of attack. The assembling of the data as part of a well-planned program has these advantages:

1. The company negotiator may have more confidence when supported by the required facts and figures
2. Negotiations may be shortened considerably
3. The data can be used effectively in influencing the union

While any one of several systems is available for putting the financial statistics and related facts in a convenient form for use, many companies use what is commonly called a "fact book." It is in the nature of a reference book. Much of the information is furnished by the controller, and a great deal may be secured by the negotiator.

Just what information should be put together in this fact book? Basically, of course, a compilation is made of statistics pertaining to the company, competing companies, and area and national related factors. Some suggested data to be included, and an indication as to what portion the controller may secure, are as follows:

Company Data	External Data

INFORMATION FURNISHED BY THE CONTROLLER

Financial Condition and Operating Results:

1. Recent financial statements	1. Information as to returns on investment for industry generally
2. Breakdown of annual earnings to show share of income, in total and percentagewise, which was allocated for:	2. Net profit as a per cent of net sales for industry, competitors, etc.

2. Breakdown of annual earnings to show share of income, in total and percentagewise, which was allocated for:
   a. Suppliers and subcontractors
   b. Employees, salaries and wages and other benefits
   c. Federal income taxes
   d. Depreciation, insurance, and property taxes
   e. Stockholders
   f. Retention in business
3. Estimated net profit or loss at varying production levels
4. Break-even point
5. Estimated operating results—next year
6. Estimated operating results if union demands are met
7. Salaries and/or wages as a per cent of net sales—for several past years
8. Additional sales volume required to earn cost of union demands
9. Return on investment—several past years (%)

Wage Data:

1. Total cost of wages and fringe benefits broken down by elements, viz., vacation pay, group insurance, overtime pay, shift differentials, clothing, meals, call-in pay	1. Similar data for industry, competitors, etc., to the extent available

2. Same data calculated on an hours-worked basis
3. Average straight-time hourly earnings
4. Average gross and take-home pay per employee—weekly, annually
5. Range of average hourly rates, weekly earnings, etc.
6. Per cent increase in average take-home pay, gross wages, etc., from selected base periods
7. Comparable data for several years to reveal trends
8. Wages paid by classifications—in total and per hour worked
9. Amount of funds to be set aside for employees' pension plan—by age groups

Company Data	External Data

Hour Data:

1. Total man-hours worked, by job classification
2. Average weekly, monthly, and yearly hours worked
3. Range of hours worked—weekly, monthly, annually
4. Same data as above, by job classification
5. Analysis of hours worked by pay—straight, time and one half, double, etc.
6. Lost hours—in total and by cause

1. Comparable data for industry, competitors, etc., to extent available

Union Demands:

1. Each item priced to determine total annual cost
2. Similar data on a cents-per-hour basis
3. Estimated costs of extending similar benefits to non-union groups

Productivity:

1. Per man-hour
2. Per machine-hour

General Information:

1. Number of employees
2. Average turnover, and turnover by age groups and length of service
3. Age distribution of employees
4. Seniority status
5. Estimated cost of work stoppages

INFORMATION FURNISHED BY THE PERSONNEL MANAGER

1. Comparison of company and competitors as to:
   a. Pension plans, including benefits
   b. Vacation policy
   c. Fringe benefits
2. Analysis of union demands on other companies, and settlements
3. Comparative workweeks, hourly earnings, etc., from own sources, and supplementary data secured by controller—BLS data, etc.
4. Cost of living data
5. Comparative data on personnel practices
6. Job descriptions
7. Union statements regarding various subjects: wages, hours, ability to pay, profits, pensions, productivity, etc.
8. Company demands
9. History of previous negotiations

PRESENTING FACTS DURING NEGOTIATIONS

One responsibility of the controller is to provide financial facts and fig ures for the company representatives during labor negotiations. In addi tion, he should assist in making decisions as to information to be furnished to the union representatives. Several problems arise in this latter connection, but the ones of primary concern to the controller are these:

1. Should any facts or figures be provided?
2. What type of information should be made available?
3. What form should the presentation take, and should the figures be interpreted?
4. Who should explain or present the data?

Circumstances under which data need not be presented to the union might include situations such as:

1. *Where the settlement will be governed primarily by patterns already established.* Under such conditions, facts relative to company operations hardly would seem pertinent.
2. *If the fundamental issues at stake are not matters which lend themselves to factual presentation.* For example, the issue might be the rights of each party regarding safety inspections or the nature of a job change. Perhaps facts would be of little value in such instances.
3. *Where the presentation of facts would not influence the results.* Several conditions might exist where this situation would obtain. Thus, it might be clearly evident that the settlement would be by arbitration. Full presentation might give the union some advantages. Or, the union leaders may be of such temperament or training as to be unwilling to listen to or unable to comprehend the facts of business operations.
4. *Where the factual presentation would injure the company.* Such injury might result at the bargaining table, or it might result in other ways:
   a. Through disclosure of costs which might reach competition
   b. Through dissemination of information concerning secret elements of income
   c. By presentation of fragments of data susceptible to misinterpretation unless the background is thoroughly understood
   d. Where the stockholders would regard such action as a sign of management weakness
   e. Where some information might be the entering wedge for other questions which could not be answered convincingly

These reasons need not be construed as intentions to withhold vital and necessary facts, or as an attempt to hide information. Rather, experience sometimes indicates practical limitations which, if exceeded, weaken the bargaining position.

There are also circumstances or reasons for presenting financial facts to the unions. For example:

1. *Where the facts are already available.* Reports to the SEC are public information which the union may secure. Reports to stockholders and proxy statements can be grouped in the same category. Under such circumstances, the company may have much to gain by a further interpretation of the data.
2. *If such presentations can strengthen the company position.* Such benefits might be for immediate bargaining or for long-term purposes. Some examples include:
   a. Instances where costs are out of line with competition
   b. Circumstances where the union claims are clearly and definitely refuted by the facts
   c. Conditions wherein the growth of mutual understanding is furthered by informing the union leaders about the business and its problems
3. *Where the facts can be used to support strong counter-demands of the company.* This may be considered as a special phase of item 2 above.

Many companies follow a middle-of-the-road policy and present only such information as will answer union arguments. Other managements use the facts in a positive or aggressive manner with good results.

SELECTING THE INFORMATION TO PRESENT

Some of the same reasons used in deciding whether to present *any* statistical or financial information to the union may be used in determining *what* to present. Whether the company negotiators are faced with requests from the union for certain data or whether on their own initiative they are selecting facts to present, the following generalizations may be useful:

1. Any information which might damage the company's competitive position should not be given.
2. Information clearly irrelevant to the union demands and beyond the scope of the union concern may be withheld. This area may change with the times.
3. Facts which are already available to the union may be presented.
4. Information, the disclosure of which is mandatory by the decision of the National Labor Relations Board or other proper authority, should be given. Thus, the NLRB has held that information was needed by the union:
   a. If it was to exercise effectively its legitimate function of representing the employees in contract negotiations, and of protecting its proper interest, or
   b. If the collection of such information by the union individually from each member would appear doubtful of accomplishment and would be attended with great difficulty and loss of time, or

The Illustrative Company
DISTRIBUTION OF EARNINGS
For the Year Ended December 31, 196–

John Doe, our average worker, produced goods which we sold to our customer, and which were valued at..		$25,000
The materials from which these goods were made cost us.........	$12,500	
John received from us as regular wages, overtime, vacation pay, and supplemental benefits in the sum of.........................	4,800	17,300
John produced earnings for us of..		7,700
We set aside for the use of machinery and equipment, paid taxes, stockholder dividends, and other expenses; and retained for future needs the sum of....		7,450
The undistributed profit John made for us was..........................		$ 250

Last year John Doe worked 2,500 hours, so that the undistributed profit is equivalent to $.10 per hour. With this amount, John helps the future success of the business; and builds a backlog which we may all need in less prosperous times.

If we can assume the same general conditions will exist next year, this 10¢ represents the amount about which we can bargain. How much do you, the union representatives, think should be set aside for future contingencies, and how much should John get?

Fig. 203—Illustrative Statement of Operating Results for Use in Labor Negotiations.

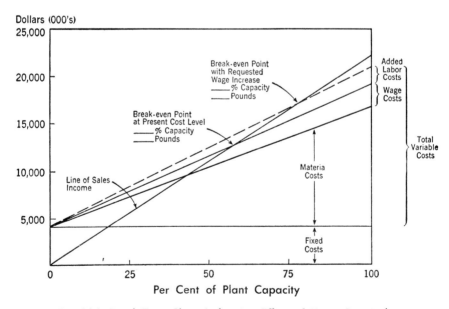

Fig. 204—Break-Even Chart Indicating Effect of Union Demands.

    c. If an employer bargaining in good faith would not have withheld the information requested.

However, the Board has held that irrelevant information, or information the furnishing of which would impose only an impossible or unreasonable burden, need not be supplied.

5. Information which will advance the company's position, or contribute to the understanding of mutual problems should be presented.

GETTING THE FACTS UNDERSTOOD

As every controller knows, it is often very difficult to get figures understood. This happens just as readily in labor matters as in anything else; and it is true as to both management and labor representatives. Under the circumstances, extreme care must be used in interpreting the facts and figures. The controller not only must furnish the accounting data, but he must assume a certain responsibility in seeing that the company representatives understand the significance as well as the limitations of the information. In some companies, the controller approves in advance any comments to be made regarding the operating position.

In dealings with the labor representatives perhaps even greater effort must be made to avoid misinterpretations. While the controller may sometimes present the figures at the request of the personnel manager, usually he does not directly handle this phase of the discussions.

The subject of annual reports to employees was reviewed in Chapter 31, and many of the same general comments presented there are applicable in connection with collective bargaining. The presentation must be simple; and graphs and tables are effective. It is preferable that written statements be made rather than simply oral ones in order (1) to have the subject a matter of record and (2) to permit further study.

The enlightened management is using simplified and personalized financial reporting in a significant degree. No standard formulas are necessarily applicable. An example of a company statement which might be effective in labor negotiations, and which can be reconciled with the published statement is illustrated in Fig. 203. This permits the union to compare the results with other companies; and it might serve as a means of getting joint action to increase low productivity.

A somewhat more technical graph of the break-even point and the effect of union demands is illustrated in Fig. 204. Whether this should be used for management or both management and labor depends on the circumstances. If the union has any doubts about the accuracy or factual basis of the figures, the services of an independent accountant agreeable to both company and union might be utilized.

45

Some General Considerations

RELATION OF CONTROLLER AND PUBLIC ACCOUNTANT

An audit of the accounting records by an independent accountant is an important function in modern business. Such examinations may be made pursuant to requirements of the Securities and Exchange Commission, the stock exchanges, or state regulations. Aside from any legal or contractual requirements, such a review is helpful where credit and banking arrangements are under discussion, where management and ownership are divorced and either party wants an accounting, where labor unions desire an independent check on profits, and in many other circumstances. By and large, independent audits are recognized as an essential protective device and a part of good management.

Obviously there is a very close relationship between the work of the public accountant and that of the controller. However, each has his own separate tasks and functions; and one cannot assume the duties and responsibilities of the other. There is perhaps a need for setting out or delineating the work of each. On the one hand the controller or chief accountant is primarily responsible for developing, installing, and operating an efficient and economical system of record keeping and internal control. The controller, and management as a group, are primarily responsible for the statements issued—and not the independent accountant. A controller cannot transfer his responsibility for the accuracy of financial statements to the public accountants.

On the other hand the work of the independent public accountant should complement and supplement the work of the controller with a minimum duplication of effort. Management expects, or should expect, the independent auditor to assure it that the statements of income and expense and financial condition are based on accepted accounting principles; that the accounting systems and internal control are adequate; and that the controller and his staff are reasonably competent and trustworthy. Management and investors expect the public accountant to be a truly independent consultant when expressing opinions on these matters.

While the auditor is in a certain sense checking on the controller, nevertheless there must be a high degree of cooperation between the two. The controller may well consider the review as a test of the adequacy of his administration. In securing this high degree of cooperation but independence of audit, the following comments are applicable:

1. Although cooperation is necessary between the internal accounting staff and the public accountant, the latter is expected to perform the examination in an impartial and objective manner. The controller should see, perhaps, that such a relationship is maintained by discouraging joint participation of these groups in purely social activities.
2. The internal audit program should be reviewed and discussed with the public accountants so that any duplication of effort is reduced to the very minimum. Thus, if the internal auditors are making certain plant audits, the work of the outside auditors may be reduced in scope as to that plant. The working papers of the internal audit as well as a copy of the internal audit report should be made available to the public accountants.
3. To the extent possible, the controller's staff should prepare working papers for the public accountants in the form prescribed. This may help in reducing the audit cost. Such papers may include:
   a. General ledger trial balance
   b. Subsidiary ledger trial balances (accounts receivable—aged, accounts payable, factory ledger, etc.)
   c. Account analyses (reserves, fixed assets, expenses, and other asset, liability, and income accounts)
   d. Inventory pricing schedules
   e. Procedure summaries
4. Major changes in accounting policy may be reviewed with the independent accountant prior to adoption.
5. The preliminary copy of the audit report may be jointly reviewed to be sure that the recommendations, if any, are practical and can be carried out.

The controller cannot and should not prescribe the independent audit program. It would appear proper, however, that any undue amount of time seemingly spent on a particular phase of the audit would at least bear questioning. If, for example, a great deal of time is being spent on fixed assets and this does not appear material to the examination, the controller should know why. If the controller is fortunate enough to have had some experience as a public accountant, this may be of value to him in judging such matters.

In some instances the controller will have a voice in selecting the firm of auditors.

A MANAGEMENT AUDIT

Another type of audit which the controller may suggest, if the circumstances warrant, is one by management consultants. In a certain sense, such audits begin where the balance sheet audits stop. This kind of review is not concerned with the verification of financial statements; rather, it is an examination of the efficiency of operations—any operations whether in the factory, in the sales organization, or in the office. Such occasional examination can prove valuable where management suspects that certain operations or methods are too costly or inefficient. In effect, the company is buying time and experience and an outside viewpoint when these consultants are hired. Through their engineering and sales experience they may suggest changes to effect considerable savings. Their work necessarily involves the matter of coordinating the accounting work incident to organizational and other changes. With respect to purely accounting routines, the systems departments of the public accounting firms are available for reviews if the controller has neither the time nor the staff with the necessary training.

THE CONTROLLER AND GOVERNMENTAL REGULATIONS

The multitude of governmental regulations, both federal and state, have influenced business accounting systems by reason of the record and reporting requirements. The trend toward even more such regulation is increasing the cost of doing business, and is adding to the work load of the controller. There are, of course, a vast number of regulations which do not directly concern the accounting staff. About the best to be said is that the controller should accept the chore of constantly being on the alert for regulations which do affect his company. In this he will have the assistance of the specialists on his staff and of legal counsel.

Other than this, the suggestion is made that friendly relations be maintained with the various government representatives who have official business with the company. There is little to be gained by antagonizing them. But on the other hand the controller should always be ready to resist any unreasonable demand.

POLICY MAKING AND LONG-TERM PLANNING

Much of the information gathered by the controller is needed for intelligent policy decisions. How he interprets the data can have a significant influence on policies, whether they be sales policies, production policies, or financial policies. For this reason the controller should attempt to maintain a broad viewpoint, the management viewpoint, in presenting and interpreting the facts and figures at the top level. He should truly operate as a member of top management.

Something often overlooked because of day-to-day operating problems is the absolute need for long-range planning. Most businesses must attempt to look ahead for a period of from three to ten years in making plans. The controller can encourage this approach, and can give effect to such plans through the medium of forecasted statements of income and expense and financial condition.

THE OUTLOOK FOR CONTROLLERSHIP

The tremendous growth in the size and complexity of modern business has brought with it a recognition of the need for more adequate accounting control and the desirability of segregating the accounting function from other duties of a secretarial or financial nature. The authors have attempted to portray the controller as the skilled business analyst who, by training and experience, is the best qualified to keep the financial records of the business and to interpret these for the guidance of management.

In any organization made up of human beings there are bound to be favoritism and prejudices. Often the controller may feel that his work or importance is not fully appreciated. He must recognize that he is a staff man, and that the opinions of the operating executives will sometimes take precedence over his proposals. His position will not be established or strengthened by any artificial forcing. In the long run, his contribution to the business will depend on the extent to which he can command the respect of his associates. This will depend in large part on his personal qualifications and his ability to make the figures useful. He must be technically competent, possess good judgment and common sense, develop an efficient staff, and have the intestinal fortitude to stand his ground on important matters.

Above all the controller cannot be a mere historian. Present-day controllership demands a forward approach—demands preventive management. The position needs more than the usual understanding of other jobs. In many companies the position of controller is proving to be a training ground for even greater management responsibility.

Index